Drugs and Society

Seventh Edition

Drugs and Society

Glen R. Hanson

Department of Pharmacology and Toxicology
University of Utah
Salt Lake City, Utah
Director of the Division of Neuroscience and Behavioral Research
National Institute on Drug Abuse, NIH

Peter J. Venturelli

Department of Sociology
Valparaiso University
Valparaiso, Indiana

Annette E. Fleckenstein

Department of Pharmacology and Toxicology
University of Utah
Salt Lake City, Utah

JONES AND BARTLETT PUBLISHERS
Sudbury, Massachusetts
BOSTON   TORONTO   LONDON   SINGAPORE

World Headquarters
Jones and Bartlett Publishers
40 Tall Pine Drive
Sudbury, MA 01776
978-443-5000
info@jbpub.com
www.jbpub.com

Jones and Bartlett Publishers Canada
2406 Nikanna Rd.
Mississauga, Ontario L5C 2W6
CANADA

Jones and Bartlett Publishers International
Barb House, Barb Mews
London W6 7PA
UK

Library of Congress Cataloging-in-Publication Data
Hanson, Glen (Glen R.)
    Drugs and society / Glen R. Hanson, Peter J. Venturelli,
        Annette E. Fleckenstein. — 7th ed.
        p. cm.
    Includes bibliographical references and index.
    ISBN 0-7637-1572-7
        1. Drugs. 2. Drugs—Toxicology. 3. Drug Abuse.
        I. Venturelli, Peter J., II. Fleckenstein, Annette E. III.
    Title.
RM301.W58 2002
615'.1—dc21   2001038968

Chief Executive Officer: Clayton Jones
Chief Operating Officer: Don W. Jones, Jr.
Executive Vice President and Publisher: Robert Holland
V.P., Manufacturing and Inventory Control: Therese Bräuer
V.P., Design and Production: Anne Spencer
Editor-in-Chief, College: J. Michael Stranz
Acquisitions Editor: Laurie A. Klausner
Production Editor: Julie C. Bolduc
Manufacturing Buyer: Amy Duddridge
Editorial Assistant: Corinne Hudson
Marketing Manager: Taryn Wahlquist
Text Design and Composition: Nesbitt Graphics, Inc.
Cover Design: Anne Spencer
Cover Photo: © PhotoDisc, Ken Usami
Printing and Binding: Courier
Cover Printing: Courier

Printed in the United States of America
05 04 03 02 01   10 9 8 7 6 5 4 3 2 1

Brief Contents

■ CHAPTER 1   Introduction to Drugs and Society   2

■ CHAPTER 2   Explaining Drug Use and Abuse   34

■ CHAPTER 3   Drug Use, Regulation, and the Law   64

■ CHAPTER 4   Addictive Behavior and Treating Drug Dependence   90

■ CHAPTER 5   Homeostatic Systems and Drugs   112

■ CHAPTER 6   How and Why Drugs Work   132

■ CHAPTER 7   CNS Depressants: Sedative-Hypnotics   158

■ CHAPTER 8   Alcohol: Pharmacological Effects   180

■ CHAPTER 9   Alcohol: A Behavioral Perspective   200

■ CHAPTER 10   Narcotics (Opioids)   236

■ CHAPTER 11   Stimulants   262

■ CHAPTER 12   Tobacco   300

■ CHAPTER 13   Hallucinogens (Psychedelics)   334

■ CHAPTER 14   Marijuana   362

■ CHAPTER 15   Inhalants   394

■ CHAPTER 16   Over-the-Counter (OTC), Prescription, and Herbal Drugs   406

■ CHAPTER 17   Drug Use Within Major Subcultures   440

■ CHAPTER 18   Drug Use/Abuse Prevention   492

Contents

Preface xiii

CHAPTER 1

Introduction to Drugs and Society 2

Introduction 4

The Dimensions of Drug Use 4
Most Commonly Abused Drugs 7

An Overview of Drugs in Society 10
How Widespread Is Drug Use? 10
Extent and Frequency of Drug
   Use in Society 11
Types of Drug Users/Abusers 15
Mass Media Influences on Drug
   Use in Everyday Life 15

**Attraction and Patterns of
Drug Use and Abuse 17**
When Does Use Lead to Abuse? 18
Drug Dependence 19

The Costs of Drug Use to Society 20
Drugs, Crime, and Violence 21
Drugs in the Workplace: A Costly Affliction 26

**Venturing to a Higher Level: A Holistic
Self-Awareness Approach to Drug Use 28**

CHAPTER 2

Explaining Drug Use and Abuse 34

Introduction 36

Drug Use: A Timeless Affliction 36

Biological Explanations 38
Abused Drugs Are Positive Reinforcers 38
Drug Abuse and Psychiatric Disorders 39
Genetic Explanations 39

Psychological Explanations 40
Distinguishing Between Substance Abuse
   and Mental Disorders 41

The Relationship Between Personality
   and Drug Use 41
Theories Based on Learning Processes 42
Social Psychological Learning Theories 43

Sociological Explanations 43
Social Influence Theories 44
Structural Influence Theories 53

Danger Signals of Drug Abuse 57
Low-Risk and High-Risk Choices 58

CHAPTER 3

Drug Use, Regulation, and the Law 64

Introduction 66

Cultural Attitudes About Drug Use 66

The Road to Regulation and the FDA 67
Prescription versus OTC Drugs 67
The Rising Demand for Effectiveness
   in Medicinal Drugs 69
Regulating the Development of
   New Drugs 69
The Effects of the OTC Review on
   Today's Medications 72

The Regulation of Drug Advertising 72
Prescription Advertising 73
Federal Regulation and Quality Assurance 73

Drug Abuse and the Law 74
Drug Laws and Deterrence 76
Factors in Controlling Drug Abuse 78

Strategies for Preventing Drug Abuse 79
Supply Reduction Strategy 79
Demand Reduction Strategy 81
Inoculation Strategy 82

Current and Future Drug Use 82
Drug Legalization Debate 83
Drug Testing 85
Pragmatic Drug Policies 86

CHAPTER 4

Addictive Behavior and Treating Drug Dependence   90

Introduction   92

The Origin and Nature of Addiction   92
Defining Addiction   92
Models of Addiction   93
Factors Contributing to Addiction   94

The Vicious Cycle of Addiction   96
Nondrug Addictions?   96

Treatment of Addiction   97

Drug Addiction Treatment in the United States   100
Alcoholics Anonymous   100
Rehabilitation Facilities   102
Detoxification Units   102
Therapeutic Communities   103
Outpatient Treatment   103
Current Trends in Providing
    Treatment Services   105

CHAPTER 5

Homeostatic Systems and Drugs   112

Introduction   114

1: Overview of Homeostasis and Drug Actions   114

Introduction to Nervous Systems   114

2: Comprehensive Explanation of Homeostatic Systems   116

The Building Blocks of the Nervous System   116
The Neuron: The Basic Structural Unit
    of the Nervous System   116
The Nature of Drug Receptors   118
Agonistic and Antagonistic Effects
    on Drug Receptors   119
Neurotransmitters: The Messengers   119

Major Divisions of the Nervous System   123
The Central Nervous System   123

The Autonomic Nervous System   124

The Endocrine System and Drugs   126
Endocrine Glands and Regulation   126
The Abuse of Hormones: Anabolic Steroids   128

Conclusion   128

CHAPTER 6

How and Why Drugs Work   132

Introduction   134

The Intended and Unintended Effects of Drugs   134

The Dose-Response Relationship of Therapeutics and Toxicity   136
Margin of Safety   136
Potency versus Toxicity   137

Drug Interaction   137
Additive Effects   138
Antagonistic (Inhibitory) Effects   138
Potentiative (Synergistic) Effects   138
Dealing with Drug Interactions   139

Pharmacokinetic Factors That Influence Drug Effects   140
Forms and Methods of Taking Drugs   140
Distribution of Drugs in the Body and
    Time-Response Relationships   142
Inactivation and Elimination of Drugs
    from the Body   144
Physiological Variables That Modify
    Drug Effects   145
Pathological Variables That Modify
    Drug Effects   145

Adaptive Processes and Drug Abuse   146
Tolerance to Drugs   147
Drug Dependence   149

Psychological Factors   150
The Placebo Effect   151

Addiction and Abuse: The Significance of Dependence   152
Hereditary Factors   152
Drug Craving   153
Other Factors   153

CHAPTER 7

CNS Depressants: Sedative-Hypnotics   158

Introduction   160

An Introduction to CNS Depressants   160
The History of CNS Depressants   160
The Effects of CNS Depressants:
Benefits and Risks   161

Types of CNS Depressants   162
Benzodiazepines: Valium-Type Drugs   163
Barbiturates   167
Other CNS Depressants   170

Patterns of Abuse with CNS Depressants   173
Treatment for Withdrawal   175

CHAPTER 8

Alcohol: Pharmacological Effects   180

Introduction   182

The Nature and History of Alcohol   182

Alcohol as a Drug   183
Alcohol as a Social Drug   184
Impact of Alcohol   184

The Properties of Alcohol   184

The Physical Effects of Alcohol   185
Alcohol and Tolerance   188
Alcohol Metabolism   188
Polydrug Use   188
Short-term Effects   189
Dependence   191

Effects of Alcohol on Organ Systems and Bodily Functions   191
Brain and Nervous System   191
Liver   191
Digestive System   193
Blood   194
Cardiovascular System   194
Sexual Organs   194
Endocrine System   195
Kidneys   195
Mental Disorders and Damage to the Brain   195
The Fetus   195
Malnutrition   196

CHAPTER 9

Alcohol: A Behavioral Perspective   200

Introduction   202

Our Alcohol Consuming Society   202

Current Statistics and Trends in Alcohol Consumption   202
Drinking Population Percentages   203
Economic Costs of Alcohol Abuse   207

History of Alcohol in America   208
Drinking Patterns   208
Historical Considerations   208

Defining Alcoholics   212
Cultural Differences   212
Alcohol Abuse and Alcoholism   213
Types of Alcoholics   215

Cultural Influences   216
Culture and Drinking Behavior   216
Culture and Disinhibited Behavior   217
Culture Provides Rules for Drinking Behavior   218
Cultures Provide Ceremonial Meaning for Alcohol Use   218
Culture Provides Models of Alcoholism   218
Cultural Stereotypes of Drinking May Be Misleading   219
Culture Provides Attitudes Regarding Alcohol Consumption   220

College and University Students and Alcohol Use   220
Binge Drinking   221
Gender and Collegiate Alcohol Use   222

Women and Alcohol Consumption Patterns   222
The Role of Alcohol in Domestic Violence   224
Alcohol and Sex   225

Alcohol and the Family: Destructive Support and Organizations for Victims of Alcoholics   225
Codependency and Enabling   225
Children of Alcoholics (COAs) and Adult Children of Alcoholics (ACOAs)   226

Treatment of Alcoholism   226
Getting Through Withdrawal   227
Helping the Alcoholic Family Recover   227

CHAPTER 10

Narcotics (Opioids)   236

Introduction   238

What Are Narcotics?   238

The History of Narcotics   238
Opium in China   238
American Opium Use   240

Pharmacological Effects   241
Narcotic Analgesics   241
Other Therapeutic Uses   242
Mechanisms of Action   243
Side Effects   243

Abuse, Tolerance, Dependence, and Withdrawal   244
Heroin Abuse   244
Treatment of Heroin and Other Narcotic
    Dependence   251

Other Narcotics   253
Morphine   253
Methadone   254
Fentanyls   255
Hydromorphone   255
Meperidine   255
Codeine   256
Pentazocine   256
Propoxyphene   256

Narcotic-Related Drugs   256
Dextromethorphan   257
Clonidine   257
Naloxone   257

CHAPTER 11

Stimulants   262

Introduction   264

Major Stimulants   264
Amphetamines   264
Cocaine   274
Current Attitudes and Patterns of Abuse   278

Minor Stimulants   287
Caffeinelike Drugs (Xanthines)   287
OTC Sympathomimetics   292
Herbal Stimulants   292

CHAPTER 12

Tobacco   300

Introduction   302

Tobacco Use: Scope of the Problem   302
Current Tobacco Use in the United States   302
The History of Tobacco Use   303
Popularity in the Western World   304
History of Tobacco Use in America   304

Phamacology of Nicotine   308
Nicotine Administration   308
Effects on the Central Nervous System   314
Other Effects of Nicotine   314
Clove Cigarettes   315

Cigarette Smoking: A Costly Addiction   315
Mortality Rates   315
Chronic Illnesses   316
Effects Without Smoking   317
Effects on the Fetus   318
Tobacco Use Without Smoking   318
Environmental Tobacco Smoke   320

Who Smokes?   323
Reasons for Smoking   323

Relapse or Readdiction   326

The Motivation Not to Smoke   326
Alternative Activities for Successfully Quitting   326
Smoking Cessation Aids   328

Social Issues: Looking to the Future   329
Tobacco as a Gateway Drug   329
Smoking Prohibition versus Smokers' Rights   330

CHAPTER 13

Hallucinogens (Psychedelics)   334

Introduction   336

The History of Hallucinogen Use   336
The Native American Church   337
Timothy Leary and the League of
    Spiritual Discovery   337

Hallucinogen Use Today   338

The Nature of Hallucinogens   338
Sensory and Psychological Effects   338
Mechanisms of Action   341

Types of Hallucinogenic Agents 341
Traditional Hallucinogens: LSD Types 341
Phenylethylamine Hallucinogens 350
Anticholinergic Hallucinogens 353
Other Hallucinogens 354

CHAPTER 14

Marijuana   362

Introduction 364

History and Trends in Marijuana Use 365

Current Use of Marijuana 368

Marijuana Use and Youth 369
Trends in Use 369
Perceived Risk 369
Disapproval 369
Availability 371

Marijuana: Is It the Assassin of Youth? 371
Peer Influences 371

The Role of Marijuana as a Gateway Drug 372

Misperceptions of Marijuana Use 372

Characteristics of Cannabis 373

The Behavioral Effects of Marijuana Use 375
The "High" 375
Subjective Euphoric Effects 376
Driving Performance 377
Critical Thinking Skills 378
The Amotivational Syndrome 379

**Therapeutic Uses and the Controversy
over Medical Marijuana Use 381**

The Physiological Effects of Marijuana Use 384
Effects on the Central Nervous System 384
Effects on the Respiratory System 385
Effects on the Cardiovascular System 385
Effects on Sexual Performance and
    Reproduction 386
Tolerance and Dependence 387
Chronic Use 387

CHAPTER 15

Inhalants   394

Introduction 396

History of Inhalants 396

Types of Inhalants 398
Volatile Substances 398
Anesthetics 400
Nitrites 401

Current Patterns and Signs of Abuse 401
Adolescent and Teenage Usage 401
Gender, Race, Socioeconomics, and Abuse 402
Signs of Inhalant Abuse 403

Dangers of Inhalant Use 403

Treatment of Abuse 404

CHAPTER 16

Over-the-Counter (OTC),
Prescription, and Herbal Drugs 406

Introduction 408

OTC Drugs 408
Abuse of OTC Drugs 408
Federal Regulation of OTC Drugs 410
OTC Drugs and Self-Care 410
Types of OTC Drugs 412
OTC Herbal (Natural) Products 422

Prescription Drugs 425
Prescription Drug Abuse 425
Proper Doctor-Patient Communication 426
Drug Selection: Generic Versus Proprietary 427
Common Categories of Prescription Drugs 428

Common Principles of Drug Use 435

CHAPTER 17

Drug Use Within Major
Subcultures   440

Introduction 442

Athletes and Drug Abuse 443
Drugs Used by Athletes 444
Prevention and Treatment 451

Drug Use Among Women 452
Women More Concerned About
    Drug Use Than Men 452
Patterns of Drug Use: Comparing
    Females with Males 452
Female Roles and Drug Addiction 454

Women's Response to Drugs 455
Treatment of Drug Dependency in Women 458

Drug Use in Adolescent Subcultures 459
Why Adolescents Use Drugs 460
Patterns of Drug Use in Adolescents 461
Adolescent versus Adult Drug Abuse 462
Consequences and Coincidental Problems 462
Prevention, Intervention, and Treatment
of Adolescent Drug Problems 468
Summary of Adolescent Drug Abuse 470

Drug Use in College Student Subcultures 470

Reasons for College Students' Drug Use 473
Additional Noteworthy Findings Regarding Drug
Use by College Students 473

HIV and AIDS: The Disease 475
Nature of HIV Infection and Related
Symptoms 475
Diagnosis and Treatment 476
Who Is at Risk for AIDS? 477
AIDS and Drugs of Abuse 480
Adolescents and AIDS 481
What to Do about HIV and AIDS 481

**The Entertainment Industry
and Drug Use 482**
More Recent Promoter of Drug Use:
The Internet 484

CHAPTER 18

Drug Use/Abuse Prevention 492

Introduction 494

Drug Prevention Programs 495

Considering the Audience and Approach 496
An Example of Drug Prevention at
Central High in Elmtown 498

**Comprehensive Prevention Programs
for Drug Use and Abuse 500**
Community-based Drug Prevention 500
School-based Drug Prevention 501
Family-based Prevention Programs 504

**Drug Prevention Programs in Higher
Education 505**
Overview and Critique of Existing
Prevention Programs 505

**Examples of Several Current Large-scale
Drug Prevention Programs 506**
BACCUS and GAMMA Peer
Education Network 506
Fund for the Improvement of Post-secondary
Education Drug Prevention Programs 507
D.A.R.E. (Drug Abuse Resistance Education) 508
Drug Courts 509

**Problems with Assessing Successes
of Drug Prevention Programs 511**

Other Alternatives to Drug Use 511
Meditation 512
The Natural Mind Approach 512

Appendices   **519**

Appendix A
**Federal Agencies with Drug
Abuse Missions 519**

Appendix B
**Some National Organizations in
the Addictions 521**

Appendix C
Drug Use and Abuse 522

Index 529

Preface

This heavily revised edition of *Drugs and Society* is intended to convey to students the impact of drug use and/or abuse on the lives of ordinary people. The authors have combined their expertise in the fields of drug abuse, pharmacology, and sociology with their extensive experiences in research, teaching, drug policy-making, and drug policy implementation to improve this edition.

To make the seventh edition of *Drugs and Society* an exceptional text on drug-related problems, this book is written at a personal level and directly addresses college students by incorporating personal drug use and abuse experiences and perspectives throughout the chapters. These significant improvements make *Drugs and Society* truly unique. The approach was implemented in response to suggestions from readers, students, and instructors to further stimulate students' comprehension and assimilation of this information.

Drugs and Society was written to assist university students from a wide range of disciplines to gain a realistic perspective of drug-related problems in our society. Students in nursing, physical education and other health sciences, psychology, social work, and sociology will find that our text provides useful current information and perspectives to help them understand:

- why and how drug use and abuse occurs;

- the results of drug use and abuse;

- how to prevent drug use and abuse;

- how drugs can be used effectively for therapeutic purposes.

To achieve this goal, we have presented the most current and authoritative views on drug abuse in an objective and easily understood manner. To help students appreciate the multifaceted nature of drug-related problems, this edition exposes the issues from pharmacological, psychological, and sociological perspectives. Besides including the most current information concerning drug use and abuse topics, each chapter also includes helpful learning aids for students. These include:

- **Holding the Line:** Vignettes intended to help the readers assess governmental efforts to deal with drug-related problems.

- **Case in Point:** Examples of relevant clinical issues that arise from the use of each major group of drugs discussed.

- **Here and Now:** Current events that illustrate the personal and social consequences of drug abuse.

- **Highlighted definitions:** Definitions of new terminology are conveniently located adjacent to their discussion in the text.

- **Learning objectives:** Goals for learning listed at the beginning of each chapter to help students identify the principal concepts being taught.

- **Summary statements:** Concise summaries found at the end of each chapter that correlate with the learning objectives.

- **Chapter questions:** Provocative questions at the end of each chapter designed to encourage students to discuss, ponder, and critically analyze their own feelings and biases about the information presented in the book.

- **Concise and well-organized tables and figures:** Updated features found throughout the book present the latest information to students in an easily understood format.

- **New color photographs and drawings:** These additions graphically illustrate important concepts and facilitate comprehension as well as retention of information.

Because of these new and updated features, we believe that this edition of *Drugs and Society* is much more "user friendly" than the previous editions and will encourage student motivation and learning.

The new topical coverage in the seventh edition of *Drugs and Society* includes:

- extensive, updated material and references with many citations from studies published between 1994 and 2000;

- updated information on Ecstasy and tobacco legislation;

- expanded coverage of natural products and herbal medicines; and

- current information on "club drugs," including GHB.

The material in the text encompasses biomedical, sociological, and social-psychological views. Chapter 1 introduces an overview: the current dimensions of drug use (statistics and trends) and the most commonly abused drugs at the turn of the century. Chapter 2 comprehensively explains drug use and abuse from multidisciplined theoretical standpoints. The latest biological, psychological, social-psychological, and sociological perspectives are explained. Chapter 3 discusses how the law deals with drug use and abuse of both licit (alcohol, OTC, and prescription) and illicit (marijuana, hallucinogens, and cocaine) drugs. Chapter 4 focuses on addictive behavior and treating drug dependence, because the addicting properties of most, if not all, substances of abuse are due to the effects of drugs on the reward centers of the brain. Chapter 5 helps the student understand the basic biochemical operations of the nervous and endocrine systems and explains how psychoactive drugs and anabolic steroids alter such functions. Chapter 6 instructs students about the factors that determine how drugs affect the body. This chapter details the physiological and psychological variables that determine how and why people respond to drugs used for therapeutic and recreational purposes.

Chapters 7 through 15 deal with specific drug groups that are commonly abused in this country. Those drugs that depress brain activity are discussed in Chapters 7 (sedative/hypnotic agents), 8 and 9 (alcohol), and 10 (opioid narcotics). The drugs that stimulate brain activity are covered in Chapters 11 (amphetamines, cocaine, and caffeine) and 12 (tobacco and nicotine). The last main category of substances of abuse is hallucinogens. Such drugs alter the senses and create hallucinatory and/or distorted experiences. These substances are discussed in Chapters 13 (hallucinogens such as LSD, mescaline, Ecstasy, and PCP) and 14 (marijuana). Chapter 15 discusses inhalants, substances

that are growing in popularity with youth. Although most drugs that are abused cause more than one effect (for example, cocaine can be a stimulant and have some hallucinatory properties), the classification we have chosen for this text is frequently used by experts and pharmacologists in the drug abuse field and is based on the most likely drug effect. All of the chapters in this section are similarly organized. They discuss:

- the historical origins and evolution of the agents so students can better understand society's attitudes toward, and regulation of, these drugs;

- previous and current clinical uses of these drugs to help students appreciate distinctions between therapeutic use and abuse;

- patterns of abuse and distinctive features that contribute to each drug's abuse potential;

- nonmedicinal and medicinal therapies for drug-related dependence, withdrawal, and abstinence.

Chapter 16 explores the topic of drugs and therapy. As with illicit drugs, nonprescription and prescription drugs can be misused if not understood. This chapter helps the student to appreciate the uses and benefits of proper drug use as well as appreciate that licit (legalized) drugs can also be problematic.

Chapter 17 explores drug use in five major subcultures: sport/athletic, women, adolescent, college student, HIV-positive, and entertainment. Included in this chapter is a discussion of a new media "electronic" drug subculture that has recently arisen.

Chapter 18 of *Drugs and Society* acquaints students with the treatment, rehabilitation, and prevention of the major drugs of abuse. This final chapter describes the principal sociological, psychological, and pharmacological strategies used to treat and prevent substance abuse and details their advantages and disadvantages. This chapter helps students to better understand why drug abuse occurs, how society currently deals with this problem on an individual and group basis, and the challenges in rehabilitating drug-dependent people.

The Appendix in this seventh edition includes an explanation of federal agencies with drug abuse missions as well as a detailed description of schedules for drugs of abuse and the penalties for their illicit manufacturing, selling, or administration.

Instructor's Aids

The ancillary package for the seventh edition includes the most contemporary technology. For instructors who adopt the seventh edition, an Instructor's ToolKit CD-ROM is available. Designed for classroom use, this CD contains lecture outlines in PowerPoint format, a computerized TestBank, and an instructor's manual. Other instructor resources such as web exercises, a transition guide, and lecture outlines can be found on Drugs and Society Online (http://drugsandsociety.jbpub.com). Interactive summaries, animated flashcards, and an online glossary are also available for students. For distance learning options or additional information, call your Jones and Bartlett Publishers Representative.

About the Authors

Dr. Glen R. Hanson, a Professor in the Department of Pharmacology and Toxicology at the University of Utah, has researched the neurobiology of drug abuse for almost 20 years and authored many scientific papers and book chapters on the subject. Dr. Hanson has lectured on drug abuse topics throughout the country and currently serves as the Director of the Division of Neuroscience and Behavioral Research at the National Institute on Drug Abuse (NIDA). NIDA is the world's premier science organization dealing with drug abuse issues and funds 85 percent of the drug abuse–related research in the world.

Dr. Peter J. Venturelli has been the coauthor of this text since the second edition of *Drugs and Society* in 1988. In addition to revising this text every three years, Dr. Venturelli's experiences and qualifications in academia and professional life include: publishing research in drug and ethnic anthologies, other drug texts, and scholarly journals; authoring more than 36 conference papers at national professional sociological meetings; serving in elected and administrative positions in professional drug research associations; recipient of several research grants involving drug use and ethnicity; authoring the latest drug research in sociological encyclopedias; and full-time teaching of undergraduate and graduate students for the past 20 years.

Dr. Annette E. Fleckenstein, a new author to *Drugs and Society,* is an Associate Professor in the Department of Pharmacology and Toxicology at the University of Utah. Dr. Fleckenstein is a scientist and lecturer widely recognized for her expertise in the neurochemistry of drug abuse. Her fresh, new perspectives greatly add to the value of the seventh edition of *Drugs and Society.*

Acknowledgments

The many improvements that have made this the best edition yet of the *Drugs and Society* series could not have occurred without the hard work and dedication of numerous people.

We are indebted to the many reviewers who evaluated the manuscript at different stages of development. Much of the manuscript was reviewed and greatly improved by comments from:

Scott Alpert
University of Maryland

Karamarie Fecho
University of North Carolina – Chapel Hill

Myrna Hewitt
University of Massachusetts – Amherst

Keith King
University of Cincinnati

Robin Lewis
Allan Hancock College

Susan Cross Lipnickey
Miami University

Michael Maina
Valdosta University

Jennifer McLean
Corning Community College

James Pahz
Central Michigan University

Ray Tricker
Oregon State University

The authors would like to express, once again, their gratitude for the comments and suggestions of users and reviewers of previous editions of *Drugs and Society.*

Dr. Fleckenstein acknowledges the support of her family in her participation in the preparation of this revised text.

At Valparaiso University, Professor Venturelli is first and foremost deeply grateful to Nancy Young and her unending motivation and persistence in continuously searching the web and producing literally hundreds of text pages for each of Venturelli's chapters detailing the latest information from these web sites. Additionally, her proofreading and editing work during the final stages of this manuscript

were as remarkable. Also gratefully acknowledged are the countless other students and working people who were interviewed for hours on end regarding their observations, knowledge, personal use, and experiences with drugs. Finally, noteworthy appreciation also goes to Valparaiso University's Moellering Library reference specialists Patricia Hogan-Vidal, and additional assistance from Ruth Mannel. Both of these patient women spent many hours searching for incomplete references when Dr. Venturelli became weary of reaching chapter deadlines involving several dozen out of hundreds of bibliographic citations.

At our respective institutions, the authors would like to thank a multitude of people too numerous to list individually but who have given us invaluable assistance.

Dr. Hanson is particularly indebted to his wife, Margaret, for her loving encouragement. Without her patience and support this endeavor would not have been possible.

Drugs and Society

Introduction to Drugs and Society

Did You Know?

- The popular use of legal drugs, particularly alcohol and tobacco, has caused far more deaths, sickness, violent crimes, economic loss, and other social problems than the use of all illegal drugs combined.

- The effect a drug has depends on multiple factors: (1) the ingredients of the drug and its effect on the body, (2) traditional use of the drug, (3) individual motivation, and (4) social and physical surroundings in which the drug is taken.

- Attempts to regulate drug use were made as long ago as 2240 B.C.

- Ancient literature is filled with references regarding the use of mushrooms, *datura*, hemp, marijuana, opium, poppies, and so on.

- In the past, the penalty for cigarette smoking was having the nose cut off in Russia, lips sliced off in Hindustan (India), and hand chopped off in China (Thio 1983; Thio 1995).

- Today, drug abuse is a more acute problem and more widespread than in any previous era.

- Designer drugs are instantly created from existing illicit-type drugs both for profit and to circumvent the laws against drugs.

- Drug use—both licit and illicit drugs—is an "equal opportunity affliction." This means that drug consumption is found across all income levels, social classes, genders, races, ethnicities, lifestyles, and age groups.

- Between $94 and $102 billion in sales per year of prescription drugs has been reported in the United States.

- In 1998, approximately 36% of the U.S. population aged 12 and older reported using illicit drugs at some point in their lives.

- There is a tendency to eventually become addicted with repeated use of most psychoactive drugs.

- Eighty-two percent of local jail and state prison inmates self-reported that they used drugs at some point in their lives.

- Approximately 70% to 75% of drug users in the United States are employed full time.

- Health and wellness can only be achieved when the mind, body, and spirit are free from the unnecessary use and abuse of nonprescribed psychoactive substances.

Chapter 1

Learning Objectives

**On completing this chapter
you will be able to:**

▶ Explain how drug use is affected by pharmacological, cultural, social, and contextual factors.

▶ Recognize the key terms for initially understanding drug use.

▶ Explain when drugs were first used and under what circumstances.

▶ Indicate how widespread drug use is and who the potential drug abusers are.

▶ List four reasons why drugs are used.

▶ Rank in descending order, from most common to least, the most commonly used licit and illicit drugs.

▶ Name three types of drug users, and explain how they differ.

▶ Describe how the mass media promotes drug use.

▶ Explain when drug use leads to abuse.

▶ List and explain the phases of drug addiction.

▶ List the major findings regarding drugs and crime.

▶ Define employee assistance programs and explain their role in resolving productivity problems.

▶ Explain the holistic self-awareness approach.

Introduction

E ach year the world undergoes a transformation—a form of technological evolution.
Technology drives social change more than
ever. The way we interact and conduct our business
constantly changes. Your great grandparents wrote
letters on manual typewriters. Your grandparents
wrote letters on electric typewriters. Your parents
started writing letters on electric typewriters then
changed to computers. You may one day write letters
by talking into a microphone attached to a computer then pressing a button, sending what you said
by e-mail. Soon you will also be able to have a live
visual conversation over your cell phone with a
friend living thousands of miles away.

This example illustrates how the way we do
things is in a continuous state of flux. Life is changing so rapidly that constant pressure is exerted to
keep pace and remain current with rapidly changing technological advancements. To cope with such
pressures to change, or to delay or avoid these
changes, many people turn to using and often abusing drugs. Despite our knowledge about the dangers of drug use and abuse, the many new laws
prohibiting drug manufacture and consumption
and the stiff penalties for violating drug laws, many
more people today than in the past use legal and
illegal types of drugs without any medical advice or
approved necessity.

Abuse and addiction to any type of drug can
happen to anyone. The use of drugs before the onset
of potential addiction is easily as seductive and
nondiscriminating as its users. This attraction can be
readily explained; drugs alter body chemistry by
interfering with its proper functioning and by altering the reception and transmission of reality. Many
argue that our "reality" would become perilous and
unpredictable if people were legally free to dabble in
their drugs of choice. Many do not realize, however,
that if abused, even legal drugs can alter our perception of reality, become severely addicting, and destroy
our social relationships with loved ones.

Before delving into more detailed information,
which is presented in other chapters, we begin by
informing and answering some key questions
related to drug use:

1. What constitutes a drug?
2. What are the most commonly abused drugs?
3. What are designer drugs?
4. How widespread is drug abuse?
5. What is the extent and frequency of drug use in our society?
6. What are the current statistics on and trends in drug use?
7. What types of drug users exist?
8. How do the media influence drug use?
9. What attracts people to drug use?
10. When does drug use lead to drug dependence?
11. When does drug addiction occur?
12. What are the costs of drug addiction to society?
13. What can be gained by learning about the complexity of drug use and abuse?

The Dimensions of Drug Use

To determine the perception of drug use in our
country, we asked several interviewees, "What do
you think of drug use in our society?" The following are three of the more typical responses:

> I think it is a big problem, especially when there
> are so many people doing drugs. Just think how
> many people are on drugs right now, this very
> minute, throughout the United States. How
> many drug users are in the workplace, driving
> trucks, making investment transactions, and even
> performing surgery? It's downright horrifying
> when you think about it. How many kids are not
> learning much, if anything, in classrooms across
> the nation because they are flying high while the
> teacher is talking? *(From Venturelli's research files,
> 28-year-old female newspaper reporter in a Mid-
> western city, October 8, 1996.)*

A second response to the same question:

> Every effort by the government to stop illegal
> drug use has failed miserably. Even legal drug
> use, like alcohol and cigarettes, continues despite
> what the governmental public health media say.
> People should be left alone about their drug use
> unless such drug use is potentially harmful to
> others. I know that if I ever quit using both legal

and illegal drugs it will be my own decision, not because the law can punish me. Yes, drug use is a problem for the addicted, but all throughout our history, drug use has been there. So why worry about it now? *(From Venturelli's research files, 24-year-old male graduate student, October 3, 1996.)*

A third response to the same question:

My drug use? Whose business is it anyway? As long as I don't affect your life when I do drugs, what business is it but my own? We come into the world alone and leave this world alone. I don't bother anyone else about whether or not so and so uses drugs, unless of course, their drug use puts me in jeopardy (like a bus driver or pilot high on drugs). On certain days when things are slow, I even get a little high on cocaine while trading stocks. These are the same clients that I have had for years and who really trust my advice. Ask my clients whether or not they are happy with my investment advice. I handle accounts with millions of dollars for corporations and even the board of education! Never was my judgment impaired or adversely affected because of too much coke. In fact, I know that I work even better under a little buzz. Now, I know this stuff has the potential to become addictive, but I don't let it. I know how to use it and when to lay off for a few weeks. *(From Venturelli's research files, 48-year-old male investment broker working in a major metropolitan city in California, June 2, 2000.)*

These three interviews reflect vastly contrasting views and attitudes about drug use. The first and second interviews show the most contrast, whereas the third interview, from an insider's perspective, shows the strong determination and belief that this man maintains about his drug use. Overall, this individual perceives his drug use as under control. Although much about these viewpoints can be debated, an interesting finding is that such vastly different views about drug use often divide users and non-drug users. Drug users are often considered "insiders" with regard to their drug use, while non-users are "outsiders." These two designations create very different values and attitudes about drug usage. Such great differences of opinion and views about drugs and drug use often result from (1) prior socialization experiences, such as family upbringing and peer group relationships, (2) the amount of exposure to drug use and drug users, and (3) the age of initial exposure to drug use (this is discussed further in Chapter 2).

Keep in mind that in its entirety, this book views the following four principal factors as affecting how a drug user experiences a drug: pharmacological, cultural, social, and contextual.

Pharmacological factors. The ingredients of a particular drug affect the functions of the body and the nervous system and in turn affects social behavior.

Cultural factors. Society's views of drug use, as determined by custom and tradition, affect our initial approach and use of a particular drug.

Social factors. The motivation for taking a particular drug is affected by needs such as diminishing physical pain; curing an illness; providing relaxation; relieving stress or anxiety; trying to escape reality; self-medicating; heightening awareness; wanting to distort and change visual, auditory, or sensory inputs; or strengthening confidence. Included in the category of social factors is the belief that attitudes about drug use develop from the values and attitudes of other drug users, the norms in their communities, subcultures, peer groups, and families, as well as the drug user's personal experiences with using drugs. These are also known as *influencing social factors*.

Contextual factors. Specific contexts define and determine personal dispositions toward drug use, as demonstrated by moods and attitudes about such activity. Specifically, the factors involve the drug-taking social behavior that develops from the physical surroundings where the drug is used. For example, drugs may be taken at fraternity parties, out-of-doors in a secluded area with other drug users, in private homes, secretly at work, or at rock concerts.

KEY TERMS

insiders
people on the inside; those who use drugs

outsiders
people on the outside; those who do not use drugs

Paying attention to the cultural, social, and contextual factors of drug use leads us to explore the sociology and psychology of drug use. Equally as important are the pharmacological factors and consequences that directly focus on how the drugs taken affect the body (primarily the central nervous system [CNS]) and the mind.

Though the common term for substances that affect both mind and body functioning is drug, researchers in the drug field use a more precise term: *psychoactive drugs* or *psychoactive substances*. Why the use of this term? Because it more precisely explains *how* drugs affect the body. The term psychoactive drugs refers to the effect these substances have on the CNS and how they alter consciousness and our perceptions. Because of their effects on the brain, psychoactive drugs can be used to treat physical or mental illness. Since the body can tolerate increasingly larger doses, many psychoactive drugs are used in progressively greater and more uncontrollable amounts to achieve the same level of effect. For many substances, a user is at risk of moving from occasional to more regular use or from moderate use to heavy and chronic use. A chronic user may then risk addiction and withdrawal symptoms whenever the drug is not supplied—that is, made available—to the body.

Generally speaking, any substance that modifies the nervous system and states of consciousness is a drug. Such modification enhances, inhibits, or distorts the functioning of the body, thus also affecting patterns of behavior and social functioning. Psychoactive drugs are classified as either licit (legal) or illicit (illegal). For example, coffee, tea, cocoa, alcohol, tobacco, and over-the-counter (OTC) drugs are licit. When licit drugs are used in moderation, they often are socially acceptable. Marijuana, cocaine, and lysergic acid diethylamide (LSD) are examples of illicit drugs. No amount of these drugs is generally socially acceptable by the majority of society or especially legally allowed.

Researchers have made some interesting findings about legal and illegal drug use:

1. The use of such legal substances as alcohol and tobacco is much more common than is the use of illegal drugs such as marijuana, heroin, and LSD. Other legal drugs, such as depressants and stimulants, although less popular than alcohol and tobacco, are still more widely used than heroin and LSD.

2. The popular use of licit drugs, particularly alcohol and tobacco, has caused far more deaths, sickness, violent crimes, economic loss, and other social problems than the combined use of all illicit drugs.

3. Societal reaction to various drugs changes with time and place. Opium today is an illegal drug and widely condemned as a *pan-pathogen* (a cause of all ills), but in the 18th and 19th centuries, it was a legal drug and was popularly praised as a *panacea* (a cure of all ills). Alcohol use was widespread in the United States in the early 1800s, became illegal during the 1920s, and then was legalized a second time and has been widely used since the 1930s. Cigarette smoking is legal in all countries today. In the 17th century, it was illegal in most countries, and in several countries, smokers were harshly punished. For example, in Russia, smokers could lose their noses; in Hindustan (India), they could lose their lips; and in China, they could lose their heads (Thio 1983; Thio 1995). Today, new emphasis in the United States on the public health hazards from cigarettes again is leading some people to consider new measures to restrict or even outlaw tobacco smoking.

Table 1.1 introduces some of the terminology that you will encounter throughout this text. It is important that you understand how the definitions vary.

KEY TERMS

drug
any substance that modifies body functions, such as the nervous system

psychoactive drugs
substances that affect the central nervous system and alter consciousness and/or perceptions

licit drugs
legal drugs, such as coffee, alcohol, and tobacco

illicit drugs
illegal drugs, such as marijuana, cocaine, and LSD (other commonly used terminology for drug use is highlighted in Table 1.1)

(OTC)
over-the-counter drugs

■ MOST COMMONLY ABUSED DRUGS

In looking at drug use, this book examines the following: (1) OTC drugs (the drugs most subject to abuse), (2) prescription drugs, (3) other drugs and compounds not taken for a medical need or necessity but for pleasure or relief from boredom, stress, or anxiety, and (4) some of the most important information that results from drug use (for example, theories of why drugs are used, legality of drugs, addiction, bodily effects of drug use, lifestyles of drug users, and drug abuse treatment and prevention).

To begin, we will now briefly examine the major drugs of use and often abuse. The drugs

TABLE 1.1 Commonly Used Terms

TERM	DESCRIPTION
Gateway drugs	The word *gateway* suggests a path leading to something else. Alcohol, tobacco, and marijuana are the most commonly used drugs. Almost all abusers of more powerfully addictive drugs have first experimented with these three substances.
Medicines	Generally, they are drugs prescribed by a physician to prevent or treat the symptoms of an illness.
Prescription medicines	These are drugs that are prescribed by a physician. Common examples include antibiotics, antidepressants, and drugs prescribed to relieve pain, induce stimulation, or induce relaxation. These drugs are taken under a physician's recommendation because they are more potent than OTC drugs. The amount spent on prescription medicines is approximately $94 billion a year. Approximately 2.5 billion prescriptions are dispensed by physicians to their patients (Goode 1999, 141).
Over-the-counter (OTC)	These drugs are sold without a prescription. Recently, OTC drugs accounted for $15 billion a year in retail sales (Goode 1999). OTC drugs can be purchased at will, without first seeking medical advice. Examples include aspirin, laxatives, diet pills, cough suppressants, and sore throat medicines. Often, these drugs are misused or abused (overused).
Drug misuse	The unintentional or inappropriate use of prescribed or OTC drugs. Misuse includes, but is not limited to, (1) taking more drugs than prescribed; (2) using OTC or psychoactive drugs in excess without medical supervision; (3) mixing drugs with alcohol or other drugs, often to accentuate euphoric effects; (4) using old medicines to self-treat new symptoms of an illness or ailment; 5) discontinuing certain prescribed drugs at will or against a physician's recommendation; and (6) administering prescription drugs to family members or friends without medical consultation and supervision.
Drug abuse	Also known as *chemical* or *substance abuse*. The willful misuse of either licit or illicit drugs for recreation, perceived necessity, or convenience. Drug abuse differs from drug use in that *drug use* is taking or using drugs, whereas *drug abuse* is a more intense and often willful misuse of drugs, often to the point of addiction.
Drug addiction	Drug addiction involves noncasual or nonrecreational drug use. A frequent symptom includes intense psychological preoccupation with obtaining and consuming drugs. Most often psychological and in some cases, depending on the drug, physiological symptoms of withdrawal are often manifested when the craving for the drug is not satisfied. Today, more emphasis is placed on defining the psychological craving (mental attachment) to the drug than on the more physiological-based withdrawal symptoms of addiction. (See Chapter 4 for more detailed information regarding addiction and the addiction process.)

Source: Goode, E. *Drugs in American Society*, 5th ed. Boston, MA: McGraw-Hill College, 1999.

examined next are stimulants, hallucinogens and other similar compounds, depressants, alcohol, nicotine, cannabis (marijuana and hashish), anabolic steroids, inhalants/ organic solvents, narcotics/opiates, and designer drugs. A brief overview is provided here, and these same drugs will be discussed in much more detail in separate chapters throughout this book.

Stimulants

Though some of these drugs can be considered to be gateway drugs (see definition in Table 1.1), these substances act on the CNS by increasing alertness, excitation, euphoria, pulse rate, and blood pressure. Insomnia and loss of appetite are common outcomes. The user initially experiences pleasant effects, such as a sense of increased energy and a state of euphoria, or "high." In addition, users feel restless and talkative and have trouble sleeping. High doses used over the long-term can produce personality changes. Some of the psychological risks include violent, erratic, or paranoid behavior. Other effects can include confusion, anxiety and depression, and loss of interest in sex or food. Major stimulants include amphetamines, cocaine and crack, methamphetamine, and methylphenidate. Minor stimulants include caffeine, tea, chocolate, and nicotine.

Hallucinogens and Other Similar Compounds

Either man-made or grown naturally, these drugs produce very intense alteration of perceptions, thoughts, and feelings. They most certainly influ-ence the complex inner working of the human mind, causing users to refer to these drugs as *psychedelics* (because they cause hallucinations or distortion of reality and thinking). For example, while under their influence, these drugs can affect the sense of taste, smell, hearing, and vision. Tolerance to hallucinogens builds very rapidly, which means that increasing amounts of this drug are needed for similar effects. Hallucinogens include LSD, mescaline, phencyclidine (PCP), and psilocybin or "magic mushrooms," more potent varieties of marijuana, hashish, and tetrahydrocannabinol (THC).

Depressants

These drugs depress the CNS. If taken in a high enough quantity, they produce insensibility or stupor. Also taken for some of the same reasons as hallucinogens, such as to relieve boredom, stress, and anxiety. The effects of both opioids and morphine derivatives appeal to many people who are struggling with emotional problems and looking for physical and emotional relief and, in some cases, to induce sleep. Depressants include alcohol (ethanol), barbiturates, benzodiazepines (such as diazepam [Valium]), and methaqualone (Quaalude).

Alcohol

Known as a gateway drug , ethanol is a colorless, volatile, and pungent liquid resulting from fermented grains, berries, and other fruits. Alcohol is a depressant that mainly affects the CNS. Excessive amounts of alcohol often cause a progression in the loss of inhibitions, flushing and dizziness, loss of coordination, impaired motor skills, blurred vision, slurred speech, sudden mood swings, vomiting, irregular pulse, and memory impairment. Chronic heavy use may lead to high blood pressure, *arrhythmia* (irregular heart beat), and *cirrhosis* (severe liver deterioration).

Nicotine

Nicotine is considered a gateway drug. It is an addictive, colorless, highly volatile liquid alkaloid found in all tobacco products such as cigarettes, chewing tobacco, pipe tobacco, and cigars. Because nicotine is highly addictive and tobacco use is still socially acceptable under certain circumstances, smokers often start young and have a very difficult

---

KEY TERMS

gateway drugs
alcohol, tobacco, and marijuana—types of drugs that some believe lead to using other drugs such as hallucinogens and cocaine-type drugs

ethanol
pharmacological term for alcohol

designer drugs
new categories of hybrid drugs

structural analogs
drugs resulting from altered chemical structures of current illicit-type(s) drugs.

time quitting. Long-term use of tobacco products can lead to several different chronic respiratory ailments and cancers.

Cannabis, or Marijuana and Hashish

This drug is the most widely used illicit drug in the United States. Marijuana consists of the dried and crushed leaves, flowers, stems, and seeds of the *cannabis sativa* plant, which grows readily in many parts of the world. THC (Delta 9-tetrahydro-cannabinol) is the primary psychoactive, mind-altering ingredient in marijuana that produces euphoria (or a high). Plant parts are usually dried, crushed, and smoked much like tobacco products. Other ways of ingesting marijuana include crushing the leaves into cookie or brownie batter and baking the batter. Hashish is another cannabis derivative, which contains the purest form of resin and the highest amount of THC.

Anabolic Steroids

Steroids are a synthetic form of the male hormone, testosterone. They are often used to increase muscle size and strength. Medically, steroids are used to increase body tissue or to treat allergies. Steroids are available either in liquid or pill form. Athletes have a tendency to use and abuse these drugs because dramatic results can occur with regard to body mass and muscle tissue. Some side effects include heart disease, liver cancer, high blood pressure, septic shock, impotence, genital atrophy, manic episodes, depression, violence, and mood swings.

Inhalants/Organic Solvents

Inhalants and organic solvents are also often considered gateway drugs and are very attractive and popular to preteens and younger teenagers. Products used include gasoline, airplane glue, and paint thinner. When inhaled, the vapors from these solvents can produce euphoric effects. Organic solvents can also refer to certain foods, herbs, and vitamins, such as "herbal ecstasy." (Appendix C lists the most commonly abused drugs in society, outlines their street names, medical uses, and routes of administration, Drug Enforcement Administration (DEA) schedules, and duration of detection in the body.)

Inhalants. These volatile chemicals, which include many common household substances, are often the most dangerous drugs, per dose, that a person can take. In addition, inhalants are most often used by young preteens and younger teenagers.

Narcotics/Opiates

These drugs also depress the CNS and if taken in a high enough quantity, they produce insensibility or stupor. Narcotics include opium, morphine, codeine, and meperidine (Demerol).

Designer Drugs

In addition to the most commonly abused illicit drug categories just described, innovations in technology have produced new categories known as designer drugs . These relatively new types are created as structural analogs of substances already scheduled as forbidden under the Controlled Substances Act (CSA). The term structural analogs refers to drugs that result from altered chemical structures of already existing illicit drugs. Generally, underground chemists, whose goal is to make a profit by creating compounds that mimic the psychoactive effects of controlled substances, prepare these drugs. The number of designer drugs that are created and sold illegally is very large. Anyone with knowledge of college-level chemistry can alter the chemical ingredients and produce new designer drugs, although it may be nearly impossible to predict their properties or effects except by trial and error. Currently, three major types of synthetic analog drugs are available through the illicit drug mar-

Designer pills made from the illicit drug ecstasy. This drug has some stimulant properties like amphetamines as well as hallucinogenic properties like LSD.

ket: analogs of PCP; analogs of fentanyl and meperidine (both synthetic narcotic analgesics) such as Demerol; MPPP (called *MPTP*); PEPAP; and analogs of amphetamine and methamphetamine (which have stimulant and hallucinogenic properties) such as MDMA , known as "Ecstasy" or "Adam," which is widely used on college campuses as a euphoriant and, to some extent, by clinicians as an adjunct to psychotherapy. The arrival of these high-technology psychoactive substances is a sign of the new high levels of risk and unpredictable outcomes faced by drug users today. As the pace of such substance use risks increases, the need for a broader, more well informed view of drug use becomes even more important than in the past.

An Overview of Drugs in Society

Many people think that problems with drugs are unique to this era. In reality, however, drug use and abuse have always been part of nearly all human societies. For example, the Grecian oracles of Del-

phi used drugs, Homer's Cup of Helen induced sleep and provided freedom from care, and the mandrake root mentioned in the first book of the Bible, Genesis, produced a hallucinogenic effect. In Genesis 30:14–16, the mandrake is mentioned in association with bartering for lovemaking:

> In the time of wheat harvest Reuben went out, found some mandrakes in the open country, and brought them to his mother Leah. Then Rachel asked Leah for some of her son's mandrakes, but Leah said, "Is it so small a thing to have taken away my husband, that you should take my son's mandrakes as well?" But Rachel said, "Very well, let him sleep with you tonight in exchange for your son's mandrakes." So when Jacob came in from the country in the evening, Leah went out to meet him and said, "You are to sleep with me tonight; I have hired you with my son's mandrakes." That night he slept with her.

Ancient literature is filled with references to the use of mushrooms, datura, hemp, marijuana, opium poppies, and so on. Under the influence of some of these drugs, many people experienced extreme ecstasy or sheer terror. Some old pictures of demons and devils look very much like those described by modern drug users during so-called bummers, or bad trips. The belief that witches could fly may also have been drug-induced because many natural preparations used in so-called witches' brews induced the sensation of disassociation from the body, as in flying or floating.

As far back as 2240 B.C., attempts were made to regulate drug use. For instance, in that year, problem drinking was addressed in the Code of Hammurabi, where it was described as "a problem of men with too much leisure time and lazy dispositions." Nearly every culture has experienced drug abuse, and as part of its historical record, laws were enacted in order to control the use of certain types of drugs.

■ HOW WIDESPREAD IS DRUG ABUSE?

As mentioned earlier, drug abuse today is more acute and widespread than in any previous age. The evidence for this development is how often large quantities of illicit drugs are seized in the United States as well as throughout the world. Media exposure about illicit drug use is more likely to occur today than in the past. On any given day, you can scan most major national and international newspapers and undoubtedly run across stories about illegal drug manufacture, storage and distribution, use and/or abuse, and convictions.

Drug use is an "equal-opportunity affliction." This means that no one is immune from the use and/or abuse of both licit and illicit drugs. Research shows that drug consumption is found across income, social classes, genders, races, ethnic groups, lifestyles, and age groups. To date, no immunity from drug usage exists. (See "Here and Now," regarding how widespread is the use of drugs, on pages 22–23.)

Many of us, for example, are a little dismayed when we discover that certain individuals we admire—celebrities, politicians, athletes, clergy, law enforcement personnel, physicians, academics, and even the polite man or woman next door—admits to or is identified and apprehended for abusing illicit drugs. We are also taken aback when we hear that cigarettes, alcohol, and marijuana abuse are commonplace in many public and private junior high schools. Furthermore, most of us know of at least one (and many times more than one) close friend or family member who appears to secretly and not so secretly to use drugs.

▪ EXTENT AND FREQUENCY OF DRUG USE IN SOCIETY

Erich Goode (1999), a much-respected sociologist, lists four types of drug use:

1. *Legal instrumental use.* Taking prescribed drugs and OTC drugs to relieve or treat mental or physical symptoms.

2. *Legal recreational use.* Using such licit drugs as tobacco, alcohol, and caffeine to achieve a certain mental or psychic state.

3. *Illegal instrumental use.* Taking drugs without a prescription to accomplish a task or goal, such as taking nonprescription amphetamines to drive through the night or relying excessively on barbiturates to get through the day.

4. *Illegal recreational use.* Taking illicit drugs for fun or pleasure to experience euphoria, such as abusing prescribed methylphenidate (Ritalin) as a substitute for cocaine.

Why has the prevalence of licit and illicit drug use remained consistent since 1988? Why has this trend occurred, when expenditures for fighting the drug war by the federal, state, and local governments have been increasing at the same time? There are several possible answers, none of which, by itself, offers a satisfactory response. One perspective notes that practically all of us use drugs in some form, with what constitutes "drug use" being merely a matter of degree. A second explanation is that more varieties of both licit and illicit drugs are available today. One source estimated that approximately 80% of all currently marketed drugs were either unknown or unavailable 20 years ago (Critser 1996). Another source stated, "The retail sales of OTC drugs (aspirin, Tylenol, NōDōz, and so on) totaled $15 billion in 1995"… [with regard to prescriptions] "… over $90 billion worth of pharmaceutical prescription drugs were sold in 1997; a total of 2.5 billion prescriptions were written in that year" (Goode 1999, p. 141). A third explanation is that "… in the modern age, increased sophistication has brought with it techniques of drug production and distribution that have resulted in a worldwide epidemic of drug use" (Kusinitz 1988, p. 149).

In the 1980s and 1990s, for example, illicit drug cartels proliferated, and varieties of marijuana with ever-increasing potency infiltrated all urban and rural areas as well as throughout the world. Many of these varieties are crossbred with ultrasophisticated techniques and equipment available everywhere.

Finally, even coffee with high caffeine content (mentioned earlier) has become available worldwide. This trend has led to the phenomenal growth of the following: (1) franchise duplication of gourmet coffee bars in the United States (such as Starbucks and Three Brothers Coffee), (2) the phenomenal growth in the sale of espresso coffee makers for home use, and (3) sales of specialized coffee and tea through

---

KEY TERMS

MDMA
a type of illicit drug known as "Ecstasy" or "Adam" having stimulant and hallucinogenic properties

equal-opportunity affliction
drug use, in that it cuts across all members of society regardless of income, social class, and age

e-mail and coffee clubs. Twenty years ago, it was difficult to purchase a cup of espresso or cappuccino in a typical restaurant; today, availability of such types of coffees is commonplace. Even at airports, shopping malls, and inner city coffee shops, it is not unusual to see people lined up waiting to order and purchase their special flavored coffee or tea. This is just one example of how caffeine (often seen as a benign drug) maintains its own impressive history of growth and progression.

Drug Use: Statistics and Trends

An incredible amount of money is spent each year for licit (legal) and illicit (illegal) chemicals that alter consciousness, awareness, or mood. Four classes of these legal chemicals exist:

1. *Social drugs.* Approximately $104 billion for alcohol; $51.9 billion for tobacco products, of which 95% comes from cigarette sales. The other 5% accounts for the $2 billion or so spent on cigars, chewing tobacco, pipe tobacco, roll-your-own tobacco, and snuff tobacco; $5.7 billion is spent on coffee, tea, and cocoa.

2. *Prescription drugs.* There is $251 billion in worldwide sales; between $94 and $102 billion in the United States. The United States is the world's largest pharmaceutical market (Morrow 1999).

3. *Over-the-counter (patent) drugs.* There is $23.5 billion in sales, including cough and cold items, external and internal analgesics, antacids, laxatives, antidiarrhea products, sleep aids, sedatives, and so on.

4. *Others.* The amount spent on miscellaneous drugs such as nutmeg, morning glory seeds, and aerosols cannot be determined.

How much is spent on illicit drugs? The White House Office of National Drug Control Policy conducted a study to determine the amount Americans spent on illicit drugs. They found that between 1988 and 1995, Americans spent $57.3 billion on drugs: $38 billion on cocaine, $9.6 billion on heroin, $7 billion on marijuana, and $2.7 billion on other illegal drugs and on legal drugs that were misused (NIDA 1998).

Further, regarding the extent of drug use, studies carried out by the Social Research Group of George Washington University, the Institute for Research in Social Behavior in Berkeley, California, and others provide detailed, in-depth data showing that drug use is universal. A major purpose of their studies was to determine the level of psychoactive drug use among people aged 18 through 74, excluding those people hospitalized or in the armed forces. Data were collected to identify people using specific categories of drugs (that is, caffeine, sleeping pills, nicotine, alcohol, and other psychoactive drugs). Other studies have shown that people in the 18- to 25-year-old age groups are by far the heaviest users and experimenters in terms of past-month and past-year usage (see Table 1.2).

More than 80% of respondents in the studies reported that they drank coffee during the previous year, and over 50% said that they drank tea. In addition, nearly one-third of the population reported consuming more than five cups of caffeine-containing beverages each day.

In 1995, 395 billion doses of caffeine were consumed in the United States. Other research data support the findings of the Social Research Group of George Washington University. For example, an estimated 60 million Americans aged 12 and older smoked tobacco in 1998, or 28% of the total U.S. population (SAMHSA 1998). Statistics also reveal that, in 1998, 113 million Americans aged 12 and older had used alcohol in the past month (52% of the population) (SAMHSA 1998).

Illicit drug use is also an ongoing problem. For example, in 1998 marijuana remained the most commonly used illicit drug, with approximately 81% of current illicit drug users indicating marijuana or hashish use. Also in 1998, about 72 million individuals, or 33%, reported marijuana use in their lifetime, 19 million (9%) reported use in the past year, and 11 million (5%) reported current use (in the past month) (SAMHSA 1998).

Finally, other reliable estimates report that in 1998, 35.8% of the U.S. population aged 12 and older reported using illicit drugs at some point in their lives. Leading illicit drugs, from highest to lower percentages, were marijuana (33%), cocaine (10.6%), and hallucinogens (9.9%) (see Table 1.3, page 14).

The average household owns about 45 drugs, of which one out of five is a prescription drug, and the other four are OTC drugs. Of the many prescriptions written by physicians, approximately one-fourth modifies moods and behaviors in one way or another. Surveys report that over 50% of adults in the United States have, at some time in their lives, taken a *psychoactive drug* (one that affects mood or consciousness). More than one-third of adults has used or is using depressants or sedatives.

A National Institute on Drug Abuse (NIDA) study and other research indicate drug use trends

TABLE 1.2 Trend Data on the Prevalence of Illicit Drug Use, 1991–1998

	1991[a]	1992[b]	1994[c]	1995[c]	1997[d]	1998[d]
Used in Past Month						
All ages 12+	6.3%	5.5%	6.0%	6.1%	6.4%	6.2%
12–17	6.8%	6.1%	8.2%	10.9%	11.4%	9.9%
18–25	15.4%	13.0%	13.3%	14.2%	14.7%	16.1%
26–34	9.0%	10.1%	8.5%	8.3%	7.4%	7.0%
35+	3.1%	2.2%	3.2%	2.8%	3.6%	3.3%
Used in Past Year						
All ages 12+	12.7%	11.1%	10.8%	10.7%	11.2%	10.6%
12–17	14.8%	11.7%	15.5%	18.0%	18.8%	16.4%
18–25	29.1%	26.4%	24.6%	25.5%	25.3%	27.4%
26–34	18.4%	18.3%	14.8%	14.6%	14.3%	12.7%
35+	6.4%	5.1%	5.7%	5.0%	6.1%	5.5%
Used in Lifetime (Ever Used)						
All ages 12+	37.0%	36.2%	34.4%	34.2%	35.6%	35.8%
12–17	20.1%	16.5%	20.3%	22.2%	23.7%	21.3%
18–25	54.7%	51.7%	46.3%	45.8%	45.4%	48.1%
26–34	61.8%	60.8%	56.1%	54.8%	50.8%	50.6%
35+	27.3%	28.0%	27.7%	27.9%	31.5%	31.8%

Note: This table shows mixed findings. Generally however, although some slight declines and increases have occurred throughout the years, drug use continues to remain stable, with very few dramatic increases or decreases. Note also that throughout the three time periods, the heaviest drug use occurred between 18 and 25 years of age.

Note: These figures include use of marijuana, cocaine, hallucinogens, inhalants (except in 1982), heroin, and nonmedical use of sedatives, tranquilizers, stimulants, and analgesics. Data on inhalant use were not collected in 1982, which may lower overall prevalence figures for that year, especially for 12- to 17-year-olds.

[a]*Source of figures in this column:* National Institute on Drug Abuse, *National Household Survey on Drug Abuse*. Rockville, MD: NIDA, 1992.
[b]*Source of figures in this column:* National Institute on Drug Abuse (NIDA), *National Household Survey on Drug Abuse*. Rockville, MD: NIDA, 1993.
[c]*Source of figures in these two columns:* Substance Abuse and Mental Health Services Administration (SAMHSA), Office of Allied Studies (OAS). *Preliminary Estimates from the 1995 National Household Survey on Drug Abuse*. Rockville, MD: U.S. Department of Health and Human Services, August 1996.
[d]*Source of figures in these two columns:* Substance Abuse and Mental Health Services Administration (SAMHSA). *Summary of Findings from the 1998 National Household Survey on Drug Abuse*. Rockville, MD: Office of Applied Studies (OAS) and SAMHSA, 1999.

based on gender. Men are most likely to use stimulants in their thirties, depressants in their forties and fifties, and sedatives from age 60 on. Women however, are most likely to use stimulants from age 21 through age 39 and depressants more frequently in their thirties. Women's use of sedatives shows a pattern similar to use by men, with the frequency of use increasing with age. Women tend to use pills to cope with problems, whereas men tend to use alcohol for this purpose. In addition, people older than 35 are more likely to take pills, whereas younger people

prefer alcohol. Among those using pills, younger people and men are more likely to use stimulants than older people and women, who take sedatives.

The actual figures for use of all psychoactive drugs are probably 35% higher than reported. This discrepancy exists partly because a large number of people obtain psychoactive drugs on the "black market" and from friends and relatives who have legitimate prescriptions. An estimated 70% of all psychoactive prescription drugs used by people under 30 are obtained without the user having a pre-

TABLE 1.3 **National Household Survey on Drug Abuse, 1998**

Percentage of population and estimated number of alcohol, tobacco, and illicit drug users in the United States.

	LIFETIME*		PAST MONTH	
	Percentage	Number of Users	Percentage	Number of Users
Alcohol	81.3	177,512,000	51.7	112,850,000
Cigarettes	69.7	152,313,000	27.7	60,406,000
Any illicit drug	**35.8**	**78,123,000**	**6.2**	**13,615,000**
Marijuana	33.0	72,070,000	5.0	11,016,000
Smokeless tobacco	17.2	37,667,000	3.1	6,730,000
Cocaine	10.6	23,089,000	0.8	1,750,000
Hallucinogens	9.9	21,607,000	0.7	1,514,000
Nonmedical use of any psychotherapeutic†	9.2	20,193,000	1.1	2,477,000
LSD	7.9	17,223,000	not available	
Inhalants	5.8	12,589,000	0.3	713,000
Analgesics	5.3	11,595,000	0.8	1,709,000
Stimulants	4.4	9,614,000	0.3	633,000
PCP	3.5	7,640,000	not available	
Tranquilizers	3.5	7,726,000	0.3	655,000
Sedatives	2.1	4,640,000	0.1	210,000
Crack	2.0	4,476,000	0.2	437,000

* Lifetime refers to ever used.
† Nonmedical use of any prescription stimulant, sedative, tranquilizer, or analgesic.

Source: National Household Survey on Drug Abuse: Population Estimates 1998. Rockville, MD: U.S. Department of Health and Human Services, Substance Abuse and Mental Health Services Administration (SAMHSA), 1999.

scription. Pharmacists' records show that about $102 billion is spent on psychoactive drug prescriptions (Ananth et al. 2000), with the rate of increase estimated at about 9% each year. Such figures indicate that it may be more difficult to find people who do not use psychoactive drugs than individuals who do.

■ TYPES OF DRUG USERS/ABUSERS

Just as a diverse set of personality traits (for example, introverts, extroverts, type A, obsessive-compulsive, and so on) exists, drug users vary according to their general approach or orientation, frequency of use, and types and amount of the drugs they consume. Some are occasional or moderate users, whereas others display much stronger attachment to drug use. In fact, some display such obsessive-compulsive behavior that they cannot let a morning, afternoon, and evening pass without using drugs. Some researchers have classified such variability in the frequency and extent of usage as fitting into three basic patterns: experimenters, compulsive users, and "floaters" or "chippers" (members of the last category drift between experimentation and compulsive use).

Experimenters begin using drugs largely because of peer pressure and curiosity, and they confine their use to recreational settings. Generally, they more often enjoy peers who also recreationally use drugs. Alcohol, tobacco, marijuana, hallucinogens, and many of the major stimulants comprise most of the drugs they are likely to use. They are usually able to set limits on when these drugs are taken (often socially), and they are more likely to know the difference between light, moderate, and chronic use.

Compulsive users, in contrast, ". . . devote considerable time and energy to getting high, talk incessantly (sometimes exclusively) about drug use, and become connoisseurs of street drugs" (Beschner 1986, p. 7). For compulsive users, recreational fun is impossible without getting high. Other characteristics of these users include the need to escape or postpone personal problems, to avoid stress and anxiety, and to enjoy the sensation of the drug's euphoric effects. Often, they have difficulty assuming personal responsibility and suffer from low self-esteem. Many compulsive users are from dysfunctional families, have persistent problems with the law, and have serious psychological problems underlying their drug-taking behavior. Problems of personal identity,

KEY TERMS

experimenters
type of drug user: experimenters are novel users

compulsive users
type of drug user: compulsive users are often addicted users

floaters (chippers)
type of drug user: floaters or chippers are users who vacillate between the need to seek pleasure and the need to relieve serious psychological problems

sexual orientation, boredom, family discord, childhood sexual and/or mental abuse, academic pressure, and chronic depression all contribute to the inability to cope with issues without drugs (see "Case in Point," Ignoring the Signs of Drug Abuse: A Hard Lesson Learned, on page 16).

Floaters or chippers focus more on using other people's drugs without maintaining as much of a personal supply. Nonetheless, chippers, like experimenters, are generally light to moderate consumers of drugs. Chippers vacillate between the need for pleasure seeking and the desire to relieve moderately serious problems. As a result, they drift between experimental drug-taking peers to chronic drug-using peers. In a sense, these drug users are marginal individuals who do not strongly identify with experimenters or compulsive users. (An example of how the various types of drug users are often adversely affected by peers is discussed in more detail in Chapters 2 and 4.)

■ MASS MEDIA INFLUENCES ON DRUG USE IN EVERYDAY LIFE

Studies continually show that the majority of young drug users comes from homes in which drugs are liberally used (Goode 1999; SAMHSA 1996b). These children frequently witness drug use at home. For instance, parents may consume large quantities of coffee to wake up in the morning and other forms of medication throughout the day: cigarettes with morning coffee, antacid tablets for an upset stomach, vitamins for stress, or aspirin for a headache. Finally, before going to bed, the grown-ups may take a few "night caps" or a sleeping pill to relax. The following is an interview related to the overuse of drugs:

Yea, I always saw my mom smoking early in the morning while reading the newspaper and slowly sipping nearly a full pot of coffee. She took prescription drugs for asthma, used an inhaler, and took aspirin for headaches. When she accused me of using drugs at concerts, I would pick up her pack of cigarettes and several prescription bottles and while she was raging on me, I would quietly wave all her drugs close up in front of her face. She would stop nagging within seconds and actually one time I think she wanted to laugh but turned away toward the sink and just started washing cups and saucers. The way I figure it, she has her drugs, and I have mine. She may not agree with my use of my drugs but then she is not better either. It's great to have a drug using family ain't it? *(From Venturelli's research files, male, age 20, college student, June 12, 2000.)*

Some social scientists believe that everyday consumption of legal drugs—caffeine, prescription, or OTC drugs, and alcohol—is fueled by the pace of modern lifestyles and greatly accelerated by the influence of today's increasingly sophisticated mass media.

CASE IN POINT

Ignoring the Signs of Drug Abuse: A Hard Lesson Learned

Michael Alig missed all of the warning signs of the dangers of drug abuse and addiction. He states, "There is no excuse for killing someone, no reason to justify being wholly or even partly responsible for the death of another human being. I have never been a violent person. I don't even like sports." Now in prison for the accidental death of a friend, Michael recalls the following warning signs he refused to note:

1. Michael was living without any real boundaries. Now that he looks back at his life, he says it was out of control, and his friends were out of control.

2. Michael overdosed many times on many different drugs and would often wake up unaware of where he was, where he had been, who he was with, what he was doing with whomever he was with, what took place while he was on drugs and so on.

3. One time Michael regained consciousness and was in the presence of ". . . an entire dinner of cocaine on the floor!" which he admits was too tempting to pass up.

4. People around Michael were constantly warning him to stop using drugs, and these were the same people with whom he was annoyed.

5. Just before his arrest, Michael had overdosed numerous times with naloxone, barely escaping death several times.

6. Michael used heroin with the false sense of euphoric security that all was good.

Now Michael, who was called the King of the Club Kids, believes he has finally learned to accept responsibilities as an adult. After solitary confinement for several months to stop using heroin in prison, he says that his approach to life has completely changed. Michael says, "A smile or a laugh isn't just a reaction to the most extreme situations anymore, but to my average daily experiences like eating a piece of sour candy, or seeing a fat boy in the prison yard with the crack of his butt exposed for everyone to see." Michael believes it will take a lot of time for his brain to rewire itself toward enjoying the simple pleasures of life. He states, "Now it will be the small, subtle life experiences that will be my reinforcements . . . [besides] parties in jail are dangerous." Today, Michael is approximately 34 years of age.

Reconstructed by author from source: Michiana Point of View/Michael Alig. "Alig Missed Signs Along the Road to Tragedy." *The South Bend Tribune* (10 January 1999): B-3.

If you look around your classroom building, the dormitories at your college, or your own homes, evidence of mass media and electronic equipment can be found everywhere. Cultural knowledge and information is transmitted via media through electronic gadgets we simply "can't live without" to the point at which they help us define *and* shape our everyday reality.

Although over 70% of adults are regular newspaper readers, television remains the most influential medium. Ninety-eight percent of households have at least one television set and 74% have two or more television sets. In the average American household, a television is on 7 hours and 12 minutes per day (Nielsen 1998). Advertisers invest huge amounts of money in television commercials because of the popularity of the medium. For example, the alcohol industry spends more than $1 billion on yearly advertising (Critser 1996; Kilbourne 1989). "The advertising budget for one beer—Budweiser—is more than the entire budget for research on alcoholism and alcohol abusers" (Kilbourne 1989, p. 13).

Although the media is often accredited for glamorizing dangerous drug use, many successful prevention campaigns have used TV, radio, and print mediums as outlets. Since the Advertising Council began the campaign "Friends Don't Let Friends Drive Drunk," 79% of Americans have stopped an intoxicated friend from getting behind the wheel.

Amanda Geiger never saw the drunk driver.

Friends Don't Let Friends Drive Drunk.

Photo by Michael Mazzeo

U.S. Department of Transportation

Ad Council

In 1995, this advertising resulted in spirits, wine, and beer sales totaling $103.9 billion with the largest sales—those of beer—reaching $62.6 billion (Critser 1996). Such sales figures clearly indicate that advertising is both highly effective and very lucrative in promoting drinking.

Radio, newspapers, and magazines are also saturated with advertisements for OTC drugs, that constantly offer relief from whatever illness you may have. There are pills for inducing sleep and those for staying awake, as well as others for treating indigestion, headache, backache, tension, constipation, and the like. Using these medicinal compounds can significantly alter mood, level of consciousness, and physical discomfort. Experts warn that such drug advertising is likely to increase.

In the early 1990s, the Food and Drug Administration (FDA) lifted a 2-year ban on consumer advertising of prescription drugs; since then, there has been an onslaught of new sales pitches. In their attempts to sell drugs, product advertisers use the authority of a physician or health expert or the seemingly sincere testimony of a product user. Adults are strongly affected by testimonial advertising because these drug commercials can appear authentic and convincing to large numbers of viewers, listeners, or readers.

The constant barrage of commercials, including many for OTC drugs, relay the message that, if you are experiencing restlessness or uncomfortable symptoms, taking drugs is an acceptable and normal response. As a result, television viewers, newspaper and magazine readers, and radio listeners are led to believe or unconsciously select the particular brand advertised when confronted with dozens upon dozens of drug choices for a particular ailment. In effect, all this advertising reaffirms the belief that drugs are necessary when taken for a real *or* an imagined symptom.

Attraction and Patterns of Drug Use and Abuse

Why are so many people attracted to drugs and the effects of recreational drug use? Like the ancient Assyrians, who sucked on opium lozenges, and the Romans, who ate hashish sweets some 2000 years ago, many users claim to be bored, in pain, frustrated, unable to enjoy life, or alienated. Such people turn to drugs in the hope of finding oblivion, peace, inner connections, outer connections (togetherness), or euphoria. The fact that many OTC drugs never really cure the ailment, especially if taken for social and psychological reasons, and the fact that frequent use of most drugs increases the risk of addiction do not seem to be deterrents. People continue to take drugs for many reasons, including the following:

1. Searching for pleasure and using drugs to heighten good feelings.

2. Taking drugs to temporarily relieve stress or tension or provide a temporary escape for people with anxiety.

3. Taking drugs to temporarily forget one's problems and avoid or postpone worries.

4. Viewing certain drugs (such as alcohol, marijuana, and tobacco) as necessary in order to relax after a tension-filled day at work.

5. Taking drugs to fit in with peers, especially when peer pressure is strong during early and late adolescence; seeing drugs as a *rite of passage.*

6. Taking drugs to enhance religious or mystical experiences (very few cultures teach children how to use specific drugs for this purpose).

7. Taking drugs to relieve pain and some symptoms of illness.

It is important to understand why historically many people have been unsuccessful in eliminating the fascination with drugs. To reach such an understanding, we address questions dealing with (1) why people are attracted to drugs, (2) how experiences with the different types of drugs vary (here many attitudes will be conveyed from the inside—the users themselves), (3) how each of the major drugs affect the body and the mind, (4) patterns of use among different groups, and (5) what forms of treatment are available for the addicted. These questions are addressed at a theoretical explanatory level in Chapter 2, and at the level of specific substances in each chapter from Chapters 8 through 16.

■ WHEN DOES USE LEAD TO ABUSE?

Views about the use of drugs depend on one's perspective. For example, from a pharmacological perspective, if a patient is suffering severe pain because of injuries sustained from an automobile accident, high doses of a narcotic such as morphine or Demerol should be given to control discomfort. While someone is in pain, no reason exists not to take the drug. From a medical standpoint, once healing has occurred and pain has been relieved, drug use should cease. If the patient continues using the narcotic because it provides a sense of well-being or has become a habit, the pattern of drug intake would then be considered abuse. Thus, the amount of drug taken or the frequency of dosing does not necessarily determine abuse (although individuals who abuse drugs usually consume frequent high doses). Rather, the *motive* for taking the drug is the principal factor in determining the presence of abuse.

Initial drug abuse symptoms include excessive use, constant preoccupation about the availability and supply of the drug, refusal to admit excessive use and reliance on the drug, all of which are early symptoms of withdrawal whenever the user attempts to stop taking the drug, and neglect of important goals or ambitions in favor of using the drug. Even the legitimate use of a drug can be controversial. Often physicians cannot decide even among themselves what constitutes legitimate use of a drug. For example, MDMA ("Ecstasy") is currently prohibited for therapeutic use, but in 1985, when the DEA was deciding MDMA's status, some 35 to 200 physicians (mostly psychiatrists) were using the drug in their practice. These clinicians claimed that MDMA relaxed inhibitions and enhanced communication and was useful as a psychotherapeutic adjunct to assist in dealing with psychiatric patients (Levinthal 1996; Schecter 1989). From the perspective of these physicians, Ecstasy was a useful medicinal tool. However, the DEA did not agree and made Ecstasy a Schedule I drug (see Chapter 3). This classification excludes any legitimate use of the drug in therapeutics; consequently, according to this ruling, anyone taking Ecstasy is guilty of drug abuse (Goode 1994).

If the problem of drug abuse is to be understood and solutions are to be found, identifying what causes the abuse is most important. When a drug is being abused, it is not legitimately therapeutic; that is, it does not improve the user's physical or mental health. If such drug use is not for therapeutic purposes, what is the motive for using it?

There are many possible answers to this question. Most drug abusers perceive some psychological advantage when using these compounds, at least initially. For many, the psychological lift is significant enough that they are willing to risk social exclusion, health problems, dramatic changes in personality, arrest, incarceration, and fines in order to have their drug. The psychological effects that these drugs cause may entail an array of diverse feelings. Different types of drugs have different psychological effects. The type of drug an individual selects to abuse may ultimately reflect his or her own mental state.

For example, people who experience chronic depression, feel intense job pressures, are unable to focus on accomplishing goals, or have a sense of inferiority may find that a stimulant such as cocaine or amphetamines appears to provide a solution to such dilemmas. These drugs cause a spurt of energy, a feeling of euphoria, a sense of superiority, and imagined confidence. In contrast, people who experience nervousness and anxiety and want instant relief from the pressures of life may choose a depressant such as alcohol or barbiturates. These agents sedate, relax, provide relief, and even have some amnesiac properties, allowing users to suspend or forget their problems. People who perceive themselves as creative or who have artistic talents may select hallucinogenic types of drugs to "expand" their minds, heighten their senses, and distort the confining nature of reality. As individuals come to rely more on drugs to inhibit, deny, accelerate, or distort their realities, they run the risk of becoming psychologically dependent on drugs—a process described in detail in Chapters 4 and 6.

Now some have argued that taking a particular drug to meet a psychological need, especially if a person is over 21 years of age, is not very different from taking a drug to cure an ailment. The belief here is that physical needs and psychological needs are really indistinguishable. In fact, several drug researchers and writers including Szasz (1992) and Lenson (1995) believe that drug taking is a citizen's right and a personal matter involving individual decision-making. They see drug taking as simply a departure from consciousness. Just an additional form of diversity among many other acceptable forms of diversity,

such as racial, religious, gender, and sexual orientation. (For additional elaboration on these views, see Venturelli 2000.) Obviously, within drug use research, this topic remains debatable.

■ DRUG DEPENDENCE

Although Chapters 2 and 4 discuss addiction and drug dependence in detail, here we introduce some underlying factors that lead to drug dependence. Our discussion emphasizes *drug dependence* instead of *addiction* because the term *addiction* is both controversial and relative (an issue that came to the forefront during the 1996 presidential election, for example). Even when drug dependence becomes full-fledged, addiction remains debatable, with many experts unable to agree on one set of characteristics that comprises addiction. Furthermore, the term *addiction* is also viewed by some as a pejorative word that adds to the labeling process (see Chapter 2, labeling theory).

The main characteristics necessary for drug dependence are:

- Both physical and psychological factors precipitate drug dependence. Recently, closer attention has been focused on the mental (psychological) attachments more so than physical addiction to drug use as principally indicative of addiction—mostly, the craving aspect in wanting the drug for consumption.

- More specifically, *psychological dependence* refers to the need that a user may feel for continued use of a drug in order to experience its effects. *Physical dependence* refers to the need to continue taking the drug to avoid withdrawal symptoms, which often include feelings of discomfort and illness.

- There is a tendency to eventually become addicted with repeated use of most psychoactive drugs.

- Generally, addiction refers to mind and body dependence. In the process of dependence, addiction can be viewed as one stage within the dependence phase.

The process of addiction involves five separate phases (see Figure 1.1, page 20): relief, increased use, preoccupation, dependency, and withdrawal. Ini-

relief → increased use → preoccupation → dependency → withdrawal

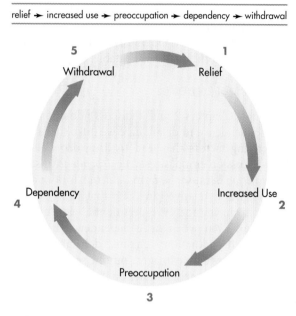

FIGURE 1.1
Stages of drug dependence.

tially, the relief phase refers to the relief from using a drug, which allows a potential addict to escape one or more of the following feelings: boredom, loneliness, tension, fatigue, anger, and anxiety. The increased use phase involves taking greater quantities of the drug. The preoccupation phase consists of a constant concern with the substance—that is, taking the drug becomes "normal" behavior. The dependency phase is synonymous with addiction. More of the drug is sought despite the presence of physical symptoms, such as coughing in cases of cigarette and marijuana addiction or blackouts from advanced alcohol addiction. The withdrawal phase involves such symptoms as itching, chills, tension, stomach pain, or depression from the nonuse of the addictive drug and/or an entire set of psychological concerns mainly involving an insatiable craving for the drug (Monroe 1996).

The Costs of Drug Use to Society

Society pays a high price for drug addiction. Many of the costs are immeasurable—for example, broken homes, illnesses, shortened lives, and loss of good minds from industries and professions. The dollar costs are also enormous. The NIDA has estimated that the typical narcotic habit costs the user $100 a day or more to maintain, depending on location, availability of narcotics, and other factors. If a heroin addict has a $100-a-day habit, this addict would need about $36,500 a year just to maintain the drug supply. It is impossible for most addicts to get this amount of money legally; therefore, many support their habits by resorting to criminal activity or working as or for drug dealers.

Most crimes related to drugs involve theft of personal property—primarily, burglary and shoplifting—and less commonly, assault and robbery (mugging). Estimates are that a heroin addict must steal three to five times the actual cost of the drugs to maintain the habit, or roughly $100,000 a year. Especially with crack and heroin use, a large number of addicts resort to pimping and prostitution. No accurate figures are available regarding the cost of drug-related prostitution, although some law enforcement officials have estimated that prostitutes take in a total of $10 to $20 billion per year. It has also been estimated that nearly three out of every four prostitutes in major cities has a serious drug dependency.

Another significant concern arises from the recent increase in clandestine laboratories throughout the country which are involved in synthesizing or processing illicit drugs. Such laboratories produce amphetamine-type drugs, heroin-type drugs, designer drugs, and LSD and process other drugs of abuse such as cocaine. The DEA reported 390 laboratories seized in 1993, a figure that increased to 967 in 1995. Another example of the phenomenal growth of methamphetamine laboratories can be found in Missouri. From 1995 to 1997, seizures of such labs in Missouri increased by 535% (Steward and Sitarmiah 1997). The reasons for such dramatic increases relate to the enormous profits and relatively low risk associated with these operations. As a rule, clandestine laboratories are fairly mobile and relatively crude (often operating in a kitchen, basement, or garage) and operated by individuals with only elementary chemical skills. Because of a lack of training, the chemical procedures are performed crudely, sometime resulting in adulterants and impure products. Such contaminants can be very toxic, causing severe harm or even death to the unsuspecting user (Drug Strategies 1995). Fortunately, when looking at all the illicit drugs produced by such underground laboratories, such outbreaks of physically harmful drugs does not occur very often. Partial proof of this is found in the small number of news media stories of deaths or poisonings from illicit drugs. Nevertheless, because profit drives these clandestine labs, which obviously have no government supervision, impurities or "cheap fillers" are always possible so that greater profits can be made. Here, caution is very advisable in that drug purchasers do not have any guarantees when purchasing powerful illicit drugs.

Society continues paying a large sum even after addicts and dealers are caught and sentenced because it takes from $75 to $1500 per day to keep one person incarcerated. Supporting programs such as methadone maintenance costs much less. New York officials estimate that methadone maintenance costs about $2000 per year per patient. Some outpatient programs, such as those in Washington, D.C., claim a cost as low as $5 to $10 per day (not counting cost of staff and facilities), which is much less than the cost of incarceration.

A more long-term effect of drug abuse that has substantial impact on society is the medical and psychological care often required by addicts due to disease resulting from their drug habit. Particularly noteworthy are the communicable diseases spread because of needle sharing within the drug-abusing population, such as hepatitis and HIV. An estimated 1 million Americans today are infected with HIV, which eventually causes AIDS. The current worldwide estimate is that 34.3 million adults and children were infected with HIV by the end of 1997 (UNAIDS 2000).

In the United States, HIV is spread primarily through unprotected sexual intercourse and sharing needles used for injecting drugs. HIV in the injecting drug user subpopulation appears to be transmitted in small amounts of contaminated blood left on shared needles. The likelihood of a member of the drug-abusing population contracting HIV correlates with the frequency of injection and the amount of needle sharing (NIDA 1990; NIDA 1995). Care for these AIDS patients lasts from months to years in intensive care units at a cost to the public of billions of dollars. Many cities throughout the United States now have publicly funded programs that distribute new uncontaminated needles to drug addicts free of charge in order to prevent spreading HIV and hepatitis B and C with contaminated needles.

Also of great concern is drug abuse by women during pregnancy. Some psychoactive drugs can have profound, permanent effects on a developing fetus. The best documented is fetal alcohol syndrome (FAS), which can affect the offspring of alcoholic mothers (see Chapter 8). Cocaine and amphetamine-related drugs can also cause irreversible congenital changes when used during pregnancy (see Chapter 11). All too often, the affected offspring of addicted mothers become the responsibility of welfare organizations.

In addition to the costs to society just mentioned, other costs of drug abuse include drug-related deaths, emergency room visits and hospital stays, and automobile fatalities.

■ DRUGS, CRIME, AND VIOLENCE

There is a long-established close association between drug abuse and criminality. The beliefs (hypotheses) for this association range between two opposing views: (1) criminal behavior develops as a means to support addiction, and (2) criminality is inherently linked to the user's personality and occurs independently of drug use (Kokkevi et al. 1993; Drug Strategies 1995). In other words, does addiction to drugs cause a person to engage in criminal behavior such as burglary, theft, and larceny in order to pay for the

HERE AND NOW

In the 1990s, a variety of factors came together in the United States to extend drug abuse beyond just the very rich or the urban poor. The ease of brewing cheaper, more potent strains of speed (methamphetamine, or "meth") and heroin, coupled with the fact that enforcement officials tended to focus on drug abuse and traffic in urban areas on the East and West Coasts, left middle class and rural populations throughout the country largely overlooked. (See "Youth Drug Use" illustration in the next column.) Suddenly, the illicit drug market was booming where no one had been looking.

By the late 1990s, speed—which had gained popularity in the 1970s among outlaw bikers, college students facing exams, all-night party-goers, and long-haul truckers—was more sought after than ever. Teenagers, middle-class workers, and suburbanites joined the ranks of methamphetamine users. "We've been fighting it really strongly for nearly seven years," Edward Synicky, a special agent with California's Bureau of Narcotics Enforcement, told *Time* magazine in early 1996. "But cocaine gets all the publicity because it's glamorous. And law enforcement in general doesn't put the resources into meth that it should."

Increasingly, the illegal substance was produced in clandestine labs set up by both major drug dealers and individual users. By January 1996, John Coonce, head of the U.S. Drug Enforcement Administration's (DEA's) meth-lab task force, said methamphetamine use was "absolutely epidemic." The surge was attributed largely to powerful Mexican drug syndicates and motorcycle gangs that sold their goods on street corners. Speed acquired the nickname "crank" because it was frequently concealed in motorcycle crankcases.

Clandestine manufacture and use of speed were especially high in the West and Southwest. Speed kitchens flourished in California because it was relatively easy for the Mexican syndicates to smuggle in ephedrine, a key ingredient that is tightly controlled in the United States. From the mid-1980s to the mid-1990s, methamphetamine-related hospitalizations in California rose approximately 366%. In Arizona's Maricopa County, methamphetamine-linked crimes jumped nearly 400% over a 3-year period in the early 1990s (see the sections, The Costs of Drug Use to Society and Drugs, Crime, and Violence in this chapter).

Soon this easy-access drug began spreading across the United States. In 1994, DEA field offices in Houston, Denver, Los Angeles, New

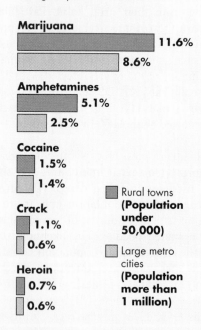

Youth Drug Use
Rural eighth-grade students are more likely to use drugs than their peers in large cities. Here are the results of a survey conducted of the percentage of eighth-graders who used drugs during the previous month.

Marijuana
11.6%
8.6%

Amphetamines
5.1%
2.5%

Cocaine
1.5%
1.4%

Crack
1.1%
0.6%

■ Rural towns **(Population under 50,000)**

Heroin
0.7%
0.6%

■ Large metro cities **(Population more than 1 million)**

Source: National Center on Addiction and Substance Abuse at Columbia University. *Monitoring the Future Survey*, Ann Arbor, MI: University of Michigan 1999.

Orleans, Phoenix, St. Louis, San Diego, and San Francisco were responsible for approximately 86% of the methamphetamine laboratory seizures in the country. By 1996, however, officials were seizing huge shipments of methamphetamine that originated in Mississippi and Tennessee.

But speed was not the only drug barreling its way across the country. Use of heroin ran rampant as well. In a southeastern Massachusetts fishing community, at least 50 fishermen died of AIDS or other drug-related causes between 1991 and 1996. The captain of one scalloper told a local newspaper, "As a wild guess, I would say that if the fishing industry were to run a blood test and eliminate the people that had drug problems, there would be very few boats sailing with a full crew" (Associated Press 1996). Many skippers cited the ease with which drug users and dealers could find jobs on board ships as one reason for the alarming rise in drug abuse among their ranks.

Even crack cocaine, which was first seen primarily in New York and Los Angeles, infiltrated rural areas. Headlines report that in many U.S. counties, eighth-graders in rural areas are using more drugs than urban youth (Briske 2000). According to the DEA, a combination of factors forced some crack distributors to develop new markets in smaller towns and rural areas; Pike County, Mississippi, was hit especially hard. Enforcement officials believed most of the crack in Mississippi came from New Orleans, but some drug shipments originating in South America were flown to remote landing strips in the middle of Mississippi farmland.

Whatever people's reasons for using these dangerous substances, it is clear that an important step toward stemming abuse is to dry up the supply lines to middle America. To accomplish that goal, the law enforcement community must look beyond traditional hotbeds of activity among the urban poor.

Sources: Associated Press. "Survey: Drug Use Pervading New Bedford Fleet." *Maine Sunday Telegram* (21 July 1996).
Briske, P. "Rural Eighth-graders Using More Drugs Than Urban Kids." *The Times* (27 January 2000): 3. Available at http://www.thetimesonline.com.
National Narcotics Intelligence Consumers Committee. *The NNICC Report, 1994.* Washington, DC: U.S. Drug Enforcement Agency, 1994: 70.
National Public Broadcast (NPR). "All Things Considered." *PM News* (18 September 1996).
Toufonio, A., et al. "There Is No Safe Speed." *Time* (8 January 1990).
Wilkie, C. "Crack Cocaine Moves South." *Boston Globe* (23 June 1996).

drug habit? Or, does criminal behavior stem from an already existing criminal personality and drugs are used as an adjunct to commit such acts? In other words, are drugs used in conjunction with crime to sedate and give the extra-added confidence to commit daring law violations?

This has never been clear because findings that contradict one view in favor of the other continue to mount on both sides. Part of the reason for the controversy about the relationship between criminal activity and drug abuse is that studies have been conducted in different settings and cultures, employing different research methods, and focusing on different addictive drugs. Part of the response to this dilemma is that perhaps too many factors are involved. We know that each type of drug has unique addictive potential and that interpretation of exactly when a deviant act is an offense (violation of law) varies. Furthermore, we know that people think differently while under the influence of drugs. Whether or not criminalistic behavior is *directly* caused by the drug use or whether prior socialization and peer influence work in concert to cause criminal behavior remains unclear. Certainly, we think it would be safe to view prior socialization, law-violating peers, and drugs as strong contributing factors for causing criminalistic behavior.

Nevertheless, although this controversy about the drugs and crime connection continues to challenge our thinking, the following findings are clear:

1. The National Institute of Justice's (NIJ's) Arrestee Drug Abuse Monitoring (ADAM) program conducted urine tests on males in 23 cities and on females in 21 cities. Male arrestees who tested positive for an illicit drug at the time of arrest ranged from 51.4% in San Jose to 80.5% in Manhattan. Female arrestees who tested positive ranged from 37.6% in San Antonio to 80.5% in Manhattan. Juvenile male detainees ranged from 41.6% in Indianapolis to 65.6% in Washington, D.C. What we see here is that approximately 50% of arrestees used drugs immediately before committing an offense. Corroborating this is the fact that the 1997 Bureau of Justice Statistics (BJS) Survey of State and Federal Prison Inmates reported that 51% of prison inmates committed their offense while under the influence of drugs or alcohol (Schmidt 1999).

2. The same survey indicates that 82% of inmates in local jails self-reported that they used a drug at some point in their lives.

3. Twenty-eight percent of state and federal prison inmates reported being under the influence of drugs at the time of their offense in 1997 (see Table 1.4). Thirty-three percent were incarcerated for drug offenses, 27% for violent offenses, 24% for property offenses, and 19% for public-order offenses—loitering, disturbing the peace, public intoxication, etc. One outcome of these findings is that approximately one out of every four major crimes committed—violent offenses, property, and drug offenses—involves an offender who is under the influence of drugs.

4. Table 1.5 shows the percentage of federal and state prison inmates who committed their offense to obtain money to buy drugs. The total number of incarcerated inmates who did this was approximately 14% in 1991. Eighteen percent of the crimes involved property offenses,

16% involved drug offenses, 15% involved violent crimes to purchase drugs, and 6% involved public-order offenses. Approximately one out of every seven major crimes is committed because of the offender's need to obtain money for drugs.

TABLE 1.4 Percentage of State and Federal Prison Inmates Who Reported Being Under the Influence of Drugs at the Time of Their Offense, 1997

TYPE OF OFFENSE	PERCENTAGE*
Total of all inmates	**28**
Violent Offense	27
Murder	
Sexual assault	
Robbery	
Assault	
Property Offense	24
Burglary	
Larceny/theft	
Motor vehicle theft	
Fraud	
Other	
Drug Offenses	33
Possession	
Trafficking	
Other	
Public-order Offenses	19
Weapons	
Other	

Source: BJS, *Substance Abuse and Treatment*, State and Federal Prisoners, Washington, DC: U.S. Government Printing Office 1997.

*Percentage compiled by averaging the percentages of federal and state prison inmates.

5. In 1998, out of a total of 14,088 homicides, 4.8% were drug-related (Spiess and Fallow 2000).

In regard to the connection between drug use and crime, the following findings can be safely summized: (1) drug users in comparison to non–drug users are more likely to commit crimes; (2) arrestees are often under the influence of a drug while committing crimes; and (3) drugs and violence often go hand-in-hand. Drug-related crimes are undoubtedly overwhelming our judicial system. According to the U.S. Department of Justice, alcohol consumption is associated with 27% of all murders, almost 33% of all property offenses, and more than 37% of robberies committed by young people. In fact, nearly 40% of the young people in adult correctional facilities reported drinking before committing a crime.

Cartels

Here are some recent trends in the world of drugs, violence, and crime:

> Shortly before 10:00 p.m. on August 3, 1997, as fans gathered in the bars and eateries near the Plaza Monumental bullring in Ciudad Juarez [in Chihuahua, Mexico], four suspected drug traffickers strolled into the popular Max Fim restaurant, pulled out their guns, and squeezed off 130 rounds into the post-fight Sunday night crowd, killing three men and two women and wounding another four people. On their way out, the assailants paused long enough to claim another victim—an off-duty law enforcement officer who had run into the street from the bar next door, gun drawn, to check out the commotion (Rylander, 1999, p. 1).

In another news report:

> . . . one indication of the export of money laundering, more than $53 million in cash was seized by U.S. Customs agents at Southwest border checkpoints between 1994 and 1996. The U.S. government suggested that drug profits of as much as $50 billion a year—$6 billion more than was appropriated in fiscal 1998 for Texas state government—flowed through Texas into Mexico. The estimate included electronic transfers, exchangehouse operation, and bulk cash (Rylander 1999, p. 3).

And in another news report:

> Drugs present the leading crime challenge in the border region, but other crimes are also a problem. Every 24 hours in 1997, an average of 60 violent crimes and 654 property offenses were committed in the border region (Rylander 1999, p. 3).

TABLE 1.5 Percentage of Federal and State Prison Inmates Who Committed Their Offenses to Obtain Money to Buy Drugs, 1991

TYPE OF OFFENSE	PERCENTAGE*
Total of all inmates	**14**
Violent Offenses	15
Homicide	
Sexual assault	
Robbery	
Assault	
Property Offenses	18
Burglary	
Larceny theft	
Fraud	
Other	
Drug Offenses	16
Possession	
Trafficking	
Other	
Public-Order Offenses	6

Source: BJS, *Comparing Federal and State Prison Inmates*, 1991. Washington, DC: U.S. Government Printing Office.

*Percentage compiled by averaging the percentages of federal and state prison inmates.

And finally,

> Bogotá, Columbia—A car bomb exploded Thursday in an affluent Bogotá neighborhood, killing at least eight people and injuring more than 30. It was the worst terrorist act in the Columbian capital since the downfall of the Medellin drug cartel in 1993. No one immediately claimed responsibility for the explosion, but political analyst Alejo Vargas said the style of the attack—with no apparent targets other than civilian—had all the markings of the drug cartels (Brodzinsky 1999).

These news briefs are just a small sampling of the types of crimes and violence perpetrated by drug dealers. It is clear that production, merchandising, and distribution of illicit drugs have developed into a worldwide operation worth hundreds of billions of dollars (Goldstein 1994). These enormous profits have attracted organized crime, in both the United States and abroad, and all too frequently even corrupt law enforcement agencies (McShane 1994). For the participants in such operations, drugs can mean incredible wealth and power. For example, dating back to 1992, Pablo Escobar was recognized as a drug kingpin and leader of the cocaine cartel in Colombia, and he was acknowledged as one of the world's richest men and Colombia's most powerful man (Wire Services 1992). With his drug-related wealth, Escobar financed a private army to conduct a personal war against the government of Colombia (Associated Press 1992) and until his death in 1993, he was a serious threat to his country's stability.

In December 1999, the notorious Juarez drug cartel is believed to be responsible for burying more than 100 bodies (22 Americans) in a mass grave at a ranch in Mexico. All of the deaths were believed to be drug-related. Vincente Carrillo Fuentes is one among dozens of drug lords and lieutenants wanted by U.S. law enforcement agents (Associated Press 1999). This same news release indicated that the drug trade would not end until drug cartels are eliminated. Such occurrences, which are often reported by the mass media, indicate the existence of powerful and dangerous drug cartels that are responsible for the availability of illicit drugs around the world.

Violence takes its toll at all levels, as rival gangs fight to control their "turf" and associated drug operations. Innocent bystanders often become unsuspecting victims of the indiscriminate violence. For example, a Roman Catholic cardinal was killed on May 24, 1993, when a car he was a passenger in, was inadvertently driven into the middle of a drug-related shootout between traffickers at the international airport in Guadalajara, Mexico. Five other innocent bystanders were killed in the incident (Associated Press 1993). Others are injured or killed by drug users who, while under the influence of drugs, commit violent criminal acts.

▪ DRUGS IN THE WORKPLACE: A COSTLY AFFLICTION

> "He was a good, solid worker, always on the job—until he suddenly backed his truck over a 4-inch gas line." If the line had ruptured, there would have been a serious explosion, according to the driver's employer. The accident raised a red flag. ". . . under the company's standard policy, the employee was tested for drugs and alcohol. He was positive for both" (Edelson 2000).

Most adults spend the majority of hours per day in some type of family environment. For most adults employed full-time, the second greatest number of hours is spent in the workplace. Generally, once drug use becomes habitual, drug use often continues at

"HE'S THE TYPICAL AMERICAN MOUSE— LIKES A DRINK BEFORE DINNER, SMOKES A LITTLE, WATCHES TV..."

Source: ® Sidney Harris, *American Scientist* magazine. Used with permission.

work. The National Household Surveys, for example, found evidence of significant drug use in the workplace. In the surveys, 65.6% of full-time workers reported alcohol use within the past month. Some 9.7% of full-time workers reported marijuana use within the past year. Part-time employees did not differ much in their use of alcohol and marijuana (SAMHSA 1996a). Based on studies of drug use within a 30-day period before being surveyed, approximately 64% of full-time employees report alcohol use, while 7% reported illicit drug use (see Figure 1.2) (NORC 1999). This costs American businesses billions of dollars annually in lost productivity and increased health care costs. Over the past several years, many large businesses have instituted substance abuse programs to respond to the problems created by alcohol and other drugs in the workplace. Highlights from the National Council on Alcoholism and Drug Dependence, Inc. (1999) indicate the following:

1. *Men* in the following occupations reported the highest rates of illicit drug use: entertainers, food preparation and service, cleaning services, and construction. Among *women,* workers involved in food preparation, social work, and the legal professions, including lawyers and legal assistants, reported the highest rates of illicit drug use. Heavy alcohol use followed similar patterns, although automobile mechanics, vehicle repairers, light truck drivers, and laborers also have high rates of alcohol use but not necessarily high rates of illicit drug use.

2. The lowest rates of illicit drug use are found among workers in the following occupations: police and detectives, administrative support personnel, teachers, and child care workers. The lowest rates of heavy alcohol use are among data clerks, personnel specialists, and secretaries. Here we find that workers in occupations that require a considerable amount of public trust, as just listed (police officers, teachers, and child care workers), report the lowest rates of illicit drug use.

3. More specifically, 70% of all current adult illegal drug users ages 18 through 49 are employed full-time. Ninety percent of alcoholics work. This means that one out of every six employees use alcohol and/or other illicit drugs.

4. Approximately 70% of large companies test for drug use. Approximately 50% of medium companies drug test, and approximately 22% of small companies drug test. Of those companies that drug test, over 90% use urine analysis, less than 20% use blood analysis, and less than 3% use hair analysis.

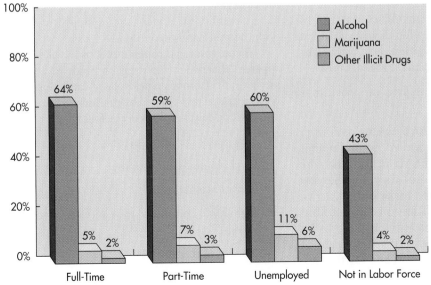

FIGURE 1.2

Percentage of working-age population reporting substance use in the past month by employment status.

Source: National Opinion Research Center (NORC). Substance Abuse and Mental Health Characteristics by Employment Status. Substance Abuse and Mental Health Services Administration (SAMHSA and Office of Applied Studies (OAS). Rockville, MD: National Clearinghouse for Alcohol and Drug Information (NCADI), June 1999.

5. Most companies that administer drug tests test for marijuana, cocaine, opiates, amphetamines, and PCP.

6. Age was the most significant predictor of marijuana and cocaine use. Younger employees (18 to 24 years old) were more likely to report drug use than older employees (25 years or older).

7. With regard to marijuana and cocaine use among younger employees (ages 18 to 34), no significant differences in marijuana and cocaine use rates were found across educational categories.

8. In general, unmarried workers reported roughly twice as much illicit drug and heavy alcohol use as married workers. Among food preparation workers, transportation drivers, and mechanics, and in industries such as construction and machinery (not electrical), the discrepancy between married and unmarried workers was especially notable.

9. Workers who reported having three or more jobs in the previous five years were twice as likely to be current or past-year illicit drug users as those who held two or fewer jobs over the same period.

10. Workers in occupations that affect public safety, including truck drivers, firefighters, and police officers, report the highest rate of participation in drug testing.

11. Seventy-five percent of workers paid on an hourly basis at one manufacturing plant reported that it was easy for them to drink at their workstations. This group included assembly line workers, electricians, and machinists.

12. Most youths do not cease drug use when they begin working.

In summarizing this research on employees who abuse alcohol or other drugs, five major findings emerge: (1) they are three times more likely than the average employee to be late to work; (2) they are three times more likely to receive sickness benefits; (3) they are 16 times more likely to be absent from work; (4) they are five times more likely to be involved in on-the-job accidents (note that many of these hurt others, not themselves); and (5) they are five times more likely to file compensation claims.

Employee Assistance Programs

Many industries have responded to drugs in the workplace by creating drug testing and employee assistance programs (EAPs). Drug testing generally involves urine screening that is undertaken to identify which employees are using drugs and which employees may have current or potential drug problems. EAPs are employer-financed programs administered by a company or through an outside contractor. More than 400,000 EAPs have been established in the United States. These programs are designed to aid in identifying and resolving productivity problems associated with employees' emotional or physical concerns, such as those related to health, marital, family, financial, and substance abuse. EAPs have also expanded their focus to combat employee abuse of OTC and prescription drugs in addition to illicit psychoactive substances. Overall, the programs attempt to formally reduce problems associated with impaired job performance.

Venturing to a Higher Level: A Holistic Self-Awareness Approach to Drug Use

Throughout this book, we continually emphasize a unique combination of pharmacological, psychological, and sociological understandings of the most commonly used licit and illicit drugs. Most chapters discuss and explain the major drugs and their common usage and abuse patterns and emphasize varied approaches for understanding how drugs affect both the mind and the body.

As you proceed through this book, it will become apparent that whenever drug use leads to abuse, it rarely results from a single, isolated cause. Instead, it is often caused or preceded by multiple factors, which may include combinations of the following:

- Hereditary (genetic) factors

- Psychological conditioning

- Peer group pressures

- Inability to cope with stress and anxiety of daily living

- Quality of role models

- Degree of attachment to a family structure

- Level of security with gender identity and sexual orientation

- Personality traits

- Perceived ethnic and racial compatibility with larger society and socioeconomic status (social class)

Gaining knowledge of the reasons for drug use, the effects of drugs, and their addictive potential comprises the valuable information in this text. As authors, we strongly endorse and advocate a holistic self-awareness approach that emphasizes a healthy balance among mind, body, and spirit. Health and wellness can only be achieved when these three domains of existence are free from any unnecessary use of psychoactive substances. The holistic philosophy is based on the idea that the mind has a powerful influence on maintaining health. All three—mind, body, and spirit—work as a unified whole to promote health and wellness.

This book works toward this direction by presenting a blend of different perspectives about drug information in order to more fully comprehend how drugs work. The different perspectives prevent limited and narrow points of view so that drug information can be perceived and understood from pharmacological, psychological, and sociological perspectives.

As mentioned earlier, understanding drug use is not only important for comprehending our own health but also for understanding (1) why others are attracted to drugs; (2) how to detect drug use in others; (3) what to do (remedies and solutions) when friends or family members abuse drugs; (4) how to help and advise drug abusers about the pitfalls of substance use; (5) what are the best educational, preventive, and treatment options available for victims of drug abuse; and (6) what are the danger signals that can arise in yourself and others you care about when drug use exceeds normal and necessary use.

In concluding this chapter, the authors find that once knowledge is gained about drug use and/or abuse, holistic health awareness results in self-awareness. Self-awareness initially begins by understanding your own drug-use practices as well as those of close family and friends. Such an understanding promotes not only healthy self-maintenance but also the ability to help others. By practicing a healthy approach to the use of psychoactive substances, you will be better equipped to understand yourself and others.

KEY TERMS

drug test
urine, blood screening, or hair analysis used to identify those who may be using drugs

Employee Assistance Programs (EAPs)
drug assistance programs for employees

holistic self-awareness approach
holistic philosophy that advocates that the mind, body, and spirit work best when drug free

Discussion Questions

1. Give an example of a drug-using friend and describe how he or she may be affected by pharmacological, cultural, social, and contextual factors.

2. Discuss and debate whether marijuana is or is not addictive.

3. In reviewing the ancient historical uses of drugs, do you think drug use today is different from back then? If so, how is usage different today? If not, how does use differ today?

4. Why do Americans use so many legal drugs (for example, alcohol, tobacco, and OTC drugs)? What aspects of our society promote extensive drug use?

5. Cite three reasons why you think that throughout the years, the use of illicit drugs, listed in Table 1.3, has not dramatically declined despite the negativity of such drug use promoted by costly campaigns against drug use by community and law enforcement officials?

6. Because many experimental drug users do not gravitate toward excessive drug use, should experimenters be left alone or perhaps just given legal warnings or fines?

7. Does the mass media really promote drug use, or do they merely reflect our extensive use of drugs? Provide some evidence for your position.

8. When do you think drug use leads to abuse? When do you think drug use does not lead to abuse?

9. What do you believe is the relationship between excessive drug use and crime? Does drug use *cause* crime or is crime simply a manifestation of personality?

10. What principal factors are involved in the relationship between drugs and crime?

11. Should all employees be randomly tested for drug use?

12. Should all students be randomly drug tested at their schools and universities? Why or why not?

13. Do you think the approach advocated by the authors regarding a holistic self-awareness approach toward drug use is a viable perspective and can be successfully used for stopping drug use? Why or why not? What, if any, improvements can be made to strengthen this approach?

Key Terms

insiders 5

outsiders 5

drug 6

psychoactive drugs 6

licit 6

illicit 6

over-the-counter (OTC) 6

gateway drugs 8

ethanol 8

designer drugs 9

structural analogs 9

MDMA 10

equal-opportunity affliction 11

experimenters 15

compulsive users 15

floaters (chippers) 15

relief phase 20

increased use phase 20

preoccupation phase 20

dependency phase 20

withdrawal phase 20

NIDA 20

DEA 20

drug test 28

employee assistance programs (EAPs) 28

holistic self-awareness approach 29

Summary

1 Pharmacological, cultural, social, and contextual issues are the four principal factors responsible for determining how a drug user experiences drug use. Pharmacological factors take into account how a particular drug affects the body. Cultural factors examine how society's views, as determined by custom and tradition, affect use of a particular drug. Social factors include the specific reasons why a drug is taken and how drug use develops from social factors, such as family upbringing, peer group alliances, subcultures, and communities. Contextual factors account for how drug use behavior develops from the physical surroundings in which the drug is taken.

2 Initial understanding of drug use includes the following key terms: drug, gateway drugs, medicines and prescription medicines, over-the-counter (OTC), drug misuse, drug abuse, and drug addiction.

3 Mentions of drug use date back to the Bible, including ancient literature dated 2240 B.C. Under the influence of drugs, many people experienced feelings ranging from extreme ecstasy to sheer terror. At times, drugs were used to induce sleep and provide freedom from care.

4 Drug users are found in all occupations and professions, at all income and social class levels, and in all age groups. No one is immune to drug use. Thus, drug use is an equal-opportunity affliction.

5 According to sociologist Erich Goode (1999), drugs are used for four reasons: (1) legal instrumental use, (2) legal recreational use, (3) illegal instrumental use, and (4) illegal recreational use.

6 The most commonly used licit and illicit drugs, rated from highest to lowest frequency, are alcohol, cigarettes, marijuana, smokeless tobacco, nonmedical use of any psychotherapeutic (prescription stimulant, sedative, tranquilizer, or analgesic), cocaine, hallucinogens, stimulants, inhalants, and analgesics. The most commonly abused illicit drugs are cannabis (marijuana), stimulants, hallucinogens, narcotics, depressants, and organic solvents.

7 The three types of drug users are experimenters, compulsive users, and floaters. Experimenters try drugs because of curiosity and peer pressure. Compulsive users use drugs on a full-time basis and seriously desire to escape from or alter reality. Floaters or "chippers" vacillate between experimental drug use and chronic drug use.

8 The mass media tend to promote drug use through advertising. The constant barrage of OTC drug commercials relays the message that, if you are experiencing some symptom, taking drugs is an acceptable option.

9 The following are the major findings of the connection between drugs and crime: (1) drug users are more likely to commit crime, (2) arrestees are often under the influence of a drug or drugs while committing their crimes, and (3) drugs and violence often go hand-in-hand.

10 The five phases of drug addiction are relief, increased use, preoccupation, dependency, and withdrawal.

11 The employee assistance programs (EAPs) are employer-financed programs administered by a company or through an outside contractor. They are designed to aid in identifying and resolving productivity problems associated with employees' emotional or physical concerns, such as those related to health, marriage, family, finances, and substance abuse. Recently, EAPs have expanded their focus to combat employee abuse of OTC and prescription drugs as well as illicit psychoactive substances.

12 The holistic self-awareness philosophy is based on the idea that the mind has a powerful influence on maintaining health. The three domains—mind, body, and spirit—work best when unobstructed by unnecessary drug use, and all three domains work as a unified whole to promote health and wellness.

References

Ananth, P., C. Annis, C. Gonzalez, K. McRae, R. Longoria, and A. Medina. "Prescription Smoothies?" Stanford Learning Lab, *Web Journal*, Department of Human Biology, 2000. Available http://sll-8Stanford.edu /webjournal.

Associated Press. "Program to Fight Drug Smuggling Costs U.S. a Lot, Produces Little." *Salt Lake Tribune* 244 (17 August 1992): A-1.

Associated Press. "Mexican Cardinal, Six Others Killed in Cross-Fire as Drug Battles Erupt in Guadalajara." *Salt Lake Tribune* 246 (25 May 1993): A-1.

Associated Press. "Discovery of Mexican Graves Unlikely to Slow Flow of Drugs." *The Times*, (5 December 1999): A-13.

Beschner, G. "Understanding Teenage Drug Use." In *Teen Drug Use*, edited by G. Beschner and A. Friedman. Lexington, MA: D. C. Heath, 1986: 1–18.

Briske, P. "Rural Eighth-Graders Using More Drugs Than Urban Kids." *The Times*, (27 January 2000): 3. Available http://www.thetimesonline.com.

Brodzinsky, S. "Car Bomb Kills 8 in Columbia Neighborhood." *USA Today*, Arlington edition, (12 November 1999).

Critser, G. "Oh, How Happy We Will Be: Pills, Paradise, and the Profits of the Drug Companies." *Harper's Magazine* (June 1996): 39–48.

Drug Strategies. *Keeping Score: What We Are Getting for Our Federal Drug Control Dollars 1995*. Washington, DC: 1995. Available 080/edres/colleges/boss/depts/cesar/drugs/ks1995.

Edelson, E. "Drug Use in the Workplace Plummets." *APB News, Inc.* (7 February 2000). Available http://www.apbnews.com/safetycenter/business/2000/02/07/drugtests0207_01.html.

Goldstein, A. "Lessons from the Street." In *Addiction from Biology to Drug Policy*. New York: Freeman, 1994.

Goode, E. *Deviant Behavior*, 4th ed. Englewood Cliffs, NJ: Prentice Hall, 1994.

Goode, E. *Drugs in American Society*, 5th ed. Boston, MA: McGraw-Hill College, 1999.

Kilbourne, J. "Advertising Addiction: The Alcohol Industry's Hard Sell." *Multinational Monitor* (June 1989): 13–16.

Kokkevi, A., J. Liappas, V. Boukouvala, V. Alevizou, E. Anastassopoulou, and C. Stefanis. "Criminality in a Sample of Drug Abusers in Greece." *Drug and Alcohol Dependence* 31 (1993): 111–21.

Kusinitz, M. "Drug Use Around the World." In *Encyclopedia of Psychoactive Drugs,* edited by S. Snyder. Series 2. New York: Chelsea House, 1988.

Lenson, D. *On Drugs.* Minneapolis, MN: University of Minnesota Press, 1995.

Levinthal, C. F. *Drugs, Behavior, and Modern Society.* Boston, MA: Allyn and Bacon, 1996.

McShane, L. "Cops Are Crooks in N.Y.'s 30th Precinct." *Salt Lake Tribune* 238 (18 April 1994): A-5.

Monroe, J. "What Is Addiction?" *Current Health* 2 (January 1996): 16–19.

Morrow, D. J. "Worldwide Drug Sales Up 4% in '98." *New York Times* (23 March 1999), C5.

National Council on Alcoholism and Drug Dependence, Inc. (NCADD). *Alcohol and Other Drugs in the Workplace: An Overview.* New York: National Council on Alcoholism and Drug Dependence, Inc. August 1999. Available http://www.ncadd.org.

National Institute on Drug Abuse (NIDA). "Costs to Society." *NIDA Infofax.* Bethesda, MD: U.S. Department of Health and Human Services, 1998. Available at http://www.nida.nih.gov.

National Institute on Drug Abuse (NIDA). *Drug Abuse and Addiction Research: The Sixth Triennial Report to Congress.* Rockville, MD: Department of Health and Human Services (DHHS), 1999. Available http://www.nida.nih.gov/strc/role3.html.

National Opinion Research Center (NORC). *Substance Abuse and Mental Health Characteristics by Employment Status.* Substance Abuse and Mental Health Services Administration (SAMHSA) and Office of Applied Studies (OAS). Rockville, MD: National Clearinghouse for Alcohol and Drug Information (NCADI), June 1999.

Nielsen Media Research. *1998 Report on Television.* Northbrook, IL: Nielsen, 1998.

Rylander, C. K. (Texas Comptroller of Public Accounts). "Bordering the Future: Crime—Line of Fire." *Window on State Government.* (7 April 1999). Available http://www.window. state.tx.us/borer/ch10/ch10html.

Schecter, M. "Serotonergic-Dopaminergic Mediation of 3, 4-Methytenedioxy-Methamphetamine (MDMA, Ectasy)." *Pharmacology, Biochemistry and Behavior* 31 (1989): 817–24.

Schmidt, G. *Drug Data Summary.* Office of National Drug Control Policy (ONDCP). Rockville, MD: Drug Policy Information Clearinghouse, NCJ-172873, April 1999.

Spiess, M., and D. Fallow. *Drug Related Crime.* Rockville, MD: Office of National Drug Control Policy (ONDCP). Drug Policy Information Clearinghouse, NCJ-181056, March 2000.

Steward, P. and G. Sitarmiah. "America's Heartland Grapples with Rise of Dangerous Drug." *The Christian Science Monitor* (13 November 1997) 1, 18.

Substance Abuse and Mental Health Services Administration (SAMHSA). *National Household Survey on Drug Abuse: Population Estimates 1998.* Rockville, MD: U.S. Department of Health and Human Services: 1–73.

Substance Abuse and Mental Health Services Administration (SAMHSA). *National Household Survey on Drug Abuse; Fact Sheet, August 1999.* Available www.samhsa.gov/ PRESS/99/990818fs.htm

Substance Abuse and Mental Health Services Administration (SAMHSA), Office of Applied Studies (OAS). *National Household Survey on Drug Abuse: Main Findings 1994.* Rockville, MD: NIDA, 1996a.

Substance Abuse and Mental Health Services Administration (SAMHSA), Office of Applied Studies (OAS). *The Relationship Between Family Structure and Adolescent Substance Use.* Rockville, MD: U.S. Department of Health and Human Services, July 1996b.

Szasz, T. *Our Right to Drugs: The Case for a Free Market.* Westport, CT: Praeger, 1992.

Thio, A. *Deviant Behavior,* 2nd ed. Boston: Houghton Mifflin, 1983: 332–333.

Thio, A. *Deviant Behavior,* 4th ed. New York: HarperCollins College, 1995.

UNAIDS. *Global Estimates of the HIV/AIDS Epidemic as of End of 1999.* Available 2000. http://www.unaids.org/epidemic_update/report/index.html#map.

USA Today. "Seven in 10 Drug Users Work Full-Time." M. Combs, 8 September 1999. Available http://www.usa today.com/life/health/addictin/lhadd021.htm.

Venturelli, P. J. "Drugs in Schools: Myths and Reality." *Annals of the American Academy of Political and Social Science* 567, edited by W. Hinkle and S. Henry, Thousand Oaks, CA: Sage Publications, 2000: 72–87.

Explaining Drug Use and Abuse

Did You Know?

- There exists an excessive amount of variation in values and attitudes regarding drug use.
- Like the United States, nearly all other countries are experiencing increasing amounts of drug use within certain sub-cultures of people who use or abuse drugs.
- Every culture has experienced problems with drug use or abuse.
- As far back as 2240 B.C., Hammurabi the Babylonian king and lawgiver addressed the problems associated with excessive use of alcohol.
- Today, drugs are more potent than they were years ago.
- Drug use and especially drug dealing is becoming a major factor in the growth of crime among the young.
- Seven in 10 drug users work full-time.
- According to biological theories, drug abuse has an innate physical beginning stemming from physical characteristics that cause certain individuals either to experiment with or to crave drugs to the point of abuse.
- Abuse of drugs by some people may represent an attempt to relieve underlying psychiatric disorders.

- "Addiction to pleasure" theory assumes that it is biologically normal to continue a pleasure stimulus (such as drug use), when once begun.
- A strong relationship exists between severe drug addiction and mental illness.
- Sigmund Freud believed that addiction to drugs was an outgrowth of habitual (compulsive) masturbatory activity.
- Such personality traits as extreme forms of introversion and extroversion may explain why many people abuse drugs.
- Drug use is generally always learned from others.
- When drug use becomes consistent and habitual, it usually occurs in the peer group setting, with people we like.
- Drugs are sometimes used to compensate for a lack of self-confidence.
- No single theory can explain why most people use drugs.
- Some theories advocate that an individual's alliance with drug-using peers largely results from an inability to cope with rapid societal change.
- People who perceive themselves as drug users are more likely to develop serious drug abuse problems.

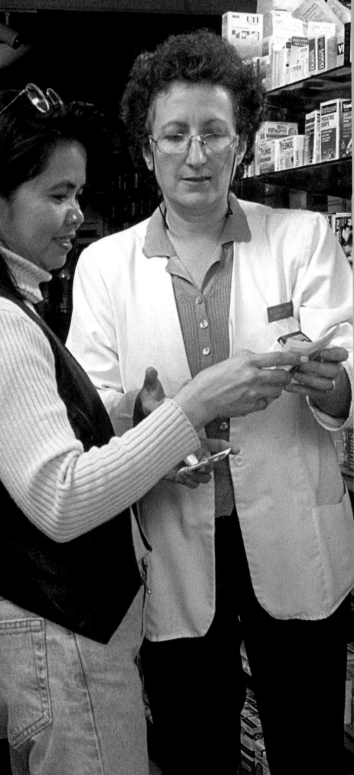

Chapter 2

Learning Objectives

On completing this chapter you will be able to:

▶ List six reasons why drug use or abuse is a more serious problem today than it was in the past.

▶ List and briefly describe the genetic and biophysical theories, as they biologically explain drug use that often leads to abuse.

▶ Explain how drugs of abuse act as positive reinforcers.

▶ Explain the relationships between some mental disorders and possible effects of certain drugs.

▶ Explain four ways that genetic factors directly or indirectly contribute to drug abuse.

▶ Explain the relationship between introverted or extraverted personality patterns and possible effects of stimulants or depressants.

▶ Briefly define and explain reinforcement or learning theory and some of its applications to drug use and abuse.

▶ List and briefly describe the four sociological theories broadly known as social influence theories.

▶ Describe symptoms and indicators of possible drug use or abuse in childhood behavior patterns.

▶ List and describe three factors in the learning process that Howard Becker believes first-time users go through before they become attached to using illicit psychoactive drugs.

▶ Define the following concepts as they relate to drug use: primary and secondary deviance, master status, and retrospective interpretation.

▶ Explain how Reckless's containment theory accounts for the roles of both internal and external controls regarding the attraction to drug use.

▶ Understand how making low-risk and high-risk drug choices regarding drug use directly affects drug use.

Introduction

Chapter 1 introduced a preliminary overview of drug use. In this chapter, we focus on the major explanations of drug use and/or abuse. The questions we explore are: Why would anyone voluntarily consume drugs when they are not medically needed or required? Why are some people attracted to altering their minds? Why are others uneasy and uncomfortable with the euphoric effects of recreational drug use? Why do people subject their bodies and minds to the harmful effects of repetitive drug use, eventual addiction, and relapse back into drug use? What logical reasons could explain such apparently irrational behavior?

Following are three perspectives regarding drug use:

> Yes, I use a lot of drugs. I like the high from weed [marijuana], the buzz from coke [cocaine], and liquor also. I like psychedelic drugs but can't do them often because one, they are harder to get, and two, I work all the time and go to school at night. Psychedelics require big time commitment and I just don't have that amount of time anymore to play around with intense mind trips. I think I am biologically attracted to drugs. What else would explain the desire to get high all the time? Some of my friends are worse than me. They don't just hang with the desire to continually want to get high, they just do it. One friend of mine does not accomplish much, my other two friends are coke addicts but they say they are not addicted, they claim to just like it. I don't think a day goes by, unless I am sick with the flu or something, that I don't get at least a little buzzed on some drug. My wife does not do any drugs, but hey, she's cool with my drug use as long as I keep working every day. *(From Venturelli's research files, graduate student and full time insurance claims adjuster, age 28, July 12, 2000.)*

> You are asking the wrong person about drug use. I am against such drugs as marijuana, cocaine, tobacco, and LSD. My friends feel the same. I occasionally drink when I am with friends or at a party, but even one or two drinks make me feel out of it. I just don't like to feel as if I am losing control of reality, I like reality too much. . . . I think people who use drugs liberally are in some way addicted to the feeling of being high. They are not aware of

how great it is to be in control of their thinking. *(From Venturelli's research files, male graduate university student, age 28, March 6, 1996.)*

> Yes, I have friends who try to tell me to slow down when we are smoking weed and drinking. I just like to get high until I am about to pass out. If I could, I would be high all day without any time out. Never think about quitting or slowing down when it comes to drugs. The only time I am happy is when I am completely zonked out. I guess I am a little attached to these drugs—I am addicted to them! *(From Venturelli's research files, male public high school student in a small Midwestern city, age 15, September 9, 1996.)*

The above excerpts show extensive variation of values and attitudes regarding drug use. The first interviewee represents a type of drug user who is powerfully attracted to drug use. He appears to believe that his attraction to drugs has a biological basis and he would like to feel the effects of drugs on a daily basis. The second interviewee represents a type of user who shuns any alteration of his reality. The third interviewee represents a type of drug user who is unaware of the pitfalls of drug addiction and is recklessly involved with substance abuse. These three views represent only a small fraction of the reasons and motivations that push people to either use or not use drugs.

Why the differences in drug use? In this chapter, we offer answers to this question by examining the motivations underlying drug use. We offer different major theoretical explanations about what causes people to initially use and often eventually abuse drugs.

To accomplish these goals, this chapter frames the different explanations within major theoretical perspectives. Like the United States, nearly all other countries are experiencing increasing amounts of drug use within certain subcultures. Moreover, as we attempt to offer major theoretical and scientific explanations for drug use, we should be able to develop an understanding of why drugs are so seductive not only in our society but also globally.

Drug Use: A Timeless Affliction

Historical records document drug use as far back as 2240 B.C., when Hammurabi, the Babylonian king and lawgiver, addressed the problems associated with drinking alcohol. Even before then, the Sumerian people of Asia Minor, who created the cuneiform (wedge-shaped alphabet), included references to a "joy plant" that dates from about 5000 B.C. Experts indicate that the plant was an opium poppy used as a sedative (O'Brien et al. 1992).

As noted in Chapter 1, virtually every culture has experienced problems with drug use or abuse. Today's drug use problems are part of a very long and rich tradition.

> These [intoxicating] substances have formed a bond of union between men of opposite hemispheres, the uncivilized and the civilized; they have forced passages which, once open, proved of use for other purposes; they produced in ancient races characteristics which have endured to the present day, evidencing the marvelous degree of intercourse that existed between different peoples just as certainly and exactly as a chemist can judge the relations of two substances by their reactions. (Louis Lewin, *Phantasica,* in Rudgley 1993, p. 3)

The quest for explaining drug use is more important than ever as the problem continues to evolve. There are many reasons why drug use and abuse are even more serious issues now than they were in the past, thus these current findings are:

1. From 1960 to the present, drug use has become a widespread phenomenon.

2. Today, drugs are much more potent than they were years ago. The drug content of marijuana in 1960 was 1% to 2%; today, due to new cultivation techniques, it varies from 4% to 6%.

3. Crack and other manufactured drugs offer potent effects at low cost, vastly multiplying the damage potential of drug abuse (Inciardi et al. 1993).

4. Whether they are legal or not, drugs are extremely popular. Their sale is a multibillion dollar a year business, with a major influence on many national economies.

5. Drug use endangers the future of a society by harming its youth and potentially destroying the lives of many young men and women. When gateway drugs, such as alcohol and tobacco are used at an early age, a strong probability exists that the use will progress to other drugs, such as marijuana, cocaine, and amphetamines. Early drug use will likely lead to a lifelong habit, which usually has serious implications for the future.

6. Drug use and especially drug dealing is becoming a major factor in the growth of crime rates among the young. Violent delinquent gangs are increasing at an alarming rate. Violent gun shootings, drive-by killings, carjacking, and "wilding" occur frequently in cities (and increasingly in small towns).

7. The fact that 7 in 10 drug users work full-time (*USA Today* 1999) increases the possibility of near or serious accidents caused by workers, especially because today we have become completely dependent on technology. For example, the operation of sophisticated machines and electronic equipment requires that workers and professionals be free of the effects of mind-altering drugs. Imagine if, on a daily basis, a certain percentage of air traffic controllers were under the influence of mind-altering drugs while working or if a certain percentage of school-bus drivers were high on cocaine each day.

With remarkable and unsurpassed excellence in scientific, technological, and electronic accomplishments, one might think that in the United States, drug use and abuse would be considered irrational behavior. One might also think that the allure of drugs would diminish on the basis of the statistically high proportions of accidents, crimes, domestic violence, relationship strife, and early deaths that result from the use and abuse of licit and illicit drugs. Yet, as the latest drug use figures show (see Chapter 1) knowledge of these effects is often not a deterrent to drug use.

Considering these costs, what explains the continuing use and abuse of drugs? What could possibly sustain and feed the attraction to use mind-altering drugs? Why are drugs used when the consequences are so well documented?

In answering these questions, we need to recall from Chapter 1 some basic reasons why people take drugs:

1. People may be searching for pleasure.

2. Drugs may relieve stress or tension or provide a temporary escape for people with excessive anxieties or severe depression.

3. Peer pressure is a strong influence, especially for young people.

4. In some cases, drugs may enhance religious or mystical experiences.

5. Drugs are used for enhancing recreational pursuits such as the popular use of Ecstasy at raves and music festivals.

6. Some believe that illicit use of drugs can enhance work performance, such as the use of cocaine by stockbrokers, office workers, and lawyers.

7. Drugs can relieve pain and symptoms of an illness.

Although these reasons may indicate some underlying causes of excessive or abusive drug use, they also suggest that the variety and complexity of explanations and motivations are almost infinite. For any one individual, it is seldom clear when the drug use shifts from nondestructive use to abuse and addiction. When we consider the wide use of such licit drugs as alcohol, nicotine, and caffeine, we find that over 88% of the U.S. population use different types of drugs on a daily basis (Drug Strategies 1995; SAMHSA 1998). Further, as we see in later chapters, some drugs can mimic many of the hundreds of moods people can experience.

We can therefore begin to understand why the explanations for drug use and abuse are complicated and cannot be forced into one or two theories. Researchers have tackled the drug use and abuse question from three major theoretical positions, namely, biological, psychological, and sociological perspectives. The remainder of this chapter discusses these three major explanations.

Biological Explanations

As noted in Chapter 1, biological explanations have tended to use genetic theories and the disease model to explain drug addiction. The view that alcoholism is a sickness dates back approximately 200 years (Conrad and Schneider 1980; Heitzeg 1996). The disease perspective is upheld by Jellinek's (1960) view that alcoholism largely involves a loss of control over drinking and that the

drinker experiences clearly distinguishable phases in his or her drinking patterns. For example, concerning alcoholism, the illness affects the abuser to the point of loss of control. Thus, the disease model views drug abuse as an illness in need of treatment or therapy.

According to biological theories, drug abuse has a beginning stemming from physical characteristics that cause certain individuals either to experiment with or to crave drugs to the point of abusive use. Genetic and biophysiological theories explain addiction in terms of genetics, brain dysfunction, and biochemical patterns.

Biological explanations emphasize that the central nervous system (CNS) reward sensors in some people are more sensitive to drugs, making the drug experience more pleasant and more rewarding for these individuals (Jarvik 1990; Mathias 1995). In contrast, others find the effects of drugs of abuse very unpleasant; such people are not likely to be attracted to these drugs (Farrar and Kearns 1989).

Most experts acknowledge that biological factors play an essential role in drug abuse. These factors likely determine how the brain responds to these drugs and why such substances prove addictive. It is thought that by identifying the nature of the biological systems that contribute to drug abuse problems, improved prevention and treatment methods can be developed (Koob 2000).

All the major biological explanations related to drug abuse assume that these substances exert their psychoactive effects by altering brain chemistry or *neuronal* (basic functional cell of the brain) activity. Specifically, the drugs of abuse interfere with the functioning of neurotransmitters, chemical messengers used for communication between brain regions (see Chapter 5 for details). The following are three principal biological theories that help explain why some drugs are abused and why certain people are more likely to become addicted when using these substances.

■ ABUSED DRUGS ARE POSITIVE REINFORCERS

Biological research has shown that stimulating some brain regions with an electrode causes very pleasurable sensations. In fact, laboratory animals would rather self-administer stimulation to these brain areas than eat or engage in sex. It has been demonstrated that drugs of abuse also activate these same pleasure centers of the brain (Weiss 1999).

It is generally believed that most drugs with abuse potential enhance pleasure centers by causing the release of specific brain neurotransmitters such as dopamine (Bespalov et al. 1999). Brain cells become accustomed to the presence of these neurotransmitters and crave them when they are absent, leading the person to seek more drugs (Spanagel and Weiss 1999). In addition, it has been proposed that overstimulation of these brain regions by continual drug use "exhausts" these dopamine systems, and leads to depression and an inability to experience normal pleasure (Volkow 1999).

■ DRUG ABUSE AND PSYCHIATRIC DISORDERS

Biological explanations are thought to be responsible for the substantial overlap that exists between drug addiction and mental illness. Because of the similarities, severe drug dependence itself is classified as a form of psychiatric disorder by the American Psychiatric Association (see the discussion of *Diagnostic and Statistical Manual*, fourth edition revised [DSM IV-TR] classifications later in this chapter). For example, abuse of drugs can in and of itself cause mental conditions that mimic major psychiatric illness, such as schizophrenia, severe anxiety disorders, and suicidal depression (APA 2000). It is believed that these similarities occur as a result of common chemical factors that are altered both by drugs of abuse and during episodes of psychiatric illness (NIDA 1993). Several important potential consequences of this relationship may help us understand the nature of drug abuse problems.

1. *Psychiatric disorders and drug addiction often occur simultaneously.* This conclusion is supported by the fact that substance abuse–related problems often coexist with other mental diseases such as conduct disorder, schizophrenia, and mood disorders (APA 2000). Due to the common mechanisms, drug abuse is likely to expose or worsen psychiatric illnesses, making management of these problems considerably more difficult (APA 2000).

> ### KEY TERMS
>
> **genetic and biophysiological theories**
> explanations of addiction in terms of genetic brain dysfunction and biochemical patterns
>
> **central nervous system**
> one of the major divisions of the nervous system, composed of the brain and the spinal cord
>
> **psychoactive effects**
> how drug substances alter and affect the brain's mental functions
>
> **neurotransmitters**
> chemical messengers released by neurons (nerve cells) for communication with other cells
>
> **dopamine**
> the brain transmitter believed to mediate the rewarding aspects of most drugs of abuse

2. *Therapies that are successful in treating psychiatric disorders may be useful in treating mental problems caused by drugs of abuse.* It is likely that many of the therapeutic lessons we learn about dealing with psychiatric illnesses can be useful in drug abuse treatment, and vice versa.

3. *Abuse of drugs by some people may represent an attempt to relieve underlying psychiatric disorders.* Such people commonly use CNS depressants such as alcohol to relieve anxiety, whereas CNS stimulants such as cocaine are frequently used by patients with depression disorders (Grinspoon 1993). In such cases, if the underlying psychiatric problem is relieved, the likelihood of successfully treating drug abuse disorder improves substantially.

■ GENETIC EXPLANATIONS

One biological theory receiving scrutiny suggests that inherited traits can predispose some individuals to drug addiction. Such theories have been supported by the observation that increased frequency of alcoholism and drug abuse exists among children of alcoholics and drug abusers (APA 2000; Uhl et al.

1993). Using adoption records of some 3000 individuals from Sweden, researchers Cloninger, Gohman, and Sigvardsson conducted one of the most extensive research studies examining genetics and alcoholism. They found that ". . . children of alcoholic parents were likely to grow up to be alcoholics themselves, even in cases where the children were reared by nonalcoholic adoptive parents almost from birth" (Doweiko 1996, p. 217). Such studies estimate that drug vulnerability due to genetic influences accounts for approximately 38% of all cases, whereas environmental and social factors account for the balance (Uhl et al. 1993).

Other studies attempting to identify the specific genes that may predispose the carrier to drug abuse problems have suggested that a brain target site (called a *receptor*—see Chapter 5 for details) for dopamine is altered in a manner that increases the drug abuse vulnerability (Wyman 1997). Studies that test for genetic factors in complex behaviors such as drug abuse are very difficult to conduct and interpret. It is sometimes impossible to design experiments that distinguish among genetic, social, environmental, and psychological influences in human populations. For example, inherited traits are known to be major contributors to psychiatric disorders, such as schizophrenia and depression. Many people with one of these illnesses also have a substance abuse disorder (APA 2000). A high incidence of an abnormal gene in a cocaine-abusing population, for example, not only may be linked to drug abuse behavior but also may be associated with depression or another psychiatric disorder (Uhl et al. 1992).

Theoretically, genetic factors can directly or indirectly contribute to drug abuse vulnerability in several ways:

1. Psychiatric disorders that are genetically determined may be relieved by drugs of abuse, thus encouraging their use.

2. In some people, reward centers of the brain may be genetically determined to be especially sensitive to addictive drugs; thus, the use of drugs by these people would be particularly pleasurable and would lead to a high rate of addiction.

3. Character traits, such as insecurity and vulnerability, that often lead to drug abuse behavior may be genetically determined, causing a high rate of addiction in these people.

4. Factors that determine how difficult it is to break away from drug addiction may be genetically determined, causing severe craving or very unpleasant withdrawal effects. People with this predisposition are less likely to abandon their drug of abuse.

The appeal of the genetic theories for explaining drug abuse may help us to understand the reasons that drug addiction occurs in some individuals but not in others. In addition, if genetic factors play a major role in drug abuse, it might be possible to use genetic screening to identify people who are especially vulnerable to drug abuse problems and to help such individuals avoid exposure to these substances.

Psychological Explanations

Psychological theories mostly deal with mental or emotional states, often associated with or exacerbated by social and environmental factors. Psychological explanations of addiction include one or more of the following: escape from reality, boredom (Burns 1997), inability to cope with anxiety, destructive self-indulgence to the point of constantly desiring intoxicants, blind compliance with drug-abusing peers, self-destructiveness, and conscious and unconscious ignorance regarding the harmful effects of abusing drugs.

Freud established early psychological theories. He linked "primal addictions" with masturbation and postulated that all later addictions, including alcohol and other drugs, were caused by ego impairments. Freud said that drugs fulfill insecurities that stem from parental inadequacies, causing difficulty in adequately forming bonds of friendships. He claimed that alcoholism (see Chapter 9) is an expression of the death instinct, as are self-destruction, narcissism, and oral fixations. Although Freud's views represent interesting intuitive insights often not depicted in other theories, his theoretical concerns are difficult to observe and test, and do not generate enough concrete data for verification.

■ DISTINGUISHING BETWEEN SUBSTANCE ABUSE AND MENTAL DISORDERS

The American Psychiatric Association has established widely accepted categories of diagnosis for behavioral disorders, including substance abuse. As standardized diagnostic categories, the characteristics of mental disorders have been analyzed by professional committees over many years and today are summarized in their revised fourth generation of development in a widely accepted book called the *DSM IV-TR,* or *Diagnostic and Statistical Manual, Revised,* fourth edition. In addition to categories for severe psychotic disorders and more common neurotic disorders, experts in the field of psychiatry have established specific diagnostic criteria for various forms of substance abuse. All patterns of drug abuse that are described in this text have a counterpart description in the DSM IV-TR manual for medical professionals. For example, the DSM IV-TR discusses the mental disorders resulting from the use or abuse of sedatives, hypnotics, or antianxiety drugs; alcohol; narcotics; amphetamine-like drugs; cocaine; caffeine; nicotine (tobacco); hallucinogens; phencyclidine (PCP); inhalants; and cannabis (marijuana). This manual of psychiatric diagnoses discusses in detail the mental disorders related to the drug use, the side effects of medications, and the consequence of toxic exposure to these substances (APA 2000).

Because of the similarities between, and the coexistence of substance-related mental disorders and primary psychiatric disorders, it is sometimes difficult to distinguish between the two problems; however, in order for proper treatment to be rendered, the cause of psychological symptoms must be determined. According to DSM-IV criteria, substance use (or abuse) disorders can be identified by the occurrence and consequence of dependence, abuse, intoxication, and withdrawal. These important distinguishing features of substance abuse disorders are discussed in detail in Chapter 6 and in conjunction with each drug group.

According to the DSM IV-TR, the following information can also help distinguish between substance-induced and primary mental disorders: (1) personal and family medical, psychiatric, and drug histories; (2) physical examinations; and (3) laboratory tests to assess physiological functions and determine the presence or absence of drugs. However, the possibility of a primary mental disorder should not be excluded just because the patient is using drugs—remember, many drug users use drugs to self-medicate their primary psychiatric problems. The coexistence of underlying psychiatric problems in a drug user is suggested by the following circumstances: (1) the psychiatric problems do not match the usual drug effects (e.g., use of marijuana usually does not cause severe psychotic behavior); (2) the psychiatric disorder was present before the patient began abusing substances; and (3) the mental disorder persists for more than 4 weeks after substance use ends. The DSM IV-TR makes it clear that the relationship between mental disorders and substances of abuse is important for proper diagnosis, treatment, and understanding (APA 2000).

■ THE RELATIONSHIP BETWEEN PERSONALITY AND DRUG USE

Since medieval times, personality theories of increasing sophistication have been used to classify long-term behavioral tendencies or traits that appear in individuals, and these traits have long been considered to be influenced by biological or chemical factors. Although such classification systems have varied widely, nearly all have shared two commonly observed dimensions of personality: introversion and extraversion. Individuals who show a predominant tendency to turn their thoughts and feelings inward rather than to direct attention outward have been considered to show the trait of *introversion.* At the opposite extreme, a tendency to seek outward activity and sharing feelings with others has been called *extroversion.* Of course, every individual shows a mix of such traits in varying degrees and circumstances.

In some research studies, introversion and extroversion patterns have been associated with levels of neural arousal in brainstem circuits (Apostolides 1996; Carlson 1990; Gray 1987) and these forms of arousal are closely associated with effects caused by drug stimulants or depressants. Such research hypothesizes that people whose systems produce high levels of sensitivity to neural arousal

social learning theory
theory that places emphasis on how an individual learns patterns of behavior from the attitudes of others, society, and peers

habituation
repeating certain patterns of behavior until they become established or habitual

"addiction to pleasure" theory
theory assuming that it is biologically normal to continue a pleasure stimulus once begun

sensation-seeking individuals
types of people who characteristically are continually seeking new or novel thrills in their experiences

differential reinforcement
ratio between reinforcers, both favorable and disfavorable, for sustaining drug use behavior

may find high-intensity external stimuli to be painful, and may react by turning inward. With these extremely high levels of sensitivity, such people may experience neurotic levels of anxiety or panic disorders. At the other extreme, individuals whose systems provide them with very low levels of sensitivity to neural arousal may find that moderate stimuli are inadequate to produce responses. To reach moderate levels of arousal, they may turn outward to seek high-intensity external sources of stimulation (Eysenck and Eysenck 1985; Gray 1987; Rousar et al. 1995).

Because high- and low-arousal symptoms are easy to create by using stimulants, depressants, or hallucinogens, it is possible that these personality patterns of introversion or extroversion will affect how a person reacts to substances. For people whose experience is predominantly introverted or extraverted, extremes of high or low sensitivity may lead them to seek counteracting substances that become important methods of bringing experience to a level that seems bearable.

■ **THEORIES BASED ON LEARNING PROCESSES**

How are abuse patterns learned? Research on learning or conditioning explains how human beings acquire new patterns of behavior by the close association or pairing of one significant reinforcing stimulus with another less significant or neutral stimulus. Also known as social learning theory (Bandura 1977) (explained more fully later), this theory emphasizes that learned associations occur in the presence of other people using drugs coupled with other, often preconceived associations with the attitudes of society and friends about drug use (Gray 1999). In this method of learning, people form expectations and become used to certain behavior patterns. This specific process of learning is known as *conditioning*, and it explains why pleasurable activities may become intimately connected with other activities that are also pleasurable, neutral, or even unpleasant. In addition, people can turn any new behavior into a recurrent and permanent one by the process of habituation —repeating certain patterns of behavior until they become established or habitual.

The basic process by which learning mechanisms can lead a person into drug use is also described in Bejerot's "addiction to pleasure" theory (Bejerot 1965, 1972, 1975). The theory assumes that it is biologically normal to continue a pleasure stimulus once started. Several research findings support this theory, indicating that "a strong, biologically based need for stimulation appears to make sensation-seeking young adults more vulnerable to drug abuse" (Mathias 1995, p. 1). A second research finding complementing this theory states, "Certain areas of the brain, when stimulated, produce pleasurable feelings. Psychoactive substances are capable of acting on these brain mechanisms to produce these sensations. These pleasurable feelings become reinforcers that drive the continued use of the substances" (Gardner 1992, p. 43). People at highest risk for drug use and addiction are those who maintain a constant preoccupation with getting high, seek new or novel thrills in their experiences, and are known to have a relentless desire to pursue physical stimulation or dangerous behaviors and are classified as sensation-seeking individuals .

Drug use may also be reinforced when it is associated with receiving affection or approval in a social setting, such as within a peer group relationship. Initially, the use of drugs may not be very important or pleasurable to the individual. However, eventually the affection and social rewards experienced when drugs are used becomes associated with the drug. In this example, drug use and intimacy may become perceived as very worthwhile.

> I don't know how to explain why but an attractive part of cocaine use is the instant feeling of intimacy with others who are also snorting this drug. You just don't want to leave the scene when the lines are cut on the glass surface and people are taking turns snorting coke. Even after I have had four or five lines and the conversation is very friendly and engaging, leaving the scene because someone is waiting for you at home or even if you have to meet with someone that night does not matter. Usually, everyone is feeling high, a lot of feelings of togetherness, and open to intimate conversation. I never saw anyone getting violent or anything like that, but I hear that it can happen especially if you have a grudge against someone before doing the coke. I think that coke just makes you more open and if you are an angry person then it will just bring it out in you. My experiences have been that everyone is just so friendly and everyone just pretends not to be overly anxious to do the next line. Actually, everyone is kind of pretending, because what they really want is more powder up their nose and an unending amount of time for talking the night away. *(From Venturelli's research files, 26-year-old male graduate student, residing in Chicago, Illinois, May 18, 2000.)*

By the conditioning process, a pleasurable experience such as drug taking may become associated with a comforting or soothing environment. When this happens, two different outcomes may result. First, the user may feel uncomfortable taking the drug in any other environment. Second, the user may become very accustomed or habituated to the familiar environment as part of the drug experience. The user may not experience the same level of rush or high in this environment and in response may take more drugs or seek a different environment.

Finally, through this process of conditioning and habituation, a drug user becomes accustomed to unpleasant effects of drug use such as withdrawal symptoms. Such unpleasant effects and experiences may become *habituated*—neutralized or less severe in their impact—so that the user can continue taking drugs without feeling or experiencing the negative effects of the drug.

■ SOCIAL PSYCHOLOGICAL LEARNING THEORIES

Other extensions of reinforcement or learning theory focus on how positive social influences by drug-using peers reinforce the attraction to drugs. Social interaction, peer camaraderie, social approval, and drug use work together as positive reinforcers to sustain drug use (Akers 1992). Thus, if the effects of drug use become personally rewarding, "or become reinforcing through conditioning, the chances of continuing to use are greater than for stopping" (Akers 1992, p. 86). It is through learned expectations, or association with others who reinforce drug use, that individuals learn the pleasures of drug taking (Becker 1963, 1967). Similarly, if drug use leads to poor and disruptive social interactions, drug use may cease.

Note that positive reinforcers, such as peers, other friends and acquaintances, family members, and drug advertisements, do not act alone in inciting and sustaining drug use. Learning theory as defined here also relies on some variable amounts of imitation and trial-and-error learning methods.

Finally, differential reinforcement —defined as the ratio between reinforcers favorable and disfavorable for sustaining drug use behavior—must be considered. The use and eventual abuse of drugs can vary with certain favorable or unfavorable reinforcing experiences. The primary determining conditions are listed:

1. The amount of exposure to drug-using peers versus non–drug-using peers.

2. The general preference for drug use in a particular neighborhood or community.

3. The age of initial use (younger adolescents are more greatly affected than older adolescents).

4. The frequency of drug use among peers.

Sociological Explanations

Sociological explanations for drug use share important commonalities with psychological explanations under social learning theories. The main distinguishing features determining psychological and sociological explanations are that psychological explanations focus more on how the *internal states* of the drug user are affected by social relationships within families, peers, and other close and more distant relationships, whereas sociological explanations focus on how factors *external to the drug user* affect drug use. Such outside forces include the types of families, adopted lifestyles of peer groups, or types of neighborhoods and communities in which avid drug users reside. The sociological perspective views the motivation for drug use as largely determined by the types and quality of bonds (attachment versus detachment) that the drug user or potential drug user has with significant others and with the social environment in general. The degree of influence and involvement with external factors affecting the individual compared with the influence exerted by internal states distinguishes sociological from psychological analyses.

As previously stated, no one biological and psychological theory can adequately explain why most people use drugs. People differ from one another in terms of personality, motivational factors, upbringing, learned priority of values and attitudes, and problems faced. Because of these differences, many responses and reasons exist why people take drugs and this results in a plurality of theoretical explanations. Further, the diverse perspectives of biology, psychology, and sociology offer their own explanations for drug use and abuse.

There are two sets of sociological theories: social influence and social structural. Social influence theories focus on microscopic explanations that concentrate on the roles played by significant others and their impact on an individual. Structural influence theories focus on macroscopic explanations of drug use and the assumption that the

organizational structure of society has a major independent impact on an individual's use of drugs. The next sections examine these theories.

■ SOCIAL INFLUENCE THEORIES

The theories presented in this section are known as (1) social learning, (2) role of significant others in socialization, (3) labeling, and (4) subculture theories. The basis of these theories is that an individual's motivation to seek drugs is caused by social influences or social pressures.

Social Learning Theory

Social learning theory explains drug use as learned behavior. Conventional learning occurs through imitation, trial and error, improvisation, rewarded behavior, and cognitive mental associations and processes (Liska and Messner 1999). Social learning theory focuses directly on how drug use and abuse are learned through interaction with other drug users.

This theory emphasizes the pervasive influence of *primary groups*, that is, groups that share a high amount of intimacy and spontaneity and whose members are emotionally bonded. Families and long-term friends are examples of primary groups. In contrast, *secondary groups* are groups that share segmented relationships where interaction is based on prescribed role patterns. An example of a secondary group would be the relationship between you and a sales clerk in a grocery store or relationships between employees scattered throughout a corporation. Social learning theory addresses a type of interaction that is highly specific. This type of interaction involves learning specific motives, techniques, and appropriate meanings that are commonly attached to a particular type of drug.

The following are examples of first-time users learning drug-using techniques from their social circles:

> The first time I tried smoking weed, nothing much happened. I always thought it was like smoking a cigarette. When the joint came around the first time, I refused it. The next time it came around, I noticed everyone was looking at me. So, I took the joint and started to inhale, then exhale.

KEY TERMS

social influence theories
mainly social psychological theories that view a person's day-to-day social relations as a primary cause for drug use

structural influence theories
theories that view the structural organization of a society, peer group, or subculture as directly responsible for drug use

My friend sitting next to me said something to the effect, "Dude, hold it in; don't waste it. This is good weed and we don't have that much between us." Right after that, we did some "shotguns." This is where someone exhales directly into your mouth—lips to lips. My friend filled my lungs with his exhaled weed breath. After the first comment about holding it in, I started to watch how everyone was inhaling and realized that you really don't smoke weed like an ordinary cigarette; you have to hold in the smoke. *(From Venturelli's research files, male, age 16, second year high school student in a small Midwestern town, February 15, 1997.)*

I first started using drugs, mostly alcohol and pot, because my best friend in high school was using drugs. My best friend Tim [a pseudonym] learned from his older sister. Before I actually tried pot, Tim kept telling me how great it was to be high on dope; he said it was much better than beer. I was really nervous the first time I tried pot with Tim and another friend even though I heard so much detail about it from Tim. The first time I tried it, it was a complete letdown. The second time (the next day, I think it was), I remember I was talking about a teacher we had and in the middle of the conversation, I remember how everything appeared different. I started feeling happy and while listening to Tim as he poked jokes about the teacher, I started to hear the background music more clearly than ever before. By the time the music ended and a new CD started, I knew I was high. *(From Venturelli's research files, 22-year-old male student at a private liberal arts college in the Midwest, February 15, 1997.)*

First time I tried acid [LSD] I didn't know what to expect. Schwa [a pseudonym] told me it was a very different high from grass [marijuana]. After munching on one "square" [one dose of LSD]— after about 20 minutes—I looked at Schwa and he started laughing and said, "Feelin' the effects, Ki-ki?" I said, "Is this it?! Is this what it feels like? I feel weird."

With a devious grin . . . Schwa said, "Yep. We are now on the runway, ready to take off. Just wait a little while longer, it's going to get better and better. Fasten your seat belts!" (*From Venturelli's files, male, age 33, May 6, 1996.*)

Learning to perceive the effects of the drug is the second major outcome in the process of becoming a regular user. Here, the ability to feel the authentic effects of the drug is being learned. The more experienced drug users in the group impart their knowledge to naive first-time users. The coaching information they provide describes how to recognize the euphoric effects of the drug.

I just sat there waiting for something to happen, but I really didn't know what to expect. After the fifth "hit" [a hit consists of deeply inhaling a marijuana cigarette as it is being passed around and shared in a group], I was just about ready to give up ever getting high.

Then suddenly, my best buddy looked deeply into my eyes and said, "Aren't you high yet?" Instead of just answering the question, I immediately repeated the same words the exact way he asked me. In a flash, we both simultaneously burst out laughing. This uncontrollable laughter went on for what appeared to be over 5 minutes. Then he said, "You silly ass, it's not like an alcohol high, it's a 'high high.' Don't you feel it? It's a totally different kind of high."

At that very moment, I knew I was definitely high on the stuff. If this friend would not have said this to me, I probably would have continued thinking that getting high on the hash was impossible for me. *(From Venturelli's files, 17-year-old male attending a small, private liberal arts college in the Southeast, May 15, 1984.)*

Once drug use has begun, continuing the behavior involves learning the following sequence: (1) where and from whom the drug can be purchased, (2) maintaining steady contact with drug dealers, (3) preoccupation with maintaining the secrecy of use from authority figures and casual non-drug using acquaintances, (4) reassuring yourself that the drug use is pleasurable, (5) using with more frequency, and (6) replacing non-drug-using friends with drug-using friends.

Role of Significant Others

Once a pattern of drug use has been established, the learning process plays a role in sustaining drug-taking behavior. Edwin Sutherland (1947; Liska and Messner 1999), a pioneering criminologist in sociology, believed that the mastery of criminal behavior depended on the frequency, duration, priority, and intensity of contact with others who are involved in similar behavior (Heitzeg 1996). This theory can also be applied to drug-taking behavior.

In applying Sutherland's principles of social learning to drug use, which he called *differential association theory*, the focus is on how other members of social groups reward criminal behavior and under what conditions this deviance is perceived as important and pleasurable.

Becker and Sutherland's theories explain why adolescents may use psychoactive drugs. Essentially, both theories say that the use of drugs is learned during intimate interaction with others who serve as a primary group. (See "Here and Now," Symptoms of Drug and Alcohol Abuse, for information on how the role of significant others can determine a child's disposition toward or away from illicit drug use.)

Learning theory also explains how adults and the elderly are taught the motivation for using a particular type of drug. This learning occurs through influences such as drug advertising, with its emphasis on testimonials by avid users, by medical experts, and by actors and actresses portraying physicians or nurses. Listeners, viewers, and readers who experience such commercials promoting a particular brand name of over-the-counter drugs, are bombarded with the necessary motives, preferred techniques, and appropriate attitudes for consuming drugs. When drug advertisements and medical experts recommend a particular drug for specific ailments, in effect they are authoritatively persuading viewers, listeners, or readers that taking a drug will soothe or cure the medical problem presented.

Are Drug Users More Likely to Be Devious?

Social scientists—primarily sociologists and social psychologists—believe that many social develop-

ment patterns are closely linked to drug use. Based on the age when an adolescent starts to consume alcohol and other drugs, predictions can be made about his or her sexual behavior, academic performance, and other behaviors, such as lying, cheating, fighting, and using marijuana. Similar predictions can be made when the adolescent begins using marijuana. A more detailed study (SAMHSA 2000) shows that there is a strong relationship between adolescent behavior problems and alcohol use. Figure 2.1 shows that often, past-month adolescent heavy drinking and emotional/behavioral problems occurred concurrently. Adolescents who drink heavily between the ages of 12 to 17 are more likely to report behavior problems (aggressiveness, and delinquent and criminal behaviors) (SAMHSA 2000).

Other studies show that early intense use of alcohol or marijuana represents a move toward less conventional behavior, greater susceptibility to peer influence, increased delinquency, and lower achievement in school. In general, drug abusers have 14 characteristics in common:

1. Their drug use usually follows clear-cut developmental steps and sequences. Use of legal drugs, such as alcohol and cigarettes, almost always precedes use of illegal drugs.

2. Use of certain drugs, particularly habitual use of marijuana, is linked to the amotivational syndrome , which some researchers believe is a general change in personality.* This change is characterized by apathy, lack of interest, and inability or difficulty accomplishing goals. The latest research also clearly shows that marijuana use is often responsible for attention and memory impairment (NIDA 1996).

3. Immaturity, maladjustment, or insecurity usually precede the use of marijuana and other illicit drugs.

---

*Some argue that perhaps a general lack of ambition (also known as *lethargic behavior*) may *precede* rather than *result from* marijuana use or that the amotivational syndrome is present in some heavy marijuana users even before the initial use of this drug, and when the drug is used, the syndrome is more pronounced. In any case, some researchers believe that the steady use of marijuana and the amotivational syndrome occur together.

HERE AND NOW

Symptoms of Drug and Alcohol Abuse

Following are profiles of children who are less likely and more likely, respectively, to use and abuse drugs.

Less Likely to Use Drugs:

- Child comes from a strong family.
- Family has a clearly stated policy toward drug use.
- Child has strong religious convictions.
- Child is an independent thinker, not easily swayed by peer pressure.
- Parents know the child's friends and the friends' parents.
- Child often invites friends into the house and their behavior is open, not secretive.
- Child is busy and productive and pursues many interests.
- Child has a good, secure feeling of self.
- Parents are comfortable with their own use of alcohol, drugs, and pills, set a good example in using these substances, and are comfortable in discussing their use.
- Parents set a good example in handling crisis situations.
- Child maintains at least average grades and good working relationships with teachers.

Symptoms Exhibited by the Child Who May Be Using Drugs

EDITOR'S NOTE: A child will usually display more than one of the symptoms below when experimenting with drugs. Please remember that any number of the symptoms could also be the result of a physical impairment or disorder.

More Likely to Use Drugs:

- Abrupt change in behavior (for example, from very active to passive, loss of interest in previously pursued activities such as sports or hobbies).
- Diminished drive and ambition.
- Moodiness.
- Shortened attention span.
- Impaired communication such as slurred speech, jumbled thinking.
- Significant change in quality of school work.
- Deteriorating judgment and loss of short-term memory.
- Distinct lessening of family closeness and warmth.
- Suddenly popular with new friends who are older and unknown to family members.
- Isolation from family members (hiding in bedroom or locking bedroom door).
- Sneaking out of the house.
- Sudden carelessness regarding appearance.
- Inappropriate overreaction to even mild criticism.
- Secretiveness about whereabouts and personal possessions.
- Friends who avoid introduction or appearance in the child's home.
- Use of words that are odd and unfamiliar.
- Secretiveness or desperation for money.
- Rapid weight loss or appetite loss.
- "Drifting off" beyond normal daydreaming.
- Extreme behavioral changes such as hallucination, violence, unconsciousness, and so on that could indicate a dangerous situation close at hand and needing fast medical attention.
- Unprescribed or unidentifiable pills.
- Strange "contraptions" (e.g. smoking paraphernalia) or hidden articles.
- Articles missing from the house. Child could be stealing to receive money to pay for drugs.

Sources: L.A.W. Publications, *Let's All Work to Fight Drug Abuse* (Addison, TX: C & L Printing Company, 1985) 38. Used with permission of the publisher. Santa Barbara Alcohol and Drug Program, 1996.

FIGURE 2.1

Adolescent behavior problems and substance use in past month.

....

Source: SAMHSA. "Study Shows Strong Relationship Between Adolescent Behavior Problems and Alcohol Use." (1 March 2000). Available www.samhsa.gov/news/docsshowone.cfm?newsid=175.

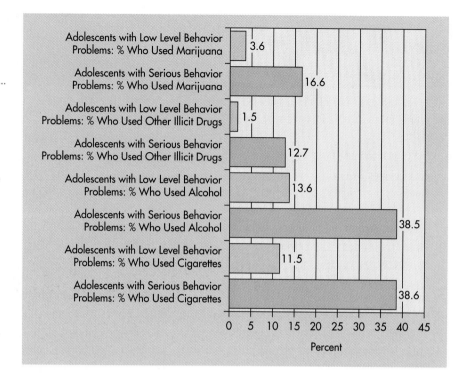

4. Those more likely to try illicit drugs, especially before age 12, usually have a history of poor school performance and classroom disobedience.

5. Delinquent or repetitive deviant activities usually precede involvement with illicit drugs.

6. A set of values and attitudes that facilitates the development of deviant behavior exists before the person tries illicit drugs.

7. A social setting in which drug use is common, such as communities and neighborhoods where peers use drugs indiscriminately, is likely to reinforce and increase the predisposition to drug use.

8. Drug-induced behaviors and drug-related attitudes of peers are usually among the strongest predictors of subsequent drug involvement.

9. Children who feel their parents are distant from their emotional needs are more likely to become drug addicted (see "Here and Now," Does Divorce Affect Adolescent Drug Use?).

10. The *younger* people are when they begin using drugs, the greater the probability of continued and accelerated drug use. Likewise, the *older* people are when they start using drugs, the less the probability of accelerated use and addiction. The period of greatest risk of initiation and habitual use of illicit drugs is usually over by the early 20s.

11. The family structure has changed, with substantially more than half the women in the United States now working outside the home. A higher divorce rate has led to many children being raised in single parent households. How the lack of a stay-at-home parent or how a single family household affects the quality of child care and nurturing is difficult to assess.

12. Mobility obstructs a sense of permanency, and it contributes to a lack of self-esteem. Often, when children are moved from one location to another, their community easily becomes nothing more than a group of strangers. They may have little pride in their home or community and have no commitment to society.

13. Among minority members, a major factor involved in drug dependence is a feeling of powerlessness due to discrimination based on race, social standing, or other attributes. Groups

subject to discrimination have a disproportionately high rate of unemployment and below-average income. Approximately 15 million U.S. children are reared in poverty (Henslin 2001). The adults they have as role models may be unemployed and experience feelings of powerlessness. Higher rates of delinquency and drug addiction occur in such settings.

14. Abusers who become highly involved in selling drugs begin by witnessing that drug trafficking is a lucrative business, especially in rundown neighborhoods. In some communities, selling drugs seems to be the only available alternative to real economic success (Jones 1996; Siegel and Senna 1994; Wilson 1990).

Labeling Theory

Although the controversy continues whether labeling is a theory or perspective (Akers 1968, 1992; Heitzeg 1996; Plummer 1979), this text takes the position that labeling is a theory (Cheron 2001; Hewitt 1994; Liska and Messner 1999), for it

HERE AND NOW   Does Divorce Affect Adolescent Drug Use?

As an example of how drug users may be affected by socialization, a study conducted by Dr. Needle (Needle, Su, and Doherty 1990; NIDA 1990; Siegel and Senna 1994) found higher drug use among adolescents whose parents divorce. According to the study, children who are adolescents when their parents divorce are associated with more extensive drug use and experience more drug-related health, legal, and other problems than their peers. This study linked the extent of teens' drug use to their age at the time of their parents' divorce. Teenagers whose parents divorce were found to use more drugs and experience more drug-related problems than two other groups of adolescents: those who were aged 10 or younger when their parents divorced, and those whose parents remained married.

This study has important implications for drug abuse prevention efforts. Basically, it says that not everyone is at the same risk for drug use. People at greater risk can be identified, and programs should be developed to meet their special needs.

In this research project, drug use among all adolescents increased over time. However, drug use was higher among adolescents whose parents had divorced, either when their children were preteens or teenagers. Drug use was highest for those teens whose parents divorced during their children's adolescent years. Such families also reported more physical problems, family disputes, and arrests.

The research results also showed that distinct gender differences existed in the way that divorce affected adolescent drug use, whether the divorce occurred during the offspring's childhood or adolescent years. Males whose parents divorced reported more drug use and drug-related problems than females. Females whose care-taking parents remarried experienced increased drug use after the remarriage. By contrast, males whose care-taking parents remarried reported a decrease in drug-related problems following the remarriage.

The researchers caution that these findings may have limited applicability, as most of the families were white and had middle to high income levels. Dr. Needle also notes that the results should not be interpreted as an argument in favor of the nuclear family. Overall, divorce affects adolescents in complex ways and remarriage can influence drug-using behavior, particularly when disruptions occur during adolescence; such turmoil can "trigger" a desire for extensive recreational licit and illicit drug use, often leading to drug abuse.

explains something very important with respect to drug use. Although labeling theory does not so much explain why initial drug use occurs, it does detail the processes by which many people come to view themselves as socially deviant from others. Note that the terms *deviant* (in cases of individuals) and *deviance* (in cases of behavior) are sociologically defined as involving the violation of significant social norms held by conventional society. The terms neither are used in a judgmental manner nor are the individuals judged to be immoral or "sick"; instead, the terms refer to an absence from expected patterns of behavior by conventional society.

Labeling theory says that other people whose opinions we value have a determining influence over our self-image (Best 1994; Goode 1997; Liska and Messner 1999). (For an example of how labeling theory applies to real-life situations, see "Case in Point.")

Implied in this theory is that we exert only a small amount of control over the image we portray. In contrast, members of society, especially those we consider to be significant others, have much greater influence and power in defining or redefining our self-image. The image we have of ourselves is vested in the people we admire and look to for guidance and advice. If these people come to define our

actions as deviant, then their definition becomes incorporated as a "fact" of our reality.

We can summarize labeling theory by saying that the labels we use to describe people have a profound influence on their self-perceptions. For example, imagine a fictitious individual known as Billy. Initially, Billy does not see himself as a compulsive drug user but as an occasional recreational drug user. Let us also assume that Billy is very humorous, unpretentious, and very outspoken about his drug use and likes to exaggerate the amount of marijuana he smokes on a daily basis. Slowly Billy's friends begin to perceive him as a "real stoner." According to labeling theory, what happens to Billy? Because of being noticed when "high," his self-presentation, and the comments he makes about the pleasures of drug use, his friends may begin to reinforce the exaggerated drug use image. At first, Billy may enjoy the reflected image of a "big-time" drug user, but after nearly all of his peers maintain a constant exaggerated image, his projected image may turn negative, especially when his friends show disrespect for his opinions. In this example, labeling theory predicts that Billy's perception of himself will begin to mirror the consistent perception expressed by his accusers. If he is unsuccessful in eradicating the addict image or, in this example, the "stoner" image, Billy will reluctantly concur with the label that has been thrust on him. Or, to strive for a self-image as an occasional marijuana user, Billy may abandon his peers so that he can become acceptable once more in the eyes of other people.

An important originator of labeling theory is Edwin Lemert (Hewitt 1994, 255; Lemert 1951; Liska and Messner 1999), who distinguished between two types of deviance: primary and secondary deviance. Primary deviance is inconsequential deviance, which occurs without having a lasting impression on the perpetrator. Generally, most first-time violations of law, for example, are primary deviations. Whether the suspected or accused individual has committed the deviant act does not matter. What matters is whether the individual identifies with the deviant behavior.

Secondary deviance develops when the individual begins to identify and perceive himself or herself as deviant. The moment this transition occurs, deviance shifts from being primary to sec-

---

KEY TERMS

labeling theory
theory emphasizing that other people's perceptions directly influence one's self-image

primary deviance
any type of initial deviant behavior in which the perpetrator does not identify with the deviance

secondary deviance
any type of deviant behavior in which the perpetrator identifies with the deviance

master status
major status position in the eyes of others that clearly identifies an individual, for example, doctor, professor, alcoholic, heroin addict

retrospective interpretation
social psychological process of redefining a person in light of a major status position, for example, homosexual, physician, professor, alcoholic, convicted felon, or mental patient

CASE IN POINT

This excerpt, from the author's files, illustrates labeling theory.

After my mom found out, she never brought it up again. I thought the incident was over—dead, gone, and buried. Well, . . . it wasn't over at all. My mom and dad must have agreed that I couldn't be trusted anymore. I'm sure she was regularly going through my stuff in my room to see if I was still smoking dope. Even my grandparents acted strangely whenever the news on television would report about the latest drug bust in Chicago. Several times that I can't ever forget was when we were together and I could hear the news broadcast on TV from my room about some drug bust. There they all were whispering about me. My grandma asking if I "quitta the dope." One night, I overheard my mother reassure my dad and grandmother that I no

longer was using dope. You can't believe how embarrassed I was that my own family was still thinking that I was a dope fiend. They thought I was addicted to pot like a junkie is addicted to heroin! I can tell you that I would never lay such a guilt trip on my kids if I ever have kids. I remember that for two years after the time I was honest enough to tell my mom that I had tried pot, they would always whisper about me, give me the third degree whenever I returned late from a date, and go through my room looking for dope. They acted as if I was hooked on drugs. I remember that for a while back then I would always think that if they think of me as a drug addict, I might as well get high whenever my friends "toke up." They should have taken me at my word instead of sneaking around my personal belongings. I should have left syringes laying around my room!

Source: Interview with a 20-year-old male college student at a private university in the Midwest, conducted by Peter Venturelli on November 19, 1993.

ondary. Many adolescents casually experiment with drugs. If, however, they begin to perceive themselves as drug users, then this behavior is virtually impossible to eradicate. The same holds true with OTC drug abuse. The moment an individual believes that he or she feels better after using a particular drug, the greater the likelihood that he or she will consistently use the drug .

Howard Becker (1963) believed that certain negative status positions (such as alcoholic, mental patient, ex-felon, criminal, drug addict, and so on) are so powerful that they dominate others (Pontell 1996). In the earlier example, if people who are important to Billy call him a "druggie," this name becomes a powerful label that will take precedence over any other status positions Billy may occupy. This label becomes Billy's master status —that he is a mindless "stoner." Even if Billy is also an above-average biology major, an excellent musician, and a

dependable and caring person, such factors become secondary because his primary status has been *recast* as a "druggie." Furthermore, once a powerful label is attached, it becomes much easier for the individual to uphold the image dictated by members of society and simply act-out the role expected by significant others. Master status labels distort an individual's public image because other people expect consistency in role performance.

Once a negative master status has been attached to an individual's public image, labeling theorist Edwin Schur asserted that retrospective interpretation occurs. Retrospective interpretation is a form of "reconstitution of individual character or identity" (Schur 1971, p. 52). It largely involves *redefining* a person's image within a particular social stereotype, category, or group (see cartoon as an illustration). In the eyes of his peers, Billy is now an emotional, intelligent yet weird or eccentric "stoner."

This cartoon illustrates the reflective process in retrospective interpretation that often occurs in daily conversations when we think that our unspoken thoughts are undetectable and hidden. In reality, however, these innermost thoughts are clearly conveyed through body language and nonverbal gestures.

Source: Reproduced with permission of Alex Silvestri.

Finally, William I. Thomas's (1923) contribution to labeling theory can be summarized in the following theorem: "If men define situations as real, they are real in their consequences" (p. 19). Thus, according to this dictum, when someone is perceived as a drug user, the perception functions as the reality of that person's character and in turn shapes his or her self-perception.

Subculture Theory

The subculture theory speaks to the role of peer pressure and the behavior resulting from peer group influences. In all groups, there are certain members who are more popular and respected and, as a result, exert more social influence than other peer members. Often, these more socially endowed members are group leaders, task leaders, or emotional leaders, who possess greater ability to influence others. Drug use that results from peer pressure demonstrates the extent to which these more popular and respected leaders can influence and pressure others to initially use or abuse drugs. These three excerpts from interviews illustrate subculture theory:

> When I was 9 or 10 three of my best friends would all take turns sneaking alcohol out of our parents' houses. Then in one of our garages, we would drink the liquor and smoke cigarettes. It was like a street corner thing but it was in a garage. In high school, we would look for the "party-people" and hang out with them. Usually on a Friday or some other school day, we would cut classes and drink and get high at someone's house that would be available. We were a tight-ass group—the goal would be to find a party somewhere. In high school we just hung-out together and were known on campus as "the party animals." *(From Venturelli's research files, 21-year-old male college student in a small town in the Midwest, November 23, 2000.)*

> I first started messing around with alcohol in high school. In order to be part of the crowd, we would sneak out during lunchtime at school and get "high." About 6 months after we started drinking, we moved on to other drugs. . . . Everyone in high school belongs to a clique, and my clique was heavy into drugs. We had a lot of fun being "high" throughout the day. We would party constantly. Basically, in college, it's the same thing. *(From Venturelli's research files, 19-year-old male student at a small, religiously affiliated private liberal arts college in the Southeast, February 9, 1985.)*

The third interview illustrates how friendship, coupled with subtle and not-so-subtle peer pressure, influences the novice drug enthusiast:

> There I was on the couch with three of my friends, and as the joint was being passed around, everyone was staring at me. I felt they were saying, "Are you going to smoke with us or will you be a holdout again?" *(From Venturelli's research files, 20-year-old male university student, April 10, 1996.)*

In sociology, charismatic leaders are viewed as possessing *status and power*, defined as distinction in the eyes of others. In drug-using peer groups,

KEY TERMS

subculture theory
explains drug use as peer-generated activity

such leaders have power over inexperienced drug users. Members of peer groups are often persuaded to experiment with drugs if the more popular members say, "Come on, try some, it's great" or "Trust me, you'll really get-off on this, come on, just try it." In groups where drugs are consumed, the extent of peer influence coupled with the art of persuasion and camaraderie are powerfully persuasive and cause the spread of drug use.

A further extension of subculture theory is the *social and cultural support perspective*. This perspective explains drug use and abuse in peer groups as resulting from an attempt by peers to solve problems collectively. In the neoclassic book, *Delinquent Boys: The Culture of the Gang* (1955), Cohen pioneered a study that showed for the first time that delinquent behavior is a collective attempt to gain social status and prestige within the peer group (Liska and Messner 1999; Siegel and Senna 1994). Members of certain peer groups are unable to achieve respect within the larger society. Such status-conscious youths find that being able to commit delinquent acts and yet evade law enforcement officials is admirable in the eyes of their delinquent peers. In effect, Cohen believed, delinquent behavior is a subcultural solution for overcoming feelings of status frustration and low self-esteem largely determined by lower class status.

Although the emphasis of Cohen's perspective is on explaining juvenile delinquency, his notion that delinquent behavior is a subcultural solution can easily be applied to drug use and abuse primarily in members of lower class peer groups. Underlying drug use and abuse in delinquent gangs, for example, results from sharing common feelings of alienation and escape from a society that appears noncaring, noninclusive, distant, and hostile.

Consider the current upsurge in violent gang memberships (see Chapter 17, "Drug Use Within Major Subcultures," for more detail on adolescents and gangs). In such groups, not only is drug dealing a profitable venture but also drug use serves as a collective response to alienation and estrangement from conventional middle class society. In cases of violent minority gang members, the alienation results from racism, increasing poverty, effects of migration and acculturation, and effects of minority status in a white male–dominated society such as the United States (Glick and Moore 1990; Moore 1978 and 1993; Sanders 1994; Thornberry 2001).

■ STRUCTURAL INFLUENCE THEORIES

These theories focus on how the *organization* of a society, group, or subculture is largely responsible for drug abuse by its members. The belief is that it is not any individual element in the society, group, or subculture that is causing the behavior—in this case, drug use—but that the organization itself or the lack of an organization largely causes the resulting behavior.

Social disorganization and social strain theories (Liska and Messner 1999; Werner and Henry 1995) identify the different kinds of social change that are disruptive and how, in a general sense, people are affected by such change. Social disorganization theory asks, What in the social order (the larger social structure) causes people to deviate? Social strain theory attempts to answer the question, What in family, peer, and employee social structures would cause someone to deviate? This theory believes that frustration results from being unable to secure the means to achieve sought-after goals, such as the goal of securing good income without much education, a well paying job without prior training, and so on. Such perceived shortcomings compel an individual to deviate to achieve desired goals.

Overall, social disorganization theory describes a situation in which, because of rapid social change, previously affiliated individuals no longer find themselves integrated into a community's social, commercial, religious, and economic institutions. When this type of alienation occurs, community members whose parents were perhaps more affiliated find themselves more disconnected and feel a lack of effective attachment to the social order. As a result, these disconnected or "disaffiliated" people find deviant behavior to be an acceptable substitute.

Developing trusting relationships, stability, and continuity are essential for proper socialization. As is discussed later in this chapter, when major identity development and transformation occur in the teen years, a stable environment is very important. Yet, in a technological society, more destabilizing and disorienting forces often result because technological development causes rapid social change (Gergen 2000; Ritzer 1999, 2000).

Although on the surface, most people appear to have little or no difficulty adapting to rapid technological social change, many people find themselves forced to maintain a frantic pace merely to "keep up" on a daily basis. The need to keep pace with social and technological innovation is increasingly more demanding today than ever (Gergen 2000). The constant need to keep pace with change and the increasing multiplicity of realities produced by such change often appears barely controllable. Still others—who are unable to cope with the constant demand for change and the required adjustment to all this change—have difficulty securing a stable identity. For example, consider the large numbers of people who need psychological counseling and therapy because they find themselves unable to cope with personal, family, and work-related problems and conflicts. In a recent study, a prediction was made that "32% of all American adults will experience some form of mental disorder during their lives" (Cohen 1997, p. 47). The following two interviews show how such confusion and lack of control lead to drug use.

Interviewee: The world is all messed up.

Interviewer: Why? In what way?

Interviewee: Nobody gives a damn anymore about anyone else.

Interviewer: Why do you think this is so?

Interviewee: It seems like life just seems to go on and on . . . I know that when I am under the influence, life is more mellow. I feel great! When I am high, I feel relaxed and can take things in better. Before I came to Chalmers College [a pseudonym], I felt home life was one great big mess; now that I am here, this college is also a big pile of crap. I guess this is why I like smoking dope. When I am high, I can forget my problems. My surroundings are friendlier; I am even more pleasant! Do you know what I mean? *(From Venturelli's research files, interview with a 19-year-old male marijuana user attending a small, private, liberal arts college in the Southeast, February 12, 1984.)*

KEY TERMS

conventional behavior
behavior largely dictated by custom and tradition, which is often disrupted by the forces of rapid technological change

---

Similarly, an interview illustrates how a work environment can affect drug use:

> I had one summer job once where it was so busy and crazy that a group of us workers would go out on breaks just to get high. We worked the night shift and our "high breaks" were between 2:00 and 5:00 in the mornings. *(From Venturelli's research files, first-year female college student, age 20, July 28, 1996.)*

Current Social Change in Most Societies

Does social change per se cause people to use and abuse drugs? In response to this question, *social change*—defined as any measurable change caused by technological advancement that disrupts cultural values and attitudes—does not by itself cause widespread drug use. In most cases, social change materialistically advances a culture by profoundly affecting how things are accomplished. At the same time, however, rapid social change disrupts day-to-day behavior preserved by tradition, which has a tendency to fragment such conventional social groups as families, neighborhoods, and communities. By conventional behavior , we mean behavior that is largely dictated by custom and tradition, which evaporates or goes into a state of flux under rapid social change.

Examples include the number of youth subcultures that proliferated during the 1960s (Yinger 1982) and other more recent lifestyles and subcultures such as right-to-life groups, prochoice groups, Mothers Against Drunk Driving (MADD), gay rights groups, rappers, punk rockers, metalers, grunge, taggers, skinheads, satanists, new wave, and rave (Wooden 1995). Furthermore, two other subcultures, teenagers and the elderly, both have become increasingly independent and, in some subgroups, alienated from other age groups in society (see Figure 2.2).

Simply stated, today's social institutions no longer embrace and influence people as they did in the past. Consequently, people are free to explore different means of expression and types of recreation. For many, this is a liberating experience leading to new and exciting outcomes; for others, this freedom from conventional societal norms and attitudes leads to an attraction to drug use and abuse.

The following two excerpts, gathered from interviews, illustrate social disorganization and strain theory:

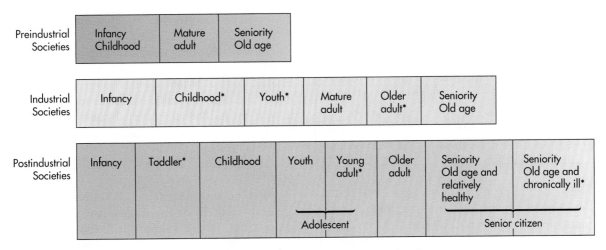

*Represents a newly developed and separate stage of identification and expression from the prior era.

FIGURE 2.2
Levels of technological development and corresponding subcultures.

Honest to God, I know things occur much faster than they did 20 years ago. Change is happening faster and occurs more often. What helps is doing some drugs at night at home. I either drink alcohol or do lines of coke. Two different highs but I like them both. This is about the only recreation I have except for the TV at night after working all darn day nonstop writing letters, answering phone calls, attending meetings, having to go onsite for inspections, and many other things I do each day. (*From Venturelli's research files, interview with a 29-year-old male home security systems manager, Chicago, Illinois, June 23, 2000.*)

I am into my own life because everyone is doing this. I see nearly everyone doing well around here. It's only those who are too stupid to succeed who are poor. I have had a rough time making it lately. Cocaine and speed help, but I know it's not the answer to all my problems. For now, drugs help me to put up with all the shit going on in my life. (*From Venturelli's research files, interview with a 25-year-old male residing in the Southeast and receiving various forms of Welfare, March 10, 1985.*)

There is no direct link between social change and drug use. However, plenty of proof exists that cer-

tain dramatic changes occur in the organization of society, and many eventually lead certain groups to use and abuse drugs. Figure 2.1 illustrates how the number of life cycle stages increases, depending on a society's level of technological development. Overall, it implies that, as societies advance from preindustrial to industrial to our current postindustrial-type of society, new subcultures are more numerous. (See Fischer 1976, for similar thinking.) In contrast to industrial and postindustrial societies, preindustrial societies do not have as many separate and distinct periods and cycles of social development. What is implied here is that the greater the number of distinct life cycles, the greater the fragmentation between the members of different stages of development. *Generation gaps* (conflicting sets of values and attitudes between age cohorts) cause much ignorance and lack of insight between age group subcultures. This often leads to separation and fragmentation across age groups who develop distinct lifestyle patterns that can easily conflict.

Control Theory

This last structural influence theory we are reviewing places most of its primary emphasis on influences outside the self as the primary cause for

KEY TERMS

control theory
theory that emphasizes when people are left without bonds to other groups (peers, family, social groups) they generally have a tendency to deviate from upheld values and attitudes

socialization
the growth and development process responsible for learning how to become a responsible, functioning human being

deviating to drug use and/or abuse. Control theory places importance on positive socialization. Socialization is defined as the process by which individuals learn to internalize the attitudes, values, and behaviors needed to become participating members of conventional society. Generally, control theorists believe that human beings can easily become deviant if left without the social controls provided by groups and organizations. Thus, theorists who specialize in control theory emphasize the necessity of maintaining *bonds* to family, school, peer groups, and other social, political, and religious organizations (Liska and Messner 1999; Thio 1998).

In the 1950s and 1960s, criminologist Walter C. Reckless (1961; Liska and Messner 1999; Siegel and Senna 1994) developed containment theory. According to this theory, the socialization process results in the creation of strong or weak internal and external control systems.

The degree of self-control, high or low frustration tolerance, positive or negative self-perception, successful or unsuccessful goal achievement, and either resistance or adherence to deviant behavior determines internal control. Environmental pressures, such as social conditions, may limit the accomplishment of goal-striving behavior; such conditions include poverty, minority group status, inferior education, and lack of employment.

The external, or outer, control system consists of effective or ineffective supervision and discipline, consistent or inconsistent moral training, positive or negative acceptance, identity, and self-worth. Many believe that latchkey children have a higher risk of becoming delinquent due to their sporadic supervision and the uneven levels of attention they receive. Alcoholic parents may also be at risk for raising children with delinquent tendencies because

these parents are more apt to be inconsistent with discipline.

In applying this theory to the use or abuse of drugs, we could say that if an individual has a weak external control system, the internal control system must take over to handle external pressure. Similarly, if an individual's external control system is strong, his or her internal control system will not be seriously challenged. If, however, either the internal or external control system is too mismatched, the possibility of drug abuse increases.

If an individual's external and internal controls are both weak, he or she is most likely to use and abuse drugs. Table 2.1 shows the likelihood of drug use resulting from either strong or weak internal and external control systems. It indicates that, if both internal and external controls are strong, the use and abuse of drugs is not likely to occur.

Travis Hirschi (1971; Liska and Messner 1999), a much respected sociologist and social control theorist, believed that delinquent behavior tends to occur when people lack (1) attachment to others, (2) commitment to goals, (3) involvement in conventional activity, and (4) belief in a common value system. If a child or adolescent is unable to become circumscribed within the family setting, school, and nondelinquent peers, then the drift to delinquent behavior is most likely inevitable.

We can apply Hirschi's theories to drug use as follows:

1. Drug users are less likely than nonusers to be closely tied to their parents.

TABLE 2.1 Likelihood of Drug Use

INDIVIDUAL INTERNAL CONTROL	EXTERNAL SOCIAL CONTROL	
	Strong	**Weak or Nonexistent**
Strong	Least likely (almost never)	Less likely (probably never)
Weak	More likely (probably will)	Most likely (almost certain)

Source: Reproduced with permission of Peter J. Venturelli.

2. Good students are less likely to use drugs.

3. Drug users are less likely to participate in social clubs and organizations and engage in team sport activities.

4. Drug users are very likely to have friends whose activities are congruent with their own attitudes.

The following excerpt illustrates how control theory works:

> I was 15 when my mother confronted me with drug use. I nearly died. We have always been very close and she really cried when she found my "dug out" [paraphernalia that holds a quantity of marijuana] and a "one hitter," [a device for smoking this drug] in her car. My fear was that she would inquire about my drug use with our next-door neighbors, whose children were my best friends. One neighbor residing on the left of our house was one of my high school teachers who knew me from the day I was born. The neighbor on the right side of our house was our church pastor. For a while after she confronted me, I just sneaked around more whenever I wanted to get high. After a few months, I became so paranoid of how my mother kept looking at me when I would come in at night that I eventually stopped smoking weed. Our family is very close and the town I live in (at that time the population was 400) was filled with gossip. I could not handle the pressure, so I quit. *(From Venturelli's research files, female postal worker, age 22, residing in a small Midwestern town, February 9, 1997.)*

In conclusion, control theory depicts how conformity with supportive groups may prevent deviance. It suggests that control is either internally or externally enforced by family, school, and peer group expectations. In addition, individuals who are either not equipped with an internal system of self-control reflecting the values and beliefs of conventional society or feel personally alienated from major social institutions may deviate without feeling guilty for their actions, often because of peer pressure resulting in a suspension or modification of internal beliefs.

Danger Signals of Drug Abuse

How does one know when the use of drugs moves beyond normal use? Many people are prescribed drugs that affect their moods. Using these drugs wisely can be important for both physical and emotional health. Sometimes, however, it may be difficult to decide when use of drugs to handle stress or anxiety becomes inappropriate. It is important that your use of drugs does not result in addiction. The following are some danger signals that can help you evaluate your drug-use behavior:

1. Do people who are close to you often ask about your drug use? Have they noticed any changes in your moods or behavior?

2. Do you become defensive when a friend or relative mentions your drug or alcohol use?

3. Do you believe you cannot have fun without alcohol or other drugs?

4. Do you frequently get into trouble with the law, school officials, family, friends, or significant others because of your alcohol or other drug use?

5. Are you sometimes embarrassed or frightened by your behavior under the influence of drugs or alcohol?

6. Have you ever switched to a new doctor because your regular physician would not prescribe the drug you wanted?

7. When you are under pressure or feel anxious, do you automatically take a sedative, a drink, or both?

8. Do you turn to drugs after becoming upset, after confrontations or arguments, or to relieve uncomfortable feelings?

9. Do you take drugs more often or for purposes other than those recommended by your doctor?

10. Do you mix drugs and alcohol?

11. Do you drink or take drugs regularly to help you sleep or even to relax?

12. Do you take a drug to get going in the morning?

13. Do you find yourself not wanting to be around friends who do not use drugs or drink on a regular basis?

14. Have you ever seriously thought that you may have a drug addiction problem?

15. Do you make promises to yourself or others that you'll stop getting drunk or using drugs?

16. Do you drink and/or use drugs alone?

If you answer "yes" to several of these questions, you are abusing drugs or alcohol. Many places offer help at the local level, such as programs in your community listed in the phone book under "Drug Abuse." Other resources include community crisis centers, telephone hotlines, and the National Mental Health Association.

■ LOW-RISK AND HIGH-RISK DRUG CHOICES

As will become more readily apparent throughout this text, some very real risks are associated with recreational drug use. Low-risk and high-risk drug choices refer to two major levels of alcohol and other drug use. Low-risk drug choices refer to values and attitudes that keep the use of alcohol and other drugs in control. High-risk drug choices refer to values and attitudes that lead to using drugs habitually and addictively resulting in emotional, psychological, and physical health problems.

Low-risk choices include abstinence from all drugs or remaining in true control of the quantity and frequency of drugs taken. Low-risk choices require self-monitoring your consumption of alcohol and other drugs in order to reduce your risk of an alcohol and other drug-related problem. Both "low-risk" and "high-risk" are appropriate descriptive concepts that allow us to focus on the health and safety issues involved in drug use and refer to developing and maintaining completely different values and attitudes in your approach to alcohol and other drugs.

In this chapter, we found that there are numerous factors and reasons why people start using or abusing drugs. There are also numerous theories that attempt to explain initial and habitual use. Some people can easily become addicted to alcohol and other drugs because of inherited characteristics, personality, mental instability or illness, and vulnerability to present situations. Others who have more resistance to alcohol and drug addiction may have stronger convictions and abilities to cope with different situations.

Maintaining a Low-Risk Approach

In order minimize the risk of alcohol and drug-related problems, we suggest you remain aware of the following:

1. Investigate your family drug history. Does anyone in your family have a history of alcohol or drug abuse? How many members of your family who have alcohol or drug problems are blood relatives? In other words, are you more likely to become dependent on alcohol or drugs because of inherited genes or the values and attitudes you are exposed to?

2. Do you particularly enjoy the effects of alcohol and other drugs? Do you spend a lot of time thinking about how "good" it feels to be high?

3. Does it seem as if the only time you really have fun is when you are using alcohol and other drugs?

4. Keep in mind the following, which will be covered throughout this text:

   - *Body size*—a small person typically becomes more impaired by drug use than a larger person.

   - *Gender*—women typically become more impaired than men of the same size, especially with regard to alcohol use.

   - *Other drugs*—taking a combination of drugs generally increases the risk of impairment and, in some combinations, accidental death.

KEY TERMS

low-risk drug choices
developing values and attitudes that lead to controlling the use of alcohol and drugs

high-risk drug choices
developing values and attitudes that lead to using drugs both habitually and addictively

- *Fatigue or illness*—fatigue increases impairment from alcohol and increases the risk for impairment.
- *Empty stomach*—an empty stomach increases impairment from most drugs.

Also keep in mind that most excessive drug use is unlawful and against school policy. Excessive alcohol and other drug use can easily lead to time in jail, fines, forced rehabilitation programs, and community service work. In addition, the defense costs involved in even simple drug possession charges are often well beyond several thousand dollars. A criminal record is a public record and can be accessed by employers and other community members. Is drug use still worth such risks? The more drugs consumed, the greater potential for damage to health, well-being, family relationships, and community respect.

Discussion Questions

1. In addition to better cultivation techniques, cite several other possible reasons why the potency of the average marijuana joint has increased since 1960.

2. Given that over 88% of the U.S. population members are daily drug users of some form, do you think we need to reexamine our strict drug laws, which may be punishing a sizable number of drug users in our society who simply want to use illicit drugs?

3. Is there any way to combine biological and sociological explanations for why people use drugs so that the two perspectives do not conflict? (Sketch out a synthesis between these two sets of theoretical explanations.)

4. What is the relationship between mental illness and drug abuse? Why is this relationship important?

5. Do you accept the "rats in a maze" concept that psychology offers for explaining why people come to abuse drugs? (This view primarily states that people are like automatons or robots and that reinforcement explains why certain people become addicted to drugs.) Explain your answer.

6. In reviewing the psychological and sociological drug use theories, which theories best explain drug use? Defend your answer.

7. Does differential association theory take into account non–drug-using individuals whose socialization environment was drug-infested?

8. Do you believe drug users are socialized differently and that these alleged differences account for drug use? Defend your answer.

9. Can divorce be blamed for adolescent drug use? Why or why not? If so, to what extent?

10. Do the current and alarming drug abuse statistics reflect the failure of social change in our society? Why do you agree or disagree with this statement?

11. Is making low-risk choices regarding drug use a more realistic approach for drug moderation than advocating, "just say no" to drug use? Why or why not?

Key Terms

genetic and biophysiological theories **38**

central nervous system **38**

psychoactive effects **38**

neurotransmitters **38**

dopamine **39**

social learning theory **42**

habituation **42**

"addiction to pleasure" theory **42**

sensation-seeking individuals **42**

differential reinforcement **43**

social influence theories **44**

structural influence theories **44**

amotivational syndrome **46**

labeling theory **50**

primary deviance **50**

secondary deviance   50

master status   51

retrospective interpretation   51

subculture theory   52

conventional behavior   54

control theory   56

socialization   56

low-risk drug choices   58

high-risk drug choices   58

Summary

1 Drug use is more serious today than in the past because (1) drug use and abuse have increased dramatically since 1960; (2) today, illicit drugs are more potent than in the past; (3) the media presents drug use as rewarding; (4) drug use physically harms members of society; and (5) drug use and dealing by violent gangs are increasing at an alarming rate.

2 Genetic and biophysiological theories explain addiction in terms of genetics, brain dysfunction, and biochemical patterns.

3 Drugs of abuse interfere with the functioning of neurotransmitters, chemical messengers used for communication between brain regions. These drugs with abuse potential enhance the pleasure centers by causing the release of a specific brain neurotransmitter such as dopamine, which acts as a positive reinforcer.

4 The American Psychiatric Association classifies severe drug dependence as a form of psychiatric disorder. Drug abuse can cause mental conditions that mimic major psychiatric illnesses such as schizophrenia, severe anxiety disorders, and suicidal depression.

5 The following four genetic factors can contribute to drug abuse: (1) Many genetically determined psychiatric disorders are relieved by drugs of abuse, which in turn encourages their use; (2) high rates of addiction result from people who are genetically sensitive to addictive drugs; (3) such character traits as insecurity and vulnerability, which are often genetically determined, can lead to drug abuse behavior; and (4) the inability to break from a particular type of drug addiction may be genetically determined, especially when severe raving or very unpleasant withdrawal effects dominate.

6 Introversion and extroversion patterns have been associated with levels of neural arousal in brain stem circuits. These forms of arousal are closely associated with effects caused by drug stimulants or depressants.

7 Reinforcement or learning theory says that the motivation to use or abuse drugs stems from how the "highs" from alcohol and other drugs reduce anxiety, tension, and stress. Positive social influences by drug-using peers also promote drug use.

8 Social influence theories include social learning, the role of significant others, labeling, and subculture theories. Social learning theory explains drug use as a form of learned behavior. Significant others play a role in the learning process involved in drug use and/or abuse. Labeling theory says that other people we consider important can influence whether drug use becomes an option for us. If key people we admire or fear come to define our actions as deviant, then the definition becomes the "fact" of our reality. Subculture theories trace original drug experimentation, use, and/or abuse to peer pressure.

9 There are a number of consistencies in socialization patterns found among drug abusers ranging from immaturity, maladjustment, and/or insecurity to exposure and belief that selling drugs is a very lucrative business venture.

10 Sociologist Howard Becker believes that first-time drug users become attached to drugs because of three factors: (1) they learn the techniques of drug use; (2) they learn to perceive the pleasurable effects of drugs; (3) and they learn to enjoy the drug experience.

11 Primary deviance is deviant behavior that the perpetrator does not identify with; hence, it is inconsequential deviant behavior. Secondary deviance is deviance that one readily identifies with.

12 Both internal and external social control should prevail concerning drug use. Internal control deals with internal psychic and internalized social attitudes; external control is exemplified by living in a neighborhood and community where drug use and abuse are severely criticized or not tolerated as a means to seek pleasure or avoid stress and anxiety.

13 Low-risk and high-risk drug-use choices refer to developing values and attitudes toward alcohol and other drugs. Low-risk drug choices refer to developing values and attitudes leading to a controlled use of alcohol and drugs—from total abstinence to very moderate use. High-risk choices refer to developing values and attitudes leading to using drugs both habitually and addictively.

References

Akers, R. L. "Problems in the Sociology of Deviance: Social Definition and Behavior." *Social Forces* 6 (June 1968): 455–65.

Akers, R. L. *Drugs, Alcohol, and Society: Social Structure, Process, and Policy.* Belmont, CA: Wadsworth, 1992.

American Psychiatric Association. DSM IV-TR. "Substance-Related Disorders." *Diagnostic Statistic Manual,* 4th ed. Revised. A. Francis, Chair. Washington, DC: American Psychiatric Association, 2000: 191–295.

Apostolides, M. "Special Report: The Addiction Revolution: Old Habits Get New Choices." *Psychology Today* 29 (September/October 1996): 33–43, 75–6.

Bandura, A. *Social Learning Theory.* Englewood Cliffs, NJ: Prentice Hall, 1977.

Becker, H. S. *Outsiders: Studies in the Sociology of Deviance.* New York: Free Press, 1963.

Becker, H. S. "History, Culture, and Subjective Experience: An Exploration of the Social Basis of Drug-Induced Experiences." *Journal of Health and Social Behavior* 8 (1967): 163–76.

Bejerot, N. "Current Problems of Drug Addiction." *Lakartidingen* (Sweden) 62, 50 (1965): 4231–38.

Bejerot, N. *Addiction: An Artificially Induced Drive.* Springfield, IL: Thomas, 1972.

Bejerot, N. "The Biological and Social Character of Drug Dependence." In *Psychiatrie der Gegenwart, Forschung und Praxis,* 2nd ed., edited by K. P. Kisker, J. E. Meyer, C. Muller, and E. Stromogrew, Vol. 3: 488–518. Berlin: Springer-Verlag, 1975.

Bespalov, A., A. Lebedev, G. Panchenko, and E. Zvartau. "Effects of Abused Drugs on Thresholds and Breaking Points of Intracranial Self-Stimulation in Rats." *European Neuropsychopharmacology: The Journal of the European College of Neuropharmacology,* 9 (1999): 377–83.

Best, J., and D. F. Luckenbill. *Organizing Deviance,* 2nd ed. Englewood Cliffs, NJ: Prentice-Hall, 1994.

Burns, D. B. "The Web of Caring: An Approach to Accountability in Alcohol Policy." In *Designing Alcohol and Other Drug Prevention Programs in Higher Education.* U.S. Department of Education. Newton, MA: The Higher Education Center for Alcohol and Other Drug Prevention, 1997. Available http://www.edc.org/hec/pubs/theory book/burns.html.

Carlson, N. *Psychology: The Science of Behavior,* 3rd ed. Boston: Allyn and Bacon, 1990.

Cheron, J. M. *Symbolic Interactionism: An Introduction, an Interpretation, an Integration,* 7th ed. Englewood Cliffs, NJ: Prentice-Hall, 2001.

Cohen, A. K. *Delinquent Boys: The Culture of the Gang.* Glencoe, IL: Free Press, 1955.

Cohen, G. D. "No Job for a Grown-Up." *Utne Reader* (January/February 1997): 47.

Conrad, P., and J. W. Schneider. *Deviance and Medicalization.* St. Louis, MO: Mosby, 1980.

Dowieko, H. E. *Concepts of Chemical Dependency,* 3rd ed. Pacific Grove, CA: Brooks/Cole, 1996: 217–18.

Drug Strategies. "Keeping Score: What We Are Getting for Our Federal Drug Control Dollars 1995." Washington, DC: 1995. Available 080/edres/colleges/boss/depts/cesar/drugs/ks1995.

Eysenck, H. J., and M. W. Eysenck. *Personality and Individual Differences: A Natural Science Approach.* New York: Plenum Press, 1985.

Farrar, H., and G. Kearns. "Cocaine: Clinical Pharmacology and Toxicology." *Journal of Pediatrics* 115 (1989): 665–75.

Fischer, C. S. *The Urban Experience.* New York: Harcourt Brace Jovanovich, 1976.

Gardner, E. L. "Brain Reward Mechanisms." In *Substance Abuse: A Comprehensive Textbook,* 2nd ed., edited by J. H. Lowinson, P. Ruiz, R. B. Millman, and J. G. Langrod. Baltimore: Williams & Wilkins, 1992.

Gergen, K. *The Saturated Self: Dilemmas of Identity in Contemporary Life.* New York, NY: Basic Books, Inc., 2000.

Glick, R., and J. Moore, eds. *Drugs in Hispanic Communities.* New Brunswick, NJ: Rutgers University Press, 1990.

Goode, E. *Deviant Behavior,* 5th ed. Upper Saddle River, NJ: Prentice-Hall, 1997.

Gray, J. A. *The Psychology of Fear and Stress,* 2nd ed. Cambridge, UK: Cambridge University Press, 1987.

Gray, P. *Psychology,* 3rd ed. New York: Worth, 1999.

Grinspoon, L. "Update on Cocaine." *Harvard Mental Health Letter* 10 (September 1993): 1–4.

Heitzeg, N. A. *Deviance: Rulemakers and Rulebreakers.* Minneapolis: West Publishing, 1996.

Henslin, J. M. *Sociology: A Down-to-Earth Approach*, 5th ed. Boston: Allyn and Bacon, 2001.

Hewitt, J. P. *Self and Society: A Symbolic Interactionist Social Psychology*, 6th ed. Boston: Allyn and Bacon, 1994.

Hirschi, T. *Causes of Delinquency*, 2nd ed. Los Angeles: University of California Press, 1971.

Inciardi, J. A., D. Lockwood, and A. E. Pottieger. *Women and Crack-Cocaine.* New York: MacMillian, 1993.

Jones, J. *Hep-Cats, Narcs, and Pipe Dreams: A History of America's Romance with Illegal Drugs.* Baltimore, MD: The Johns Hopkins University Press, 1996.

Jarvik, M. "The Drug Dilemma: Manipulating the Demand." *Science* 250 (1990): 387–92.

Jellinek, E. M. *The Disease Concept of Alcoholism.* New Haven, CT: Hillhouse Press, 1960.

Koob, G. "Drug Addiction." in *Neurobiology of Disease* 7 (5) (October 2000): 543–5.

Lemert, E. M. *Social Psychology: A Systematic Approach to the Theory of Sociopathic Behavior.* New York: McGraw–Hill, 1951.

Liska, A. E., and S. F. Messner. *Perspectives on Crime and Deviance.* Upper Saddle River, NJ: Prentice Hall, 1999.

Mathias, R. "Novelty Seekers and Drug Abusers Tap Same Brain Reward System, Animal Studies Show." *NIDA Notes* 10, 4 (July/August 1995): 1–5.

Moore, J. "Gangs, Drugs, and Violence. In *Gangs: The Origins and Impact of Contemporary Youth Gangs in the United States*, edited by S. Cummings and D. J. Monti, 27–46. Albany: State University of New York Press, 1993.

Moore, J. *Homeboys: Gangs, Drugs and Prison in the Barrios of Los Angeles.* Philadelphia: Temple University Press, 1978.

National Institute on Drug Abuse (NIDA). "Study Finds Higher Use Among Adolescents Whose Parents Divorce." *NIDA Notes* 5 (Summer 1990): 10.

National Institute on Drug Abuse (NIDA). "Double Trouble: Substance Abuse and Psychiatric Disorders." *NIDA Notes* 8 (November/December 1993): 20.

National Institute on Drug Abuse (NIDA). "Attention and Memory Impaired in Heavy Users of Marijuana." Rockville, MD: Office of the National Institute on Drug Abuse (20 February 1996). Available http://www.health.org/pressrel/heavymar/html.

Needle, R. H., S. S. Su, and W. J. Doherty. "Divorce, Remarriage, and Adolescent Substance Use: A Prospective Longitudinal Study." *Journal of Marriage and the Family* 52 (1990): 157–9.

O'Brien, R., S. Cohen, G. Evans, and J. Fine. *The Encyclopedia of Drug Abuse*, 2nd ed. New York: Facts on File, 1992.

Plummer, K. "Misunderstanding Labelling Perspectives." *Deviant Interpretations*, edited by D. Downes and P. Rock, 85–121. London: Robertson, 1979.

Pontell, H. N. *Social Deviance*, 2nd ed. Upper Saddle River, NJ: Prentice-Hall, 1996.

Reckless, W. C. "A New Theory of Delinquency." *Federal Probation* 25 (1961): 42–6.

Ritzer G. *The McDonaldization of Society*, 3rd ed. Thousand Oaks, CA: Pine Forge Press, 2000.

Ritzer, G. *Enchanting a Disenchanted World: Revolutionizing the Means of Consumption.* Thousand Oaks, CA: Pine Forge Press, 1999.

Rousar, E., K. Brooner, M. W. Regier, and G. E. Bigelow. "Psychiatric Distress in Antisocial Drug Abusers: Relation to Other Personality Disorders." *Drug and Alcohol Dependence* 34 (1995): 149–54.

Rudgley, R. *Essential Substances: A Cultural History of Intoxicants in Society.* New York: Kodansha International, 1993.

Sanders, W. B. *Gangbangs and Drive-bys: Grounded Culture and Juvenile Gang Violence.* New York: 1994, Aldine De Gruyter.

Schur, E. M. *Labeling Deviant Behavior.* New York: Harper & Row, 1971.

Siegel, L. J., and J. J. Senna. *Juvenile Delinquency: Theory, Practice and Law.* St. Paul, MN: West Publishing, 1994.

Spanagel, R., and Weiss, F. "The Dopamine Hypothesis of Reward: Past and Current Status." *Trends in Neuroscience* 22 (1999): 521–27.

Substance Abuse and Mental Health Services Administration (SAMHSA), *National Household Survey on Drug Abuse: Fact Sheet* (August 1998). Available http://www.samhsa.gov/PRESS/99/990818fs.htm.

Substance Abuse and Mental Health Services (SAMHSA). *Study Shows Strong Relationship Between Adolescent Behavior Problems and Alcohol Use.* Rockville, MD: U.S. Department of Health and Human Services Press Release (1 March 2000). Available http://www.health.org/PRESSREL/mar00/1.htm.

Sutherland, E. *Principles of Criminology*, 4th ed. Philadelphia: Lippincott, 1947.

Thio, A. *Deviant Behavior*, 5th ed. New York: Addison Wesley Longman, 1998.

Thomas, W. I., with D. S. Thomas. *The Child in America.* New York: Knopf, 1923.

Thornberry, T. P. "Risk Factors for Gang Membership." In *The Modern Gang Reader*, 2nd ed., edited by J. Miller, C. L. Maxson, and M. W. Klein, 32-42. Los Angeles: Roxbury, 2001.

Uhl, G., K. Blum, E. Noble, and S. Smith. "Substance Abuse Vulnerability and D-2 Receptor Genes." *Trends in Neurological Sciences* 16 (1993): 83–8.

Uhl, G., A. Persico, and S. Smith. "Current Excitement with D-2 Dopamine Receptor Gene Alleles in Substance Abuse." *Archives of General Psychiatry* 49 (February 1992): 157–60.

USA Today. "Seven in 10 Drug Users Work Full-Time." 1999. Available http://www.usatoday.com/life/health/addiction/lhadd021.htm.

Volkow, N. *Changes in Human Brain Systems After Long-term Cocaine Use* (1 February 1999). Available http://165.112.78.61/meetsum/ccb/volkow.html.

Weiss, F. *Cocaine Dependence and Withdrawal: Neuroadaptive Changes in Brain Reward and Stress Systems.* Available http://165.112.78.61/meetsum/ccb/weiss.html.

Werner, E., and S. Henry. *Criminological Theory: An Analysis of Its Underlying Assumptions.* Fort Worth, TX: Harcourt Brace College Publishers, 1995.

Wilson, W. J. *The Truly Disadvantaged.* Chicago: University of Chicago Press, 1990.

Wooden, W. S. *Renegade Kids, Suburban Outlaws: From Youth Culture to Delinquency.* Belmont, CA: Wadsworth, 1995.

Wyman, J. "Promising Advances Toward Understanding the Fenetic Roots of Addiction." *NIDA Notes* 12 (July/August 1997): 1–5.

Yinger, M. J. *Countercultures: The Promise and the Peril of a World Turned Upside Down.* New York: Free Press, 1982.

Drug Use, Regulation, and the Law

Did You Know?

- ► At the turn of the century, drug laws in the United States were more concerned with protecting the secret formulas of patent medicines than with protecting the public from the dangers of these products.

- ► Some patent medicines sold at the turn of the century contained opium and cocaine and were highly addictive.

- ► Before World War II, all drugs, except those classified as narcotics, were available without prescription.

- ► Before 1938, drugs did not need to be proven safe before distribution.

- ► Enforcement of drug use policies and drug laws differs across different countries.

- ► The United States spends nearly $2 billion per year on drug interdiction.

- ► The number of current illicit drug users is about half its 1979 peak, when there were 25 million users.

- ► Although statistics indicate that overall drug usage is decreasing, 52,000 Americans still die annually, as a result.

- ► The economic cost to society of drug abuse runs into the hundreds of billions of dollars. Between 1988 and 1995, Americans spent $57.3 billion on illegal drugs that would otherwise support legitimate savings or spending by the user.

Chapter 3

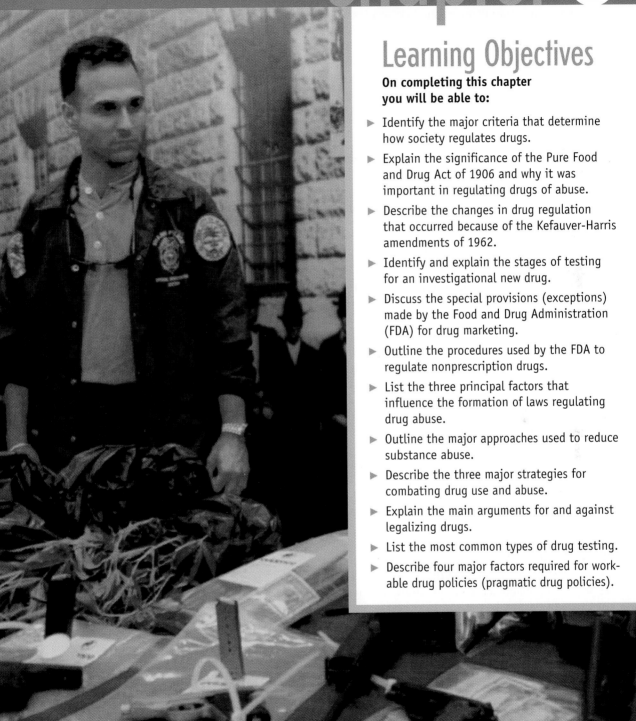

Learning Objectives

**On completing this chapter
you will be able to:**

► Identify the major criteria that determine
how society regulates drugs.

► Explain the significance of the Pure Food
and Drug Act of 1906 and why it was
important in regulating drugs of abuse.

► Describe the changes in drug regulation
that occurred because of the Kefauver-Harris
amendments of 1962.

► Identify and explain the stages of testing
for an investigational new drug.

► Discuss the special provisions (exceptions)
made by the Food and Drug Administration
(FDA) for drug marketing.

► Outline the procedures used by the FDA to
regulate nonprescription drugs.

► List the three principal factors that
influence the formation of laws regulating
drug abuse.

► Outline the major approaches used to reduce
substance abuse.

► Describe the three major strategies for
combating drug use and abuse.

► Explain the main arguments for and against
legalizing drugs.

► List the most common types of drug testing.

► Describe four major factors required for work-
able drug policies (pragmatic drug policies).

Introduction

S ociety mandates that it maintain control over which drugs are permissible and which drugs are prohibited. Through legislation we decide which drugs are licit and illicit. We decide which licit drugs are readily available "over-the-counter" (OTC) and which can be obtained "by prescription only." Thus, drug laws prohibit indiscriminate use of what society defines as a drug. As we saw in Chapter 1, licit and illicit drugs can produce vastly different effects on both the mental and bodily functions. Chapters 5 and 6 focus on how and why different types of drugs affect our bodies. In this chapter, you will come to better understand how our society attempts to control drug use and abuse.

Drug regulation brings to mind numerous questions. For example, why are the laws against drug use so controversial? When were these laws first created? In regulating and prohibiting the free marketing of either licit or illicit drug use, how does U.S. society compare with other societies? Do these other societies have fewer drug users as a result of being more lenient or restrictive toward drug abusers? Do our drug laws coincide with the opinions of most U.S. citizens? Are nonpunitive approaches toward drug use feasible? Do drug laws realistically diminish drug use? What common attitudes prevail regarding the enactment and enforcement of drug laws?

This chapter attempts to respond to many of these questions by delving into the relationship between drug use and the law. We examine the development of drug regulations in the United States as it applies to both the manufacture of drugs and the control of their use. Although many think that the regulation of drug manufacturing and drug abuse lie at the opposite ends of the spectrum, regulation of drug manufacturing and abuse of drugs actually evolved from the same process.

Cultural Attitudes About Drug Use

Currently, the cultural attitudes in the United States regarding the use of drugs blend beliefs in individuals' rights to live their lives as they desire with society's obligation to protect its members from burdens due to uncontrolled behavior. The history of drug regulation consists of regulatory swings due to attempts by government to balance these two factors while responding to public pressures and perceived public needs. For example, 100 years ago, most people expected the government to protect citizens' rights to produce and market new foods and substances; they did not expect or desire the government to regulate product quality or claims. Instead, the public relied on private morals and common sense to obtain quality and protection in an era of simple technology. Unfortunately, U.S. society had to learn by tragic experience that its trust was not well placed; many unscrupulous entrepreneurs were willing to risk the safety and welfare of the public in order to maximize profits and acquire wealth. In fact, most medicines of these earlier times were not merely ineffective but often dangerous.

Because of the advent of high technology and the rapid advancements society has made, we now rely on highly trained experts and government "watchdog" agencies for consumer information and protection. Out of this changing environment have evolved two major guidelines for controlling drug development and marketing:

1. Society has the right to protect itself from the damaging impact of drug use. This concept not only is closely aligned with the emotional and highly visible issues of drug abuse but also includes protection from other drug side effects. Thus, although we expect the government to protect society from drugs that can cause addiction, we also expect it to protect us from drugs that cause cancer, cardiovascular disease, or other threatening medical conditions.

2. Society has the right to demand that drugs approved for marketing be safe and effective to the general public. If drug manufacturers promise that their products relieve pain, those drugs should be analgesics; if they promise that their products relieve depression, those drugs should be antidepressants; if they promise that their products relieve stuffy noses, those drugs should be decongestants.

The public, through regulatory agencies and statutory enactments, has attempted to require that drug manufacturers produce safe and effective pharmaceutical products. Closely linked is the fact that society uses similar strategies to protect itself from the problems associated with the specific drug side effect of dependence or addiction, which is associated with drug abuse.

The Road to Regulation and the FDA

The decline of patent medicines began with the 1906 Pure Food and Drug Act, which required manufacturers to indicate the amounts of alcohol, morphine, opium, cocaine, heroin, and marijuana extract on the label of each product. It became obvious at this time that many medicinal products on the market labeled "nonaddictive" were, in fact, potent drugs "in sheep's labeling" and could cause severe dependence. However, most government interest at the time centered on regulation of the food industry, not drugs.

Even though federal drug regulation was based on the free-market philosophy that consumers could select for themselves, it was decided that the public should have information about possible dependence-producing drugs to ensure that they understood the risks associated with using these products. The Pure Food and Drug Act made misrepresentation illegal, so that a potentially addicting patent drug could not be advertised as "non–habit forming." This step marked the beginning of new involvement by governmental agencies in drug manufacturing.

Shortcomings in the Pure Food and Drug law were quickly obvious. For example, the law did not allow the government to stop the distribution of dangerous preparations, including those designed to reduce weight. One such product contained dinitrophenol, a compound that purportedly increased metabolic rate and was responsible for many deaths (FDA History Office 2000).

The Pure Food and Drug Act was modified, although not in a consumer-protective manner, by the Sherley Amendment in 1912. The distributor of a cancer "remedy" was indicted for falsely claiming on the label that the contents were effective. The case was decided in the U.S. Supreme Court in 1911. Justice Holmes, writing for the majority opinion, said that, based on the 1906 act, the company

had not violated any law because legally all it was required to do was accurately state the contents and their strength and quality. The accuracy of the therapeutic claims made by drug manufacturers was not controlled. Congress took the hint and passed the Sherley Amendment to add to the existing law the requirement that labels should not contain "any statement . . . regarding the curative or therapeutic effect . . . which is false and fraudulent." However, the law required that the government prove fraud, which turned out to be difficult (and in fact is still problematic). This amendment did not improve drug products but merely encouraged pharmaceutical companies to be more vague in their advertisements (Temin 1980).

■ PRESCRIPTION VERSUS OTC DRUGS

The distinction between prescription and OTC drugs is relatively new to the pharmaceutical industry. All nonnarcotic drugs were available OTC before World War II. It was not until a drug company unwittingly produced a toxic product that killed 107 people that the FDA was given control over drug safety in the 1938 Federal Food, Drug, and Cosmetic Act (Hunter et al. 1993). The bill had been debated for several years in Congress and showed no promise of passage. Then a pharmaceutical company decided to sell a liquid form of a sulfa drug (one of the first antibiotics) and found that the drug would dissolve well in a chemical solvent, diethylene glycol (presently used in antifreeze products). The company marketed the antibiotic as Elixir Sulfanilamide without testing the solvent for toxicity. Under the 1906 Pure Food and Drug Act, the company could not be prosecuted for the toxicity of this form of drug or for not testing the formulation of the drug on animals first. It could only be prosecuted for mislabeling the product on the technicality that *elixir* refers to a solution in alcohol, not a solution in diethylene glycol. Again, it was apparent that the laws in place provided woefully inadequate protection for the public.

The 1938 act differed from the 1906 law in several ways. It defined *drugs* to include products that affected bodily structure or function even in the absence of disease. Companies had to file applications with the government for all new drugs showing that they were safe (not effective, just safe) for use as described. The drug label had to list all ingredients and include the quantity of each, as well as provide instructions regarding correct use of the drug and warnings about its dangers. In addition, the Act eliminated a Sherley Amendment requirement to prove intent to defraud in drug misbranding cases (FDA Backgrounder 1999).

Before passage of the 1938 act, you could go to a doctor and obtain a prescription for any nonnarcotic drug or go to the pharmacy directly if you had already decided what was needed. The labeling requirement in the 1938 act allowed drug companies to create a class of drugs that could not be sold legally without a prescription. It has been suggested that the actions by the FDA were motivated by the frequent public misuse of two classes of drugs developed before passage of the 1938 law: sulfa antibiotics and barbiturates. People often took too little of the antibiotics to cure an infection and too much of the barbiturates and became addicted.

The 1938 Food, Drug, and Cosmetic Act allowed the manufacturer to determine whether a drug was to be labeled *prescription* or *nonprescription*. The same product could be sold as prescription by one company and as OTC by another. After the Durham-Humphrey Amendment was passed in 1951, almost all new drugs were placed in the prescription-only class. The drugs that were patented and marketed after World War II included potent new antibiotics and phenothiazine tranquilizers such as Thorazine. Both the FDA and the drug firms thought these products were potentially too dangerous to sell OTC. The Durham-Humphrey Amendment established the criteria, which are still used today, for determining whether a drug should be classified as prescription or nonprescription. Basically, if a drug does not fall into one of the following three categories, it is considered nonprescription:

1. The drug is habit-forming.

2. The drug is not safe for self-medication because of its toxicity.

3. The drug is a new compound that has not been shown to be completely safe.

In 1959, Senator Estes Kefauver initiated hearings concerned with the enormous profit margins earned by drug companies due to the lack of competition in the market for new, patented drugs.

Testimony by physicians revealed that an average doctor in clinical practice often was not able to evaluate accurately the efficacy of the drugs he or she prescribed. The 1938 law did not give the FDA authority to supervise clinical testing of drugs; consequently, the effectiveness of drugs being sold to the public was not being determined. Both the Kefauver and Harris Amendments in the House were intended to deal with this problem but showed no likely signs of becoming law until the thalidomide tragedy occurred.

During the Kefauver hearings, the FDA received an approval request for Kevadon, a brand of thalidomide that the William Merrell Company hoped to market in the United States. Thalidomide had been used in Europe as a sedative for pregnant women. Despite ongoing pressure from the firm, medical officer Frances Kelsey refused to allow the request to be approved because of insufficient safety data (FDA History Office 2000). By 1962, the horrifying

Characteristic limb deformities caused by thalidomide.

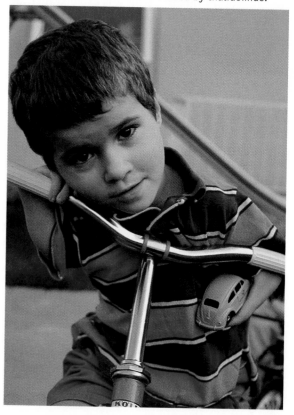

effects of thalidomide on developing fetuses became known. There are two approximately 24-hour intervals early in pregnancy when thalidomide can alter the development of the arms and legs of an embryo. If a woman takes thalidomide on one or both of these days, the infant could be born with abnormally developed arms and/or legs (called phocomelia , from the Greek words for flippers, or "seal-shaped limbs"). Even though Kevadon was never approved for marketing, Merrell had distributed more than 2 million tablets in the United States for investigational use, use that the law and regulations left mostly unchecked. Once thalidomide's deleterious effects became known, the FDA moved quickly to recover the supply from physicians, pharmacists, and patients. For her efforts, Kelsey received the President's Distinguished Federal Civilian Service Award in 1962, the highest civilian honor available to government employees.

Although standard testing probably would not have detected the congenital effect of thalidomide and the tragedy would likely have occurred anyway, these debilitated infants stimulated passage of the 1962 Kefauver and Harris Amendment. They strengthened the government's regulation of both the introduction of new drugs and the production and sale of existing drugs. The amendments required, for the first time, that drug manufacturers demonstrate the efficacy as well as the safety of their drug products. The FDA was empowered to withdraw approval of a drug that was already being marketed. In addition, the agency was permitted to regulate and evaluate drug testing by pharmaceutical companies and mandate standards of good drug-manufacturing policy.

■ THE RISING DEMAND FOR EFFECTIVENESS IN MEDICINAL DRUGS

To evaluate the effectiveness of the more than 4000 drug products that were introduced between 1938 and 1962, the FDA contracted with the National Research Council to perform the Drug Efficacy Study. This investigation started in 1966 and ran for 3 years. The council was asked to rate drugs as either effective or ineffective. Although the study was supposed to be based on scientific evidence, this information often was not available, which meant that conclusions were sometimes founded on the clinical experience of the physicians on each panel; this judgment was not always based on reliable information.

A legal challenge resulted when the FDA took an "ineffective" drug off the market and the manufacturer sued. This action finally forced the FDA to define what constituted an adequate and well-controlled investigation. Adequate, documented clinical experience was no longer satisfactory proof that a drug was safe and effective. Each new drug application now had to include information about the drug's performance in patients compared with the experiences of a carefully defined control group. The drug could be compared with (1) a placebo, (2) another drug known to be active based on previous studies, (3) the established results of no treatment, or (4) historical data about the course of the illness without the use of the drug in question. In addition, a drug marketed before 1962 could no longer be grandfathered in. If the company could not prove the drug had the qualifications to pass the post-1962 tests for a new drug, it was considered a new, unapproved drug and could not legally be sold.

■ REGULATING THE DEVELOPMENT OF NEW DRUGS

The amended Federal Food, Drug, and Cosmetic Act in force today requires that all new drugs be registered with and approved by the FDA. The FDA is mandated by Congress to (1) ensure the rights and safety of human subjects during clinical testing of experimental drugs; (2) evaluate the safety and efficacy of new treatments based on test results and information from the sponsors (often health-related companies); and (3) compare potential benefits and risks to determine if a new drug should be approved and marketed. Because of FDA

KEY TERMS

thalidomide
a sedative drug that, when used during pregnancy, can cause severe developmental damage to a fetus

phocomelia
a birth defect; impaired development of the arms, legs, or both

regulations, all pharmaceutical companies must follow a series of steps when seeking permission to market a new drug (see Figure 3.1).

Regulatory Steps for New Prescription Drugs

Step 1: Preclinical Research and Development A chemical must be identified as having potential value in the treatment of a particular condition or disease. The company interested in marketing the chemical as a drug must run a series of tests on at least three animal species. Careful records must be kept of side effects, absorption, distribution, metabolism, excretion, and the dosages of the drug necessary to produce the various effects. Carcinogenic, mutagenic, and teratogenic variables are tested. The dose-response curve must be determined along with potency, and then the risk and benefit of the substance must be calculated (see Chapter 6). If the company still believes there is a market for the substance, it will forward the data to the FDA to obtain an investigational new drug (IND) number for further tests.

Step 2: Clinical Research and Development Animal tests provide some information, but ultimately tests must be done on the species for which the potential drug is intended—that is, humans. These tests usually follow three phases (Simonsen 1993).

Phase 1 is called the *initial clinical stage.* Small numbers of volunteers (usually 20–100), both healthy people and patients, are recruited to establish drug safety and dose range for effective treatment and to examine side effects. Formerly, much of this research was done on prison inmates, but because of bad publicity and the possibility of coercion, fewer prisoners are used today. Medical students, paid college student volunteers, and volunteers being treated at free clinics are more often used after obtaining informed consent. The data are collected, analyzed, and sent to the FDA for approval before beginning the next phase of human subject testing.

Phase 2 testing is called the *clinical pharmacological evaluation stage.* The effects of the drug are tested to eliminate investigator bias and to determine side effects and the effectiveness of the treatment. Because the safety of the new drug has not been thoroughly established, a few patients (perhaps 100–300 volunteers) with the medical problem the drug is intended to treat are used for these studies. Statistical evaluation of this information is carried out before proceeding with Phase 3 testing.

Phase 3 is the *extended clinical evaluation stage.* By this time, the pharmaceutical company has a good idea of both drug effectiveness and dangers. The drug can be offered safely to a wider group of participating clinics and physicians, who cooperate

FIGURE 3.1
Steps required by the FDA for reviewing a new drug.

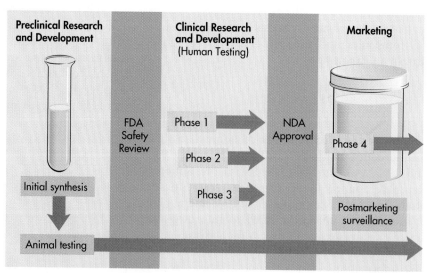

| Preclinical Research and Development | | Clinical Research and Development (Human Testing) | | Marketing |

Duration: 1–3 years   2–10 years   Variable

in the administration of the potential drug—when medically appropriate—to thousands of volunteer patients who have given informed consent.

This stage makes the drug available on a wide experimental basis. Sometimes, by this point, there has been publicity about the new drug, and people with the particular disease for which the drug was developed may actively seek physicians licensed to experiment with it.

During Phase 3 testing, safety checks are made and any side effects are noted that might show up as more people are exposed to the drug. After the testing program is over, careful analysis is made of the effectiveness, side effects, and recommended dosage. If there are sufficient data to demonstrate that the drug is safe and effective, the company will submit a new drug application (NDA) as a formal request that the FDA consider approving the drug for marketing (Hunter et al. 1993). The application usually comprises many thousands of pages of data and analysis, and the FDA must sift through it and decide whether the risks of using the drug justify its potential benefits. The FDA usually calls for additional tests before the drug is determined to be safe and effective and before granting permission to market it.

Step 3: Permission to Market At this point, the FDA can allow the drug to be marketed under its patented name. It may cost $200-$500 million and take up to 12 years to develop a new drug in the United States. The situation is similar elsewhere, although in some countries, the clinical evaluations are less stringent and require less time. Once the drug is marketed, it continues to be closely scrutinized for adverse effects. This postmarketing surveillance is often referred to as *Phase 4* and is important because, in some cases, negative effects may not show up for a long time. For example, it was determined in 1970 that diethylstilbestrol (DES), when given to pregnant women to prevent miscarriage, causes an increased risk of a rare type of vaginal cancer in their daughters when these children entered their teens and young adult years. The FDA subsequently removed from the market the form of DES that had been used to treat pregnant women. As described earlier, the thalidomide tragedy resulted in passage of the law that gave the FDA this authority.

Exceptions: Special Drug-Marketing Laws There is continual concern that the process used by the FDA to evaluate prospective drugs is laborious and excessively lengthy. Hence, an amendment was passed to accelerate the evaluation of urgently needed drugs. The so-called fast-track rule has been applied to the testing of certain drugs used for the treatment of rare cancers, AZT (zidovudine) for the treatment of AIDS (the review process only required 2 years; Hunter et al. 1993), and other similar drugs. As a result, they have reached the market after a much reduced testing program.

A second amendment, the Orphan Drug Law, allows drug companies to receive tax advantages if they develop drugs that are not very profitable because they are only useful in treating small numbers of patients, such as those who suffer from rare diseases. A *rare disease* is defined as one that affects fewer than 200,000 people in the United States or one for which the cost of development is not likely to be recovered by marketing.

The federal government and the FDA are continually refining the system for evaluating new drugs in order to ensure that new effective therapeutic substances can be made available for clinical use as soon as it is safely possible. Some of these modifications reflect the fact that patients with life-threatening diseases are willing to accept greater drug risks in order to gain faster access to potentially useful medications. Attempts to accelerate the drug review are illustrated by the Prescription Drug User Fee Act of 1992. Under this law, fees are paid by the FDA-regulated pharmaceutical companies to support additional FDA reviewers in order to decrease the average review time for drugs that will treat life-threatening and serious diseases from an average of 2 years to approximately 1 year ("A Speedier FDA" 1992).

The Regulation of Nonprescription Drugs

The Durham-Humphrey Amendment to the Food, Drug, and Cosmetic Act made a distinction between prescription and nonprescription (OTC) drugs and required the FDA to regulate OTC drug marketing. In 1972, the FDA initiated a program to evaluate the effectiveness and safety of the nonprescription drugs on the market and to ensure that they included appropriate labeling (for more details, see Chapter 16). Each so-called active ingredient in the OTC medications was reviewed by a panel of drug experts, including physicians, pharmacologists, and pharmacists. Based on the recommendations of these panels, the ingredients were placed in one of the following three categories:

I. Generally recognized as safe and effective for the claimed therapeutic indication

II. Not generally recognized as safe and effective or unacceptable indications

III. Insufficient data available to permit final classification

By 1981, the panels had made initial determinations about over 700 ingredients in more than 300,000 OTC drug products and submitted more than 60 reports to the FDA.

In the second phase of the OTC drug review, the FDA evaluated the panels' findings and submitted a tentative adoption of the panels' recommendations (after revision, if necessary), following public comment and scrutiny. After some time and careful consideration of new information, the agency issued a final ruling and classification of the ingredients under consideration.

■ THE EFFECTS OF THE OTC REVIEW ON TODAY'S MEDICATIONS

The review process for OTC ingredients has had a significant impact on the public's attitude about OTC products and their use (both good and bad) in self-medication. It was apparent from the review process that many OTC drug ingredients did not satisfy the requirements for safety and effectiveness. In fact, in 1990 alone, the FDA banned 223 uses of nonprescription drug ingredients, ruling that the ingredients were ineffective against problems ranging from acne to swimmer's ear. Consequently, it is almost certain that, in the future, there will be fewer active ingredients in OTC medicines, but these drugs will be safer and more effective than ever before.

KEY TERMS

switching policy
an FDA policy allowing the change of suitable prescription drugs to over-the-counter status.

In addition, with heightened public awareness, greater demand has been brought to bear on the FDA to make better drugs available to the public for self-medication. In response to these pressures, the FDA has adopted a switching policy , which allows it to review prescription drugs and evaluate their suitability as OTC products. The following criteria must be satisfied if a drug is to be switched:

1. The drug must have been marketed by prescription for at least 3 years.

2. Use of the drug must have been relatively high during the time it was available as a prescription drug.

3. Adverse drug reactions must not be alarming, and the frequency of side effects must not have increased during the time the drug was available to the public.

In general, this switching policy has been well received by the public. In fact, 85% of Americans believe that it is important to have OTC medications available to relieve minor problems (FDA 1996). The medical community and the FDA are generally positive about OTC switches as well. There are some concerns, however, that more effective drug products will lead to increased abuse or misuse of OTC products. Hence, emphasis is placed on adequate labeling and education to ensure that consumers have sufficient information to use OTC products safely and effectively.

The Regulation of Drug Advertising

Much of the public's knowledge and impressions about drugs, especially those available OTC, come from advertisements. It is difficult to ascertain the amount of money currently spent by the pharmaceutical industry to promote its products. Because of the intense competition among OTC drugs, it is likely that up to 15% to 20% of the dollar sales for these products is spent on advertising to the general public and that the advertising budget equals a sum of approximately $10 billion annually. For prescription drugs, it is likely that the costs of advertising, promoting, and marketing exceed $10 billion annually (Woolsey 1994).

There is no doubt that these promotional efforts by pharmaceutical manufacturers have a tremendous impact on the drug-purchasing habits of the general public and health professionals. Not surprisingly, drug use based on misleading or false advertising claims, rather than facts, can result in unsatisfactory drug therapy and can be extremely dangerous. Regulations governing the advertising of nonprescription drugs are set and enforced by the Federal Trade Commission (FTC). These rules are less stringent than those for prescription medicines (Woolsey 1994).

■ PRESCRIPTION ADVERTISING

The economics of prescription drugs are unique because a second party, the health professional, dictates what the consumer, the patient, will purchase. Currently, many pharmaceutical companies advertise medications directly to the public. Direct advertising of prescription drugs to consumers has experts concerned that patients will put pressure on physicians to prescribe inappropriately. For example, in 1992 more than $100 million was spent by pharmaceutical companies for public advertising (TV, newspapers, magazines, and so on) of nicotine patches for people trying to quit smoking. Some medical experts argue that, as a consequence, many consumers perceive the patches as a quick cure for their tobacco dependence and ignore the fact that they work only as part of a serious behavior modification program. Critics claim this lack of consumer understanding led to incorrect use of the patches and has resulted in fatal heart attacks (Hwang 1992).

The vast majority of prescription drug promotion is directed at health professionals and controlled by the FDA. The approaches employed by manufacturers to encourage health professionals to prescribe their products include advertising in prestigious medical journals, direct mail advertising, and some radio and television advertising. All printed and audio materials distributed by drug salespeople are controlled by FDA advertising regulations. Perhaps the most effective sales approach is for drug representatives to personally visit health professionals; this tactic is harder to regulate.

Many health professionals rely on drug company salespeople for the so-called latest scientific information concerning drugs and their effects.

Although these representatives of the drug industry can provide an important informational service, it is essential that health professionals remember that these people make a living by selling these products, and often their information is biased accordingly.

Many people in and out of the medical community have questioned the ethics of drug advertising and marketing in the United States and are concerned about the negative impact that deceptive promotion has on target populations. One of the biggest problems in dealing with misleading or false advertising is defining such deception. Probably the best guideline for such a definition is summarized in the Wheeler-Lea Amendment to the FTC Act:

> The term *false advertisement* means an advertisement, other than labeling, which is misleading in a material respect; and in determining whether any advertisement is misleading, there shall be taken into account not only representations . . . but the extent to which the advertisement fails to reveal facts.

Tough questions are being asked as to how much control should be exerted over the pharmaceutical industry to protect the public without excessively infringing on the rights of these companies to promote their goods. The solutions to these problems will not be simple; however, efforts to keep drug advertisements accurate, in good taste, and informative are worthwhile and are necessary if the public is expected to make rational decisions about drug use.

■ FEDERAL REGULATION AND QUALITY ASSURANCE

No matter what policy is adopted by the FDA and other drug-regulating agencies, there will always be those who criticize their efforts and complain that they do not do enough or that they do too much. On one hand, the FDA has been blamed for being excessively careful and requiring too much testing before new drugs are approved for marketing; on the other hand, when new drugs are released and cause serious side effects, the FDA is condemned for being sloppy in its control of drug marketing.

What is the proper balance, and what do we, as consumers, have the right to expect from government? These are questions each of us should ask, and we have a right to share our answers with government representatives.

Yet regardless of our individual feelings, it is important to understand that the current (and likely future) federal regulations do not ensure drug safety or effectiveness for everyone. Too many individual variables alter the way each of us responds to drugs, making such universal assurances impossible. Federal agencies can only deal with general policies and make general decisions. For example, what if the FDA determines that a given drug is reasonably safe in 95% of the population and effective in 70%? Are these acceptable figures, or should a drug be safe in 99% and effective in 90% before it is suitable for general marketing? What of the 5% or 1% of the population who will be adversely affected by this drug? What rights do they have to be protected?

There are no simple answers to these questions. Federal policies are compromises that assume that the clinician who prescribes the drug and/or the patient who buys and consumes it will be able to identify when use of that drug is inappropriate or threatening. Unfortunately, sometimes drug prescribing and drug consuming are done carelessly and unnecessary side effects occur or the drug does not work. The questions surface again: Are federal drug agencies doing all they can to protect the public? Should the laws be changed?

It is always difficult to predict the future, especially when it depends on sometimes fickle politicians and erratic public opinion. Nevertheless, with the dramatic increase in new and better drugs becoming available to the public, it is not likely that federal or state agencies will diminish their role in regulating drug use. Now more than ever, the public demands safer and more effective drugs. This public attitude will likely translate into even greater involvement by regulatory agencies in issues of drug development, assessment, and marketing.

Another reason for increased regulation in the future is that many of the larger pharmaceutical companies have become incredibly wealthy. Several of the most profitable companies have become subsidiaries of powerful corporations that are driven more by profit margins than philanthropic interests. In such an environment, governmental agencies are essential to ensure that the rights of the public are protected.

Drug Abuse and the Law

The laws that govern the development, distribution, and use of drugs in general and drugs of abuse in particular are interrelated. There are, however, some unique features concerning the manner in which federal agencies deal with the drugs of abuse that warrant special consideration. A summary of drug abuse laws in the United States is shown in Table 3.1.

Coffee, tea, tobacco, alcohol, marijuana, hallucinogens, depressants (such as barbiturates), and narcotics have been subject to a wide range of controls, varying from none to rigid restrictions. A few countries have instituted severe penalties, such as strangulation for smoking tobacco or opium, and strict bans on alcohol. In other countries, these substances have been deemed either legal or prohibited, depending on the political situation and the desires of the population. Historically, laws have been changed when so many people demanded access to a specific drug of abuse that it would have been impossible to enforce a ban (as in the revocation of Prohibition) or when the government needed tax revenues that could be raised by selling the drug (one argument for legalizing drugs of abuse today). A current example is the controversy over decriminalization or legalization of marijuana (see Chapter 14).

The negative experiences that Americans had at the turn of the 20th century with addicting substances such as opium led to the Harrison Act of 1914 . It marked the first legitimate effort by the federal government to regulate and control the production, importation, sales, purchase, and distribution of addicting substances. The Harrison Act served as the foundation and reference for subsequent laws directed at regulating drug abuse issues.

Today, the ways in which law enforcement agencies deal with substance abuse are largely determined by the Comprehensive Drug Abuse Prevention and Control Act of 1970. This act divided substances with

---

KEY TERMS

Harrison Act of 1914
the first legitimate effort by the government to regulate addicting substances

TABLE 3.1 **Federal Laws Associated with the Control of Narcotics and Other Abused Drugs**

DATE	NAME OF LEGISLATION	SUMMARY OF COVERAGE AND INTENT OF LEGISLATION
1914	Harrison Act	First federal legislation to regulate and control the production, importation, sale, purchase, and free distribution of opium or drugs derived from opium.
1922	Narcotic Drug Import and Export Act	Intended to eliminate the use of narcotics except for medical and other legitimate purposes.
1924	Heroin Act	Made it illegal to manufacture heroin.
1937	Marijuana Tax Act	Provided controls over marijuana similar to those that the Harrison Act provides over narcotics.
1942	Opium Poppy Control Act	Prohibited growing opium poppies in the United States except under license.
1956	Narcotics Control Act	Intended to impose very severe penalties for those convicted of narcotics or marijuana charges
1965	Drug Abuse Control Amendments (DACA)	Adopted strict controls over amphetamines, barbiturates, LSD, and similar substances, with provisions to add new substances as the need arises.
1966	Narcotic Addict Rehabilitation Act (NARA)	Enhanced federal efforts to treat and rehabilitate narcotic addicts through three programs provided for voluntary and pretrial civil commitment and sentencing to treatment of convicted addicts.
1970	Comprehensive Drug Abuse Prevention and Control Act	Directed the Secretary of Department of Health, Education, and Welfare (now the Department of Health and Human Services) to make scientific and medical determinations relative to scheduling of controlled substances.
1972	Drug Abuse Office and Treatment Act	Created the Special Action Office for Drug Abuse Prevention (SAODAP) within the Executive Office of the President; authorized the establishment of the National Institute on Drug Abuse (NIDA) within the National Institute of Mental Health (NIMH) to become operational in 1974 and responsible for developing a national community-based treatment system; and permitted the maintenance treatment of narcotic addicts.
1973	Methadone Control Act	Placed controls on methadone licensing.
1973	Drug Enforcement Administration (DEA)	Bureau of Narcotics and Dangerous Drugs was remodeled to become the DEA.
1974	Comprehensive Alcohol Abuse and Alcoholism Prevention, Treatment, and Rehabilitation Act Amendments	Statutorily established Alcohol, Drug Abuse and Mental Health Administration (ADAMHA), charged with supervising and coordinating the functions of NIDA, National Institute on Alcohol Abuse and Alcoholism (NIAAA) and NIMH. Programs and responsibilities of SAODAP were moved to NIDA.
1974	Narcotic Addict Treatment Act	Required separate DEA registrations for physicians who want to use approved narcotics in drug abuse treatment and separate approvals of registrants by U.S. Department of Health and Human Services and by state agencies.
1986	Analogue (Designer Drug) Act	Made illegal the use of substances similar in effects and structure to substances already scheduled.

(continued)

TABLE 3.1 *(continued)*

DATE	NAME OF LEGISLATION	SUMMARY OF COVERAGE AND INTENT OF LEGISLATION
1986	Executive Order 12564	Mandated a drug-free federal workplace program. NIDA became the lead agency, creating its Office of Workplace Initiatives.
1988	Anti-Drug Abuse Act	Established the Office of National Drug Control Policy (ONDCP) in the Executive Office of the President to oversee all federal policies regarding research about control of drug abuse.
1992	ADAMHA Reorganization Act	Transferred the three institutes that constitute ADAMHA (NIDA, NIAAA and NIMH) to the National Institutes of Health (NIH), and incorporate ADAMHA's service programs into the new Substance Abuse and Mental Health Services Administration (SAMHSA).
2000	Children's Health Act	Allowed qualified physicians to prescribe medications classified as Schedule IV and V narcotics (including buprenorphine) for treatment of addiction. Also included the Methamphetamine Anti-Proliferation Act, the Ecstasy Anti-Proliferation Act, and the SAMHSA reauthorization bill.

abuse potential into categories based on the degree of their abuse potential and their clinical usefulness. The classifications, which are referred to as *schedules,* range from I to V. *Schedule I* substances have high abuse potential and no currently approved medicinal use; they cannot be prescribed by health professionals. *Schedule II* drugs also have high abuse potential but are approved for medical purposes and can be prescribed with restrictions. The distinctions between *Schedule II through V* substances reflect the likelihood of abuse occurring and the degree to which the drugs are controlled by governmental agencies. The least addictive and least regulated of the substances of abuse are classified as Schedule V drugs (see "Here and Now"). Penalties for illegal use and/or trafficking of these agents vary according to the agent's schedule, amount possessed, and number of previous drug-associated offenses (see Table 3.2, page 78).

■ **DRUG LAWS AND DETERRENCE**

As previously discussed, drug laws often do not serve as a satisfactory deterrent against the use of illicit drugs. People have used and abused drugs for thousands of years despite governmental restrictions. It is very likely they will continue to do so despite stricter laws and greater support for law enforcement.

As the amount of addiction increased during the mid-1960s, many ill-conceived programs and laws were instituted as knee-jerk reactions, with little understanding about the underlying reasons for the rise in drug abuse. Unpopular, restrictive laws rarely work to reduce the use of illicit drugs. Even as laws become more restrictive, they usually have little impact on the level of addiction; in fact, in some cases addiction problems actually have increased. For example, during the restrictive years of the 1960s and 1980s, drugs were sold everywhere to everyone—in high schools, colleges, and probably every community. In the 1980s especially, increasingly large volumes of drugs were sold throughout the United States. Billions of dollars were paid for those drugs. Although no one knows precisely how much was exchanged, it likely approached $80 to $100 billion per year for all illegal drugs, of which the two biggest categories were an estimated $30 billion for cocaine and $24 billion for marijuana.

Because of the large sums of money involved, drugs have brought corruption to all levels. Other problems associated with the implementation of drug laws are an insufficient number of law enforcement personnel and inadequate detention facilities; consequently, much drug traffic goes unchecked. In addition, the judiciary system sometimes gets so backlogged that many cases never reach court. Plea bargaining is often used to clear the court docket. Often, dealers and traffickers are back in business the same day that they are arrested.

This apparent lack of punishment seriously damages the morale of law enforcers, legislators, and average citizens.

It is estimated that nearly 1 million drug-related arrests occur each year. This problem represents a tremendous cost to society in terms of damaged lives and family relationships; being arrested for a drug-related crime seriously jeopardizes a person's opportunity to pursue a normal life. Drug taking is closely tied to societal problems, and it will

HERE AND NOW

Controlled substances classified as Schedule I, II, III, IV, or V drugs are described below:

Schedule I

- The drug or other substance has a high potential for abuse.
- The drug or other substance has no currently accepted medical use in treatment in the United States.
- There is a lack of accepted safety for use of the drug or other substance under medical supervision.

Schedule II

- The drug or other substance has a high potential for abuse.
- The drug or other substance has a currently accepted medical use in treatment in the United States or a currently accepted medical use with severe restrictions.
- Abuse of the drug or other substance may lead to severe psychological or physical dependence.

Schedule III

- The drug or other substance has less of a potential for abuse than the drugs or other substances in Schedules I and II.
- The drug or other substance has a currently accepted medical use in treatment in the United States.

- Abuse of the drug or other substance may lead to moderate or low physical dependence or high psychological dependence.

Schedule IV

- The drug or other substance has a low potential for abuse relative to the drugs or other substances in Schedule III.
- The drug or other substance has a currently accepted medical use in treatment in the United States.
- Abuse of the drug or other substance may lead to limited physical dependence or psychological dependence relative to the drugs or other substances in Schedule III.

Schedule V

- The drug or other substance has a low potential for abuse relative to the drugs or other substances in Schedule IV.
- The drug or other substance has a currently accepted medical use in treatment in the United States.
- Abuse of the drug or other substance may lead to limited physical dependence or psychological dependence relative to the drugs or other substances in Schedule IV.

Source: U.S. Code, January 24, 1995.

remain a problem unless society provides more meaningful experiences to those most susceptible to drug abuse. Improved education and increased support should be given to preteens because that is the age when deviant behavior starts. In cases in which drug education programs have been successful in involving students, the amount of drug taking and illegal activity seems to have decreased (see Chapter 18).

■ **FACTORS IN CONTROLLING DRUG ABUSE**

Three principal issues influence laws regarding drug abuse:

1. If a person abuses a drug, should he or she be treated as a criminal or as a sick person afflicted with a disease?

2. How is the user (supposedly the victim) distinguished from the pusher (supposedly the criminal) of an illicit drug, and who should be more harshly punished—the person who creates the demand for the drug or the person who satisfies the demand?

3. Are the laws and associated penalties effective deterrents against drug use or abuse, and how is effectiveness determined?

TABLE 3.2 **Federal Trafficking Penalties**

CSA SCHEDULE	DRUGS	QUANTITY	FIRST OFFENCE	SECOND OFFENCE
I & II	Methamphetamine, Heroin, Cocaine, LSD, PCP	low	Not less than 5 years. If death or serious injury, not less than 20 years, not more than life. Fine of not more than $2 million individual.	Not more than 30 years. If death or serious injury, life. Fine $2 million individual.
I & II	Methamphetamine, Heroin, Cocaine, LSD, PCP	high	Not less than 10 years; not more than life. If death or serious injury, not less than 20 years, not more than life. Fine of not more than $4 million individual.	Not less than 20 years; not more than life. If death or serious injury, not less than life. Fine of not more than $8 million individual
I	Marijuana	high	Not less than 10 years; not more than life. If death or serious injury, not less than 20 years, not more than life. Fine of not more than $4 million individual.	Not less than 20 years, not more than life. If death or serious injury, not less than life. Fine of not more than $8 million individual.
III	All	any	Not more than 5 years. Fine not more than $250,000 individual.	Not more than 10 years. Fine not more than $500,000 individual.
IV	All	any	Not more than 3 years. Fine not more than $250,000 individual.	Not more than 6 years. Fine not more than $500,000 individual.
V	All	any	Not more than 1 year. Fine not more than $100,000 individual.	Not more than 2 years. Fine not more than $200,000 individual.

Source: adapted from "Federal Trafficking Penalties as of October, 1999." U.S. Department of Justice, Drug Enforcement Administration. Available www.usdoj.gov/dea/briefingbook/page10-11.htm.

In regard to the first issue, drug abuse may be considered both an illness and a crime. It is a psychiatric disorder, an abnormal functional state, in which a person is compelled (either physically or psychologically, see Chapter 4) to continue using the drug (American Psychiatric Association 1994). It becomes a crime when the law, reflecting social opinion, makes abuse of the drug illegal (see "Holding the Line," page 80). Health issues are clearly involved because uncontrolled abuse of almost any drug can lead to physical and psychological damage. Because the public must pay for health care costs or societal damage, laws are created and penalties implemented to prevent or correct drug abuse problems (see Table 3.2 on federal trafficking penalties).

Concerning the second issue, drug laws have always been more lenient on the user than the seller of a drug of abuse. Actually, it is often hard to separate user from pusher, as many drug abusers engage in both activities. Because huge profits are often involved, some people may not use the drugs they peddle and are only pushers; the law tries to deter use of drugs by concentrating on these persons but has questionable success. Organized crime is involved in major drug sales, and these "drug rings" have proven hard to destroy.

In regard to the third issue, considerable evidence indicates that, in the United States, criminal law has only limited success in deterring drug abuse. During 1999, approximately 42% of twelfth-graders used an illicit drug; marijuana was used by 38%, LSD by 8%, and cocaine by 6% (Johnston et al. 1999). The total number of Americans using illegal drugs in 1998 has been estimated by the National Household Survey on Drug Abuse to be 13.6 million (SAMHSA-NHSDA 1998). It is clear that the drug abuse problem is far from being resolved, and many feel that some changes should be made in how we deal with this problem.

Strategies for Preventing Drug Abuse

The U.S. government and the public became concerned about the increasing prevalence of drug use during the 1960s, when demonstrations and nationwide protests against the Vietnam War proliferated as youth (mostly college students) rebelled against what they viewed as an unnecessary and unjust war. During the 1960s and early 1970s, for the first time, large numbers of middle- and upper-middle class youth began using licit and illicit gateway drugs on a massive scale. In response, the government responded with strategies for combating drug use and abuse. The three major strategies it employed were supply reduction , demand reduction , and inoculation (Bennett 1989; Heath 1992; HHS Press Office 1996).

■ SUPPLY REDUCTION STRATEGY

Early attempts at drug abuse prevention included both the Harrison Narcotic Act of 1914 and the 18th Amendment (Prohibition) to the U.S. Constitution. Both laws were intended to control the manufacture and distribution of classified drugs, with legislators anticipating that these restrictions would compel people to stop using drugs. The laws enforced supply reduction, which involves a lessened, restrictive, or elimination of available drugs.

Supply reduction drug prevention policy attempts to curtail the supply of illegal drugs or their precursors and exert greater control over other more therapeutic drugs. Part of the supply reduction policy includes interdiction , which is defined as decreasing the amounts of these agents that are carried across U.S. borders by using foreign crop eradication measures and agreements, by imposing

KEY TERMS

supply reduction
a drug reduction policy aimed at reducing the supply of illegal drugs and controlling other therapeutic drugs

demand reduction
attempts to decrease individuals' tendency to use drugs, often aimed at youth, with emphasis on reformulating values and behaviors

inoculation
a method of abuse prevention that protects drug users by teaching them responsibility

interdiction
the policy of cutting off or destroying supplies of illicit drugs

HOLDING THE LINE

The Netherlands has implemented drug policies referred to as revolutionary by some and dangerous by others. It is an offense to sell, produce, possess, or export either "soft" or "hard" drugs. However, it is often not an offense to use drugs. *Hard drugs* are substances deemed by the Dutch to be harmful to health, such as heroin, MDMA, and cocaine. *Soft drugs* include marijuana and hashish.

Although technically illegal, the possession of soft drugs for personal use in quantities up to 30 grams is a "summary, non-indictable offence." *Coffeeshops* (defined as cafés where no alcoholic drinks can be sold) can sell "soft drugs" without prosecution to individuals aged 18 or older. (The sale is technically an offence, but shops that sell up to 5 grams are not prosecuted.) Efforts are made to curtail the sale of drugs in private homes and in public places other than coffeeshops. The possession of less than 1/2 gram of a hard drug is an indictable offence, but given "a low priority in law enforcement policy." (It should be noted that cities formulate their own local policies on coffee shops, and can ban all in their jurisdiction.) The major aim of Dutch drug policy is to prevent harm to users and those around them. For instance, coffeeshops are permitted so as to "keep soft drugs separate from hard drugs in order to protect soft-drug users, especially from youngsters who want to try them out, from exposure to hard drugs and the criminal traffic in them." The government encourages addicts to give up drugs, and believes that "the fact that (drug users) will not be prosecuted or stigmatized makes it easier to seek help." According to The Netherlands Ministry of Foreign Affairs, only a small proportion of soft-drug users become hard-drug users.

A spokesperson for the United States Office of National Drug Control Policy (ONDCP) disagrees with the Dutch policy. "If the Dutch experience with drugs is an appropriate model at all, it is because it illustrates the harms that result from increased tolerance of illegal drugs." This conclusion was drawn after ONDCP representatives traveled to the Netherlands in 1998 to gain a better understanding of the Dutch approach. When Dutch coffeeshops began selling marijuana in small quantities, its use more than doubled between 1984 and 1996 among 18- to 25-year-olds. Moreover, tolerance of drug use in the Netherlands has, in the opinion of many, created a climate that drug traffickers and manufacturers have seized upon to produce and market more dangerous and addictive drugs.

The impact of high-potency marijuana on Dutch youth has been severe. In Foreign Affairs, Dr. Ernest Bunning of the Ministry of Health has said, "there are young people who abuse soft drugs . . . particularly those that have high THC. The place that cannabis takes in their lives becomes so dominant they don't have space for other important things in life. They crawl out of bed in the morning, grab a joint, don't work, smoke another joint. They don't know what to do with their lives. I don't want to call it a drug problem because if I do, then we have to get into a discussion that cannabis is dangerous, that sometimes you can't use it without doing damage to your health or your psyche. The moment we say, 'There are people who have problems with soft drugs,' our critics will jump on us, so it makes it a little bit difficult for us to be objective on this matter."

During this period of tolerance, the Netherlands has also experienced a serious problem with other substances of abuse, in particular heroin and synthetic drugs. Increasingly, this problem is spilling over to other nations, as the Netherlands is more and more seen as Europe's synthetic drug production center by law enforcement agencies, according to the ONDCP. Hence, whether the Dutch policy is successful remains to be determined.

Sources: "Q&A: A Guide to Dutch Policy." Published by the Netherlands Ministry of Foreign Affairs Foreign Information Division, The Netherlands, 2000.

ONDCP. Testimony to Congress. Available http://www.whitehousedrugpolicy.gov/news/testimony/legalization/english/leglz%20final.htm.

stiff penalties for drug trafficking, and by controlling of alcoholic beverages through licensing.

The United States dedicates enormous resources to interdiction programs. For fiscal year 2000, former president Clinton requested $1.85 billion for drug interdiction, a decrease of nearly $500 million from 1999 enacted levels. This included funds for U.S. Customs Service, Department of Defense, U.S. Coast Guard, Immigration and Naturalization Service (USDOJ 2000). Although seizures of large caches of illicit drugs are reported routinely in the national press, there is no indication that the availability of drugs has diminished substantially. One can argue that as long as a strong demand for these psychoactive agents exists, demand will be satisfied if the price is right. Even if interdiction successfully reduces the supply of one drug of abuse, if demand persists, that drug usually will be replaced by another with similar abuse potential (for example, substitution of amphetamines for cocaine; see Chapter 11).

■ DEMAND REDUCTION STRATEGY

The demand reduction approach attempts to minimize the actual demand for drugs. Through programs and activities often aimed at youth, emphasis is placed on reformulating values, attitudes, skills, and behaviors conducive to resisting drug use. (Chapter 18, provides extensive information about methods and techniques for reducing drug use.) As part of this strategy, support for medical and group drug treatment programs for abusers is encouraged. Although this approach does not address drug supply, it does attempt to curb and eventually eliminate the need to purchase drugs by reducing the buyer's demand.

Drug abuse is a complex and very individual problem, with many causes and aggravating factors. Even so, experience has shown that prevention and demand reduction are better strategies and, in the long run, less costly than interdiction or penalties administered via the criminal justice system (Goldstein 1994).

The following are some suggestions and strategies as to how demand for drugs can be reduced:

1. The top priority of any prevention program, if it is to provide a long-term solution, is reduction of drug demand by youth. Children must be the primary focus in any substance abuse program.

To achieve success requires stabilizing defective family structures, implementing school programs that create an antidrug attitude, establishing a drug-free environment, and promoting resistance training to help youth avoid drug involvement. In addition, children should be encouraged to become involved in alternative activities that can substitute for drug-abusing activity. Potential drug abusers need to be convinced that substance abuse is personally and socially damaging and unacceptable.

2. Education about drug abuse must be carefully designed and customized for the target population or group. For example, education based on scare tactics is not likely to dissuade adolescents from experimenting with drugs. Adolescents are at a point in their lives when they feel invincible, and graphically depicting the potential health consequences of drug and alcohol abuse has little impact. A discussion about the nature of addiction and the addiction process is more likely to influence their attitudes. Adolescents need to understand why people use drugs to appreciate the behavior patterns in themselves. Other important topics that should be discussed are how drug abuse works and why it leads to dependence. To complement drug education, adolescents also should be taught coping strategies that include proper decision-making and problem-solving.

3. Attitudes toward drug abuse and its consequence must be changed. The drug use patterns of many people, both young and old, are strongly influenced by peers. If individuals believe that drug abuse is glamorous and contributes to acceptance by friends and associates, the incidence of drug abuse will remain high. In contrast, if the prevailing message in society is that drug abuse is unhealthy and not socially acceptable, the incidence will be much lower.

4. Replacement therapy has been shown to be a useful approach to weaning the individual on drugs of abuse. The most common example of this strategy is the use of the narcotic methadone to treat the heroin addict (see Chapter 10). Use of methadone prevents the cravings and severe withdrawal routinely associated with breaking the heroin habit. Unfortunately, most heroin

addicts insist that they be maintained on methadone indefinitely. Even though methadone is easier to control and is less disruptive than heroin, one drug addiction has been substituted for another, which draws criticism. Replacement therapy certainly is not the entire answer to all drug abuse problems, but it often can provide a window of opportunity for behavioral modification so that a long-term solution to the abuse problem is possible.

■ INOCULATION STRATEGY

The *inoculation* method of abuse prevention aims to protect drug users by teaching them responsibility. The emphasis is on being accountable, rational, and responsible about drug use, and informing users about the effects of drugs on both mind and bodily function. Responsible drinkers who use designated drivers, and nonalcohol parties are outcomes of applying inoculation strategy.

Current and Future Drug Use

During the administrations of former Presidents Ronald Reagan and George Bush (1980–1992), the official policy of the U.S. federal government included a "get tough" attitude about drug abuse. Slogans such as "Just Say No" and "War on Drugs" reflected the frustration of a public that had been

victimized by escalating crime (many incidents were drug-related); personally touched by drug tragedies in families, at work, or with associates and friends; and economically strained by dealing with the cost of the problem. It is no wonder that, in 1989 and 1990, drug abuse was viewed as the number one problem in this country by the majority of its citizens. Recent surveys indicate that this concern persists today (Newport 2000).

How successful has the government-declared "War on Drugs" been since its inception? What has and has not been accomplished?

Has been accomplished:

- According to the 1998 National Household Survey on Drug Abuse (SAMHSA-NHSDA 1998), an estimated 13.6 million Americans overall (6.2% of the U.S. population age 12 and older) were current users of illicit drugs. Although this is not a statistically significant change from the previous year, it represents a significant downward trend; the number of current illicit drug users is about half its peak in 1979, when there were 25 million current users.

- In general, fewer young people are using illicit drugs: in 1998, an estimated 9.9% of adolescents age 12 through 17 reported current illicit drug use, meaning they used an illicit drug at least once during the 30 days before the survey interview. This estimate represents a statistically significant decrease from the estimate of 11.4% in 1997 (SAMHSA-NHSDA 1998).

An example of the many public awareness advertisements cautions against drinking and driving.

Has not been accomplished:

- Although statistics indicate that overall drug usage is decreasing, 52,000 Americans still die each year as its result (Feldman 1999).

- The economic cost to society of drug abuse continues to be staggering. In 1992, the estimated cost of drug and alcohol abuse was $246 billion. This includes treatment and prevention costs, as well as costs associated with crime, loss of job productivity, social welfare, and lost wages. The Office of National Drug Control Policy (ONDCP) conducted a survey to determine how much money was spent on illegal drugs that might otherwise support legitimate savings or spending by the user: it estimated that between 1988 and 1995, Americans spent $57.3 billion on illegal drugs that would otherwise support legitimate savings of spending by the user (NIDA Infofax 1999).

- Although overall current usage may be decreasing, the number of first-time users remains staggering. For instance, in 1997, an estimated 2.1 million persons first used marijuana, approximately 5,800 new marijuana users per day. In addition, an estimated 81,000 persons used heroin for the first time. There were an estimated 730,000 new cocaine users and an estimated 1.1 million new hallucinogen users as well (SAMHSA Press Office 1999).

- Although millions of dollars have been spent in an attempt to educate young people regarding the dangers of substance abuse, the percentage of youths reporting that they perceived themselves to be at great risk in using cocaine once a month decreased from 63% in 1994 to 54% in 1996 (SAMHSA 2000). In addition, there was a decrease in perceived risk of marijuana use among youths 12 through 17 between 1990 and 1997 (SAMHSA Press Office 1996, SAMHSA Press Office 1998).

- Despite the introduction of "Drug-Free School Zones" throughout the country, in 1996 more than half of youths age 12 through 17 reported that marijuana was easy to obtain, and about one-quarter reported that heroin was easy to obtain. Fifteen percent of youths reported being approached by someone selling drugs in the month before the interview (SAMHSA Press Office 1996).

- Although overall drug use is decreasing, usage of several drugs including methamphetamine and "club drugs" such as methylenedioxymethamphetamine (MDMA), gamma-hydroxybutyrate (GHB), Rohypnol (flunitrazepam), ketamine and LSD are gaining popularity.

- Involvement of inmates in drugs or alcohol in the month before the offense or at the time of the offense increased during the 1990s. About half of the inmates in state and federal prisons in 1997 reported using drugs or alcohol while committing their offense, and about one in six inmates in state and federal prisons said they committed their current offense to obtain money to buy drugs. In 1998, the Federal Bureau of Investigation estimated that there were about 1.6 million state and local arrests for drug abuse violations, an increase of almost 1 million since 1980 (SAMHSA 2000).

Fighting the "War on Drugs" is clearly difficult and complex. Progress has been made. Nonetheless, significant problems still exist and require attention of politicians, clinicians, law enforcement agencies, families, councilors and all concerned citizens.

■ DRUG LEGALIZATION DEBATE

The persistence of the drug abuse problem and the high cost in dollars and frustration of waging the "War on Drugs" helps to energize the ongoing debate regarding legalizing the use of drugs of abuse. Proponents of legalization are no longer limited to libertarians and so-called academic intellectuals. Increasingly, this group includes representatives of a distressed law enforcement system. For example, discontented judges whose courts are swamped with drug cases and police officers who spend much of their on-duty time trying to trap and arrest every drug dealer and user on the street are publicly declaring that the drug laws are wasteful and futile.

Several arguments are used commonly by individuals and groups promoting the legalization of all substances of abuse (USDOJ-DEA 1994). For instance, proponents often contend that if drugs were legalized, violence and crime would become less frequent. These individuals point out that users often commit crimes to pay for drugs: if drugs were legal, then the tremendous profits associated with drugs because of their illegal status would disappear and, once gone, the black market and criminal activity associated with drugs would be eliminated. Furthermore, legalization would decrease law enforcement costs by eliminating the backlog of drug-related court cases and reduce populations in overcrowded prisons. In contrast, opponents of drug legalization believe that legalization would lead to increased availability of drugs, which would, in turn, lead to increased use. They point out that the use of drugs, especially methamphetamine, phenylcyclidine (PCP), and cocaine, is often associated with violent criminal behavior. Numerous studies demonstrate the links among drugs, violence, and crime, and the link between alcohol, a legal substance, and crime are well documented. According to legalization opponents, drug use would only increase the incidence of crime, even if the drugs were legally purchased. Accordingly, the economic (as well as social) cost to society would increase.

Legalization proponents claim that making illicit drugs licit would not cause more of these substances to be consumed, nor would addiction increase. They note correctly that many people use drugs in moderation. Furthermore, many would choose not to use drugs, just as many abstain currently from tobacco and alcohol. As noted earlier, opponents contend that if drugs were made licit and more widely available, usage and addiction rates would increase. These individuals contend that legalizing drugs sends a message that drug use (like tobacco and alcohol) is acceptable and encourages drug use among people who currently do not use drugs.

Proponents claim that drug legalization would allow users the right to practice a diversity of consciousness, ". . . the practice of getting high has existed from the dawn of time, and all efforts to eradicate it are based on an incomplete understanding of human nature" (Lenson 1995). Just as diversity of race, ethnicity, sexual orientation, religion, and other varied lifestyles are allowed, legalization of drugs would permit citizens in our society to alter their consciousness without legal repercussions as long as they do not harm or threaten the safety and security of others. Moreover, proponents argue that education, health care, road building, and a wide array of other worthwhile causes would benefit from the taxes that could be raised by legalizing and then taxing drugs. They argue that the United States has spent billions of dollars to control drug production, trafficking, and use with few, if any, positive results. They contend that the money spent on drug control should be shifted to other, more productive endeavors.

Opponents believe that health and societal costs of drug legalization would increase. It has been predicted that drug treatment costs, hospitalization for long-term drug-related diseases, and treatment of the consequences of drug-associated family violence would further burden our already strapped health care system. It would increase costs to society due to greater medical and social problems resulting from greater availability and increased use. The two most frequently abused substances, alcohol and tobacco, are both legal and readily available. These two substances cause more medical, social, and personal problems than all the illicit drugs of abuse combined. They question whether society wants to legalize additional drugs with abuse potential.

Despite some of the compelling arguments for legalization of drugs of addiction, the majority of law enforcement professionals, politicians, federal agencies, and medical associations oppose legalization of some or all drugs of abuse. In addition, polls indicate that most voters object to legalization or decriminalization of illicit drugs (Knight-Ridder News Service 1992). A major Gallup survey of public attitudes showed that 54% of respondents opposed drug legalization, and another 31% were moderately opposed to it; only 14% favored it (CNN/USA Today/Gallup Poll 1995).

Although arguments for both sides warrant consideration, extreme policies are not likely to be implemented; instead, a compromise will most probably be adopted. For example, some areas of compromise include the following (Kalant 1992):

Selective legalization. Eliminate harsh penalties for those drugs of abuse that are the safest and least likely to cause addiction, such as marijuana.

Control of substances of abuse by prescription or through specially approved outlets. Have the availability of the illegal drugs controlled by physicians and trained clinicians, rather than by law enforcement agencies.

Discretionary enforcement of drug laws. Allow greater discretion by judicial systems for prosecution and sentencing of those who violate drug laws. Such decisions would be based on perceived criminal intent.

In conclusion, the drug legalization debate remains a very divisive issue in the United States. Although legalization would lessen the number of drug violators involved in the criminal justice system, the problems associated with legalizing current illicit drugs cause most members in our society to regard this idea with disfavor. As stated earlier, opponents of legalization argue that we already have massive problems with licit drugs such as tobacco and alcohol. According to them, legalizing additional types of drugs would produce a substantial increase in the rate of addiction and in the social and psychological problems associated with drug use. Proponents favoring legalization assert that, despite the current drug laws and severe penalties for drug use, people continue to use illicit drugs.

A compromise between legalization and current criminalization of illicit drug use might include selective legalization . Such an approach would probably legalize marijuana, whereas other drugs such as heroin and cocaine would remain illegal. A second type of compromise might call medical practitioners to control drug availability instead of law enforcement agencies. A third compromise might involve discretionary enforcement of drug laws, which would allow judicial systems to exercise greater discretion in prosecution and sentencing of drug law violators, based largely on perceived criminal intent.

■ DRUG TESTING

In response to the demand by society to stop the spread of drug abuse and its adverse consequences, drug testing has been implemented in some situations to detect drug users (Catlin et al. 1992; Jaffe 1995). The most common types of drug testing use Breathalyzers and laboratory studies of urine, blood, and hair specimens. Urine and blood testing are preferred for detecting drug use. Hair specimen testing must overcome technical problems before hair can be used as a definitive proof of drug use, including

| KEY TERMS |

selective legalization
an approach that would legalize marijuana, while other drugs such as heroin and cocaine would remain illegal

complications from hair treatment (e.g., hair coloring) and environmental absorption (Jaffe 1995).

The drugs of abuse most frequently tested are marijuana, cocaine, amphetamines, narcotics, sedatives, PCP, and anabolic steroids. Drug testing is often mandatory in some professions in which public safety is a concern (such as airline pilots, railroad workers, law enforcement employees, medical personnel) or for employees of some organizations and companies as part of general policy (such as the military, many federal agencies, and some private companies). Drug testing is also often mandatory for participants in sports at all levels, in high school, college, international, and professional competition (Catlin et al. 1992) in order to prevent unfair advantages that might result from the pharmacological effects of these drugs and to discourage the spread of drug abuse among athletes. Drug testing is also used routinely by law enforcement agencies to assist in the prosecution of those believed to violate drug abuse laws. Finally, drug testing is used by health professionals to assess the success of drug abuse treatment, that is, to determine if a dependent patient is diminishing his or her drug use or has experienced a relapse in drug abuse habits.

Drug testing to identify drug offenders is usually accomplished by analyzing body fluids, in particular urine, although other approaches (such as analysis of expired air for alcohol) are also used. To understand the accuracy of these tests, several factors should be considered (Catlin et al. 1992, Jaffe 1995).

1. *Testing must be standardized and conducted efficiently.* In order to interpret testing results reliably, it is essential that fluid samples be collected, processed, and tested using standard procedures. Guidelines for proper testing procedures have been established by federal regulatory agencies as well as scientific organizations. Deviations from established protocols can result in false positives (tests that indicate a drug is present when none was used), false negatives (tests that

are unable to detect a drug that is present), or inaccurate assessments of drug levels.

2. *Sample collection and processing must be done accurately and confidentially.* In many cases, drug testing can have punitive consequences (for example, athletes cannot compete or employees are fired if results are positive). Consequently, drug users often attempt to outsmart the system. Some individuals have attempted to avoid submitting their own drug-containing urine for testing by filling specimen bottles with "clean" urine from artificial bladders hidden under clothing or in the vagina or by introducing "clean" urine into their own bladders just before collection (Catlin et al. 1992). To confirm the legitimacy of the specimen, it often is necessary to have the urine collection witnessed directly by a trustworthy observer. To ensure that the fluid specimens are not tampered with and that confidentiality is maintained, samples should be immediately coded and movement of each sample from site to site during analysis should be documented and confirmed.

Just as it is important that testing identify individuals who are using drugs, it is also important that those who have not used drugs not be wrongfully accused. To avoid false positives, all samples that test positive in screening (usually fast and inexpensive procedures) should be analyzed again using more accurate, sensitive, and sophisticated analytical procedures to confirm the results.

3. *Confounding factors that interfere with the accuracy of the testing can be inadvertently or deliberately present.* For example, normal dietary consumption of pastries containing poppy seeds is sufficient to cause a positive urine test for the narcotic morphine. The use of bicarbonate alkalinizes the urine and increases the

rate of elimination of some drugs, such as methamphetamine, and thereby diminishes the likelihood of a positive test (Catlin et al. 1992). Excessive intake of fluid or use of diuretics increases the volume of urine formed and decreases the concentration of drugs, making them more difficult to detect.

The dramatic increase in drug testing since 1985 has caused experts to question its value in dealing with drug abuse problems. Unfortunately, drug testing often is linked exclusively to punitive consequences, such as disqualification from athletic competition, loss of job, or even fines and imprisonment. Use of drug testing in such negative ways does little to diminish the number of drug abusers or their personal problems.

However, drug testing programs can have positive consequences by identifying drug users who require professional care. After being referred for drug rehabilitation, the offender can be monitored using drug testing to confirm the desired response to therapy. In addition, tests can identify individuals who put others in jeopardy because of their drug abuse habits because they perform tasks that are dangerously impaired by the effects of these drugs (for example, airline pilots, train engineers, truck drivers, and so forth).

The widespread application of drug testing to control the illicit use of drugs in the general population would be extremely expensive, difficult to enforce, and almost certainly ineffective. In addition, such indiscriminate testing would likely be viewed as an unwarranted infringement on individual privacy and declared unconstitutional. However, the use of drug testing to discourage inappropriate drug use in selected crucial professions that directly impact public welfare appears to be publicly tolerated and has been shown to be effective (Bryson 1992). Even so, it is probably worthwhile to periodically revisit the issue of drug testing and analyze its benefits and liabilities relative to "public safety" and "individual privacy" issues.

KEY TERMS

pragmatic drug policy
developing drug laws reflecting the desires of the majority of the citizenry; stressing drug education and treatment; developing nondiscriminatory policies

■ **PRAGMATIC DRUG POLICIES**

Several principles for a pragmatic drug policy emerge from a review of past drug policies and an understanding of the drug-related frustrations of today. To create drug policies that work, the following suggestions are offered:

1. It is important that the government develop programs that are consistent with the desires of the majority of the population.

2. Given the difficulties and high cost of efforts to prevent illicit drugs from reaching the market, it is logical to deemphasize interdiction and instead stress programs that reduce demand. To reduce demand, drug education and drug treatment must be top priorities.

3. Government and society need to better understand the role played by law in their efforts to reduce drug addiction. Antidrug laws by themselves do not eliminate drug problems; indeed, they may even create significant social difficulties (for example, the Prohibition laws against all alcohol use). Used properly and selectively, however, laws can reinforce and communicate expected social behavior and values (for example, laws against public drunkenness or against driving a vehicle under the influence of alcohol).

4. Finally, programs should be implemented that employ "public consensus" more effectively to campaign against drug abuse. For example, antismoking campaigns demonstrate the potential success that could be achieved by programs that alter drug abuse behavior. Similar approaches can be used to change public attitudes about drugs through education without moral judgments and crusading tactics. Our society needs to engage in more collaborative programs where drug-using individuals, their families, communities, and helping agencies work together.

Discussion Questions

1. Describe the FDA approval process for assessing the safety and efficacy of a newly developed drug. What are its advantages and disadvantages?

2. Name the principal legislative initiatives that mandate that drugs be proven safe or effective.

3. What are the principal advantages and disadvantages of switching products from prescription to OTC status?

4. What could account for the vast differences in attitudes and opinions regarding drug use and the law voiced by drug users/abusers and nonusers of drugs?

5. Would decriminalization of illicit drug use increase or decrease drug-related social problems? Justify your answer.

6. Compare and contrast supply reduction, demand reduction, and inoculation strategies for dealing with drug abuse.

7. List the principal arguments for and against legalizing drugs of abuse such as marijuana and cocaine.

Key Terms

thalidomide **68**

phocomelia **69**

switching policy **72**

Harrison Act of 1914 **74**

supply reduction **79**

demand reduction **79**

inoculation **79**

interdiction **79**

selective legalization **85**

pragmatic drug policy **86**

Summary

1 Societies have evolved to believe that they have the right to protect themselves from the damaging impact of drug use and abuse. Consequently, governments, including that of the United States, have passed laws and implemented programs to prevent social damage from inappropriate drug use.

In addition, such societies have come to expect that drugs be effective.

2 The 1906 Pure Food and Drug Act was not a strong law, but it required manufacturers to include on labels the amounts of alcohol, morphine, opium, cocaine, heroin, and marijuana extract in each product. This was the first real attempt to make consumers aware of the action contents in the drug products they were consuming.

3 The 1938 Federal Food, Drug, and Cosmetic Act gave the FDA control over drug safety.

4 The 1951 Durham-Humphrey Amendment to the Food, Drug, and Cosmetic Act made a formal distinction between prescription and nonprescription drugs.

5 The Kefauver-Harris Amendment of 1962 required manufacturers to demonstrate both efficacy and safety of their products.

6 All drugs to be considered for marketing must first be tested for safety in animals. Following these initial tests, if the drug is favorably reviewed by the FDA, it is given IND status. It then generally undergoes three phases of clinical testing before final FDA approval.

7 In 1972, the FDA initiated a program to ensure that all OTC drugs were safe and effective. Specific panels were selected to evaluate the safety and effectiveness of more than 700 OTC drug ingredients. Each of the ingredients was classified into categories: I, II, and III.

8 The switching policy of the FDA allows it to review prescription drugs and evaluate their suitability as OTC products.

9 Three of the principal factors that influence laws on drug abuse address the following questions: Should drug abusers be treated as criminals or patients? How can drug users and drug pushers be distinguished from one another? What types of laws and programs are effective deterrents against drug abuse?

10 Controversy exists as to how to best reduce substance abuse. A principal strategy used by governmental agencies to achieve this objective is interdiction; the majority of money used to fight drug abuse is spent on trying to stop and confiscate drug supplies. Experience has proved that interdiction is often ineffective. To reduce drug abuse, demand for these substances must be diminished. Youth must be a top priority in any substance abuse program. Treatment that enables drug addicts to stop their habits with minimal discomfort should be provided. Finally, education should be used to change attitudes toward drug abuse and its consequences. Potential drug abusers need to be convinced that substance abuse is personally and socially damaging and is unacceptable.

11 Three major strategies for combating drug use and abuse follow: supply reduction, demand reduction, and inoculation strategy. Supply reduction involves using drug laws to control the manufacturing and distribution of classified drugs. Demand reduction strategy aims to reduce the actual demand for drugs by working mainly with youth and teaching them to resist drugs. Inoculation strategy aims to protect drug users by teaching them responsibility and explaining the effects of drugs on bodily and mental functioning.

12 In response to the demand by society to stop the spread of drug abuse and its adverse consequences, drug testing has been implemented in some situations to detect drug users. Common drug testing uses breathalyzers and analysis of urine, blood, and hair specimens. Urine and blood testing are the preferred methods of testing for drug use. Hair specimen testing must overcome a number of technical problems before hair can be used as a definitive proof of drug use, including hair treatment and environmental absorption.

References

American Psychiatric Association. *Diagnostic and Statistical Manual of Mental Disorders*, 4th ed., [DSM-IV], chairperson Allen Frances. Washington, DC: APA, 1994: 175–272.

"A Speedier FDA." *American Druggist* (November 1992): 13.

Bennett, W. "Introduction." *National Drug Control Strategy*. Washington, DC: U.S. Government Printing Office, 1989: 12–13.

Bryson, R. "Railroads Try to Derail Drug Abuse." *Salt Lake Tribune* 244 (9 June 1992): D-5.

Catlin, D., D. Cowan, M. Donike, D. Fraisse, H. Oftebro, and S. Rendic. "Testing Urine for Drugs." *Journal of Automated Chemistry* 14 (1992): 85–92.

CNN/USA Today/Gallup Poll. "Drugs and Drug Abuse." *Gallup Poll Survey* G0105147, 14–17 September 1995.

Drug Facts and Comparisons. St. Louis, MO: Lippincott, 1991.

FDA Consumer Magazine, 1996. Available http://www.verity.fdd.gov.

FDA History Office. "A Brief History of the Center for Drug Evaluation and Research." Available http://www.fda.gov/cder/about/history/default.htm.

FDA Backgrounder. "Milestones in U.S. Food and Drug Law History." 1999. Available http://www.fda.gov/opacom/backgrounders/miles.html.

Feldman, C. "America's War on Drugs Reduces Users, but Supply Keeps Coming." *CNN.com* (9 September 1999).

Goldstein, A. "Lessons from the Street." In *Addiction from Biology to Drug Policy*. New York: Freeman, 1994.

Heath, D. B. "U.S. Drug Control Policy: A Cultural Perspective." *Daedalus* (Summer 1992): 269–91.

HHS Press Office. Substance Abuse—A National Challenge: Prevention, Treatment and Research at HHS. (6 May 1996). Available www.os.dhhs.gov/news/press/1996pres/960506b.html.

Hunter, J. R., D. L. Rosen, and R. DeChristoforo. "How FDA Expedites Evaluation of Drugs." *Welcome Trends in Pharmacy* (January 1993): 2–9.

Hwang, S. "Nicotine Patch Reignites Fight Over Drug Ads." *Wall Street Journal* 73 (30 June 1992): B1.

Jaffe, J. H., ed. *Encyclopedia of Drugs and Alcohol*. New York: Simon and Schuster, Macmillan, 1995.

Johnston, L. D., O'Malley, P. M., Bachman J. G.; National Survey on Drug Abuse, The Monitoring the Future Study, The Univ. of Michigan Institute for Social Research and the National Institute on Drug Abuse, 1999.

Kalant, H. "Formulating Policies on the Non-medical Use of Cocaine." In *Cocaine: Scientific and Social Dimensions*. Ciba Foundation Symposium 166. New York: Wiley, 1992: 261–76.

Knight-Ridder News Service. "Time to Make Drugs Legal? Many Say Yes." *Salt Lake Tribune* 244 (July 11, 1992): A1.

Lenson, D. *On Drugs*. Minneapolis, MN: University of Minnesota Press, 1995.

Newport, F. "Economy, Education, Health, Crime and Morality Most on Americans' Minds This Election Year." The Gallup Organization (22 June 2000).

NIDA Infofax. "Costs to Society." Publication 13564 (November 1999).

SAMHSA. "Substance Abuse Treatment in Adult and Juvenile Correctional Facilities." *Drug and Alcohol Services Information System Series*: S-9. (April 2000).

SAMHSA Press Office. "Perceived Risk and Availability." 1996.

SAMHSA Press Office. "Overall Drug Use Is Level, but Youth Drug Increase Persists." 1998.

SAMHSA Press Office. "Annual National Drug Survey Results Released." (August 1999).

SAMHSA-NHSDA. *Fact Sheet*. August 1998. Available www.samhsa.gov/PRESS/99/990818fs.htm.

Simonsen, L. "Medicines in Development Keep Older Americans Healthy, at Home, Longer." *Pharmacy Times*. 59, (1993) 81–85.

Temin, P. *Taking Your Medicine: Drug Regulation in the United States*. Cambridge, MA: Harvard University Press, 1980.

USDOJ. Bureau of Justice Statistics Drugs and Crime Facts: Drug Control Budget. 2000. Available www.ojp.usdoj.gov/ bjs/dcf/dcb.htm.

USDOJ-DEA. "Speaking Out Against Drug Legalization." Available http://www.usdoj.gov/dea/pubs/legaliz/contents.htm.

Woolsey, R. "A Prescription for Better Prescriptions." *Issues in Science and Technology* (Spring, 1994) 59–66.

Addictive Behavior and Treating Drug Dependence

Did You Know?

- Addiction can be described as a complex disease.
- People who are addicted to drugs come from all walks of life.
- Many addicts suffer from psychiatric or other health problems that can make their addiction difficult to treat.
- A variety of approaches to drug addiction treatment exist, including behavioral and pharmacological therapies.

- No single treatment approach is appropriate for all individuals.
- The most successful treatment programs provide a combination of therapies and other services to meet the needs of the individual abuser.

Chapter 4

Learning Objectives

On completing this chapter you will be able to:

► Provide in your own words a generally accepted definition of addiction.

► Identify and explain two biological factors that encourage chemical dependency.

► Identify and explain two social or environmental factors encouraging chemical dependency.

► Identify two models that may be used to treat chemical dependency.

► List several principles that characterize effective drug treatment.

Introduction

The Origin and Nature of Addiction

Humans can develop a very intense relationship with chemicals. Most people have chemically altered their mood at some point in their lives, if only by consuming a cup of coffee or a glass of white wine, and a majority do so occasionally. Yet for some individuals, chemicals become the center of their lives, driving their behavior and determining their priorities, even where catastrophic consequences to their health and social well-being ensue. Although the word *addiction* is an agreed-upon term referring to such behavior, little agreement exists as to the origin, nature, or boundaries of the concept of addiction. It has been classified as a very bad habit, a failure of will or morality, a symptom of other problems, or a chronic disease in its own right.

Although public perception of drug abuse and addiction as a major social problem has waxed and waned over the past 20 years, the social costs of addiction have not: the total criminal justice, health, insurance, and other costs in the United States are roughly estimated at $80 to $175 billion annually, depending on the source. Despite numerous prevention efforts, the "War on Drugs," and a fall-off in the heavy drug use of the 1960s and 1970s, lessons learned in one decade seem to quickly pass out of awareness. For example, marijuana use among young people, which had declined in every year from 1978 to 1991, has risen sharply over the past few years. In 1991, 3.2% of eighth graders reported using marijuana in the past 30 days; in 1999, this number rose to 9.7% (Johnston et al. 1999). Its use, as well as that of alcohol or cigarettes, is penetrating into younger and younger grades (Drug Strategies 1996).

Chapter 1 focused on the scope of the substance abuse problem. Chapter 2 described the major theories of why people use or abuse drugs. Chapter 3 described how drug use and abuse are viewed and regulated by the law. This chapter will introduce facts and ideas to help better define this persistent social, public health, and safety problem. Factors contributing to addiction will be described. Finally, this chapter will propose principles for effective treatment and describe a few of the most common strategies used to treat substance abuse and addiction.

■ DEFINING ADDICTION

Addiction can be described as a complex disease. In 1964, the World Health Organization (WHO) of the United Nations defined it as "a state of periodic or chronic intoxication detrimental to the individual and society, which is characterized by an overwhelming desire to continue taking the drug and to obtain it by any means." Accordingly, it is characterized as compulsive, at times uncontrollable, drug craving, seeking, and use that persist even in the face of extremely negative consequences (NIDA 1999). This relentless pursuit of a drug of choice occurs despite the fact that the drug is usually harmful and injurious to bodily and mental functions.

The word *addiction*, derived from the Latin verb *addicere*, refers to the process of binding to things. Today, the word largely refers to a chronic adherence to drugs. This can include both physical and psychological dependence. *Physical dependence* is the body's need to constantly have the drug or drugs, and *psychological dependence* is the mental inability to stop using the drug or drugs.

The *Diagnostic and Statistical Manual of Mental Disorders*, published by the American Psychiatric Association, 4th edition (DSM-IV) (1994), differentiates among intoxication by, abuse of, and addiction to drugs. Although *substance abuse* is considered maladaptive, leading to recurrent adverse consequences or impairment, it is carefully differentiated from true addiction, called *substance dependence*, the essential feature of which is continued use despite significant substance-related problems known to the user. Many of these features are usually present:

- *Tolerance:* need for increased amounts or diminished effect of same amount

- *Withdrawal:* experience of characteristic withdrawal syndrome for the specific substance, which can be avoided by taking closely related substances

- Unsuccessful attempts to cut down

• Increasing time spent in substance-related activities, such as obtaining, using, and recovering from its effects

■ MODELS OF ADDICTION

Various models attempt to describe the essential nature of drug addiction. Newspaper accounts of "inebriety" in the 19th and early 20th centuries contain an editorializing undertone that looks askance at the poor morals and lifestyle choices followed by the inebriate. This view has been dubbed the moral model , and although it may seem outdated from a modern scientific standpoint, it still characterizes an attitude among many traditionally minded North Americans and members of many ethnic groups.

The prevailing concept or model of addiction in America is the disease model . Most proponents of this concept specify addiction to be a chronic and progressive disease, over which the sufferer has no control. This model originated in part from research performed by Jellinek, one of the founders of addiction studies (1952, 1960), among members of Alcoholics Anonymous (AA). He observed a seemingly inevitable progression in his subjects, which they made many failed attempts to arrest. This philosophy is currently espoused by the recovery fellowships of AA and Narcotics Anonymous (NA) and the treatment field in general. It has even permeated the psychiatric and medical establishments' standard definitions of addiction. There are many variations within the broad rubric of the disease model. This model has, however, been bitterly debated: viewpoints range from fierce adherence to the equally fierce opposition, with intermediate views patronizing the disease concept as a convenient myth (Smith et al. 1985).

Those who view addiction as another manifestation of something gone awry with the personality system adhere to the characterological or personality predisposition model . Every school of psychoanalytic, neophychoanalytic, and psychodynamic psychotherapy has its specific "take" on the subject of addiction (Frosch 1985). Tangentially, many addicts are also diagnosed with personality disorders (formerly known as "character disorders"), such as impulse control disorders and sociopathy. Although few addicts are treated by psychoanalysis or psy-

choanalytic psychotherapy, a characterological type of model was a formative influence on the drug-free, addict–run, "therapeutic community" model, which uses harsh confrontation and time-extended, sleep-depriving group encounters. People who follow the therapeutic community model conclude that addicts must have withdrawn behind a "double wall" of encapsulation where they failed to grow, making such techniques necessary.

Others view addiction as a "career"—a series of steps or phases with distinguishable characteristics. One career pattern of addiction includes six phases (Clinard and Meier 1992; Waldorf 1983):

1. Experimentation or initiation

2. Escalation (increasing use)

3. Maintenance or "taking care of business" (optimistic use of drugs coupled with successful job performance)

KEY TERMS

moral model
the belief that people abuse alcohol because they choose to do so

disease model
the belief that people abuse alcohol because of some biologically caused condition

characterological or personality predisposition model
view of chemical dependency as a symptom of problems in the development or operation of the system of needs, motives, and attitudes within the individual

personality disorders
a broad category of psychiatric disorders, formerly called "character disorders," that includes the antisocial personality disorder, borderline personality disorder, schizoid personality disorder, and others. These serious, ongoing impairments are difficult to treat.

psychoanalysis
a theory of personality and method of psychotherapy originated by Sigmund Freud, focused on unconscious forces and conflicts and a series of psychosexual stages

"double wall" of encapsulation
an adaption to pain and avoidance of reality, in which the individual withdraws emotionally and further anesthetizes himself or herself by chemical means

4. Dysfunction or "going through changes" (problems with constant use and unsuccessful attempts to quit)

5. Recovery or "getting out of the life" (arriving at a successful view about quitting and receiving drug treatment)

6. Ex-addict (actually having successfully quit)

■ FACTORS CONTRIBUTING TO ADDICTION

Many, perhaps millions, of individuals use or even occasionally abuse drugs without compromising their basic health, legal, and occupational status and social relationships. Why do a significant minority become caught up in abuse and addictive behavior? The answer stems from the fact that many (i.e., not a single) factors generally contribute to an individual becoming addicted. Table 4.1 represents a compilation of factors identified as complicit in the origin or "etiology" of addiction, taken from the fields of psychology, sociology, and addiction studies.

In addition to the social and cultural factors listed in Table 4.1, other "cultural" risk factors for development of abuse include the following:

- Drinking at times other than at meals

- Drinking alone

- Drinking defined as an antistress and antianxiety potion

- Patterns of solitary drinking

- Drinking defined as a rite of passage into an adult role

- Recent introduction of a chemical into a social group with insufficient time to develop informal social control over its use (Marshall 1979)

It is important to recall that the "mix" of risk factors differs for each person. It varies according to social, cultural, and age groups and individual and family idiosyncrasies. Most addiction treatment professionals believe that it is difficult, if not impossible, to tease out these factors before treatment, when the user is still "talking to a chemical," or during early treatment, when the brain and body are still recuperating from the effects of long-term abuse. Once a stable sobriety is established, one can begin to address any underlying problems. An exception would be the mentally ill chemical abuser, whose treatment requires special considerations from the outset.

In addition to the factors just listed, a number of age-dependent stressors and conflicts sometimes promote drug misuse. Risk factors that apply especially to adolescents include the following:

- Peer norms favoring use

- Misperception of peer norms (users set the tone)

- Power of age group (peer norms versus other social influences)

- Conflicts that generate anxiety or guilt, such as dependence versus independence, adult maturational tasks versus fear, new types of roles versus familiar safe roles

- Teenage risk-taking, sense of omnipotence or invulnerability

- Use defined as a rite of passage into adulthood

- Use perceived as glamorous, sexy, facilitating intimacy, fun, and so on

Risk factors that apply especially to middle-aged individuals include the following:

- Retirement: loss of meaningful role or occupational identity

- Loss, grief, or isolation: loss of parents, divorce, departure of children ("empty nest syndrome")

- Loss of positive body image

- Disappointment when life expectations are not met

Even in each of these age groups, a mix of factors is at play. The adolescent abuser might have risk factors that were primary neurological vulnerabilities, such as undiagnosed attention-deficit hyperactivity disorder. Or he or she may experience failure and rejection at school, disappoint his or her parents, or be labeled odd, lazy, or unintelligent (Kelly and Ramundo 1993).

In response to the information presented in Table 4.1, a student who was a recovering alcoholic commented: "You're an alcoholic because you

TABLE 4.1 Risk Factors for Addiction

RISK FACTOR	LEADING TO THIS EFFECT
Biologically Based Factors (genetic, neurological, biochemical, and so on):	
• A less subjective feeling of intoxication	• More use to achieve intoxication (warning signs of abuse absent)
• Easier development of tolerance; liver enzymes adapt to increased use	• Easier to reach the addictive level
• Lack of resilience or fragility of higher (cerebral) brain functions	• Easy deterioration of cerebral functioning, impaired judgment, and social deterioration
• Difficulty in screening out unwanted or bothersome outside stimuli (low stimulus barrier)	• Feeling overwhelmed or stressed
• Tendency to amplify outside or internal stimuli (stimulus augmentation)	• Feeling attacked or panicked; need to avoid emotion
• Attention-deficit hyperactivity disorder and other learning disabilities	• Failure, low self-esteem, or isolation
• Biologically based mood disorders (depression and bipolar disorders)	• Need to self-medicate against loss of control or pain of depression; inability to calm down when manic or to sleep when agitated
Psychosocial/Developmental "Personality" Factors:	
• Low self-esteem	• Need to blot out pain, gravitate to outsider groups
• Depression rooted in learned helplessness and passivity	• Need to blot out pain; use of a stimulant as an anti-depressant
• Conflicts	• Anxiety and guilt
• Repressed and unresolved grief and rage	• Chronic depression, anxiety, or pain
• Post-traumatic stress syndrome (as in veterans and abuse victims)	• Nightmares or panic attacks
Social and Cultural Environment:	
• Availability of drugs	• Easy frequent use
• Chemical-abusing parental model	• Sanction; no conflict over use
• Abusive, neglectful parents; other dysfunctional family patterns	• Pervasive sense of abandonment, distrust, and pain; difficulty in maintaining attachments
• Group norms favoring heavy use and abuse	• Reinforced, hidden abusive behavior that can progress without interference
• Misperception of peer norms	• Belief that most people use or favor use or think it's "cool" to use
• Severe or chronic stressors, as from noise, poverty, racism, or occupational stress	• Need to alleviate or escape from stress via chemical means
• "Alienation" factors: isolation, emptiness	• Painful sense of aloneness, normlessness, rootlessness, boredom, monotony, or hopelessness
• Difficult migration/acculturation with social disorganization, gender/generation gaps, or loss of role	• Stress without buffering support system

Peer influence combined with teenage risk-taking can lead to problems with drugs and/or alcohol.

drink!" He had a good point: the mere presence of one, two, or more risk factors does not create addiction. Drugs must be available, they must be used, and they must become a pattern of adaptation to any of the many painful, threatening, uncomfortable, or unwanted sensations or stimuli that occur in the presence of genetic, psychosocial, or environmental risk factors. Prevention workers often note the presence of multiple messages encouraging use: the medical use of minor tranquilizers to offset any type of psychic discomfort; the marketing of alcohol as sexy, glamorous, adult, and facilitative of social interaction; and so forth.

The Vicious Cycle of Addiction

> First the man takes a drink, then the drink takes a drink, then the drink takes the man.
> *(Traditional Chinese proverb)*

Drug addiction develops as a process: it is not a sudden occurrence. The body makes simple physiological adaptations to the presence of alcohol and other drugs. For instance, brain cell tolerance and increased metabolic efficiency of the liver can develop, necessitating consumption of more of the chemical to achieve the desired effect. Physical dependence can also develop, in which cell adaptations cause withdrawal syndromes to occur in the absence of the chemical.

Other factors can promote the cycle of addiction. For instance, abuse impairs cerebral functioning, including memory, judgment, behavioral organization, ability to plan, ability to solve problems, and motor coordination. Thus, poor decision-making, impaired and deviant behavior, and overall dysfunction result in adverse social consequences, such as accidents, loss of earning power and relationships, and impaired health. Such adverse social and health consequences cause pain, depression, and lowered self-esteem, which may result in further use as an emotional and physical anesthetic. The addict often adapts to this chronically painful situation by erecting a defense system of denial, minimization, and rationalization; this denial of reality may be exacerbated by the chemical blunting of reality. It is unlikely, at this point, that the addict or developing addict will feel compelled to cease or cut back on drug use on his or her own (Tarter et al. 1983).

Family, friends, and colleagues often unwittingly "enable" the maintenance and progression of addiction by making excuses for addicts, literally and figuratively bailing them out, taking up the slack, denying and minimizing their problems, and otherwise making it possible for addicts to avoid facing the reality and consequences of what they are doing to themselves and others. Although these friends may be motivated by simple naiveté, embarrassment, or misguided protectiveness, there are often hidden gains in taking up this role, known popularly as "codependency" (Beattie 1987). A variety of cultural and organizational factors also operate in the workplace or school that allow denial of the existence or severity of abuse or dependency. This triad of personal denial, peer and kin denial and codependency, and institutional denial represents a formidable impediment to successful intervention and recovery (Myers 1990).

■ NONDRUG ADDICTIONS?

The addictive disease model and the twelve-step recovery model followed by AA and NA have seemed so successful to both addicts and their families and friends that other unwanted syndromes have been added to the list. The degree to which the concept of addiction fits these syndromes varies. Gambling, for example, shows progressive worsening, loss of control, relief of tension from the activity, and continuance despite negative consequences known to the user. Some recovering gamblers even claim to have experienced a form of withdrawal. Gamblers Anonymous is a fellowship that has formed to assist its members. Clearly, gambling as an activity has much in common with chemical addictions, but it is debatable whether it belongs in the category of addiction (the DSM-IV does not include it, for example).

Many other groups have followed in the footsteps to Gamblers Anonymous including those related to eating (Overeaters Anonymous) and sexual relationships (The Augustine Fellowship, Sex and Love Addicts Anonymous). In recent years, any excessive or unwanted behaviors, including excess shopping, chocolate consumption, and even Internet use, have been labeled "addictions," which has led to satirical reporting in the press. Addictions professionals lament the overdefinition, which they feel trivializes the seriousness and suffering of rigorously defined addictions.

Treatment of Addiction

People who are addicted to drugs come from all walks of life. Many suffer from occupational, social, or psychiatric or other health problems that can make their addictions difficult to treat. Even in the absence of such complicating problems, the severity of addictions varies widely. Moreover, there are many types of addictive drugs, and the use and abuse of several drugs concurrently is common. See Table 4.2 for percentages of addicts who enter different treatment programs for drug abuse only, alcohol abuse only, and drug and alcohol abuse combined. As a consequence and by necessity, treatments for specific drug dependencies often differ.

A variety of approaches to drug addiction treatment exist. Some include behavioral therapy, such as counseling, psychotherapy or cognitive therapy. Others include medications, ranging from treatment medications (i.e., methadone, LAAM [l-α-acetyl-methadol], nicotine patches, and nicotine gum) to those intended to treat co-occurring mental disorders (i.e., antidepressants or mood stabilizers). The most successful drug abuse treatment programs provide a combination of therapies and other services to meet the needs of the individual

abuser. These include adequate assessment of treatment needs required not only as a direct consequence of the physiological and psychological effects of the drug but also from indirect problems, such as the need for housing, legal and financial services, educational and vocational assistance, and family/child care services. Such needs are often shaped by the gender, age, race, culture, and sexual orientation of the abuser.

In the United States, more than 11,000 specialized treatment facilities provide rehabilitation, counseling, behavioral therapy, medication, case management, and other types of services to people dealing with substance abuse. Treatment can take various lengths of time and can occur in many different forms in a variety of settings. Because drug addiction is generally a chronic disorder characterized by occasional relapses, a one-time, short-term treatment is often inadequate. Research has shown that good outcomes are contingent on adequate lengths of treatment. Generally, for residential or outpatient treatment, participation for fewer than 90 days is of limited or no effectiveness; treatments lasting significantly longer are needed (NIDA 1999). For methadone maintenance, 12 months of treatment is often the minimum needed, and some individuals who are addicted to opiates require extended treatment lasting several years. Many individuals who enter treatment drop out before receiving all of its benefits; hence, successful treatment often requires more than one treatment experience.

To best target treatment for an individual, the type and goals of treatment must be determined. Consideration must be given to the fact that both the type and the goals of treatment largely depend on the view one holds of addiction. For example, if the disease model is applied to addiction, total abstinence is required because this model views drug abuse as a biological condition that is largely uncontrollable. The user is perceived as "sick" and thus irrational about continued drug use. On the other hand, if responsible drug use is the goal, then occasional and moderate drug use are the intended end results.

Effective treatment allows addicts to stop abusing drugs, returns them to a drug-free state of existence, and transforms them into employable and productive members of society. Measures of effectiveness typically include assessing levels of family

TABLE 4.2 Substance Abuse Treatment Clients by Substance of Abuse, According to Facility Ownership and Organizational Setting: October 1, 1998

Ownership and Organizational Setting	Total	SUBSTANCE OF ABUSE		
		Both Alcohol and Drug Abuse (%)	Drug Abuse Only (%)	Alcohol Abuse Only (%)
Total Number of Clients	1,038,378	49.4	26.9	23.8
Ownership				
Private non-profit	556,191	51.5	26.2	22.2
Private for-profit	252,369	43.3	31.7	25.0
Local, county, or community government	115,774	48.0	26.4	25.6
State government	62,771	58.1	24.4	17.5
Federal government	41,627	44.5	15.8	39.7
Department of Veterans Affairs	33,518	49.8	17.6	32.6
Department of Defense	6,922	18.7	8.6	72.7
Indian Health Service	873	47.0	4.4	48.7
Other	314	44.6	9.9	45.5
Tribal government	9,646	63.3	7.0	29.8
Organizational Setting				
Specialty substance abuse treatment	486,424	44.9	33.8	21.4
Outpatient	388,368	40.5	37.0	22.4
Residential (including halfway house, therapeutic community)	59,289	63.7	21.2	15.1
Outpatient and residential	38,767	59.3	20.3	20.4
Community mental health center/other mental health facility	154,459	50.7	19.7	29.6
Solo or group practice	48,640	51.3	15.6	33.1
General hospital (including Veterans Affairs)	89,810	48.7	22.9	28.4
Psychiatric or other specialized hospital	63,654	53.1	24.2	22.7
Criminal justice	81,950	57.8	23.4	18.7
Community or religious agency/organization	17,478	63.9	17.2	18.9
Community health center	6,999	57.9	17.3	24.7
Multiple or unknown settings	88,964	57.3	19.6	23.1

Changes in the distribution from figures reported in earlier publications may be because the questionnaire response order was changed in 1998.

Adapted from: Office of Applied Studies, Substance Abuse and Mental Health Services Administration, Uniform Facility Data Set (UFDS) survey, October 1, 1998. Available at http://dasis3.samhsa.gov/98ufds/table_4_3.htm

functioning, employability, criminal behavior, and medical condition. Overall, treatment of addiction is as successful as treatment of other chronic diseases such as diabetes, hypertension, and asthma (NIDA 1999). Results show that addicts who receive treatment for more than 3 months remain drug-free a year later; when treatment lasts a year or longer, two-thirds remain drug-free many years later (Drug Strategies 1996). Findings clearly show that treatment is much less expensive than continuing addiction. It costs society $43,200 a year to let one addict remain untreated, compared with an average of $16,000 a year for residential care or $1500 a year for an outpatient program. Treatment is also less expensive than simply incarcerating addicts. For example, the average cost for 1 full year of methadone maintenance treatment is approximately $4700 per patient, whereas 1 full year of imprisonment costs approximately $18,400 per person (NIDA 1999). According to several estimates, every $1 invested in addiction treatment programs yields a return of between $4 and $7 in reduced drug-related crime, criminal justice costs, and theft (NIDA 1999). Major savings to the individual and society also come from significant drops in interpersonal conflicts, improvements in workplace productivity, and reductions in drug-related incidents.

Successful outcomes depend on retaining the person in treatment long enough to gain the full benefit. Several factors influence retention, including individual motivation to change drug-using behavior and degree of support from family and friends. Pressure from employers, the criminal justice system, or extensions of the court (i.e., child protective services) can also be important. Because individual problems such as mental illness or criminal involvement decrease the likelihood of retaining patients in treatment, broad-ranging programs (i.e., with medical and legal services) are important. It is also important for providers to ensure a transition to continuing care or "aftercare" following a patient's completion of formal treatment (NIDA 1999).

NIDA has recently delineated 13 overarching principles that characterize effective addiction treatment (NIDA 1999). These tenets, similar to those described by the majority of treatment researchers and providers, include the following:

1. *No single treatment is appropriate for all individuals.* As described earlier, treatment settings, interventions, and services must be matched to each individual's particular problems and needs.

2. *Treatment needs to be readily available.* Individuals who are addicted to drugs are often uncertain about whether to seek treatment. Hence, it is crucial that services be available as soon as an individual makes the decision to seek help for his or her addiction. Opportunities for treatment can be lost if it is not immediately available or is not readily accessible.

3. *Effective treatment attends to multiple needs of the individual, not just his or her drug use.* To be effective, treatment must address the individual's drug use and any associated medical, psychological, social, vocational, and legal problems.

4. *An individual's treatment and services plan must be assessed continually and modified as necessary to ensure that the plan meets his or her changing needs.* A person undergoing treatment may require varying combinations of services and treatment components during the course of treatment and recovery. In addition to counseling or psychotherapy, medication, other medical services, family therapy, parenting instruction, vocational rehabilitation, and social and legal services may be required. Hence, continual monitoring is important.

5. *Remaining in treatment for an adequate period is critical for treatment effectiveness.* The appropriate duration for an individual depends on his or her problems and needs. As noted earlier, research indicates that for most patients, the threshold of significant improvement is reached at about 3 months in treatment.

6. *Counseling (individual and/or group) and other behavioral therapies are critical components of effective treatment for addiction.* In behavioral therapy, patients address issues of motivation, build skills to resist drug use, replace drug-using activities with constructive and rewarding nondrug-using activities, and improve problem-solving abilities.

7. *Medications are an important element of treatment for many patients, especially when combined with counseling and other behavioral therapies.* Methadone, LAAM, naltrexone, and

nicotine patches are just some examples of medications that can be effective treatments. For patients with mental disorders, medications (i.e., antidepressants, anxiolytics) can be especially important.

8. *Addicted or drug-abusing individuals with coexisting mental disorders should have both disorders treated in an integrated way.* Because addictive and mental disorders often occur in the same individual, patients presenting for either condition should be assessed and treated for the co-occurrence of the other.

9. *Medical detoxification is only the first stage of addiction treatment and by itself does little to change long-term drug use. Medical detoxification* or the process of safely managing the acute physical symptoms of withdrawal associated with stopping drug use can be an important first step toward abstinence. However, detoxification alone is rarely sufficient to help addicts achieve long-term abstinence.

10. *Treatment does not need to be voluntary to be effective.* Strong motivation can facilitate the treatment process. Sanctions or enticements in the family, criminal justice system, or employment setting can facilitate treatment entry and increase both retention rates and success of drug treatment interventions.

11. *Possible drug use during treatment must be monitored continuously.* Backsliding into drug use often occurs during addiction treatment. The objective of monitoring a patient's drug and alcohol use during treatment is that it can help the patient withstand urges to use drugs. Such monitoring also can provide early evidence of drug use so that the individual's treatment plan can be adjusted. Feedback to patients who test positive for illicit drug use is an important element of monitoring.

12. *Treatment programs should provide assessment for HIV/AIDS, hepatitis B and C, tuberculosis, and other infectious diseases and counseling to help patients modify or stop behaviors that place them or others at risk of infection.*

13. *Recovery from drug addiction can be a long-term process and frequently requires multiple episodes of treatment.* As with other chronic illnesses, relapses to drug use can occur during or after successful treatment episodes. Addicted individuals may require prolonged and multiple episodes of treatment to achieve long-term abstinence and fully restored functioning. Participation in self-help support programs during and following treatment often is helpful in maintaining abstinence.

Many treatment programs apply one or more of these listed principles as part of their therapeutic strategy.

Drug Addiction Treatment in the United States

In the branch of the addiction field that strives for total abstinence from drugs, it is often difficult to separate self-help approaches from other forms of treatment, because their histories are interwoven. In the next section, selected self-help recovery movements, the main treatment modalities that they influenced, and the settings in which drug-free treatment takes place will be described. Drug maintenance and innovative treatment techniques will then be presented.

■ ALCOHOLICS ANONYMOUS

Founded in the mid-1930s, AA is now an international organization. The desire to stop drinking is the sole criterion required to join. The original founders of AA were strongly influenced by a religious movement known as the "Oxford Group" and the psychoanalyst Carl Jung. The "Twelve Steps for Recovery" espoused by AA are cited in the accompanying "Case in Point," AA's Twelve Steps for Recovery.

AA calls itself a "fellowship" of recovering alcoholics. It is perhaps the prototype for the self-help group movement, in which nonprofessional, ordinary citizens with problems form a caring community with supportive healing qualities. "Twelve Step groups" offer a simple, concrete program for recovery from addictions. Members always emphasize that they are not "ex-alcoholics" but are merely holding their alcoholic disease in abeyance "a day at a time." Meetings are nonthreatening, noncon-

CASE IN POINT

AA's Twelve Steps for Recovery

1. We admitted we were powerless over alcohol—that our lives had become unmanageable.

2. Came to believe that a Power greater than ourselves could restore us to sanity.

3. Made a decision to turn our will and our lives over to the care of God *as we understood Him.*

4. Made a searching and fearless moral inventory of ourselves.

5. Admitted to God, to ourselves, and to another human being the exact nature of our wrongs.

6. Were entirely ready to have God remove all these defects of character.

7. Humbly asked Him to remove our shortcomings.

8. Made a list of all persons we had harmed, and become willing to make amends to them all.

9. Made direct amends to such people wherever possible, except when to do so would injure them or others.

10. Continued to take personal inventory and when we were wrong promptly admitted it.

11. Sought through prayer and meditation to improve our conscious contact with God *as we understood Him*, praying only for knowledge of His will for us and the power to carry that out.

12. Having had a spiritual awakening as the result of these steps, we tried to carry this message to alcoholics, and to practice these principles in all our affairs.

Source: Alcoholics Anonymous World Services, Inc., *Alcoholics Anonymous: The Story of How Many Thousands of Men and Women Have Recovered from Alcoholism*, 3rd ed. New York: Alcoholics Anonymous (1976): 59–60. Permission to reprint this material does not mean that AA has reviewed or approved the contents of this chapter, nor that AA agrees with the views expressed herein. AA is a program of recovery from alcoholism—use of the Twelve Steps in connection with programs and activities which are patterned after AA, but which address other problems, does not imply otherwise.

frontational, and noncoercive. AA in particular, and Twelve Step groups in general, have an extremely loose, nonhierarchical organizational structure. NA, founded in 1951, is less well known but has grown tremendously in recent years, particularly in urban communities.

It is difficult to assess AA's success for four reasons:

1. AA insists on anonymity; it does not reveal names of members.

2. Membership is strictly voluntary. Those who want to join become members when they vow to give up drinking. Controlled studies are impossible.

3. Members are a homogeneous group. They tend to be middle class and socially conservative.

4. Some addiction researchers are of the opinion that the more severe, hard-core alcoholics who refuse to seek help generally do not go to AA, whereas a smaller percentage of problem drinkers who come to view themselves as addicted to alcohol take this path (see Rudy 1994 for further discussion of this and other related findings). In part, this self-selection may be responsible for the group's high success rate.

Regardless, AA has been, and continues to be, a very important method for treating many recovering alcoholics.

Common alcohol abuse-related problems are shared at AA meetings.

AA has two types of meetings: open and closed. Open meetings are open to anyone who has an interest in attending and witnessing these meetings, and they last approximately 45 minutes to 1 hour. Closed meetings are for alcoholics who have a serious desire to completely stop drinking. These meetings are not open to viewers or "shoppers." At closed meetings, recovering alcoholics address, through testimonials, how alcohol has diminished their quality of life.

Some outgrowths of AA include Al-Anon, Adult Children of Alcoholics (ACOA), and Alateen. These are parallel organizations supporting AA. Al-Anon is for spouses and other close relatives of alcoholics, and Alateen is exclusively for teenage children of alcoholic parents. Both relatives and teen members of alcoholic families learn means and methods for coping with destructive behaviors exhibited by alcoholic members.

■ REHABILITATION FACILITIES

The first rehabilitation programs grew out of the work that AA members did with other active alcoholics. Known as "Twelfth Stepping," it involves reaching out to others in need and attempting to draw them in. This movement began in the early days of AA when the organization's founder, Bill W., had alcoholics trying to stop drinking or "dry out" living at his house in Brooklyn. At that time, "[his] home was stuffed, from cellar to attic, with alco-

holics in all stages of recovery" (Al-Anon 1970). It was a natural transition to opening up "drying out houses" in the 1940s and 1950s.

Also during the 1950s, the Minnesota model, an inpatient rehabilitation model, was developed. It combined the AA philosophy with a multidisciplinary treatment team. A treatment plan was used, based on assessment of the individual and prioritization of goals. This model, which borrows from social work practice, is still used in treatment programs. Due to the vagaries of insurance reimbursement in Minnesota, the program lasted 28 days because that was the length covered by insurance; therefore, alcoholism programs traditionally were roughly 1 month long.

The 1970s and 1980s were a golden era for rehabilitation, when many costly, long-term programs flourished. Recently, and in the context of reimbursement concerns, the need for such a long-term inpatient stay has been questioned in several studies (Holder et al. 1991). Under the pressure of managed care and new insurance guidelines, many inpatient programs have closed or been converted to other forms of treatment. These forms include:

- *Intensive outpatient rehabilitation programs* are partial hospitalization or day programs that allow the client to work or attend school while spending from 15 to 30 hours per week at the treatment center.

- *Halfway houses* are residential therapeutic environments where individuals who have completed a rehabilitation program may live while pursuing employment or working. They should not be confused with psychiatric halfway houses and board-and-care settings.

- *Long-term care facilities* are residential settings for individuals who are socially and psychologically unprepared to be self-supporting in the community. Many are religious in nature, such as the Salvation Army Adult Rehabilitation Programs.

■ DETOXIFICATION UNITS

Since the 1960s, it has been recognized that an alcoholic needs special medical attention and social support to get through the rigors of physical withdrawal.

Special facilities known as "detoxes" (detoxification units) evolved to serve this need. Some are hospital-based. Others, known as "social detoxes" or "sobering-up stations," are freestanding, nonmedical AA-related units; these units have fallen out of favor in recent years. Finally, these special facilities can be adjuncts to full-fledged rehabilitation programs. Detoxification programs, lasting from 3 to 7 days, are misunderstood as treatment programs or modalities and are even statistically compared with rehabilitation programs and treatment facilities. Treatment professionals of all persuasions recognize that addiction is a syndrome that often involves relapse and that an individual may go through treatment more than once. Detoxification is not considered anything more than the first stage of treatment by any chemical dependency professional, and, by itself, detoxification will certainly fail. (We are not including the heavily involved AA member who undergoes detoxification). Patients typically cycle through the program many times, often at moments of crisis, or, if homeless, during cold weather.

■ THERAPEUTIC COMMUNITIES

Another major model of treatment for chemical dependency came from a different branch of the self-help movement. Although the term originated with patient government and other forms of "milieu therapy" in the psychiatric hospital setting, the therapeutic community (TC) is known today as a residential treatment program for drug dependency. TCs are programs with planned lengths of stay of 6 to 12 months. These programs focus on "resocializing" the individual; use the program's entire "community," including other residents and staff members, and integrate social context as active components of treatment (NIDA 1999). Treatment often uses confrontational methods, hard work, and a status system as rehabilitation aids. It focuses on establishing personal accountability. The main goal of TCs is a complete change in lifestyle: abstinence from drugs, elimination of criminal behavior, and development of employable skills, self-reliance, personal honesty, and responsibility.

Compared with patients in other forms of drug treatment, the typical TC resident has more severe problems, including more co-occurring mental health problems and more criminal involvement

KEY TERMS

open meetings
meetings to which anyone having an interest in attending and witnessing is invited

closed meetings
meetings to which only alcoholics having a serious desire to completely stop drinking are invited

Minnesota model
a major model in the treatment of alcohol and drug abuse, involving a month-long stay in an inpatient rehabilitation facility, a multidisciplinary treatment team, systematic assessment, and a formal treatment plan with long- and short-term goals

therapeutic community
a program that advocates a complete change in lifestyle, such as complete abstinence from drugs, elimination of deviant behavior, and development of employable skills

(NIDA 1999). More recently, some TCs have been developed to serve criminal justice clients almost exclusively (McNeece and DiNitto 1994). Others have been tailored to treat adolescents, women, or people with severe mental disorders. Drug addicts referred to TCs are placed in appropriate settings where delinquent or criminal peers and the adverse effects of crime-ridden neighborhoods, and by extension communities, are physically distant, and the temptations of peers and environment are excluded.

■ OUTPATIENT TREATMENT

The term *outpatient treatment* denotes a nonresidential setting where treatment takes place (see "Case in Point," Using Support Groups to Counter Life Stress and Alcohol Abuse, on page 104). It can involve any number of individual, group, or family sessions that the client attends one or more times per week. Treatment may use any of a number of approaches, including Twelve Step–style groups, interactive group therapy, confrontational groups, support and relapse prevention, occupational counseling, and so on. Outpatient treatment in which the client is present 10 to 30 hours per week is usually called *intensive outpatient treatment, day treatment,* or *partial hospitalization.*

If only because it is the least expensive option, most addiction treatment takes place on an outpa-

CASE IN POINT

Using Support Groups to Counter Life Stress and Alcohol Abuse

Although Marie was never quite alone with her abuse problem, it took a personal confrontation for her to realize that she needed support. Marie is the adult child of two alcoholics. Her mother died of complications from alcoholism when she was 20, and her father died 15 years later from a similar fate. When she was about 13, Marie began to make the association between the beverages her parents drank and the subsequent moods that followed, and she made a vow that she would never follow that path. As often happens, peer pressure in college changed her position. Weekend keg parties and "booze cruise" road trips seemed to be a part of college life that she could not avoid if she was to be accepted, and more than anything else, deep inside she desired to be accepted.

Growing up as the child of two alcoholic parents, Marie never knew what to expect when she got home from school—in what condition the house would be, or in what state of mind she would find her parents. For this reason, she never invited any friends over for fear that she would be humiliated in front of them because her mother or father was inebriated and abusive. Marie kept to herself, but still longed for the acceptance of friends she felt she could never have while she lived at home. When the time came to go to college, she applied to schools far away. As luck would have it, she was accepted to a school 500 miles away.

Weekend social drinking habits in college became a daily behavior for Marie after graduation. When asked, she would say that she liked the buzz she got from alcohol, but, she said, she was always in control. In her mind, Marie might have been in control, but her body's physiology told a different story. The end result was that Marie was a full-fledged alcoholic by age 25. Rather than an occasional beer on weekends, she was downing a gallon of vodka every two days, a source of inspiration she kept hidden in her knapsack.

When confronted by her older brother, Marie at first vehemently denied she had a drinking problem. Within hours, however, she admitted she was powerless and needed help—desperately. An alcoholic seizure and subsequent coma the next week made the message abundantly clear. Ironically, what attracted her to alcohol, social acceptance, soon became her saving grace—Alcoholics Anonymous (AA). Beginning an alcohol rehabilitation program called Day One, Marie attended her first AA meeting and soon learned that she was not alone with her problem. Although her situation was unique, her predicament was quite common.

Researchers now know that support groups are one of the most effective ways to deal with the stress of life. No matter what the affliction, engaging in the community of friends, colleagues, and even strangers with similar issues, problems, or concerns diminishes levels of stress. Members of our circle of friends, particularly people who have "been there," tend to help buffer the effects of stress. As Marie will attest, alcoholism is definitely a stressor:

Having something control your life makes you feel powerless, completely helpless. Alcohol offers such an illusion. It makes you think as if you are in complete control, but the truth is, with each sip, you freely give your power away. I was scared shitless with my first AA meeting. It's one thing to admit to yourself that you have a drinking problem. It's quite another when you have to admit to a room full of strangers how weak you are and how much control this substance has over you. But what I learned from AA is that these people don't pass judgment. They accept you as you are. This has made all the difference in my life now. my friends in AA are my new family.

Marie is now happily married with two children. She has been sober for many years. The pieces of her life are firmly back in place after being shattered in her early to late 20s. As she says, "Every day is a struggle, but it's a good struggle. I have been through the dark night of my soul. You only have to do that trip once to realize it's not a place you want to stay very long." Marie beams, "I am very grateful to this family and my family and friends in AA."

tient basis. In fact, participation in an outpatient program can be undertaken for the following purposes:

- For initial assessment and referral into inpatient care

- As a follow-up to inpatient or intensive outpatient rehabilitation, called *continuing care*

- As the entire course of treatment in cases in which addiction is not overly severe

■ CURRENT TRENDS IN PROVIDING TREATMENT SERVICES

Certifying Qualified Counselors

The separate treatment models that evolved for drug addicts and alcoholics led to separate governmental and certification entities. Over the past decade, most of these bodies have been merged into single-chemical dependency or addictions authorities and certification boards, although New York state accomplished this step in 1995–1996. Most recently, the recognition of the terrible health costs of tobacco consumption has led to the addition of nicotine to the responsibility of addictions authorities and to the knowledge areas required of counselors.

Although qualifications for becoming addictions counselors once included merely being a recovering addict and having the enthusiasm, energy, and empathy to work with other addicts, the credentialing requirements became more rigorous in the 1970s. From the mid-1970s on, a credentialing system evolved that demanded increased levels of competency. Today, most states operate certification boards, which are linked in a national consortium, and certification is also provided by the national addiction counselors' association (see Appendix B, page 521).

Certification requirements include taking classes, passing a written examination, and undertaking service experience. The certification consortium generally requires an oral and written case presentation as well. Although minor variations in the state credentialing systems exist, counselors must be able to perform the following tasks:

- Screen candidates for eligibility and appropriateness.

- Follow intake procedures.

- Handle patient orientation and education.

- Practice case management.

- Assess patient strengths and weaknesses.

- Develop and implement a treatment plan in collaboration with the patient.

- Handle cases involving addiction-specific individual, group, and family counseling.

- Understand the pharmacology of addictive substances and the dynamics of addiction.

- Maintain ethical practices and patient confidentiality.

- Understand the role of the addictions counselor and how it differs from that of other professional roles.

One of the most important advances in the field has been the development of a subfield for addicts with concurrent psychiatric disabilities (mentally ill chemical abusers [MICAs]) (Kelly and Ramundo 1993). This field is particularly complex because many symptoms of mental illness share similarities with chemically induced organic brain syndromes (early in the days of crack cocaine, many patients were overdiagnosed with "paranoid schizophrenia" in public hospitals in New York City—especially by newly arrived, out-of-town physicians).

Patient Placement Criteria Today

Treatment professionals use `patient placement criteria` to match the severity of the addiction to the level of care needed, ranging from medical inpatient care, nonmedical inpatient care, and intensive outpatient care, to outpatient care (CSAT 1993). Unfortunately, the new managed care guidelines established by many health insurance carriers simply do not allow for treatment beyond outpatient care or brief inpatient detoxification. Moreover,

---

KEY TERMS

patient placement criteria
a system that allows the referring professional to match the assessed level of addictive severity with an appropriate intensity and level of care, ranging from an outpatient clinic to a medical center

matching the client's profile to a treatment modality is more likely to achieve lasting success. A person with severe attention-deficit hyperactivity disorder, for example, tends to be disorganized and forgetful and is unsuited for the strict behavioral expectations of the TC. Likewise, an emotionally fragile individual is unsuited to confrontational groups.

Special Focus Programs

Programs have been created that are similar to AA and NA but without the spiritual emphasis that some potential members find difficult to accept. These programs include Rational Recovery, which evolved from Albert Ellis's Rational-Emotive Therapy (Ellis et al. 1988), and the similar programs Smart Recovery and Secular Organizations for Sobriety (Christopher 1988). One of the principles behind these programs is early intervention. In contrast to past practices, in which the early addict was scooped up off the street (fitting the description of

A patient receives individual counseling in an alcoholism treatment center.

the addict "hitting rock bottom"), treatment begins at an earlier phase of addiction.

There has also been a recent shift to mandated or involuntary treatment. Two components of this practice include the following:

- Originally called *industrial alcoholism programs*, these programs have existed for some time. Their goal is to identify and refer addicted employees to treatment programs. This model has been adapted for use in school settings (*student assistance programs*, [SAPs]) and in organizational settings such as labor unions or consortia of unions (*member assistance programs*). Some states now fund SAPs and certify SAP professionals.

- The TC has always counted many court-mandated clients, but the trend accelerated tremendously in the 1990s, with demonstration programs established in Colorado, Texas, and New Mexico for collaborative planning of criminal justice and addictions treatment systems. Many treatment programs have retooled to accommodate convicts paroled or serving out their sentences, and treatment programs have been instituted in prisons (see "Holding the Line").

Maintenance Programs

Maintenance programs (which offer support to those addicted to morphine, methadone, and heroin) are based on the principle that, if past treatment programs have not been successful, "incurable" addicts should be able to register and receive drugs, such as narcotics, under supervision. Proponents of these programs contend that many addicts are forced into a life of crime to support their habits but would become law-abiding and useful citizens if they received narcotics (usually a less euphoric type, such as methadone) legally. Moreover, it is argued, the illicit narcotics trade would be eliminated due to the loss of these customers. Opponents of maintenance programs say that sufficient treatment programs exist to cure many addicts and that providing addicts with substitute narcotics does not solve the basic problem causing drug dependence.

The concept of maintenance using a non-euphoric opiate is now widely accepted in the United States as one way to help treat drug abusers.

HOLDING THE LINE

A National Institute on Drug Abuse (NIDA)-funded treatment research program allows offenders imprisoned in the Delaware correctional system to participate in a 2-year rehabilitation program. During phase one, the offenders live for 12 months in a therapeutic community in prison, known as KEY, which is separated from the general prison population. During phase two, offenders stay in a therapeutic community for 6 months, called the CREST outreach center, which is a work-release facility. In the final 6-month phase, offenders participate in counseling and group therapy while they are on parole or other supervised release. According to Dr. Peter Delaney of NIDA's Services Research Branch,

this program differs from other therapeutic prison treatment in including a work-release component.

The KEY-CREST program has proved effective at reducing both drug use and recidivism in participant offenders. Eighteen months after release from prison, the KEY-CREST participants were 76% drug-free and 71% arrest-free, compared with 19% drug-free and 30% arrest-free for offenders from the general population.

This research demonstrates the importance of a therapeutic prison environment coupled with a community-based work program in preventing additional drug abuse and criminal activity in criminal offenders.

Source: Mathias, R. "Correctional Treatment Helps Offenders Stay Drug and Arrest Free." *NIDA Notes* (July/August 1995) http://www.nida.nihgov/NIDA_NOTES.

Methadone Maintenance Vincent Dole and Marie Nyswander were the first doctors to use the synthetic narcotic methadone in a rehabilitation program with heroin addicts in the mid-1960s. Methadone maintenance treatment (MMT) involves replacing street heroin with methadone, a synthetic opiate that allows clients to stabilize physiologically so that they can explore alternative ways of functioning. This type of treatment is usually provided on an outpatient basis.

MMT is used to reduce illegal heroin use. Although it can be used to detoxify heroin addicts, most such individuals return to heroin. Methadone is most effective when used as an adjunct to reduce or, in a minority of cases, eliminate heroin use by stabilizing addicts as long as it takes to reassemble their lives and avoid returning to previous patterns of drug use. Further, even after 20 to 30 years of methadone use, research shows that ". . . almost no negative health consequences are experienced" (Nadelmann 1996).

How successful is methadone treatment? A recent California study found that $1 spent on treatment saves taxpayers $7. The savings occur as a result of reductions in crime and in the need for medical care (Swan 1995). Another study showed that "over a six-month period, the costs to society for an untreated heroin abuser is $21,500, $20,000 for an imprisoned drug abuser, and $1,750 for someone undergoing methadone maintenance treatment" (Swan 1994).

Once stabilized on methadone, the addict faces a crucial period of adjustment. After being devoted to maintaining a heroin habit 24 hours a day, 365

KEY TERMS

noneuphoric opiate
a drug used in maintenance programs that satisfies the craving but does not produce the euphoric effect, such as methadone

days a year, the addict must be transformed into a self-supporting, socially acceptable person. MMT establishes the potential for such a change, but it is the person's motivation and capabilities that determine the success of the rehabilitation effort. A range of medical, psychiatric, social, and vocational services are usually available during this phase of treatment.

One supervisor of a methadone clinic associated with a Brooklyn, New York, hospital explains the process it employs:

> First of all, we test for alcohol, benzodiazepines [Valium-like substances] and other drugs. Clients with positive tox [who text positive for drugs] are administratively discharged. They come in at 6:30 for their dose, and then the vast majority go off to work! Methadone, job counseling, and GED classes allow them to get their lives together. Our goal is to taper them off to zero.

Although many criticisms have been levied against the use of methadone, other research findings contradict this skepticism. Recent research findings show that, since the 1980s, 65% to 85% of methadone-treated patients not only remain in treatment for a year or more but also dramatically cease or strongly curtail their criminal behavior and have strong records of gainful employment while receiving the drug (Swan 1994). In addition, methadone is reported to reduce the risk of AIDS infection. This benefit alone is believed to lower the costs to society, especially those associated with providing health care to AIDS patients.

The relatively new long-acting methadone analogue, LAAM, need only be taken three times a week and is being used experimentally in some programs. Initially, addicts participate in intensive daily counseling. Later in the program, they come in for the maintenance drug and follow-up treatment less frequently. Addicts may be treated with

daily methadone first to increase the probability that they will at least attend counseling sessions and then be switched to LAAM when they reach an appropriate point in the program.

Opiate Antagonists

An antagonist is a compound that suppresses the actions of a drug. Narcotic antagonists have properties that make them important tools in the clinical treatment of narcotic drug dependence. For instance, they counteract the central nervous system–depressant effects in opioid drug overdoses.

Opiate antagonists are occasionally used as adjuncts to inpatient treatment; they are more typically associated with the emergency treatment of opiate poisoning (overdose), however. Some physicians claim to perform instant detoxification with the use of an opiate antagonist during sedation. Two opiate antagonists, naltrexone and cyclazocine, block heroin from having an effect on the heroin addict. Further, naloxone (Narcan) is often used as an antidote for opioid overdose (commonly known as "narcotic poisoning"). Narcotic antagonists are generally best suited for opioid-dependent patients who want to leave TCs and MMT programs.

Antagonists were developed as a byproduct of research in analgesics. Scientists were interested in dissociating the dependence-producing and necessary pain-relieving properties of substances that could replace morphine. This research led to the development of nalorphine, the first specific opiate antagonist. Although its short duration of action and frequent unpleasant side effects limited its clinical usefulness, its properties stimulated further research into this class of drugs (Archer 1981; Palfai and Jankiewicz 1991).

As will be discussed in more detail later, clonidine (Catapres) is useful in treating opiate-dependent people during the difficult withdrawal stages (Ginzburg 1986). Studies thus far show the value of this drug for withdrawal from heroin, morphine, codeine, and methadone. Clonidine is not addictive and does not cause euphoria, but it does block cravings for drugs. It also makes the person feel better compared with the depression experienced by addicts using other methods of withdrawal.

Antabuse, which goes by the trade name disulfiram, is a drug used for treating alcoholics. This drug is perceived as a deterrent drug—it makes people violently ill if alcohol is used. "Antabuse interferes with the normal metabolism of alcohol, resulting in serious physical reaction if even a small amount of alcohol is ingested" (McNeece and DiNitto 1994, 113). The greatest asset in using this drug is its ability to deter impulsive drinking (McNeece and DiNitto 1994).

Discussion Questions

1. Define the terms *addiction, tolerance, dependence,* and *withdrawal.*

2. Describe and contrast the disease and characterological (or personality predisposition) models of addiction.

3. List several biological, social, and cultural factors that may predispose someone to addiction.

4. List several principles that characterize effective addiction treatment.

5. Describe Alcoholics Anonymous and its approach to assisting individuals addicted to alcohol.

6. Describe the therapeutic community approach to treating substance abuse.

Key Terms

moral model **93**

disease model **93**

characterological or
personality predisposition model **93**

personality disorders **93**

psychoanalysis **93**

"double wall" of encapsulation **93**

open meetings **102**

closed meetings **102**

Minnesota model **102**

therapeutic community **103**

patient placement criteria **105**

noneuphoric opiate **106**

antagonist **108**

Summary

1 Chemical dependence has been considered a major social problem throughout U.S. history.

2 People define chemical addiction in many ways. The essential feature is a chronic adherence to drugs despite significant negative consequences.

3 The major models of addiction are the moral model, the disease model, and the characterological or personality predisposition model.

4 Transitional periods, such as adolescence and middle age, are associated with particular sets of risk factors.

5 Addiction is a gradual process during which abusers become caught up in vicious cycles that worsen their situation, cause pain, and increase their drug use. Addiction tends to progress, although this step is not inevitable.

6 One of the earliest real alcoholism recovery efforts was Alcoholics Anonymous (AA). Programs modeled on AA, known as Twelve Step fellowships, are major routes to recovery.

7 Modern addictions treatment includes screening; intake; assessment; formulation of a treatment plan; individual, group, and family treatment; and vocational reentry.

8 Addiction counseling has now become a true profession, governed by national and state certification.

9 A major approach to heroin and other opiate addiction has involved the provision of methadone, a synthetic opiate.

References

Al-Anon. *Al-Anon's Favorite Forum Editorials.* New York: Al-Anon Family Group Headquarters, 1970.

American Psychiatric Association. *Diagnostic and Statistical Manual of Mental Disorders,* 4th ed. Washington, DC: APA, 1994.

Archer, S. "Historical Perspective on the Chemistry and Development of Naltrexone." In *Narcotic Antagonists: Naltrexone Pharmaco-Chemistry and Sustained-Release Preparations,* edited by R. E. Willette and G. Barnett. NIDA Research Monograph 28. Washington, DC: National Institute on Drug Abuse, 1981.

Beattie, M. *Codependent No More.* San Francisco: Harper, 1987.

Christopher, J. *Unhooked: Staying Sober and Drug-Free.* Buffalo, NY: Prometheus Books, 1988.

Clinard, M. B., and R. F. Meier. *Sociology of Deviant Behavior,* 8th ed. Fort Worth, TX: Harcourt, Brace, Jovanovich, 1992.

CSAT *Guidelines for the Treatment of Alcohol and Other Drug-Abusing Adolescents.* Treatment Improvement Protocol (TIP) Series 4. Rockville, MD: U.S. HHS, PHS, SAMHSA, Center for Substance Abuse Treatment, 1993.

Drug Strategies. *Keeping Score: What Are We Getting for Our Federal Drug Control Dollars, 1996,* edited by H. Milkman and H. Shaffer. Washington, DC: Drug Strategies, 1996. Available 080/res/colleges/bsos/depts/cesar/drugs/ks 1996.

Ellis, A., J. F. McInerney, R. DiGiuseppe, and R. J. Yeager. *Rational-Emotive Therapy with Alcoholics and Substance Abusers.* Boston: Allyn and Bacon, 1988.

Frosch, W. A. "An Analytic Overview of the Addictions." In *The Addictions: Multidisciplinary Perspectives and Treatments,* edited by H. Milkman and H. Shaffer. Lexington, MA: Lexington Books/D.C. Heath, 1985.

Ginzburg, H. M. *Naltrexone: Its Chemical Utility.* Rockville, MD: National Institute on Drug Abuse, 1986.

Holder, H., R. Longabaugh, W. R. Miller, and A. V. Rubonis. "The Cost Effectiveness of Treatment for Alcoholism: A First Approximation." *Journal of Studies on Alcohol* 52 (1991): 517–40.

Jellinek, E. M. "Phases of Alcohol Addiction." *Quarterly Journal of Studies on Alcohol* 13 (1952): 673–84.

Jellinek, E. M. *The Disease Concept of Alcoholism.* Highland Park, NJ: Hillhouse Press, 1960.

Johnston, L. D., O'Malley, P. M., Bachman, J. G. University of Michigan News and Information Services; 17 Dec. 1999, citing the *National Survey on Drug Abuse, The Monitoring the Future Study.* The University of Michigan Institute for Social Research, National Institute on Drug Abuse, U.S. Department of Human Services, National Institutes of Health, 1999.

Kelly, K., and P. Ramundo. *You Mean I'm Not Lazy, Stupid, or Crazy?!* New York: Scribner, 1993.

Marshall, M. "Conclusions." In *Beliefs, Behavior, and Alcoholic Beverages—A Cross-Cultural Survey,* edited by M. Marshall, 451–7. Ann Arbor, MI: University of Michigan Press, 1979.

McNeece, C. A., and D. M. DiNitto. Chemical Dependency: A Systems Approach. Englewood Cliffs, NJ: Prentice-Hall, 1994.

Myers, P. L. "Sources and Configurations of Institutional Denial." *Employee Assistance Quarterly* 5(B) (1990): 43–54.

Nadelmann, E. A. *Methadone Maintenance Treatment.* New York: The Lindesmith Center, 1996.

NIDA. *Principles of Drug Addiction Treatment.* National Institutes of Health Publication No. 99-4180, October 1999.

Rudy, D. "Perspectives on Alcoholism: Lessons from Alcoholics and Alcohologists." In *Drug Use in America: Social, Cultural, and Political Perspectives,* edited by P. J. Venturelli, 23–29. Boston: Jones and Bartlett, 1994.

Smith, D. E., H. Milkman, and S. Sunderwirth. "Addictive Disease: Concept and Controversy." In *The Addictions: Multidisciplinary Perspectives and Treatments,* edited by H. Milkman and H. J. Shaffer. Lexington, MA: Lexington Books/D.C. Heath, 1985.

Swan, N. "Research Demonstrates Long-Term Benefits of Methadone Treatment." *NIDA Notes* 9 (November/December 1994): http://www.nida.nihgov/NIDA_NOTES.

Swan, N. "California Study Finds $1 Spent on Treatment Saves Taxpayers $7." *NIDA Notes* 10 (March/April 1995): http://www.nida.nihgov/NIDA_NOTES.

Tarter, R. E., A. Alterman, and K. L. Edwards. "Alcoholic Denial: A Biopsychosociological Interpretation." *Journal of Studies on Alcohol* 45 (1983): 214–18.

Waldorf, D. "Natural Recovery from Opiate Addiction: Some Social-Psychological Processes of Untreated Recovery." *Journal of Drug Issues* 13 (1983): 237–80.

Homeostatic Systems and Drugs

Did You Know?

▶ The brain is composed of more than 10 billion neurons that communicate with one another by releasing chemical messengers called *neurotransmitters*.

▶ Many drugs exert their effects by interacting with specialized protein regions in cell membranes called *receptors*.

▶ Some natural chemicals produced by the body have the same effect as narcotic drugs; these chemicals are called *endorphins*.

▶ The body likely produces natural substances that have effects like marijuana and diazepam (Valium).

▶ Drugs that affect the neurotransmitter dopamine usually alter both mental state and motor activity.

▶ The pleasant sensations that encourage continual use of most drugs of abuse are due to stimulation of dopamine activity in the limbic system.

▶ The hypothalamus is the principal brain region for control of endocrine systems.

▶ The anabolic steroids often abused by athletes are chemically related to testosterone, the male hormone, and stimulate increased muscle mass.

▶ Anabolic steroids are considered controlled drugs by the Drug Enforcement Administration and have been classified as Schedule III substances.

Chapter 5

Learning Objectives

**On completing this chapter
you will be able to:**

► Explain the similarities and differences
between the nervous and endocrine systems.

► Describe how a neuron functions.

► Describe the role of receptors in mediating
the effects of hormones, neurotransmitters,
and drugs.

► Distinguish between receptor agonists
and antagonists.

► Describe the different features of the
principal neurotransmitters.

► Outline the principal components of the
central nervous system, and explain their
general functions.

► Identify which brain areas are most likely
to be affected by drugs of abuse.

► Distinguish between the sympathetic and
parasympathetic nervous systems.

► Identify the principal components of the
endocrine system.

► Explain how and why anabolic steroids
are abused and the health impact attributed
to abuse.

Introduction

Why is your body susceptible to the influence of drugs and other substances? Part of the answer is that your body is constantly adjusting and responding to its environment in order to maintain internal stability and balance. This delicate process of dynamic adjustments— homeostasis —is necessary to optimize body functions and is essential for survival. These continual compensations help to maintain physiological and psychological balances and are mediated by the release of endogenous regulatory chemicals (such as neurotransmitters from neurons and hormones from glands). Many drugs exert intended or unintended effects by altering the activity of these regulatory substances, which changes the function of the nervous or endocrine system . For example, all drugs of abuse profoundly influence mental states by altering the chemical messages of the neurotransmitters in the brain, and some alter endocrine function by affecting the release of hormones. By understanding the mechanisms of how drugs alter these body processes, we are able to recognize drug benefits and risks and devise therapeutic strategies to deal with ensuing problems.

This chapter is divided into two sections. The first is a brief overview to introduce the basic concept of how the body is controlled by nervous systems and explain why drugs influence the elements of these systems. The second section is intended for readers who desire a more in-depth understanding of the anatomical, physiological, and biochemical basis of homeostatic functions. In this second section, the elements of the nervous system are discussed in greater detail, followed by an examination of its major divisions: the central, peripheral, and autonomic nervous systems (CNS, PNS, and ANS). The components and operation of the endocrine system are also discussed in specific relation to drugs. The use of anabolic steroids is given as an example.

1: Overview of Homeostasis and Drug Actions

The body continuously adjusts to both internal and external changes in the environment. To cope with these adjustments, the body systems include elaborate self-regulating mechanisms. The name given to this compensatory action is *homeostasis*, which refers to the maintenance of internal stability or equilibrium. For example, homeostatic mechanisms control the response of the brain to changes in the physical, social, and psychological environments, as well as regulate physiological factors such as body temperature, metabolism, nutrient utilization, and organ functions. The two principal systems that help human beings maintain homeostasis are the nervous system and the endocrine system (described in Section 2, page 116). They greatly influence each other and work together closely.

Introduction to Nervous Systems

All nervous systems consist of specialized nerve cells called neurons . The neurons are responsible for conducting the homeostatic functions of the brain and other parts of the nervous system by receiving and sending information. The transfer of

KEY TERMS

homeostasis
maintenance of internal stability; often biochemical in nature

neurotransmitters
chemical messengers released by neurons

hormones
chemical messengers released into the blood by glands

endocrine system
relating to hormones, their functions, and sources

neurons
specialized nerve cells that make up the nervous system and release transmitters

axons
an extension of the neuronal cell body along which electrochemical signals travel

receptors
special proteins in a membrane that are activated by natural substances or drugs to alter cell function

psychoactive
drugs that affect mood or alter the state of consciousness

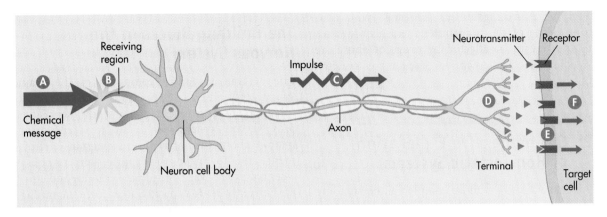

FIGURE 5.1

The process of sending messages by neurons. The receiving region (B) of the neuron is activated by an incoming message (A) near the neuronal cell body. The neuron sends an electricity-like impulse down the axon to its terminal (C). The impulse causes the release of neurotransmitter from the terminal to transmit the message to the target (D). This is done when the neurotransmitter molecules activate the receptors on the membranes of the target cell (E). The activated receptors then cause a change in intracellular functions to occur (F).

messages by neurons includes chemical and electrical processes that consist of the following steps (see Figure 5.1):

1. The *receiving region* of the neuron (B) is affected by a chemical message (A) that either excites (causes the neuron to send its own message) or inhibits (prevents the neuron from sending a message) it.

2. If the message is excitatory, an impulse (much like electricity) moves from the receiving region of the neuron, down its wirelike processes (called axons) to the sending region (called the *terminal*) (C). When the electricity-type impulse reaches the terminal, chemical messengers called *neurotransmitters* are released (D) (see Table 5.1, page 116).

3. The neurotransmitters travel very short distances and attach to specialized and specific receiving proteins called receptors on the outer membranes of their target cells (E).

4. Activation of receptors by their associated neurotransmitters causes a change in the activity of the target cell (F). The target cells can be other neurons or cells that make up organs (such as heart, lungs, kidneys, and so on), muscles, or glands.

Neurons are highly versatile and, depending on their functions, can send discrete excitatory or inhibitory messages to their target cells. Neurons are distinguished by the types of chemical substances they release as neurotransmitters to send their messages. The neurotransmitters represent a wide variety of molecules that are classified according to their functional association as well as their ability to stimulate or inhibit the activity of target neurons, organs, muscles, and glands. They are discussed in greater detail in Section 2.

An example of a common neurotransmitter used by neurons in the brain to send messages is the substance dopamine. When released from neurons associated with the pleasure center in the brain, dopamine causes substantial euphoria by activating its receptor on target neurons (Wyman 1997). This effect is relevant to drugs of abuse because most (if not all) of these substances' addictive properties stem from their ability to stimulate dopamine release from these neurons (for example, amphetamine or cocaine) and thus cause pleasant euphoric effects in the user (Swan 1998).

It is important to understand that many of the desired and undesired effects of psychoactive drugs (which alter the mental functions of the brain), such as the drugs of abuse, are due to their ability to alter the neurotransmitters associated with neurons. Some of the transmitter messenger systems most likely to be affected by drugs of abuse are listed in Table 5.1 and are discussed in greater detail in Section 2.

2: Comprehensive Explanation of Homeostatic Systems

For those desiring a more complete understanding of the consequences of drug effects on the homeostatic systems of the body, this section provides an in-depth discussion of the anatomical and physiological nature and biological arrangements of the nervous and endocrine systems. Because drugs of abuse are most likely to exert their psychoactive effects on neurons and their receptor targets, the nervous system is presented first and in greater depth, followed by a less detailed description of endocrine function.

The Building Blocks of the Nervous System

The nervous system is composed of the brain, spinal cord, and all the neurons that connect to other organs and tissues of the body (see Figure 5.7). Nervous systems enable one to receive information about the internal and external environment and to make the appropriate responses essential to survival. Considerable money and effort are currently being dedicated to explore the mechanisms whereby the nervous system functions and processes information resulting in frequent new and exciting discoveries.

■ THE NEURON: THE BASIC STRUCTURAL UNIT OF THE NERVOUS SYSTEM

The building block of the nervous system is the nerve cell, or *neuron*. Each neuron in the CNS (brain and spinal cord) is in close proximity with

TABLE 5.1 Common Neurotransmitters of the Brain Affected by Drugs of Abuse

NEUROTRANSMITTER	TYPE OF EFFECT	MAJOR CENTRAL NERVOUS SYSTEM CHANGES	DRUGS OF ABUSE THAT INFLUENCE THE NEUROTRANSMITTER (DRUG ACTION)
Dopamine	Inhibitory–excitatory	Euphoria Agitation Paranoia	Amphetamines, cocaine (activate)
GABA (gamma-aminobutyric acid)	Inhibitory	Sedation Relaxation Drowsiness Depression	Alcohol, diazepam-type, barbiturates (activate)
Serotonin	Inhibitory	Sleep Relaxation Sedation	LSD (activate)
Acetylcholine	Excitatory–inhibitory	Mild euphoria Excitation Insomnia	Tobacco, nicotine (stimulate)
Endorphins	Inhibitory	Mild euphoria Blockage of pain Slow respiration	Narcotics (activate)

other neurons, forming a complex network. The human brain contains more than 10 billion neurons, each of which is composed of similar parts but with different shapes and sizes. Neurons do not form a continuous network. They always remain separate, never actually touching, although they are very close. The typical point of communication between one neuron and another is called a synapse. The gap (called the synaptic cleft) between neurons at a synapse may be only 0.00002 millimeter, but it is essential for proper functioning of the nervous system (see Figure 5.2).

The neuron has a cell body with a nucleus and receiving regions called dendrites, which are short, treelike branches that pick up information from the environment and surrounding neurons.

The axon of a neuron is a threadlike extension that receives information from the dendrites near the

> ### KEY TERMS
>
> **synapse**
> site of communication between a message-sending neuron and its message-receiving target cell
>
> **synaptic cleft**
> a minute gap between the neuron and target cell, across which neurotransmitters travel
>
> **dendrites**
> short branches of neurons that receive transmitter signals

cell body, in the form of an electrical impulse; then, like an electrical wire, it transmits the impulse to the cell's terminal. Although most axons are less than 1 inch in length, some may be quite long; for example, some axons extend from the spinal cord to the toes.

FIGURE 5.2

(A) Each neuron may have many synaptic connections. They are designed to deliver short bursts of a chemical transmitter substance into the synaptic cleft, where the substance can act on the surface of the receiving nerve cell membrane. Before release, molecules of the chemical neurotransmitter are stored in numerous vesicles, or sacs. (B) A closeup of the synaptic terminals, showing the synaptic vesicles and mitochondria. *Mitochondria* are specialized structures that help supply the cell with energy. The gap between the synaptic terminal and the target membrane is the *synaptic cleft*.

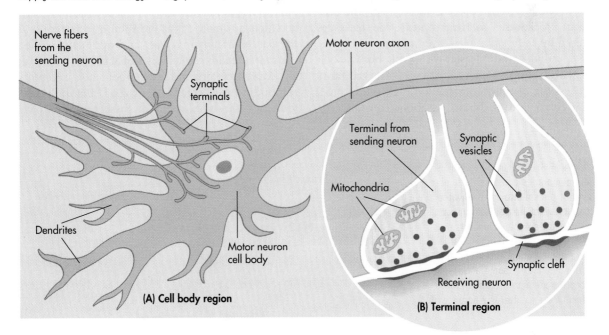

As discussed, at the synapse, information is transmitted chemically to the next neuron, as shown in Figure 5.1. A similar synaptic arrangement also exists at sites of communication between neurons and target cells in organs, muscles, and glands; that is, neurotransmitters are released from the message-sending neurons and activate receptors located in the membranes of message-receiving target cells.

There are two types of synapses: (1) the *excitatory synapse*, which initiates an impulse in the receiving neuron when stimulated, thereby causing release of neurotransmitters or increasing activity in the target cell; and (2) the *inhibitory synapse*, which diminishes the likelihood of an impulse in the receiving neuron or reduces the activity in other target cells. A receiving neuron or target cell may have many synapses connecting it to neurons and their excitatory or inhibitory information (see Figure 5.2, part A). The final cellular activity is a summation of these many excitatory and inhibitory synaptic signals.

■ THE NATURE OF DRUG RECEPTORS

Receptors are special proteins located in the membranes of receiving neurons and other target cells (see Figure 5.3). They help regulate the activity of cells in the nervous system and throughout the body. These selective protein sites on specific cells act as transducers to communicate the messages caused by *endogenous messenger substances* (chemicals produced and released within the body), such as neurotransmitters and hormones. The receptors process the complex information each cell receives as it attempts to maintain metabolic constancy, or

homeostasis, and fulfill its functional role (Kandel et al. 2000a). Many drugs used therapeutically and almost all drugs of abuse exert their effects on the body by directly or indirectly interacting (either to activate or antagonize) with these receptors.

Understanding how receptors interact with specific drugs has led to some interesting results. For example, opiate receptors (sites of action by narcotic drugs, such as heroin and morphine) are naturally present in animal and human brains (Snyder 1977). Why would human and animal brains have receptors for opiate narcotics, which are plant chemicals? Discovery of the opiate receptors suggested the existence of internal (endogenous) neurotransmitter substances in the body that normally act at these receptor sites and have effects like narcotic drugs, such as codeine and morphine. This finding led to the identification of the body's own opiates, the endorphins (Kandel et al. 2000b). Specific receptors have also been found for other drugs such as the CNS depressant diazepam (Valium) (Kandel et al. 2000a) and the active ingredient in marijuana (Fattore et al. 1999). Because of these discoveries, it is speculated that endogenous substances exist that mimic the effects of Valium and marijuana and help provide natural sedation and relaxation for the body (Hobbs, Rall, and Verdoorn 1995; O'Brien 1995). Presently, several research laboratories are attempting to identify the natural chemical messengers that normally act at the Valium (referred to as the *benzodiazepine receptor*) and marijuana (called the *cannabinoid receptor*) sites of activity.

Much remains unknown about how receptors respond to or interact with drugs. Using molecular biology techniques, many of these receptors have

FIGURE 5.3

Cell membranes consist of a double layer of phospholipids. The water-soluble layers are pointed outward and the fat-soluble layers are pointed toward each other. Large proteins, including receptors, float in the membrane. Some of these receptors are activated by neurotransmitters to alter the activity of the cell.

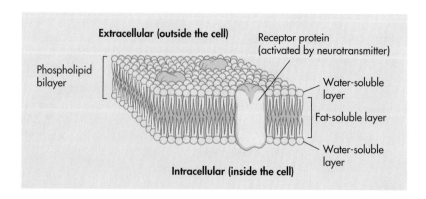

been found to initiate a cascade of linked chemical reactions, which can change intracellular environments to produce either activation or inactivation of cellular functions and metabolism (Kandel et al. 2000c).

Receptors that have been isolated and identified are protein molecules; it is believed that the shape of the protein is essential in regulating a drug's interaction with a cell. If the drug is the proper shape and size and has a compatible electrical charge, it may substitute for the endogenous messenger substance and activate the receptor protein by causing it to change its shape, or conform. This process is like a "lock-and-key" arrangement, with only certain shapes of chemicals (the keys) being able to interact and activate a receptor (the "lock") (Goldstein 1994).

■ AGONISTIC AND ANTAGONISTIC EFFECTS ON DRUG RECEPTORS

A drug may have two different effects on a receptor when interaction occurs: agonistic or antagonistic . As shown in Figure 5.4, an agonistic drug interacts with the receptor and produces some type of cellular response, whereas an antagonistic drug interacts with the receptor but prevents that response. By analogy, using the lock-and-key model, a key can be used to open a lock (agonistic effect), whereas another key that fits in the lock but does not work can jam it (antagonistic effect).

An agonistic drug mimics the effect of a messenger substance (such as a neurotransmitter) that is naturally produced by the body and interacts with the receptor to cause some cellular change. For

example, narcotic drugs are agonists that mimic the endorphins and activate opiate receptors. An antagonist has the opposite effect: it inhibits the sequence of metabolic events that a natural substance or an agonist drug can stimulate, usually without initiating an effect itself. Thus, the drug naloxone (created to treat heroin overdoses) is an antagonist at the opiate receptors and blocks the effects of narcotic drugs, such as heroin, as well as the effects of the naturally occurring endorphins.

■ NEUROTRANSMITTERS: THE MESSENGERS

Many drugs affect the activity of neurotransmitters by altering their synthesis, storage, release, or deactivation. By changing these steps, a drug may modify or block information transmitted by these neurochemical messengers. Thus, by altering the amount of neurotransmitter, such drugs can act indirectly, like agonists and antagonists, even though they do not directly change neurotransmitter receptors.

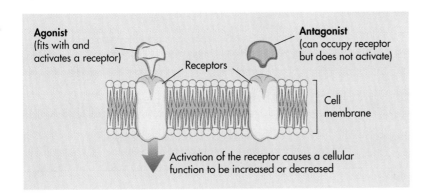

FIGURE 5.4

Interaction of agonist and antagonist with membrane receptor. When this receptor is occupied and activated by an agonist, it can cause cellular changes.

Agonist (fits with and activates a receptor)

Antagonist (can occupy receptor but does not activate)

Receptors

Cell membrane

Activation of the receptor causes a cellular function to be increased or decreased

Experimental evidence shows that many different neurotransmitters exist, although much remains to be learned about their specific functions. These biochemical messengers are released from specific neurons. The transmitters most likely altered by drugs of abuse include acetylcholine (ACh), norepinephrine, epinephrine, dopamine, serotonin, gamma-aminobutyric acid (GABA), and the endorphins (peptides). Because of the unique shapes, each neurotransmitter affects only its specific receptors (Bloom 1995). Drugs can also affect these receptors if they are sufficiently similar in shape to the neurotransmitters. Figure 5.5 summarizes some of the important features about the common neurotransmitters.

Acetylcholine

Large quantities of ACh are found in the brain. This neurotransmitter is synthesized in the neuron by combining molecules of choline (provided by diet and also manufactured in the body) and acetyl coenzyme A (CoA) (a product of glucose metabolism). ACh is one of the major neurotransmitters in the autonomic portion of the PNS, which will be discussed later in the chapter.

Neurons that respond to ACh are distributed throughout the brain. Depending on the region, ACh can have either excitatory or inhibitory effects. The receptors activated by ACh have been divided into two main subtypes based on the response to two drugs derived from plants: muscarine and nicotine. Muscarine (a substance in mushrooms that causes mushroom poisoning) and similarly acting drugs activate muscarinic receptors. Nicotine, whether experimentally administered or inhaled by smoking tobacco, stimulates nicotinic receptors.

Neurotransmitters are inactivated after they have done their job by removal, metabolism (by

FIGURE 5.5
Features of common neurotransmitters.

Acetylcholine
Chemical type: Choline product
Location: CNS—Basal ganglia, cortex, reticular activating system
PNS—Neuromuscular junction, parasympathetic system
Action: Excitatory and inhibitory

Norepinephrine
Chemical type: Catecholamine
Location: CNS—Limbic system, cortex, hypothalamus, reticular activating system, brain stem, spinal cord
PNS—Sympathetic nervous system
Action: Usually inhibitory; some excitation

Epinephrine
Chemical type: Catecholamine
Location: CNS—Minor
PNS—Adrenal glands
Action: Usually excitatory

Dopamine
Chemical type: Catecholamine
Location: CNS—Basal ganglia, limbic system, hypothalamus
Action: Usually inhibitory

Serotonin (S-HT)
Chemical type: Tryptophan-derivative
Location: CNS—Basal ganglia, limbic system, brain stem, spinal cord, cortex
Other—Gut, platelets, cardiovascular
Action: Inhibitory

GABA
Chemical type: Amino acid
Location: CNS—Basal ganglia, limbic system, cortex
Action: Inhibitory

Endorphins
Chemical type: Peptide (small protein)
Location: CNS—Basal ganglia, hypothalamus, brain stem, spinal cord
Other—Gut, cardiovascular system
Action: Inhibitory (narcotic-like effects)

Key: CNS—Central nervous system
PNS—Peripheral nervous system

enzymes), or reabsorption into the neuron. If a deactivating enzyme is blocked by a drug, the effect of the transmitter may be prolonged or intensified. For example, ACh stimulates nicotinic receptors that cause strong contraction of muscles. The ACh is metabolized by the deactivating enzyme, acetylcholinesterase, into the choline and acetate molecules, and the muscles relax. Some nerve gases developed by the military for chemical warfare purposes, for example, block the acetylcholinesterase enzyme. The target receptors in the presence of these drugs continue to be stimulated because the ACh is not inactivated by metabolism. This continual firing of electrical impulses causes muscle paralysis due to the persistent muscle contraction.

Catecholamines

Catecholamines include the neurotransmitter compounds norepinephrine, epinephrine, and dopamine, and have similar chemical structures. Neurons that synthesize catecholamines convert the amino acids phenylalanine or tyrosine to dopamine. In some neurons, dopamine is further converted to norepinephrine, and finally to epinephrine.

Unlike ACh, after acting at their receptors, most of the catecholamines are taken back up into the neurons that released them, to be used over again; this process is called *reuptake*. An enzymatic breakdown system also metabolizes the catecholamines to inactive compounds. The reuptake process and the activity of metabolizing enzymes, especially monoamine oxidase (MAO), can be greatly affected by some of the drugs of abuse. If these deactivating enzymes or reuptake systems are blocked, the concentration of norepinephrine and dopamine may build up in the brain, causing a significantly increased effect. Cocaine, for example, prevents the reuptake of norepinephrine and dopamine in the brain, resulting in continual stimulation of neuron catecholamine receptors.

Norepinephrine and Epinephrine Although norepinephrine and epinephrine are structurally very similar, their receptors are selective and do not respond with the same intensity to either transmitter or to sympathomimetic drugs. Just as the receptors to ACh can be separated into muscarinic and nicotinic types, the norepinephrine and epinephrine receptors are classified into the categories of

alpha and beta. Receiving cells may have alpha- or beta-type receptors, or both. Norepinephrine acts predominantly on alpha receptors and with less action on beta receptors.

The antagonistic (blocking) action of many drugs that act on these catecholamine receptors can be selective for alpha, whereas others block only beta receptors. This distinction can be therapeutically useful. For example, beta receptors tend to stimulate the heart, whereas alpha receptors constrict blood vessels; thus, a drug that selectively affects beta receptors can be used to treat heart ailments without directly altering the state of the blood vessels.

Dopamine As has been mentioned, dopamine is a catecholamine transmitter that is particularly influenced by drugs of abuse (Swan 1998; Wyman 1997). Most, if not all, drugs that elevate mood, have abuse potential, or cause psychotic behavior, enhance the activity of dopamine in some way, particularly in brain regions associated with limbic structures and regulating mental states. In addition, dopamine is an important transmitter in controlling movement and fine muscle activity, as well as endocrine functions. Thus, because many drugs of abuse affect dopamine neurons, they can also alter all of these functions.

Serotonin

Serotonin (5-hydroxytryptamine, or 5HT) is synthesized in neurons and elsewhere (for example, in the gastrointestinal tract and platelet-type blood cells) from the dietary source of tryptophan. Tryp-

---

KEY TERMS

muscarinic
a receptor type activated by ACh; usually inhibitory

nicotinic
a receptor type activated by ACh; usually excitatory

catecholamines
a class of biochemical compounds including the transmitters norepinephrine, epinephrine, and dopamine

sympathomimetic
agents that mimic the effects of norepinephrine or epinephrine

tophan is an essential amino acid, meaning that human beings do not have the ability to synthesize it and must obtain it through diet. Like the catecholamines, serotonin is degraded by the enzyme MAO; thus, drugs that alter this enzyme affect levels of not only catecholamines but also serotonin.

Serotonin is also found in the upper brain stem, which connects the brain and the spinal cord (see Figure 5.6). Axons from serotonergic neurons are distributed throughout the entire CNS. Serotonin generally inhibits action on its target neurons. One important role of the serotonergic neurons is to prevent overreaction to various stimuli, which can cause

aggressiveness, excessive motor activity, exaggerated mood swings, insomnia, and abnormal sexual behavior. Serotonergic neurons also help regulate the release of hormones from the hypothalamus.

Alterations in serotonergic neurons, serotonin synthesis, and degradation have been proposed to be factors in mental illness and to contribute to the side effects of many drugs of abuse. In support of this hypothesis is the fact that drugs such as psilocybin and lysergic acid diethylamide (LSD), which have serotonin-like chemical structures, are frequently abused because of their hallucinogenic properties and can cause psychotic effects (see Chapter 13).

FIGURE 5.6

Functional components of the central nervous system. Limbic structures include the hypothalamus, thalamus, medial forebrain bundle, and frontal lobe of the cerebrum and are important for controlling mental states.

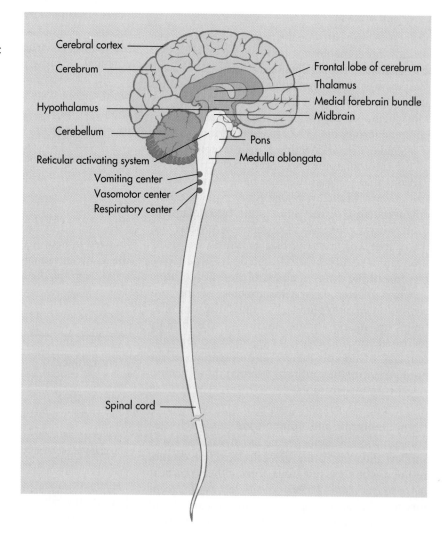

Major Divisions of the Nervous System

The nervous system can be divided into two major components: the central (CNS) and peripheral (PNS) nervous systems. The CNS consists of the brain and spinal cord (see Figure 5.6), which receive information through the input nerves of the PNS. This sensory information allows the CNS to evaluate the specific status of all organs and the general status of the body. After receiving and processing this information, the CNS reacts by regulating muscle and organ activity through the output nerves of the PNS (Lefkowitz et al. 1995).

The PNS is comprised of neurons whose cell bodies or axons are located outside the brain or spinal cord. It consists of input and output nerves to the CNS. The PNS input to the brain and spinal cord conveys sensory information such as pain, pressure, and temperature, whereas its output activities are separated into somatic types (control of voluntary muscles) and autonomic types (control of unconscious functions, such as essential organ and gland activity).

■ THE CENTRAL NERVOUS SYSTEM

The human brain is an integrating (information processing) and storage device unequaled by the most complex computers. It can not only handle a great deal of information simultaneously from the senses but also evaluate and modify the response to the information rapidly. Although the brain weighs only 3 pounds, its more than 10 billion neurons give it the potential to perform a multitude of functions. The following are some important brain regions influenced by drugs of abuse.

The Reticular Activating System

The reticular activating system (RAS) is an area of the brain that receives input from all of the sensory systems as well as from the cerebral cortex. The RAS is at the junction of the spinal cord and the brain (see Figure 5.6). One of the major functions of the RAS is to control the brain's state of arousal (sleep versus awake).

Because of its complex, diffuse network structure, the RAS is very susceptible to the effects of

> **KEY TERMS**
>
> **CNS**
> the central nervous system, including the brain and spinal cord
>
> **PNS**
> the peripheral nervous system, including neurons outside the CNS
>
> **anticholinergic**
> agents that antagonize the effects of acetylcholine

drugs. The RAS is sensitive to the effects of LSD, potent stimulants such as cocaine and amphetamines, and CNS depressants such as alcohol and barbiturates.

Norepinephrine and ACh are important neurotransmitters in the RAS. High levels of epinephrine, norepinephrine, or stimulant drugs, such as amphetamines, activate the RAS. In contrast, drugs that block the actions of another transmitter, ACh, called anticholinergic drugs (for example, antihistamines), suppress RAS activity, causing sleepiness.

The Basal Ganglia

The basal ganglia are the primary centers for involuntary and fine-tuning of motor functions involving, for example, posture and muscle tone. Two important neurotransmitters in the basal ganglia are dopamine and ACh. Damage to neurons in this area may cause *Parkinson's disease*, the progressive yet selective degeneration of the main dopaminergic neurons in the basal ganglia.

A close association exists between control of motor abilities and control of mental states. Both functions rely heavily on the activity of dopamine-releasing neurons. Consequently, drugs that affect dopamine activity usually alter both systems, resulting in undesired side effects. For example, heavy use of tranquilizers (such as chlorpromazine [Thorazine], trifluoperazine [Stelazine], and so on) in the treatment of psychotic patients produces Parkinson-like symptoms. If such drugs are administered daily over several years, problems with motor functioning may become permanent. Drugs of abuse, such as stimulants, increase dopamine activity, causing enhanced motor activity as well as psychotic behavior.

The Limbic System

The limbic system includes an assortment of linked brain regions located near to and including the hypothalamus (see Figure 5.6). Besides the hypothalamus, the limbic structures include the thalamus, medial forebrain bundle, and front portion of the cerebral cortex. Functions of the limbic and basal ganglia structures are inseparably linked; drugs that affect one system often affect the other as well.

The primary roles of limbic brain regions include regulating emotional activities (such as fear, rage, and anxiety), memory, modulation of basic hypothalamic functions (such as endocrine activity), and activities such as mating, procreation, and caring for the young. In addition, reward centers are also believed to be associated with limbic structures. It is almost certain that the mood-elevating effects of drugs of abuse are mediated by the limbic systems of the brain.

For example, studies have shown that, when given the option, laboratory animals will self-administer most stimulant drugs of abuse (such as amphetamines and cocaine) through a cannula surgically placed into limbic structures (such as the medial forebrain bundle and frontal cerebral cortex). This self-administration is achieved by linking injection of the drug into the cannula with a lever press or other activity by the animal (Winsauer et al. 2000). It is thought that the euphoria or intense "highs" associated with these drugs result from their effects on these brain regions. Some of the limbic system's principal transmitters include dopamine, norepinephrine, and serotonin; dopamine activation appears to be the primary reinforcement that accounts for the abuse liability of most drugs (Swan 1998).

The Cerebral Cortex

The unique features of the human cerebral cortex gives human beings a special place among animals. The cortex is a layer of gray matter made up of nerves and supporting cells that almost completely surrounds the rest of the brain and lies immediately under the skull (see Figure 5.6). It is responsible for receiving sensory input, interpreting incoming information, and initiating voluntary motor behavior. Many psychoactive drugs, such as psychedelics, dramatically alter the perception of sensory information by the cortex and cause hallucinations that result in strange behavior.

The most developed part of the cortex is called the *associative cortex*. The associative areas of the brain do not directly receive input from the environment nor do they directly initiate output to the muscles or the glands. Instead, these cortical areas may store memories, control complex behaviors, and help process information. Some psychoactive drugs disrupt the normal functioning of these areas and thereby interfere with an individual's ability to deal with complex issues.

The Hypothalamus

The hypothalamus (see Figures 5.6 and 5.7) is located near the base of the brain. It integrates information from many sources and serves as the CNS control center for the ANS and many vital support functions. It also serves as the primary point of contact between the nervous and the endocrine systems. Because the hypothalamus controls the ANS, it is responsible for maintaining homeostasis in the body; thus, drugs that alter its function can have a major impact on systems that control homeostasis. The catecholamine transmitters are particularly important in regulating the function of the hypothalamus, and most drugs of abuse that alter the activity of norepinephrine and dopamine are likely to alter the activity of this brain structure.

The Autonomic Nervous System

Although the cell bodies of the neurons of the ANS are located within the brain or spinal cord, their axons project outside of the CNS to involuntary muscles, organs, and glands; thus, the ANS is considered part of the PNS. The ANS is an integrative, or regulatory, system that does not require conscious control (that is, you do not have to think about it to make it function). It is usually consid-

KEY TERMS

ANS
the autonomic nervous system, controls the unconscious functions of the body

ered primarily a motor or output system. A number of drugs that cannot enter the CNS because of the blood-brain barrier are able to affect the ANS only. The ANS is divided into two functional components, the sympathetic and the parasympathetic nervous systems (Lefkowitz et al. 1995). Both systems include neurons that project to most visceral organs and to smooth muscles, glands, and blood vessels (see Figure 5.7).

The two components of the ANS generally have opposite effects on an organ or its function. The working of the heart is a good example of sympathetic and parasympathetic control. Stimulation of the parasympathetic nervous system slows the heart

FIGURE 5.7

Autonomic pathways of the parasympathetic and sympathetic nervous systems and the organs affected.

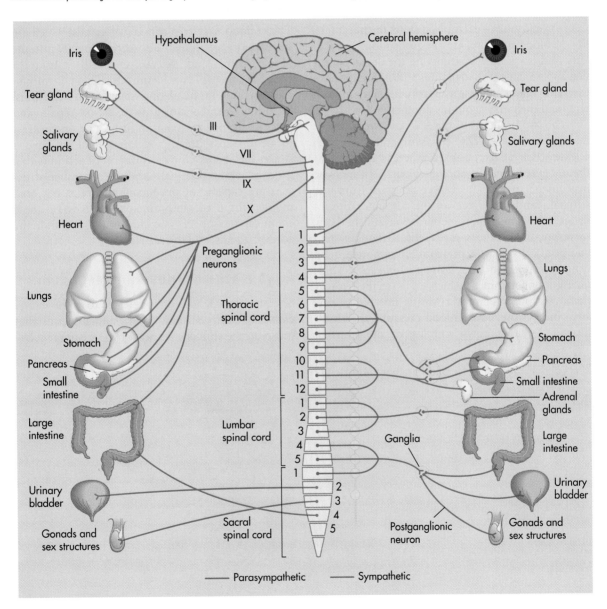

rate, whereas stimulation of the sympathetic nerves accelerates it. These actions constitute a constant biological check-and-balance, or regulatory system. Because the two parts of the ANS work in opposite ways much of the time, they are considered physiological antagonists. These two systems control most of the internal organs, the circulatory system, and the secretory (glandular) system. The sympathetic system is normally active at all times; the degree of activity varies from moment to moment and from organ to organ. The parasympathetic nervous system is organized mainly for limited, focused activity and usually conserves and restores energy rather than expends it. For example, it slows the heart rate, lowers blood pressure, aids in absorption of nutrients, and is involved in emptying the urinary bladder. Table 5.2 lists the structures and/or functions of the sympathetic and parasympathetic nervous systems and their effects on one another.

The two branches of the ANS use two different neurotransmitters. The parasympathetic branch releases ACh at its synapses, whereas the sympathetic neurons release norepinephrine. An increase in epinephrine in the blood released from the adrenal glands (see later) or the administration of drugs that mimic norepinephrine causes the body to respond as if the sympathetic nervous system had been activated. As previously mentioned, such drugs are referred to as *sympathomimetics.* Thus, taking amphetamines (which enhance the sympathetic nervous system by releasing norepinephrine and epinephrine) raises blood pressure, speeds up heart rate, slows down motility of the stomach walls, and may cause the pupils of the eyes to enlarge; other so-called "uppers," such as cocaine, have similar effects.

Drugs that affect ACh release, metabolism, or interaction with its respective receptor are referred to as *cholinergic* drugs. They can either mimic or antagonize the parasympathetic nervous system, according to their pharmacological action.

The Endocrine System and Drugs

The endocrine system consists of glands, which are ductless (meaning that they secrete directly into the bloodstream) and release chemical substances called hormones (see Figure 5.8). These hormones are essential in regulating many vital functions, including metabolism, growth, tissue repair, and sexual behavior, to mention just a few. In contrast to neurotransmitters, hormones tend to have a slower onset and a longer duration of action with a more generalized target. Although a number of tissues are capable of producing and releasing hormones, three of the principal sources of these chemical messengers are the pituitary gland, the adrenal glands, and the sex glands.

■ ENDOCRINE GLANDS AND REGULATION

The pituitary gland is often referred to as the *master gland.* It controls many of the other glands that make up the endocrine system by releasing regulat-

TABLE 5.2 Sympathetic and Parasympathetic Control

STRUCTURE OR FUNCTION	SYMPATHETIC	PARASYMPATHETIC
Heart rate	Speeds up	Slows
Breathing rate	Speeds up	Slows
Stomach wall	Slows motility	Increases
Skin blood vessels (vasomotor function)	Constricts	Dilates
Iris of eye	Constricts (pupil enlarges)	Dilates
Vomiting center	Stimulates	—

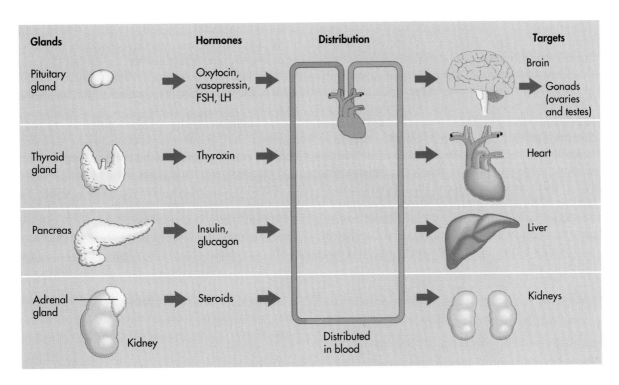

Glands	Hormones	Distribution	Targets

Pituitary gland → Oxytocin, vasopressin, FSH, LH → → Brain, Gonads (ovaries and testes)

Thyroid gland → Thyroxin → → Heart

Pancreas → Insulin, glucagon → → Liver

Adrenal gland, Kidney → Steroids → → Kidneys

Distributed in blood

FIGURE 5.8

Examples of some glands in the endocrine system.

ing factors and growth hormone. Besides controlling the brain functions already mentioned, the hypothalamus helps control the activity of the pituitary gland and thereby has a very prominent effect on the endocrine system.

The adrenal glands are located near the kidneys and are divided into two parts: the outer surface, called the *cortex,* and the inner part, called the *medulla.* The adrenal medulla is actually a component of the sympathetic nervous system and releases adrenaline (another name for *epinephrine*) during sympathetic stimulation. Other important hormones released by the adrenal cortex are called *corticosteroids* or, frequently, just steroids . Steroids help the body respond appropriately to crises and stress. In addition, small amounts of male sex hormones, called androgens , are also released by the adrenal cortex. The androgens produce anabolic effects that increase the retention and synthesis of proteins, causing growth in the mass of tissues such as muscles and bones.

Sex glands are responsible for the secretion of male and female sex hormones that help regulate the development and activity of the respective reproductive systems. The organs known as *gonads* include the female ovaries and the male testes. The activity of the gonads is regulated by hormones released from the pituitary gland (see Figure 5.8) and, for the most part, remains suppressed until puberty. After activation, estrogens and progesterones are released from the ovaries and the androgens (principally testosterone) are released from the testes. These hormones are responsible for the

KEY TERMS

hormones
regulatory chemicals released by endocrine systems

steroids
hormones related to the corticosteroids released from the adrenal cortex

androgens
male sex hormones

development and maintenance of the secondary sex characteristics. They influence not only sex-related body features but also emotional states, suggesting that these sex hormones enter the brain and significantly affect the functioning of the limbic systems.

For the most part, drugs prescribed to treat endocrine problems are intended as replacement therapy. For example, diabetic patients suffer from a shortage of insulin produced by the pancreas, so therapy consists of insulin injections. Patients who suffer from dwarfism receive insufficient growth hormone from the pituitary gland; thus, growth hormone is administered to stimulate normal growth. Because some hormones can affect growth, muscle development, and behavior, they are sometimes abused.

■ THE ABUSE OF HORMONES: ANABOLIC STEROIDS

Androgens are the hormones most likely to be abused in the United States (Mathias 1997). Testosterone, the primary natural androgen, is produced by the testes. Naturally produced androgens are essential for normal growth and development of male sex organs as well as secondary sex characteristics such as male hair patterns, voice changes, muscular development, and fat distribution. The androgens are also necessary for appropriate growth spurts during adolescence (*Drug Facts and Comparisons* 2000). Accepted therapeutic use of the androgens is usually for replacement in males with abnormally functioning testes. In such cases, the androgens are administered before puberty and for prolonged periods during puberty to stimulate proper male development.

Androgens clearly have an impressive effect on development of tissue (Karch 1996); in particular, they cause pronounced growth of muscle mass and a substantial increase in body weight in young men with deficient testes function. Because of these effects, androgens are classified as anabolic (able to stimulate the conversion of nutrients into tissue mass) steroids (they are chemically similar to the steroids).

In addition, many athletes and trainers have assumed that, in very high doses, androgens can enhance muscle growth and increase strength above that achieved by normal testicular function. Because of this effect, male and female athletes, as well as nonathletes who are into body building and sports, have been attracted to these drugs in hopes of enlarging muscle size, improving their athletic performances, and enhancing their physiques (see Chapter 17) (see "Case in Point," Home Runs and Doping).

Several studies have demonstrated that anabolic hormones particularly affect the limbic structures of the brain. Consequently, these drugs can cause excitation and a sense of superior strength and performance in some users. These effects, coupled with increased aggressiveness, could encourage continual use of these drugs. Other CNS effects, however, may be disturbing to the user. Symptoms that may occur with very high doses include uncontrolled rage (referred to as "roid rage"), headaches, anxiety, insomnia, and perhaps paranoia (*Drug Facts and Comparisons* 2000). Because of concern about the abuse potential and side effect profile of the anabolic steroids, these drugs are controlled as Schedule III substances.

Conclusion

All psychoactive drugs affect brain activity by altering the ability of neurons to send and receive messages. Consequently, drugs of abuse exert their addicting effects by stimulating or blocking the activity of CNS neurotransmitters or their receptors. Thus, to understand why these drugs are abused and the nature of their dependence, how neurons and their neurotransmitter systems function must be studied. In addition, many scientists believe that elucidating how substances of abuse affect nervous systems will lead to new and more effective methods for treating drug addiction.

KEY TERMS

anabolic steroids
compounds chemically like the steroids that stimulate production of tissue mass

CASE IN POINT

Home Runs and Doping

Use of steroids to enhance performance is often done blatantly by those considered to be athletic heroes. Mark McGwire established a new Major League Baseball home run record in 1998 while acknowledging the use of an over-the-counter product containing androstenedione. This substance is classified as a "food supplement" but is metabolized by the body into testosterone, a male hormone. Like other steroids, it increases muscle mass and strength. Although legal in the United States, this steroid is a banned substance for Olympic competition, in the NFL, and in the NCAA. After announcing McGwire's use of this supplement, sales of the product increased fivefold. In August of 1999 McGwire announced that he was no longer taking androstenedione. McGwire cited his discomfort with the knowledge that his actions may have encouraged kids to start taking the supplement as his reason for discontinuing its use.

Mark McGwire

Source: Smith, C. "Doping Battle Aims to Win Kids' Hearts." *Salt Lake Tribune* 259 (2000): 1A.

Discussion Questions

1. How are neurotransmitters and hormones alike, and how are they different?

2. Why is it important for the body to have chemical messengers that can be quickly released and rapidly inactivated?

3. Why are receptors so important in understanding the effects of drugs of abuse?

4. Why do many drugs of abuse affect motor behavior?

5. What are some mechanisms whereby a drug of abuse can increase the activity of dopamine transmitter systems in the brain?

6. Some drugs of abuse are described as "sympathomimetics" and some as "anticholinergic." What features distinguish these two pharmacological properties?

7. Was classifying anabolic steroids as Schedule III drugs justified? What do you think will be the long-term consequence of this action?

Key Terms

homeostasis **114**

neurotransmitters **114**

hormones **114**

endocrine system **114**

neurons `114`

axons `115`

receptors `115`

psychoactive `115`

synapse `117`

synaptic cleft `117`

dendrites `117`

opiate receptors `118`

endorphins `118`

agonistic `119`

antagonistic `119`

muscarinic `120`

nicotinic `120`

catecholamines `121`

sympathomimetic `121`

CNS `123`

PNS `123`

anticholinergic `123`

ANS `124`

hormones `126`

steroids `127`

androgens `127`

anabolic steroids `128`

Summary

1 The nervous and endocrine systems help mediate internal and external responses to the body's surroundings. Both systems release chemical messengers in order to achieve their homeostatic functions. These messenger substances are called *neurotransmitters* and *hormones,* and they exert their functions through receptors. Many drugs exert their effects by influencing these chemical messengers.

2 The neuron is the principal cell type in the nervous system. This specialized cell consists of dendrites, a cell body, and an axon. It communicates with other neurons and organs by releasing neurotransmitters, which can cause either excitation or inhibition at their target sites.

3 The chemical messengers from glands and neurons exert their effects by interacting with special protein regions in membranes called *receptors.* Because of their unique construction, receptors interact only with molecules that have specific construction. Activation of receptors can initiate a chain of events within cells, resulting in changes in gene expression, enzyme activity, or metabolic function.

4 *Agonists* are substances or drugs that stimulate receptors. *Antagonists* are substances or drugs that attach to receptors and prevent them from being activated.

5 A variety of different substances are used as neurotransmitters by neurons in the body. The classes of transmitters include the catecholamines, serotonin, acetylcholine, GABA, and peptides. These transmitters are excitatory, inhibitory, or sometimes both, depending on which receptor is being activated. Many drugs selectively act to either enhance or antagonize these neurotransmitters and their activities.

6 The central nervous system consists of the brain and spinal cord. Regions within the brain help to regulate specific functions. The hypothalamus controls endocrine and basic body functions. The basal ganglia are primarily responsible for controlling motor activity. The limbic system regulates mood and mental states. The cerebral cortex helps interpret, process, and respond to input information.

7 The limbic system and its associated transmitters, especially dopamine, are major sites of action for the drugs of abuse. Substances that increase the activity of dopamine cause a sense of well-being and euphoria, which encourages psychological dependence.

8 The autonomic nervous system is composed of the sympathetic and parasympathetic systems; neurons associated with these systems release noradrenalin and acetylcholine as their

transmitters, respectively. These systems work in an antagonistic fashion to control unconscious, visceral functions such as breathing and cardiovascular activity. The parasympathetic nervous system usually helps conserve and restore energy in the body, whereas the sympathetic nervous system is continually active.

9 The endocrine system consists of glands that synthesize and release hormones into the blood. Distribution via blood circulation carries these chemical messengers throughout the body, where they act on specific receptors. Some of the principal structures include the pituitary, adrenals, and gonads (testes and ovaries).

10 Anabolic steroids are structurally related to the male hormone testosterone. They are often abused by both male and female athletes trying to build muscle mass and enhance performance. The continual use of high doses of anabolic steroids can cause annoying and dangerous side effects. The long-term effects of low, intermittent doses of these drugs have not been determined. Because of concerns voiced by most medical authorities, anabolic steroids are controlled substances and have been classified as Schedule III substances.

References

Bhasin, S., T. W. Storer, N. Berman, C. Callegari, B. Clevenger, J. Phillips, T. Bunnell, R. Tricker, A. Shirazi and R. Casaburi. "The Effects of Supraphysiologic Doses of Testosterone on Muscle Size and Strength in Normal Men." *New England Journal of Medicine* 335 (1996): 1–7.

Bloom, F. "Neurotransmission and the Central Nervous System." In *The Pharmacological Basis of Therapeutics,* 9th ed., edited by J. Harman and T. Limbird, 267–93. New York: McGraw–Hill, 1995.

Drug Facts and Comparisons. St. Louis: J. B. Lippincott, 2000.

Fattore, L., M. Martellotta, G. Cossu, M. Mascia, W. Fratta, "CB-1 Cannabinoid Receptor Agonist WIN55,212-2 Decreases Intravenous Cocaine Self-Administration in Rats." *Behavioral Brain Research* 104 (1999): 141–46.

Goldstein, A. *Addiction from Biology to Drug Policy,* 15–60. New York: Freeman, 1994.

Hobbs, W., T. Rall, T. Verdoorn. "Hypnotics and Sedatives: Ethanol." In *The Pharmacological Basis of Therapeutics,* 9th ed., edited by J. Hardman and T. Limbird, 361–96. New York: McGraw–Hill, 1995.

Kandel, E., J. Schwartz, T. Jessell. "Overview of Synaptic Transmission." In *Principles of Neural Science,* 4th ed., 175–86. New York: McGraw–Hill, 2000a.

Kandel, E., J. Schwartz, T. Jessell. "The Perception of Pain." In *Principles of Neural Science,* 4th ed., 207–52. New York: McGraw–Hill, 2000b.

Kandel, E., J. Schwartz, T. Jessell. "Modulation of Synaptic Transmission: Second Messengers." In *Principles of Neural Science,* 4th ed., 229–52. New York: McGraw–Hill, 2000c.

Karch, S. "Anabolic Steroids." In *The Pathology of Drug Abuse,* 2nd ed., 409–29. New York: CRC, 1996.

Lefkowitz, R., B. Hoffman, P. Taylor. "Neurotransmission, the Autonomic and Somatic Motor Nervous Systems." In *The Pharmacological Basis of Therapeutics,* 9th ed., edited by J. Hardman and T. Limbird, 361–96. New York: McGraw–Hill, 1995.

Mathias, R. "Steroid Prevention Program Scores with High School Athletes." *NIDA Notes* (July/August, 1997): 14, 15.

O'Brien, C. "Drug Addiction and Drug Abuse." In *The Pharmacological Basis of Therapeutics,* 9th ed., edited by J. Hardman and T. Limbird, 557–77. New York: McGraw–Hill, 1995.

Smith, C. "Doping Battle Aims to Win Kids' Hearts." *Salt Lake Tribune* 259 (2000): 1A.

Snyder, S. H. "Opiate Receptors in the Brain." *New England Journal of Medicine* 296 (1977): 266–71.

Swan, N. "Like Other Drugs of Abuse, Nicotine Disrupts the Brain's Pleasure Circuit." *NIDA Notes* 13 (1998): 12.

Winsauer, P., K. Silvester, J. Moerschbaecher, C. France. "Cocaine Self-Administration in Monkeys: Effects on the Acquisition and Performance of Response Sequences." *Drug and Alcohol Dependence* 59 (2000): 51–61.

Wyman, J. "Promising Advances Toward Understanding the Genetic Roots of Addiction." *NIDA Notes* 12 (July/August 1997): 11, 12.

How and Why Drugs Work

Did You Know?

▶ Twenty percent of the total hospital costs in the United States are due to medical care for health damage caused by substances of abuse.

▶ Side effects and reactions to prescription drugs seriously injure as many as 2 million people and kill 100,000 people in the United States each year.

▶ The same dose of a drug does not have the same effect on everyone.

▶ In excessive doses, almost any drug or substance can be toxic.

▶ Sixty-five percent of the strokes among young Americans are related to cigarette, cocaine, or amphetamine use.

▶ Many people who abuse cocaine also abuse alcohol to counter unpleasant side effects.

▶ Use of some drugs can dramatically enhance the effects of others.

▶ Smoking cocaine, methamphetamine, and heroin is as addicting and dangerous as administering these drugs intravenously.

▶ Many drugs are unable to pass from the blood into the brain.

▶ Most drugs cross the placental barrier from the mother to the fetus.

▶ Physical dependence is characterized by withdrawal effects when use of the drug is stopped.

▶ Tolerance to one drug can often cause tolerance to other similar drugs; this effect is called *cross-tolerance*.

▶ Placebos can have significant effects in relieving symptoms such as pain.

▶ The body produces natural narcotic substances called *endorphins*.

▶ Hereditary factors may predispose some individuals to becoming psychologically dependent on drugs with abuse potential.

Chapter 6

Learning Objectives

**On completing this chapter
you will be able to:**

- ▶ Describe some of the common unintended drug effects.

- ▶ Explain why the same dose of a drug may affect individuals differently.

- ▶ Explain the difference between potency and toxicity.

- ▶ Describe the concept of a drug's "margin of safety."

- ▶ Identify and give examples of additive, antagonistic, and potentiative (synergistic) drug interactions.

- ▶ Identify the pharmacokinetic factors that can influence the effects caused by drugs.

- ▶ Cite the physiological and pathological factors that influence drug effects.

- ▶ Explain the significance of the blood-brain barrier to psychoactive drugs.

- ▶ Define *threshold dose, plateau effect,* and *cumulative effect.*

- ▶ Discuss the role of the liver in drug metabolism and the consequences of this process.

- ▶ Define *biotransformation.*

- ▶ Describe the relationships among tolerance, withdrawal, rebound, physical dependence, and psychological dependence.

- ▶ Discuss the significance of placebos in responding to drugs.

- ▶ Describe drug craving and how it affects drug abuse.

Introduction

A common belief is that drugs are the solution for life's physical and emotional problems. Although medications are essential to treatment for many diseases, excessive reliance on drugs causes unrealistic expectations that may lead to dangerous, even fatal, consequences. For example, drug addiction and dependence often follow from such unrealistic expectations. Obviously, not every person who uses drugs inappropriately becomes a drug addict, nor are patients who use drugs as prescribed by the doctor immune from becoming physically and mentally dependent on their medications. In fact, because of individual variability, it is difficult to predict accurately which drug users will or will not have drug problems such as addiction and dependence.

In this chapter, we consider the factors that account for the variability of drug responses—that is, what determines how the body responds to drugs and why some drugs work while others do not. First we review the general effects of drugs, both intended and unintended. The correlation between the dose and response of a drug is addressed next, followed by a discussion of how drugs interact with one another. The section on *pharmacokinetic* factors considers how drugs are introduced into, distributed throughout, and eliminated from the body, along with physiological and pathological variables that modify how drugs affect the body. The final sections in the chapter consider concepts important to understanding drug abuse, such as tolerance, physical versus psychological dependence, and addiction.

The Intended and Unintended Effects of Drugs

When physicians prescribe drugs, their objective is usually to cure or relieve symptoms of a disease. Frequently, however, drugs cause unintended effects that neither the physician nor the patient expected.

The intended responses produced by a drug are called main effects , whereas those that are unintended are called side effects . The distinction between main and side effects depends on the therapeutic objective. A response that is considered unnecessary or undesirable in one situation may, in fact, be the intended effect in another. For example, antihistamines found in many over-the-counter (OTC) drugs have an intended main effect of relieving allergy symptoms, but they often cause annoying drowsiness as a side effect; in fact, their labels include warnings that they should not be used while driving a car. These antihistamines are also included in OTC sleep aids, where their sedating action is the desired main effect because it encourages sleep in people suffering from insomnia.

Side effects can influence many body functions and occur in any organ (see Figure 6.1). Side effects of prescription and nonprescription drugs are estimated to seriously injure 2.1 million people and kill 100,000 people in the United States each year (MacDonald 1998). The following are basic kinds of side effects that can result from drug use:

Nausea or vomiting. Almost any drug can cause an upset stomach; in fact, this is a common complaint with narcotics.

Changes in mental alertness. Some medications can cause sedation and drowsiness (for example, antihistamines in OTC allergy medications) or nervousness and insomnia (for example, caffeine in OTC stay-awake products).

Dependence. This phenomenon compels people to continue using a drug because they want to achieve a desired effect or because they fear unpleasant reactions, called withdrawal , that occur when the drug is discontinued. Dependence has been associated with such apparently benign OTC drugs as nasal decongestant sprays and laxatives, as well as more potent drugs such as alcohol (see Chapters 8 and 9), narcotics (see Chapter 10), and stimulants (see Chapter 11).

Allergic reactions (hypersensitive reactions or sensitization). Allergic reactions occur when the body becomes sensitized to a drug and attempts to destroy and dispose of it. During an allergic reaction, the drug can cause tissue reactions such as rashes, hives, and itching or cause very serious conditions such as shock and breathing difficulty.

Changes in cardiovascular activity. Many drugs that are available OTC or by prescription or that are used illicitly can alter the activity of the heart

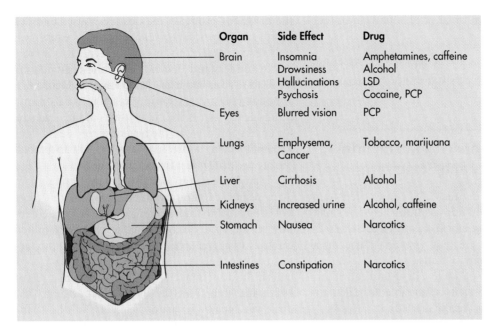

Organ	Side Effect	Drug
Brain	Insomnia	Amphetamines, caffeine
	Drowsiness	Alcohol
	Hallucinations	LSD
	Psychosis	Cocaine, PCP
Eyes	Blurred vision	PCP
Lungs	Emphysema, Cancer	Tobacco, marijuana
Liver	Cirrhosis	Alcohol
Kidneys	Increased urine	Alcohol, caffeine
Stomach	Nausea	Narcotics
Intestines	Constipation	Narcotics

FIGURE 6.1

Common side effects with drugs of abuse. Almost every organ or system in the body can be negatively affected by the substances of abuse.

and change the state of the blood vessels. The results of these side effects include changes in blood pressure, fainting, heart attack, and stroke.

This partial list of side effects demonstrates the types of risk involved whenever any drug (prescription, nonprescription, illicit, and even some herbal products) is used. Consequently, before taking a drug, whether for therapeutic or recreational use, you should understand its potential problems and determine whether the benefits justify the risks. For example, it is important to know that morphine is effective for relieving severe pain, but it also depresses breathing and retards intestinal activity, causing constipation. Likewise, amphetamines can be used to suppress appetite for losing weight, but they also increase blood pressure and stimulate the heart. Cocaine is a good local anesthetic, but it can be extremely addicting and can cause tremors or even seizures. The greater the danger associated with using a drug, the less likely that the benefits will warrant its use.

Adverse effects of drugs of abuse are particularly troublesome in the United States. Studies have suggested that billions of dollars are spent each year in the United States on medical care and premature deaths due to the use of addicting substances (Rice 1999). Other statistics illustrating the major nega-

tive health impact of adverse unintended effects caused by drugs of abuse include the following ("Trends, Policy and Research" 1993):

- Patients who abuse alcohol, tobacco, and other drugs are hospitalized twice as long as other patients with the same diagnosis.

- Seventy-five percent of the chronic pancreatitis (damaged pancreas) cases in the United States are due to alcohol abuse.

- Sixty-five percent of the strokes among young Americans are related to cigarette, cocaine, or amphetamine use.

- Youth under 15 years of age are hospitalized three to four times longer, regardless of their

KEY TERMS

main effects
intended drug responses

side effects
unintended drug responses

withdrawal
unpleasant effects that occur when use of a drug is stopped

illness, if they have an alcohol, tobacco, or other drug problem.

- More than 50% of the pediatric AIDS cases are the result of injecting drugs of abuse.

The Dose-Response Relationship of Therapeutics and Toxicity

All effects—both desired and unwanted—are related to the amount of drug administered. A small concentration of drug may have one effect, whereas a larger dose may create a greater effect or a different effect entirely. Because some correlation exists between the response to a drug and the quantity of the drug dose, it is possible to calculate dose-response curves (see Figure 6.2).

Once a dose-response curve for a drug has been determined in an individual, it can be used to predict how that person will respond to different doses of the drug. For example, the dose-response curve for user B in Figure 6.2 shows that 600 mg of aspirin will only relieve 50% of his or her headache. It is important to understand that not everyone responds the same to a given dose of drug. Thus, in Figure 6.2, although 600 mg of aspirin gives 50% relief from a headache for user B, it relieves 100% of the headache for user A and none of the headache for user C. This variability in response makes it difficult to predict the precise drug effect from a given dose.

Many factors can contribute to the variability in drug responses (Bourne 1998). One of the most important is tolerance, or reduced response over time to the same dosage, an effect that is examined carefully in a later section of this chapter. Other factors include the size of the individual, stomach contents if the drug is taken by mouth, different levels of enzymatic activity in the liver (which changes the drug via metabolic action), acidity of the urine (which affects the rate of drug elimination), time of day, and state of the person's health. Such multiple interacting factors make it difficult to calculate accurately the final drug effect for any given individual.

■ MARGIN OF SAFETY

An important concept for developing new drugs for therapy, as well as for assessing the probability of serious side effects for drugs of abuse, is called the margin of safety. The margin of safety is determined by the difference between the doses necessary to cause the intended (therapeutic or recreational) effects and the toxic unintended effects. The larger the margin of safety, the less likely that serious adverse side effects will occur when using the drug to treat medical problems or even when abusing it. Drugs with relatively narrow margins of safety, such as phencyclidine (PCP) or cocaine, have a very high rate of serious reactions in populations who abuse these substances.

There is no such thing as the perfect drug that goes right to the target in the body, has no toxicity, produces no side effects, and can be removed or neutralized when not needed. Unfortunately, most effective drugs are potentially dangerous if the doses are high enough. Pharmacologists refer to a perfect drug as a "magic bullet"; so far, no magic bullets have been discovered. Even relatively safe drugs available OTC can cause problems for some

FIGURE 6.2

Dose-response curve for relieving a headache with aspirin in three users. User A is the most sensitive and has 100% headache relief at a dose of 600 mg. User B is the next most sensitive and experiences 50% headache relief with a 600-mg dose. The least sensitive is user C: with a 600-mg dose, user C has no relief from a headache.

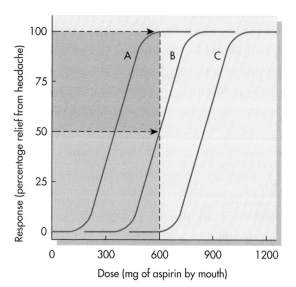

prospective users. Not surprisingly, all drugs of abuse can cause very serious side effects, especially when self-administered by users unfamiliar with the potential toxicities of these substances. The possibility that adverse effects will occur should always be considered before using any drug.

■ POTENCY VERSUS TOXICITY

Most of us know that some drugs of abuse are more dangerous than others. For example, it is common knowledge that abuse of the narcotic drug heroin is more likely to be lethal than abuse of another narcotic drug, codeine. One important feature that makes heroin more dangerous than codeine is its high potency. Potency is a way of expressing how much of a drug is necessary to cause an effect, whether it be desired or toxic. The smaller the dose required to achieve a drug action, the greater the drug potency.

The concept of potency can also be used to describe a drug's ability to create a therapeutic effect. More potent medications require lower doses to be effective. Knowledge of a drug's potency is essential if it is to be used properly and safely.

Toxicity is the capacity of a drug to upset or even destroy normal body functions. Toxic compounds are often called *poisons*, although almost any compound—including sugar, table salt, aspirin, and vitamin A—can be toxic at sufficiently high doses. If a foreign chemical is introduced into the body, it may disrupt the body's normal functions. In many instances, the body can compensate for this disruption, perhaps by metabolizing and rapidly eliminating the chemical, and little effect is noted. Sometimes, however, the delicate balance is altered and the person becomes sick or even dies. If the body's functional balance is already under stress from disease, the introduction of a drug may have a much more serious effect than its use in a healthy person who can adjust to its toxicity.

A drug with high potency often is toxic even at low doses; therefore, the amount given must be carefully measured and the user closely monitored. If caution is not taken, serious damage to the body or death can occur. Very potent drugs that are abused, such as heroin, are particularly dangerous because they are often consumed by unsuspecting users who are ignorant of the drug's extreme toxic-

KEY TERMS

dose-response
correlation between the amount of a drug given and its effects

tolerance
changes in the body that decrease response to a drug even though the dose remains the same

margin of safety
range in dose between the amount of drug necessary to cause a therapeutic effect and that needed to create a toxic effect

potency
amount of drug necessary to cause an effect

toxicity
capacity of one drug to damage or cause adverse effects in the body

drug interaction
presence of one drug alters the action of another drug

ity (see "Here and Now," Killer Cocktail in Melbourne, page 138). Potency depends on many factors, such as the drug's absorption, its distribution in the body, individual metabolism, the form of excretion, the rate of elimination, and its activity at the site of action (Nicholas and Benet 1998).

Drug Interaction

A drug's effects can be dramatically altered when other drugs are also present in the body: this effect is known as drug interaction (Klaasen 1995). A typical example of multiple drug use occurs when you treat your common cold. Because of your many cold-related symptoms, you may consume an assortment of pain relievers, antihistamines, decongestants, and anticough medications all at the same time.

Multiple drug use can create a serious medical problem because many drugs influence the actions of other drugs (Correia 1998). Even physicians may be baffled by unusual effects when multiple drugs are consumed. Frequently, drug interactions are misdiagnosed as symptoms of a disease. Such errors in diagnosis can lead to inappropriate treatment and serious health consequences. Complications can

HERE AND NOW   `Killer Cocktail in Melbourne`

A fatal cocktail of extremely potent heroin killed more than 30 drug addicts in one of the worst heroin overdose outbreaks in Melbourne, Australia. The lethal epidemic was apparently due to a new super-potent batch of heroin. The cocktail caused users to collapse on sidewalks, in night-clubs, on hotel stairs, and in railway stations. Ambulance teams were called out from all over the city to deal with the deadly epidemic. Doctors successfully revived 31 of the collapsed heroin users with the anti-heroin drug, naloxone (Narcan).

Source: Giles, R. "Australia: Killer Cocktail Fear for Addicts." *Melbourne Herald Sun* (April 18, 1998). Available hseditor@ozemail.com.au.

arise that are dangerous, even fatal. The interacting substance may be another drug, or it may be some substance in the diet or in the environment, such as a pesticide. Because of the increasing popularity of herbal products, we are also observing that herbs can interact with both prescription and nonprescription drugs. These interactions are not surprising because some of the herbs themselves contain drugs that occur naturally. Consequently, an herb that causes sedation almost certainly will enhance the depressing effects of either prescription or nonprescription sleep aids. Drug interaction is an area in which more research and public education are greatly needed.

Depending on the effect on the body, drug interaction may be categorized into three types: *additive, antagonistic (inhibitory),* and *potentiative (synergistic).*

■ ADDITIVE EFFECTS

Additive interactions are the combined effects of drugs taken concurrently. An example of an additive interaction results from using aspirin and acetaminophen (Tylenol) at the same time. The pain relief provided is equal to the sum of the two analgesics, which could be achieved by a comparable dose of either drug alone. Thus, if a 300-mg tablet of Bayer aspirin were taken with a 300-mg tablet of Tylenol, the relief would be the same as if two tablets of either Bayer Aspirin or Tylenol were taken instead.

■ ANTAGONISTIC (INHIBITORY) EFFECTS

Antagonistic interactions occur when one drug cancels or blocks the effect of another. For example, if you take antihistamines to reduce nasal congestion, you may be able to antagonize some of the drowsiness often caused by these drugs by using a central nervous system (CNS) stimulant such as caffeine.

It is likely that drug abusers who use two drugs at the same time often are trying to antagonize the unpleasant side effects of the first drug by administering the second. It has been reported that many of those currently abusing cocaine also use alcohol (Prevention Online 1998). The combined use of these two drugs may be a major factor in drug-related problems and death in emergency rooms (Karch 1996). Nevertheless, it appears that some users may coadminister these drugs in order to antagonize the disruptive effects of alcohol with the stimulant action of the cocaine (O'Brien 1995).

■ POTENTIATIVE (SYNERGISTIC) EFFECTS

The third type of drug interaction is known as *potentiation,* or synergism. Synergism occurs when the effect of a drug is enhanced by the presence of another drug or substance. A common example is the combination of alcohol and diazepam (Valium) (see Table 6.1). It has been estimated that as many as 3000 people die each year from mixing alcohol

TABLE 6.1 Common Interactions with Substances of Abuse

DRUG	COMBINED WITH	CONSEQUENCE OF INTERACTION
Sedatives		
Diazepam (Valium), triazolam (Halcion)	Alcohol, barbiturates	Increase sedation
Stimulants		
Amphetamines, cocaine	Insulin Antidepressants	Decrease insulin effect Cause hypertension
Narcotics		
Heroin, morphine	Barbiturates, Valium Anticoagulant Antidepressants Amphetamines	Increase sedation Increase bleeding Cause sedation Increase euphoria
Tobacco		
Nicotine	Blood-pressure medication Amphetamines, cocaine	Elevate blood pressure Increase cardiovascular effects
Alcohol	Cocaine	Produces cocaethylene, which enhances euphoria and toxicity

with CNS depressants such as Valium. Alcohol, like Valium, is a CNS depressant. When depressants are taken together, CNS functions become impaired and the person becomes groggy. A person in this state may forget that he or she has taken the pills and repeat the dose. The combination of these two depressants (or other depressants, such as antihistamines) can interfere with the CNS to the point where vital functions such as breathing and heartbeat are severely impaired.

Although the mechanisms of interaction among CNS depressants are not entirely clear, these drugs likely enhance one another's direct effects on inhibitory chemical messengers in the brain (see Chapter 5). In addition, interference by alcohol with liver-metabolizing enzymes also contributes to the synergism that arises with the combination of alcohol and some depressants, such as barbiturates (Hobbs et al. 1995).

■ DEALING WITH DRUG INTERACTIONS

Although many drug effects and interactions are not very well understood, it is important to be

aware of them. Increasing amounts of evidence indicate that many of the drugs and substances we deliberately consume will interact and produce unexpected and sometimes dangerous effects (see Table 6.1). It is alarming to know that many of the foods we eat and some chemical pollutants also interfere with and modify drug actions. Pesticides, traces of hormones in meat and poultry, traces of metals in fish, nitrites and nitrates from fertilizers, and a wide range of chemicals—some of which are used as food additives—have been shown, under

KEY TERMS

additive interactions
effects created when drugs are similar and add together
antagonistic interactions
effects created when drugs cancel one another
synergism
ability of one drug to enhance the effect of another; also called *potentiation*

certain conditions, to interact with some drugs (Correia 1998).

As the medical community has become aware of the frequent complications arising from multiple drug use, efforts have been made to reduce the incidence as well as the severity of the problem. It is essential that the public be educated about interactions most likely to occur with drugs that are prescribed, self-administered legitimately (for example, OTC drugs and herbal products), or taken recreationally (for example, drugs of abuse). People need to be aware that OTC and herbal drugs are as likely to cause interaction problems as prescription drugs. For example, an OTC or herbal decongestant (for example, ephedra), that contains mild CNS stimulants taken with potent CNS stimulants, such as cocaine and amphetamines, can cause interactions fatally affecting the heart and brain. If any question arises concerning the possibility of drug interaction, individuals should talk to their physicians, pharmacists, or other health care providers.

Most drug abusers are multiple drug (polydrug) users with little concern for the dangerous interactions that could occur. It is common, for example, for drug abusers to combine multiple CNS depressants to enhance their effects, to combine a depressant with a stimulant to *titrate* a CNS effect (to determine the smallest amount that can be taken to achieve the desired "high"), or to experiment with a combination of stimulants, depressants, and hallucinogens just to see what happens. The effects of such haphazard drug mixing are impossible to predict, difficult to treat in emergency situations, and all too frequently fatal.

Pharmacokinetic Factors That Influence Drug Effects

Although it is difficult to predict precisely how any single individual will be affected by drug use, the following major factors represent different aspects of the body's response that should be considered when attempting to anticipate a drug's effects (Correia 1998; Nicholas and Benet 1998).

1. How does the drug enter the body? (administration)

2. How does the drug move from the site of administration into the body's system? (absorption)

3. How does the drug move to various areas in the body? (distribution)

4. How and where does the drug produce its effects? (activation)

5. How is the drug inactivated, metabolized, and/or excreted from the body? (biotransformation and elimination)

These issues relate to the pharmacokinetics of a drug and are important considerations when predicting the body's response.

■ FORMS AND METHODS OF TAKING DRUGS

Drugs come in many forms. How a drug is formulated—solution, powder, capsule, or pill—influences the rate of passage into the bloodstream and consequently its efficacy.

The means of introducing the drug into the body will also affect how quickly the drug enters the bloodstream and how it is distributed to the site of action, as well as how much will ultimately reach its target and exert an effect (Mathias 1997) (see Figure 6.3). The principal forms of drug administration are *oral ingestion, inhalation, injection,* and *topical application.*

Oral Ingestion

One of the most common and convenient ways of taking a drug is orally. This type of administration usually introduces the drug into the body by way of the stomach or intestines.

Following oral administration, it is difficult to control the amount of drug that reaches the site of action, for three reasons:

1. The drug must enter the bloodstream after passing through the wall of the stomach or

---

KEY TERMS

pharmacokinetics
the study of factors that influence the distribution and concentration of drugs in the body

Method of Administration	Onset	Duration	Effect
Smoking			
cocaine	fast (~15 sec)	brief (10–15 min)	potent and strong
heroin	fast (~20 sec)	short (1–2 hr)	potent and strong
Intravenous			
cocaine	fast (20 sec)	short (30 min)	potent and strong
heroin	fast (1–2 min)	short (1–2 hr)	potent and strong
Snorting			
cocaine	moderate (~10 min)	short (45 min)	less potent
heroin	moderate (~15 min)	short (1–2 hr)	less potent
Oral			
cocaine (coca leaf)	slow (30 min)	moderate (~2–4 hr)	minor
methadone	slow (30–60 min)	long (24 hr)	less euphoria/ used for treatent

FIGURE 6.3

Relationship between the method of drug administration and drug effects.

intestines without being destroyed or changed to an inactive form. From the blood, the drug must diffuse to the target area and remain there in sufficient concentration to have an effect.

2. Materials in the stomach or intestines, such as food, may interfere with the passage of some drugs through the gut lining and thus prevent drug action. For example, food in your stomach will diminish the effects of alcohol because food interferes with alcohol's absorption.

3. The liver might metabolize orally ingested drugs too rapidly, before they are able to exert an effect. The liver is the major detoxifying organ in the body, which means it removes chemicals and toxins from the blood and usually changes them into an inactive form that is easy for the body to excrete. This function is essential to survival, but it creates a problem for the pharmacologist developing effective drugs. The liver is especially problematic to oral administration because the substances absorbed from the digestive tract usually go to the liver before being distributed to other parts of the body and their site of action. For this reason, cocaine taken orally is not very effective.

Inhalation

Some drugs are administered by inhalation into the lungs through the mouth or nose. The lungs include large beds of capillaries, so chemicals capable of crossing membranes can enter the blood as rapidly as intravenous (IV) injection and can be equally as dangerous (Meng et al. 1999). Ether, chloroform, and nitrous oxide anesthetics are examples of drugs that are therapeutically administered by inhalation. Nicotine, cocaine, methamphetamine, and heroin are drugs of abuse that can be inhaled as smoke (Mathias 1997). One serious problem with inhalation is the potential for irritation to the mucous membrane lining of the lungs; another is that the drug may have to be continually inhaled to maintain the concentration necessary for an effect. Inhalation of illicit drugs of abuse is common to prevent contracting AIDS, which can be transmitted by IV injection with contaminated needles (Meng 1999; NIDA Notes 1999).

Injection

Some drugs are given by injection: intravenously (IV), intramuscularly (IM), or subcutaneously (SC). A major advantage of administering drugs by IV is the speed of action; the dosage is delivered rapidly and directly, and often less drug is needed because it reaches the site of action quickly. This method can be very dangerous if the dosage is calculated incorrectly. Additionally, impurities in injected materials may irritate the vein; this issue is a particular problem in the drug abusing population, where needle sharing frequently occurs. The injection itself injures the vein by leaving a tiny point of scar tissue where the vein is punctured. If repeated injections are administered into the same area, the elasticity of the vein is gradually reduced, causing the vessel to collapse.

Intramuscular injection can damage the muscle directly if the drug preparation irritates the tissue or indirectly if the nerve controlling the muscle is damaged. If the nerve is destroyed, the muscle will degenerate (atrophy). An SC injection may kill the skin at the point of injection if a particularly irritating drug is administered. Another danger of drug injections occurs when contaminated needles are shared by drug users. This danger has become a serious problem in the spread of infectious diseases such as AIDS and hepatitis.

Topical Application

Those drugs that readily pass through surface tissue such as the skin, the lining of the nose, and the mouth can be applied topically, for systemic (whole-body) effects. Although most drugs do not appreciably diffuse across these tissue barriers into the circulation, there are notable exceptions. For example, a product to help quit smoking, a nicotine transdermal patch (Nicoderm), is placed on the skin; the drug passes through the skin and enters the body to prevent tobacco craving and withdrawal.

■ DISTRIBUTION OF DRUGS IN THE BODY AND TIME-RESPONSE RELATIONSHIPS

Following administration (regardless of the mode), most drugs are distributed throughout the body in the blood. The circulatory system consists of many miles of arteries, veins, and capillaries and includes 5 to 6 liters of blood. Once a drug enters the bloodstream by passing through thin capillary walls, it is rapidly diluted and carried to organs and other body structures. It requires approximately 1 minute for the blood, and consequently the drugs it contains, to circulate completely throughout the body.

Factors Affecting Distribution

Drugs have different patterns of distribution depending on their chemical properties (Nicholas and Benet 1998; Correia 1998):

- Their ability to pass across membranes and through tissues

- Their molecular size (large versus small molecules)

- Their solubility properties (do they dissolve in water or in fatty [oily] solutions?)

- Their tendency to attach to proteins and tissues throughout the body

These distribution-related factors are very important because they determine whether a drug can pass across tissue barriers in the body and reach its site of action. By preventing the movement of

---

KEY TERMS

intravenously (IV)
drug injection into a vein

intramuscularly (IM)
drug injection into a muscle

subcutaneously (SC)
drug injection beneath the skin

blood-brain barrier
selective filtering between the cerebral blood vessels and the brain

threshold
minimum drug dose necessary to cause an effect

plateau effect
maximum drug effect, regardless of dose

acute
immediate or short-term effects after taking a single drug dose

chronic
long-term effects, usually after taking multiple drug doses

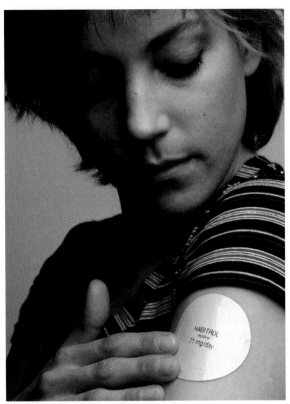

Nicoderm patches contain topical nicotine to help smokers stop their drug habit.

drugs into organs or across tissues, these barriers may interfere with drug activity and limit the therapeutic usefulness of a drug if they do not allow it to reach its site of action. Such barriers may also offer protection by preventing entry of a drug into a body structure where it can cause problems.

Blood is carried to the nerve cells of the brain in a vast network of thin-walled capillaries. Drugs that are soluble in fatty (oily) solutions are most likely to pass across these capillary membranes (known as the blood-brain barrier) into the brain tissue. Most psychoactive drugs, such as the drugs of abuse, are able to pass across the blood-brain barrier with little difficulty. However, many water-soluble drugs cannot pass through the fatty capillary wall; such drugs are not likely to cross this biological barrier and affect the brain.

A second biological barrier, the placenta, prevents the transfer of certain molecules from the mother to the fetus. A principal factor that determines passage of substances across the placental barrier is molecule size. Large molecules do not usually cross the placental barrier, whereas small molecules do. Because most drugs are relatively small molecules, they usually cross from the maternal circulation into the fetal circulation; thus, most drugs (including the drugs of abuse) taken by a woman during pregnancy enter and affect the fetus.

Required Doses for Effects

Most drugs do not take effect until a certain amount has been administered and a crucial concentration has reached the site of action in the body. The smallest amount of a drug needed to elicit a response is called its threshold .

The effectiveness of some drugs may be calculated in a *linear* (straight-line) fashion—that is, the more drug that is taken, the more drug distributes throughout the body and the greater the effect. However, many drugs have a maximum possible effect, regardless of dose; this is called the plateau effect . OTC medications, in particular, have a limit on their effects. For example, use of the nonprescription analgesic aspirin can effectively relieve your mild to moderate pain, but aspirin will not effectively treat your severe pains, regardless of dose. Other drugs may cause distinct or opposite effects, depending on the dose. For example, low doses of alcohol may appear to act like a stimulant, whereas high doses usually cause sedation.

The Time-Response Factors

An important factor that determines responses is the time that has elapsed between when a drug was administered and the onset of its effects. The delay in effect after administering a drug often relates to the time required for the drug to disseminate from the site of administration to the site of action. Consequently, the closer a drug is placed to the target area, the faster the onset of action.

The drug response is often classified as immediate, short-term, or acute , referring to the response after a single dose. The response can also be chronic , or long-term, a characteristic usually associated with repeated doses. The intensity and quality of a drug's acute effect may change considerably within a short period of time. For example, the main intoxicating effects of a large dose of alcohol generally peak in less than 1 hour and then gradually taper off. In addition, an initial stimulating effect by alcohol may later change to sedation and depression.

The effects of long-term, or chronic, use of some drugs can differ dramatically from their short-term, or acute, use. The administration of small doses may not produce any immediately apparent detrimental effect, but chronic use of the same drug (frequent use over a long time) may yield prolonged effects that do not become apparent until years later. Although for most people there is little evidence to show any immediate damage or detrimental response to short-term use of small doses of tobacco, its chronic use has damaging effects on heart and lung functions. Because of these long-term consequences, research on tobacco and its effects often continues for years, making it difficult to unequivocally prove a correlation between specific diseases or health problems and use of this substance. Thus, the results of tobacco research are often disputed by tobacco manufacturers with vested financial interests in the substance and its public acceptance.

Another important time factor that influences drug responses is the interval between multiple administrations. If sufficient time for drug metabolism and elimination does not separate doses, a drug can accumulate within the body. This drug buildup due to relatively short dosing intervals is referred to as a cumulative effect . Because of the resulting high concentrations of drug in the body, unexpected prolonged drug effects or toxicity can occur when multiple doses are given within short intervals. This situation occurs with cocaine or methamphetamine addicts who repeatedly administer these stimulants during "binges" or "runs," increasing the likelihood of dangerous effects.

■ INACTIVATION AND ELIMINATION OF DRUGS FROM THE BODY

Immediately after drug administration, the body begins to eliminate the substance in various ways. The time required to remove half of the original amount of drug administered is called the half-life of the drug. The body will eliminate the drug either directly without altering it chemically or (in most instances) after it has been metabolized (chemically altered) or modified. The process of changing the chemical or pharmacological properties of a drug by metabolism is called biotransformation (Correia 1998). Metabolism usually (but not always) makes it possible for the body to inactivate, detoxify, and excrete drugs and other chemicals.

The liver is the primary organ that metabolizes drugs in the body. It is a complex biochemical laboratory containing hundreds of enzymes that continuously synthesize, modify, and deactivate biochemical substances such as drugs. The healthy liver is also capable of metabolizing many of the chemicals that occur naturally in the body (such as hormones). After the liver enzymes metabolize a drug (the resulting chemicals are called metabolites), the products usually pass into the urine or feces for final elimination. Drugs and their metabolites can appear in other places as well, such as sweat, saliva, or expired air.

The kidneys are probably the next most important organ for drug elimination because they remove metabolites and foreign substances from the body. The kidneys constantly eliminate substances from the blood. The rate of excretion of some drugs by the kidneys can be altered by making the urine more acidic or more alkaline. For example, nicotine and amphetamines can be cleared faster from the body by making the urine slightly more acidic, and salicylates and barbiturates can be cleared more rapidly by making it more alkaline. Such techniques are used in emergency rooms and can be useful in the treatment of drug overdosing.

The body may eliminate small portions of drugs through perspiration and exhalation. Approximately 1% of consumed alcohol is eliminated in the breath and thus may be measured with a Breathalyzer; this apparatus is used by police officers in evaluating suspected drunk drivers. Most people are aware that consumption of garlic will change body odor because garlic is excreted through perspiration. Some drugs are handled in the same way. The mammary glands are modified sweat glands, so it is not surprising that many drugs are concentrated and excreted in milk during lactation, including antibiotics, nicotine, barbiturates, caffeine, and alcohol. Excretion of drugs in a mother's milk can pose a particular concern during nursing, as the excreted drugs can be consumed by and affect the infant.

The Breathalyzer takes advantage of the fact that alcohol is partially eliminated from the body in the breath.

■ PHYSIOLOGICAL VARIABLES THAT MODIFY DRUG EFFECTS

As previously mentioned, individuals' responses to drugs vary greatly, even when the same doses are administered in the same manner. This variability can be especially troublesome when dealing with drugs that have a narrow margin of safety. Many of these variables reflect differences in the pharmacokinetic factors just discussed and are associated with diversity in body size, composition, or functions. They include the following (Nies and Spielberg 1995):

Age Changes in body size and makeup occur throughout the aging process, from infancy to old age. Changes in the rates of drug absorption, biotransformation, and elimination also arise as a consequence of aging. As a general rule, young children and elderly people should be administered lower drug doses (calculated as drug quantity per unit of body weight) due to immature or compromised body processes.

Gender Variations in drug responses due to gender usually relate to differences in body size, composition, or hormones (male versus female types—for example, androgens versus estrogens). Most clinicians find many more similarities than differences between males and females relative to their responses to drugs.

Pregnancy During the course of pregnancy, unique factors must be considered when administering drugs. For example, the physiology of the mother changes as the fetus develops and puts additional stress on organ systems, such as the heart, liver, and kidneys. This increased demand can make the woman more susceptible to the toxicity of some drugs. In addition, as the fetus develops, it can be very vulnerable to drugs with teratogenic (causing abnormal development) properties. Consequently, it is usually advisable to avoid taking any drugs during pregnancy, if possible.

■ PATHOLOGICAL VARIABLES THAT MODIFY DRUG EFFECTS

Individuals with diseases or compromised organ systems need to be particularly careful when taking drugs (Nies and Spielberg 1995) (see "Here and Now," Marijuana Use Promotes Tumor Growth and May Impair Defenses Against Cancer, page 146). Some diseases can damage or impair organs that are vital for appropriate and safe responses to drugs. For example, *hepatitis* (inflammation and damage to the liver) interferes with the metabolism and disposal of many drugs, resulting in a longer duration of drug action and increased likelihood of side effects. Similar concerns are associated with kidney disease, which causes compromised renal activity and diminished excretion capacity. Because many drugs

KEY TERMS

cumulative effect
buildup of a drug in the body after multiple doses taken at short intervals

half-life
time required for the body to eliminate and/or metabolize half of a drug dose

biotransformation
process of changing the chemical properties of a drug, usually by metabolism

metabolism
chemical alteration of drugs by body processes

metabolites
chemical products of metabolism

teratogenic
something that causes physical defects in the fetus

HERE AND NOW

Marijuana Use Promotes Tumor Growth and May Impair Defenses Against Cancer

Reports in the July 2000 issue of the *Journal of Immunology* demonstrated that tetrahydrocannabinol (THC), the major psychoactive ingredient in marijuana, may promote cancer by interfering with the body's ability to produce antitumor immune responses. A research group from UCLA's Jonsson Comprehensive Cancer Center observed that administration of THC to mice stimulated the production of two types of cytokines that are potent immune suppressors capable of interfering with the body's ability to fight the growth of tumors, such as cancer. This observation demonstrates that receptors activated by THC (called *cannabioid* receptors) are important in regulating the body's immune system. These findings suggest that regular inhalation of marijuana smoke may significantly increase the user's likelihood of developing cancer.

Source: NIDA News Release (July 17, 2000). Available www.nida.nih.gov/MedAdv/00/NR6-20.html.

affect the cardiovascular system (especially drugs of abuse, such as stimulants, tobacco, and alcohol), patients with a history of cardiovascular disease (heart attack, stroke, hypertension, or abnormal heart rhythm) should be particularly cautious when using drugs. They should be aware of medicines that stimulate the cardiovascular system, especially those that are self-medicated, such as OTC decongestants. These drugs should either be avoided or used only under the supervision of a physician.

Adaptive Processes and Drug Abuse

Your body systems are constantly changing so that they can establish and maintain balance in their physiological and mental functions; such balance is necessary for optimal functioning of all organ systems, including the brain, heart, lungs, gastrointestinal tract, liver, and kidneys. Sometimes drugs interfere with the activity of the body's systems and compromise their normal workings. These drug-induced disruptions can be so severe that they can even cause death. For example, stimulants can dangerously increase the heart rate and blood pressure and cause heart attacks, while CNS depressants can diminish brain activity, resulting in unconsciousness and a loss of breathing reflexes.

To protect against potential harm, the organ systems of the body can adjust to disruption. Of particular relevance to drugs of abuse are adaptive processes known as *tolerance* and dependence (both psychological and physical types) and the related phenomenon of *withdrawal* (see Figure 6.4).

Tolerance and dependence are closely linked, most likely to result from multiple drug exposures, and thought to be caused by similar mechanisms. Tolerance occurs when the response to the same dose of a drug decreases with repeated use (Goldstein 1994). Increasing the dose can sometimes compensate for tolerance to a drug of abuse. For the most part, the adaptations that cause the tolerance phenomenon are also associated with altered physi-

KEY TERMS

dependence
physiological and psychological changes or adaptations that occur in response to the frequent administration of a drug

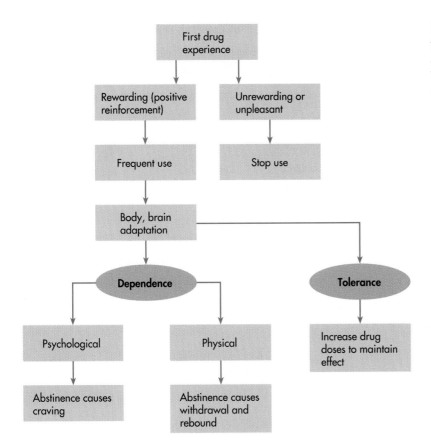

FIGURE 6.4
The relationship and consequences of adaptive processes to drug use. The processes discussed in the text are highlighted in the figure.

cal and psychological states that lead to dependence. These altered states reflect the efforts of the body and brain to reestablish balance in the continual presence of a drug. The user develops dependence in the sense that if the drug is no longer taken, the symptoms of the body become overcompensated and unbalanced, causing withdrawal. In general, withdrawal symptoms are opposite in nature to the direct effects of the drug that caused the dependence (Goldstein 1994).

Although tolerance, dependence, and withdrawal are all consequences of adaptation by the body and its systems, they are not inseparable processes. It is possible to become tolerant to a drug without developing dependence and vice versa (see Table 6.2). The following sections provide greater detail about these adaptive drug responses, which are very important for many therapeutic drugs and almost all drugs of abuse (O'Brien 1995).

■ TOLERANCE TO DRUGS

The extent of tolerance and the rate at which it is acquired depends on the drug, the person using the drug, the dosage, and the frequency of administration. Some drug effects may be reduced more rapidly than others when drugs are used frequently. Tolerance to effects that are rewarding or reinforcing often causes users to increase the dosage. Sometimes, abstinence from a drug can reduce tolerance, but with renewed use, the tolerance often builds quickly.

The body does not necessarily develop tolerance to all effects of a drug equally. For example, with repeated use, a moderate degree of tolerance develops to most effects of alcohol and barbiturates. A heavy drinker may be able to consume two or three times the alcohol tolerated by an occasional drinker. Little tolerance develops, however, to the lethal toxicity of these drugs. A heavy user of sedatives is just

TABLE 6.2 **Tolerance, Dependence, and Withdrawal Properties of Common Drugs of Abuse**

DRUG	TOLERANCE	PSYCHOLOGICAL DEPENDENCE	PHYSICAL DEPENDENCE	WITHDRAWAL SYMPTOMS (INCLUDE REBOUND EFFECTS)
Barbiturates	■■	■■	■■■	Restlessness, anxiety, vomiting, tremors, seizures
Alcohol	■■	■■	■■■	Cramps, delirium, vomiting, sweating, hallucinations, seizures
Benzodiazepines	■	■■	■■	Insomnia, restlessness, nausea, fatigue, twitching, seizures (rare)
Narcotics (heroin)	■■■	■■	■■■	Vomiting, sweating, cramps, diarrhea, depression, irritability, gooseflesh
Cocaine, amphetamines	■*	■■■	■■	Depression, anxiety, drug craving, need for sleep ("crash"), anhedonia
Nicotine	■	■■	■■	Highly variable; craving, irritability, headache, increased appetite, abnormal sleep
Caffeine	■	■	■	Anxiety, lethargy, headache, fatigue
Marijuana	■	■	■	Irritability, restlessness, decreased appetite, weight loss, abnormal sleep
LSD (lysergic acid diethylamide)	■■	■	—	Minimal
PCP (phencyclidine)	■	■	■	Fear, tremors, some craving, problems with short-term memory

■■■ Intense   ■■ Moderate   ■ Some   — Not significant
*Can sensitize.

as susceptible to death by overdose as a nontolerant person, even though the heavy user has been forced to increase doses to maintain the relaxing effects of the drug. In contrast, frequent use of opiate narcotics such as morphine can cause profound tolerance, even to the lethal effects of these drugs. Heavy users have been known to use routinely up to 10 times the amount that would kill a nonuser.

The exact mechanisms by which the body becomes tolerant to different drug effects are not completely understood, but as mentioned earlier, may be related to those mechanisms that cause dependence (Goldstein 1994). Several processes have been suggested. Drugs such as barbiturates stimulate the body's production of metabolic enzymes, primarily in the liver, and cause drugs to be inactivated and eliminated faster. In addition, evidence suggests that a considerable degree of CNS tolerance to some drugs develops independent of changes in the rate of metabolism or excretion. This process reflects the adaptation of drug target sites in nervous tissue, so that the effect of the same concentration of drug decreases. If you were tolerant to alcohol, for example, you would be relatively unaffected by several glasses of wine. This situation may be due to some general molecular adaptation to the drug at the level of the individual nerve cell, or it may be caused by a specific brain response that counteracts the sedating effects and maintains normal function (for example, counterbalancing excitatory system is enhanced to compensate for the depression caused by the alcohol).

Another type of drug response that can appear to be tolerance, but is actually a learned adjustment, is called *behavioral compensation*. Drug effects that are troubling may be compensated for or hidden by the drug user. Thus, alcoholics learn to speak and walk slowly to compensate for the slurred speech and stumbling gait they usually experience. To an observer, it might appear as though the pharmacological effects of the drug are diminished, but they are actually unchanged. Consequently, this type of adaptation is not a true form of tolerance.

Other Tolerance-Related Factors

The tolerance process can affect drug responses in several ways. We have discussed the effect of tolerance that diminishes the action of drugs and causes the user to compensate by increasing the dose. The following are examples of two other ways that the tolerance process can influence drug responses.

Reverse Tolerance (Sensitization) Under some conditions, a response to a drug is elicited that is the opposite of tolerance. This effect is known as reverse tolerance , or sensitization. If you were sensitized, you would have the same response to a lower dose of a drug as you initially did to the original, higher dose. This condition seems to occur in users of marijuana and some hallucinogens, as well as amphetamines and cocaine (O'Brien 1995).

Although the causes of reverse tolerance are still unclear, some researchers believe that its development depends on how often and how much of the drug is consumed. It has been speculated that this heightened response to drugs of abuse may reflect adaptive changes in the nervous tissues (target site of these drugs). The reverse tolerance that occurs with cocaine use may be responsible for the psychotic effects or the seizures caused by chronic use of this drug (O'Brien 1995).

Cross-Tolerance Development of tolerance to a drug sometimes can produce tolerance to other similar drugs: this phenomenon, known as cross-tolerance , may be due to altered metabolism resulting from

chronic drug use. For example, a heavy drinker will usually exhibit tolerance to barbiturates, other depressants, and anesthetics because the alcohol has induced (stimulated) his or her liver metabolic enzymes. Cross-tolerance might also occur among drugs that cause similar pharmacological actions. For example, if adaptations have occurred in nervous tissue that cause tolerance to one drug, such changes might also produce tolerance to other similar drugs that exert their effects by interacting with that same nervous tissue site. This type of cross-tolerance has been shown to develop among some of the hallucinogens, such as lysergic acid diethylamide (LSD), mescaline, and psilocybin.

■ DRUG DEPENDENCE

Drug dependence can be associated with either physiological or psychological adaptations. Physical dependence reflects changes in the way organs and systems in the body respond to a drug, whereas psychological dependence is caused by changes in attitudes and expectations. In both types of dependence, the individual experiences a need (either physical or emotional) for the drug to be present in order for the body or the mind to function normally.

Physical Dependence

In general, the drugs that cause physical dependence also cause a drug withdrawal phenomenon called the rebound effect . This condition is sometimes known as the *paradoxical effect* because the symptoms associated with rebound are nearly opposite to the direct effects of the drug. For example, a person taking barbiturates or benzodiazepines will be

---

KEY TERMS

reverse tolerance
enhanced response to a given drug dose; opposite of tolerance

cross-tolerance
development of tolerance to one drug causes tolerance to related drugs

rebound effect
form of withdrawal; paradoxical effects that occur when a drug has been eliminated from the body

greatly depressed physically but during withdrawal may become irritable, hyperexcited, and nervous and generally show symptoms of extreme stimulation of the nervous system, even life-threatening seizures. These reactions constitute the rebound effect.

Physical dependence may develop with high-intensity use of such common drugs as alcohol, barbiturates, narcotics, and other CNS depressants. However, with moderate, intermittent use of these drugs, most people do not become physically dependent. Those who do become physically dependent experience damaged social and personal skills and relationships and impaired brain and motor functions.

Withdrawal symptoms resulting from physical dependency can be prevented by administering a sufficient quantity of the original drug or one with similar pharmacological activity. The latter case, in which different drugs can be used interchangeably to prevent withdrawal symptoms, is called cross-dependence . For example, barbiturates and other CNS depressants can be used to treat the abstinence syndrome experienced by the chronic alcoholic. Another example is the use of methadone, a long-acting narcotic, to treat withdrawal from heroin (Zickler 1999). Such therapeutic strategies allow the substitution of safer and more easily managed drugs for dangerous drugs of abuse and play a major role in treatment of drug dependency.

Psychological Dependence

The World Health Organization states that psychological dependence instills a feeling of satisfaction and psychic drive that requires periodic or continuous administration of the drug to produce a desired effect or to avoid psychological discomfort. This sense of dependence usually leads to repeated self-administration of the drug in a fashion described as abuse. This type of dependence may be found either independent of or associated with physical dependence. Psychological dependence does not produce the physical discomfort, rebound effects, or life-threatening consequences that can be associated with physical dependence. Even so, it does produce intense cravings and strong urges that frequently lure former drug abusers back to their habits of drug self-administration. In many instances, psychological aspects may be more significant than physical dependence in maintaining chronic drug use. Thus, the major problem with cocaine or nicotine dependence is not the physical aspect, because withdrawal can be successfully achieved in a few weeks; rather, strong urges often cause a return to chronic use of these substances because of psychological dependence.

How does psychological dependence develop? If the first drug trial is rewarding, a few more rewarding trials will follow until drug use becomes a conditioned pattern of behavior. Continued positive psychological reinforcement with the drug leads, in time, to primary psychological dependence. Primary psychological dependence, in turn, may produce uncontrollable compulsive abuse of any psychoactive drug in certain susceptible people and cause physical dependence. The degree of drug dependence is contingent on the nature of the psychoactive substance, the quantity used, the duration of use, and the characteristics of the person and his or her environment. It is often not possible to make a sharp distinction between use and abuse when it comes to developing dependence; many shades of gray separate the drug user and the drug addict.

Even strong psychological dependence on some psychoactive substances does not necessarily result in injury or social harm. For example, typical dosages of mild stimulants such as coffee usually do not induce serious physical, social, or emotional harm. Even though the effects on the CNS are barely detectable by a casual observer, strong psychological dependence on stimulants like tobacco and caffeine-containing beverages may develop; however, the fact that their dependence does not typically induce antisocial behavior distinguishes them from most forms of dependence-producing drugs.

Psychological Factors

The general effect of most drugs is greatly influenced by a variety of psychological and environmental factors. Unique qualities of an individual's personality, his or her past history of drug and social experience, attitudes toward the drug, expectations of its effects, and motivation for use are extremely influential (see "Case in Point," Researchers Probe Which Comes First, Drug Abuse or Antisocial Behavior?). These factors are often referred to collectively as the person's mental set . The setting, or

CASE IN POINT

Researchers Probe Which Comes First, Drug Abuse or Antisocial Behavior?

A study conducted by the University of Colorado School of Medicine and directed by Thomas Crowley, a psychiatrist, asked 51 troubled substance-abusing boys, ages 14 to 19, how and when their antisocial behavior began. All the boys were diagnosed with conduct disorders and were enrolled in a Denver residential drug abuse treatment improvement program. Seventy-seven percent of the boys claimed to have engaged in their antisocial behavior (including stealing, truancy, fighting, arson, property destruction, cruelty to people or animals, lying, and running away) 1 to 13 years before regular drug use, suggesting that there is a link between antisocial behavior and a tendency to abuse drugs. (Swan 1993).

---

total environment, in which a drug is taken may also modify its effect.

The mental set and setting are particularly important in influencing the responses to psychoactive drugs (drugs that alter the functions of the brain). For example, ingestion of LSD, a commonly abused hallucinogen, can cause pleasant, even spiritual-like experiences in comfortable, congenial surroundings. In contrast, when the same amount of LSD is consumed in hostile, threatening surroundings, the effect can be frightening, taking on a nightmarish quality.

■ THE PLACEBO EFFECT

The psychological factors that influence responses to drugs, independent of their pharmacological properties, are known as placebo effects . The word *placebo* is derived from Latin and means "I shall please." The placebo effect is most likely to occur when an individual's mental set is susceptible to suggestion. A placebo drug is a pharmacologically inactive compound that the user thinks causes some therapeutic change.

In some persons or in particular settings, a placebo substance may have surprisingly powerful consequences (Nies and Spielberg 1995). For example, a substantial component of most pain is perception. Consequently, placebos administered as pain relievers and promoted properly can provide dramatic relief. Therefore, in spite of what appears to be a drug effect, the placebo is not considered a pharmacological agent because it does not directly alter any body functions by its chemical nature.

The bulk of medical history may actually be a history of confidence in the cure—a history of placebo medicine—because many effective cures of the past have been shown to be without relevant pharmacological action, suggesting that their effects were psychologically mediated. In fact, even today, some people argue that placebo effects are a significant component of most drug therapy, particularly when using OTC medications or herbal products. Medical researchers currently are investigating so-called psychological cures, attempting to identify which factors contribute to this interesting

KEY TERMS

cross-dependence
dependence on a drug can be relieved by other similar drugs

psychological dependence
dependence that results because a drug produces pleasant mental effects

mental set
the collection of psychological and environmental factors that influence an individual's response to drugs

placebo effects
effects caused by suggestion and psychological factors independent of the pharmacological activity of a drug

phenomenon. It is important when testing new drugs for effectiveness that drug experiments be conducted in a manner that allows a distinction between pharmacological and placebo effects. Such studies can usually be done by treating one group with the real drug and another group with a placebo that looks like the drug and then comparing the responses to both treatments.

In some situations, perhaps placebos, or perhaps the power of suggestion, activate endogenous systems that help relieve medical problems or associated symptoms (Sherman 1992). The activation of such endogenous systems most likely explains the effectiveness of placebos against pain. A family of *peptides* (called *endorphins*) produced by the body acts similar to morphine and other opiate narcotics (Hughes 1975). The endorphins, among other things, are potent *endogenous analgesics* (substances that block pain) that provide the means for the body to defend itself against the debilitating effects of extreme pain. Research has shown that placebos cause the release of the endorphins to control pain. Other placebo effects may have similar biochemical bases in that they cause the release of endogenous substances that influence the body's functions and alter the course of disease. Just as the placebo effect can alter therapeutic responses, it may also influence responses to drugs of abuse.

Addiction and Abuse: The Significance of Dependence

The term *addiction* has many meanings (see Chapter 4). It is often used interchangeably with *dependence,* either physiological or psychological in nature; other times, it is used synonymously with the term *drug abuse* (drug addiction).

The traditional model of the addiction-producing drug is based on opiate narcotics and requires the individual to develop tolerance and both physical and psychological dependence. This model often is not satisfactory because only a few commonly abused drugs fit its parameters. It is clearly inadequate for many other drugs that can cause serious dependency problems but that produce little tolerance, even with extended use (see Table 6.2).

Because it is difficult to assess the contribution of physical and psychological factors to drug dependency, determining whether all psychoactive drugs truly cause drug addiction poses a challenge. To alleviate confusion, it has been suggested that the term *dependence* (either physical or psychological) be used instead of *addiction.* However, because of its acceptance by the public, the term *addiction* is not likely to disappear from general use.

Some have speculated that the only means by which drug dependence can be eliminated from society is to prevent exposure to those drugs that have the potential to be abused. Because some drugs are such powerful, immediate reinforcers (i.e., they cause a rapid reward), it is feared that rapid dependence (psychological) will occur when anyone uses them. Although it may be true that most people, under certain conditions, could become dependent on some drug with abuse potential, in reality, most people who have used psychoactive drugs do not develop significant psychological or physical dependence. For example, approximately 87% of those who use alcohol experience minimal personal injury and few negative social consequences. Of those who have used stimulants, depressants, or hallucinogens for illicit recreational purposes, only 10% to 20% become dependent (O'Brien 1995). The following sections discuss some possible reasons for the variability.

■ HEREDITARY FACTORS

The reasons why some people readily develop dependence on psychoactive drugs and others do not are not well understood. One factor may be heredity, which predisposes some people to drug abuse (Wyman 1997). For example, studies of identical and fraternal twins have revealed that a greater similarity in the rate of alcoholism for identical twins than for fraternal twins occurs if alcohol abuse begins before the age of 20 years (McGue et al. 1992; Vanyukov and Tarter 2000). Because identical twins have 100% of their genes in common whereas fraternal twins share only 50%, these results suggest that genetic factors can be important in determining the likelihood of alcohol dependence (Wyman 1997). It is possible that similar genetic factors contribute to other types of drug dependence as well (Vanyukov and Tarter 2000).

■ DRUG CRAVING

Frequently, a person who becomes dependent develops a powerful, uncontrollable desire for drugs during or after withdrawal from heroin, cocaine, alcohol, nicotine, or other addicting substances: this desire for drugs is known as *craving*. Because researchers do not agree as to the nature of craving, there does not exist a universally recognized scientific definition or an accepted method to measure this psychological phenomenon. Some drug abuse experts claim that craving is the principal cause of drug abuse; others believe that it is not a cause but a side effect of drugs that produce dependence. Craving is often assessed by (1) questioning patients about the intensity of their drug urges; (2) measuring physiological changes such as increases in heart and breathing rates, sweating, and subtle changes in the tension of facial muscles; and (3) determining patients' tendency to relapse into drug-taking behavior (Swan 1993).

Evidence indicates that at least two levels of craving can exist. For example, cocaine users experience an acute craving when using the drug itself, but the ex-cocaine abuser can have chronic cravings that are triggered by familiar environmental cues that elicit positive memories of cocaine's reinforcing effects.

Although it is not likely that craving itself causes drug addiction, it is generally believed that, if pharmacological or psychological therapies could be devised that reduced or eliminated drug craving, treatment of drug dependence would be more successful. Thus, many researchers are attempting to identify drugs or psychological strategies that interfere with the development and expression of the craving phenomenon.

■ OTHER FACTORS

If a drug causes a positive effect in the user's view, it is much more likely to be abused than if it causes an aversive experience (see Figure 6.4). Perhaps genetic factors influence the brain or personality so that some people find taking drugs an enjoyable experience (at least initially), whereas others find the effects very unpleasant and uncomfortable (dysphoric). Other factors that could also contribute significantly to drug use patterns include (1) peer pressure (especially in the initial drug experimentation); (2) home, school,

dysphoric
characterized by unpleasant mental effects; the opposite of euphoric

and work environment (Mello and Griffith 1987); and (3) mental state. It is estimated that 30% to 60% of drug abusers have some underlying psychiatric illness such as personality disorder, major depression, bipolar disorder, or schizophrenia (Leshner 1999). In some cases, the drug user may be attempting to relieve symptoms associated with the mental disorder by self-medicating with the substance of abuse (Addington 1997). Consequently, it is not surprising that one treatment for cocaine abuse has been the antidepressant desipramine (O'Brien 1995).

It is difficult to identify all of the specific factors that influence the risk of drug abuse for each individual. (Some of the possible influences are discussed in Chapter 2.) If such factors could be identified, treatment would be improved and those at greatest risk for drug abuse could be determined and informed of their vulnerability.

Discussion Questions

1. What is the significance of drug "potency" in the therapeutic use and the abuse of drugs?

2. How can drug interactions be both detrimental and beneficial? Give examples of each.

3. Why would a drug with a relatively narrow "margin of safety" be approved by the Food and Drug Administration for clinical use?

4. What are possible explanations for the fact that you (for example) may require twice as much of a drug to get an effect as does your friend?

5. What significance would the blood-brain barrier have on drugs with abuse potential?

6. Contrary to your advice, a friend is going to spend $20 on cocaine. What significance will the pharmacokinetic concepts of threshold,

half-life, cumulative effect, and biotransformation have on your friend's drug experience?

7. How would the factors of tolerance, physical dependence, rebound, and psychological dependence affect a chronic heroin user?

8. Why would the lack of physical dependence on LSD for some drug abusers make it preferable to cocaine, which does cause physical dependence?

Key Terms

main effects **134**

side effects **134**

withdrawal **134**

dose-response **136**

tolerance **136**

margin of safety **136**

potency **137**

toxicity **137**

drug interaction **137**

additive interactions **138**

antagonistic interactions **138**

synergism **138**

pharmacokinetics **140**

intravenously (IV) **142**

intramuscularly (IM) **142**

subcutaneously (SC) **142**

blood-brain barrier **143**

threshold **143**

plateau effect **143**

acute **143**

chronic **143**

cumulative effect **144**

half-life **144**

biotransformation **144**

metabolism **144**

metabolites **144**

teratogenic **145**

dependence **146**

reverse tolerance **149**

cross-tolerance **149**

rebound effect **149**

cross-dependence **150**

psychological dependence **150**

mental set **150**

placebo effects **151**

dysphoric **153**

Summary

1 All drugs have intended and unintended effects. The unintended actions of drugs can include effects such as nausea, altered mental states, dependence, a variety of allergic responses, and changes in the cardiovascular system.

2 Many factors can affect the way an individual responds to a drug: dose, inherent toxicity, potency, and pharmacokinetic properties such as the rate of absorption into the body, the way it is distributed throughout the body, and the manner in which and rate at which it is metabolized and eliminated. The form of the drug as well as the manner in which it is administered can also affect the response to a drug.

3 *Potency* is determined by the amount of a drug necessary to cause a given effect. *Toxicity* is the ability of the drug to affect the body adversely. A drug that is very toxic is very potent in terms of causing a harmful effect.

4 A drug's *margin of safety* relates to the difference in the drug doses that cause a therapeutic or a toxic effect; the bigger the difference, the greater the margin of safety.

5 *Additive* interactions occur when the effects of two drugs are combined; for example, the analgesic effects of aspirin plus acetaminophen are additive. Antagonistic effects occur when the effects of two drugs cancel; for example, the stimulant effects of caffeine tend to antagonize the drowsiness caused by antihistamines. *Synergism* (potentiation) occurs when one drug enhances the effect of another; for example, alcohol enhances the CNS depression caused by Valium.

6 Pharmacokinetic factors include absorption, distribution, biotransformation, and elimination of drugs.

7 Many physiological and pathological factors can alter the response to drugs. For example, age, gender, and pregnancy are all factors that should be considered when making drug decisions. In addition, some diseases can alter the way in which the body responds to drugs. Medical conditions associated with the liver, kidneys, and cardiovascular system are of particular concern.

8 In order for psychoactive drugs to influence the brain and its actions, they must pass through the blood-brain barrier. Many of these drugs are fat-soluble and able to pass through capillary walls from the blood into the brain.

9 The *threshold* dose is the minimum amount of a drug necessary to have an effect. The *plateau effect* is the maximum effect a drug can have, regardless of dose. The *cumulative effect* is the buildup of drug concentration in the body due to multiple doses taken within short intervals.

10 The liver is the primary organ for the metabolizing of drugs and many naturally occurring substances in the body, such as hormones. By altering the molecular structure of drugs, the metabolism usually inactivates drugs and makes them easier to eliminate through the kidneys.

11 *Biotransformation* is the process that alters the molecular structure of a drug. Metabolism contributes to biotransformation.

12 *Drug tolerance* causes a decreased response to a given dose of a drug. It can be caused by increasing metabolism and elimination of the drug by the body or by a change in the systems or targets that are affected by the drug.

13 *Physical dependence* is characterized by the adaptive changes that occur in the body due to the continual presence of a drug. These changes are often chemical in nature and reduce the response to the drugs and cause *tolerance.* If drug use is halted after physical dependence has occurred, the body is overcompensated, causing a *rebound* response. Rebound effects are similar to the *withdrawal* that occurs because drug use is stopped for an extended period. *Psychological dependence* occurs because drug use is rewarding, bringing euphoria, increased energy, and relaxation, or because stopping drug use produces craving.

14 Suggestion can have a profound influence on a person's drug response. Health problems with significant psychological aspects are particularly susceptible to the effects of placebos. For example, because the intensity of pain is related to its perception, a placebo can substantially relieve pain discomfort. This *placebo effect* may relate to the release of natural pain-relieving substances, such as endorphins. Other placebo responses may likewise be due to the release of endogenous factors in the body.

15 A powerful, uncontrollable desire (craving) for drugs can occur with chronic use of some drugs of abuse. Although craving by itself may not cause drug addiction, if it can be eliminated, treatment of substance abuse is more likely to be successful.

References

Addington, J. and V. Duchak. "Reasons for Substance Use in Schizophrenia." *Acta Psychiatry Scandinavia* 96 (1997): 329–33.

Bourne, H. R. "Drug Receptors and Pharmacodynamics." In *Basic and Clinical Pharmacology*, 7th ed., edited by B. Katzung, 9–33. Stamford, CT: Appleton and Lange, 1998.

Correia, M. "Drug Biotransformation." In *Basic and Clinical Pharmacology*, 7th ed., edited by B. Katzung, 50–61. Stamford, CT: Appleton and Lange, 1998.

Goldstein, A. *Addiction from Biology to Drug Policy.* New York: Freeman, 1994.

Hobbs, W. R., T. Rall, and T. Verdoorn. "Hypnotics and Sedatives: Ethanol." In *The Pharmacological Basis of Therapeutics,* 9th ed., edited by J. Hardman and L. Limbird, 386–96. New York: McGraw–Hill, 1995.

Hughes, J. "Isolation of an Endogenous Compound from the Brain with Pharmacological Properties Similar to Morphine." *Brain Research* 88 (1975): 295–308.

Karch, S. "Cocaine." In *The Pathology of Drug Abuse,* 39–44. New York: CRC Press, 1996.

Klaasen, C. D. "Principles of Toxicology and Treatment of Poisoning." In *The Pharmacological Basis of Therapeutics,* 9th ed., edited by J. Hardman and L. Limbird, 63–75. New York: McGraw–Hill, 1995.

Leshner, A. "Drug Abuse and Mental Disorder: Comorbidity Is Reality." *NIDA Notes* 14 (1999): 3,4.

MacDonald, S. "Use with Care: Medicines Can Cure or Kill." *Salt Lake Tribune* (September 3, 1998): B-1.

Mathias, R. "Rate and Duration of Drug Activity Play Major Roles in Drug Abuse, Addiction and Treatment." *NIDA Notes* 12 (March/April, 1997): 8–11.

McGue, M., R. Pickens, and D. Svikis. "Sex and Age Effects on the Inheritance of Alcohol Problems: A Twin Study." *Journal of Abnormal Psychology* 101 (January 1992): 3–17.

Mello, K., and R. Griffith. "Alcoholism and Drug Abuse: An Overview." In *Psychopharmacology: The Third Generation of Progress,* edited by H. Meltzer, 1511–20. New York: Raven Press, 1987.

Meng, Y., M. Dukat, D. Bridgen, B. R. Martin, and A. H. Lichtman. "Pharmacological Effects of Methamphetamine and Other Stimulants Via Inhalation Exposure." *Drugs and Alcohol Dependence* 53 (1999): 111–20.

Nicholas, H., and L. Benet. "Pharmacokinetics and Pharmacodynamics: Dose Selection and the Time Course of Drug Action." In *Basic and Clinical Pharmacology,* 7th ed., edited by B. Katzung, 34–49. Stamford, CT: Appleton and Lange, 1998.

NIDA Notes. "Infectious Diseases and Drug Addiction." 14 (1999): 15.

Nies, A., and S. Spielberg. "Principles of Therapeutics." In *The Pharmacological Basis of Therapeutics,* 9th ed., edited by J. Hardman and L. Limbird, 43–62. New York: McGraw–Hill, 1995.

O'Brien, C. "Drug Addiction and Drug Abuse." In *The Pharmacological Basis of Therapeutics,* 9th ed., edited by J. Hardman and L. Limbird, 557–77. New York: McGraw–Hill, 1995.

Prevention Online. "Information About Cocaine from ONDCP Pulse Check: National Trends in Drug Abuse." *Prevline, SAMSHA* (June 1998). Available www.health.org/pubs/qdocs/cocaine/index.htm.

Rice, D. P. "Economic Costs of Substances of Abuse, 1995." *Proceedings of the Association of American Physicians* 111 (1999): 119–25.

Sherman, M. "The Placebo Effect." *American Druggist* (January 1992): 39–42.

Swan, N. "Despite Advances, Drug Craving Remains an Elusive Research Target." *NIDA Notes* (May/June 1993): 1–4.

"Trends, Policy and Research." *Prevention Pipeline* [Center for Substance Abuse Prevention] (November/December 1993): 27.

Vanyukov, M. M., and R. E. Tarter. "Genetic Studies of Substance Abuse." *Drug and Alcohol Dependence* 59 (2000): 101–23.

Wyman, J. "Promising Advances Toward Understanding the Genetic Roots of Addiction." *NIDA Notes* 12 (July/August, 1997) 11,12.

Zickler, P. "High-dose Improves Treatment Outcome." *NIDA Notes* 14 (1999): 4,5.

CNS Depressants: Sedative-Hypnotics

Did You Know?

▶ Alcohol temporarily relieves anxiety and stress because of its central nervous system (CNS) depressant effects.

▶ At low doses, a CNS depressant relieves anxiety, and at high doses, it becomes a sleep aid.

▶ The benzodiazepines (Valium-like drugs) are much safer than the barbiturates.

▶ Benzodiazepines are by far the most frequently prescribed CNS depressants.

▶ Most people dependent on benzodiazepines obtain their drugs legally by prescription.

▶ Long-term users of Valium can experience severe withdrawal symptoms if drug use is stopped abruptly.

▶ Our bodies probably produce a natural antianxiety substance that functions like drugs such as Valium, triazolam (Halcion) and alprazolam (Xanax).

▶ Antihistamines are CNS depressants and the principal active ingredients in over-the-counter (OTC) sleep aids.

▶ The short-acting CNS depressants are the most likely to be abused.

▶ GHB (gamma hydroxybutyrate) is an abused "club drug" that occurs naturally in the body and has been classified as a Schedule I substance.

Learning Objectives

**On completing this chapter
you will be able to:**

- ▶ Identify the primary drug groups used for CNS depressant effects.

- ▶ Explain the principal therapeutic uses of the CNS depressants and how the effects relate to drug dose.

- ▶ Explain why CNS depressant drugs are commonly abused.

- ▶ Identify the differences and similarities between benzodiazepines and barbiturates.

- ▶ Relate how benzodiazepine dependence usually develops.

- ▶ Describe the differences in effects between short- and long-acting CNS depressants.

- ▶ Describe the CNS depressant properties of antihistamines, and compare their therapeutic usefulness to that of benzodiazepines.

- ▶ List the four principal types of people who abuse CNS depressants.

- ▶ Identify the basic principles in treating dependence on CNS depressants.

- ▶ Explain why GHB is abused and why it has been classified a Schedule I substance.

Introduction

Central nervous system (CNS) depressants are some of the most widely used and abused drugs in the United States. Why? Taken at low doses they all produce a qualitatively similar "high" by their disinhibitory effects on the brain. In addition, they relieve stress and anxiety and even induce sleep—effects that appeal to many people, particularly those who are struggling with problems and looking for a break, physically and emotionally. CNS depressants also can cause a host of serious side effects, including problems with tolerance and dependence. Ironically, many individuals who become dependent on depressants obtain them through legitimate means: a prescription given by a physician. Depressants are also available on the street, although this illicit source is not the bulk of the problem.

In this chapter, we briefly review the history of CNS depressants, in terms of both development and use, and then discuss the positive and negative effects these drugs can produce. Each of the major types of depressant drugs are then reviewed in detail: *benzodiazepines* (Valium-like drugs), *barbiturates,* and other *minor* categories. We conclude with an examination of abuse patterns of depressant drugs, and discuss how drug dependence and withdrawal are treated.

An Introduction to CNS Depressants

Henry* lived with his wife and two children. He claimed to be a nonsmoker and denied any use of illegal drugs; however, he did have a history of daily coffee consumption and admitted to occasionally consuming moderate amounts of alcohol. Despite no history of mental illness, his behavior changed over the course of several months; he experienced insomnia, depression, difficulty concentrating, nightmares, irritability, loss of job, and marital discord. His problems culminated one summer afternoon after drinking beer with a friend, when he got into an argument with the manager of his apartment. Acting in an

_____
*Not his real name.

incoherent manner, Henry picked up a kitchen knife and small hand ax from his apartment, proceeded to the manager's office, and tried to chop down the door, while yelling at both the manager and witnesses in the hallway. He was apprehended by police and charged with criminal behavior. When questioned, Henry had no recollection of the incident. A medical history revealed that he had been prescribed Rivotril (a Valium-type CNS depressant) for insomnia and stress as well as clomipramine (Anafranil), an antidepressant that can cause CNS depression or excitation. Psychotherapists concluded that his aberrant personal and criminal behavior were directly caused by the effects of the prescribed CNS depressants taken in combination with alcohol. Given the conclusions of the clinicians, the city prosecutor offered Henry a plea bargain to reduce the charge to a misdemeanor and a suspended sentence (Pagliaro and Pagliaro 1992).

This actual case study illustrates several reasons why CNS depressants can be problematic. First, in contrast to most other substances of abuse, CNS depressants are usually not obtained illicitly and self-administered but are prescribed under the direction of a physician. Second, use of CNS depressants can cause very alarming, even dangerous, behavior if not monitored closely; most problems associated with these drugs occur due to insufficient professional supervision. Third, several seemingly unrelated drug groups have some ability to cause CNS depression. When these drugs are combined, bizarre and dangerous interactions can result (see Chapter 6 for a discussion on drug interactions). Particularly problematic is the combination of alcohol with other CNS depressants. Finally, CNS depressants can cause disruptive personality changes that are unpredictable and sometimes very threatening. This chapter will help you understand the nature of the CNS depressant effects experienced by Henry as well as other important features of these drugs. In addition, the similarities and differences among the commonly prescribed CNS depressant drugs are discussed.

▪ THE HISTORY OF CNS DEPRESSANTS

Before the era of modern drugs, the most common depressant used to ease tension, cause relaxation, and help forget problems was alcohol. These effects undoubtedly accounted for the immense popularity of alcohol and help explain why this traditional depressant is the most commonly abused drug of all time. (Alcohol is discussed in detail in Chapters 8 and 9.)

Attempts to find CNS depressants other than alcohol that could be used to treat nervousness and anxiety began in the 1800s with the introduction of bromides. These drugs were very popular until their toxicities became known. In the early 1900s, bromides were replaced by barbiturates . Like bromides, barbiturates were initially heralded as safe and effective depressants; however, problems with tolerance, dependence, and lethal overdoses became evident. It was learned that the doses of barbiturates required to treat anxiety also could cause CNS depression, affecting respiration and impairing mental functions (Hobbs et al. 1995). The margin of safety for barbiturates was too narrow, so research for a safer CNS depressant began again.

It was not until the 1950s that the first benzodiazepines were marketed as substitutes for the dangerous barbiturates. Benzodiazepines were originally viewed as extremely safe and free from the problems of tolerance, dependence, and withdrawal that occurred with the other drugs in this category (Mondanaro 1988). Unfortunately, benzodiazepines also have been found to be less than ideal antianxiety drugs. Although relatively safe when used for short periods, long-term use can cause dependence and withdrawal problems much like those associated with their depressant predecessors (Trevor and Lay 1998). These problems have become a major concern of the medical community, as is discussed in greater detail later in the chapter.

Many of the people who become dependent on CNS depressants such as benzodiazepines began using the drugs under the supervision of a physician. Some clinicians routinely prescribe CNS depressants for patients with stress, anxiety, or apprehension without trying nonpharmacological approaches, such as psychotherapy or counseling. This practice sends an undesirable and often detrimental message to patients—that is, CNS depressants are a simple solution to their complex, stressful problems. The following quote illustrates the danger of this practice:

> I am still, unfortunately, lost in " 'script addiction." . . . I have gone on-line asking for pills. I could really identify with the one posting about doctors who continue to write the 'scripts to

increase/continue the patient "flow." This is exactly what is happening with me and my doctor. (From America Online Alcohol and Drug Dependency and Recovery message board.)

Consequently, during the 1970s and 1980s, there was an epidemic of prescriptions for CNS depressants. For example, in 1973, 100 million prescriptions were written for benzodiazepines alone. Approximately twice as many women as men were taking these drugs at this time; a similar gender pattern continues today. During this period, many homemakers made CNS depressants a part of their household routine, as described in the lyrics of the song "Mother's Little Helper" on the Rolling Stones' album *Flowers*:

> Things are different today
> I hear every mother say
> "Mother needs something today to calm
>   her down"
> And though she's not really ill,
> There's a little yellow pill.
> She goes running for the shelter
> Of her "mother's little helper"
> And it helps her on her way,
> Gets her through her busy day.

As the medical community became more aware of the problem, the use of depressants declined (Latner 2000). Today, efforts are being made by pharmaceutical companies and scientists to find new classes of CNS depressants that can be used to relieve stress and anxiety without causing serious side effects such as dependence and withdrawal.

■ THE EFFECTS OF CNS DEPRESSANTS: BENEFITS AND RISKS

The CNS depressants are a diverse group of drugs that share an ability to reduce CNS activity and diminish the brain's level of awareness. Besides the benzodiazepines, barbiturate-like drugs, and alcohol,

---

KEY TERMS

barbiturates
potent CNS depressants, usually not preferred because of their narrow margin of safety

benzodiazepines
the most popular and safest CNS depressants in use today

depressant drugs also include antihistamines and opioid narcotics such as heroin (see Chapter 10).

Depressants are usually classified according to the degree of their medical effects on the body. For instance, sedatives cause mild depression of the CNS and relaxation. This drug effect is used to treat extreme anxiety and often is referred to as anxiolytic . Many sedatives also have muscle-relaxing properties that enhance their relaxing effects.

Depressants are also used to promote sleep. Hypnotics (from the Greek god of sleep, *Hypnos*) are CNS depressants that encourage sleep by inducing drowsiness. Often when depressants are used as hypnotics, they produce amnesiac effects as well. As already mentioned, the effects produced by depressants can be very enticing and encourage inappropriate use.

The effects of the CNS depressants tend to be dose-dependent (see Figure 7.1). Thus, if you were to take a larger dose of a sedative, it might have a hypnotic effect. Often, the only difference between a sedative and a hypnotic effect is the dosage; consequently, the same drug may be used for both purposes by varying the dose. By increasing the dose still further, an anesthetic state can be reached. Anesthesia , a deep depression of the CNS, is used to achieve a controlled state of unconsciousness so that a patient can be treated, usually by surgery, in relative comfort and without memory of an unpleasant experience. With the exception of benzodiazepines, if the dose of most of the depressants is increased much more, coma or death will ensue because the CNS becomes so depressed that vital centers controlling breathing and heart activity cease to function properly (Trevor and Lay 1998).

As a group, CNS depressant drugs used in a persistent fashion cause tolerance. Because of the diminished effect due to the tolerance, users of these drugs continually escalate their doses. Under such conditions, the depressants alter physical and psychological states, resulting in dependence. The dependence can be so severe that abrupt drug abstinence results in severe withdrawals that include life-threatening seizures (American Psychiatric Association 1994). Because of these dangerous pharmacological features, treatment of dependence on CNS depressants must proceed very carefully (Goldstein 1995). This issue is discussed in greater detail at the end of this chapter and in Chapter 6.

Types of CNS Depressants

It is important for you to realize that all CNS depressants are not "created equal." Some have wider margins of safety; others have a greater potential for nonmedicinal abuse. These differences are important when considering the therapeutic advantages of each type of CNS depressant. In addition, unique features of the different types of depressants make them useful for treatment of other medical problems. For example, some barbiturates and benzodiazepines are used to treat forms of epilepsy or acute seizure activity, whereas opioid narcotics are used to treat many

FIGURE 7.1
Dose-dependent effects of CNS depressants.

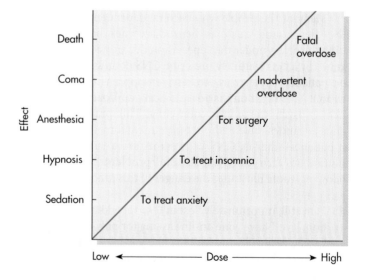

CNS depressants can be used as hypnotics to initiate sleep.

antihistamines
drugs that often cause CNS depression and are used to treat allergies

sedatives
CNS depressants used to relieve anxiety, fear, and apprehension

anxiolytic
drug that relieves anxiety

hypnotics
CNS depressants used to induce drowsiness and encourage sleep

amnesiac
causing the loss of memory

anesthesia
a state characterized by loss of sensation or consciousness

types of pain. Some of these unique features will be dealt with in greater detail when the individual drug groups are discussed. The benzodiazepines, barbiturate-like drugs, antihistamines, and the naturally occurring gamma hydroxybutyrate (GHB) are discussed in this chapter. Other CNS depressants, such as alcohol and opiates are covered in Chapters 8, 9, and 10. Finally, the unique features of the CNS depressants help determine the likelihood of abuse. For example, abuse is more likely to occur with the short-acting depressant agents than with those agents that have long-lasting effects. Currently, non-medicinal use of the sedatives occurs in 3% to 5% of the population. This abuse is most likely to be caused by the benzodiazepines that have a short half-life ("Common Substances of Abuse" 2000).

■ BENZODIAZEPINES: VALIUM-TYPE DRUGS

Benzodiazepines are by far the most frequently prescribed CNS depressants for anxiety and sleep. In fact, 4 of the top-selling 100 prescription drugs in the United States during 1999 were benzodiazepines (Latner 2000). Because of their wide margin of safety (death from overdose is rare), benzodiazepines have replaced barbiturate-like drugs for use as sedatives and hypnotics (Goldstein 1995). Benzodiazepines were originally referred to as the *minor tranquilizers*, but this terminology erroneously implied that they had pharmacological properties similar to those of antipsychotic drugs (the *major tranquilizers*), when

in fact they are very different. Consequently, the term *minor tranquilizer* is usually avoided by clinicians.

The first true benzodiazepine, chlordiazepoxide (Librium), was developed for medical use and marketed about 1960; the very popular drug Valium came on the market about the same time. In fact, Valium was so well received that from 1972 to 1978 it was the top-selling prescription drug in the United States. Its popularity, however, has since dropped considerably, and in 1999 sales of its generic form, diazepam, ranked only 96th in the United States (Latner 2000).

Because of dependence problems, the benzodiazepines are now classified as Schedule IV drugs. In recent years, considerable concern has arisen that benzodiazepines are overprescribed because of their perceived safety; it has been said, somewhat facetiously, that the only way a person could die from using the benzodiazepines would be to choke on them. Clinicians and even consumer organizations ("High Anxiety" 1993) are concerned about this overconfident attitude toward benzodiazepines and warn patients against prolonged and unsupervised administration of these drugs.

Medical Uses

Benzodiazepines are used for an array of therapeutic objectives, including the relief of anxiety, treatment of neurosis, relaxation of muscles, alleviation of lower back pain, treatment of some convulsive disorders, induction of sleep (hypnotic), relief from withdrawal symptoms associated with narcotic and alcohol dependence, and induction of amnesia, usually for preoperative administration (administered just before or during surgery or very uncomfortable medical procedures) (Longo and Johnson 2000).

Mechanisms of Action

In contrast to barbiturate-type drugs, which cause general depression of most neuronal activity, benzodiazepines selectively affect those neurons that have receptors for the neurotransmitter gamma aminobutyric acid (GABA) (Hobbs et al. 1995). GABA is a very important inhibitory transmitter in several brain regions: the limbic system, the reticular activating system, and the motor cortex (see Chapter 5). In the presence of benzodiazepines, the inhibitory effects of GABA are increased. Depression of activity in these brain regions likely accounts for the ability of benzodiazepines to alter mood (a limbic function), cause drowsiness (a reticular activating system function), and relax muscles (a cortical function). The specific GABA-enhancing effect of these drugs explains the selective CNS depression caused by benzodiazepines.

Of considerable interest is the observation that these Valium-like drugs act on specific receptor sites that are linked to the GABA receptors in the CNS. As yet, no endogenous substance has been identified that naturally interacts with this so-called benzodiazepine site. It is very likely, however, that a natural benzodiazepine does exist that activates this same receptor population and serves to reduce stress and anxiety by natural means. Because benzodiazepines have specific target receptors, it has been possible to develop a highly selective antagonist drug, flumazenil (Romazicon). This drug is used to treat benzodiazepine overdoses, but must be used carefully because its administration can precipitate withdrawal in people taking benzodiazepines (Hebel 2000).

Types of Benzodiazepines

Because benzodiazepines are so popular and thus profitable, new related drugs are routinely released into the pharmaceutical market. Currently, approximately 14 benzodiazepine compounds are available in the United States.

Benzodiazepines are distinguished primarily by their duration of action (see Table 7.1). As a general rule, the short-acting drugs are used as hypnotics to treat insomnia, thus allowing the user to awake in the morning with few after-effects (such as a hangover). The long-acting benzodiazepines tend to be prescribed as sedatives, giving prolonged relaxation and relief from persistent anxiety. Some of the long-acting drugs can exert a relaxing effect for as long as 2 to 3 days. One reason for the long action in some benzodiazepines is that they are converted by the liver into metabolites that are as active as the original drug. For example, Valium has a half-life of 20 to 80 hours and is converted by the liver into several active metabolites, including oxazepam (which itself is marketed as a therapeutic benzodiazepine; see Table 7.1).

Side Effects

Reported side effects of benzodiazepines include drowsiness, lightheadedness, lethargy, impairment of mental and physical activities, skin rashes, nausea, diminished libido, irregularities in the menstrual cycle, blood cell abnormalities, and increased sensitivity to alcohol and other CNS depressants (McEvoy 2000). In contrast to barbiturate-type drugs, only very high doses of benzodiazepines have a significant impact on respiration. There are actually few verified instances of death resulting from overdose of benzodiazepines alone (Longo and Johnson 2000). Almost always, serious suppression of vital functions occurs when these drugs are combined with other depressants, most often alcohol (Hobbs et al. 1995).

There is no clear evidence of permanent, irreversible damage to neurological or other physiological processes, even with long-term benzodiazepine use (Woods et al. 1992). Benzodiazepines have less effect on REM sleep (rapid eye movement, the restive phase) than do barbiturates. Consequently, sleep under the influence of benzodiazepines is more likely to be restful and satisfying. However, prolonged use of hypnotic doses of benzodiazepines may cause rebound (see Chapter 6) increases in REM sleep and insomnia when the drug is stopped.

KEY TERMS

REM sleep
the restive phase of sleep associated with dreaming

paradoxical
an unexpected effect

TABLE 7.1 Half-lives of Various Benzodiazepines

DRUG	HALF-LIFE (HOURS)
Alprazolam (Xanax)	12–15
Chlordiazepoxide (Librium)	5–30
Clonazepam (Klonopin)	18–50
Clorazepate (Tranxene)	30–100
Diazepam (Valium)	20–80
Estazolam (ProSom)	10–24
Flurazepam (Dalmane)	2–4
Halazepam (Paxipam)	14
Lorazepam (Ativan)	10–20
Midazolam (Versed)	1–12
Oxazepam (Serax)	5–20
Quazepam (Doral)	39
Temazepam (Restoril)	10–17
Triazolam (Halcion)	1.5–5.5
Zolpidem (Ambien; not a true benzodiazepine)	2–5

Source: Adapted from W. Hobbs, T. Rall, and T. Verdoorn. "Hypnotics and Sedatives." In *The Pharmacological Basis of Therapeutics*, 9th ed., edited by J. Hardman and L. Limbird, 361–96. New York: McGraw-Hill, 1995; and *Drugs Facts and Comparisons*, 876–83. St. Louis, MO: Wolters Kluwer, 2000.

On rare occasions, benzodiazepines can have paradoxical effects, producing unusual responses such as nightmares, anxiety, irritability, sweating, and restlessness (McEvoy 2000). Bizarre, uninhibited behavior—extreme agitation with hostility, paranoia, and rage—may occur as well. One such case was reported in 1988 in Utah. A 63-year-old patient who was taking Halcion (a relatively short-acting benzodiazepine) murdered her 87-year-old mother. The suspect claimed that the murder occurred because of the effects of the drug and that she was innocent of committing a crime. Her defense was successful, and she was acquitted of murder. After her acquittal, the woman initiated a $21 million lawsuit against Upjohn Pharmaceuticals for marketing Halcion, which she claimed is a dangerous drug. The lawsuit was settled out of court for an undisclosed amount. This tragic episode came to a surprising conclusion in 1994 when the daughter committed suicide (Associated Press 1994).

Critics' complaints that Halcion causes unacceptable "amnesia, confusion, paranoia, hostility and seizures" (Associated Press 1994) prompted the Food and Drug Administration (FDA) to closely evaluate this benzodiazepine. Despite the fact that several other countries have banned Halcion, the FDA concluded that its benefits outweigh the reported risks; however, the FDA also concluded that "In no way should this [the FDA's conclusion] suggest that Halcion is free of side effects. It has long been recognized and emphasized in Halcion's labeling that it is a potent drug that produces the same type of adverse effects as other CNS sedative hypnotic drugs" ("New Halcion Guidelines" 1992; *PDR* 1997). Although the FDA did not require that Halcion be withdrawn, it did negotiate changes in the labeling and package inserts with Halcion's manufacturer, Upjohn Pharmaceuticals. These changes emphasize appropriate Halcion use in treatment of insomnia and additional information about side effects, warnings, and dosage. As a result of these concerns, the sales of Halcion plummeted, causing it to fall from the 18th largest-selling prescription drug in 1987 to not even being 1 of the top 200 most-prescribed drugs in 1999 (Latner 2000).

There is no obvious explanation for the strange benzodiazepine-induced behaviors. It is possible that, in some people, the drugs mask inhibitory centers of the brain and allow expression of antisocial behavior that is normally suppressed and controlled.

Related concerns have also been made public about another very popular benzodiazepine, alprazolam (Xanax). In 1990, Xanax became the first drug approved for the treatment of *panic disorder* (repeated, intense attacks of anxiety that can make life unbearable). Reports that long-term use of Xanax can cause severe withdrawal effects and a stubborn dependency on the drug ("High Anxiety" 1993) raised public concerns about use of benzodiazepines in general. For example, how many people are severely dependent on these CNS depressants? What is the frequency of side effects such as memory impairment, serious mood swings, and cognitive problems? And how many patients using the benzodiazepines would be better served with non-drug psychotherapy? Clearly, use of the benzodiazepines to relieve acute stress or insomnia can be beneficial, but these drugs should be prescribed at the lowest dose possible and for the shortest time possible or withdrawal problems can result, as illustrated in the following quote:

> I was put on alprazolam (Xanax) two and a half years ago by [my] doctor. Now told by another doctor that it is for short-term use only and I am trying to get off slowly, but having difficulty. [I] have never used other drugs and do not have any information on the withdrawal process. (From America Online Alcohol and Drug Dependency and Recovery message board.)

Tolerance, Dependence, Withdrawal, and Abuse

As with most CNS depressants, frequent, chronic use of benzodiazepines can cause tolerance, dependence (both physical and psychological), and withdrawal (McEvoy 2000; Trevor and Lay 1998). Such side effects are usually not as severe as those of most other depressants, and they occur only after using the drugs for prolonged periods (Kosten and Hollister 1998). In addition, for most people, the effects of the benzodiazepines are not viewed as reinforcing; thus, compared with other depressants, such as barbiturates, benzodiazepines are not especially addicting (Kosten and Hollister 1998). However, these drugs should be prescribed with caution for patients with a history of drug abuse (Longo and Johnson 2000).

Withdrawal can mimic the condition for which the benzodiazepine is given; for example, withdrawal symptoms can include anxiety or insomnia. In such cases, a clinician may be fooled into thinking that the underlying emotional disorder is still present and may resume drug therapy without realizing that the patient has become drug-dependent. This can happen after as little as 1 month of treatment ("Common Substances of Abuse" 2000). In situations in which users have consumed high doses of benzodiazepine over the long term, more severe, even life-threatening withdrawal symptoms may occur (Goldstein 1995); depression, panic, paranoia, and convulsions (Gatzonis 2000) have been reported (see Table 7.2). Severe withdrawal can often be avoided by gradually weaning the patient from the benzodiazepine ("Common Substances of Abuse" 2000). Long-term use of benzodiazepines (periods exceeding 3 to 4 months) to treat anxiety or sleep disorders has not been shown to be therapeutically useful for most patients. Even so, this approach is a common indiscriminate practice and has been suggested by some clinicians to be responsible for the largest group of prescription drug-dependent people in the United States. As one user explains:

> I went through a trauma 4 years ago, and the doctor prescribed a very high dose of Ativan. Well, I soon became addicted, both emotionally

TABLE 7.2 Abstinence Symptoms That Occur When Long-term Users of Benzodiazepines Abruptly Stop Taking the Drug

DURATION OF ABSTINENCE	SYMPTOMS
1–3 days	Often no noticeable symptoms
3–4 days	Restlessness, agitation, headaches, problems eating, and inability to sleep
4–6 days	The preceding symptoms plus twitching of facial and arm muscles and feeling of intense burning in the skin
6–7 days	The preceding symptoms plus seizures

Source: W. Hobbs, T. Rall, and T. Verdoorn. "Hypnotics and Sedatives." In *The Pharmacological Basis of Therapeutics,* 9th ed., edited by J. Hardman and L. Limbird, 361–96. New York: McGraw-Hill, 1995.

and physically . . . How do I get off? . . . This stuff is very addicting and my body can't really function without it. (From America Online Alcohol and Drug Dependency and Recovery message board.)

It is very unusual to find nontherapeutic drug-seeking behavior in a patient who has been properly removed from benzodiazepines, unless that individual already has a history of drug abuse (Longo and Johnson 2000). Research has shown that when benzodiazepines are the primary drug of abuse, these CNS depressants are usually self-administered to prevent unpleasant withdrawal symptoms in dependent users. If benzodiazepine-dependent users are properly weaned from the drugs and withdrawal has dissipated, there is no evidence that craving for the benzodiazepines occurs because people usually do not consider the benzodiazepines particularly pleasant (Woods and Winger 1992). An exception to this conclusion appears to be former alcoholics. Many people with a history of alcoholism find the effects of benzodiazepines rewarding; consequently, nearly 21% of prior alcoholics use benzodiazepines chronically (Woods and Winger 1992).

Benzodiazepines are commonly used as a secondary drug of abuse and combined with illicit drugs (O'Brien 1995). For example, narcotic users frequently combine benzodiazepines with weak heroin to enhance the narcotic effect. It is very common to find heroin users who are dependent on depressants as well as narcotics (O'Brien 1995).

Another frequent combination is the use of benzodiazepines with stimulants such as cocaine. Some addicts claim that this combination enhances the pleasant effects of the stimulant and reduces the "crashing" that occurs after using high doses. (More is said about benzodiazepine abuse later in this chapter.)

It should also be mentioned that benzodiazepines are occasionally used to make people vulnerable to sexual assaults referred to as *date rapes*. The use of CNS depressants to commit these acts of violence is discussed in greater detail later in the chapter, but such assaults have sometimes involved the use of the club drug Rohypnol. Rohypnol (sometimes called *Rophie, Roche,* or *Forget Me*) is the proprietary name for the benzodiazepine, fluni-

trazepam. Rohypnol, which has been outlawed in the United States, comes as a tablet that can be dissolved in beverages without leaving an odor or taste and impairs short-term memory, making victims unable to recall details of the assault (NIDA Notes 2000).

■ BARBITURATES

Barbiturates are defined as barbituric acid derivatives used in medicine as sedatives and hypnotics. Barbituric acid was first synthesized by A. Bayer (of aspirin fame) in Germany in 1864. The reason that he chose the name *barbituric acid* is not known. Some have speculated that the compound was named after a girl named Barbara whom Bayer knew. Others think that Bayer celebrated his discovery on the Day of St. Barbara in a tavern that artillery officers frequented. (St. Barbara is the patron saint of artillery soldiers.)

The first barbiturate, barbital (Veronal), was used medically in 1903. The names of the barbiturates all end in *-al*, indicating a chemical relationship to barbital, the first one synthesized. Historically, barbiturates have played an important role in therapeutics because of their effectiveness as sedative-hypnotic agents, which allowed them to be routinely used in the treatment of anxiety, agitation, and insomnia. However, because of their narrow margin of safety and their abuse liability, barbiturates have been largely replaced by safer drugs, such as benzodiazepines.

Uncontrolled use of barbiturates can cause a state of acute or chronic intoxication. Initially, there may be some loss of inhibition, euphoria, and behavioral stimulation, a pattern often seen with moderate consumption of alcohol. When taken to relieve extreme pain or mental stress, barbiturates may cause delirium and produce other side effects that can include nausea, nervousness, rash, and diarrhea. The person intoxicated with barbiturates may have difficulty thinking and making judgments, may

KEY TERMS

club drugs
drugs used at all-night raves, parties, dance clubs, and bars to enhance sensory experiences

be emotionally unstable, may be uncoordinated and unsteady when walking, and may slur speech (not unlike the drunken state caused by alcohol).

When used for their hypnotic properties, barbiturates cause an unnatural sleep. The user awakens feeling tired, edgy, and quite unsatisfied, most likely because barbiturates markedly suppress the REM phase of sleep. (REM sleep is necessary for the refreshing renewal that usually accompanies a good sleep experience.) Because benzodiazepines suppress REM sleep (as do all CNS depressants) less severely than barbiturates, use of these agents as sleep aids is generally better tolerated.

Continued misuse of barbiturate drugs has a cumulative toxic effect on the CNS that is more life-threatening than misuse of opiates. In large doses or in combination with other CNS depressants, barbiturates may cause death from respiratory or cardiovascular depression. Because of this toxicity, barbiturates have been involved in many drug-related deaths, both accidental and suicidal. Repeated misuse induces severe tolerance of and physical dependence on these drugs. Discontinuing use of short-acting barbiturates in people who are using large doses can cause dangerous withdrawal

effects such as life-threatening seizures. Table 7.3 summarizes the range of effects of barbiturates and other depressants on the mind and body.

Concern about the abuse potential of barbiturates caused the federal government to include some of these depressants in the Controlled Substances Act. Consequently, the short-acting barbiturates, such as pentobarbital and secobarbital, are classified as Schedule II drugs, whereas the long-acting barbiturates, such as phenobarbital, are less rigidly controlled as Schedule IV drugs.

Effects and Medical Uses

Barbiturates have many pharmacological actions. They depress the activity of nerves and skeletal, smooth, and cardiac muscles and impact the CNS in several ways, ranging from mild sedation to coma, depending on the dose. At sedative or hypnotic dosage levels, only the CNS is significantly affected. Higher anesthetic doses cause slight decreases in blood pressure, heart rate, and flow of urine. The metabolizing enzyme systems in the liver are important in inactivating barbiturates; thus, liver damage may result in exaggerated responses to barbiturate use.

TABLE 7.3 Effects of Barbiturates and Other Depressants on the Body and Mind

	BODY	MIND
Low dose	Drowsiness	Decreased anxiety, relaxation
	Trouble with coordination	Decreased ability to reason and solve problems
	Slurred speech	
	Dizziness	Difficulty in judging distance and time
	Staggering	
	Double vision	Amnesia
	Sleep	
	Depressed breathing	Brain damage
	Coma (unconscious and cannot be awakened)	
	Depressed blood pressure	
High dose	Death	

Low doses of barbiturates relieve tension and anxiety, effects that give several barbiturates substantial abuse potential. The drawbacks of barbiturates are extensive and severe:

- They lack selectivity and safety

- They have a substantial tendency to create tolerance, dependence, withdrawal, and abuse

- They cause problems with drug interaction

As a result, barbiturates have been replaced by benzodiazepines in most treatments; however, they are still included in a number of combination products for the treatment of an array of medical problems, such as gastrointestinal disorders, hypertension, asthma, and pain (Hobbs et al. 1995). Their use in such preparations is very controversial. The long-acting phenobarbital is still frequently used for its CNS depressant activity to alleviate or prevent convulsions in some epileptic patients and seizures caused by strychnine, cocaine, and other stimulant drugs. Thiopental (Pentothal) and other ultrashort- and short-acting barbiturates are used as anesthesia for minor surgery and as preoperative anesthetics in preparation for major surgery.

Mechanism of Action and Elimination

The precise mechanism of action for barbiturates is unclear. Like benzodiazepines, they likely interfere with activity in the reticular activating system, the limbic system, and the motor cortex. However, in contrast to benzodiazepines, barbiturates do not seem to act at a specific receptor site; they probably have a general effect that enhances the activity of the inhibitory transmitter GABA. Because benzodiazepines also increase GABA activity (but in a more selective manner), these two types of drugs have overlapping effects. Because the mechanisms whereby they exert their effects are different, it is not surprising that these two types of depressants also have different pharmacological features.

Like the benzodiazepines, barbiturates can be classified in terms of duration of action (see Table 7.4). In general, the more fat-soluble the barbiturate is, the more easily it enters the brain, the faster it will act, and the more potent it will be as a depressant. Barbiturates are eliminated by the kidneys at varying rates. The rate of removal depends primarily on how quickly the barbiturate is metabolized in the liver to a fat-insoluble metabolite. Excretion of barbiturates occurs more rapidly when the urine is alkaline, a characteristic that can be manipulated to treat barbiturate poisoning.

Because barbiturates are not completely removed from the body overnight, even the short-acting ones used for insomnia can cause subtle distortions of mood and impaired judgment and motor skills the following day (Julien 1992). The user may have mild withdrawal symptoms such as hyperexcitability, nausea, and vomiting even after short-term use. The long-acting barbiturates such as phenobarbital are metabolized more slowly and cause an extended drug hangover.

The fat solubility of barbiturates is also an important factor in the duration of their effects.

TABLE 7.4 Details on the Most Frequently Abused Barbiturates

DRUG	NICKNAMES	EFFECTS
Amobarbital (Amytal Sodium)	Blues, blue heavens, blue devils	Moderately rapid action
Pentobarbital (Nembutal Sodium)	Nembies, yellow jackets, yellows	Short-acting
Phenobarbital (Luminal Sodium)	Purple hearts	Long-acting barbiturate particularly well-suited for treatment of epilepsy
Secobarbital (Seconal Sodium)	Reds, red devils, red birds, Seccy	Short-acting with a prompt onset of action
50% amobarbital and 50% secobarbital (Tuinal)	Tooeys, double trouble, rainbows	Results in a rapidly effective, moderately long-acting sedative

Barbiturates that are the most fat-soluble move in and out of body tissues (such as the brain) rapidly and are likely to be shorter-acting. Fat-soluble barbiturates also are more likely to be stored in fatty tissue; consequently, the fat content of the body can influence the effects on the user. Because women have a higher body-fat ratio than men, their reaction to barbiturates may be slightly different.

Continual use of barbiturates results in both tolerance and dependence. Development of physical dependence on barbiturates is a relatively slow process, requiring weeks or months of use before withdrawal symptoms occur during drug abstinence.

Withdrawal from barbiturates after dependence has developed causes hyperexcitability because of the rebound of depressed neural systems. Qualitatively (but not quantitatively), the withdrawal symptoms are similar for all sedative-hypnotics (Trevor and Lay 1998).

Table 7.4 gives details on the barbiturates abused most frequently.

■ OTHER CNS DEPRESSANTS

Although benzodiazepines and barbiturates are by far used most frequently to produce CNS depressant effects, many other agents, representing an array of distinct chemical groups, can similarly reduce brain activity. Although the mechanisms of action might be different for some of these drugs, if any CNS depressants (including alcohol) are combined, they will interact synergistically and can suppress respiration in a life-threatening manner. Thus, it is important to avoid such mixtures if possible. Even some over-the-counter (OTC) products, such as cold and allergy medications, contain drugs with CNS depressant actions.

Nonbarbiturate Drugs with Barbiturate-like Properties

This category of depressants includes agents that are not barbiturates but have barbiturate-like effects. All of these drugs cause substantial tolerance, physical and psychological dependence, and withdrawal symptoms. The therapeutic safety of these CNS depressants more closely resembles that of barbiturates than benzodiazepines; consequently, like barbiturates, these agents have been replaced by the safer and easier-to-manage benzodiazepines.

Because these drugs have significant abuse potential, they are restricted much like other CNS depressants. In this group of depressants, methaqualone is a Schedule II drug; glutethimide and methyprylon are Schedule III drugs; and chloral hydrate is a Schedule IV drug. The basis for the classification is the relative potential for physical and psychological dependence. Abuse of Schedule II drugs may lead to severe or moderate physical dependence or high psychological dependence, and abuse of Schedule III drugs may cause moderate physical and psychological dependence. Schedule IV drugs are considered much less likely to cause either type of dependence.

Chloral Hydrate   Chloral hydrate (Noctec), or "knock-out drops," has the unsavory reputation of being a drug that is slipped into a person's drink to make him or her unconscious. In the late 1800s, the combination of chloral hydrate and alcohol was given the name *Mickey Finn* on the waterfront of the Barbary Coast of San Francisco when sailors were in short supply. As legend has it, the name of one of the bars dispensing unwanted knockout drops was Mickey Finn's. An unsuspecting man would have a friendly drink and wake up as a crew member on an outbound freighter to China.

Chloral hydrate is a good hypnotic, but it has a narrow margin of safety. This compound is a stomach irritant, especially if given repeatedly and in fairly large doses. Addicts may take enormous doses of the drug; as with most CNS depressants, chronic, long-term use of high doses will cause tolerance and physical dependence (Hobbs et al. 1995).

Glutethimide   Glutethimide (Doriden) is another example of a barbiturate-like drug that can be abused and that causes severe withdrawal symptoms. It also induces blood abnormalities in sensitive individuals, such as a type of anemia and abnormally low white cell counts. Nausea, fever, increased heart rate, and convulsions occasionally occur in patients who have been taking this sedative regularly in moderate doses. Doriden seems to have a smaller margin of safety than barbiturates. Continual use causes tolerance and physical dependence. Doriden was used more commonly as a "street" drug before it was definitely proved to be addictive and tighter controls were instituted.

Methyprylon Methyprylon (Noludar) is a short-acting nonbarbiturate that is used as a sedative and hypnotic. Its effects are similar to those of Doriden, and it is capable of causing tolerance, physical dependence, and addiction, much like barbiturates.

Methaqualone Few drugs have become so popular so quickly as methaqualone. This barbiturate-like sedative-hypnotic was introduced in India in the 1950s as an antimalarial agent. Its sedative properties, however, were soon discovered. It then became available in the United States as Quaalude, Mequin, and Parest.

After several years of street abuse, methaqualone was classified as a Schedule II drug. Since 1985, methaqualone has not been manufactured in the United States because of adverse publicity. It is interesting to note, however, that large amounts of illegal methaqualone are still imported into the United States from Colombia, Mexico, and Canada. It is referred to by street names such as *Ludes, Sopors,* or *714s.*

Common side effects of methaqualone include fatigue, dizziness, anorexia, nausea, vomiting, diarrhea, sweating, dryness of the mouth, depersonalization, headache, and paresthesia of the extremities (a pins-and-needles feeling in the fingers and toes). Hangover is frequently reported. High doses of methaqualone can cause psychological and physical dependence and dangerous withdrawal symptoms when drug use is stopped.

Antihistamines

Antihistamines are drugs used in both nonprescription and prescription medicinal products. The most common uses for antihistamines are to relieve the symptoms associated with the common cold, allergies, and motion sickness (see Chapter 16). Although frequently overlooked, many antihistamines cause significant CNS depression and are used both as sedatives and hypnotics (Trevor and Lay 1998). For example, the agents hydroxyzine (Visteril) and promethazine (Phenergan) are prescribed for their sedative effects, whereas diphenhydramine is commonly used as an OTC sleep aid.

The exact mechanism of CNS depression caused by these agents is not totally known but appears to relate to their blockage of acetylcholine receptors in the brain (they antagonize the mus-

carinic receptor types). This anticholinergic activity (see Chapter 5) helps cause relaxation and sedation and can be viewed as a very annoying side effect when these drugs are being used to treat allergies or other problems.

Therapeutic Usefulness and Side Effects Antihistamines are viewed as relatively safe agents. Compared with other more powerful CNS depressants, antihistamines do not appear to cause significant physical or psychological dependence or addiction problems, although drugs with anticholinergic activity, such as the antihistamines, are sometimes abused, especially by children and teenagers (Carlini 1993). However, tolerance to antihistamine-induced sedation occurs quite rapidly. Reports of significant cases of withdrawal problems when use of the antihistamines is stopped are rare. This situation may reflect the fact that these agents are used as antianxiety drugs for only minor problems and for short periods of time (often only for a single dose).

One significant problem with antihistamines is the variability of responses they produce. Different antihistamines work differently on different people.

Antihistamines are found in OTC medicines used to relieve cold and allergy symptoms.

Usually therapeutic doses will cause decreased alertness, relaxation, slowed reaction time, and drowsiness. But it is not uncommon for some individuals to be affected in the opposite manner, that is, an antihistamine can cause restlessness, agitation, and insomnia. There are even cases of seizures caused by toxic doses of antihistamine, particularly in children (Serafin and Babe 1995). Side effects of antihistamines related to their anticholinergic effects include dry mouth, constipation, and inability to urinate. These factors probably help to discourage high-dose abuse of these drugs. However, OTC antihistamines are still sometimes taken for recreational purposes despite the unpleasant side effects (Hughes et al. 1999).

Even though antihistamines are relatively safe in therapeutic doses, they can contribute to serious problems if combined with other CNS depressants. Because of this potentially dangerous interaction, patients who have been prescribed other sedative-hypnotics should be aware of consuming drugs that contain antihistamines. For example, many OTC cold, allergy, antimotion, and sleep aid products contain antihistamines and should be avoided by patients using the potent CNS depressants.

GHB (gamma hydroxybutyrate): The *Natural* Depressant

GHB is a natural substance in the body resulting from the metabolism of the inhibitory neurotransmitter, GABA (see Chapter 5) (Lingenhoehl et al. 1999). It was first synthesized nearly 30 years ago by a French researcher who intended to study the CNS effects of GABA (Poldrugo and Addolorato 1999). It was initially believed that GHB exerted its effects by enhancing CNS GABA systems, although this mechanism has recently been questioned. There is some evidence that GHB is itself a neuromodulator with its own receptor targets in the brain (Lingenhoehl et al. 1999). Because of its central depressant effects, GHB has been used in Europe as an adjunct for general anesthesia, a treatment for insomnia and narcolepsy (a daytime sleep disorder), and a treatment for alcoholism and alcohol withdrawal (see "Case in Point," GHB Use by an Ex-alcoholic) and narcotic dependence (Kam and Yoong 1998). During the 1980s, GHB became available without a prescription in health food stores and was used principally by body builders to stimulate the release of growth hormone with the intent to reduce fat and build muscle

("Club Drugs" 2000). More recently, this substance has been gaining popularity for recreational use due to what has been described as a pleasant, alcohol-like, hangover-free high with aphrodisiac properties (Morgenthaler and Joy 1994). Because of its frequent use by young people at nightclubs and bars, GHB has become known as a *club drug* ("Club Drugs" 2000).

Due to concerns about GHB abuse and side effects, an advisory warning that this substance is unsafe was first issued by the FDA in 1990. In 1997, the FDA released another warning that GHB was not approved for clinical use in the United States and was a potentially dangerous substance. Finally, due to the rising illicit use of GHB and resultant problems, this drug was made a Schedule I Controlled Substance by the DEA in March 2000 ("Gamma Hydroxybutyric Acid" 2000).

Despite concerns, many questions remain regarding the potential risks of using GHB. Those who defend its use refer to a "scientific consensus" concerning its benign nature and the fact that no deaths have been reported due to its overdose (Morgenthaler and Joy 1994). However, evidence is mounting that in high doses, GHB can be dangerous and even deadly. There have been more than 60 documented deaths attributed to GHB overdoses ("Gamma Hydroxybutyric Acid" 2000; Kam and Yoong 1998). It has been reported that GHB use can cause significant side effects, such as hormonal problems, sleep abnormalities, drowsiness, nausea, vomiting, and changes in blood pressure (Gallimberti et al. 1989). Both users and clinicians seem to agree that GHB is most dangerous when combined with other drugs, especially other CNS depressants such as alcohol ("Gamma Hydroxybutyric Acid" 2000).

Because GHB is illegal in the United States, it is currently available only through the underground "gray market" as a "bootleg" product manufactured by kitchen chemists and with suspicious quality and purity. As of the year 2000, the FDA had investigated 124 cases involving large-scale interstate manufacture and distribution of GHB (Leshner 2000). The lack of reliability of these GHB-containing products and the highly variable responses of different people to this substance increase the likelihood of problems when using this depressant.

There is some debate whether the use of GHB can cause dependence and withdrawal. There is evidence suggesting that chronic high-dose use of GHB may lead to prolonged abuse and a with-

CASE IN POINT

GHB Use by an Ex-alcoholic

I have been doing some self-experimentation with GHB. . . . The literature shows results . . . using it as treatment for . . . alcoholics. I am an alcoholic with a perpetual fight to keep control. . . . I tried it (GHB) out of curiosity and found the psychoactive effect to be extremely pleasant. Dizziness and disruption of motor control are equivalent to or worse than alcohol. . . . It lacks the aggressive quality that seems to make one feel capable (e.g., to drive) with alcohol. This lack of aggressive content is a very distinguishing feature. . . . It definitely acts as a disinhibitor similarly to alcohol. Talking is facilitated . . . I am also a good listener when I am on GHB. It has an empathogenic quality. Not nearly as profound as MDMA . . . but in the same vein. No shaking, no sweating, no weak knees or any of the symptoms we alcoholics have come to know and love. And . . . no hangover. It comes on pretty fast, under a half an hour. . . . It is long-lasting, 4 hours of motor impairment. . . . It is fairly soporific and fairly relaxing with a time dilating effect similar to mushrooms, but less profound . . . when my supply is removed . . . there is no excessive craving or nervousness. It is much like being cut off from marijuana. . . . It should not be mixed with alcohol. They each enhance the other and one feels very inebriated very fast. . . .

Source: GHB, Internet address: alt.psychoactives.alt.drugs.alt.psychobiology.sci.med.pharmacy.

drawal syndrome consisting of insomnia, anxiety and tremors that typically resolves in 3 to 12 days (Craig et al. 2000; Galloway et al. 1997). Another major concern with this substance is its use in cases of date rape. Because GHB can be stored as a clear, colorless, odorless liquid, it easily is added undetected to a beverage such as an alcoholic drink (NIDA Notes 2000). Its amnesiac and sedative properties disable users and make them vulnerable to sexual assault (Leshner 2000). Despite attempts to vigorously prosecute these cases, because the victims frequently are unable to recall details of the attack and the drug disappears so quickly from the bloodstream (its half-life is 2 to 3 hours) date rape with GHB can be difficult to prove.

Another substance related to GHB is gamma butyrolactone (GBL). GBL is the solvent precursor for GHB and because of its rapid conversion to GHB in the body after ingestion, it is being used as a substitute for GHB. In January 1999, the FDA requested a voluntary recall of all GBL-containing products sold in health food stores and health clubs and warned of its potential dangers. It is expected that use of GBL causes adverse effects similar to those associated with GHB use (Leshner 2000).

Patterns of Abuse with CNS Depressants

The American Psychiatric Association (APA) considers dependence on CNS depressants to be a psychiatric disorder. According to its widely used *Diagnostic and Statistical Manual of Mental Disorders, Fourth Edition (DSM-IV)*, (American Psychiatric Association 1994), a *substance dependence disorder* is present when three of the following criteria are satisfied at any time in a 12-month period:

1. The person needs greatly increased amounts of the substance to achieve the desired effect or experiences a markedly diminished effect with continued use of the substance.

2. Characteristic withdrawal occurs when drug use is stopped, which encourages continued use of the substance to avoid the unpleasant effects.

3. The substance is consumed in larger amounts over a longer period of time than originally intended.

4. The person shows persistent desire or repeated unsuccessful efforts to decrease or control substance use.

5. A great deal of time is spent obtaining and using the substance or recovering from its effects.

6. All daily activities revolve around the substance—important social, occupational, or recreational activities are given up or reduced because of substance use.

7. The person withdraws from family activities and hobbies to use the substance privately or spend more time with substance-using friends.

8. The person continues use of the substance despite recognizing that it causes social, occupational, legal, or medical problems.

A review of the previous discussion about the properties of CNS depressants reveals that severe dependence on these drugs can satisfy all these DSM-IV criteria; thus, according to the APA, dependence on CNS depressants is classified as a form of mental illness.

The principal types of people who are most inclined to abuse CNS depressants include the following:

1. Those who seek sedative effects to deal with emotional stress, to try to escape from problems they are unable to face. Sometimes these individuals are able to persuade clinicians to administer depressants for their problems; at other times, they self-medicate with depressants that are obtained illegally.

2. Those who seek the excitation that occurs, especially after some tolerance has developed; instead of depression, they feel exhilaration and euphoria.

3. Those who try to counteract the unpleasant effect or withdrawal associated with other drugs of abuse, such as some stimulants, and lysergic acid diethylamide (LSD), and other hallucinogens.

4. Those who use sedatives in combination with other depressant drugs such as alcohol and heroin. Alcohol plus a sedative gives a faster high but can be dangerous because of the multiple depressant effects and synergistic interaction. Heroin users often resort to barbiturates if their heroin supply is compromised.

As mentioned earlier, depressants are commonly abused in combination with other drugs (Trevor and Lay 1998). In particular, opioid narcotic users take barbiturates, benzodiazepines, and other depressants to augment the effects of a weak batch of heroin or a rapidly shrinking supply. Chronic narcotic users also claim that depressants help to offset tolerance to opioids, thereby requiring less narcotic to achieve a satisfactory response by the user. It is not uncommon to see joint dependence on both narcotics and depressants.

Another common use of depressants is by alcoholics to soften the withdrawal from ethanol or to help create a state of intoxication without the telltale odor of alcohol. Interestingly, similar strategies are also used therapeutically to help detoxify the alcoholic. For example, long-acting barbiturates or benzodiazepines are often used to wean an alcohol-dependent person away from ethanol. Treatment with these depressants helps to reduce the severity of withdrawal symptoms, making it easier and safer for alcoholics to eliminate their drug dependence.

Finally, as already mentioned, CNS depressants are often used in conjunction with alcohol to commit sexual assaults. Because these drugs are sedating, remove inhibitions, and can induce a temporary state of amnesia, they are sometimes secretly added to an alcoholic beverage in order to incapacitate the intended victim of a date rape. Recent statistics suggest that about 40% of women who are sexually assaulted have alcohol in their blood, 20% have cannabinoids (from marijuana use), 8% have cocaine, 8% have a benzodiazepine, 4% have amphetamines, 4% have GHB, less than 2% have opioid narcotics, and 1% have barbiturates (Elsohly and Salamone 1999).

In general, those who chronically abuse the CNS depressants prefer (1) the short-acting barbiturates, such as pentobarbital and secobarbital, (2) the barbiturate-like depressants, such as glutethimide, methyprylon, and methaqualone; (3) the faster-acting benzodiazepines, such as diazepam (Valium), alprazolam (Xanax), or lorazepam (Ativan). However, most nonabusing people do not find the benzodiazepines particularly reinforcing (Woods et al. 1992).

Dependence on sedative-hypnotic agents can develop insidiously. Often, a long-term patient is treated for persistent insomnia or anxiety with daily exposures to a CNS depressant. When an attempt to withdraw the drug is made, the patient becomes agitated, unable to sleep, and severely anxious; a state of panic may be experienced when deprived of the drug. These signs are frequently mistaken for a resurgence of the medical condition being treated and are not recognized as part of a withdrawal syndrome to the CNS depressant. Consequently, the patient is restored to his or her supply of CNS depressant, and the symptoms of withdrawal subside. Such conditions generally lead to a gradual increase in dosage as tolerance to the sedative-hypnotic develops. The patient becomes severely dependent on the depressant, both physically and psychologically, and the drug habit becomes an essential feature in the user's daily routines. Only after severe dependence has developed does the clinician often realize what has taken place. The next stage is the unpleasant task of trying to wean the patient from the drug (detoxification) with as little discomfort as possible.

Because of the similarities between alcohol and barbiturate-like drugs, it is common to see individuals who abuse both types of depressants. One danger is that these people use both drugs together. Due to the synergism that exists between CNS depressants in general, such a mixture can severely suppress respiration and cardiovascular function, often with deadly consequences (Trevor and Lay 1998). Knowledge of this dangerous interaction is quite common among the drug-using population; consequently, many suicide attempts are made by self-administering high doses of barbiturate-like drugs with a chaser of ethanol.

The prevalence of abuse of illicit CNS depressants appeared to peak in the early 1980s for 12th graders. Illegal use of these drugs then decreased dramatically until 1992, at which time abuse appears to have rebounded (see Table 7.5).

Detoxification of patients who are severly dependent on CNS depressants can be very unpleasant and even life-threatening.

anorexia, nausea, vomiting, seizures, delirium, and maniacal activity.

The duration and severity of withdrawal depends on the particular drug taken. With short-acting depressants, such as pentobarbital, secobarbital, and methaqualone, withdrawal symptoms tend to have a faster onset of action and be more severe. They begin 12 to 24 hours after the last dose and peak in intensity between 24 and 72 hours later. Withdrawal from longer-acting depressants, such as phenobarbital, diazepam, and chlordiazepoxide, develops more slowly and is less intense; symptoms peak on the fifth to eighth day (Trevor and Lay 1998).

Not surprisingly, the approach to detoxifying a person who is dependent on a sedative-hypnotic depends on the nature of the drug itself (that is, to which category of depressants it belongs), the severity of the dependence, and the duration of action of the drug. The general objectives of detoxification are to eliminate drug dependence (both physical and psychological) in a safe manner while minimizing discomfort. Having achieved these objectives, it

■ TREATMENT FOR WITHDRAWAL

All sedative-hypnotics, including alcohol and benzodiazepines, can produce physical dependence and a barbiturate-like withdrawal syndrome if taken in sufficient dosage over a long period. Withdrawal symptoms include anxiety, tremors, nightmares, insomnia,

detoxification
elimination of a toxic substance, such as a drug, from the body and its effects

TABLE 7.5 **Lifetime Prevalence of Abuse of CNS Depressants for 12th-graders**

	1990	1992	1995	1998	1999
Any illicit drug	47.9%	40.7%	48.4%	54.1%	54.7%
Barbiturates	6.8%	5.5%	7.4%	8.7%	8.9%
Methaqualone	2.3%	1.6%	1.2%	1.6%	NA
All depressants (including benzodiazepines)	7.5%	6.1%	7.6%	9.2%	NA

Source: L. Johnston. *Drug Abuse Survey.* Lansing, MI: University of Michigan, 2000.

is hoped that the patient will be able to remain free of dependence on all CNS depressants.

Often the basic approach for treating severe dependence on sedative-hypnotics is substitution with either pentobarbital or the longer-acting phenobarbital for the offending, usually shorter-acting, CNS depressant. Once substitution has occurred, the long-acting barbiturate dose is gradually reduced. Using a substitute is necessary because abrupt withdrawal for a person who is physically dependent can be dangerous and can cause life-threatening seizures. This substitution treatment uses the same rationale as the treatment of heroin withdrawal by methadone replacement. Detoxification also includes supportive measures such as vitamins, restoration of electrolyte balance, and prevention of dehydration. The patient must be watched closely during this time because he or she will be apprehensive, confused, and unable to make logical decisions (O'Brien 1995).

If the person is addicted to both alcohol and barbiturates, the phenobarbital dosage must be increased to compensate for the double withdrawal. Many barbiturate addicts who enter a hospital to be treated for withdrawal are also dependent on heroin. In such cases, the barbiturate dependence should be addressed first because the associated withdrawal can be life-threatening. Detoxification from any sedative-hypnotic should take place under close medical supervision, typically in a hospital (O'Brien 1995).

It is important to remember that elimination of physical dependence does not necessarily result in a cure. The problem of psychological dependence can be much more difficult to handle. If an individual is

abusing a CNS depressant because of emotional instability, personal problems, or a very stressful environment, eliminating physical dependence alone will not solve the problem and drug dependence is likely to recur. These types of patients require intense psychological counseling and must be trained to deal with their difficulties in a more constructive and positive fashion. Without such psychological support, benefits from detoxification will only be temporary, and therapy will ultimately fail.

DEPRESSANTS

Natural Substances

Some plants that contain naturally occuring CNS depressants are included in herbal products or made into herbal teas for relaxation or as treatment for sleep problems. Probably the best known of this group is the kava kava plant (*piper methysticum*). Drinks and bars containing extract from kava kava root are legally available in many health food stores and are especially popular in Polynesian populations and sometimes used in religious ceremonies. The extract is prepared from the part of the kava plant beneath the surface of the ground. Small amounts of kava kava can produce euphoria and increased sociability, while larger doses cause substantial relaxation, lethargy, relaxed lower limbs and eventually sleep. For some users there may be visual and auditory hallucinations that can last up to 1–2 hours. Some users report that kava drinks can make the mouth numb much like topical local anesthetics used by dentists.

A second type of common herb that contains CNS depressants belong to the Datura family of plants. Although these botanicals are typically associated with hallucinogenic effects, in lower amounts they sometimes can also cause sedation and even induce sleep. Examples of these plants include *Datura inoxia* (Devil's Weed) and *Datura strammonium* (Jimson Weed or Thornapple). The active ingredients in these plants are typically anticholinergic drugs such as atropine or scopolamine. In lower doses, these herbs, especially if they contain scopolamine, have been used to encourage sleep. In fact, the actions of the herbs are somewhat similar to the OTC antihistamine-contained sleepaids which also work due to their anticholinergic actions. In higher doses, both atropine and scopolamine can cause hallucinogenic effects. The anticholinergic actions of these herbs can be quite annoying and include constipation, dry mouth, and blurred vision, just to mention a few.

Discussion Questions

1. Why have benzodiazepine drugs replaced the barbiturates as the sedative-hypnotic drugs most prescribed by physicians?

2. Which features of CNS depressants give them abuse potential?

3. Why is long-term use of the benzodiazepines more likely to cause dependence than short-term use?

4. Why are some physicians careless when prescribing benzodiazepines for patients suffering from severe anxiety?

5. Currently, sleep aid products are available OTC. Should the FDA also allow sedatives to be sold without a prescription? Support your answer.

6. Are there any real advantages to using barbiturates as sedatives or hypnotics? Should the FDA remove them from the market?

7. What types of people are most likely to abuse CNS depressants? Suggest ways to help these people avoid abusing these drugs.

8. What is the appeal for using GHB? Why is it used to commit sexual assaults?

9. What dangers are associated with treating individuals who are severely dependent on CNS depressants?

Key Terms

barbiturates **161**

benzodiazepines **161**

antihistamines **162**

sedatives **162**

anxiolytic **162**

hypnotics **162**

amnesiac **162**

anesthesia **162**

REM sleep **164**

paradoxical **165**

club drugs **167**

detoxification **175**

Summary

1 Several unrelated drug groups cause CNS depression, but only a few are actually used clinically for their depressant properties. The most frequently prescribed CNS depressants are benzodiazepines, which include drugs such as Klonopin, Ambien, and Xanax. Barbiturates once were popular but, because of their severe side effects, they are no longer used by most clinicians. Much like barbiturates, drugs such as chloral hydrate, glutethimide, and methaqualone are little used today. Finally, some OTC and prescription antihistamines, such as diphenhydramine, hydroxyzine, and promethazine, are still used for their CNS-depressant effects.

2 The clinical value of CNS depressants is dose-dependent. At low doses, these drugs relieve anxiety and promote relaxation (*sedatives*). At higher doses, they can cause drowsiness and promote sleep (*hypnotics*). At even higher doses, some

of the depressants cause anesthesia and are used for patient management during surgery.

3 Because CNS depressants can relieve anxiety and reduce stress, they are viewed as desirable by many people. If used frequently over long periods, however, they can cause tolerance that leads to dependence.

4 The principal reason benzodiazepines have replaced barbiturates in the treatment of stress and insomnia is that benzodiazepines have a greater margin of safety and are less likely to alter sleep patterns. Benzodiazepines enhance the GABA transmitter system in the brain through a specific receptor, whereas the effects of barbiturates are less selective. Even though benzodiazepines are safer than barbiturates, dependence and significant withdrawal problems can result if the drugs are used indiscriminately.

5 Often, benzodiazepine dependence occurs in patients who suffer stress or anxiety disorders and are under a physician's care. If the physician is not careful and the cause of the stress is not resolved, drug treatment can drag on for weeks or months. After prolonged benzodiazepine therapy, tolerance develops to the drug; when benzodiazepine use is stopped, withdrawal occurs, which itself causes agitation. A rebound response to the drug might resemble the effects of emotional stress (agitation), so use of benzodiazepine is continued. In this way, the patient becomes severely dependent.

6 The short-acting CNS depressants are preferred for treatment of insomnia. These drugs help the patient get to sleep and then are inactivated by the body; when the user awakens the next day, he or she is less likely to experience residual effects than with long-acting drugs. The short-acting depressants are also more likely to be abused because of their relatively rapid onset and intense effects. In contrast, the long-acting depressants are better suited to treating persistent problems such as anxiety and stress. The long-acting depressants are also used to help wean dependent people from their use of short-acting compounds such as alcohol.

7 Although at one time very popular, methaqualone is no longer legally available in the United States due to abuse problems. Even so, it continues to be found on the street because it is smuggled across the Mexican and Canadian borders into the United States.

8 Many antihistamines cause sedation and drowsiness due to their anticholinergic effects. Several of these agents are useful for short-term relief of anxiety and are available in OTC sleep aids. The effectiveness of these CNS depressants is usually less than that of benzodiazepines. Because of their anticholinergic actions, antihistamines can cause some annoying side effects. These agents are not likely to be used for long periods; thus, dependence or serious abuse usually does not develop.

9 The people most likely to abuse CNS depressants include individuals who (1) use drugs to relieve continual stress; (2) paradoxically feel euphoria and stimulation from depressants; (3) use depressants to counteract the unpleasant effects of other drugs of abuse, such as stimulants; and (4) combine depressants with alcohol and heroin to potentiate the effects.

10 The basic approach for treating dependence on CNS depressants is to detoxify in a safe manner while minimizing discomfort. This state is achieved by substituting a long-acting barbiturate or benzodiazepine, such as phenobarbital or Valium, for the offending CNS depressant. The long-acting drug causes less severe withdrawal symptoms over a longer period of time. The dependent person is gradually weaned from the substitute drug until depressant-free.

11 GHB is a naturally occurring substance related to the neurotransmitter GABA that has been used for its sedating, euphorigenic and muscle-building properties. It has also been used to debilitate victims of date rape during sexual assaults. Because of concerns that this substance is frequently abused, GHB was classified as a Schedule I drug in 2000.

References

American Psychiatric Association. "Substance Related Disorders." In *Diagnostic and Statistical Manual of Mental Disorders,* 4th ed., [DSM-IV], chair Allen Frances. 175–272. Washington, DC: APA, 1994.

Associated Press. "Woman Who Used Halcion Defense Hangs Self." *Salt Lake Tribune* 248 (1994): D-3.

Carlini, E. "Preliminary Note: Dangerous Use of Anticholinergic Drugs in Brazil." *Drug and Alcohol Dependence* 32 (1993): 1–7.

"Club Drugs." NINA Infofax (22 May 2000). Available http://165.112.78.61/Infofax/clubdrugs.html.

"Common Substances of Abuse." *Diagnosis and Treatment of Drug Abuse in Family Practice* (22 May 2000). Available www.165.112.78.61/Diagnosis-Treatment/substances .html.

Craig, K., H. Gomez, J. McMannus, and T. Bania. "Severe Gamma-hydroxybutyrate Withdrawal: A Case Report and Literature Review." *Journal of Emergency Medicine* 18 (2000): 65–70.

Elsohly, M. and S. Salamone. "Prevalence of Drugs Used in Cases of Alleged Sexual Assault." *Journal Analytical Toxicology* 23 (1999): 141–6.

Gallimberti, L., M. Ferri, S. Ferrara, F. Fadda, and G. Gessa. "Gamma-hydroxybutyric acid for the treatment of alcohol withdrawal syndrome." *Lancet* 30 (1989): 787–9.

Galloway, G., S. Frederick, F. Staggers, M. Gonzales, S. Stalcup, and D. Smith. "Gamma-hydroxybutyrate: An Emerging Drug of Abuse That Causes Physical Dependence." *Addiction* 92 (1997): 89–96.

"Gamma Hydroxybutyric Acid (GHB, Liquid X, Goop, Georgia Home Boy)." *DEA Bulletin* DEA/ODE# (000612), (12 June 2000).

Gatzonis, S., E. Angelopoulos, E. Daskalopoulou, V. Mantouvalos, A. Chioni, C. Zournas, and A. Siafanas. "Convulsive Status Epilepticus Following Abrupt High-Dose Benzodiazepine Discontinuation." *Drug and Alcohol Dependence* 59 (2000): 95–7.

Goldstein, A. "Pharmacological Aspects of Drug Abuse." In *Remington's Pharmaceutical Sciences,* 19th ed., edited by A. R. Gennaro, 780–93. Easton, PA: 1995.

Hebel, S. "Antidotes, Flumazenil." *Facts and Comparisons.* St. Louis, MO: Wolters Kluwer, 2000: 386–7.

"High Anxiety." *Consumer Reports* (January 1993): 19–24.

Hobbs, W., T. Rall, and T. Verdoorn. "Hypnotics and Sedatives." In *The Pharmacological Basis of Therapeutics,* 9th ed., edited by J. Hardman and L. Limbird, 361–96. New York: McGraw–Hill, 1995.

Hughes, G., J. McElnay, C. Hughes, and P. McKenna. "Abuse/Misuse of Non-prescription Drugs." *Pharmacy World Science* 21 (1999): 251–5.

Julien, R. "General Nonselective Central Nervous System Depressants." In *A Primer of Drug Action,* 6th ed., 51–70. New York: Freeman, 1992.

Kam, P. and F. Yoong. "Gamma-hydroxybutyric Acid: An Emerging Recreational Drug." *Anesthesia* 53 (1998): 1195–8.

Kosten, T. and L. Hollister. "Drugs of Abuse." In *Basic and Clinical Pharmacology,* 7th ed., edited by B. Katzung, 516–31. Samford, CT; Appleton & Lange, 1998.

Latner, A. "The Top 200 Drugs of 1999." *Pharmacy Times* 66 (2000): 16–32.

Leshner, A. E. "Club Drug Alert." *NIDA Notes.* 14 (2000); 3 (posted 22 May 2000). Available www.165.112.78.61/ NIDA_Notes/NNVOL14N6/DirRepVol14N6.html.

Lingenhoehl, K., R. Brom, J. Heid, P. Beck, W. Froestl, K. Kaupman, B. Bettler, and J. Mosbacher. "Gamma-hydroxybutyrate Is a Weak Agonist Against Recombinant GABA (B) Receptors." *Neuropharmacology* 38 (1999): 1667–73.

Longo, L. and B. Johnson. "Addiction: Part I. Benzodiazepines, Side Effects, Abuse Risks and Alternatives." *American Family Physician* 61 (2000): 2121–8.

McEvoy, G., ed. *American Hospital Formulary Service Drug Information.* Bethesda, MD: American Society of Hospital Pharmacists, 2000.

Mondanaro, J. *Chemically Dependent Women.* Lexington, MA: Lexington Books/Heath, 1988.

Morgenthaler, J. and D. Joy. *Special Report on GHB.* Petaluma, CA: Smart Publication, 1994.

"New Halcion Guidelines." *American Druggist* (January 1992): 14.

NIDA Notes. "What Are Club Drugs?" *NIDA Notes* 14 (22 May 2000). Available http://165.112.78.61/NIDA_Notes/ Nnvol14N6/whatare.html.

O'Brien, C. "Drug Addiction and Drug Abuse." In *The Pharmacological Basis of Therapeutics,* 9th ed., edited by J. Hardman and L. Limbird, 557–77. New York: McGraw–Hill, 1995.

Pagliaro, L. and A. Pagliaro. "Drug Induced Aggression." *Medical Psychotherapist* (Newsletter of the American Board of Medical Psychotherapists) 8 (Fall 1992): 1.

Physician's Desk Reference. 50th ed., (PDR) Montvale, NJ: Medical Economics, 1997.

Poldrugo, F. and G. Addolorato. "The Role of Gamma-hydroxybutyrate Acid in the Treatment of Alcoholism: From Animal to Clinical Studies." *Alcohol, Alcoholism* 34 (1999): 15–34.

Serafin, W. and Babe, K. "Histamine, Bradykinin and Their Antagonists." In *The Pharmacological Basis of Therapeutics,* 9th ed., edited by J. Hardman and L. Limbird, 581–600. New York: McGraw–Hill, 1995.

Trevor, A. and W. Lay. "Sedative-hypnotic Drugs." In *Basic and Clinical Pharmacology,* 7th ed., edited by B. Katzung, 354–71. Samford, CT, 1998.

Woods, J., J. Katz, and G. Winger. "Benzodiazepines: Use, Abuse and Consequences." *Pharmacological Reviews* 44 (1992): 155–323.

Alcohol: Pharmacological Effects

Did You Know?

- ▶ Ethanol leads all other substances of abuse in treatment admissions.
- ▶ Ethanol is the only alcohol used for human consumption; the other alcohols are poisonous.
- ▶ Some wild animals and insects become drunk after seeking out and consuming alcohol-containing fermented fruit.
- ▶ The first recorded beer brewery was in existence in 3700 B.C.
- ▶ Alcohol-related deaths outnumber deaths related to other drugs of abuse (except tobacco) by a four to one margin.
- ▶ Low daily consumption of alcohol can reduce cardiovascular disease in older men and postmenopausal women.

- ▶ Women reach a higher blood alcohol level than men when consuming the same amount of alcohol per body weight.
- ▶ The lethal level of alcohol is between 0.4% and 0.6% by volume in the blood.
- ▶ The liver metabolizes alcohol at a constant rate, unaffected by the amount ingested.
- ▶ Among alcoholics, liver disorders account for approximately 10% to 15% of deaths.
- ▶ Fetal alcohol syndrome (FAS) is characterized by facial deformities, growth deficiencies, and mental retardation.
- ▶ The incidence of FAS is one in three infants born to alcoholic mothers.
- ▶ Alcoholism is commonly associated with severe malnutrition.

Learning Objectives

**On completing this chapter
you will be able to:**

▶ Explain how common alcohol (ethanol)
is a drug.

▶ Explain the pharmacokinetic properties of
alcohol.

▶ Explain the role of alcohol in "polydrug"
abuse.

▶ Name the possible physical effects of
prolonged heavy ethanol consumption.

▶ Explain the potential cardiovascular benefits
of moderate alcohol use.

▶ Describe FAS and its effects.

▶ Explain how prolonged consumption of
alcohol affects the brain and nervous
system, liver, digestive system, blood,
cardiovascular system, sexual organs,
endocrine systems, and kidneys, and how
it leads to mental disorders and damage
to fetuses.

▶ Explain why malnutrition is so common in
alcoholics.

Introduction

In this chapter and the next, we examine several aspects of alcohol use. This chapter focuses on how alcohol affects the body from a pharmacological perspective. Chapter 9 studies the social effects of this drug, mainly, the effects and consequences of alcohol on an individual's personal and social life.

As a licit drug, alcohol is extensively promoted socially through advertising. But more important, drinking is perceived as acceptable. The popularity of this drug was recently shown in the 1999 Monitoring the Future Study: in 1998, 88% of U.S. college students had used alcohol sometime during their life; 85% used it during the preceding year; 68% used it during the preceding month; 4% used it daily; and 39% consumed at least five drinks in a row sometime during the preceding 2 weeks (Johnston et al. 1999).

This chapter focuses on the many adverse effects of alcohol on the human body. Overall, it provides you with a foundation to understand the pharmacological nature of alcohol. We hope that such an understanding of how this drug affects the various organ systems of the body will lead to more responsible use and less abuse of alcohol. Because of its widespread consumption, alcohol leads all other addicting substances for treatment admissions. Almost 50% of the patients entering treatment for drug dependence in 1997 had abused alcohol (SAMHSA News 2000).

Because of frequent advertising, use of alcohol is perceived as normal and acceptable.

The Nature and History of Alcohol

Alcohol has been part of human culture since the beginning of recorded history. The technology for alcohol production is ancient. Several basic ingredients and conditions are needed: sugar, water, yeast, and warm temperatures.

The process of making alcohol, called fermentation, is a natural one. It occurs in ripe fruit and berries and even in honey that bees leave in trees. These substances contain sugar and water and are found in warm climates, where yeast spores are transported through the air. Animals such as elephants, baboons, birds, wild pigs, and bees will seek and eat fermented fruit. Elephants under the influence of alcohol have been observed bumping into one another and stumbling around. Intoxicated bees fly an unsteady beeline toward their hives. Birds eating fermented fruit become so uncoordinated that they cannot fly, or if they do, they crash into windows or branches. In fact, fermented honey, called mead, may have been the first alcoholic beverage.

The Egyptians had breweries 6000 years ago; they credited the god Osiris with introducing wine to humans. The ancient Greeks used large quantities of wine and credited a god, Bacchus (or Dionysus), with introducing the drink. Today, we use the words bacchanalia and dionysian to refer to revelry and drunken events. The Hebrews were also heavy users of wine. The Bible mentions that Noah, just nine generations removed from Adam, made wine and became drunk.

Alcohol is produced by a single-celled microscopic organism, one of the yeasts, that breaks down sugar by a metabolic form of combustion, thereby releasing carbon dioxide and forming water and ethyl alcohol as a waste product. Carbon dioxide creates the foam on a glass of beer and the fizz in champagne. Fermentation continues until the sugar supply is exhausted or the concentration of alcohol reaches the point at which it kills the yeast (12%–14%). Thus, 12% to 14% is the natural limit of alcohol found in fermented wines or beers.

The distillation device, or *still*, was developed by the Arabs around A.D. 800 and was introduced into medieval Europe around A.D. 1250. By boiling the fermented drink and gathering the condensed vapor in a pipe, a still increases the concentration of alcohol, potentially to 50% or higher. Because distillation made it easier for people to get drunk, it greatly intensified the problem of alcohol abuse. However, even before the arrival of the still, alcoholic beverages had been known to cause problems in heavy users that resulted in severe physical and psychological dependence. But not until the past century did the concept of alcoholism as a disease develop (Mann et al. 2000). (See "Here and Now," A Century of Alcohol.)

Alcohol as a Drug

Alcohol (more precisely designated as ethanol), as a natural product of fermentation, is an extremely popular social beverage, the second most widely used and abused of all the psychoactive drugs (next to caffeine), and widely misunderstood (Quindien 2000). This psychoactive substance depresses the central nervous system (CNS) while influencing almost all major organ

systems of the body. Alcohol is also an addictive drug in that it may produce a physical and behavioral dependence. Although tradition and attitude are important factors in determining the use patterns of this substance, the typical consumer rarely appreciates the diversity of pharmacological effects caused by alcohol, the drug. The pharmaco-

HERE AND NOW   A Century of Alcohol

An overwhelming need to consume alcohol (known today as alcoholism) was first described in the literature by Benjamin Rush in 1784, but the concept that excessive use of alcohol is a disease didn't really evolve until the past 100 years. This perspective was encouraged by the "temperance movement" of the late 19th century. Because of the ill effects of alcohol, temperance legally became "prohibition" in 1919. *Prohibition* (alcohol made illegal) was initially successful in reducing consumption, but consumption began to rebound in the late 1920s. However, it has been suggested that prohibition was repealed in 1933 not because it failed to reduce alcohol use but

because of shifting policy during the Great Depression that argued liquor manufacturing would create jobs and provide taxes on alcoholic beverages that could fund government programs.

The second half of the 20th century saw the emergence of the belief that genetics plays a major role in alcoholism. This concept suggests that because of inherited traits, some families and individuals are more vulnerable to alcohol addiction than others. Researchers today are energetically moving forward to identify which genes might contribute to the development and expression of the addiction in order to improve prevention and treatment for alcoholism.

Source: Quindien 2000.

logical action of alcohol accounts for both its pleasurable and CNS effects as well as its hazards to health and public safety.

■ ALCOHOL AS A SOCIAL DRUG

Why is alcohol often perceived as an acceptable adjunct to such celebrations as parties, birthdays, weddings, and anniversaries, and as a way of relieving stress and anxiety? Social psychologists refer to the perception of alcohol as a social lubricant . This term implies that drinking is misconceived as safely promoting conviviality and social interaction, and as an activity that bolsters confidence by repressing inhibitions and strengthening extraversion. Why do many people have to be reminded that alcohol is a drug like marijuana or cocaine and may have serious consequences for some people (Quindien 2000)? Four reasons explain this misconception:

1. The use of alcohol is legal.

2. Through widespread advertising, the media promote the notion that alcohol consumption is as normal and safe as drinking fruit juices and soft drinks.

3. The distribution or the sale of alcoholic beverages is widely practiced.

4. Alcohol use has a long tradition, dating back to 30,000 B.C. (Royce 1989).

KEY TERMS

social lubricant
belief that drinking (misconceived as safe) that represses inhibitions and strengthens extraversion leads to increased sociability

methyl alcohol
wood alcohol or methanol

ethylene glycol
alcohol used as antifreeze

isopropyl alcohol
rubbing alcohol, sometimes used as an antiseptic

anesthetic
a drug that blocks sensitivity to pain

blood alcohol concentration (BAC)
concentration of alcohol found in the blood, often expressed as a percentage

■ IMPACT OF ALCOHOL

Although many consider the effects of alcohol enjoyable and reassuring, the adverse pharmacological impact of this drug is extensive, and its effects are associated with more than 100,000 deaths each year in the United States (Special Report 1997). It is estimated that at some time during their lives, almost 50% of all Americans will be involved in an alcohol-related traffic accident. The pharmacological effects of alcohol abuse cause severe dependence, which is classified as a psychiatric disorder according to *The Diagnostic and Statistical Manual of Mental Disorders*, fourth edition (DSM IV) criteria (Hoffman and Tabakoff 1996). These effects also disrupt personal, family, social, and professional functioning and frequently result in multiple illnesses and accidents, violence, and crime (Eronen et al. 1996). Alcohol consumed during pregnancy can lead to devastating damage to offspring and is a principal cause of mental retardation in newborns (Larroque and Kaminski 1998). Next to tobacco, alcohol is the leading cause of premature death in America. Experts have estimated that in the United States, approximately $167 billion is spent annually dealing with social and health problems resulting from the pharmacological effects of alcohol (Quindien 2000). However, such estimates fall short of assessing the emotional upheaval and human suffering caused by this drug ("Centerpiece" 1993).

Despite all of the problems that alcohol causes, our free society has demanded that access to this drug be preserved. However, it is unthinkable to ignore the tremendous negative social impact of this drug. There are no simple answers to this dichotomy, yet clearly governmental and educational institutions could do more to protect members of society against the dangers of alcohol. The best weapons we have against the problems caused by alcohol are education, prevention, and treatment (see Chapter 4).

The Properties of Alcohol

Technically, alcohol is a chemical structure that has a hydroxyl group (OH, for one oxygen and one hydrogen atom) attached to a carbon atom. Of the many types of alcohol, several are important in this context. The first is methyl alcohol (*methanol* or *wood alcohol*), so called because it is made from wood products. Its metabolites are poisonous. Small amounts (4 mL) cause blindness by affecting the retina, and larger amounts (80–150 mL) are usually fatal (Klaasen 1995). Methyl alcohol is added to ethyl alcohol (*ethanol* or *grain alcohol*, the drinking type) intended for industrial use so that people will not drink it. A similar mixture is also sometimes added to illegally manufactured ("bootleg") liquor.

Another type of poisonous alcohol, ethylene glycol, is used in antifreeze, and a third type, isopropyl alcohol, is commonly used as rubbing alcohol and as an *antiseptic* (a solution for preventing the growth of microorganisms). These two types of alcohol are also poisonous if consumed. Pure ethyl alcohol (ethanol) is recognized as an official drug in the U.S. Pharmacopoeia, although the various alcoholic beverages are not listed for medical use.

Alcohol can be used as a solvent for other drugs or as a preservative. It is used to cleanse, disinfect, and harden the skin and to reduce sweating. A 70% alcohol solution is an effective bactericide. However, it should not be used on open wounds because it will dehydrate the injured tissue and worsen the damage. Alcohol may be deliberately injected in or near nerves to treat severe pain; it causes local anesthesia and deterioration of the nerve.

In all alcoholic beverages—beer, wine, liqueurs or cordials, and distilled spirits—the psychoactive agent is the same, but the amount of ethanol varies (see Table 8.1). The amount of alcohol is expressed either as a percentage by volume or, in the older

proof system, as a measurement based on the military assay method. To make certain that they were getting a high alcohol content in the liquor, the British military would place a sample on gunpowder and touch a spark to it. If the alcohol content exceeded 50%, it would burn and ignite the gunpowder. This test was "proof" that the sample was at least 50% alcohol. If the distilled spirits were "under proof," the water content would prevent the gunpowder from igniting. The percentage of alcohol volume is one-half the proof number. For example, 100-proof whiskey has a 50% alcohol content.

The Physical Effects of Alcohol

How does alcohol affect the body? Figure 8.1 graphically illustrates how alcohol is absorbed into the body. After a drink, alcohol has direct contact with the mouth, esophagus, stomach, and intestine, acting as an irritant and an anesthetic (blocking sensitivity to pain). In addition, alcohol influences almost every organ system in the body after entering the bloodstream. Alcohol diffuses into the blood rapidly after consumption by passing (absorption process) through gastric and intestinal walls. Once the alcohol is in the small intestine, its absorption is largely independent of the presence of food, unlike in the stomach, where food retards absorption.

The effects of alcohol on the human body depend on the amount of alcohol in the blood, known as the blood alcohol concentration (BAC). This concentration largely determines behavioral and physical responses to alcoholic beverages. Relative to behavior, circumstances in which the drinking occurs, the drinker's mood, and his or her attitude and previous experience with alcohol all contribute to the reaction to drinking. People demonstrate individual patterns of psychological functioning that may affect their reactions to alcohol, as well. For instance, the time it takes to empty the stomach may be either reduced or accelerated as a result of anger, fear, stress, nausea, and the condition of the stomach tissues.

The blood alcohol level produced depends on the presence of food in the stomach, the rate of alcohol consumption, the concentration of the alcohol, and the drinker's body composition. Fatty foods, meat, and milk slow the absorption of alco-

TABLE 8.1 The Concentration of Ethanol in Common Alcoholic Beverages

TYPE OF BEVERAGE	CONCENTRATON OF ETHANOL
U.S. beers	4%–6%
Wine coolers	10%–12%
Cocktail and dessert wines	17%–20%
Liqueurs	22%–50%
Distilled spirits	40%–50%

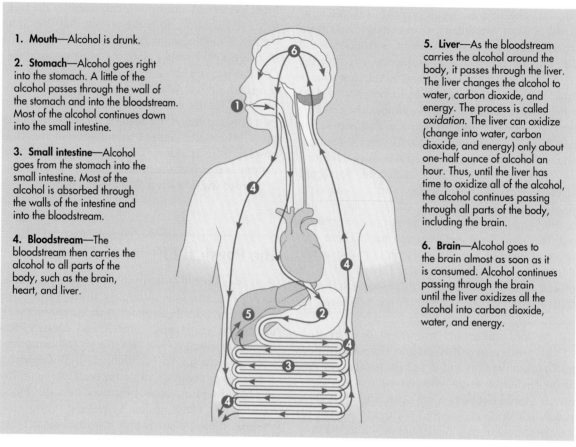

1. **Mouth**—Alcohol is drunk.

2. **Stomach**—Alcohol goes right into the stomach. A little of the alcohol passes through the wall of the stomach and into the bloodstream. Most of the alcohol continues down into the small intestine.

3. **Small intestine**—Alcohol goes from the stomach into the small intestine. Most of the alcohol is absorbed through the walls of the intestine and into the bloodstream.

4. **Bloodstream**—The bloodstream then carries the alcohol to all parts of the body, such as the brain, heart, and liver.

5. **Liver**—As the bloodstream carries the alcohol around the body, it passes through the liver. The liver changes the alcohol to water, carbon dioxide, and energy. The process is called *oxidation*. The liver can oxidize (change into water, carbon dioxide, and energy) only about one-half ounce of alcohol an hour. Thus, until the liver has time to oxidize all of the alcohol, the alcohol continues passing through all parts of the body, including the brain.

6. **Brain**—Alcohol goes to the brain almost as soon as it is consumed. Alcohol continues passing through the brain until the liver oxidizes all the alcohol into carbon dioxide, water, and energy.

FIGURE 8.1

How alcohol is absorbed in the body.

Source: National Institute on Alcohol Abuse and Alcoholism. *Alcohol Health and Research World.* Washington, DC: U.S. Department of Health and Human Services, 1988.

hol, allowing more time for its metabolism and reducing the peak concentration in the blood. When alcoholic beverages are taken with a substantial meal, peak BACs may be as much as 50% lower than they would have been had the alcohol been consumed by itself. When large amounts of alcohol are consumed in a short period, the brain and other organs are exposed to higher peak concentrations. Generally, the more alcohol in the stomach, the greater the absorption rate. There is, however, a modifying effect of very strong drinks on the absorption rate. The absorption of drinks stronger than 100 proof is inhibited. This effect may be due to blocked passage into the small intestine or irrita-

tion of the lining of the stomach, causing mucus secretion, or both. (See "Here and Now," Half-truths About Alcohol.)

Diluting an alcoholic beverage with water helps to slow down absorption, but mixing with carbonated beverages increases the absorption rate. The carbonation causes the stomach to empty its contents into the small intestine more rapidly, causing a more rapid "high." The carbonation in champagne has the same effect.

Once in the blood, distribution occurs as the alcohol uniformly diffuses throughout all tissues and fluids, including fetal circulation in pregnant women. Because the brain has a large blood supply,

HERE AND NOW   Half-truths About Alcohol

Much is known about alcohol, but much more needs to be learned in order to effectively and safely manage its use. There are several half-truths that are commonly believed by the general public that should be clarified:

Belief: Alcohol, if used in moderation, is healthy for everyone.

Fact: Typically, moderate drinking only benefits men over 50 years of age and women who are postmenopausal. Even for these populations, the benefits appear to be minimal in persons who already have healthy lifestyles.

Belief: Pound for pound, women hold their liquor as well as men.

Fact: Because women have proportionally less body water and tend to metabolize alcohol more slowly than men, women become more intoxicated with comparable dose consumption per body weight.

Belief: A drink before bed induces sleep.

Fact: After moderate drinking, onset of sleep may be faster, but the sleep itself becomes restless, marked by frequent wakings and inability to get back to sleep.

Belief: If you don't feel drunk, it is OK to drive.

Fact: People are typically unable to determine accurately how much alcohol is in their system. For most states in the United States, 0.08%–0.1% alcohol in the blood is the legal threshold for driving (i.e., it is against the law to drive with this blood alcohol content or higher), but studies have shown that driving performance is significantly impaired at half this concentration.

Sources: "Your Health: Alcohol: The Whole Truth, Seven Half-truths About Drinking, Exposed." *Consumer Reports* 64 (December 1999): 60–1; "FAQs on Alcohol Abuse and Alcoholism." NIAA (2000). Available http://silk.nih.gov/silk/niaaa1/questions/q-a.htm#questions2.

its activity is quickly affected by a high alcohol concentration in the blood. Body composition—the amount of water available for the alcohol to be dissolved in—is a key factor in BAC and distribution. The greater the muscle mass, the lower the BAC that will result from a given amount of alcohol. This relationship arises because muscle has more fluid volume than does fat. For example, if two men each weigh 180 pounds but one man has substantially more lean mass than the other man, the former will have a lower blood alcohol level after consuming 4 ounces of whiskey. The leaner man will show fewer effects. A woman of a weight equivalent to a man will have a higher blood alcohol level because women generally have a higher percentage of fat. Thus, they are affected more by identical drinks.

Alcoholic beverages contain almost no vitamins, minerals, protein, or fat—just large amounts of carbohydrates. Alcohol cannot be used by most cells; it must be metabolized by an enzyme, alcohol dehydrogenase, which is found almost exclusively in the liver. Alcohol provides more calories

KEY TERMS

alcohol dehydrogenase
principal enzyme that metabolizes ethanol

per gram than does carbohydrate or protein and only slightly less than does pure fat. Because it can provide many calories, the drinker's appetite may be satisfied, thus he or she may not eat properly, causing malnutrition (Achord 1995). The tolerance that develops to alcohol is comparable to that of barbiturates (see Chapter 7). Some people have a higher tolerance for alcohol and can more easily disguise intoxication.

■ ALCOHOL AND TOLERANCE

Repeated use of alcohol results in tolerance and in reduction in many of alcohol's pharmacological effects. As with other psychoactive drugs, tolerance to alcohol encourages increased consumption to regain its effects and can lead to severe physical and psychological dependence (O'Brien 1995). Tolerance to alcohol is similar to that seen with CNS depressants, such as the barbiturates and benzodiazepines. It consists of both an increase in the rate of alcohol metabolism (due to stimulation of metabolizing enzymes; see Chapter 6) and a reduced response by neurons and transmitter systems (particularly by increasing the activity of the inhibitory neurotransmitter, gamma-aminobutyric acid [GABA]) to this drug. Development of tolerance to alcohol is extremely variable; some users can consume large quantities of this drug with minor pharmacological effects. The tolerance-inducing changes caused by alcohol can also alter the body's response to other drugs (referred to as *cross-tolerance*; see Chapter 6) and can specifically reduce the effects of some other CNS depressants (O'Brien 1995).

> ### KEY TERMS
>
> **behavioral tolerance**
> compensation for motor impairments through behavioral pattern modification by chronic alcohol users
>
> **polydrug use**
> using multiple drugs concurrently
>
> **disinhibition**
> loss of conditioned reflexes due to depression of inhibitory centers of the brain
>
> **diuretic**
> a drug or substance that increases the production of urine

Many chronic alcohol users learn to compensate for the motor impairments of this drug by modifying their patterns of behavior. These adjustments are referred to as behavioral tolerance. Examples of this adjustment include individuals altering and slowing their speech, walking more deliberately, or moving more cautiously to hide the fact that they have consumed debilitating quantities of alcohol.

■ ALCOHOL METABOLISM

Almost 95% of consumed alcohol is inactivated by liver metabolism. The liver metabolizes alcohol at a slow and constant rate and is unaffected by the amount ingested. Thus, if one can of beer is consumed each hour, the BAC will remain constant without resulting in intoxication. If, however, more alcohol is consumed per hour, the BAC will rise proportionately because large amounts of alcohol that cannot be metabolized spill over into the bloodstream.

■ POLYDRUG USE

It is a common practice to take alcohol with other drugs; this mode of consumption is known as polydrug use. Mixing alcohol with other types of drugs can intensify intoxication. For example, alcohol taken in combination with other depressant drugs, such as barbiturates and benzodiazepines, has produced lethal interactions.

Some surveys show that as much as 50% to 60% of young adults who use marijuana also consume alcohol (Golub and Johnson 1994), whereas 30% to 60% of cocaine-dependent people have a concurrent alcohol-use disorder (Brady et al. 1995; Earleywine and Newcomb 1997). In a recent report, almost one-half of those seeking treatment for alcoholism also were treated for abuse of other drugs (SAMHSA News 2000).

The reasons why individuals combine alcohol with other drugs of abuse are not always apparent. The following explanations have been proposed (Hettema et al. 1999):

1. Alcohol enhances the reinforcing properties of other CNS depressants.

2. It decreases the amount of an expensive and difficult-to-get drug required to achieve the desired effect.

3. It helps to diminish unpleasant side effects of other drugs of abuse, such as the withdrawal caused by CNS stimulants (NIAAA 1993).

4. There is a common predisposition to use alcohol and other substances of abuse.

Clearly, coadministration of alcohol with other substances of abuse is a common practice that can be very problematic and result in dangerous interactions.

■ SHORT-TERM EFFECTS

The impact of alcohol on the CNS is most similar to that of sedative-hypnotic agents such as barbiturates. Alcohol depresses CNS activity at all doses (Hobbs et al. 1995), producing definable results.

At low to moderate doses, disinhibition occurs; this loss of conditioned reflexes reflects a depression of inhibitory centers of the brain. The effects on behavior are variable and somewhat unpredictable. To a large extent, the social setting and mental state determine the individual's response to such alcohol consumption. For example, alcohol can cause one person to become euphoric, friendly, and talkative but can prompt another to become aggressive and hostile. Low to moderate doses also interfere with motor activity, reflexes, and coordination. Often this impairment is not apparent to the affected person ("Your Health" 1999).

In moderate quantities, alcohol slightly increases the heart rate; slightly dilates blood vessels in the arms, legs, and skin; and moderately lowers blood pressure. It stimulates appetite, increases production of gastric secretions, and markedly stimulates urine output.

At higher doses, the social setting has little influence on the expression of depressive actions of the alcohol. The CNS depression incapacitates the individual, causing difficulty in walking, talking, and thinking. These doses tend to induce drowsiness and cause sleep. If large amounts of alcohol are consumed rapidly, severe depression of the brain system and motor control area of the brain occurs, producing uncoordination, confusion, disorientation, stupor, anesthesia, coma, and even death.

The lethal level of alcohol is between 0.4% and 0.6% by volume in the blood. Death is caused by severe depression of the respiration center in the brain stem, although the person usually passes out before drinking an amount capable of producing this effect. Although an alcoholic may metabolize the drug more rapidly than a light drinker, the toxicity level of alcohol stays about the same. In other words, it takes approximately the same concentration of alcohol in the body to kill a nondrinker as to kill someone who drinks on a regular basis. The amount of alcohol required for anesthesia is very close to the toxic level, which is why it would not be a useful anesthetic. See Table 8.2 for a summary of the psychological and physical effects of various BAC levels.

As a general rule, it takes as many hours as the number of drinks consumed to sober up completely. Despite widely held beliefs, drinking black coffee, taking a cold shower, breathing pure oxygen, and so forth will not hasten the sobering process. Stimulants such as coffee may help keep the drunk person awake but will not improve judgment or motor reflexes to any significant extent.

The Hangover

A familiar aftereffect of overindulgence is fatigue combined with nausea, upset stomach, headache, sensitivity to sounds, and ill temper—the *hangover* ("Centerpiece" 1993). These symptoms are usually most severe many hours after drinking, when little or no alcohol remains in the body. No simple explanation exists for what causes the hangover. Theories include accumulation of acetaldehyde (a metabolite of ethanol), dehydration of the tissues, poisoning due to tissue deterioration, depletion of important enzyme systems needed to maintain routine functioning, an acute withdrawal (or rebound) response, and metabolism of the impurities in alcoholic beverages.

The body loses fluid in two ways through alcohol's diuretic action, which sometimes results in dehydration: (1) the water content, such as in beer, will increase the volume of urine, and (2) the alcohol depresses the center in the hypothalamus of the brain that controls release of a water conservation hormone (*antidiuretic hormone*). With less of this hormone, urine volume is further increased. Thus, after drinking heavily, especially the highly concentrated forms of alcohol, the person is thirsty. However, this effect by itself does not explain the symptoms of hangover.

TABLE 8.2 **Psychological and Physical Effects of Various Blood Alcohol Concentration Levels**

NUMBER OF DRINKS*	BLOOD ALCOHOL CONCENTRATION	PSYCHOLOGICAL AND PHYSICAL EFFECTS
1	0.02%–0.03%	No overt effects, slight mood elevation
2	0.05%–0.06%	Feeling of relaxation, warmth; slight decrease in reaction time and in fine muscle coordination
3	0.08%–0.09%	Balance, speech, vision, hearing slightly impaired; feelings of euphoria, increased confidence; loss of motor coordination
3–4	0.10%	Legal intoxication in all states; driving is illegal with this level (however, many states are changing or have changed the legal limit to 0.08%)
4	0.11%–0.12%	Coordination and balance becoming difficult; distinct impairment of mental faculties, judgment
5	0.14%–0.15%	Major impairment of mental and physical control; slurred speech, blurred vision, lack of motor skills
7	0.20%	Loss of motor control—must have assistance in moving about; mental confusion
10	0.30%	Severe intoxication; minimum conscious control of mind and body
14	0.40%	Unconsciousness, threshold of coma
17	0.50%	Deep coma
20	0.60%	Death from respiratory failure

Note: For each hour elapsed since the last drink, subtract 0.015% blood alcohol concentration, or approximately one drink.

*One drink = one beer (4% alcohol, 12 oz) or one highball (1 oz whiskey).

Source: Modified from data given in Ohio State Police Driver Information Seminars and the National Clearinghouse for Alcohol and Alcoholism Information, 5600 Fishers Lane, Rockville, MD 85206.

The type of alcoholic beverage you drink may influence the hangover that results. Some people are more sensitive to particular alcohol impurities than others. For example, some drinkers have no problem with white wine but an equal amount of some red wine will give them a hangover. Whiskey, scotch, and rum may cause worse hangovers than vodka or gin, given equal amounts of alcohol, because vodka and gin have fewer impurities. There is little evidence that mixing different types of drinks per se produces a more severe hangover. It is more likely that more than the usual amount of alcohol is consumed when various drinks are sampled.

A common treatment for a hangover is to take a drink of the same alcoholic beverage that caused the hangover. This practice is called "taking the hair of the dog that bit you" (from the old notion that the burnt hair of a dog is an antidote to its bite). This treatment might help the person who is physically dependent, in the same way that giving heroin to a heroin addict will ease the withdrawal symptoms. The "hair of the dog" method may work by depressing the centers of the brain that interpret pain or by relieving a withdrawal response. In addition, it may affect the psychological factors involved in having a hangover; distraction or focusing attention on something else may ease the effects.

Another remedy is to take an analgesic compound such as an aspirin-caffeine combination after drinking. This treatment is based on the belief that aspirin will help control headache; the caffeine may help counteract the depressant effect of the alcohol. In reality, however, these ingredients have no effect on the actual sobering-up process. In fact, products such as aspirin, caffeine, and Alka-Seltzer can irritate the stomach lining to the point where the person feels worse.

■ DEPENDENCE

Because of the disinhibition, relaxation, and sense of well-being mediated by alcohol, some degree of psychological dependence often develops, and the use of alcoholic beverages at social gatherings may become routine. Unfortunately, many people become so dependent on the psychological influences of alcohol that they become compulsive, continually consuming it. These individuals can be severely handicapped because of their alcohol dependence and often become unable to function normally in society. People who have become addicted to this drug are called alcoholics.

Because of the physiological effects, physical dependence also results from the regular consumption of large quantities of alcohol. This consequence becomes apparent when ethanol use is abruptly interrupted and withdrawal symptoms result. The severity of the withdrawal can vary according to the length and intensity of the alcohol habit. The prototypic withdrawal patterns are as follows (NIDA Diagnosis 2000):

Stage 1 (minor): restlessness, anxiousness, sleeping problems, agitation, tremors, and rapid heartbeat

Stage 2 (major): "minor" symptoms plus hallucinations, whole-body tremors, increased blood pressure and vomiting

Stage 3 (delirium tremens): fever, disorientation, confusion, seizures, and fatality in 3% to 5% of cases

Recovery from alcohol dependence is a long-term process. Because of the severe withdrawal and the need for behavioral adjustments, most people relapse several times before long-term abstinence is achieved. Even people who have not used alcohol for years may relapse under very stressful circumstances (NIDA Diagnosis 2000). The treatment of alcoholism is discussed in more detail in Chapter 9.

Effects of Alcohol on Organ Systems and Bodily Functions

As mentioned earlier, BAC depends on the size of the person, presence of food in the stomach, rate of drinking, amount of carbonation, and ratio of muscle mass to body fat. Furthermore, we mentioned that alcohol has pervasive effects on the major organs and fluids of the body (Worman 2000). In fact, the effect of this substance on body functions potentially can be so profound and destructive that alcoholism (*severe dependence*) is now considered a disease (Mann et al. 2000). The pervasive effects of alcohol on bodily organs are discussed in greater detail in the next section.

■ BRAIN AND NERVOUS SYSTEM

Every part of the brain and nervous system is affected and in extreme cases can be damaged by alcohol (Figure 8.2, page 192). "Initially, alcohol depresses subcortical inhibitions of the control centers of the cerebral cortex, resulting in disinhibition. In higher doses, alcohol depresses the cerebellum, resulting in slurred speech and staggering gait. In very high doses, alcohol can depress the respiratory centers of the medulla, resulting in death" (Levin 1990, p. 23). Furthermore, alcohol alters the production and functioning of transmitters such as dopamine, serotonin, GABA, and brain endorphins (Hettema et al. 1999). These neurochemical effects contribute to the fact that alcohol consumption can aggravate underlying psychiatric disorders such as depression and schizophrenia ("Centerpiece" 1993).

Heavy drinking over many years may result in serious mental disorders and irreversible damage to the brain and peripheral nervous system, leading to permanently compromised mental function and memory.

■ LIVER

Among alcoholics, liver disorders are responsible for 10% to 15% of deaths (Worman 2000). There are three stages of alcohol-induced liver disease (Worman 2000). The first stage is known as *alcoholic fatty liver*, where liver cells increase the production of fat, resulting in an enlarged liver. This

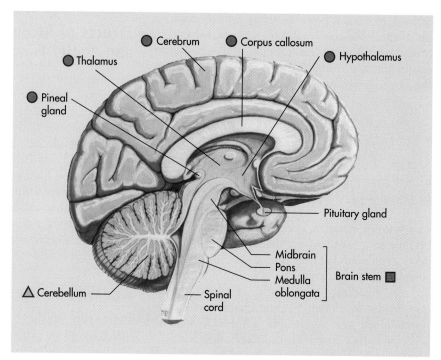

FIGURE 8.2
The principal control centers of the brain affected by alcohol consumption. Note also that all areas of the brain are interconnected.

direct toxic effect on liver tissue is known as the hepatotoxic effect . This effect is reversible and can disappear if alcohol use is stopped. Several days of drinking five or six alcoholic beverages each day produces fatty liver in males. For females, as few as two drinks of hard liquor per day several days in a row can produce the same condition. After several days of abstaining from alcohol, the liver will return to normal.

The second stage develops as the fat cells continue to multiply. Generally, irritation and swelling that result from continued alcohol intake cause alcoholic hepatitis . At this stage, chronic inflammation sets in and can be fatal. This second stage is also reversible if the intake of alcohol ceases.

Unlike stage 1 and 2, stage 3 is not reversible. Scars begin to form on the liver tissue during this stage. These scars are fibrous, and they cause hardening of the liver as functional tissue shrinks and deteriorates. This condition of the liver is known as cirrhosis and often is fatal. (See "Case in Point," Mickey Mantle Dies from Complications of Alcoholism.)

The liver damage caused by heavy alcohol consumption can cause problems when taking drugs that affect liver function. For example, the over-the-

KEY TERMS

hepatotoxic effect
when liver cells increase the production of fat, resulting in an enlarged liver

alcoholic hepatitis
the second stage of alcohol-induced liver disease in which chronic inflammation occurs; reversible if alcoholic consumption ceases

cirrhosis
scarring of the liver and formation of fibrous tissues; results from alcohol abuse; irreversible

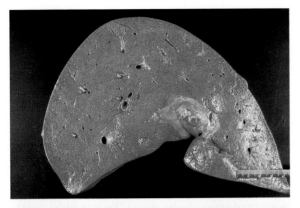

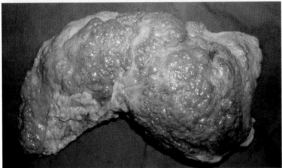

A normal liver (*top*) as it would be found in a healthy human body. An abnormal liver (*bottom*) that exhibits the effects of moderate to heavy alcohol consumption.

counter analgesic acetaminophen (Tylenol) can have a deleterious effect on the liver, especially when the function of this organ has already been compromised by alcohol.

■ DIGESTIVE SYSTEM

The digestive system consists of gastrointestinal structures involved in processing and digesting food and liquids; it includes the mouth, pharynx, esophagus, stomach, and small and large intestines. As alcohol travels through the digestive system, it irritates tissue and can even damage the tissue lining as it causes acid imbalances, inflammation, and acute gastric distress. Often, the result is *gastritis* (an inflamed stomach) and heartburn. The more frequently consumption takes place, the greater the irritation; one out of three heavy drinkers suffers from chronic gastritis. Furthermore, the heavy drinker has double the probability of developing cancer of the mouth and esophagus because alcohol passes these two organs on the way to the stomach.

Prolonged heavy use of alcohol may cause ulcers, hiatal hernia, and cancers throughout the digestive tract. The likelihood of cancers in the mouth, throat, and stomach dramatically increases

CASE IN POINT

Mickey Mantle Dies from Complications of Alcoholism

Mickey Mantle, the legendary centerfielder for the New York Yankees, died August 14, 1995, at the age of 63, from complications of alcoholism. During his heyday as a baseball star, his heavy drinking was discreetly hidden from adoring fans. It wasn't until well after his retirement from baseball that Mantle checked himself into a treatment clinic and admitted publicly that he had been severely dependent on alcohol for most of his life. He sought professional treatment only after doctors warned Mantle that his drinking habits had almost destroyed his liver. Despite heroic attempts to save Mantle's life with a liver transplant in June of the same year, a cancer from the diseased liver spread rapidly, resulting in death only two months later.

Mickey Mantle

Source: Knight-Ridder/Tribune News Service, 14 August 1995, p. 814K6829.

(15 times) if the person is also a heavy smoker ("Centerpiece" 1993). The pancreas is another organ associated with the digestive system that can be damaged by heavy alcohol consumption. Alcohol can cause pancreatitis, pancreatic cirrhosis, and alcoholic diabetes (NIAAA 1997).

■ BLOOD

High concentrations of alcohol diminish the effective functioning of the *hematopoietic* (blood-building) system. They decrease production of red blood cells, white blood cells, and platelets. Problems with clotting and immunity to infection are not uncommon among alcohol abusers. Often, the result is lowered resistance to disease. Heavy drinking appears to affect the bone marrow, where various blood cells are formed. The suppression of the bone marrow can contribute to *anemia*, in which red blood cell production cannot keep pace with the need for those cells. Heavy drinkers are also likely to develop alcoholic bleeding disorders because they have too few platelets to form clots (NIAAA 1997).

■ CARDIOVASCULAR SYSTEM

The effects of ethanol on the cardiovascular system have been extensively studied, but much remains unknown. Ethanol causes dilation of blood vessels, especially in the skin. This effect accounts for the flushing and sensation of warmth associated with alcohol consumption.

The long-term effects of alcohol on the cardiovascular system are dose-dependent. Recent studies have demonstrated that regular light to moderate drinking (two drinks or fewer of wine a day) actually reduces the incidence of heart diseases such as heart attacks, strokes, and high blood pressure by 20% to 40% in some populations. The type of alcoholic beverage consumed does not appear to be important as long as the quantity of alcohol consumed is moderate (1–2.5 ounces per day) ("Your Health" 1999). Although the precise explanation for this coronary benefit is not known, it appears to be related to the effects of moderate alcohol doses in relieving stress and increasing the blood concentration of high-density lipoproteins (HDL). An HDL is a molecular complex used to transport fat

through the bloodstream, and its levels are negatively correlated with cardiovascular disease. In addition, moderate levels of alcohol also decrease the formation of blood clots that can plug arteries and deprive tissues of essential oxygen and nutrients. Populations most likely to benefit from the protective properties of moderate levels of alcohol are men over 50 years of age and postmenopausal women. Moderate drinking on a daily average is approximately one drink (e.g., a glass of wine) for women and two drinks for men. Drinking more than this can result in increased health risks that more than offset the benefits ("Your Health" 1999).

Because of the potential for developing addiction to alcohol and the increased health risk with heavy drinking, most doctors would not encourage a nondrinker to start to consume alcohol in order to gain a health benefit. In addition, even in populations most likely to benefit from moderate alcohol consumption, the benefit is likely to disappear in persons who already have healthy lifestyles that include low-fat diets, stress and weight management techniques, and regular exercise ("Your Health" 1999). In general, most clinicians believe that alcohol use kills more people (~100,000/year) than it saves, and those it kills tend to be younger (Special Report 1997).

Chronic intense use of alcohol changes the composition of heart muscle by replacing it with fat and fiber, resulting in a heart muscle that becomes enlarged and flabby. Congestive heart failure from alcoholic cardiomyopathy often occurs when heart muscle is replaced by fat and fiber. Other results of alcohol abuse that affect the heart are irregular heartbeat or *arrhythmia*, high blood pressure, and stroke. A common example of damage is "holiday heart," so called because people drinking heavily over a weekend turn up in the emergency room with a dangerously irregular heartbeat. Chronic excessive use by people with arrhythmia causes congestive heart failure. Malnutrition and vitamin deficiencies associated with prolonged heavy drinking also contribute to cardiac abnormalities (Klatsky 1995).

■ SEXUAL ORGANS

Although alcohol lowers social inhibition, its use interferes with sexual functioning. As Shakespeare said in *Macbeth*, alcohol "provokes desire, but it takes away the performance." Continued alcohol use causes *prostatitis*, which is an inflammation of the prostate gland. This condition directly interferes with a man's ability to maintain an adequate erection during sexual stimulation. Another frequent symptom of alcohol abuse is atrophy of the testicles, which results in lowered sperm count and diminished hormones in the blood (Hobbs et al. 1995).

■ ENDOCRINE SYSTEM

As mentioned in Chapter 5, endocrine glands release hormones into the bloodstream. The hormones function as messengers that directly affect cell and tissue function throughout the body. Alcohol abuse alters endocrine functions by influencing the production and release of hormones, and affects endocrine regulating systems in the hypothalamus, pituitary, and gonads. Because of alcohol abuse, levels of *testosterone* (the male sex hormone) may decline, resulting in sexual impotence, breast enlargement, and loss of body hair in men. Women experience menstrual delays, ovarian abnormalities, and infertility (NIAAA 1997).

■ KIDNEYS

Frequent abuse of alcohol can also severely damage the kidneys. The resulting decrease in kidney function diminishes this organ's ability to screen blood and properly form urine and can result in serious metabolic problems. Another consequence of impaired kidney function in alcoholics is that they tend to experience more urinary tract infections than do nondrinkers or moderate drinkers (NIAAA 1997).

■ MENTAL DISORDERS AND DAMAGE TO THE BRAIN

Long-term heavy drinking can severely affect memory, judgment, and learning ability (NIAAA 1997). Wernicke-Korsakoff's syndrome is a characteristic psychotic condition caused by alcohol use and the associated nutritional and vitamin deficiencies. Patients who are brain-damaged (Hobbs et al. 1995) cannot remember recent events and compensate for their memory loss with *confabulation* (making up fictitious events that even the patient accepts as fact).

Fetal alcohol syndrome is characterized by facial deformities, as well as growth deficiency and mental retardation.

■ THE FETUS

In pregnant women, alcohol easily crosses the placenta and often damages the fetus in cases of moderate to excessive drinking. It can also cause spontaneous abortion due to its toxic actions. Another tragic consequence of high alcohol consumption during pregnancy is fetal alcohol syndrome (FAS), which is characterized by facial deformities, growth

---

KEY TERMS

alcoholic cardiomyopathy
congestive heart failure due to the replacement of heart muscle with fat and fiber

Wernicke-Korsakoff's syndrome
psychotic condition connected with heavy alcohol use and associated vitamin deficiencies

fetal alcohol syndrome (FAS)
a condition affecting children born to alcohol-consuming mothers that is characterized by facial deformities, growth deficiency, and mental retardation

deficiency, mental retardation, and joint and limb abnormalities (Larroque and Kaminski 1998). The growth deficiency occurs in embryonic development, and the child usually does not "catch up" after birth. The mild to moderate mental retardation does not appear to lessen with time, apparently because the growth impairment affects the functional development of the brain as well.

The severity of FAS appears to be dose-related: the more the mother drinks, the more severe the fetal damage. A safe lower level of alcohol consumption has not been established for pregnant women (Larroque and Kaminski 1998). Birth-weight decrements have been found at levels corresponding to about two drinks per day, on average. Clinical studies have established that alcohol itself clearly causes the syndrome; it is not related to the effects of smoking, maternal age, parity (number of children a woman has borne), social class, or poor nutrition. The incidence of FAS is one in three infants born to alcoholic mothers actively consuming during pregnancy (Hobbs et al. 1995).

■ MALNUTRITION

As previously mentioned, malnutrition is a frequent and extremely serious consequence of severe alcoholism that tends to occur most often in less-affluent alcoholics. It has been suggested that malnutrition exaggerates the damage that alcohol causes to the body's organs, especially the liver (Santolaria et al. 2000). Malnutrition apparently arises so frequently in this population because many alcoholics find it difficult to eat a balanced diet with adequate calorie intake. Many alcoholics consume between 300 and 1000 kilocalories per day (2000 kilocalories per day is considered normal for an average man). In addition, most of the calories consumed by alcoholics come from alcohol, which contains 7 kilocalories/gram (compared with fat, which contains 9 kilocalories/gram). The malnutrition problem is aggravated because alcohol's calories are empty—that is, alcohol does not contain other nutrients such as vitamins, minerals, protein, or fat (Achord 1995). Because alcoholics may be deriving 50% or more of their usual calorie intake from alcoholic beverages, profound deficiencies in important nutrients result, leading to serious degeneration of health.

Discussion Questions

1. What evidence indicates that alcohol is a drug like marijuana, cocaine, or heroin?

2. Explain how alcohol is manufactured.

3. In the Western world, alcohol use has a long history. List and discuss some of these historical events.

4. Explain how alcohol affects the mouth, stomach, small intestine, brain, liver, and bloodstream.

5. List at least five factors that affect the absorption rate of alcohol in the bloodstream.

6. Explain why alcohol is commonly consumed together with other drugs.

7. List three short-term effects of alcohol abuse.

8. Explain why moderate use of ethanol may prevent heart attacks.

9. Describe the symptoms and causes of a hangover.

10. What characterizes FAS?

11. Why is malnutrition a common occurrence in alcoholics, and what are its consequences?

Key Terms

fermentation **182**

mead **182**

distillation **182**

ethanol **183**

social lubricant **184**

methyl alcohol **185**

ethylene glycol **185**

isopropyl alcohol **185**

anesthetic **185**

blood alcohol concentration (BAC)   185

alcohol dehydrogenase   187

behavioral tolerance   188

polydrug use   188

disinhibition   189

diuretic   189

hepatotoxic effect   192

alcoholic hepatitis   192

cirrhosis   192

alcoholic cardiomyopathy   194

Wernicke-Korsakoff's syndrome   195

fetal alcohol syndrome (FAS)   195

Summary

1 Alcohol is a drug because it is a CNS depressant, and it affects both mental and physiological functioning.

2 Three types of poisonous alcohols are methyl alcohol, made from wood products; ethylene glycol, used as antifreeze; and isopropyl alcohol, used as an antiseptic. A fourth type, ethanol, is the alcohol used for drinking purposes.

3 The blood alcohol level produced depends on the presence of food in the stomach, the rate of alcohol consumption, the concentration of alcohol, and the drinker's body composition.

4 Alcohol depresses CNS activity at all doses. Low to moderate doses of alcohol interfere with motor activities, reflexes, and coordination. In moderate quantities, alcohol slightly increases heart rate; slightly dilates blood vessels in the arms, legs, and skin; and moderately lowers blood pressure. It stimulates appetite, increases production of gastric secretions, and at higher doses markedly stimulates urine output. The CNS depression incapacitates the individual, causing difficulty in walking, talking, and thinking.

5 Alcohol is commonly used in combination with other drugs (1) to enhance reinforcing properties; (2) to reduce the amount of expensive or hard-to-get drug required for an effect; (3) to reduce unpleasant side effects; or (4) because a common predisposition for use of alcohol and other drugs exists.

6 Moderate daily alcohol use can reduce cardio-vascular diseases in men older than 50 years and postmenopausal women.

7 Long-term heavy alcohol use directly causes serious damage to nearly every organ and function of the body.

8 Prolonged heavy drinking causes various types of muscle disease and tremors. Heavy alcohol consumption causes irregular heartbeat. Heavy drinking over many years results in serious mental disorders and permanent, irreversible damage to the brain and peripheral nervous system. Memory, judgment, and learning ability can deteriorate severely.

9 Women who are alcoholics or who drink heavily during pregnancy have a higher rate of sponta-neous abortions. Infants born to drinking mothers have a high probability of being afflicted with FAS. These children have characteristic patterns of facial deformities, growth deficiency, joint and limb irreg-ularities, and mental retardation.

10 Alcohol has pervasive effects on the major organs and fluids of the body. Every part of the brain and nervous system is affected and can be dam-aged by alcohol. Among alcoholics, liver disorders include alcoholic fatty liver, alcoholic hepatitis, and cirrhosis. Alcohol also irritates tissue and damages the digestive system. Heavy use of alcohol seriously affects the blood, heart, sexual organs, endocrine sys-tem, and kidneys.

11 Malnutrition is a common occurrence in severe alcoholism. It is the result of decreased calorie intake by alcoholics and the diminished consumption of essential nutrients due to the nutritional deficiency of alcoholic beverages.

References

Achord, J. L. "Alcohol and the Liver." *Scientific American and Medicine* 2 (1995): 16–25.

Brady, K., S. Sonne, C. Randall, B. Adinoff, and R. Malcolm. "Features of Cocaine Dependence with Concurrent Alcohol Abuse." *Drug and Alcohol Dependence* 39 (1995): 69–71.

"Centerpiece: Alcohol in Perspective." *Wellness Letter* 9 (February 1993): 4–6.

Earlywine, M. and M. Newcomb. "Concurrent Versus Simultaneous Polydrug Use: Prevalence, Correlates, Discriminant Validity, and Prospective Effects on Health Outcomes." *Experimental Clinical Psychopharmacology,* 5 (1997): 353–64.

Eronen, M. J., J. Tiihonen, and P. Hakola. "Schizophrenia and Homocidal Behavior." *Schizophrenia Bulletin* 22 (1996): 83–9.

Golub, A. and B. Johnson. "The Shifting Importance of Alcohol and Marijuana as Gateway Substances Among Serious Drug Users." *Journal of Study of Alcohol* 55 (1994): 607–14.

Hettema, J., L. Corey, and K. Kendler. "A Multivariate Genetic Analysis of the Use of Tobacco, Alcohol and Caffeine in a Population Sample of Male and Female Twins." *Drug and Alcohol Dependency* 57 (1999): 9–78.

Hobbs, W., T. Rall, and T. Verdoorn. "Hypnotics and Sedatives: Ethanol." In *The Pharmacological Basis of Therapeutics*, 9th ed., edited by J. Hardman and L. Limbird, 361–96. New York: McGraw–Hill, 1995.

Hoffman, P. L. and B. Tabakoff. "Alcohol Dependence: A Commentary on Mechanisms." *Alcohol and Alcoholism* 31 (1996): 333–40.

Johnston, L. D., P. O'Malley, and J. Bachman. University of Michigan News and Information Services; 17 December 1999; citing the *National Survey on Drug Abuse, The Monitoring the Future Study, 1999*; The University of Michigan Institute for Social Research, National Institute on Drug Abuse, U.S. Department of Human Services, National Institutes of Health.

Klatsky, A. "Cardiovascular Effects of Alcohol." *Scientific American* 2 (1995): 28–37.

Larroque, B. and M. Kaminski. "Prenatal Alcohol Exposure and Development at Preschool Age: Main Results of a French Study." *Alcoholism: Clinical and Experimental Research* 22 (1998): 295–303.

Levin, J. D. *Alcoholism: A Bi-Psycho-Social Approach.* New York: Hemisphere, 1990.

Mann, K., D. Herman, and A. Heinz. "One Hundred Years of Alcoholism: The Twentieth Century." *Alcohol and Alcoholism* 35 (2000): 10–15.

NIDA Diagnosis. "Diagnosis and Treatment of Drug Abuse in Family Practice." (May 2000). Available 165.112.78 .61/Diagnosis-treatment/Diagnosis6.html.

NIAAA. (National Institute on Alcohol Abuse and Alcoholism). Publication 21 (1997). Available http://silk.nih .gov/silk/niaaa1/publication/iss21-1.htm.

NIAAA. (National Institute on Alcohol Abuse and Alcoholism). *8th Special Report to Congress on Alcohol and Health.* (Sept. 1993): 121.

O'Brien, C. "Drug Addiction and Drug Abuse." In *The Pharmacological Basis of Therapeutics*, 9th ed., edited by J. Hardman and L. Limbird, 557–77. New York: McGraw–Hill, 1995.

Quindien, A. "America's Most Pervasive Drug Problem Is the Drug that Pretends It Isn't." *Salt Lake Tribune* (20 April 2000): A-11.

Royce, J. E. *Alcohol Problems and Alcoholism: A Comprehensive Survey.* New York: Free Press, 1989.

SAMHSA News. "Opiates Surpass Cocaine in Treatment Admissions." *SAMHSA News* 8 (Winter 2000): 1.

Santolaria, F., A. Castilla, E. Gonzalez-Reimers, J. Perez-Rodriguez, C. Rodriguez-Gonzalez, A. Lopez-Penalver, and J. DeMiguel. "Nutritional Assessment in Alcoholic Patients. Its Relationship with Alcoholic Intake, Feeding Habits, Organic Complications and Social Problems." *Drug and Alcohol Dependency* 59 (2000): 295–304.

Special Report. "Alcohol: Weighing the Benefits and Risks for You." *U.C. Berkeley Wellness Letter* 13 (August 1997): 4–5.

Worman, H. "Alcoholic Liver Disease." Columbia University (2000). Available http://cpmcnet.columbia.edu/dept/ gi/alcohol.html.

"Your Health: Alcohol: The Whole Truth, Seven Half-truths About Drinking, Exposed." *Consumer Reports.* 64 (December 1999): 60–1.

Alcohol: A Behavioral Perspective

Did You Know?

- Approximately 113 million Americans age 12 and over currently use alcohol: 5.1 million are binge drinkers, and 2.3 million are classified as heavy drinkers.

- Seventy-seven percent of the population believes that alcohol creates the most problems in our society.

- Whites have the highest rate of alcohol consumption (86%), whereas African Americans rank second (72%), and Hispanics rank third (69%).

- People have complained about fraternity drinking since 1840.

- Of all U.S. minority groups, Asian Americans have the highest rate of abstinence, the lowest rate of heavy drinking, and the lowest level of drinking-related problems.

- The use of fermentation to make alcohol dates back to 4200 B.C.

- Three years after Prohibition was in effect, the use of distilled liquors began rising and has risen every year since.

- Americans consumed twice as much alcohol in 1830 as they do now.

- Most of the economic costs of alcohol and drug problems fall on taxpayers, most of whom do not abuse alcohol and drugs.

- By 12th grade, the percentage of students using alcohol doubles to approximately 60%.

- Globally, when illnesses, accidents, and crimes are connected to alcohol, the costs add up to more than a quarter trillion dollars a year.

- On most weekend nights throughout the United States, 70% of all fatal single-vehicle crashes involve a driver who is legally intoxicated.

- Less affluent people drink less than more affluent individuals.

- Most alcoholics are secret or disguised drinkers who very much look like common working people.

- People can easily feel intoxicated by expectations and physical surroundings associated with the experience of drinking alcohol, without the alcohol itself actually affecting them.

- Cultural expectations have an effect on how we perceive and interpret alcohol consumption.

- Most people who consume alcohol do not become problem drinkers.

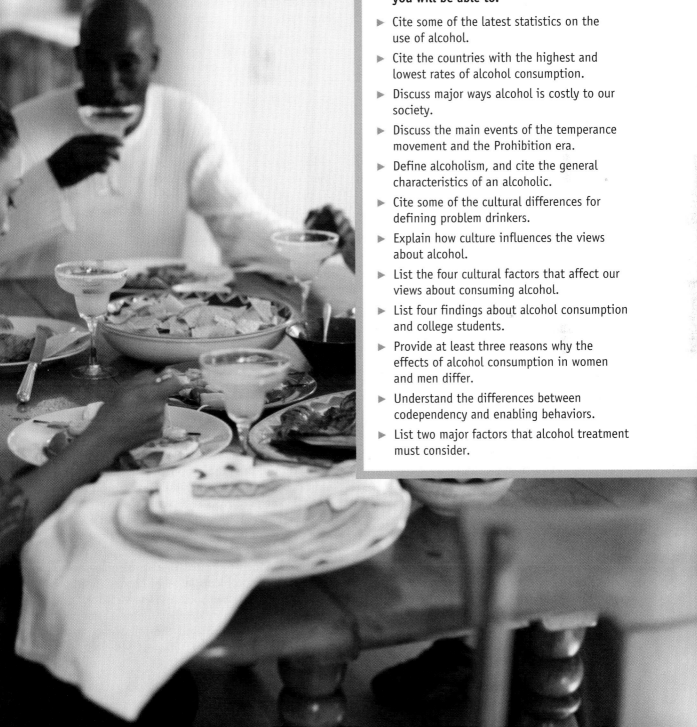

Chapter 9

Learning Objectives

On completing this chapter you will be able to:

▶ Cite some of the latest statistics on the use of alcohol.

▶ Cite the countries with the highest and lowest rates of alcohol consumption.

▶ Discuss major ways alcohol is costly to our society.

▶ Discuss the main events of the temperance movement and the Prohibition era.

▶ Define alcoholism, and cite the general characteristics of an alcoholic.

▶ Cite some of the cultural differences for defining problem drinkers.

▶ Explain how culture influences the views about alcohol.

▶ List the four cultural factors that affect our views about consuming alcohol.

▶ List four findings about alcohol consumption and college students.

▶ Provide at least three reasons why the effects of alcohol consumption in women and men differ.

▶ Understand the differences between codependency and enabling behaviors.

▶ List two major factors that alcohol treatment must consider.

Introduction

As a clerk here at this store, I see all kinds of people buying alcohol. Sometimes you can tell who more than likely have big problems with alcohol by just looking at them. One man comes in about three times a week, usually at night. He buys fifths, half gallons, and pints of vodka. He is usually well dressed and works at some office job somewhere here in town. I know someone who knows him, and this lady friend of his says that if you call him up after 10 at night, his speech is slurred, and she knows for a fact that he keeps pints under his car seat while driving during the day. This lady friend lives right next door to him and she sees him going to and from work and taking swigs from his stash so-to-speak. (*From Venturelli's research files, interview with a 50-year-old female liquor store clerk in a small Midwestern town, August 9, 1999.*)

I even knew a professor who would buy pints of whiskey as soon as we would open in the morning. He would drive off and go to your university [referring to the author's university] to teach. He was a heck of a nice fella, always ready with a joke and very pleasant to talk to, but I knew he had a problem with this stuff. (*From Venturelli's research files, interview with a 50-year-old female liquor store clerk in a small Midwestern town, August 9, 1999.*)

Finally, I vividly recall at age 10 seeing at least three or four middle-aged men arrive at my father's tavern as soon as the doors were opened at 8:00 A.M. on most mornings, desperately looking for the morning's first drink of alcohol. I recall, my dad would crack a raw egg into an 8-ounce glass. Draft beer and the raw egg filled the glass half full. The reason for the raw egg was to get some breakfast protein and the reason for the half full glass of beer was because their hands were very shaky and they had to steady the drink to their mouths. Immediately following what my dad referred to as a "full" breakfast were at least several double shots of Jim Beam whiskey. These alcoholic customers had to have the drinks so that they could feel "normal" for the rest of the day. Some would even be dressed in formal attire ready to go off to their office jobs. (*Venturelli, personal observation, May 18, 2000.*)

Our Alcohol Consuming Society

Similar to most societies, alcohol has always been a part of American society. The quotes above illustrate how an individual can consume an excessive amount of a psychoactive and addictive substance without necessarily coming to the attention of anyone except perhaps a neighbor, a lone liquor store employee, or even a bartender and his son. Furthermore, this same depressant chemical is often not perceived as a drug by many Americans. It is considered more of a social substance, something that is "always" found at social gatherings and is even expected at such gatherings.

In a 1998 survey conducted by the Substance Abuse and Mental Health Services Administration (SAMHSA), 113 million Americans age 12 and older who participated in the survey reported that they used alcohol at least once within the prior 30-day period (SAMHSA 1999). In the same survey, approximately 33 million reported engaging in binge drinking in the 30 days before the survey. A staggering 10.5% of current drinkers were under 21 in 1998. Of this underage group, 5.1 million engage in binge drinking, including 2.3 million who are classified as heavy drinkers . Despite all the laws, increased campaigns and advertisements against drug and alcohol abuse, and increased enforcement expenditures since 1994, the number of underage drinkers has not changed much (SAMHSA 1999).

Current Statistics and Trends in Alcohol Consumption

At the time of this publication, the latest Gallup Poll indicated that 64% of the adult population drinks alcohol, whereas 26% reported excessive alcohol consumption patterns (Newport 2000). An all-time high of 36% of the population reported that drinking alcohol has caused family problems, and 77% of those questioned indicated that in comparison to all other drug problems, alcohol creates the most family problems in our society (Newport 2000).

In looking at more detailed figures about consumption patterns, we find the following can be summarized largely from Newport (1999), unless otherwise designated:

- Sixty percent of men prefer to drink beer, whereas women prefer wine.

- As men age, their preference for beer steadily decreases.

- Overall, as both men and women age, they say wine is their favorite alcoholic beverage.

- Lower income drinkers prefer beer, whereas higher income drinkers prefer wine.

- The highest rate of family drinking problems is among 18- to 29-year-olds.

- Currently, 42% of the population report family disputes caused by excessive drinking; 17% reported this problem in 1996.

- Sixty-four percent claim they drink and 36% report that they abstain. In 1999 61% drank and 39% abstained.

- In 1999, 42% of all alcohol drinkers claimed to primarily drink beer, 34% wine, and 19% hard liquor.

- Of the total number of drinkers, 24% reported that they drink more than they should.

- To date, alcohol has been tried by 53% of 8th graders, 70% of 10th graders, 81% of 12th graders, and 89% of college students. Occasions of *heavy drinking* (five or more drinks in a row at least once before this survey was administered) occurred in 14% of the nation's 8th graders, 24% of the nation's 10th graders, and 32% of the nation's 12th graders.

- Estimated spending for health care services was $18.8 billion for alcohol problems and medical consequences of alcohol consumption and $9.9 billion for other types of drug problems.

- An estimated $82 billion was lost in potential productivity due to both alcohol and other drug abuse.

- Throughout the world, Luxembourg tops the list for recorded alcohol consumption a year, at 12.6 liters per person, followed by Germany at 12.1 liters, and France at 11.5 liters. The lowest levels are found in Turkey, Krygyzstan, Turkmenistan, Israel, and Armenia, which all have levels below 3 liters per person.

KEY TERMS

binge drinking
consuming five or more drinks on one occasion
heavy drinkers
five or more drinks on one occasion on 5 or more days during a given 30-day period

- When illegal imports and illicit home production of alcohol are taken into account, several countries exceed the amount of alcohol consumed in Luxembourg, Germany, and France. Latvia leads at 16 to 20 liters per person, followed by Slovenia at 18 liters per person, and in descending order from highest to lowest are Estonia, Russia, Lithuania, Macedonia, and Greece (Alcohol Concern 2000).

- Whites have the highest rate of alcohol consumption at 86%, African Americans are second at 72%, and Hispanics are third at 69% (SAMHSA/OAS 1999).

- In contrast to common assumptions, the higher the level of education attained, the higher the likelihood of current alcohol use. College graduates registered an average of 93%, those with some college 91%, high school graduates 86%, and those with less than a high school degree 76% (SAMHSA/OAS 1999).

- Drinking is commonly believed to be associated with poverty, yet according to a Gallup Poll, people most likely to drink have higher incomes, under age 65, do not attend church, live in regions of the United States other than the South, and are more likely to identify themselves as liberals.

- Finally, research shows that much of the economic burden of alcohol and drug problems falls on the population of tax payers who do not abuse alcohol and drugs. Government, private insurance, and other members of households bear most of these costs (NIDA 2000).

■ DRINKING POPULATION PERCENTAGES

What percentage of our society drinks alcohol? A pyramid can be constructed based on the amount of alcohol consumed, based on the pattern of drinking, or based on the "problem" or "illness" dimension (e.g., by attempting to calculate what proportion of Americans are "abusers" or "dependent"; the criteria for each were discussed in Chapter 8). For example, at the beginning of this chapter, the first two interviews discussed people who bought and consumed liquor and are prime examples of alcohol drinkers who probably imbibe approximately 1 quart per day. This, by most definitions, is a clear diagnostic criterion for a diagnosis of alcoholism. Interestingly, all three of the chapter opening examples indicate that the alcohol drinkers are apparently functional, or at least they manage to create this impression.

The pyramid shown in Figure 9.1 has a base of 35% who are teetotalers , then a layer of about 13% who occasionally drink, and a top 52% who drink fairly regularly. Some 11 million Americans, or 5.5% of Americans age 12 or older, had five or more drinks on the same occasion at least five different days in the past month, which is one possible definition of heavy drinking. Different definitions of what constitutes heavy drinking exist. Thus, if we define *heavy drinking* differently—for example, as more than two drinks per day—we come up with a much larger slice of the pyramid—three times as large.

Drinking Alcohol Is Hardly an Adult Problem

With regard to age, alcohol consumption does not have any boundaries. Alcohol has been tried by 53% of 8th graders, 70% of 10th graders, 81% of 12th graders, and 89% of college students (NIDA 1999). Even more alarming is that 14% of 8th graders, 24% of 10th graders, and 32% of 12th graders reported an occasion of heavy drinking within a 2-week period before a nationwide survey (NIDA 1999). (See "Point/Counterpoint," Lower the Legal Drinking Age?) Since the early 1990s, however, 8th, 9th, and 10th graders have reported marijuana to be the

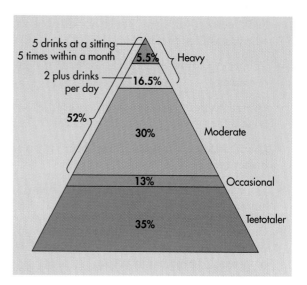

FIGURE 9.1
Broad distribution of drinking behaviors.

drug they use the most frequently, followed by alcohol. Although much more is said in Chapter 14, the noteworthy finding here is that on a daily basis for this group of minors, marijuana now exceeds alcohol usage.

Figure 9.2 presents a more precise breakdown of the three major types of alcohol (beer, wine coolers, and liquor) used by junior high and high school students (grades 9–12). Here, the most noteworthy finding is that from 9th through 12th grades, alcohol consumption increases dramatically (Pride USA Survey, 1998).

With regard to 12th graders' consumption of alcohol, white underage students are much more likely to binge drink (36%) compared with African American students (12%) and Hispanic students (28%). Finally, boys in 12th grade are more likely to drink alcohol on a daily basis compared with girls of the same grade and age: boys are reported at 6.4% whereas girls are reported at 1.4%. Boys are more likely than girls to drink large quantities of alcohol in a single sitting: 39% of 12th-grade males reported drinking five or more drinks in a row before 2 weeks prior to being surveyed, and 24% of the 12th-grade females drank the same amount. When reviewing the statistics, keep in mind that females differ from males in alcohol drinking capacities (see Chapter 8 for more details).

KEY TERMS

teetotalers
individuals who drink no alcoholic beverages whatsoever; a term in common usage in decades past

POINT/COUNTERPOINT

Lower the Legal Drinking Age?

If we look across the world, we find that the United States appears to be the only country in the world that sets the minimum legal drinking age at 21. A number of countries such as Ireland, Finland, and Sweden specify a minimum of 18, and other countries such as Germany, France, Italy, Netherlands, Portugal, and the United Kingdom specify a minimum of 16. Still other countries such as Belgium, Denmark, Greece, Spain, and Austria do not specify any legal age for alcohol consumption (Harkin and Klinkenberg, 1995).

Arguments *against* lowering the legal limit for consuming alcohol are as follows:

1. A higher minimum legal drinking age (MLDA) is effective in preventing alcohol-related deaths and injuries among youth. When the MLDA has been lowered, injury and death rates increase, and when the MLDA is increased, death and injury rates decline (Wagenaar 1993).

2. A higher MLDA results in fewer alcohol-related problems among youth, and the 21-year-old MLDA saves the lives of well over 1000 youth each year. Conversely, when the MLDA is lowered, motor vehicle crashes and deaths among youth increase. At least 50 studies have evaluated this correlation (Wagenaar 1993).

3. Research shows that when the MLDA is 21, people under age 21 drink less overall and continue to do so through their early twenties (O'Malley & Wagenaar 1991).

4. Higher MLDAs reduce traffic fatalities involving drivers in 18 to 20 years old by 13%. These laws have saved an estimated 18,220 lives since 1975 (NHTSA 1999).

Arguments *for* lowering the legal limit for consuming alcohol are as follows:

1. A study of a large sample of young people between the ages of 16 and 19 in Massa-chusetts and New York after Massachusetts raised its drinking age revealed that the average, self-reported daily alcohol consumption in Massachusetts did not decline in comparison with New York (Hanson 1999).

2. Comparison of college students attending schools in states that had maintained, for at least 10 years, a minimum drinking age of 21 with those in states that had similarly maintained minimum drinking ages below 21 revealed few differences in drinking problems (Hanson 1999).

3. A study of all 50 states and the District of Columbia found "a positive relationship between the purchase age and single-vehicle fatalities." Thus, single-vehicle fatalities were found to be more frequent in those states with high purchase ages (Hanson 1999).

4. Comparison of drinking before and after the passage of raised minimum age legislation has generally revealed little impact on behavior. For example, a study that examined college students' drinking behavior before and after an increase in the minimum legal drinking age from 18 to 19 in New York state found the law had no impact on underage students' consumption rates, intoxication rates, drinking attitudes, or drinking problems. These studies were corroborated by other researchers at a different college in the same state (Hanson 1999).

5. Finally, an examination of East Carolina University students' intentions regarding their behavior following passage of the 21-year-age drinking law revealed that only 6% intended to stop drinking, 70% planned to change their drinking location, 21% expected to use a false or borrowed

—continued on next page

—continued from previous page

identification to obtain alcohol, and 22% intended to use other drugs. Anecdotal statements by students indicated the belief by some that it "might be easier to hide a little pot in my room than a six pack of beer" (Hanson 1999).

Further, research and the information from sources in this chapter indicate that with regard to under 21 alcohol violations, the United States continues to have serious problems. Thus, we are not any better than most countries regarding the percentage of minors consuming alcohol, despite our unique minimum 21 age requirement for alcohol consumption. What about the idea that instead of prohibiting alcohol consumption to those under age 21 (which to date continues to be ineffective), we need to teach moderation at an early age so that the percentage of youth that decides to consume alcohol can learn to do so responsibly?

Because the 21 age requirement has not deterred our nation's youth from consuming alcohol and in light of younger and younger age groups consuming alcohol, do you think it is time to reconsider lowering the age limit of alcohol consumption so that:

1. We are in alignment with the remainder of the world.

2. We can eliminate costly, burdensome, and unnecessary underage drinking violations.

These infractions with the law include fines, legal costs, imprisonment, court time, legal expenses, and introducing our nation's youth into the criminal justice system, (which many believe should remain "lean and mean" so that it can effectively prohibit and prosecute serious law violators).

3. We can teach responsible drinking, drinking in moderation and alcohol consumption can be promoted and taught to be a "normal" part of behavior when eating, socializing with friends (like consuming coffee or fruit juice). Such prevention measures can clearly emphasize that excessive alcohol consumption is a sign of immaturity and lack of self-respect.

How successful do you think a campaign calling for lowering the legal drinking age would be with (1) family members, (2) your school, (3) community, (4) city/town, and (5) American society in general? Would it be successful? If yes, why? If no, why? Have you had any experiences in foreign countries where alcohol consumption was not severely restricted? If so, what did you observe?

In essence, do you think we should try to change the current drinking laws, in light of the fact that the current laws continue to be ineffective? Why are we not like other nations with regard to age limits on the use of alcohol? How important is it for the United States to be like other nations?

Sources: Hanson, D. J. "The Legal Drinking Age: Science vs. Ideology," 1999. Available http://www.student.potsdam.edu/alcohol-info/InMyOpinion/ScienceIdeology.html.

Harkin, A.M. with assistance of L. Klinkenberg. *Profiles of Alcohol in the Member States of the European Region of the World Health Organization*. Copenhagen: WHO Regional Office for Europe, May 1995.

National Highway Traffic Safety Administration (NHTSA), National Center for Statistics and Analysis. *Drunk Driving Facts*. Washington, DC: NHTSA, 1999.

O'Malley P. M., and Wagenaar, A. C. "Effects of Minimum Drinking Age Laws on Alcohol Use, Related Behaviors and Traffic Crash Involvement Among American Youth: 1976–1987." *Journal of Studies on Alcohol*. 52 (1991): 478–91.

Wagenaar, A. C. "Minimum Drinking Age and Alcohol Availability to Youth: Issues and Research Needs. In Hilton M. E., and B. Bloss, eds. Economics and the Prevention of Alcohol-Related Problems. National Institute on Alcohol Abuse and Alcoholism (NIAAA) Research Monograph No. 25, NIH Pub. No. 93-3513. Bethesda, MD: NIAAA; 1993:175–200.

A. Beer Consumption by Youths in Junior High and High School

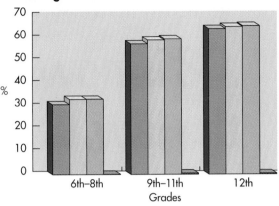

B. Wine Cooler Consumption by Youths in Junior High and High School

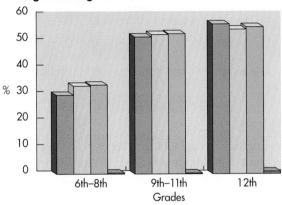

C. Liquor Consumption by Youths in Junior High and High School

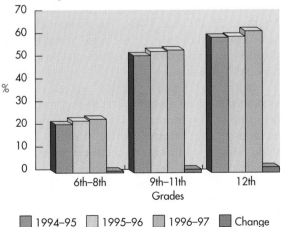

■ 1994–95   ☐ 1995–96   ▨ 1996–97   ■ Change

FIGURE 9.2

Source: Pride USA Survey, 1998. 1994–95, 1995–96, and 1996–97.
Available http://members.aol.com/_ht_a/drgedrscs/page3.html.

■ ECONOMIC COSTS OF ALCOHOL ABUSE

The economic costs of alcohol abuse to society are staggering. In summary, the following are some of the current results of alcohol abuse:

• From a global perspective, when including illness, accidents, and crimes connected to alcohol, the costs add up to more than a quarter trillion dollars yearly (Reuters Limited, 1999).

• The estimated cost of alcohol abuse and alcoholism (not including other drugs) to the United States was approximately $166.5 billion in 1995. (This cost rises approximately 12.5% yearly) (NIAAA 1995).

• Estimated total spending for health care services was $18.8 billion for alcohol problems in 1995. Specialized detoxification and rehabilitation services as well as prevention, training, and research expenditures cost $6.6 billion (NIAAA 1995).

• Yearly, more than 107,400 people die as a result of alcohol-related abuse.

• An estimated $82 billion in lost potential productivity was attributed to alcohol ($67.7 billion) and drug abuse ($14.2 billion) in 1992.

• Total costs attributed to alcohol-related motor vehicle crashes were estimated to be $24.7 billion.

• Expenditures for alcohol-related crime totaled $6.2 billion, and $17.4 billion for illicit drugs.

• Alcohol abuse is estimated to have contributed to 25% to 30% of violent crime.

• Finally, alcohol is officially linked to at least half of all highway fatalities, and that figure includes only legal intoxication. In most states, the blood alcohol level ranges from 0.08% to 0.1%. In as much as 70% of all single-vehicle fatal crashes on weekend nights, the driver was legally intoxicated, and this occurs during most weekends throughout the United States. Interestingly, this single issue has been the only alcohol problem with very vocal and effective groups to lobby for stricter enforcement of laws against alcohol-impaired automobile driving. Groups such as MADD (Mothers Against Drunk Driving) and SADD (Students Against Drunk Driving) are the largest prevention organizations in the nation (Alcoholism Kills, 2000).

Killed by a drunk driver.

.08 is now the law.

Scott Gorham. Age 17.

GOVERNOR'S OFFICE ON HIGHWAY SAFETY
RHODE ISLAND TRAFFIC SAFETY COALITION

Current advertisement used to promote lowering the minimum legally acceptable blood alcohol level (BAC) while operating a motor vehicle in the United States.

History of Alcohol in America

■ DRINKING PATTERNS

From a peak in 1830, when the amount of alcohol ingested by the average American was 7.1 gallons per year, use declined continuously until 1871–1880, when the average was 1.72 gallons. Numbers then rose to a high in 1906–1910 to 2.6 gallons, then fell to 1.96 gallons just before Prohibition, 1916–1919. Under Prohibition, less than a gallon of absolute alcohol per person was consumed, on average. During the last half of the 20th century, alcohol consumption stayed fairly constant, within the 2 to 3 gallon range. Wine and beer gained in popularity, while the popularity of "spirits" (hard liquor) declined (Lender 1985).

■ HISTORICAL CONSIDERATIONS

Alcoholic beverages have played an important role in the history of the United States as well as most countries throughout the world. Most likely, fermentation was the first method for making alcohol,

dating as early as 4200 B.C. As early as A.D. 100, it appears that brandy was the first distilled beverage. In Ireland and Scotland, whiskey was first distilled in the 1400s, and gin began appearing in the 1600s, first distilled by a Flemish physician. Other types of liquor also have distinct origins; for example, rum was first invented in Barbados in the 1650s. Finally, bourbon, in the late 1700s, was first made near Georgetown, Kentucky. In the United States, the first distillery was created in the 1600s in the area that is now New York City.

In colonial America, alcohol was viewed very favorably. From an economic standpoint, the manufacturing of rum became New England's largest and most profitable industry in the so-called triangle trade. It acquired this name because Yankee traders would sail with a cargo of rum to the West Coast of Africa, where they bargained the "demon" for slaves. From there, they sailed to the West Indies, where they bartered the slaves for molasses. Finally, they took the molasses back to New England, where it was made into rum, thus completing the triangle. For many years, New England distilleries flourished and the slave trade proved highly lucrative (see Figure 9.3).

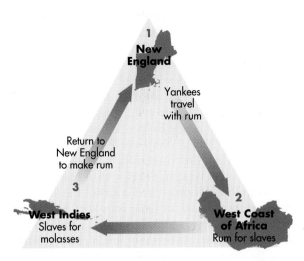

FIGURE 9.3
Slave trade triangle.

This process continued until 1807, when an act of Congress prohibited the importation of slaves.

From a social standpoint, the consumption of alcohol was seen as a part of life. The colonial tavern "was a key institution, the center of social and political life" (Levine 1983, p. 66). In the 17th and 18th centuries, alcohol flowed freely at weddings, baptisms, and funerals. Especially in the 18th century, people drank at home, at work, and while traveling. In the 19th century, largely because of the temperance movement, taverns became stigmatized and were viewed as dens where the lower classes, immigrants, and mostly men would congregate. "Any drinking, [Lyman Beecher] argued, was a step toward 'irreclaimable' slavery to liquor" (Lender and Martin 1987). People in the 19th century began to report that they were addicted to alcohol. Here is where the temperance movement had its effects in bringing about a change in attitudes regarding drinking.

From the Temperance Movement (1830–1850) to the Prohibition Era (1920–1933)

The time from the temperance movement to the Prohibition era was a very turbulent period in the history of alcohol in America. The period of heaviest drinking in America began during Jefferson's term of office (1800–1808). The nation was going through uneasy times, trying to stay out of the war between Napoleon and the British allies. The transient population increased, especially in the seaport cities, and the migration westward had begun. Heavy drinking had become a major form of recreation and a "social lubricant" at elections and public gatherings. The temperance movement never began with the intention of stopping alcohol consumption but with the goal of encouraging moderation. In fact, in the 1830s, at the peak of this early campaign, temperance leaders (many of whom drank beer and wine) recommended abstinence only from distilled spirits, not the other forms of alcohol such as beer or wine. This movement developed from several very vocal spiritual leaders who preached that alcohol harms "the health and physical energies of a nation" and that alcohol interfered with the spreading of the gospel. Later, as is explained below in more detail, the temperance movement went against all other forms of alcohol.

Because the temperance movement was closely tied into the abolitionist movement as well as the African American church, African Americans were preeminent promoters of temperance. Leaders such as Frederick Douglass stated that "it was as well to be a slave to master, as to whisky and rum. When a slave was drunk, the slaveholder had no fear that he would plan an insurrection; no fear that he would escape to the north. It was the sober, thinking slave who was dangerous, and needed the vigilance of his master to keep him a slave" (Douglass 1892, p. 133).

Over the next decades, partly in connection with religious revivals, the meaning of *temperance* was gradually altered from "moderation" to "total abstinence." All alcoholic beverages were attacked as being unnecessary, harmful to health, and inherently poisonous. Over the course of the 19th century, the demand gradually arose for total prohibition (Austin 1978).

By the late 19th and early 20th centuries, a number of countries either passed legislation or created alcohol restrictions. Most of these laws and restrictions eventually failed. In the United States, attempts to control, restrict, or abolish alcohol were made, but they all met with abysmal failure. From 1907 to 1919, 34 states passed prohibition laws. Finally, on a more national scale, the 18th Amendment to the Constitution was ratified in 1919 in an attempt to stop the

Al Capone ("Scarface") (center), the undisputed leader of Chicago's gang scene during Prohibition, made millions of dollars in his bootlegging operations until he was convicted of tax evasion in 1931 and eventually imprisoned in Alcatraz.

rapid spread of alcohol addiction. In January 1920, alcohol was outlawed. As soon as such a widely used substance became illegal, criminal activity to satisfy the huge demand for alcohol flourished. Illegal outlets developed for purchasing liquor. Numerous not-so-secret speakeasies developed as illegal establishments where people could buy and consume alcoholic beverages, despite the laws of Prohibition. Bootlegging was a widely accepted activity. In effect, such "dens of sin" filled the vacuum for many drinkers during Prohibition.

During the temperance movement and Prohibition period, doctors and druggists prescribed whiskey and other alcohol known as patent medicines (see "Case in Point," The Great American Fraud: Patent Medicines).

By 1928, doctors made an estimated $40 million per year writing prescriptions for whiskey. Patent medicines flourished, with alcohol contents as high as 50%. Whisko, a "non-intoxicating stimulant," was 55 proof (or 27.5% alcohol). Another, Kaufman's Sulfur Bitters, was labeled "contains no alcohol" but was 40 proof (20% alcohol) and did not contain sulfur. There were dozens of others, many of which contained other types of drugs, such as opium.

Both Prohibitionists and critics of the law were shocked by the violent gang wars that broke out between rivals seeking to control the lucrative black market in liquor. More important, a general disregard for the law developed. Corruption among law enforcement agents was widespread and organized crime was begun and grew to be an enormous illegitimate business. In reaction to these developments, political support rallied against Prohibition, resulting in its repeal in 1933 by the 21st Amendment. Early in the 20th century, women suffragettes had been prominent temperance organizers; paradoxically, flappers organized against Prohibition and were vital in gathering the signatures for repeal.

It appears, three main findings occurred as a result of Prohibition. First, alcohol use began to diminish for the first 2 or 3 years after Prohibition was in effect. This trend had begun several years before the law was passed, but more importantly, after 3 years of steady decline, the use of distilled liquors rose every year afterward. Further, even minors were becoming addicted to alcohol during this period.

Second, enforcement of laws against alcohol use was thwarted by corrupt law enforcement officials, enforcement was uneven (in some areas of the United States enforcement was lax while in other areas very strict), and finally, law enforcement experienced more than 50% turnover in its ranks. Corruption of law enforcement officials stands out as paramount. Reportedly, 10% of law enforcement was "on the take" and had to be continually discharged.

Third, in the nature of western Europeans who emigrated to the United States *en masse* during this period, the consumption of alcohol was culturally prescribed. Prohibition against alcohol usage to the Italian, German, French, Polish, Irish, and other European-based immigrants was perceived as unnecessary and an infringement to the right to common

KEY TERMS

speakeasies
places where alcoholic beverages were illegally sold during the Prohibition era

bootlegging
making, distributing, and selling alcoholic beverages during the Prohibition era

patent medicines
the ingredients in these uncontrolled "medicines" were secret, often composed of large amounts of colored water, alcohol, cocaine, or opiates

CASE IN POINT

The Great American Fraud: Patent Medicines

In the late 1800s and early 1900s, before the days of FDA legislation, the sales of uncontrolled medicines flourished and became widespread. Many of these products were called *patent medicines*, which signified that the ingredients were secret, not that they were patented. The law of the day seemed to be more concerned with someone's recipe being stolen than with preventing harm to the naive consumer. Some of these patent medicines included toxic ingredients such as acetanilide in Bromo-Seltzer and Orangeine and prussic (hydrocyanic) acid in Shiloh's Consumption Cure.

Most patent medicines appear to have been composed largely of either colored water or alcohol, with an occasional added ingredient such as opium or cocaine. Hostetter's Stomach Bitters with 44% alcohol could easily have been classified as liquor. Sale of Peruna (28% alcohol) was prohibited to Native Americans because of its high alcoholic content. Birney's Catarrh Cure contained 4% cocaine. Wistar's Balsam of Wild Cherry (see Figure 9.4), Dr. King's Discovery for Consumption, Mrs. Winslow's Soothing Syrup, and several others contained opiates as well as alcohol.

The medical profession of the mid- and late-19th century was ill-prepared to do battle with the ever-present manufacturers or distributors of patent medicines. Qualified physicians during this time were rare. Much more common were medical practitioners with poor training and little understanding. In fact, many of these early physicians practiced a brand of medicine what was generally useless and frequently more life-threatening than the patent medicines themselves.

In 1905, *Collier's Magazine* ran a series of articles called the "Great American Fraud," which warned of the abuse of patent medicines. This brought the problem to the public's attention of the public (Adams 1905). *Collier's* coined the phrase "dope fiend" from "dope," an African word meaning "intoxicating substance." The American Medical Association (AMA) joined in and widely distributed reprints of *Collier's* story to inform the public about the dangers of these medicines, even though the AMA itself accepted advertisements for patent medicines that physicians knew were addicting. The publicity caused mounting pressure on Congress and President Roosevelt to do something about these fraudulent products. In 1905, the President proposed that a law be enacted to regulate interstate commerce of misbranded and adulterated foods, drinks, and drugs. This received further impetus when Upton Sinclair's book *The Jungle* that was published in 1906—a nauseatingly realistic exposé detailing how immigrant laborers worked under appalling conditions of filth, disease, putrefaction, and other extreme exploitations at Chicago's stockyards.

Two substances used in patent medicines helped shape attitudes that would form the basis of regulatory policies for years to come: the opium derivatives (narcotic drugs, such as heroin and morphine) and cocaine (see Chapter 3).

FIGURE 9.4

This is a poster of one of the patent medicines that contained liberal doses of opium and a high concentration of alcohol. This medicine was widely used to treat tuberculosis ("consumption") around the turn of the century, when over 25% of all adult deaths were from this disease. The U.S. government finally forced the remedy off the market by 1920.

existence. One 93-year-old Italian-American émigré to Chicago illustrates some of these attitudes:

> Well, when we were not allowed to drink because of the government, I thought it was a stupid law. Many of us here in the neighborhood [a fading Italian-American community in Chicago's West Side and the original home of Venturelli] made lots of money as "alki cookers."
>
> We would make the alcohol in our bathtubs and sell to other people or even to those mafia types. Oh, it was horrible cheap and crappy alcohol, if the night before you drank too much, it gave you headaches sometimes for days. On Sunday afternoons, if you walked through this neighborhood in the hot summer days, you could smell the alcohol oozing from peoples' windows. Nearly everyone my mother's and father's age and older at the time made extra money as alki cookers. It was actually a good law [referring to Prohibition] for making a few bucks to help out the family expenses. No one around here gave a damn about the law, because too many were "on the take" so-to-say . . . and it was not just us [referring to the local Italian-Americans]. At least for us when we meet together and eat for fun, alcohol is like the air we breathe. Who the hell is going to change that, especially something so deep? *(From Venturelli's research files, interview with a 93-year-old male, May 26, 2000.)*

Defining Alcoholics

As we discussed in Chapter 8 and at the beginning of this chapter, creating absolute definitions or categories of behavior that represent an alcoholic *type* is very difficult because all behaviors enormously vary from one person to the next, thus most behaviors range on a continuum. Adding to this is the fact that some disagreement exists among experts on what the exact criteria should be regarding the definition of an alcoholic. In other words, when is a person an alcoholic? Is it the daily drinker or the inebriated weekend drinker? What if he or she is able to maintain a job and provide for his or her family? How does this type of alcoholic compare with an unemployed resident of skid row?

In the minds of many Americans, an alcoholic is a derelict who frequents skid rows, train stations, and bus terminals; panders for money; and sleeps on a park bench at night. Yet this stereotypical image of an alcoholic represents only a few percent of the millions of Americans who qualify as alcoholic by any of the accepted medical definitions. The more typical alcoholic, in fact, is the example of the professor or businessman purchasing alcohol at a liquor store, (given as an example at the opening of this chapter). In effect, most alcoholics are secret or hidden drinkers who very much look like common everyday working people.

■ CULTURAL DIFFERENCES

Although much more will be presented later in this chapter about the pervasive role that culture plays in drinking behavior, we begin with a quote highlighting cultural differences in interpreting alcohol consumption:

> Even definitions of a "problem drinker" differ from one culture to the next. In Poland, loss of productivity tends to demonstrate a drinking problem, while Californians emphasize drunk driving as an important and sometimes key indicator . . . [Among Italian-Americans, an inability to provide for one's family because of heavy drinking qualifies a person as an alcoholic.] . . . Some methods of assessing problem drinking looks to behavior that leads to a brush with the law. However, drunkenness may or may not lead to disruptive behavior. In the Netherlands, alcoholic beverage consumption is similar to that in Finland and Poland, but there is much less disruptive or public drinking. In these nations, the actual amount of alcohol consumed is not indicated by the arrest figures, the actual amount consumed, and the number of physical ailments caused by excessive alcohol consumption. Secondly, the social response to drunkenness may not be arrest and conviction. Ireland, for example, has traditionally used psychiatric institutions to control drunkenness (Osterberg 1986, p. 83).

Estimates vary, but it is believed that approximately three-fourths of problem drinkers are men and one-fourth are women. The proportion of women has risen in recent years. This increase occurred for two reasons: (1) women as problem drinkers are more visible and numerous because they now make up about half of the workforce, and (2) women are more likely to acknowledge the problem and seek treatment, especially if they are in white collar occupations. Thus, female problems drinkers may now be more visible and more self assured as well as more numerous.

Next, in attempting to define alcoholism, we turn to models that speak of the state of addiction. Alcoholism is a state of physical and psychological addiction to ethanol, a psychoactive substance (also see Chapter 8). It was once viewed as a vice and dismissed as sinful, but over the years, there has been a shift from this perspective to one that views alcoholism as a disease. The "sinfulness" perspective failed to focus on the fact that alcoholism is an addiction—an illness—and not the result of a lack of personal discipline and morality.

Attempts to expand the basic definition of alcoholism to include symptoms of the condition and psychological and sociological factors have been difficult; no one definition satisfies everyone. The World Health Organization defines *alcohol dependence syndrome* as a syndrome characterized by a state, psychic and usually also physical, resulting from drinking alcohol. This state is characterized by behavioral and other responses that include a compulsion to drink alcohol (like an unquenchable thirst) on a continuous or periodic basis to experience its psychic effects and sometimes to avoid the discomfort of its absence; tolerance may or may not be present (NIAAA 1980).

Another more classic explanation of alcoholism that remains popular is, "Alcoholism is a chronic behavioral disorder manifested by repeated drinking of alcoholic beverages in excess of the dietary and social uses of the community, to an extent that interferes with the drinker's health or his social or economic functioning" (Keller 1958, p. 78). Finally, another definition emphasizes, "Alcoholism is a chronic, primary, hereditary disease that progresses from an early, physiological susceptibility into an addiction characterized by tolerance changes, physiological dependence, and loss of control over drinking. [In this definition], [P]sychological symptoms are secondary to the physiological disease and not relevant to its onset" (Gold 1991, p. 99).

In summary, the definitions above either list or hint at the following major components of *alcoholism*, which follow (NIAAA "Frequently Asked Questions"):

Craving: an overwhelming compulsion to drink even when not feasible, such as at work, driving a car, mowing a lawn, and so on.

Very impaired or loss of control: an inability to limit one's drinking once drinking has begun, for example, one drink only before going to bed is impossible to control.

Physical dependence: presence of withdrawal symptoms when attempting to abstain from usage. Such symptoms as nausea, sweating, shakiness, and anxiety about the availability of alcohol are common.

Tolerance: a need to continually increase the amount of alcohol consumed to maintain its effects (or to maintain the "buzz").

■ ALCOHOL ABUSE AND ALCOHOLISM

When attempting to understand the meaning of chronic drinking, one additional clarification that should be made is the difference between alcohol abuse and alcoholism. The two explanations of drinking behavior differ as a matter of degree. When speaking of *alcohol abuse*, the craving, loss of control, and physical dependence just listed as primary manifestations are less prominent and not as pronounced as in alcoholism. There is diminished ability to fulfill obligations and goals; more occasions of drinking at the wrong time, such as while driving; legal problems such as driving under the influence; and relationship problems. Note that many of these problems that

---

KEY TERMS

alcohol abuse
uncontrollable drinking that leads to alcohol craving, loss of control, and physical dependence but with less prominent characteristics than found in alcoholism

alcoholism
a state of physical and psychological addiction to ethanol, a psychoactive substance

result from alcohol abuse are also experienced by alcoholics, but not all manifestations of alcoholics are experienced by alcohol abusers. For example, an alcoholic may repeatedly argue with family members two or three times per week, whereas an alcohol abuser may have fewer occurrences of the same type of alcohol-inspired arguments with a family member. Thus, even though the alcohol abuser has fewer occasions of uncontrollable drinking than the alcoholic, the drinking remains largely uncontrollable when it occurs. For many years, people with drinking problems were lumped together under the label *alcoholic,* and *alcohol abusers* were assumed to be suffering from the same illness. Today, as a result of greater understanding about addiction and addictive behav-iors, the distinction between the two terms leads to a more precise understanding of excessive alcohol abuse (see "Here and Now," Are You "on the Road" to Alcoholism?).

Figure 9.5 graphically illustrates the millions of men and women who are either alcohol abusers or alcoholics, and the number of both alcohol abusers and alcoholics combined for 1985, 1990, and 1995. Note that from 1985 through 1995 very little change (up or down) occurred in the numbers of both types of problem drinkers. Figure 9.5 also shows that in all 3 time periods, there were approximately 7.2 million alcohol abusers, 11 million alcoholics, and 18.1 million alcohol abusers and alcoholics (Williams et al. 1997).

HERE AND NOW   Are You "on the Road" to Alcoholism?*

Answer the following questions with either a simple "yes" or "no."

1. Do you frequently drink because you have problems or need to relax?
2. When out with friends, do you become irritated or bored when the evening does not lead to the use of alcohol and/or drugs?
3. Do you drink when you get mad at other people, such as your friends or parents?
4. Do you often prefer to drink alone?
5. Are your grades suffering because of the time you spend drinking?
6. Do you stop drinking "for good" then start again?
7. Have you begun to drink in the morning, before school or work?
8. Do you often gulp your drinks?
9. Do you have loss of memory because of your drinking?
10. Do you lie about the amount you drink?
11. Do you ever get into trouble when you are drinking?
12. Do you get drunk when you drink, even when you do not plan to?
13. Do you think you are cool when you can hold your liquor?

If you answered more than one as "yes," you may have a drinking problem that will become increasingly problematic moving in the direction of alcoholism.

*Reformulated from The A.A. Grapevine, Inc., A.A. World Services, Inc., 1988, 1998. Available at http://www.alcoholics-anonymous.org/ef9doc1.html.

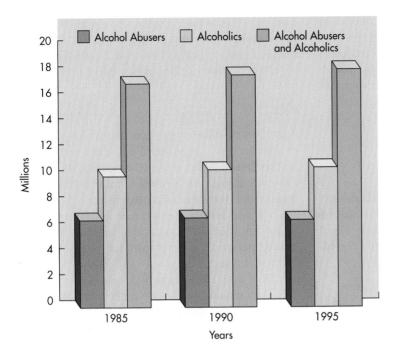

FIGURE 9.5
Alcohol use in men and women 18 years of age and over.

....

Source: William, G. D., Stinson, F. S., Parker, D. A., Hartford, T. C., and Noble, J. Epidemiologic Bulletin No. 15: Demographic Trends, Alcohol Abuse and Alcoholism, 1985–1995. *Alcohol Health & Research World* 11(3) (1997): 30–83, 92.

■ TYPES OF ALCOHOLICS

Although written more than 3 decades ago, Jellinek's (1960) original personality-typology (characterizations), differentiating the types of alcoholics remains very important for adding more preciseness in understanding alcohol abuse and its outcomes. Jellinek's categories are as follows:

Alpha alcoholism: mostly a psychological dependence on alcohol to bolster an inability to cope with life. The alpha type constantly needs alcohol and becomes irritable and anxious when it is not available.

Beta alcoholism: mostly a social dependence on alcohol. Often, although not exclusively, this type is a heavy beer drinker who continues to meet social and economic obligations. Some nutritional deficiencies can occur, including organic damage such as gastritis and cirrhosis.

Gamma alcoholism: the most severe form of alcoholism. This type of alcoholic suffers from emotional and psychological impairment. Jellinek believed this type of alcoholic suffered from a true disease and progresses from a psychological dependence to physical dependence. Loss of control over when alcohol is consumed

and how much is taken characterizes the latter phase of this type of alcoholism.

Delta alcoholics: called the maintenance drinker (Royce 1989). The person loses control over drinking and cannot abstain for even a day or two. Many wine-drinking countries such as France and Italy contain delta-type alcoholics who sip wine throughout most of their waking hours. Being "tipsy" but never completely inebriated is typical of the delta alcoholic.

Epsilon alcoholic: this type of alcoholic is characterized as a binge drinker. The epsilon-type drinker drinks excessively for a certain period (for days and sometimes weeks) then abstains completely from alcohol until the next binge period. The dependence on alcohol is both physical and psychological. Loss of control over the amount consumed is another characteristic of this type of alcoholic.

Zeta alcoholic: this category was added to Jellinek's types to describe the moderate drinker who becomes abusive and violent. Although this type is also referred to as a "pathological drinker" or "mad drunk," zeta types may not be addicted to alcohol.

Other classifications differentiate alcoholics by their reaction to the drug as quiet, sullen, friendly, or angry types. Finally, another method is to classify alcoholics according to drinking patterns: people with occupational, social, escape, and emotional disorders.

Cultural Influences

In this section, we explain how views of alcohol are culturally influenced—that is, how culture encodes the thoughts, attitudes, values, and beliefs about alcohol and how it influences our behavior regarding the use and abuse of alcohol.

> I was just drinking beer a lot and hardly ever drank the hard stuff. I was drinking about a six-pack after work each night. My wife never said anything much about my drinking. Then as time went on, I remember that I would start drinking beer earlier and earlier after work. Then came the six-pack and an extra quart of beer each night while sitting home trying to relax after a pressure-filled day at the office. Well, little did I realize then, I was having a drinking problem and it was only beer! I could not believe that I was sort of a beer alcoholic. Back then, I never thought that silly ole' beer could get a person hooked.
> *(From Venturelli's research files, male, age 32, currently in court-ordered Alcoholics Anonymous, April 12, 2000.)*

Or,

> Q: Do you consider yourself a heavy drinker?
> A: No, I only drink beer.
> Q: You were drunk when you came in here last week.
> A: No, I only had a few beers.

These two interviews illustrate a belief shared by many Americans, which is that the milder alcohols such as beer, wine, and wine coolers are often placed outside the domain of potentially addictive types of beverages. Some may even believe that the distilled spirits such as vodka, gin, and whiskey are the only types of addictive alcoholic beverages. Finally, the comment that "I don't use and never would use drugs, I only drink" can easily be heard being espoused by a large portion of Americans, (probably a majority), who place alcohol in a completely separate category from drugs. However, each 12-ounce bottle of beer is equal to 1 ounce of liquor. Thus, two beers equals a double shot of bourbon or vodka.

■ CULTURE AND DRINKING BEHAVIOR

Another way of looking at how culture has an influence on us would be to stand outside of our culture and see how people behave when intoxicated in our culture and in a variety of other cultures in order to understand the real relationship among culture, alcohol, and human beings. A major contribution to our knowledge of intoxicated behavior from an outside perspective comes from the field of cultural anthropology.

How does culture affect the way we view alcohol? Why would our culture differ from other cultures in the use and abuse of alcoholic beverages? These are two questions we will focus on in this section. Throughout the world, cultures create a climate for the development of attitudes toward most behaviors, and like other behaviors, the use of alcohol is embedded within our culture. Culture does more than contain the attitudes and feelings that people have toward alcohol use; culture dictates the variety, the attachment, and the intensity of attitudes that are held toward other peoples' behavior. For example, in the 1930s, American college students acquired a "reverence for strong drink" (Room 1984, p. 8). Although for decades many people believed that college students "majored in drinking," during the 1930s, students grew to consider heavy use as romantic and adult, resonating with the romantic, heavy-drinking expatriate community of writers in Paris, such as Ernest Hemingway.

American culture in general views ethanol-containing beverages as sexy, mature, sophisticated, facilitating socializing, and enhancing status. Today, many of these beliefs are communicated through the mass media, and advertising is a key medium of communication. Advertising uses positive images in order to persuade observers to purchase a particular brand of alcohol. For example, what messages are found in newspapers and especially magazines about drinking certain types of wine, bourbon, scotch, and the numerous types of domestic and imported beers? What attitudes are generally conveyed when a sexy, glamorous woman is dressed in formal evening attire standing next to her man in front of a perfectly glowing fireplace, smiling confidently as he stares into her eyes and sips his special-label cognac?

■ CULTURE AND DISINHIBITED BEHAVIOR

The concept of drunken comportment was first formulated by MacAndrew and Edgerton (1969). Drunken comportment refers to the behavior emitted while under the influence of alcohol within the norms and expectations of a particular culture. Instead of simply labeling drinking behavior as drunken behavior, this concept sensitizes us to how drinking behavior is influenced by cultural norms and expectations. For example, in the United States, drinking is comported to mean time out away from duties and obligations. "The symbolism of alcohol in American culture contains this motif of release and remission, as in the emergence of TGIF [Thank God It's Friday]" (Gusfield 1986, p. 203). Another example is that in some cultures, drinking occurs during celebrations and festivities, and as part of religious ceremony. In France and Italy, drinking alcohol occurs while eating with family members. Alcohol is a disinhibitor , which refers to depression of the cerebral cortex functions. When this occurs, it results in a suspension of rational or thoughtful constraints on impulsive behavior. *Inhibitions* (inner raw feelings and attitudes) are normally controlled through rationality and logical thought processes. The popular image of Christmas parties at the office where too much alcohol is consumed or any party that gets out of control because of over consumption of alcohol are examples. People at such events can easily become uncontrollable, loud, impulsive, and just simply irrational. In such situations, outbreaks of arguing and physical and verbal abuse are more likely to occur. Such behavior is disinhibited behavior.

Although all of us know that the alcohol content that is usually measured in terms of alcohol proof (see Chapter 8 for more details) has an independent effect on the user, two additional factors contribute to the effects of alcohol; set and setting (Goode 1999, Zinberg 1984; Zinberg and Robertson 1972). *Set* is the individual's expectation of what a drug will do to his or her personality. *Setting* is both the physical and social environment in which the drug is consumed. How important are these two distinctions? Some psychologists contend that both set and setting can overshadow the pharmacological effects of most drugs. In fact, set and

setting are far more influential in determining a drug user's experience even when the less immediately addictive drugs, such as alcohol and marijuana, are used, in contrast to more potent addictive drugs, such as cocaine and heroin. Good examples of this are when people who drink alcohol say "I felt that drink right away" or "I drank a lot last night but I had something on my mind and dude, I was just not in the partying mood."

A review of various ethnographic studies (Marshall 1983) reveals pseudointoxicated behavior among Tahitians, Rarotongans, Chippewa, Dakota, Pine Ridge and Teton Sioux, Aleuts, Baffin Island Inuits, and Potawatomi—that is, people *acting* drunk before or seconds after the bottle is opened, or as the drink is consumed. The frequency of use or the amount consumed have less effect on how drinkers comport themselves, but rather the cultural values, beliefs, mental maps, and norms cause a particular behavioral outcome. Using the terminology of psychology, we would say that it is not the biochemical effects on the brain alone that account for disinhibitory behavior but the belief that one has been drinking a substance that has a disinhibitory effect; that is, the mental (cognitive) appraisal of the physiological state allows disinhibited behavior. In other words, in using the terminology of sociology and revising a famous sociological axiom, we could say that "what we believe to be true (or personally define as true) is true in its consequences or in the obtained results." Thus, if you believe you are drunk, you act drunk, you are drunk.

Cultures vary in how they evaluate alcohol consumption. Some religions in the United States view drinking as evil, whereas other religions view alcohol as a gift from God and it is used in religious ceremonies. In some subcultures, excessive use of alcohol is an indication of manhood, strength, and virility, whereas in other subcultures, excessive alcohol use in public is disgusting and embarrassing. Even drug education has different perspectives. Do we emphasize total abstinence or teach people how to drink in moderation? Why such vastly different approaches? Because our culture has contradictory practices.

Similarly, the views we maintain about alcohol abuse and addiction vary. For example, is alcoholism a disease? Is it prescribed by certain customs within ethnic groups? Does it result from some type of personality flaw? The three concepts discussed in this section—drunken comportment, set and setting, and pseudointoxication—demonstrate that social and cultural contexts exert their independent influences on the effects of alcohol consumption.

CULTURE PROVIDES RULES FOR DRINKING BEHAVIOR

Many cultures, such as traditional Italian and Jewish cultures, permit moderate drinking within the family, especially at meals, but disapprove of drunken behaviors. Note that many differences separate these groups; for example, Italians use wine as a food item, whereas it has only ritual value among Orthodox Jews. In one study of Scandinavian nations, by contrast, drinking was considered absolutely separated from work. Where drinking at work was permitted, however, it was allowed to go on to the point of intoxication (Makela 1986). Finnish, Polish, and Russian cultures are associated with binge drinking, whereas French culture is linked with sipping. In the United States, we encounter a vast variety of subgroups: some heavy drinkers may live in a community where it is not considered excessive to drink with their friends out of paper bags on the street in the morning, whereas in other communities all outdoor drinking is either done in parks, restaurants, bars, or outdoor cafes. Some people may belong to a "workplace culture of drinking" at a post office, construction site, or law

firm where "three martini lunches" are not unheard of. Perhaps this type of drinking is not much different from the habits of teenage peer groups. To be "treated" for this behavior might seem as strange as going into rehab for acting "normal."

CULTURE PROVIDES CEREMONIAL MEANING FOR ALCOHOL USE

The first notable work on ceremonial use and ethnic drinking practices was undertaken by Bales (1946), who attempted to explain the different rates of drinking between Jews (low) and Irish (high) in terms of symbolic and ceremonial meanings. For Jews, drinking had familial and sacramental significance, whereas for the Irish it represented male convivial bonding.

A high rate of heavy drinking was observed among the Irish in the 1800s. It was said that these individuals drank because they were Irish. Today, some descendants of the Irish continue to live the stereotype; for them, it represents Irishness—they drink because they are Irish. A button displayed on St. Patrick's Day proclaimed, "Today I'm Irish, Tomorrow I'm Hung Over," and a New York Post supplement declared this event to be "Three Days of Drinking and Revelry." Jews, on the other hand, think that Jews cannot be alcoholic. That is, they believe that if a person is Jewish, even though he or she drinks a lot, true alcoholism is impossible. If the individual gives up denial, however, and admits alcoholism, then he or she cannot be Jewish (Blume et al. 1980).

CULTURE PROVIDES MODELS OF ALCOHOLISM

In Chapter 4, we discussed models of addiction, such as the disease model. U.S. citizens define alcoholism as a disease far more often than French Canadians or French (Babor et al. 1986). Some South Bronx Hispanics have ascribed alcoholism to "spells," spirits (Garrison and Podell 1981), the evil eye (mal ojo), or witchcraft (brujeria). The entire addiction may also be ignored or bypassed; ulcers, divorce, or car accidents that an alcohol counselor may recognize as alcoholism-based may instead be traced directly to supernatural influence. One way or another, if it is attributed to a supernatural cause, a supernatural solution may be called upon to cure this problem. Thus, many seek the help of a folk curer (*espiritista, santero,* and so on). Some African Americans interpret their problems as a punishment from God, and they may also often subscribe to a moral model that conflicts with a disease or other psychiatric or addictive model.

■ CULTURAL STEREOTYPES OF DRINKING PATTERNS MAY BE MISLEADING

African American drinking patterns run the gamut from middle-class cocktail lounges (as seen in liquor ads in *Ebony*), to blue collar wakes and birthday parties, to the "bottle-gang" of homeless poor. By class, middle-class African American women drinkers are not dramatically different from middle-class white women drinkers; they are typically moderate drinkers, with few nondrinkers and heavy drinkers. Poorer African American female groups have a larger proportion of nondrinkers; among those who do drink, more are heavy drinkers. Breaking it down further, being married, older, and church-affiliated has also been associated with nonacceptance of heavy drinking (Gary and Gary 1985; Kinney 2000). At initially established black colleges and universities, blacks have lower levels of alcohol and other types of drug consumption than colleges and universities with a majority of white students. At all colleges and universities, white students drink significantly more than African American students (Kinney 2000).

Gordon, who studied a Connecticut city in 1981, examined three Hispanic groups, all new to the United States and all blue-collar. In this group, Dominicans drank less after migration. They emphasized suave or sophisticated drinking, and they saw drunkenness as indecent (without respect). Alcoholics were seen as "sick," perhaps from some tragic experience. Guatemalans drank substantially more after migration: one-third of males were often drunk and binged most weekends. Being drunk was considered glamorous and sentimentalized—like Humphrey Bogart under the hanging lightbulb, alone in a hotel room. These individuals boasted of hangovers, even when they did not have one. The Guatemalan Alcoholics Anonymous (AA) group was alien to Puerto Ricans. Puerto Ricans broke down into middle-class American-style moderate drinkers, depressed and wife-abusing alcoholic welfare recipients, and various sorts of polydrug abusers, including those who entered into the mainland "druggie" youth culture (Gordon 1981). Among Hispanics in general, men were twice as likely to be involved in heavy drinking than both white and African American males (Kinney 2000). In fact, African American students have the lowest lifetime, annual, and 30-day prevalence rates for alcohol use; they also tend to have the lowest rates for daily drinking (NIDA 1999). Even when looking at physiological responses to alcohol, ethnicity appears to matter. The long-term effects of alcohol dependence are reported to cause more damage on the immune systems of African Americans than other ethnic groups. The greater sensitivity to alcohol and its damaging effects puts this group at an increased risk for infection and, in many cases, at a greater likelihood of death (Rostler 2000).

Blane (1977) surveyed Italian-American drinking patterns, comparing recent arrivals, (those born abroad but living in the United States for more than 10 years), children of immigrants, and grandchildren of immigrants. Among males, the percentage of daily drinkers declined from 92% to 15% as one moved through the generations, as did wine and cordial consumption. Any heavy use (five drinks at one sitting) rose from one-fifth to three-fifths, and once-a-week heavy use went from one-eighth to one-third. With women, daily drinking declined from 73% to 9%, wine and cordial use was more than halved (although still significantly "Italian"), occasional heavy use rose from 6% to 32%, and weekly heavy use increased from 3% to 10% (Blane 1977).

As information on cultural differences in alcohol use and abuse has become known throughout the alcohol abuse field, administrative agencies have attempted to incorporate these insights into professional standards of practice, under the rubric of "cultural competence." Prevention and treatment programs are to be evaluated from the standpoint of their competence in providing services to the cultural populations they serve. To avoid stereotyping, these considerations include understanding of such variables as ethnic acculturation and skills at eliciting information on the cultural background of clients (OSAP 1992). Prevention issues such as consumption of gateway drugs and media advocacy have been refined to target ethnic at-risk populations. For example, urban African American youths are bombarded with aggressive marketing of 40-ounce malt liquors, known as "40s." Consumption of 40s is celebrated in rap lyrics such as "Tap the

Bottle." The alcohol content of malt liquors ranges from 5.6% to 8%, compared with 3.5% for regular beers. This large, inexpensive bottle of potent brew offers a cheap high, often leading to alcohol abuse. Moreover, in the mid-1990s, 40s drinking increasingly became associated with marijuana smoking, going together like cookies and milk, used before school or at "hooky parties."

■ CULTURE PROVIDES ATTITUDES REGARDING ALCOHOL CONSUMPTION

Although cultures often maintain generalized (normative) attitudes regarding alcohol use and abuse, significant attitude differences also exist within cultures (Arkin and Funkhouser 1992; Inciardi 1992). The United States is characterized as culturally ambivalent regarding alcohol use (Kinney 2000). This means that alcohol consumption enormously varies across our culture. Different geographic regions, diverse religious beliefs, and racial and ethnic differences result in confusing attitudes about drinking alcohol. Other factors that contribute to diversity in attitudes include social upbringing, peer group dynamics, social class, income, education, and occupational differences.

What specific impact do such attitudes have on drinking? As just mentioned, attitudes are responsible for making alcohol consumption acceptable or unacceptable—or even relished as a form of behavior. For example, in one segment of impoverished African American groups, alcohol use and abuse is so common that it has become accepted behavior. The following excerpt describes an accepted use of alcohol consumption:

> A party without liquor or a street rap without a bottle is often perceived as unimaginable. These attitudes about drinking are shaped as youth grow up seeing liquor stores in their communities next to schools, churches, and homes. Liquor stores and bootleg dealers frequently permeate the black residential community, where in traditionally white communities they are generally restricted to commercial or business zones. With liquor stores throughout the fabric of black residential life, black youth grow up seeing men drinking in the streets and relatives drinking at home (Harper 1986).

Contrast this attitude with orthodox religious and fundamentalist communities where the use of alcohol and other drugs is strictly prohibited:

> I was raised in a very religious, Seventh-Day Adventist family. My father was a pretty strong figure in our little church of 18 members. My mother stayed home most of the time, living in a way like an Old Testament kind of biblical life, so to speak. We were strict vegetarians, and all of us in the family had to be very involved with church life. The first time I ever saw alcohol outside of always hearing how corrupting it was to the mind and the body, was when I was 7. One day the father of a friend of mine—the only non-Adventist family friend I was allowed to play with—was drinking a beer in the kitchen when we walked in. I asked, "What's that?" The father's reply was "This is beer, dear John." I looked strangely at him and pretended to be amused at the father's answer. Actually, inside I remember being very surprised and scared at the same time for I was always told that people who drink alcohol were not doing what God wanted them to do in life. *(From Venturelli's research files, 18-year-old male university student, May 21, 1993.)*

From these contrasting examples, we can see that the values expressed through group and family attitudes regarding drug use are very significant in determining the extent of alcohol consumption.

College and University Students and Alcohol Use

Over the years, alcohol use and consumption rates among college students remains stable, although other drugs show a lot more variance. For example, marijuana use has dramatically risen, fallen, and then risen again. There do exist some interesting findings about college students and alcohol consumption:

- College students drink an estimated 4 billion cans of beer annually.

- The total amount of alcohol consumed by college students each year is 430 million gallons, enough for every college and university in the United States to fill an Olympic-size swimming pool.

- As many as 360,000 of the nation's 12 million undergraduates will die from alcohol-related causes while in school. This is more than the number who will receive master's and doctorate degrees (Alcoholism Kills 2000).

- Nearly half of all college students are binge drinkers.

- The number of college women who drink to get drunk has more than tripled in the past 10 years, rising from 10% to 35%.

- On America's college campuses, alcohol is a factor in 40% of all academic problems and 28% of all dropouts.

- Seventy-five percent of male students and 55% of female students involved in acquaintance rape had been drinking or using drugs at the time.

- For college men, alcohol consumption was inversely related to the size of the institution; that is, male students at smaller institutions consumed far more than those at larger institutions. (Lack of social activities could be a precipitating factor.)

- Nearly one-quarter of students reported failing a test or project because of the after effects of drinking or doing drugs.

- A related consequence of alcohol abuse is motor vehicle accidents. For young people under the age of 25, motor vehicle accidents rate as the number one cause of death (Presley et al. 1996).

- Findings from CORE Institute (see paragraph following this list) indicate that 300,000 of today's college students will die of alcohol-related causes such as drunk driving accidents, liver disorders, various sexually transmitted diseases from improper sexual protection (lack of condoms leading to HIV), cancers from alcohol abuse, and various severely damaged organs from chronic drinking (see Chapter 8), (Phoenix House 2000).

- Although the average cost for book purchases for classes is about $450 per year, the average student spends about $900 on alcohol each year (Phoenix House 2000).

- Finally, on a positive side, there is a small but very significant downward trend in alcohol use on America's campuses. In 1985, the percentage of college students who had consumed alcohol in the previous 30 days was approximately 80%. By 1990, that number had declined to 74.5% and continues to decline each year. Keep in mind that while this is good news for alcohol consumption, the use of other illegitimate-type drugs continues to increase.

The CORE Institute survey is a validated survey instrument that has been administered to more than 1 million students—by far the largest sample of college students surveyed. The available figures from the CORE Institute survey (Presley et al. 1996) indicate that on average, approximately 83% of college students consume alcohol within the year this survey was given. The average number of drinks that students consume is 5.1 per week (Presley et al. 1996). Approximately 42% engaged in binge drinking 2 weeks before the CORE survey was administered. Of all the drugs reported, alcohol was the most heavily abused on college campuses, followed by tobacco 44% and marijuana 31%.

■ BINGE DRINKING

Binge drinking is defined as consumption of five or more drinks in one sitting or five or more drinks in short succession. The widely reported study by Wechsler and colleagues (1994) brought this issue to the public's attention. This report, which surveyed 17,592 students at 140 campuses, revealed that 44% engaged in binge drinking, which impacted on many areas of students' lives—both their own and those of others whose lives were disrupted by this behavior (giving rise to the term *second-hand drinking*). As mentioned earlier, today, 42% to 50% (depending on the diversity of survey results) of all college students often binge drink. This type of alcohol consumption remains very worrisome to anyone promoting, protecting, caring for, and responsible for the behavior of young people in this subculture. Equally, health professionals see this as a serious form of alcohol abuse.

One may question whether all five-drink episodes qualify as *binge drinking*, a term that calls to mind a weekend of drinking, or Jellinek's epsilon alcoholism. However, 11.1% of males and 7.4% of females reported three or more episodes of mem-

Alcohol consumption is routine at many social activities for college students.

ory loss during the past year due to drug or alcohol use, of which the overwhelming majority were alcohol-related, both because alcohol is the major drug consumed by students and because it produces amnesiac episodes. Amnesiac episodes are accepted as symptoms of problem drinking behavior.

Approximately 16% of students (22.6% of males and 9.5% of females) reported binge drinking on at least three occasions during the previous 2 weeks (Presley et al. 1996). Community college students were less likely to engage in binge drinking: 29.9% had binged in the previous 2 weeks compared with 40.4% of their peers at 4-year schools. Approximately one-fourth of all males enrolled at 4-year colleges reported three or more binge episodes during the previous 2 weeks.

Students who live on campus were more likely to binge drink than those who live off campus. Further, older, working, off-campus students are less likely to engage in such behavior, lowering their scores in this regard relative to the standard college student. Some 12.1% of on-campus students suffered three or more memory losses compared with 7.3% of off-campus students (this last figure is not broken down by gender). These data are corroborated by the observation that 30.3% of students younger than age 21 had memory losses during the year, as opposed to 20.1% of those over age 21. Finally, ethnically, Native American students had the highest frequency of drinking episodes, binge drinking, and memory loss, followed in order by white, Hispanic, African American, and Asian students.

■ GENDER AND COLLEGIATE ALCOHOL USE

The findings from the CORE survey consistently indicated greater frequency of male drinking, frequency of male binge drinking, and consequences of drinking. In a review of the literature addressing gender and student drinking patterns, Berkowitz and Perkins (1987) found a historic pattern of male-dominated college drinking patterns. The transition into college is associated with a doubling of the percentages of those who drink for both genders. Both men and women drink to enhance sociability or social interaction, to escape negative emotions or release otherwise unacceptable ones, and to simply get drunk. "Drinking to get drunk" was considered more of a male pursuit. Indeed, males are more frequently associated with binge drinking and negative public consequences than female drinkers. Severe drunkenness and a customary rowdiness or drunken comportment is normative for male drinkers who binge, including fighting, property damage, and troubles with authorities. The latter were twice as likely to be male problems.

Unsurprisingly, drinking is inversely related to grades. With heavier drinkers, grades suffered for both male and female students. According to the studies cited by Berkowitz and Perkins (1987) for binge drinkers, the impact on impaired academic performance is just as great for women drinkers. More recent information (De Jong 1995; Presley et al. 1996) corroborates this finding and shows similar consequences among male and female binge drinkers in terms of health problems, personal injury, and unplanned sexual activity. Over the past few decades, however, an increase in drinking similarities (amount and percentage of drinking) has been occurring between males and females.

Women and Alcohol Consumption Patterns

Women are affected by alcohol differently than men. Women possess greater sensitivity to alcohol, have a greater likelihood of addiction, and develop alcohol-related health problems sooner than men. Why do women respond differently than men to alcohol? Three reasons are (1) body size (men are generally larger than women); (2) women absorb alcohol sooner than men because on average, women possess more body fat and body fat does not dilute alcohol as well as water, which male bodies contain more of; and (3) women possess less of a metabolizing enzyme that functions to get rid of (process out) alcohol.

In Britain, for example, the proportion of women drinking has risen steadily since 1984. This increase in drinking still holds true for all age groups with the exception of women over 65 (Alcohol Concern 2000). Other notable facts regarding women and drinking can be summarized as follows (2000 About com, Inc. 1998):

- Although men begin drinking earlier in life, women are more likely than men to start drinking heavily later in life.

- Women are more easily affected by alcohol consumption, both its effects and diseases related to alcoholism: cirrhosis of the liver, stomach cancer, and so on.

- Women's alcohol consumption is often similar to that of people they are close to such as a lover or husband.

- Full-time working, professionally oriented women drink at the end of their working day, whereas women who stay at home drink alcohol throughout the day.

- More women in alcohol treatment come from sexually abusive homes (70%), in comparison to men (12%).

- Today, women are more visible and their behavior, especially alcohol consumption, is more observable (e.g., drinking in bars, purchasing alcohol, and so on).

Figure 9.6 shows the prevalence of reported alcohol consumption among women of childbearing age (18–44 years). Highest consumption of alcohol for these women was found in Wisconsin (19.4%), Iowa (18.9%), and Pennsylvania (18.8%). The lowest con-

FIGURE 9.6

Prevalence of reported frequent alcohol consumption* among childbearing-aged women (18–44 years)—United States, Behavioral Risk Factor Surveillance System, 1995.

*Consumption of an average of seven or more drinks per week or five or more drinks on at least one occasion during the preceding month. *Source:* CDC (Centers for Disease Control and Prevention) Wonder. Available at http://wonder.cdc.gov/wonder/ prevguid/moo47306/graphic.htm.

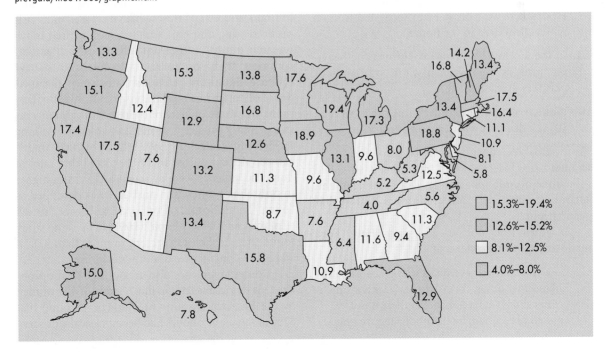

sumption was found in Tennessee (4.0%), Kentucky (5.2%), and West Virginia (5.3%). We also found that as a group, alcohol-abusing women are more likely to drink alone at home. A high incidence of alcohol abuse is found in women who are unemployed and looking for work, whereas less alcohol abuse is likely in women who are employed part-time. Divorced or separated women, women who never marry, and those who are unmarried and living with a partner are more likely to use and abuse alcohol than married women. Other high-risk groups are women in their twenties and early thirties and women with heavy-drinking husbands or partners. Other researchers (Wilsnack et al. 1986 and Williams et al. 1987) found that women who experience depression or encounter problems with fertility or menopausal changes also demonstrate heavier drinking behavior.

Looking at specific age groups, the following conclusions were drawn by the National Institute on Alcohol Abuse and Alcoholism (1990 and 1992):

1. Women in the 21- to 34-year-old age group were least likely to report alcohol-related problems if they had stable marriages and were working full-time. In other words, young mothers with full-time occupations reported less reliance on alcohol in comparison to childless women without full-time work.

2. In the 35- to 49-year-old age group, the heaviest drinkers were divorced or separated women without children in the home.

3. In the 50- to 64-year-old age group, the heaviest drinkers were women whose husbands or partners drank heavily.

4. Women 65 years and older comprised less than 10% of drinkers with drinking problems.

More alcohol consumption is also found in women who closely work in traditionally so-called masculine occupations and levels of management, such as executives and traditional blue-collar occupations.

In April 1995, former First Lady Betty Ford made the following statement:

> Today, we know that when a woman abuses alcohol or other drugs, the risk to her health is much greater than it is for a man. Yet there is not enough prevention, intervention, and treatment targeting women. It is still much harder for women to get help. That needs to change (SAMHSA 1995, p. 14).

In fact, women risk serious health consequences when they choose to use alcohol and other drugs. Alcohol, in particular, can often be devastating to women's health.

As just presented, not only does alcohol have a greater immediate effect on women but also its long-term risks are more dangerous as well. Some surveys now show that more alcohol consumption occurs among girls 12 to 17 years old than among boys the same age. This places young women at a risk of delaying the onset of puberty, a condition that can wreak havoc in terms of adolescent maturation.

Finally, women are more likely to combine alcohol with prescription drugs than men. When the use of other drugs enters into the equation, ovulation may become inhibited and fertility adversely affected. Women also risk early menopause when they consume alcohol.

■ THE ROLE OF ALCOHOL IN DOMESTIC VIOLENCE

Much attention became focused on domestic violence in the mid-1990s through high-profile criminal cases such as those involving the Menendez brothers and O. J. Simpson. The increased emphasis on decreasing domestic violence has inspired much research into its causes and effects as well as into common traits of abusers. Recent studies have found a significant relationship between the incidence of battering and the abuse of alcohol; furthermore, the abuse of alcohol overwhelmingly emerges as a primary predictor of marital violence (De Jong 1995; Drug Strategies 1999). A study of 2000 American couples conducted in 1993 showed that rates of domestic violence were as much as 15 times higher in households where the husband was described as "often" being drunk, as opposed to "never" drunk (Collins and Messerschmidt 1993). The same study found that alcohol was present in more than half of all reported incidences of domestic abuse.

Domestic violence also creates significant problems for its victims later in life. A study of 472 women by the Research Institute on Addictions found that 87% of female alcoholics had been physically or sexually abused as children (Drug Strategies 1999; Miller and Downs 1993). The insidiousness of domestic violence may exist because of the consistent abuse of alcohol that is associated with both abusers and victims. Given these disturbing statistics, more research and counseling programs focused on the prevention of alcoholism and subsequent domestic violence are necessary before the very foundations of identity, security, and happiness are forever destroyed. As one reformed alcoholic explains:

> I had gone too far. I had abused my family, I had beaten my wife. I had driven them off, all for a drink. *(From Venturelli's research files, 50-year-old male, October 1996.)*

■ ALCOHOL AND SEX

Alcohol use is linked to an overwhelming proportion of unwanted sexual behaviors, including acquaintance and date rape , unplanned pregnancies, and sexually transmitted diseases, including HIV infections (Abbey 1990; WHO/OMS 1998). Factors that immediately come to mind include disinhibition concerning restraints on sexuality, poor judgment, and unconsciousness or helplessness on the part of victims. The links between unwanted sex and substance abuse are subtler than many imagine, however. Although disinhibition, impulsivity, and helplessness are certainly major considerations, other elements come into play, as illustrated in the following paragraphs.

Recall the drunken comportment thesis that was introduced in the section on culture and drinking behavior. Some nonreligious ceremonial drinking settings incorporate expectations of disinhibited behaviors, such as at office parties at holiday times. Drinking is a signal or cue that it is acceptable to be amorous, even sexually aggressive, and that the intoxicated object of one's affections will not object and is disinhibited.

Intoxicated people are not as capable of attending to multiple cues. When cues are ambiguous, drunken men are more likely to miss the ambiguity and to interpret cues as meaning that sex will occur and should be initiated (men are generally more likely to interpret friendly cues as sexual signals, but intoxication makes this misunderstanding more likely). In addition, possible dangers implicit in a

private setting, on a date, with a drunken male will not be picked up as often or easily by the intoxicated and potentially victimized female (Abbey 1990).

Alcohol and the Family: Destructive Support and Organizations for Victims of Alcoholics

■ CODEPENDENCY AND ENABLING

Codependency and enabling generally occur together. Codependency (which some call *co-alcoholism*) refers to a relationship pattern, and enabling refers to a set of specific behaviors (Doweiko 1999). *Codependency* is defined as the behavior displayed by either addicted or nonaddicted family members (codependents) who identify with the alcohol addict and *cover up* the excessive drinking behavior. An example of codependency is when a family member remains silent when empty bottles of vodka (for example) are discovered under another family member's bed.

Enablers are those close to the alcohol addict who deny or make excuses for enabling the excessive drinking. Often, both codependency and enabling are done by the same person. An example is the husband who calmly conspires and phones his wife's place of employment and reports that his wife has stomach flu when the she is too drunk or hungover to even realize it is Monday morning.

Such a husband is both codependent and an enabler. He lies to cover up his wife's addiction and

---

KEY TERMS

acquaintance and date rape
unplanned and unwanted forced sexual attack from a friend or a date partner

codependency
behavior displayed by either addicted or nonaddicted family members (codependents) who identify with the alcohol addict and cover-up the excessive drinking behavior, allowing it to continue and letting it affect the codependent's life

enablers
those close to the alcohol addict who deny or make excuses for enabling the excessive drinking

enables her not to face the irresponsible drinking behavior. In this example, the husband is responsible for perpetuating the spouse's addiction. Even quiet toleration of the alcoholic's addiction enables the drinker to continue.

■ CHILDREN OF ALCOHOLICS (COAs) AND ADULT CHILDREN OF ALCOHOLICS (ACOAs)

It is estimated that out of 260 million Americans, 14 million are alcoholics. There are 28.6 million COAs in the United States, and 6.6 million are under the age of 18 (Alcoholism Kills, 2000; NCADI 1992). Approximately 25% of American children are exposed before the age of 18 to at least one person in the family who is either an alcoholic or alcohol abuser. Children of alcoholics are at high risk of developing the same attachment to alcohol. Alcoholics are more likely than nonalcoholics to have an alcoholic parent, sibling, or other relative.

Within the last decade, both COAs and ACOAs have been studied extensively. Here are some findings concerning these two groups:

1. COAs are two to four times more likely to develop alcoholism. In addition, both COAs and ACOAs are more likely to marry into families where alcoholism is prevalent.

2. Research studies show that approximately one-third of alcoholics come from families in which one parent was or is an alcoholic.

3. Both physiological and environmental factors appear to place COAs and ACOAs at greater risk of becoming alcoholics.

4. COAs and ACOAs exhibit more symptoms of depression and anxiety than do children of nonalcoholics.

5. Young children of alcoholics exhibit an excessive amount of crying, bed-wetting, and sleep problems, such as nightmares.

6. Teenagers display excessive perfectionism, hoarding, staying by themselves (loners), and excessive self-consciousness.

7. Phobias develop, and difficulty with school performance is not uncommon.

Treatment of Alcoholism

Chapter 4 provided an overview of treatment and rehabilitation of addicts. Although treatment of alcoholism and other addictions have somewhat separate historical roots and consequently gave rise to separate treatment systems, governmental authorities, and counselor certifications, they have now merged in most states in the United States. In addition to recognizing that alcohol is a drug addiction, it is also true that, epidemiologically, few "pure" alcoholics and drug addicts exist any more. Most addicts drink in addition to their other addictions (polydrug users); many alcoholics abuse other drugs, and some move through stages of heroin, methadone, and alcohol use, in that order. Alcoholism and its treatment have a few special features:

1. While addicts remain in denial, the socially acceptable nature of drinking, or even of heavy drinking, makes it easier to maintain denial as a psychological defense. It is harder to stay in denial of crack addiction, for example.

2. Although all addictions are relapsing syndromes and any addict may relapse, the social environment that permits or even encourages drinking and the ready availability of alcohol make it easy to relapse without a radical shift in lifestyle. Again, the alcoholic is buffered within a sociocultural cloud of use. Alcoholics Anonymous remains particularly vigilant in looking for signs of relapse, advising the alcoholic to "keep the memory green," HALT (don't get too hungry, angry, lonely, or thirsty/tired, as these are possible relapse triggers), and not to become isolated from others but to stay in the support system, making phone calls and attending "90 meetings in 90 days."

3. Alcohol rehabilitation differs from other addiction treatments mainly in its medical ramifications. Alcoholism is devastating to the liver, muscles, nutritional system, gastrointestinal system, and brain. Alcoholics who have become "dry" only recently may still suffer from pancreatitis, weakness, impaired cognitive capacities, and so forth. The fact that treatment is so structured, simplified, and sloganized ("Don't drink and go to meetings," "Keep coming: it

works") makes it possible for the bleary and confused recently dried-out alcoholic to follow (an AA term for this condition is *mokus*). Although the cognitive impairment tends to clear up somewhat over a period of 6 months (unless clear cortical wasting has occurred, a condition known as "wet brain"), the alcoholic is often physically ravaged to an extent that requires years to mend the damage, if it is ever possible.

4. The alcoholic is typically more emotionally fragile than other addicts in treatment.

5. The other major medical ramification is withdrawal. Withdrawal from alcohol and withdrawal from barbiturates are the two most severe withdrawal syndromes. Before modern medical management techniques, many individuals succumbed to acute alcohol withdrawal syndrome.

■ GETTING THROUGH WITHDRAWAL

An alcoholic who is well nourished and in good physical condition can go through withdrawal as an outpatient with reasonable safety. However, an acutely ill alcoholic needs medically supervised care. A general hospital ward is best for preliminary treatment.

The alcohol withdrawal syndrome is quite similar to that described in Chapter 7 for barbiturates and other sedative hypnotics. Symptoms typically appear within 12 to 72 hours after total cessation of drinking but can appear whenever the blood alcohol level drops below a certain point. The alcoholic experiences severe muscle tremors, nausea, and anxiety. In extremely acute alcohol syndromes, a condition known as delirium tremens occurs, where the individual hallucinates, is delirious, and suffers from a high fever and rapid heartbeat. Delirium tremens, commonly called DTs, is an uncommon but life-threatening condition.

Alcohol withdrawal syndrome reaches peak intensity within 24 to 48 hours. About 5% of the alcoholics in hospitals and perhaps 20% to 25% who suffer the DTs without treatment die. Phenobarbital, chlordiazepoxide (Librium), and diazepam (Valium) are commonly prescribed to prevent withdrawal symptoms. Simultaneously, the alcoholic may need

KEY TERMS

relapsing syndrome
returning to the use of alcohol after quitting

acute alcohol withdrawal syndrome
symptoms that occur when an individual who is addicted to alcohol does not maintain his/her usual blood alcohol level

delirium tremens
the DTs; the most severe, even life-threatening form of alcohol withdrawal, involving hallucinations, delirium, and fever

treatment for malnutrition and vitamin deficiencies (especially the B vitamins). Pneumonia is also a frequent complication.

Once the alcoholic patient is over the acute stages of intoxication and withdrawal, administration of CNS depressants may be continued for a few weeks, with care taken not to transfer dependence on alcohol to dependence on the depressants. Long-term treatment with sedatives (such as Librium or Valium) does not prevent a relapse of drinking or assist with behavioral adaptation. A prescription of disulfiram (Antabuse) may be offered to encourage patients to abstain from alcohol; it blocks metabolism of acetaldehyde, and drinking any alcohol will result in a pounding headache, flushing, nausea, and other unpleasant symptoms. The patient must decide about two days in advance to stop taking Antabuse before he or she can drink. Antabuse is an aid to other supportive treatments, not the sole method of therapy.

■ HELPING THE ALCOHOLIC
   FAMILY RECOVER

Alcoholism is a pervasive family disease. The family is a system, not of planets or subatomic particles, but of people who affect one another and who play certain roles, all maintaining a balance in the system. We are all familiar with the stereotype of families in which the oldest child is the "hero," the middle child is "forgotten," and the youngest is the "baby." Whatever the roles of the individuals, when the family includes an alcoholic, it means that a member of the

Even after the alcoholic is ready for rehabilitation, the other family members will also need treatment and support.

system is ill. The system adapts to dysfunction by rearranging itself around the problem. The family is like a mobile, a sculpture with interdependent parts that revolve around one another. We are not talking about adjusting to a person with a broken leg or diabetes, but someone who is in denial—manipulative, lying, and blaming other family members. By adjusting around the addiction, the family members enable the addict to progress further along the disease path. Roles become exaggerated and distorted. Persons may be blamed, scapegoated, or lost and forgotten. One major adaptation is related to the person who "takes up the slack" by assuming extra responsibilities and taking on the role of a parent or even spouse.

Early family therapy systems research described how the family often acts as a unit. It focused on the disturbed communication patterns within families and the process by which the family throws up a scapegoat, often in the form of a child who is presented as the "identified patient" (Kolevzon and Green 1985; Satir 1964). The concept of the "super-responsible one" was first described by Virginia Satir in 1964. In modern, popular writing on addiction in the family and codependent roles of children that are carried into adulthood, all of these roles are depicted as especially characteristic of addicted families (Wegscheider 1991). Because such roles are so common, many individuals may identify with them and ascribe a variety of ills to their being addict offspring. Many individuals do suffer

tremendously from the legacy of family addiction, and some have indeed been cast in one of these roles as a byproduct of addiction in the family. Acting as if only one kind of family or one kind of addicted family exists, which transcends cultural backgrounds, is not much better than saying that all languages or religions are the same. For example, "executive authority" over younger children can be the normal role of the eldest female child in African American families as part of a broader pattern of role flexibility (Brisbane 1985; Brisbane and Womble 1985). When an older child plays a parental part in the family, it may represent culturally routine behavior or it may be indicative of a response to addiction in the family.

There is some gain or perceived benefit to the person playing a role, and to the system as a whole, in the individual's actions, although this gain may seem very indirect and, in fact, injurious in the long run. Although the person may be overburdened and resentful, he or she also feels important, heroic, and capable. Over a period, this role solidifies. Perhaps the hero becomes unable to remember or imagine it any other way. If the alcoholic enters or promises to enter into recovery, it may threaten the benefits to the family member. One of many examples is a wife in a subservient role who relishes, at some level, the power, control, and authority she is under with an alcoholic husband or the recognition she receives in martyrdom—perhaps her only recognition in life. Another example is the child who is given executive authority, prematurely, in the family. Without knowing it, the family members may resist change, not only for what they may have to give up but also because change is always feared. Thus, they may undermine recovery.

Role systems found in alcoholic families can be enmeshed so that everyone is hyperresponsive to and dependent on one another: disorganized, chaotic, or exploded into nothingness. The old-fashioned middle-class alcoholic family is commonly enmeshed. If religion represents a barrier to divorce, and hence removal of the alcoholic, this situation is even more likely to arise.

A family counselor can help the family members understand the roles they are playing and start a process of change. This recognition allows family members to develop their own identities separate from the roles they have been playing. Two of the techniques used in understanding roles and rela-

HERE AND NOW

"The Top Tens" of Helping Alcoholics and Their Families

10 "Don'ts"

Don't "persecute" the addict. Confront lovingly.

Don't have the goal of "saving the family."

Don't start sentences with "you never," or "you always."

Don't live in the past or in the future.

Don't make excuses for the alcoholic.

Don't let the alcoholic be the center of your life.

Don't clean up after the alcoholic (literally or figuratively).

Don't protect the alcoholic from the consequences of his or her behavior.

Don't blame, excuse, justify, or rationalize.

Don't join in drinking.

10 "Do's"

Set limits, using "I" words (I need to stop).

Set limits empathetically (I know, you want me to _____, but I can't).

Detach, lovingly, from the addict's problems.

Teach parenting skills.

Concentrate on the here and now.

Talk about violence and abuse.

Remember that you didn't cause it, you can't cure it, and you can't control it.

Take life a day at a time.

Give "self" assignments, taking care of yourself.

Accept the right to have your feelings and for others to have their feelings.

10 Alcoholic Family Self-Statements

In an Actively Alcoholic Family

"Don't talk" (about how you feel, about what's going on).

"Don't trust."

"Don't feel."

"Alcoholism isn't the cause of our problems."

"Keep the status quo at all costs."

In a Family Having a Hard Time Becoming Used to Sobriety

"We liked you better drunk."

"You're always away at AA meetings."

"Who are these people you're always having coffee with?"

"I felt important feeding my brothers and sisters, Mom."

"I felt important going to the school on Open School Night, Dad."

10 Roles for Spouses of Alcoholics

Rescuer

Long-suffering martyr

Blamer, conscience

Fellow drinker

Placater

Overextended, superresponsible one

Composed computer

Sick hypochondriac

Scapegoat ("it's all your fault")

Avoider

10 Roles for Children of Alcoholics

Family hero*

Scapegoat*

Lost child*

Mascot*

Placater

Sick role

Parental child or pseudoparent to younger children

Pseudoparent to alcoholic parent

Pseudospouse to sober parent

Place of refuge (for younger children)

---

*Wegscheider, S. *Another Chance*. Palo Alto, CA: Science and Behavior Books, 1991.

Source: Inservice Training Program, Essex County, New Jersey, Professional Advisory Committee on Alcohol and Drug Abuse. November 1993. Prepared by Peter L. Myers, Ph.D. *Helping the Alcoholic Family Recover.*

KEY TERMS

psychodrama
a family therapy system developed by Jacques Moreno in which significant interpersonal and intrapersonal issues are enacted in a focused setting using dramatic techniques

role playing
a therapeutic technique in which group members play assigned parts to elicit emotional reactions

genogram
a family therapy technique that records information about behavior and relationships on a type of family tree to elucidate persistent patterns of dysfunctional behavior

post-traumatic stress disorder
a psychiatric syndrome in which an individual who has been exposed to a traumatic event or situation experiences persistent psychological stress that may manifest itself in a wide range of symptoms, including reexperiencing the trauma, numbing of general responsiveness, and hyperarousal

tionships are psychodrama (or role playing) and the genogram , a kind of family tree in which behavioral relationships as well as biological relationships are explored.

The family counselor can help the family members figure out their patterns of thinking, which involves certain modes of information processing. In the alcoholic family, these patterns typically involve denial, minimization, rationalization, shame, blame, and projection. Counselors also rely on certain self-statements (see "Here and Now," "The Top Tens" of Helping Alcoholics and Their Families, on page 229).

In addition, the family counselor can help the family members understand their patterns of communication. Alcoholic family communication is almost certainly a type of abnormal communication, characterized by either simple absence of communication (chaotic, destructive, manipulative, blaming) or a combination of communication methods. What the family does in the public view, visible to the outside world ("front stage"), differs from what goes on when the family is done ("back stage"). Some individuals may be cut off from communication or embroiled in endless argument and acrimony. Teaching people how to communicate their feelings and opinions in a direct, honest, and nonhurtful way begins the healing process.

The alcoholic family is injured, traumatized, often in debt, and collectively suffering from post-traumatic stress disorder . Impacted grief, loss, pain, and rage are present. Healing will not take place overnight and will not occur just because the alcoholic stops drinking. The child, in particular, may have been wounded by violence, neglect, and inconsistent parenting, and may have been witness to sex, violence, or depression.

Discussion Questions

1. Why do you think alcohol has almost always been part of our existence as human beings?

2. Cite five positive and five negative outcomes of alcohol use. Do you think negatives outweigh the positives? If so, why? If not, why not?

3. Look at the pyramid of drinkers shown in Figure 9.1. How do you think the percentages will change 10 years, 20 years, and 30 years from now? Support your projections.

4. In light of having read Chapters 8 and 9, what are three positive and three negative outcomes regarding lowering the legal drinking age to 18?

5. Do you personally believe the strong independent effects of set and setting and pseudointoxication? Can these psychological processes have more effect on the alcohol user than the alcohol itself? Wherever possible, give personal examples.

6. Why do you think the temperance movement and Prohibition failed? Cite three main reasons that also support the text material.

7. It is believed that gays and homeless people tend to abuse alcohol more than the straight (heterosexual) and non-homeless populations. What are three reasons why you think each of the members of these two subcultures have a tendency to over consume alcohol?

8. Why do you think children desire to consume alcohol with peers?

9. After reviewing the different definitions of what is an alcoholic, what definition do you believe suits you best? Write out a clear definition of what you think is a "real" alcoholic.

10. What specific criteria would you include when teaching college students to drink in moderation during freshman orientation?

11. Should alcohol be available on college campuses for those 21 years of age or over? Why or why not?

12. Recall and discuss the question of how you may have unknowingly acted as enabler for a family member or a friend. Can you cite reason why you acted like this?

Key Terms

binge drinking **202**

heavy drinkers **202**

teetotalers **204**

speakeasies **210**

bootlegging **210**

patent medicines **210**

alcohol abuse **213**

alcoholism **213**

drunken comportment **217**

disinhibitor **217**

set and setting **217**

pseudointoxicated **217**

acquaintance and date rape **225**

codependency **225**

enablers **225**

relapsing syndrome **226**

acute alcohol withdrawal syndrome **227**

delirium tremens **227**

psychodrama **230**

role playing **230**

genogram **230**

post-traumatic stress disorder **230**

Summary

1 In 1998, 113 million Americans age 12 and older reported that they consumed alcohol. Approximately 33 million engaged in binge drinking, and an alarming 10.5% were under 21.

2 Luxembourg ranks first for consumption of alcohol, followed by Germany, then France. The lowest levels of drinking are found in Turkey, Kyrgyzstan, Turkmenistan, Israel, and Armenia.

3 Globally, alcohol costs add up to more than a quarter-trillion dollars yearly when including illness, accidents, and crime connected to alcohol. In the U.S., on a yearly basis, more than 107,400 people die because of alcohol related abuse. An estimated $82 billion was lost in potential lost productivity because of alcohol use and abuse. Alcohol abuse is estimated to have contributed to 25% to 30% of violent crime. Finally, alcohol is officially linked to at least half of all highway fatalities.

4 The temperance movement was a response to the heaviest drinking period in America during Jefferson's term in office (1800–1808), the temperance movement occurred. The original goal of this movement was to promote moderate use of alcohol. Largely because it was unsuccessful, the temperance movement began advocating total abstinence. Over the course of the 19th century, complete prohibition was enacted into law. Shortly after Prohibition laws were created making alcohol use illegal, organized crime monopolized in the production and sale of alcohol as an illicit drug.

5 There are several accepted definitions of alcoholism. Alcohol addiction involves both a physical and psychological dependence on ethanol. Most definitions include chronic behavioral disorders, repeated drinking to the point of loss of control, health disorders, and difficulty functioning socially and economically.

6 The definition of who is a problem drinker varies from one culture to the next. In Poland, a person becomes a problem drinker when there is a loss of productivity. Californians find that drunk driving violations are a key indication. For Italian-Americans, an inability to provide for one's family because of heavy drinking qualifies a person as a problem drinker.

7 Culture influences our view of alcohol and alcohol consumption. Culture dictates the self-definition, attachment, and intensity of our behavior. For example, with regard to drinking, much of how we feel after ingesting alcohol is determined by social and psychological experiences. In addition to the amount consumed, *drunken comportment* refers to society's expectations regarding drinking behavior. *Set and setting* refer to the expectation and environment where alcohol is consumed. *Pseudointoxication* refers to the psychological belief regarding how one feels under the effects of alcohol, in effect, how inebriated the drinker imagines the effect of the consumed alcohol.

8 The broader general effects of how culture affects the consumption of alcohol are the following: (1) culture provides rules for drinking behavior, (2) culture provides ceremonial meaning for alcohol use, (3) culture provides models of alcoholism, and (4) culture provides attitudes regarding alcohol consumption.

9 Regarding alcohol and college students, we find that (1) college students consume an estimated 4 billion cans of beer annually; (2) nearly half of all college students are binge drinkers; (3) one consequence of alcohol abuse is motor vehicle accidents (the number one cause of death in people under the age of 25 is motor vehicle accidents); and (4) 75% of male students and 55% of female students involved in acquaintance rape had been drinking or using drugs at the time.

10 In comparison to men, women possess greater sensitivity to alcohol, are more likely to become addicted, and develop health problems earlier in life than men. Three main reasons why women are more sensitive and are more easily affected by alcohol use are (1) men have larger bodies than women; (2) women absorb alcohol sooner than men because women have more body fat (fat does not dilute alcohol) and men's bodies contain more water; and (3) women possess less of a metabolizing enzyme that functions to get rid of (process out) alcohol.

11 Codependency and enabling generally occur together. *Codependency* is defined as the behavior that a family member or close friend displays to cover-up the excessive drinking. Enabling refers to anyone who helps the excessive drinker deny or makes excuses for the excessive drinking.

12 Alcoholism treatment must take into consideration physical withdrawal *and* denial.

References

Abbey, A. "Sex and Substance Abuse: What Are the Links." *Eta Sigma Gamman* 22 (Fall 1990): 16–8.

Adams, S. H. "The Great American Fraud." *Collier's* 36, No. 5 (1905): 17–8; No. 10 (1905): 16–8; No. 16 (1906): 18–20.

Alcohol Concern 2000. *Alcohol Concern Fact Sheet 27*, London, 3 August 2000. Available www.alcoholconcern.org.uk/information/factsheets/factsheet27.htm.

Alcoholism Kills. "Alcoholism Facts." May 2000. Available http://www.alcoholismkills.com/alcoholi.htm.

Arkin, E. B. and J. E. Funkhouser, eds. *Communicating About Alcohol and Other Drugs: Strategies for Reaching Populations at Risk*, OSAP Prevention Monograph No. 5. Rockville, MD: Office of Substance Abuse Prevention, U.S. DHHS, 1992.

Austin, G. A. "Perspectives on the History of Psychoactive Substance Use." *National Institute on Drug Abuse Research Issues* 23. Washington, DC: U.S. Department of Health, Education, and Welfare, 1978.

Babor, T. F., M. Hesselbrock, S. Radouce-Thomas, L. Feguer, J.-P. Ferrant, and K. Choquette. "Concepts of Alcoholism Among American, French-Canadian, and French Alcoholics." In *Alcohol and Culture: Comparative Perspectives from Europe and America*, edited by T. F. Babor (98–109). New York: New York Academy of Sciences, 1986.

Bales R. F. "Cultural Differences in Rates of Alcoholism." *Quarterly Journal of Studies on Alcohol* 6 (1946): 489–99.

Berkowitz, A. D. and H. W. Perkins. "Recent Research on Gender Differences in Collegiate Alcohol Use." *Journal of American College Health* 36 (September 1987): 12–15.

Blane, H. "Acculturation and Drinking in an Italian American Community." *Journal of Studies on Alcohol* 38 (1977): 1324–44.

Blume, S., D. Dropkin, and L. Sokolow. "The Jewish Alcoholic: A Descriptive Study." *Alcohol, Health, and Research World* 4 (1980): 21–6.

Brisbane, F. L. "Understanding the Female Child Role of Family Hero in Black Alcoholic Families." *Bulletin of the NY State Chapter of the National Black Alcoholism Council* 4 (April 1985).

Brisbane, F. L. "A Self-Help Model for Working with Black Women of Alcoholic Parents." *Alcoholism Treatment Quarterly* 2 (Fall 1985b/Winter 1986): 47–53.

Collins, J. J. and M. A. Messerschmidt. "Epidemiology of Alcohol-Related Violence." U.S. DHHS NIAAA. *Alcohol, Health, and Research World* 17 (1993): 93–100.

De Jong, J. "Scope of the Problem: Gender and Drinking." *Catayst (Higher Education Center for Alcohol and Other Drug Prevention)* 1 (Spring 1995): 1.

Douglass, Frederick. *Life and Times of Frederick Douglass.* New York. Collier Books. (1967 edition) 1892: 147–8.

Doweiko, H. E. *Concepts of Chemical Dependency,* 4th ed. Monterey, CA: Brooks/Cole, 1999.

Drug Strategies. "Alcohol and Crime." *Millennium Hangover: Keeping Score on Alcohol.* Washington, DC (1999) 5. Available http://www.drugstrategies.org/keepingscore 1999/crime.html.

Garrison, V. and J. Podell. "Community Support Systems Assessment for Use in Clinical Interviews." *Schizophrenia Bulletin* 7 (1981): 1.

Gary, L. E. and R. B. Gary. "Treatment Needs of Black Alcoholic Women." *Alcoholism Treatment Quarterly* 2 (1985): 97–113.

Gold, M. S. *The Good News About Drugs and Alcohol.* New York: Villard Books, 1991.

Goode, E. *Drugs in American Society.* Boston: McGraw–Hill College, 1999.

Gordon, A. J. "The Cultural Context of Drinking and Indigenous Therapy for Alcohol Problems in Three Migrant Hispanic Cultures." *Journal of Studies on Alcohol* supplement 9 (1981): 217–40.

Gusfield, J. R. *Symbolic Crusade: Status Politics and the American Temperance Movement,* 2nd ed. Chicago: University of Illinois, 1986.

Harper, F. D. *The Black Family and Substance Abuse.* Detroit: Detroit Urban League, 1986.

Inciardi, J. A. *The War on Drugs II.* Mountain View, CA: Mayfield, 1992.

Jellinek, E. M. *The Disease Concept of Alcoholism.* New Haven, CT: College and University Press, 1960.

Keller, M. "Alcoholism: Nature and Extent of the Problem: Understanding Alcoholism." *Annals American Academy Political and Social Science* 315 (1958): 1–11.

Kinney, J. *Loosening the Grip,* 6th ed. Boston: McGraw– Hill, 2000.

Kolevzon, M. S. and R. G. Green. *Family Therapy Models.* New York: Springer, 1985.

Kolevzon, M. S. and R. G. Green. "Spirituality: A Tool in the Assessment and Treatment of Black Alcoholics and Their Families" *Alcoholism Treatment Quarterly* 2: (1986): 31–44. Fall/Winter 1985/1986.

Lender, M. E. *Drinking in America.* New York: Free Press, 1985.

Lender, M. E. and J. K. Martin. *Drinking in America,* rev. ed. New York: Free Press, 1987.

Levine, H. G. "The Good Creature of God and the Demon Rum," 111–61. In *Research Monograph No. 12: Alcohol and Disinhibition: Nature and Meaning of the Link,* by National Institute on Alcohol Abuse and Alcoholism. Rockville, MD: NIAAA 1983.

MacAndrew, C. and R. B. Edgerton. *Drunken Comportment: A Social Explanation.* Chicago: Aldine, 1969.

Makela, K. "Attitudes Towards Drinking and Drunkenness in Four Scandinavian Countries." In *Alcohol and Culture: Comparative Perspectives from Europe and America.* Annals of the New York Academy of Science 472, edited by T. F. Babor. New York: New York Academy of Sciences, 1986.

Marshall, M. "Four Hundred Rabbits": An Anthropological View of Ethanol as a Disinhibitor." In *Alcohol and Disinhibition: Nature and Meaning of the Link.* Washington, DC: U.S. HHS, PHS, ADAMHA, NIAAA Research Monograph No. 12, 1983.

Miller, B. A. and W. R. Downs, "The Impact of Family Violence on the Use of Alcohol by Women." *Alcohol, Health, and Research World* 17 (1993): 137–43.

National Clearinghouse for Alcohol and Drug Information (NCADI). *The Fact Is . . . Alcoholism Tends to Run in Families.* OSAP Prevention Resource Guide. Rockville, MD: NCADI, 1992.

National Institute on Alcohol Abuse and Alcoholism (NIAAA). "Frequently Asked Questions on Alcohol Abuse and Alcoholism." Available http://silk.nih.gov/silk/niaaa1/questions /q-a.htm.

National Institute on Alcohol Abuse and Alcoholism (NIAAA). *Facts About Alcohol and Alcoholism.* Washington, DC: U.S. Government Printing Office, 1980.

National Institute on Alcohol Abuse and Alcoholism (NIAAA). *Apparent Per Capita Alcohol Consumption: National, State and Regional Trends, 1977–1987.* Surveillance Report No. 13. Washington, DC: U.S. Government Printing Office, 1989.

National Institute on Alcohol Abuse and Alcoholism (NIAAA). *Seventh Special Report to the U.S. Congress on Alcohol and Health.* Washington, DC: U.S. Government Printing Office, 1990.

National Institute on Alcohol Abuse and Alcoholism (NIAAA). *Alcohol Alert: Moderate Drinking.* Rockville, MD: U.S. DHHS, Report No. 16, PH315m, April 1992.

National Institute on Alcohol Abuse and Alcoholism (NIAAA). *Alcohol Alert: Estimating the Economic Cost of Alcohol Abuse.* Rockville, MD: U.S. DHHS AAMHA, Report No. 11, PH293, January 1995.

National Institute on Drug Abuse (NIDA) and National Institute of Alcohol Abuse and Alcoholism (NIAAA). 30 May 2000. Available http://www.nida.nih.gov/Economic Costs/Chapter1.

National Institute on Drug Abuse (NIDA). *National Survey Results on Drug Use from the Monitoring the Future Study, 1975–1998.* Volume 1: Secondary School Students. U.S. DHHS. Washington, DC: U.S. Government Printing Office, 1999.

National Institute on Drug Abuse (NIDA). "Presenter's Comments." In *Alcohol and Disinhibition: Nature and Meaning of the Link.* Washington, DC: U.S. HHS, PHS, ADAMHA, NIAAA Research Monograph No. 12, 1983.

NIDA Notes. Available http://www.nida.nigov/NIDA_ NOTES.

National Institute on Drug Abuse (NIDA). *National Survey Results on Drugs from the Monitoring the Future Study, 1975–1992.* Volume 1: Secondary School Students, 137. Rockville, MD: NIDA, 1993.

National Institute on Drug Abuse (NIDA) and National Institute on Alcohol Abuse and Alcoholism (NIAAA). "The Economic Costs of Alcohol and Drug Abuse in the United States—1992, Executive Summary." Available http://www.nida.nih.gov/EconomicCosts/Chapter1.html.

Newport, F. "Alcohol and Drinking." Princeton: *The Gallup Organization.* November 13–15, 2000. Available at http://www.gallup.com/poll/indicators/indalcohol.asp.

OSAP. *Cultural Competence for Evaluators.* Washington, DC: Office for Substance Abuse Prevention, U.S. HHS, PHS, ADAMHA, DHHS Publication No. (ADM) 92-1884, 1992.

Osterberg, E. "Alcohol-Related Problems in Cross-National Perspective." In *Alcohol and Culture: Comparative Perspectives from Europe and America. Annals of the New York Academy of Sciences,* 472 (1986): 10–21.

Phoenix House. *School Daze? 2000.* Available http://www.factsontap.org/collexp/Stats.htm

Presley, C., P. Meilman, and R. Lyerla. *Recent Statistics on Alcohol and Other Drug Use on American College Campuses: 1995–1996.* Carbondale, IL: CORE Institute, Southern Illinois University at Carbondale, 1996. Available http://www.siu.edu/departments/coreinst/public_html/recent.html.

Pride USA Survey, 1994–95, 1995–96, and 1996–97, 1998. Available http://members.aol.com/_ht_a/drgedrscs/page3.html.

Reuters Limited. "Global Costs of Alcohol Abuse Top $250 Billion." *Yahoo News.* Health Headlines, 27 December 1999, 1–2. Available http://dailynews.yahoo.com/h/nm/19991227/hl/adb_3.html.

Room, R. " 'A Reverence for Strong Drink': The Lost Generation and the Elevation of Alcohol in American Culture." *Journal of Studies on Alcohol* 43 (1984): 540–45.

Rostler, S. "Alcoholism Put Blacks at Greater Risk of Infection." *Reuters Health Headlines,* 28 April 2000. Available http://dailynews.yahoo.com/h/nm/a2000048/hl/alcoholism_1.html.

Royce, James E. *Alcohol Problems and Alcoholism* (rev. ed.) New York: Free Press, 1989.

Satir, V. *Conjoint Family Therapy.* Palo Alto, CA: Science and Behavior Books, 1964.

Substance Abuse and Mental Health Services Administration (SAMHSA). *1998 Fact Sheet. National Household Survey on Drug Abuse,* August 1999. Available http://samhsa.gov/press/99/990818fs.htm.

Substance Abuse and Mental Health Services Administration (SAMHSA)/Office of Applied Studies (OAS). *National Household Survey on Drug Abuse: Main Findings 1997.* DHHS, 1999. Available http://silk.niaaa1database/dkpat2.txtsilk/niaaa/database/dkpat2.txt.

Substance Abuse and Mental Health Services Administration (SAMHSA). *Making the Link: Alcohol, Tobacco, and Other Drugs and Women's Health.* Rockville, MD: U.S. DHHS Publication No. ML011, Spring 1995.

2000 About com, Inc., "Alcoholism: Greater Risks for Women." November 4, 1998. Available at http://alcoholism.about.com/health/alcoholism/library/weekly/aa981104.htm

Wechsler, H., A. Davenport, G. Dowdall, B. Moeykens, and S. Castillo. "Health and Behavioral Consequences of Binge Drinking in College: A National Survey of Students at 140 Campuses." *Journal of the American Medical Association* 272 (December 7, 1994).

Wegscheider, S. *Another Chance.* Palo Alto, CA: Science and Behavior Books, 1991.

WHO/OMS. Trends in Substance Use and Associated Health Problems." *Trends in Substance Use. Fact Sheet No. 127.* 1998. Available at http://www.who.int/inf-fs/en/fact127.html.

Williams, G. D., F. S. Stinson, D. A. Parker, T. C. Harford, and V. Noble. "Demographic Trends, Alcohol Abuse and Alcoholism, 1985–1995." *Epidemiologic Bulletin No. 15. Alcohol, Health, and Research World* 11 (1997): 80–3.

Wilsnack, S. C., R. W. Wilsnack, and A. D. Klassen. "Epidemiological Research on Women's Drinking, 1978–1984." In *Women and Alcohol: Health-Related Issues.* Research Monograph No. 16. DHHS Pub. No. (ADM). Washington, DC: U.S. Government Printing Office, 1986.

Zinberg, N. E. *Drug, Set, and Setting: The Basis for Controlled Intoxicant Use.* New Haven, CT: Yale University Press, 1984.

Zinberg, N. E. and J. A. Robertson. *Drugs and the Public.* New York: Simon & Schuster, 1972.

Narcotics (Opioids)

Did You Know?

▶ The release of natural substances called *endorphins* can mimic the effects of narcotics such as heroin.

▶ By the end of the 19th century, almost 1 million Americans were addicted to opiates, primarily due to the use of patent medicines that contained opium products.

▶ Narcotics are the most potent analgesics available today.

▶ A narcotic antagonist has been shown to effectively reduce craving for alcohol in some alcoholics.

▶ Extreme tolerance to the narcotics can develop with continual use, causing as much as a 35-fold increase in dosage to maintain the effects.

▶ Almost one-half of all heroin addicts have been exposed to the AIDS virus.

▶ Heroin supplies today are more potent and cheaper than those available in the 1980s.

▶ Many young people believe that heroin is safe as long as it is not injected.

▶ Only 10% of heroin addicts receive adequate treatment for their drug dependence.

▶ One designer drug, made from the narcotic fentanyl, is 6000 times more potent than heroin.

▶ Some heroin addicts have to be treated with the narcotic methadone for the rest of their lives.

▶ One contaminant of illegal narcotic manufacturing, called *MPTP*, can cause irreversible, severe Parkinson's Disease in a matter of days.

▶ Dextromethorphan (a common over-the-counter cough medicine chemically related to codeine) in high doses can cause phencyclidine (PCP)-like hallucinations.

Chapter 10

Learning Objectives

On completing this chapter you will be able to:

► Describe the principal pharmacological effects of narcotics and their main therapeutic uses.

► Identify the major side effects of the narcotics.

► Identify the abuse patterns for heroin.

► Outline the stages of heroin dependence.

► Describe the association of AIDS with heroin abuse.

► List the withdrawal symptoms that result from narcotic dependence, and discuss the significance of tolerance.

► Describe the use of methadone and other long-acting narcotics in treating narcotic addiction.

► Identify the unique features of fentanyl that make it appealing to illicit drug dealers but dangerous to narcotic addicts.

► Describe how "designer" drugs have been associated with the narcotics.

► Describe the abuse potential for dextromethorphan.

Introduction

T he term *narcotic* in general means central nervous system (CNS) depressant that produces insensibility or stupor. The term has also come to designate those drugs and substances with pharmacological properties related to opium and its drug derivatives. All opioid narcotics activate opioid receptors and have abuse potential. In addition, the narcotics are effective pain relievers (analgesics) and anticough medications and are effective in the treatment of diarrhea.

In this chapter we introduce the opioid narcotics with a brief historical account. The pharmacological and therapeutic uses of these drugs are discussed, followed by a description of their side effects and problems with tolerance, withdrawal, and addiction. Narcotic abuse is presented in detail, with special emphasis on heroin. In addition, treatment approaches for narcotic addiction and dependence are included. This chapter concludes with descriptions of other commonly used opioid narcotics and related drugs.

What Are Narcotics?

The word *narcotic* has been used to label many substances, from opium to marijuana to cocaine. The translation of the Greek word *narkoticos* is "benumbing or deadening." The term *narcotic* is sometimes used to refer to a CNS depressant, producing insensibility or stupor, and at other times to refer to an addicting drug. Most people would not consider marijuana among the narcotics today, although for many years it was included in this category. Although pharmacologically cocaine is not a narcotic either, it

is still legally classified as such. Perhaps part of this confusion is due to the fact that cocaine, as a local anesthetic, can cause a numbing effect.

For purposes of the present discussion, the term *narcotic* is used to refer to those naturally occurring substances derived from the opium poppy and their synthetic substitutes. These drugs are referred to as the opioid (or opiate) narcotics because of their association with opium. They have similar pharmacological features, including abuse potential, pain-relieving effects (referred to as *analgesics*), cough suppression (antitussive), and reduction of intestinal movement often causing constipation. Some of the most commonly used opioid narcotics are listed in Table 10.1.

The History of Narcotics

The opium poppy, *Papaver somniferum*, from which opium and its naturally occurring narcotic derivatives are obtained, has been cultivated for millenia. A 6000-year-old Sumerian tablet has an ideograph for the poppy shown as "joy" plus "plant," suggesting that the addicting properties of this substance have been appreciated for many centuries. The Egyptians listed opium along with approximately 700 other medicinal compounds in the famous Ebers Papyrus (~1500 B.C.).

The Greek god of sleep, Hypnos, and the Roman god of sleep, Somnus, were portrayed as carrying containers of opium pods, and the Minoan goddess of sleep wore a crown of opium pods.

During the so-called Dark Ages that followed the collapse of the Roman Empire, Arab traders actively engaged in traveling the overland caravan routes to China and to India, where they introduced opium. Eventually, both China and India grew their own poppies.

■ OPIUM IN CHINA

The opium poppy had a dramatic impact in China, causing widespread addiction (Karch 1996). Initially, the seeds were used medically, as was opium later. However, by the late 1690s, opium was being smoked and used for diversion. The Chinese government, fearful of the weakening of national vital-

---

KEY TERMS

analgesics
drugs that relieve pain without affecting consciousness

opioid
relating to the drugs that are derived from opium

antitussive
drugs that block coughing

TABLE 10.1 Commonly Used Opioid Narcotic Drugs and Products

NARCOTIC DRUGS	COMMON NAMES	MOST COMMON USES
Heroin	Horse, smack, junk (street names)	Abuse
Morphine	(Several)	Analgesia
Methadone	Dolophine	Treat narcotic dependence
Meperidine	Demerol	Analgesia
Oxycodone	Percodan	Analgesia
Propoxyphene	Darvon	Analgesia
Codeine	(Several)	Analgesia, antitussive
Loperamide	Imodium A-D	Antidiarrheal
Diphenoxylate	Lomotil	Antidiarrheal
Opium tincture	Paregoric	Antidiarrheal

ity by the potent opiate narcotic, outlawed the sale of opium in 1729. The penalty for disobedience was death by strangulation or decapitation.

Despite these laws and threats, the habit of opium smoking became so widespread that the Chinese government went a step further and forbade its importation from India, where most of the opium poppy was grown. In contrast, the British East India Company (and later the British government in India) encouraged cultivation of opium. British companies were the principal shippers to the Chinese port of Canton, which was the only port open to Western merchants. During the next 120 years, a complex network of opium smuggling routes developed in China with the help of local merchants, who received substantial profits, and local officials, who pocketed bribes to ignore the smugglers.

Everyone involved in the opium trade, particularly the British, continued to profit until the Chinese government ordered the strict enforcement of the edict against importation. Such actions by the Chinese caused conflict with the British government and helped trigger the Opium War of 1839 to 1842. Great Britain sent in an army, and by 1842, 10,000 British soldiers had won a victory over 350 million Chinese. Because of the war, the island of Hong Kong was ceded to the British, and an indem-

nity of $6 million was imposed on China to cover the value of the destroyed opium and the cost of the war. In 1856, a second Opium War broke out. Peking was occupied by British and French troops, and China was compelled to make further concessions to Britain. The importation of opium continued to increase until 1908, when Britain and China made an agreement to limit the importation of opium from India (Austin 1978).

Famous cartoon, showing a British sailor shoving opium down the throat of a Chinese man, which dates back to the Opium War of 1839–1842.

▪ AMERICAN OPIUM USE

Meanwhile, in 1803, a young German named Frederick Serturner extracted and partially purified the active ingredients in opium. It was 10 times more potent than opium itself and was named *morphine* after Morpheus, the Greek god of dreams. This discovery increased worldwide interest in opium, and by 1832, a number of different active substances had been isolated from the raw material. In 1832, the second compound was purified and named *codeine*, after the Greek word for "poppy capsule" (Maurer and Vogel 1967).

The opium problem was aggravated further in 1853, when Alexander Wood perfected the hypodermic syringe and introduced it first in Europe and then in America. Christopher Wren and others had worked with the idea of injecting drugs directly into the body by means of hollow quills and straws, but the approach was never successful or well received. Wood perfected the syringe technique with the intent of preventing morphine addiction by injecting the drug directly into the veins rather than by oral administration (Golding 1993). Unfortunately, just the opposite happened: injection of morphine increased the potency and the chance of dependence (Maurer and Vogel 1967).

The hypodermic syringe was used extensively during the Civil War to administer morphine to treat pain, dysentery, and fatigue (Kosten and Hollister 1998). A large percentage of the men who returned from the war were addicted to morphine. Opiate addiction became known as the "soldier's disease" or "army disease."

With the development of the hypodermic needle and its use during the Civil War, heroin addiction became more likely and more severe.

By 1900, an estimated 1 million Americans were dependent on the opiates (Abel 1980). This drug problem was made worse because of (1) Chinese laborers, who brought with them to the United States opium to smoke (it was legal to smoke opium in the United States at that time); (2) the availability of purified morphine and the hypodermic syringe; and (3) the lack of controls on the large number of patent medicines that contained opium derivatives (Karch 1996). Until 1914, when the Harrison Narcotic Act was passed (regulating opium, coca leaves, and their products), the average opiate addict was a middle-aged, Southern, white woman who functioned well and was adjusted to her role as a wife and mother. She bought opium or morphine legally by mail order from Sears and Roebuck or at the local store, used it orally, and caused very few problems. A number of physicians were addicted as well. One of the best-known morphine addicts was William Holsted, a founder of Johns Hopkins Medical School.

Chinese laborers often smoked heroin at the turn of the 20th century.

Holsted was a very productive surgeon and innovator, although secretly an addict for most of his career. He became dependent on morphine as a substitute for his cocaine dependence (Brecher 1972).

Looking for better medicines, chemists found that modification of the morphine molecule resulted in a more potent compound. In 1898, diacetylmorphine was placed on the market as a cough suppressant by Bayer. It was to be a "heroic" drug, without the addictive potential of morphine—it thus received the name *heroin*.

Heroin was first used in the United States as a cough suppressant and to combat addiction to other substances (Hubbard 1998). However, its inherent abuse potential was quickly discovered. When injected, heroin is more addictive than other narcotic because of its ability to enter the brain rapidly and cause a euphoric surge (DiChiara and

North 1992). Heroin was banned from U.S. medical practice in 1924, although it is still used legally as an analgesic in other countries (Karch 1996).

The Vietnam War was an important landmark for heroin use in the United States (Hubbard 1998). It has been estimated that as many as 40% of the U.S. soldiers serving in Southeast Asia at this time used heroin to combat the frustrations and stress associated with this unpopular military action. Although only 7% of the soldiers continued to use heroin after returning home, those who were addicted to this potent narcotic became a major component of the heroin-abusing population in this country (Golding 1993).

Heroin smoking became popular in the mid-1980s in response to the AIDS epidemic. This was due to a fear of HIV infection when using infected needles to administer the drug intravenously (Hubbard 1998). The effect resulting from inhalation is as intense as that caused by injection, although very pure drug is required for smoking. Smoking continues to be a favorite form of heroin administration today.

Bayer Pharmaceutical introduced two new products in the late 1800s: aspirin and heroin.

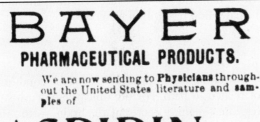

Pharmacological Effects

Even though opioid narcotics have a history of being abused, they continue to be important therapeutic agents.

■ NARCOTIC ANALGESICS

The most common clinical use of the opioid narcotics is as analgesics to relieve pain. These drugs are effective against most varieties of pain, including *visceral* (associated with internal organs of the body) and *somatic* (associated with skeletal muscles, bones, skin, and teeth) types. Used in sufficiently high doses, narcotics can even relieve the intense pain associated with some types of cancer (Way et al. 1998).

The opioid narcotics relieve pain by activating the same group of receptors that are controlled by the endogenous substances called *endorphins* (Way et al. 1998). As discussed in Chapter 5, the endorphins are peptides (small proteins) that are released in the brain, in the spinal cord, and from the adrenal glands in response to stress and painful experiences. When released, the endorphins serve as transmitters and stimulate receptors designated as opioid types. Activation of opioid receptors by either the naturally released endorphins or administration of the narcotic analgesic drugs blocks the transmission of pain through the spinal cord or brain stem and alters the perception of pain in the "pain center" of the brain. Because the narcotics work at all three levels of pain transmission, they are potent analgesics against almost all types of pain.

Interestingly, the endorphin system appears to be influenced by psychological factors as well. It is possible that pain relief caused by administration of placebos or nonmedicinal manipulation such as acupuncture is due in part to the natural release of endorphins. This relationship suggests that physiological, psychological, and pharmacological factors are intertwined in pain management through the opioid system, which makes it impossible to deal with one without considering the others.

Although the narcotics are very effective analgesics, they do cause some side effects that are particularly alarming; thus, their clinical use usually is limited to the treatment of moderate to severe pain (Reisine and Pasternak 1995). Other, safer drugs, such as the aspirin-type analgesics (see Chapter 16), are preferred for pain management when possible. Often, the amount of narcotic required for pain relief can be reduced by combining a narcotic, such as codeine, with aspirin or acetaminophen (the active ingredient in Tylenol). Such combinations reduce the chance of significant narcotic side effects while providing adequate pain relief (Reisine and Pasternak 1995).

Morphine is a particularly potent pain reliever and often is used as the analgesic standard by which other narcotics are compared (Medical Letter 1998). With continual use, tolerance develops to the analgesic effects of morphine and other narcotics, sometimes requiring a dramatic escalation of doses to maintain adequate pain control (Reisine and Pasternak 1995).

Because pain is expressed in different forms with many different diseases, narcotic treatment can vary considerably. Usually, the convenience of oral narcotic therapy is preferred but often is inadequate for severe pain. For short-term relief from intense pain, narcotics are effective when injected subcutaneously or intramuscularly. Narcotics can also be given intravenously for persistent and potent analgesia or administered by transdermal patches for sustained chronic pain (Karch 1996). Despite the fact that most pain can be relieved if enough narcotic analgesic is properly administered, physicians frequently underprescribe narcotics. Because of fear of causing narcotic addiction or creating legal problems with federal agencies such as the Drug Enforcement Administration (DEA), it is estimated that less than 50% of the cancer patients in the United States receive enough narcotics for adequate pain relief (Nowak 1992). An important rule of narcotic use is that adequate pain relief should not be denied because of concern about the abuse potential of these drugs (Reisine and Pasternak 1995). Despite the fact that addiction to narcotics is rare in patients receiving these drugs for therapy unless they have a history of drug abuse or have an underlying psychiatric disorder (Medical Letter 1998). Occasionally there are outbreaks of abuse of commonly prescribed narcotic products (see "Holding the Line," The Law and Prescription Narcotics).

■ OTHER THERAPEUTIC USES

Opioid narcotics are also used to treat conditions not related to pain. For example, these drugs suppress the coughing center of the brain, so they are effective antitussives. Codeine, a natural opioid narcotic, is commonly included in cough medicine. In addition, opioid narcotics slow the movement of materials through the intestines, a property that can be used to relieve diarrhea or can cause the side effect of constipation (Way et al. 1998). Paregoric contains an opioid narcotic substance and is commonly used to treat severe diarrhea.

When used carefully by the clinician, opioid narcotics are very effective therapeutic tools. Some precautions for avoiding unnecessary problems with these drugs include the following (Way and Way 1992):

1. Before beginning treatment, therapeutic goals should be clearly established.

2. Doses and duration of use should be limited as much as possible while permitting adequate therapeutic care.

HOLDING THE LINE

The Law and Prescription Narcotics

Recently, law enforcement agencies have faced the difficult chore of trying to control the trafficking of prescription opioid pain-relievers to narcotic addicts. Because opioid narcotics are considered some of our best analgesics, they can be a critical element in the management of the severe pain frequently associated with terminal cancer. In the past, most clinicians believed that despite the fact that the potent forms of these drugs have significant abuse potential, when controlled by prescription, they were rarely a significant abuse issue. However, the addiction problems caused by prescription narcotic analgesics have become particularly evident with the abuse and illegal trafficking of the painkiller known as OxyContin. This product includes the opiate, oxycodone, which has the approximate narcotic potency of morphine and can be obtained with relative ease. Authorities claim that the illegal pills come from doctors' offices, from dealers who fake illness to get legal prescriptions or who are writing phony orders, and from others who steal the supplies from pharmacies. OxyContin has been called "oxys," "O.C.," and "killers" on the street and is popular with narcotic abusers because of its rapid and potent effect. On the street, the drug can cost 10 times its prescription price. Because of its potent ability to suppress respiration, OxyContin appears to have been involved in numerous overdose deaths throughout the country.

---

3. If other, safer drugs (for example, nonnarcotic analgesics such as ibuprofen or aspirin) adequately treat the medical condition, narcotics should be avoided.

■ MECHANISMS OF ACTION

As mentioned, the opioid receptors are the site of action of the naturally occurring endorphin peptide transmitters and are found throughout the nervous system, intestines, and other internal organs. Because narcotic drugs such as morphine and heroin enhance the endorphin system by stimulating opioid receptors, these drugs have widespread influences throughout the body.

For example, the opioid receptors are present in high concentration within the limbic structures of the brain. Stimulation of these receptors by narcotics causes release of the transmitter, dopamine, in limbic brain regions. This effect contributes to the rewarding actions of these drugs and leads to dependence and abuse (Reisine and Pasternak 1995).

■ SIDE EFFECTS

One of the most common side effects of the opioid narcotics is constipation. Other side effects of these drugs include drowsiness, mental clouding, respiratory depression (suppressed breathing is usually the cause of death from overdose), nausea and vomiting, itching, inability to urinate, a drop in blood pressure, and constricted pupils ("Opioids" 1996). This array of seemingly unrelated side effects is due to widespread distribution of the opioid receptors throughout the body and their involvement in many physiological functions (O'Brien 1995). With continual use, tolerance develops to some of these undesirable narcotic responses (Way et al. 1998).

Drugs that selectively antagonize the opioid receptors can block the effects of natural opioid systems in the body and reverse the effects of narcotic opiate drugs (Way et al. 1998). When an opioid antagonist such as the drug naloxone is administered alone, it has little noticeable effect. The antiopioid actions of naloxone become more apparent when the antagonist is injected into someone who has taken a narcotic opioid drug. For example, naloxone will cause (1) a recurrence of pain in the patient using a narcotic for pain relief, (2) the restoration of consciousness and normal breathing in the addict who has overdosed on heroin, and (3) severe withdrawal effects in the opioid abuser who has become dependent on narcotics ("Opioids" 1996).

An interesting recent use of opioid antagonists is to treat alcohol dependence. The Food and Drug Administration (FDA) has approved the use of naltrexone (a narcotic antagonist) to relieve the craving of alcoholics for excessive alcohol consumption (*Drug Facts and Comparisons* 2000). Early research suggests that this drug may have a dramatic effect on the future therapeutic approach for alcoholism. Only time and experience will reveal whether the benefits are truly as dramatic as originally thought. These findings suggest that the natural opioid (endorphin) system likely contributes to the dependence seen in alcoholics.

Abuse, Tolerance, Dependence, and Withdrawal

All the opioid narcotic agents that activate opioid receptors have abuse potential and are classified as scheduled drugs (see Table 10.2). Their patterns of abuse are determined by the ability of these drugs to cause tolerance, dependence, and withdrawal effects.

The process of tolerance literally begins with the first dose of a narcotic, but tolerance does not become clinically evident until after 2 to 3 weeks of frequent use (either therapeutic- or abuse-related). Tolerance occurs most rapidly with high doses given in short intervals. Doses can be increased as much as 35 times so as to regain the narcotic effect. Physical dependence invariably accompanies severe tolerance (Reisine and Pasternak 1995). Psychological dependence can also develop with continual narcotic use because these drugs can cause euphoria and relieve stress. Such psychological dependence leads to compulsive use (Way and Way 1992). Because all narcotics affect the same opioid systems in the body, developing tolerance to one narcotic drug means the person has cross-tolerance to all drugs in this group.

TABLE 10.2 Schedule Classification of Some Common Narcotics

NARCOTIC	SCHEDULE*
Heroin	I
Morphine	II, III
Methadone	II
Fentanyl	II
Hydromorphone	II
Meperidine	II
Codeine	II, III, V
Pentazocine	IV
Propoxyphene	IV
Narcotics combined with nonsteroidal anti-inflammatory drugs	III

*According to the Drug Enforcement Administration classification, Controlled Substances Act.

The development of psychological and physical dependence makes breaking the narcotic habit very difficult. Abstinence from narcotic use by a long-term addict can cause severe withdrawal effects such as exaggerated pain responses, agitation, anxiety, stomach cramps and vomiting, joint and muscle aches, runny nose, and an overall flu-like feeling. Although these withdrawal symptoms are not fatal, they are extremely aversive and encourage continuation of the narcotic habit (Colapinto 1996; Reisine and Pasternak 1995). Overall, the narcotics have similar actions; there are differences, however, in their potencies, severity of side effects, likelihood of being abused, and clinical usefulness.

■ HEROIN ABUSE

Heroin is currently classified as a Schedule I drug by the DEA. It is not approved for any clinical use in the United States, it is one of the most widely abused illegal drugs in the world (Best et al. 1996), and it is reported to account for more than 110 billion dollars in global sales each year (Gannett News Service 1997). It is also thought to be associated with the highest mortality and most emergency room visits of any of the illegal drugs of abuse in the United States (Zickler 1999). Heroin was illicitly used more than any other drug of abuse in the United States (except for marijuana) until 20 years ago, when it was replaced by cocaine (DiChiara and North 1992), although a recent resurgence in its use, especially in adolescents and young adults (Epstein and Gfroerer 1998) has caused great concern with the authorities.

From 1970 through 1976, most of the heroin reaching the United States originated from the Golden Triangle region of Southeast Asia, which includes parts of Burma, Thailand, and Laos. During that period, the United States and other nations purchased much of the legal opium crop from Turkey in order to stop opium from being converted into heroin. From 1975 until 1980, the major heroin supply came from opium poppies grown in Mexico. The U.S. government furnished the Mexican government with helicopters, herbicide sprays, and financial assistance to destroy the poppy crop. Changes in political climates have shifted the source of supply back to the Golden Triangle and Latin American countries (e.g., Peru, Bolivia, and Columbia) (Gannett News Service 1997), and much of the supplies are currently brought into the United States by Chinese criminal societies (Maas 1994) and Mexican drug organizations (National Trends in Drug Abuse 2000).

Heroin Combinations

Pure heroin is a white powder. Other colors, such as brown Mexican heroin, result from unsatisfactory processing of morphine or from adulterants (DEA 2000). Heroin is usually "cut" (diluted) with lactose (milk sugar) to give it bulk and thus increase profits (DEA 2000). When heroin first enters the United States, it may be up to 95% pure, but by the time it is sold to users, its purity may be as low as 3% or (recently) as high as 60% (Epstein and Gfroerer 1998). If users are unaware of the variance in purity and do not adjust doses accordingly, the results can be extremely dangerous and occasionally fatal (Leland 1996).

Crude heroin is dark, while purified heroin is a white powder.

Heroin has a bitter taste, so sometimes it is cut with quinine, a bitter substance, to disguise the fact that the heroin content has been reduced. Quinine can be a deadly adulterant. Part of the "flash" from direct injection of heroin may be caused by this contaminant. Quinine is an irritant, and it causes vascular damage, acute and potentially lethal disturbances in heartbeat, depressed respiration, coma, and death from respiratory arrest. Opiate poisoning causes acute pulmonary edema as well as respiratory depression. To counteract the constipation caused by heroin, sometimes mannitol is added for its laxative effect.

Another potentially lethal combination is when heroin is laced with the much more potent artificial narcotic fentanyl. This adulterated heroin is known on the streets as *Tango and Cash* or *Goodfellas* and can be extremely dangerous due to its unexpected potency (Treaster and Halloway 1994). In February 1991, a batch of heroin cut with fentanyl sold for $10 a bag in a South Bronx neighborhood and killed 22 people, while sending more than 200 other users to area hospitals (Greenhouse 1992).

Frequently, heroin is deliberately combined with other drugs when self-administered by addicts (National Trends in Drug Abuse 2000). According to the National Institute on Drug Abuse (NIDA)-sponsored Drug Abuse Warning Network (DAWN) survey of emergency rooms in the United States, 41% of the reported heroin abuse cases included other drugs of abuse in combination with this narcotic. Heroin is most frequently used with alcohol, but, it is often combined with CNS stimulants, such as cocaine (National Trends in Drug Abuse 2000). Some crack cocaine smokers turn to heroin to ease the jitters caused by the CNS stimulant (Leland 1996). Such users often "chase the dragon" by smoking a heroin and crack mixture called *moon rock* or *parachute rock* ("Heroin '96" 1996). It also has been reported that heroin addicts use cocaine to withdraw or detoxify themselves from heroin by gradually decreasing amounts of heroin while increasing amounts of cocaine. This drug combination is called speedballing , and addicts claim the cocaine provides relief from the unpleasant withdrawal effects that accompany heroin abstinence in a dependent user.

Profile of Heroin Addicts

There are an estimated 600,000 active heroin addicts in the United States, a figure that has remained relatively stable despite changes in the number of infrequent and moderate users (NIDA Infofax 2000). Heroin addicts often search for a better and purer drug; however, if they do find an unusually potent batch of heroin, there is a good chance they will get more than they bargained for. Addicts are sometimes found dead with the needle still in the vein after injecting heroin (Thompson 1995). In such cases, as described earlier, the unsuspecting addict may have died in reaction to an unusually concentrated dose of this potent narcotic. Approximately 3000 to 4000 deaths occur annually in the United States from heroin overdoses (Leland 1996). Death associated with heroin injection is usually due to concurrent use of alcohol or barbiturates, and not the heroin alone.

It is typical for hard-core addicts to share a common place where they can stash supplies and equipment for their heroin encounters. These locations, called *shooting galleries*, serve as gathering places for addicts (Bourgois 1999). Shooting galleries can be set up in homes, but are usually located in less-established locations such as abandoned cars,

cardboard lean-tos, and weed-infested vacant lots. An entrance charge often is required of the patrons. Conditions in shooting galleries are notoriously filthy, and these places are frequented by intravenous heroin users with blood-borne infections that can cause AIDS or hepatitis. Because of needle sharing and other unsanitary practices, shooting galleries have become a place where serious communicative diseases are spread to a wide range of people of different ages, races, genders, and socioeconomic statuses (Bearak 1992; Bourgois 1999). Some addicts become resigned to their fate, such as one user who, after testing positive for HIV, responded, "I've seen lots of guys die already. They turned into skeletons and their teeth fell out . . . I hope I die before I get that far. Maybe I'll be lucky and just die one night up in the gallery" (Bearak 1992).

The heroin in shooting galleries is typically prepared by adding several drops of water to the white powder in an improvised container (such as a metal bottle cap), and lightly shaking the container while heating it over a small flame to dissolve the powder. The fluid is then drawn through a tiny wad of cotton to filter out the gross contaminants into an all-too-often used syringe where it is ready for injection (Bearak 1992).

Some addicts become fixated on the drug's paraphernalia, especially the needle. They can get a psychological "high" from playing with the needle

Heroin paraphernalia is usually simple and crude but effective: a spoon on which to dissolve the narcotic and a makeshift syringe with which to inject it.

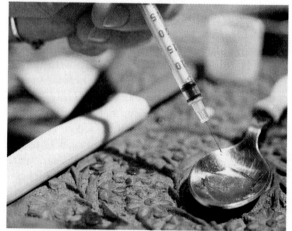

KEY TERMS

speedballing
combining heroin and cocaine

and syringe. The injection process and syringe plunger action appear to have sexual overtones for them. As one reformed user explained, "I think what I miss more than heroin sometimes is just the ritual of shooting up." A current user concurred, explaining, "You get addicted to the needle . . . Just the process of sticking something into your vein, having such a direct involvement with your body . . ." ("Mary" 1996).

Heroin and Crime

In 1971, the Select Committee on Crime in the United States released a report on methods used to combat the heroin crisis that arose in the 1950s and 1960s. This report was a turning point in setting up treatment programs for narcotic addicts. The report stated that drug arrests for heroin use had increased 700% since 1961, that there were as many as 4000 deaths per year from heroin, and that the cost of heroin-related crimes to U.S. society was estimated to exceed $3 billion per year. Other studies since that time have linked heroin addiction with crime (Gossop et al. 2000).

Although many young heroin addicts come from affluent or middle-class families (Weiss 1995), research shows most heavy users are poorly educated with minimal social integration. Because of these disadvantages, heroin addicts often have a low level of employment, exist in unstable living conditions, and socialize with other illicit drug users (Bourgois 1999; Hall et al. 1993). Clearly, such undesirable living conditions encourage criminal activity; however, three other factors also likely contribute to the association between heroin use and crime.

1. The use of heroin and its pharmacological effects encourage antisocial behavior that is crime-related. Depressants such as heroin diminish inhibition and cause people to engage in activities they normally would not. The effects of heroin and its withdrawal makes addicts self-centered, demanding, impulsive, and governed by their "need" for the drug.

2. Because heroin addiction is expensive, the user is forced to resort to crime to support the drug habit (Weiss 1995).

3. A similar personality is driven to engage in both criminal behavior and heroin use. Often, heroin addicts start heroin use about the same time they begin to become actively involved in criminal activity. In most cases, the heroin user has been taking other illicit drugs, especially marijuana, years before trying heroin (Hall et al. 1993).

These findings suggest that for many heroin addicts, the antisocial behavior causes the criminal behavior rather than the criminal behavior resulting from the heroin use. Thus, the more a drug such as heroin is perceived as being illegal, desirable, and addictive, the more likely it will be used by deviant criminal populations. One user explained how he got caught up in criminal activity to support his addiction:

> I lost everything, financially and emotionally . . . I was literally walking up and down Hollywood Boulevard with one pair of tennis shoes, looking to steal a handbag off some old lady to get another fix. (*Newsweek* 1996, p. 54.)

Patterns of Heroin Abuse

It has become apparent that problems with narcotics are no longer confined to the inner cities, but have infiltrated suburban areas and small towns and afflict both rich and poor. Although the use of heroin appeared to decline each year from 1989 to 1991 (see Table 10.3), several disturbing trends have since caused authorities to become concerned. These trends include the following:

- Heroin use continues to increase in many parts of the United States and among most age groups, especially adolescents and young adults (National Trends in Drug Abuse 2000; see Table 10.3).

- Heroin has become purer (60%–70% purity) and cheaper ($0.37 per milligram) than ever before (Leland 1996; National Trends in Drug Abuse 2000).

- With greater purity, new users are able to administer heroin in less efficient ways, such as smoking and snorting, and avoid the dangers of intravenous use (National Trends in Drug Abuse 2000).

- Many youth believe that heroin can be used safely if it is not injected (Epstein and Gfroerer 1998).

TABLE 10.3 **Prevalence of Heroin and Other Opioid Abuse Among High School Seniors**

Year	ANNUAL USE		LIFETIME USE	
	Heroin	Other Opioids	Heroin	Other Opioids
1989	0.6%	4.4%	1.3%	8.3%
1992	0.6%	3.3%	1.2%	6.1%
1995	1.1%	4.7%	1.6%	7.2%
1999	1.1%	6.7%	2.0%	10.2%

Source: L. Johnston, "University of Michigan Annual National Survey of Secondary School Students." Lansing, MI: University of Michigan News and Information Services, 17 December 2000.

- Because of its association with popular fashions and entertainment (see "Here and Now," Heroin and Junkie Musicians), heroin is viewed as glamorous and chic, especially by many young people, despite its highly publicized lethal consequences ("Heroin '96" 1996; Kennedy 1996).

- Emergency room visits due to narcotic overdoses have significantly increased since the beginning of the 1990s (NIDA 2000).

The reasons for these disturbing changes in heroin use patterns and attitude are not immediately apparent. It has been speculated that because antidrug efforts in the late 1980s and early 1990s targeted cocaine, they inadvertently encouraged drug users to replace cocaine with heroin. Another possible reason for increased heroin use is that many drug dealers previously selling cocaine switched to heroin to make greater profits ("Heroin '96" 1996), making heroin even more readily available. Whatever the reasons, it has become imperative to educate all populations about the dangers of this potent drug and reverse the present trend of escalating use and complacency about the dangers.

Stages of Dependence

Initially, the effects of heroin are often unpleasant, especially after the first injection (May 1998). It is

not uncommon to experience nausea and vomiting after administration; gradually, however, the euphoria overwhelms the aversive effects (Goldstein 1994). There are two major stages in the development of a psychological dependence on heroin or other opioid narcotics.

1. In the rewarding stage, euphoria and positive effects occur in at least 50% of users. These positive feelings and sensations increase with continued administration and encourage use.

2. Eventually, the heroin or narcotic user must take the drug to avoid withdrawal symptoms that start about 6 to 12 hours after the last dose. At this stage, it is said that "the monkey is on his back." This stage is psychological dependence. If one grain of heroin (about 65 milligrams) is taken over a two-week period on a daily basis, the user becomes physically dependent on the drug.

Methods of Administration

Many heroin users start by sniffing the powder or injecting it into a muscle (intramuscular) or under the skin ("skin popping"). Because of the increased purity and decreased cost, today's heroin users are administering their drug by smoking and snorting (Epstein and Gfroerer 1998).

Most established heroin addicts still prefer to mainline the drug (intravenous injection) (NIDA 2000). The injection device can be made from an eyedropper bulb, part of a syringe, and a hypodermic needle. Mainlining drugs causes the thin-walled veins to become scarred, and if done

KEY TERMS

mainline
to inject a drug of abuse intravenously

HERE AND NOW   Heroin and Junkie Musicians

Heroin abuse has been particularly visible among popular musical artists. For example, the 1994 and 1995 suicide deaths of Kurt Cobain and Shannon Hoon. Although neither rock star actually died from a narcotic overdose, friends and associates agree that the tragic endings to their lives were precipitated by severe addiction to heroin and their inability to escape drug dependence despite repeated attempts. Although the most visible victims, Cobain and Hoon were only two of a long list of rock and roll artists who died because of the allure of heroin and the life-shortening impact of its addiction. Other artistic notables who have succumbed to this tragic dependence include Hole's Kristen Pfaff, Skinny Puppy's Dwayne Goettel, and the Replacements' Bob Stinson.

Kurt Cobain

Source: Colapinto, J. "Rock and Roll Heroin." *Rolling Stone* (30 May 1996): 15–20.

frequently, the veins will collapse. Once a vein is collapsed, it can no longer be used to introduce the drug into the blood. Addicts become expert in locating new veins to use: in the feet, the legs, the neck, even the temples. When addicts do not want "needle tracks" (scars) to show, they inject under the tongue or in the groin (NIDA Infofax 2000; "Opioids" 1996).

A heroin addict "mainlining" his drug.

Heroin Addicts and AIDS

As noted already, because needle sharing is common among heavy heroin users, the transmission of deadly communicable diseases such as AIDS is a major problem (see Chapter 18). Over 50% of intravenous heroin users have been exposed to the AIDS virus. Fear of contracting this deadly disease has contributed to the increase of administering this drug by smoking and snorting (Hubbard 1998); however, many heroin users who start by smoking and snorting eventually progress to intravenous administration due to its more intense effects (Leland 1996).

Heroin and Pregnancy

In some places, heroin alone or in combination with methadone represents the drug of choice for approximately 80% of addicted pregnant women (Fabris et al. 1998). In the United States, as many as 10,000 infants are born each year to women who chronically used either heroin or other opioid drugs during their pregnancies (Paule 1998). There is no evidence that prenatal exposure to opioid drugs causes overt structural damage, although incidents of smaller birth weights or even reduced head size have been reported in infants born to mothers using opioid drugs; however, these findings have not been universally confirmed (Bennett 1999; Paule 1998). The most devastating consequence of heroin or opioid use during pregnancy appears to be physical dependence in the newborn, resulting in withdrawal symptoms usually immediately after birth. Treatment for such withdrawal problems generally includes low doses of a long-lasting opioid narcotic to reduce the intensity of the symptoms and then a gradual tapering of the dose in order to eventually wean the infant from the drug. For heroin, this typically takes up to 2 weeks (Paule 1998).

Withdrawal Symptoms

After the effects of the heroin wear off, the addict usually has only a few hours in which to find the next dose before severe withdrawal symptoms begin.

A single "shot" of heroin only lasts 4 to 6 hours. It is enough to help addicts "get straight" or relieve the severe withdrawal symptoms called *dope sickness* but is not enough to give a desired "high" (Bearak 1992). Withdrawal symptoms start with a runny nose, tears, and minor stomach cramps. The addict may feel as if he or she is coming down with a bad cold (Hubbard 1998; NIDA Infofax 2000). Between 12 and 48 hours after the last dose, the addict loses all of his or her appetite, vomits, has diarrhea and abdominal cramps, feels alternating chills and fever, and develops goose pimples all over (going "cold turkey"). Between 2 and 4 days later, the addict continues to experience some of the symptoms just described, as well as aching bones and muscles and powerful muscle spasms that cause violent kicking motions ("kicking the habit"). After 4 to 5 days, symptoms start to subside, and the person may get his or her appetite back (NIDA Infofax 2000). However, attempts to move on in life will be challenging because compulsion to keep using the drug remains strong.

The severity of the withdrawal varies according to the purity and strength of the drug used and to the personality of the user. The symptoms of withdrawal from heroin, morphine, and methadone are summarized in Table 10.4. Withdrawal symptoms from opioids such as morphine, codeine, meperidine, and others are similar, although the timeframe and intensity vary (O'Brien 1995).

TABLE 10.4 Symptoms of Withdrawal from Heroin, Morphine, and Methadone

Symptoms	TIME IN HOURS		
	Heroin	Morphine	Methadone
Craving for drugs; anxiety	4	6	24–48
Yawning, perspiration, runny nose, tears	8	14	34–48
Pupil dilation, goose bumps, muscle twitches, aching bones and muscles, hot and cold flashes, loss of appetite	12	16	48–72
Increased intensity of preceding symptoms, insomnia, raised blood pressure, fever, faster pulse, nausea	18–24	24–36	≥72
Increased intensity of preceding symptoms, curled-up position, vomiting, diarrhea, increased blood sugar, foot kicking ("kicking the habit")	26–36	36–48	—

■ TREATMENT OF HEROIN AND OTHER NARCOTIC DEPENDENCE

The ideal result of treatment for dependency on heroin or other narcotics is to help the addict live a normal, productive, and satisfying life without drugs. Unfortunately, less than 10% of the heroin addicts receive adequate treatment for their addiction (Maxwell 1998). Of those who are treated, relatively few heroin users become absolutely "clean" from drug use; thus, therapeutic compromise is often necessary (Millstein 1992; Payte 1998) (see Figure 10.1). In the real world, treatment of heroin dependency is considered successful if the addict does the following:

1. Stops using heroin

2. No longer associates with dealers or users of heroin

3. Avoids dangerous activities often associated with heroin use (such as needle sharing, injecting unknown drugs, and frequenting shooting galleries)

FIGURE 10.1

Treatment of Heroin Addiction

The principal aspects of treating heroin addiction include minimizing the very aversive withdrawal effect (usually with drug adjuncts); preventing relapse (usually with behavioral modification); and if necessary, providing maintenance support with other opioid-like drugs that have longer action than heroin.

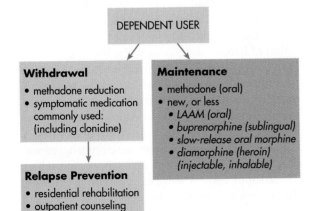

4. Improves employment status

5. Refrains from criminal activity

6. Is able to enjoy normal family and social relationships (McLellan et al. 1993).

For more than 30 years, many heroin addicts have achieved these goals by substituting a long-lasting synthetic narcotic, such as methadone, for the short-acting heroin (Zickler 1999). The maintenance ("substitute") narcotic is made available to heroin-dependent people through drug treatment centers under the direction of trained medical personnel. The dispensing of the substitute narcotic is tightly regulated by governmental agencies. The rationale for the substitution is that a long-acting drug such as methadone can conveniently be taken once a day (Medical Letter 1998) to prevent the unpleasant withdrawal symptoms that occur within 4 hours after each heroin use (see Table 10.4). Although the substitute narcotic may also have abuse potential and be scheduled by the DEA (see Table 10.2), it is given to the addict in its oral form; thus, its onset of action is too slow to cause a rush like that associated with heroin use, which means that its abuse potential is substantially less (Medical Letter 1998). In addition, the cost to society is dramatically reduced; according to one study, an untreated heroin addict costs the community $21,000 for 6 months, but the cost of methadone maintenance for a person dependent on heroin is only $1750 for the same period (Grinspoon 1995; Hubbard 1998) (see "Here and Now," The Cycle of Relapse Without Drug Maintenance, on page 252).

Currently, methadone is approved by the FDA for "opiate maintenance therapy" in the treatment of heroin (or other narcotic) dependency (Hubbard 1998). Proper use of methadone has been shown to effectively decrease illicit use of narcotics and other undesirable behavior related to drug dependence (Lucky 1998). Another drug called LAAM (1-alpha-acetyl-methadol) has been clinically tested and also approved to treat narcotic addiction (Eissenberg et al. 1999). LAAM is a very long-acting narcotic and is more convenient because it requires only three administrations per week to block heroin withdrawal symptoms (Eissenberg et al. 1999). A third narcotic, buprenorphine, which is currently used as an analgesic, also is being tested in the treatment of narcotic dependence (Buprenorphine Update 2000;

HERE AND NOW   The Cycle of Relapse Without Drug Maintenance

The lack of supportive drug maintenance with long-acting narcotics, such as methadone or LAAM, to relieve withdrawal for patients severely dependent on heroin often results in a cycle of events during treatment that eventually causes relapse of addiction and tremendous frustration. For example, L.S., a long-term heroin addict, 3 months after completing a withdrawal program manifested a dramatic elevation in mood. This sudden and unexpected improvement in behavior contrasted with the irritability and impulsivity expressed, since stopping the heroin use. L.S. ap-peared stable and pleasant. What appeared to the casual observer to be a therapeutic success was actually a bad sign suggesting L.S. was returning to his heroin habit. This positive phase was short-lived as L.S. began selling his possessions, missed work, and stayed home for extended periods due to an escalating heroin dependence. Oftentimes this relapse cycle seen in L.S. is repeated several times before the patient finally realizes that his or her life will not stabilize without maintenance drug therapy with methadone or LAAM to help manage withdrawal from heroin.

Source: Payte, J. T. "The Evolution of Methadone Treatment Programs." *Connection* (a semiannual newsletter published by the Association for Health Services Research) (June 1998): 1–2.

Lewis 1999). Its minimal potential for dependence makes this drug a desirable substitute for heroin (Best et al. 1996; Swan 1993). See Table 10.5 for a comparison of these three drugs. Other drugs used for similar maintenance therapy of heroin addicts include slow-release oral morphine and even heroin itself for addicts who do not respond to the other maintenance opioid drugs (Bammer 1999).

Some people, including some professionals involved in drug abuse therapy, view heroin or narcotic addiction as a "failure of the will" and see methadone treatment as substituting one addiction for another (Goldstein 1994). As a result, unrealistic treatment expectations are sometimes imposed on heroin addicts, leading to high failure rates. For example, many methadone treatment programs may distribute inadequate methadone doses to maintain heroin or narcotic abstinence (Strain et al. 1999); alternatively, narcotic-dependent patients may be told their methadone will be terminated within 6 months regardless of their progress in the program. Such ill-advised policies often drive clients back to their heroin habits and demonstrate that many professionals who treat heroin and narcotic dependency do not understand that methadone is not a cure for heroin addiction but is a means to achieve a healthier, more normal lifestyle (Millstein 1992; Swan 1994).

It also is essential to understand that even proper use of methadone does not guarantee resolution of heroin or narcotic addiction (see "Case in Point," Tragic Ending to Heroin Addiction). To maximize the possibility of successful treatment, the clients must also participate in regular counseling sessions to help modify the drug-seeking behavior and receive on-site care from professionals, including job training, career development, education, general medical care, and family counseling. These supplemental services dramatically improve the success rate of narcotic dependence treatment (Grinspoon 1995; McLellan et al. 1993).

TABLE 10.5 Comparison of Narcotic Substitutes Used in Opiate Maintenance Therapy

PROPERTIES	METHADONE	LAAM	BUPRENOPHINE
Administration	Oral	Oral	Oral or sublingual
Frequency of doses	Daily	Three times per week	Daily
Other uses	Analgesic	None	Analgesic
Physical dependence	Yes	Yes	Little
Causes positive subjective effects	Yes	Some	Yes
Abuse potential	Yes	Limited	Limited

Source: Swan, N. "Two NIDA-Tested Heroin Treatment Medications Move Toward FDA Approval." *NIDA Notes* (March/April 1993): 45.

CASE IN POINT

Tragic Ending to Heroin Addiction

Michael Douglas, 29, and his 25-year-old fiancée, Mora McGowan, hung themselves from the Steel Bridge before downtown Portland commuters. This startling double suicide occurred after previous attempts to take their own lives by heroin overdose or cutting their wrists failed. The account in a 13-page journal helped to explain this disturbing gesture of despair. Both Douglas and his fiancée experienced a loss of hope as the addiction to heroin became all consuming and thoughts of rehabilitation and treatment were replaced by a need to escape even at the cost of their own lives. The price of heroin addiction can be very high, not only in terms of money but also in human tragedy.

Source: Roberts, M. "Heroin's Grasp on Portland." *The Sunday Oregonian* (12 July 1998): A-1.

Other Narcotics

A large number of nonheroin narcotics are used for medical purposes. However, many are also distributed in the streets, such as morphine, methadone, codeine, hydromorphone (Dilaudid), meperidine (Demerol), and other synthetics. A few of the most commonly abused opioids are discussed briefly in the following sections. Except where noted, they are all Schedule II drugs.

■ MORPHINE

As noted earlier, morphine is the standard by which other narcotic analgesic agents are measured (Way et al. 1998). It has been used to relieve pain since it was first isolated in 1803. Morphine has about half the analgesic potency of heroin but 12 times the potency of codeine. Morphine is commonly used to relieve moderate to intense pain that cannot be controlled by less potent and less dangerous narcotics. Because of its potential for serious side effects, morphine is generally used in a hospital setting where emergency care can be rendered, if necessary. Most pain can be relieved by morphine if high enough doses are used (Reisine and Pasternak 1995; Way et al. 1998); however, morphine is most effective against continuous dull pain.

The side effects that occur when using therapeutic doses of morphine include drowsiness, changes in mood, and inability to think straight. In addition, therapeutic doses depress respiratory activity; thus, morphine decreases the rate and depth of breathing and produces irregular breathing patterns. Like the other narcotics, it can create an array of seemingly unrelated effects throughout the body, including nausea and vomiting, constipation, blurred vision, constricted pupils, and flushed skin (Way et al. 1998).

The initial response to morphine is varied. In normal people who are not suffering pain, the first exposure can be unpleasant, with nausea and vomiting being the prominent reactions. However, continual use often leads to a euphoric response and encourages dependence. When injected subcutaneously, the effects of heroin and morphine are almost identical; this situation occurs because heroin is rapidly metabolized in the body into morphine. After intravenous administration, the onset of heroin's effects is more rapid and more intense than that of morphine because heroin is more lipid-soluble and enters the brain faster. Because heroin is easier to manufacture and is more potent, it is more popular in illicit trade than morphine. Even so, morphine also has substantial abuse potential and is classified as a Schedule II substance (McEvoy 1993).

Tolerance to the effects of morphine can develop very quickly if the drug is used continuously. For example, an addict who is repeatedly administering the morphine to get a "kick" or maintain a "high" must constantly increase the dose. Such users can build up to incredible doses. One addict reported using 5 grams of morphine daily; the normal analgesic dose of morphine is 50 to 80 *milligrams* per day (Jaffe and Martin 1990). Such high doses are lethal in a person without tolerance to narcotics.

■ METHADONE

Methadone was first synthesized in Germany in 1943, when natural opiate analgesics were not available because opium could not be obtained from the Far East during World War II. Methadone was first called *Dolophine*, after Adolph Hitler; one company still uses that trade name. (On the street, methadone pills are often called *dollies*.) As previously described, methadone is often substituted for heroin in the treatment of narcotic-dependent people. It is an effective analgesic, equal to morphine if injected and more potent if taken orally (Way et al. 1998).

The physiological effects of methadone are the same as those of morphine and heroin. As a narcotic, methadone produces psychological dependence, tolerance, and then physical dependence if repeated doses are taken. It is effective for about 24 to 36 hours; therefore, the addict must take methadone daily to avoid narcotic withdrawal. It is often considered as addictive as heroin if injected; consequently, because methadone is soluble in water, it is formulated with insoluble, inert ingredients to prevent it from being injected by narcotic addicts.

Among methadone's most useful properties are cross-tolerance with other narcotic drugs and a less intense withdrawal response. If it reaches a sufficiently high level in the blood, methadone blocks heroin euphoria. In addition, withdrawal symptoms of patients physically dependent on heroin or morphine and the postaddiction craving can be suppressed by oral administration of methadone. The effective dose for methadone maintenance is 50 to 100 milligrams per day to treat severe withdrawal symptoms (Way et al. 1998; Zickler 1999).

The value of substituting methadone for heroin lies in its longer action. Because addicts no longer need heroin to prevent withdrawal, they often can be persuaded to leave their undesirable associates, drug sources, and dangerous lifestyles. The potential side effects from methadone are the same as those from morphine and heroin, including constipation and sedation; yet if properly used, methadone is a safe drug (Way et al. 1998).

When injecting methadone, some people feel the same kind of euphoria that can be obtained from heroin. Methadone addicts receiving maintenance treatment sometimes become euphoric if the dose is increased too rapidly. There are cases of people who injected crushed methadone pills and developed serious lung conditions from particles that lodged in the tissue, creating a condition somewhat like emphysema. The number of deaths from methadone overdose has been higher than those from heroin in some major cities like New York. Many of these deaths involved young children who took methadone that parents in maintenance programs had brought home or teenagers who tried to shoot up with street methadone or methadone in combination with other drugs. Methadone overdoses can be reversed by the antagonist naloxone if the person is treated in time.

■ FENTANYLS

The fentanyls belong to a family of very potent narcotic analgesics (>200 times the potency of morphine) that are often administered intravenously for general anesthesia. These synthetic opioid narcotics include drugs such as sufentanil and alfentanil (Way et al. 1998). Fentanyls are also used in transdermal systems (patches on the skin) in the treatment of chronic pain (Duragesic); occasionally, reports surface of individuals abusing a fentanyl patch by licking, swallowing, or even smoking it (Marquardt and Tharratt 1994).

It is estimated that some 100 different active forms of fentanyl could be synthesized; up to now, about 10 derivatives have appeared on the street. They are considered to be "designer" drugs (see Chapter 1); because of their great potency and ease of production, they have sometimes been used to replace heroin. Fentanyl-type drugs can appear in the same forms and colors as heroin, so there is nothing to alert users that they have been sold a heroin substitute (Henderson 1988). Due to their powerful effects, these drugs are especially dangerous, and incredibly small doses can cause fatal respiratory depression in an unsuspecting heroin user (Greenhouse 1992). (One "designer" fentanyl, 3-methyl fentanyl, is 6000 times more potent than heroin.) More than 100 deaths have been reported in the United States due to overdoses from fentanyl-related drugs. Most have occurred in California and New York (Karch 1996; Way et al. 1998). Because these drugs are sometimes very difficult to detect in the blood owing to the small quantities used, there is no reliable information regarding the extent of fentanyl abuse.

■ HYDROMORPHONE

Hydromorphone (Dilaudid) is prepared from morphine and used as an analgesic and cough suppressant. It is a stronger analgesic than morphine and is used to treat moderate to severe pain. Nausea, vomiting, constipation, and euphoria may be less marked with hydromorphone than with morphine (Karch 1996; Way et al. 1998). On the street, it is taken in tablet form or injected.

■ MEPERIDINE

Meperidine (Demerol) is a synthetic drug that frequently is used as an analgesic for treatment of moderate pain; it can be taken in tablet form or injected. Meperidine is about one-tenth as powerful as morphine, and its use can lead to dependence (Way et al. 1998). This drug is sometimes given too freely by some physicians because tolerance develops, requiring larger doses to maintain its therapeutic action. With continual use, it causes physical dependence. Meperidine addicts may use large daily doses (3–4 grams per day). Repeated use of high doses of meperidine can cause seizures (Way et al. 1998)

MPTP, a "Designer" Tragedy

Attempts to synthesize illicit designer versions of meperidine by street chemists have proved tragic for some unsuspecting drug addicts. In 1976, a young drug addict with elementary laboratory skills attempted to make a meperidine-like drug by using shortcuts in the chemical synthesis. Three days after self-administering his untested drug product, the drug user developed a severe case of tremors and motor problems identical to Parkinson's Disease, a neurological disorder generally occurring in the elderly. Even more surprising to attending neurologists was that this young drug addict improved dramatically after treatment with levodopa, a drug that is very effective in treating the symptoms of traditional Parkinson's Disease. After 18 months of treatment, the despondent addict committed suicide. An autopsy revealed he had severe brain damage that was almost identical to that occurring in classical Parkinsonian patients (Davies et al. 1979). It was concluded that a byproduct resulting from the sloppy synthesis of the meperidine-like designer narcotic was responsible for the irreversible brain damage.

This hypothesis was confirmed by a separate and independent event on the West Coast in 1981 when a cluster of relatively young heroin addicts (ages 22–42) in the San Francisco area also developed symptoms of

Parkinson's Disease. All of these patients had consumed a new "synthetic heroin," obtained on the streets, which was produced by attempting to synthesize meperidine-like drugs (Aminoff 1998; Langston et al. 1983). Common to both incidents was the presence of the compound MPTP, which was a contaminant resulting from the careless synthesis. MPTP is metabolized to a very reactive molecule in the brain that selectively destroys neurons containing the transmitter dopamine in the motor regions of the basal ganglia (see Chapter 5). Similar neuronal damage occurs in classical Parkinson's Disease over the course of 50 to 70 years, whereas ingestion of MPTP dramatically accelerates the degeneration to a matter of hours (Goldstein 1995). As tragic as the MPTP incident was, it was heralded as an important scientific breakthrough: MPTP is now used by researchers as a tool to study why Parkinson's Disease occurs and how to treat it effectively (Aminoff 1998).

■ CODEINE

Codeine is a naturally occurring constituent of opium and the most frequently prescribed of the narcotic analgesics. It is used principally as a treatment for minor to moderate pain and as a cough suppressant. Maximum pain relief from codeine occurs with 30 to 50 milligrams. Usually, when prescribed for pain, codeine is combined with either a salicylate (such as aspirin) or acetaminophen (Tylenol). Aspirin-like drugs and opioid narcotics interact in a synergistic fashion to give an analgesic equivalence greater than what can be achieved by aspirin or codeine alone. Although not especially powerful, codeine may still be abused. Codeine-containing cough syrup is currently classified as a Schedule V drug. Because the abuse potential is considered minor, the FDA has ruled that codeine cough products can be sold without a prescription; however, the pharmacist is required to keep them behind the counter and must be asked in order to obtain codeine-containing cough medications. Despite the FDA ruling, about 50% of the states have more restrictive regulations and require that codeine-containing cough products be available only by prescription (Way et al. 1998).

Although codeine dependence is possible, it is not very common; most people who abuse codeine developed narcotic dependence previously with one

of the more potent opioids. In general, large quantities of codeine are needed to satisfy a narcotic addiction; therefore, it is not commonly marketed on the street.

■ PENTAZOCINE

Pentazocine (Talwin) was first developed in the 1960s in an effort to create an effective analgesic with low abuse potential. When taken orally, its analgesic effect is slightly greater than that of codeine. Its effects on respiration and sedation are similar to those of the other opioids, but it does not prevent withdrawal symptoms in a narcotic addict. In fact, pentazocine will precipitate withdrawal symptoms if given to a person on methadone maintenance (Reisine and Pasternak 1995). Pentazocine is not commonly abused because its effects can be unpleasant, resulting in dysphoria. It is classified as a Schedule IV drug.

■ PROPOXYPHENE

Propoxyphene (Darvon, Dolene) is structurally related to methadone, but it is a much weaker analgesic, about half as potent as codeine (Way et al. 1998). Like codeine, propoxyphene is frequently given in combination with aspirin or acetaminophen. Although it was once an extremely popular analgesic, the use of propoxyphene has declined as questions about its potency have been raised. Some research suggests this narcotic is no more effective in relieving pain than aspirin (Reisine and Pasternak 1995). To a large extent, new, more effective non-narcotic analgesics have replaced propoxyphene. In very high doses, it can cause delusions, hallucinations, and convulsions. Alone, propoxyphene causes little respiratory depression; however, when combined with alcohol or other CNS depressants, this drug can depress respiration.

Narcotic-Related Drugs

Although not classified as narcotics, the following drugs are either structurally similar to narcotics (dextromethorphan) or are used to treat narcotic withdrawal (clonidine) or overdose (naloxone).

■ DEXTROMETHORPHAN

Dextromethorphan is a synthetic used in cough remedies since the 1960s and can be purchased without prescription. Although its molecular structure resembles that of codeine, this drug does not have analgesic action nor does it cause typical narcotic dependence (Way et al. 1998).

Although not considered a major drug abuse problem, sporadic recreational use of dextromethorphan-containing cough medicines has been reported in the United States and other countries. The abuse typically occurs among adolescents and young adults. The relatively few cases of addiction reveal a pattern of high-dose use for months to even years. The principal symptoms of abuse include altered perceptions, sense of floating, hallucinations, visual distortions, and even paranoia and psychotic reactions. Its effects have been described to be similar to those of phencyclidine (PCP) and the general anesthetic, ketamine (Cranston 1999). There is some suggestion that both physical and psychological dependence can occur to dextromethorphan resulting in withdrawal when use is discontinued (Cranston 1999). Dextromethorphan is sometimes mixed with drugs such as alcohol, amphetamines, and cocaine to give unusual psychoactive interactions. As of 2000, the DEA had taken no steps to restrict the use of dextromethorphan in over-the-counter (OTC) products.

Some people are becoming aware of dextromethorphan abuse potential from worldwide websites on the Internet. There are a growing number of these sites that promote dextromethorphan as a "powerful" OTC mind-altering drug. Included on these sites are personal experiences of users as well as directions on how to use the drug, what to expect, warning signs of adverse reactions, and instructions as to how to extract dextromethorphan from OTC cough medicines (Cranston 1999).

■ CLONIDINE

Clonidine (Catapres) was created in the late 1970s. It is not a narcotic analgesic and has no direct effect on the opioid receptors; instead, it stimulates receptors for noradrenaline, and its principal use is as an oral antihypertensive (Benowitz 1998). Clonidine is mentioned here because it is a nonaddictive, non-

euphoriagenic prescription medication with demonstrated efficacy in relieving some of the physical effects of opiate withdrawal (such as vomiting and diarrhea). However, clonidine does not alter narcotic craving or generalized aches associated with withdrawal (O'Brien 1995). The dosing regimen is typically a 7- to 14-day inpatient treatment for opiate withdrawal. Length of treatment can be reduced to 7 days for withdrawal from heroin and short-acting opiates; the 14-day treatment is needed for the longer-acting methadone-type opiates. Because tolerance to clonidine may develop, opiates are discontinued abruptly at the start of treatment. In this way, the peak intensity of withdrawal will occur while clonidine is still maximally effective (Kleber 1998; McEvoy 1993).

One of the most important advantages of clonidine over other treatments for opiate withdrawal detoxification is that it shortens the time for withdrawal to 14 days compared with several weeks or months using standard procedures, such as methadone treatment (Kleber 1998). The potential disadvantage of taking clonidine is that it can cause serious side effects of its own, the most serious being significantly lowered blood pressure, which can cause fainting and blacking out (Benowitz 1998). Overall, its lack of abuse potential makes clonidine particularly useful in treating narcotic dependence.

■ NALOXONE

Naloxone is a relatively pure narcotic antagonist. The drug attaches to opiate receptors in the brain and throughout the body and does not activate them, but rather prevents narcotic drugs, such as heroin and morphine, from having an effect. By itself, naloxone does not cause much change, but it potently blocks or reverses the effects of all narcotics. Because of its antagonistic properties, naloxone is a useful antidote in the treatment of narcotic overdoses; thus, administration of naloxone reverses life-threatening, narcotic-induced effects on breathing and the cardiovascular system. However, if not used carefully, this antagonist will also block the analgesic action of the narcotics and initiate severe withdrawals in narcotic-dependent people (Way et al. 1998). Its use has been proposed to prevent addicts from experiencing the effects of heroin; however, most individuals dependent on heroin are not interested in using this drug because it can also precipitate withdrawal symptoms. Recently, there has been interest in employing this drug to reduce the craving for alcohol in the treatment of chronic alcoholism. It has been approved by the FDA for this purpose (Way et al. 1998).

Narcotics

Although there are many herbal preparations that can cause drowsiness or have some analgesic properties, few of these actually contain opioid narcotic drugs. The naturally occurring opioid drugs include morphine, codeine, heroin, papaverine, and thebaine and are only found in the opium poppy, *Papaver somniferum* as discussed in this chapter. Although several varieties of opium-yielding poppies exist, they all are typically winter crops in the Southern hemisphere and do best in climates that have warm days and cool nights. All of the plants thrive in sandy soil. Most of the active drugs are found in the seepage from the seed heads located beneath the flower petals of the poppy flowers, although small amounts of these active ingredients are also found in other parts of the plant such as the stem and leaves. The poppy flowers persist until the end of October in the Southern regions. Although this species of plant can survive in the United States if the environment is rigidly controlled, the vast majority of the supplies of the naturally occurring narcotic drugs are brought into the country, either legally and sold as legitimate pharmaceuticals, or smuggled across borders and sold as illicit narcotics.

Discussion Questions

1. What effects of narcotics cause them to have abuse potential?

2. What are the principal clinical uses of the opioid narcotics?

3. What is the relationship between endorphin systems and the opioid narcotics?

4. Why has there recently been an increase in heroin abuse in the United States?

5. Why does heroin addiction contribute to criminal activity?

6. What are the principal withdrawal effects when heroin use is stopped in addicts?

7. How does "methadone maintenance" work for the treatment of narcotic dependence? Explain a possible drawback to this approach.

8. What is considered to be successful treatment for heroin addiction?

9. How does morphine compare with heroin?

10. Why is dextromethorphan potentially addicting and what should the federal government do to stop its abuse?

Key Terms

analgesics   **238**

opioid   **238**

antitussive   **238**

speedballing   **246**

mainline   **248**

Summary

1 The term *narcotic* refers to naturally occurring substances derived from the opium poppy and their synthetic substitutes. These drugs are referred to as the opioid (or opiate) narcotics because of their association with opium. For the most part, the opioid narcotics possess abuse potential, but they also have important clinical value and are used to relieve all kinds of pain (they are analgesic), suppress coughing (they are antitussive), and stop diarrhea.

2 The principal side effects of the opioid narcotics, besides their abuse potential, include drowsiness, respiratory depression, nausea and vomiting,

constipation, inability to urinate, and sometimes a drop in blood pressure. These side effects can be annoying or even life-threatening, so caution is required when using these drugs.

3 Heroin is the most likely of the opioid narcotics to be severely abused; it is easily prepared from opium and has a rapid, intense effect.

4 When narcotics such as heroin are first used by people not experiencing pain, the drugs can cause unpleasant, dysphoric sensations. However, euphoria gradually overcomes the aversive effects. The positive feelings increase with narcotic use, leading to psychological dependence. After psychological dependence, physical dependence occurs with frequent daily use, which reinforces the narcotic abuse. If the user stops taking the drug after physical dependence has occurred, severe withdrawal symptoms result.

5 Tolerance to narcotics can occur rapidly with intense use of these drugs. This tolerance can result in the use of incredibly large doses of narcotics that would be fatal to a nontolerant person.

6 Methadone and LAAM are frequently used to help narcotic addicts stop using heroin or one of the other, highly addicting drugs. Oral methadone relieves the withdrawal symptoms that would result from discontinuing narcotics. Methadone can also cause psychological and physical dependence, but it is less addicting than heroin and easier to control. Another long-acting narcotic, buprenorphine, is also being used in narcotic maintenance programs.

7 Fentanyls are very potent synthetic opioid narcotics. They can be easily synthesized and converted into drugs that are as much as 3000 to 6000 times more potent than heroin itself. Detection and regulation of these fentanyl derivatives by law enforcement agencies are very difficult. The fentanyl-type drugs are being used as heroin substitutes and have already killed many narcotic addicts because of their unexpected potency.

8 Attempts to create designer narcotics have led to the synthesis of very potent fentanyl-like drugs that are responsible for a number of overdose deaths. In addition, attempts to synthesize a meperidine (Demerol) designer drug resulted in the inadvertent creation of MPTP, a very reactive compound that causes dramatic Parkinson's Disease in its users.

9 Dextromethorphan is a codeine-related drug used as an antitussive in OTC cough medicines. In very high doses, dextromethorphan can cause PCP-like hallucinations and sensory distortions. The sporadic abuse of this drug has not been substantial enough to result in its removal or special control by federal agencies.

References

Abel, E. L. *Marijuana: The First Twelve Thousand Years.* New York: Plenum, 1980.

Aminoff, M. "Pharmacologic Management of Parkinsonism and Other Movement Disorders." In *Basic and Clinical Pharmacology*, 7th ed., edited by Bertram Katzung, 450–63. Stamford, CT: Appleton and Lange: 1998.

Austin, G. A. *Perspective on the History of Psychoactive Substance Use.* NIDA Research Issues No. 24. Washington, DC: U.S. Department of Health, Education, and Welfare, 1978.

Bammer, G. A., Dobler-Mikola, M. Fleming, J. Strang, and A. Uchtenhagen. "The Heroin Prescribing Debate: Integrating Science and Politics." *Science* 284 (1999): 1277–8.

Bearak, B. "Junkies Playing Roulette with Needles." *Salt Lake Tribune* (29 November 1992): A-4.

Bennett, A. "Perinatal Substance Abuse and the Drug-exposed Neonate." *Advanced Nurse Practitioner* 7 (1999): 32–6.

Benowitz, N. "Antihypertensive Agents." In *Basic and Clinical Pharmacology*, 7th Edition, edited by Bertram Katzung, 153–78. Stamford, CT: Appleton and Lange, 1998.

Best, S., A. Oliveto, and T. Kosten. "Opioid Addiction: Recent Advances in Detoxification and Maintenance Therapy." *CNS Drugs* 6 (October 1996): 301–14.

Bourgois, P. "Participant Observation Study of Indirect Paraphernalia Sharing/HIV Risk in a Network of Heroin Injection." NIDA website (17 November 1999). Available http://165.112.78.61/CEWG/ethno.html.

Brecher, E. M. *Licit and Illicit Drugs.* Boston: Little, Brown, 1972.

"Buprenorphin Update." NIDA website (2000). Available www.nida.nih.gov/Bupupdata.html.

Colapinto, J. "Rock and Roll Heroin." *Rolling Stone* (30 May 1996): 15–20, 58–60.

Cranston, J. "Abuse of Dextromethorphan." *Archives of Family Medicine* 8 (1999): 99.

Davies, G., A. Williams, S. Markey, M. Ebert, E. Caine, C. Reickert, and I. Kopin. "Chronic Parkinsonism Secondary to Intravenous Injection of Meperidine Analogues." *Psychiatry Research* 1 (1979): 249–54.

DiChiara, G. and A. North. "Neurobiology of Opiate Abuse." *Trends in Pharmacological Sciences* 13 (May 1992): 185–93.

Drug Facts and Comparisons. St. Louis: Wolters Kluwer, (2000): 382.

DEA. "Heroin." Chapter from *Drugs of Abuse.* (2000). Available www.health.org/pubs/qdocs/heroin/doaher.html.

Eissenberg, T., M. Stitzer, G. Bigelow, A. Buchalter, and S. Walsh. "Relative Potency of Levo-alpha-acetylmethadol and Methadone in Humans Under Acute Dosing Conditions." *Journal of Pharmacology and Experimental Therapeutics* 289 (1999): 936–45.

Epstein, J. and J. Gfroerer. "Data Point to Increase in Numbers of Young Heroin Users." *Connection* (a semiannual newsletter published by the Association for Health Services Research) (June 1998): 3.

Fabris, C., G. Prandi, C. Perathoner, and A. Soldi. "Neonatal Drug Addiction." *Panminerva Medica* (1998): 239–43.

Gannett News Service. "Addiction Fueling $400 Billion Global Illegal Drug Industry." *Salt Lake Tribune* 255 (14 November 1997): A-15.

Golding, A. "Two Hundred Years of Drug Abuse." *Journal of the Royal Society of Medicine* 86 (May 1993): 282–6.

Goldstein, A. *Addiction from Biology to Drug Policy,* 137–54. New York: Freeman, 1994.

Gossop, M., J. Marsden, D. Stewart, and A. Rolfe. "Reductions in Acquisitive Crime and Drug Use After Treatment of Addiction Problems: 1-Year Follow-up Outcomes." *Drug and Alcohol Dependence* 58 (2000): 165–72.

Greenhouse, C. "NIDA Lays Plans for Quicker Response to Drug Crises." *NIDA Notes* 7 (January/February 1992): 20.

Grinspoon, L. "Psychotherapy for Methadone Patients—Part II." *Harvard Mental Health Letter* 12 (October 1995): 7.

Hall, W., J. Bell, and J. Carless. "Crime and Drug Use Among Applicants for Methadone Maintenance." *Drug and Alcohol Dependence* 31 (1993): 123–9.

Henderson, G. "Designer Drugs: Past History and Future Prospects." *Journal of Forensic Sciences* 33 (1988): 569–75.

"Heroin '96: What Americans Need to Know." *Prevention Pipeline* 8 (November/December, 1996): 20.

Hubbard, R. "Focus on Heroin: Increase in Users and Changing Treatment System Present New Challenges for Services Researchers." *Connection* (a semiannual newsletter published by the Association for Health Services Research) (June 1998): 1–2.

Jaffe, J. and M. Martin. "Opioid Analgesics and Antagonists." *The Pharmacological Basis of Therapeutics,* 8th ed., edited by A. Gilman, T. Rall, A. Nies, and P. Taylor. 522–73. New York: Pergamon, 1990.

Lewis, D. C. "Access to Narcotic Addiction Treatment and Medical Care: Prospects for the Expansion of Methadone Maintenance Treatment." *Journal of Addiction Disease* 18 (1999): 5–21.

Karch, S. "Narcotics." *The Pathology of Drug Abuse,* 281–408. New York: CRC, 1996.

Kennedy, D. "Flirting with Disaster." *Entertainment Weekly* (9 August 1996): 18–26.

Kleber, H. "Detoxification." *National Conference on Drug Addiction Treatment: From Research to Practice.* Abstract. (21 April 1998). Available http://165.112.78.61/Meetsum/Tx/Txinfo31.html.

Kosten, T. and L. Hollister. "Drugs of Abuse." In *Basic and Clinical Pharmacology,* 7th ed., edited by Bertram Katzun, 516–31. Stamford, CT: Appleton & Lange, 1998.

Langston, J., P. Ballard, J. Tetrud, and I. Irwin. "Chronic Parkinsonism in Humans Due to a Product of Meperidine-Analogue Synthesis." *Science* 219 (1983): 979–80.

Leland, J. "The Fear of Heroin Is Shooting Up." *Newsweek* (26 August 1996): 55–6.

Lucky, B. "MTQS Study Highlights Possibilities and Challenges for Performance Measurement." *Connection* (a semiannual newsletter published by the Association for Health Services Research) (June 1998): 4.

Maas, P. "The Menace of China White." *Parade Magazine* (18 September 1994): 4.

Marquardt, K. and R. S. Tharratt. "Inhalation Abuse of Fentanyl Patch." *Clinical Toxicology* 32 (1994): 75–8.

"Mary." *Rolling Stone* 30 (1996): 42–3.

Maurer, D. and V. Vogel. *Narcotics and Narcotic Addiction,* 3rd ed. Springfield, IL: Thomas, 1967.

Maxwell, J. "Unmet Treatment Needs Among Heroin Addicts Raise Ethical Issues." *Connection* (a semiannual newsletter published by the Association for Health Services Research) (June 1998): 5.

May, H. "Heroin Easy to Get in S.L., but Hard to Leave Behind." *Salt Lake Tribune* 257 (1998): D-1.

McEvoy, G., ed. "Opiate Agonists." In *American Hospital Formulary Service Drug Information.* Bethesda, MD: American Society of Hospital Pharmacists, 1993.

McLellen, T., O. Arndt, D. Metzger, G. Woody, and C. O'Brien. "The Effects of Psychosocial Services in Substance Abuse Treatment." *Journal of the American Medical Association* 269 (21 April 1993): 1953–9.

Medical Letter. Opioid Analgesics. 40 (1998): 81–2.

Millstein, R. "Methadone Revisited" *NIDA Notes* 7 (July/August 1992): 3–4.

National Trends in Drug Abuse. "Information About Heroin from ONDCP Pulse Check." Available www.health.org/pubs/ondcptrends/heroin.html (April 6, 2000). *Newsweek* (26 August 1996): 54.

NIDA. "The Sixth Triennial Report to Congress." Available www.nida.nih.gov/STRC/Forms.html#Heroin (6 April 2000).

NIDA Infofax. "Heroin." *National Institute on Drug Abuse Infofax.* (April 2000) Available http://165.112.78.61/Infofax/heroin.html.

Nowak, R. "Cops and Doctors: Drug Busts Hamper Pain Therapy." *Journal of NIH Research* 4 (May 1992): 27–9.

O'Brien, C. "Drug Addiction and Drug Abuse." In *The Pharmacological Basis of Therapeutics*, 9th ed., edited by J. Hardman and L. Limbird, 557–77. New York: McGraw–Hill, 1995.

"Opioids." *Medical Letter* 38 (10 May 1996).

Paule, M. G. "Maternal Drug Abuse and Adverse Effects on Neurobehavior of Offspring." In *Handbook of Developmental Neurotoxicology*, edited by W. Slikker and L. Chang, 617–29. New York: Academic Press, 1998.

Payte, J. T. "The Evolution of Methadone Treatment Programs." *Connection* (a semiannual newsletter published by the Association for Health Services Research) (June 1998): 1–2.

Reisine, T. and G. Pasternak. "Opioid Analgesics and Antagonists." *The Pharmacological Basis of Therapeutics*, 9th ed., edited by J. Hardman and L. Limbird, 521–55. New York: McGraw–Hill, 1995.

Roberts, M. "Heroin's Grasp on Portland." *The Sunday Oregonian* (12 July 1998): A-1.

Strain, E., G. Bigelow, I. Liebson, and M. Stitzer. "Moderate- vs. High-dose Methadone in the Treatment of Opioid Dependence: A Randomized Trial." *Journal of the American Medical Association* 281 (1999): 1000–5.

Swan, N. "Two NIDA-Tested Heroin Treatment Medications Move Toward FDA Approval." *NIDA Notes* (March/April 1993): 45.

Swan, N. "Research Demonstrates Long-Term Benefits of Methadone Treatment." *NIDA Notes* 9 (1994): 1, 4–5.

Thompson, C. "Deadly, Super-Pure Heroin Spreading." *Salt Lake Tribune* 250 (22 June 1995): A-13.

Treaster, J. and L. Halloway. "Potent New Blend of Heroin Ends Eight Very Different Lives." *New York Times* 143 (1994): 1, 13.

Way, W. and E. Way. "Opioid Analgesics and Antagonists." In *Basic and Clinical Pharmacology*, 5th ed., edited by B. Katzung, 420–36. Norwalk, CT: Appleton & Lange, 1992.

Way, W., H. Fields, and E. L. Way. "Opioid Analgesics and Antagonists." In *Basic and Clinical Pharmacology*, 7th ed., edited by Bertram Katzung, 496–515. Stamford, CT: Appleton & Lange, 1998.

Weiss, E. "Seattle Scene Represents Nation's Rising Heroin Use." *All Things Considered*, National Public Radio (2 January 1995).

Zickler, P. "High-dose Methadone Improves Treatment Outcomes." *NIDA Notes* 14 (1999): 81–2.

Stimulants

Did You Know?

- The first therapeutic use of amphetamines was in inhalers to treat nasal congestion.
- Methylphenidate (Ritalin) is a type of amphetamine used to treat hyperactive (attention deficit hyperactivity disorder) children.
- The most common Food and Drug Administration (FDA)-approved use of amphetamines is as a diet aid to treat obesity.
- Illegal methamphetamine can be easily made from drugs found in common over-the-counter (OTC) decongestants and some herbal products.
- Methamphetamine labs use extremely toxic and explosive chemicals as part of the synthesis process.
- The original Coca-Cola was a cocaine-containing tonic developed in the late 1800s.
- Ecstasy is referred to as a "club drug" owing to its frequent use at "raves," nightclubs, and bars.

- In the early 1980s, cocaine was viewed as a relatively harmless, glamorous substance by the media and some medical experts in this country.
- Smoking "freebased" or "crack" cocaine is more dangerous and more addicting than other forms of administration.
- Many people who abuse cocaine or methamphetamine have underlying mental illness.
- Caffeine is the most frequently used stimulant in the world.
- OTC decongestant drugs usually contain mild central nervous system (CNS) stimulants that can be habit-forming.
- Herbal stimulants promoted as "natural highs" contain CNS stimulants that can cause high blood pressure, seizures, and strokes.

Chapter 11

Learning Objectives

**On completing this chapter
you will be able to:**

► Explain how amphetamines work.

► Identify the FDA-approved uses for
amphetamines.

► Recognize the major side effects of
amphetamines on brain and cardiovascular
functions.

► Identify the terms *speed, ice, run, high,* and
tweaking as they relate to amphetamine use.

► Explain what "designer" amphetamines
are and how Ecstasy compares to
methamphetamine.

► Explain what "club drugs" are.

► Identify the three cocaine eras.

► Trace the changes in attitude toward
cocaine abuse that occurred in the 1980s
and explain why they occurred.

► Compare the effects of cocaine with those
of amphetamines.

► Identify the different stages of cocaine
withdrawal.

► Discuss the different approaches to treating
cocaine dependence.

► Identify and compare the major sources
of the caffeine-like xanthine drugs.

► List the principal physiological effects
of caffeine.

► Compare caffeine dependence and
withdrawal to that associated with the
major stimulants.

► Understand the possible consequences of
using herbal stimulants such as ephedra.

► Identify the role of the FDA in regulating
herbal stimulants.

Introduction

Stimulants are substances that cause the user to feel pleasant effects such as a sense of increased energy and a state of euphoria, or "high." This effect is likely due to the ability of these drugs to release dopamine (Nash 1997). The user may also feel restless and talkative and have trouble sleeping. High doses administered over the long-term can produce personality changes or even induce violent, dangerous behavior. The following is a quote from a former methamphetamine user: "Meth produces the same high as cocaine, but for longer time at a cheaper price . . . You get very violent coming down. And you get violent trying to get the drug. Users tend to take guns—they tend to carry guns." (Prevention Pipeline 1997).

Many users self-medicate psychological conditions (for example, depression) with stimulants. Because the initial effects of stimulants are so pleasant, these drugs are frequently abused, leading to dependence.

In this chapter, you will learn about two principal classifications of stimulant drugs. Major stimulants, including amphetamines and cocaine, are addressed first, given their prominent role in current drug abuse problems in the United States. The chapter concludes with a review of minor stimulants—in particular, caffeine. The stimulant properties of over-the-counter (OTC) sympathomimetics and "herbal highs" are also discussed. (Because nicotine has unique stimulant properties, it is covered in Chapter 12, "Tobacco.")

Major Stimulants

All major stimulants increase alertness, excitation, and euphoria; thus, these drugs are referred to as uppers . The major stimulants are classified as either Schedule I ("designer" amphetamines) or Schedule II (amphetamine and cocaine) controlled substances because of their abuse potential. Although these drugs have properties in common, they also have unique features that distinguish them from one another. The similarities and differences of the major stimulants are discussed in the following sections.

■ AMPHETAMINES

Amphetamines are potent synthetic central nervous system (CNS) stimulants capable of causing dependence due to their euphorigenic properties and ability to eliminate fatigue. Despite their addicting effects, amphetamines can be legally prescribed by physicians. Consequently, amphetamine abuse occurs in people who acquire their drugs by both legitimate and illicit means (McCafferty 1999).

The History of Amphetamines

The first amphetamine was synthesized by the German pharmacologist L. Edeleano in 1887, but it was not until 1910 that this and several related compounds were tested in laboratory animals. Another 17 years passed before Gordon Alles, a researcher looking for a more potent substitute for ephedrine (used as a decongestant at the time), self-administered amphetamine and gave a firsthand account of its effects. Alles found that when inhaled or taken orally, amphetamine dramatically reduced fatigue, increased alertness, and caused a sense of confident euphoria (Grinspoon and Bakalar 1978).

Because of Alles' impressive findings, the Benzedrine (amphetamine) inhaler became available in 1932 as a nonprescription medication in drugstores across America. The Benzedrine inhaler, marketed for nasal congestion, was widely abused for its stimulant action but continued to be available OTC until 1949. Because of a loophole in a law that was passed later, not until 1971 were all potent amphetamine-like compounds in nasal inhalers withdrawn from the market (Grinspoon and Bakalar 1978; McCafferty 1999).

Owing to the lack of restrictions during this early period, amphetamines were sold to treat a variety of different ailments, including obesity, alcoholism, bed-wetting, depression, schizophrenia, morphine and codeine addiction, heart block, head injuries, seasickness, persistent hiccups, and caffeine mania. Today, most of these uses are no longer approved as legitimate therapeutics but would be considered forms of drug abuse.

World War II provided a setting in which both the legal and "black market" use of amphetamines flourished (Grinspoon and Bakalar 1978). Because of their stimulating effects, amphetamines were widely used by the Germans, Japanese, and British in World War II to counteract fatigue. By the end of World War II, large quantities of amphetamines were readily available without prescription in seven different types of nasal inhalers.

In spite of warnings about these drugs' addicting properties and serious side effects, the U.S. armed forces issued amphetamines on a regular basis during the Korean War. Veterans of this war, going back to college, used amphetamine tablets to stay awake and cram for examinations, and other students quickly adopted the practice. Amphetamine use became widespread among truck drivers making long hauls; in fact, it is believed that among the earliest distribution systems for illicit amphetamines were truck stops along major U.S. highways. High achievers under continuous pressure in the fields of entertainment, business, and industry often relied on amphetamines to counteract fatigue. Homemakers used them to control weight and to combat boredom from unfulfilled lives. At the height of the U.S. epidemic in 1967, some 31 million prescriptions were written for anorexiants (diet pills) alone.

Today, a variety of related drugs and mixtures exist, including amphetamine substances such as dextroamphetamine (Dexedrine), methamphetamine (Desoxyn), and amphetamine itself. Generally, if doses are adjusted, the psychological effects of these various drugs are similar, so they will be discussed as a group. Other drugs with some of the same pharmacological properties are phenmetrazine (Preludin), and methylphenidate (Ritalin). Common slang terms for the amphetamines include *speed, crystal, meth, bennies, dexies, uppers, pep pills, diet pills, jolly beans, copilots, hearts, footballs, white crosses, crank,* and *ice.*

How Amphetamines Work

Amphetamines are synthetic chemicals that are similar to natural neurotransmitters such as norepinephrine (noradrenaline), dopamine, and the stress hormone epinephrine (adrenaline). The amphetamines exert their pharmacological effect by increasing the release and blocking the metabolism of these catecholamine substances as well as serotonin (see Chapter 5), both in the brain and nerves associated with the sympathetic nervous system. Because amphetamines cause release of norepinephrine from

sympathetic nerves, they are classified as sympathomimetic drugs. The amphetamines generally cause an arousal or activating response (also called the *fight-or-flight response*) that is similar to the normal reaction to emergency situations or crises.

Amphetamines also cause alertness so that the individual becomes aroused, hypersensitive to stimuli, and feels "turned on." These effects occur even without external sensory input. This activation may be a very pleasant experience in itself, but a continual high level of activation may convert to anxiety, severe apprehension, or panic.

Amphetamines have potent effects on dopamine in the reward (pleasure) center of the brain (see Chapter 5). This action probably causes the "flash" or sudden feeling of intense pleasure that occurs when amphetamine is taken intravenously. Some users describe the sensation as a "whole body orgasm," and many associate intravenous methamphetamine use with sexual feelings. The actual effect of these drugs on sexual behavior is quite variable and dependent on dose (McCafferty 1999).

What Amphetamines Can Do

A curious condition commonly reported with heavy amphetamine use is behavioral stereotypy , or getting *hung up*. This term refers to a simple activity that is done repeatedly. An individual who is "hung up" will get caught in a repetitious thought or act for hours. For example, he or she may take objects apart, like radios or clocks, and carefully categorize all the parts, or sit in a tub and bathe all day, persistently sing a note, repeat a phrase of music, or repeatedly clean the same object. This phenomenon seems to be peculiar to potent stimulants such as the amphetamines and cocaine. Similar patterns of repetitive behavior also occur in psychotic condi-

KEY TERMS

uppers
CNS stimulants

anorexiants
drugs that suppress appetite for food

behavioral stereotypy
meaningless repetition of a single activity

tions, which suggests that the intense use of stimulants such as amphetamines or cocaine alters the brain in a manner like that causing psychotic mental disorders (DSM-IV-TR 2000) and can lead to violent behavior.

Chronic use of high doses of amphetamines causes dramatic decreases in the brain content of the neurotransmitters dopamine and serotonin that persist for months, even after drug use is stopped (Gygi et al. 1996). These decreases have been shown to reflect damage to the CNS neurons that release these transmitters. It is not clear why this neuronal destruction occurs, although there is evidence that the amphetamines can stimulate production of very reactive molecules, called *free radicals*, which in turn damage brain cells (Fumagalli et al. 1999).

Approved Uses

Until 1970, amphetamines were prescribed for a large number of conditions, including depression, fatigue, and long-term weight reduction. In 1970, the Food and Drug Administration (FDA), acting on the recommendation of the National Academy of Sciences, restricted the legal use of amphetamines to three medical conditions: (1) narcolepsy, (2) attention deficit hyperactivity disorder, and (3) short-term weight reduction programs (DSM-IV-TR 2000).

Narcolepsy Amphetamine treatment of narcolepsy is not widespread because this condition is a relatively rare disorder. The term narcolepsy comes from the Greek words for "numbness" and "seizure." A person who has narcolepsy falls asleep as frequently as 50 times a day if he or she stays in one position for very long. Taking low doses of amphetamines helps keep narcoleptic people alert.

Attention Deficit Hyperactivity Disorder This common behavioral problem in children and adolescents involves an abnormally high level of physical activity, an inability to focus attention, and frequent disruptive behavior. About 4 out of every 100 grade-school children and 40% of schoolchildren referred to mental health clinics because of behavioral disturbances are hyperactive. The drug commonly used to treat children with attention deficit hyperactivity disorder is the amphetamine-related methylphenidate or Ritalin (discussed later in this chapter).

Weight Reduction By far the most common use of amphetamines is for the treatment of obesity. Amphetamines and chemically similar compounds are used as anorexiants to help obese or severely overweight people control appetite. Amphetamines are thought to act by affecting the appetite center in the hypothalamus of the brain which causes the user to decrease food intake. The FDA has approved short-term use of amphetamines for weight loss programs but has warned of their potential for abuse. Many experts feel that the euphoric effect of amphetamines is the primary motivation for their continued use in weight reduction programs. It is possible that many obese people have a need for gratification that can be satisfied by the euphoric feeling this drug produces. If the drug is taken away, these individuals return to food to satisfy their need and sometimes experience "rebound," causing them to gain back more weight than they lost. Some persons who become addicted to amphetamine-like substances begin illicit use of this drug by trying to prevent weight gain or to lose weight on their own without the guidance of a physician (DSM-IV-TR 2000).

Side Effects of Therapeutic Doses

The two principal side effects of therapeutic doses of amphetamines include (1) abuse, which has already been discussed at length, and (2) cardiovascular toxicities. Many of these effects are due to the amphetamine-induced release of epinephrine from the adrenal glands and norepinephrine from the nerves associated with the sympathetic nervous system. The effects include increased heart rate, elevated blood pressure, and damage to vessels, especially small veins and arteries (Max 1991; Swan 1996). In users with a history of heart attack, coronary arrhythmia, or hypertension, amphetamine toxicity can be severe or even fatal.

Current Misuse

Because amphetamine drugs can be readily and inexpensively synthesized in makeshift laboratories for illicit sale, can be administered by several routes, and cause a more sustained effect, these drugs are more popular than cocaine in many parts of the United States (Johnston 1999; McCafferty 1999). Surveys suggest that there was a decline in the abuse of amphetamines in the late 1980s and early 1990s in parallel with a similar trend in cocaine abuse (Johnston 1996). However, in 1993, the declines were replaced by a rise in the number of persons abusing amphetamines. By 1999, approximately 4.5% of high school seniors used amphetamines at least each month (Johnston 1999). The surge in the abuse of high doses of methamphetamine and its frightening social impact caused the U.S. Attorney General, Janet Reno, to propose a "national methamphetamine strategy" in 1996; it included plans to deal with methamphetamine-related criminal activity, violence, and law enforcement problems (Reno 1996).

Because of the potential for serious side effects, U.S. medical associations have asked all physicians to be more careful about prescribing amphetamines. In fact, presently, use is recommended only for narcolepsy and some cases of hyperactivity in children (Hoffman and Lefkowitz 1995). In spite of FDA approval, most medical associations do not recommend the use of amphetamines for weight loss. Probably less than 1% of all prescriptions now written are for amphetamines, compared with 8% in 1970.

Amphetamine abusers commonly administer a dose of 10 to 30 milligrams. Besides the positive effects of this dose—the "high"—it can cause hyperactive, nervous, or jittery feelings that encourage the use of a depressant such as a benzodiazepine, barbiturate, or alcohol to relieve the discomfort of being "wired" (Hoffman and Lefkowitz 1995).

A potent and commonly abused form of amphetamine is speed , an illegal methamphetamine available as a white, odorless, bitter tasting crystalline powder for injection. Methamphetamine is a highly addictive stimulant that is cheaper and much longer lasting than cocaine (Swan 1996). The profit for the speed manufacturer is substantial enough to make illicit production financially attractive. Because the cost ranges from $60 to $200 per gram it is sometimes known as the "poor man's cocaine" (Prevention Pipeline 1997). Methamphetamine is relatively easy and inexpensive to make. The illicit manufacturers are usually individuals without expertise in chemistry. Such people, referred to as "cookers," produce methamphetamine batches by using cookbook-style recipes (often obtained in jail or over the Internet). The most popular recipe uses common OTC ingredients—ephedrine, pseudoephedrine, and phenylpropanolamine—as precursor chemicals for the

methamphetamine. To discourage the illicit manufacture of this potent stimulant, the Comprehensive Methamphetamine Control Act was passed in October 1996. This law increases penalties for trafficking in methamphetamine and in the precursor chemicals used to create this drug and gives the government authority to regulate and seize these substances (Hatch 1999).

Due to the ease of production and the ready availability of chemicals used to prepare methamphetamine, this drug has become particularly problematic in the United States. Traditional methamphetamine users have been white, male, blue-collar workers over 26 years of age, although currently there also is a disturbingly high rate of use in adolescents (3%–5% annual use; Johnston 1999). There is higher abuse of this drug in the western United States, illustrated by the fact that 33% of all arrestees during 1998–1999 in San Diego, California, tested positive for methamphetamine. In contrast, methamphetamine abuse is much less common on the East coast; thus, none of the arrestees in New York during this same time period had evidence of this stimulant in their blood or urine (McCafferty 1999). In general, production and trafficking is rampant throughout the West and Midwest areas, with the highest levels occurring in California, Arizona, and Utah. However, the methamphetamine problem is moving across the country with Iowa and Missouri particularly affected and there are increasing reports of its use in the South and some Northeast areas (McCafferty 1999).

Today, so-called meth or speed labs are frequently raided by law enforcement agencies across the country as local drug entrepreneurs try to grab a share of the profits. In 1998, the law enforcement agencies shut down almost 6000 illegal metham-

---

KEY TERMS

narcolepsy
a condition causing spontaneous and uncontrolled sleeping episodes

speed
an injectable methamphetamine used by drug addicts

precursor chemicals
chemicals used to produce a drug

phetamine labs, most of which were in the western United States (USIS Washington File 1999). The laboratory operators are usually well armed, and the facilities are frequently booby-trapped with explosives. Not surprisingly, these operations pose a serious threat to their neighbors (Reno 1996) and to residents, especially children, in the structure that contains the lab (Vigh 2000). Law enforcement personnel and firefighters are also at risk when dealing with methamphetamine labs owing to ignitable, corrosive, reactive, and toxic chemicals at the site that might explode, start a fire, emit toxic fumes, or cause serious injury. The toxic chemicals can create fumes that contaminate neighboring buildings, water supply, or soil. These labs are especially dangerous when set up in poorly ventilated rooms (Kennedy 1999) (see "Here and Now," Chemical Toxins Associated with Meth Labs).

Patterns of High-Dose Use Amphetamines can be taken orally, intravenously, or by smoking. The intensity and duration of effects vary according to the mode of administration. The "speed freak" uses chronic, high doses of amphetamines intravenously and is often infected with HIV (see Chapter 17) (NIDA Research Report 2000). Another approach to administering amphetamines is smoking ice, which can cause effects as potent, but perhaps more prolonged and erratic, than intravenous doses. The initial effect (after 5–30 minutes) of these potent stimulants is called the rush and includes racing heartbeat and elevated blood pressure, metabolism, and pulse. During this phase the user has powerful impressions of pleasure and enthusiasm. The next stage is the high (4–16 hours after drug use) when the person feels aggressively smarter, energetic, talkative, and powerful and may initiate and complete highly ambitious tasks. The amphetamine addict tries to maintain the high for as long as possible with continual drug use leading to extended mental and physical hyperactivity; this is referred to as a run or binge and can persist from 3 to 15 days. Persistent use of these drugs, such as methamphetamine, to maintain the high for long periods of time

HERE AND NOW   Chemical Toxins Associated with Meth Labs

Methamphetamine labs can be set up almost anywhere and pose a serious threat to occupants as well as to law officers and emergency personnel. The following are some of the chemicals often present and their toxic potentials.

Chemicals	Toxic Reactions
sodium hydroxide	irritant to skin and eyes
ammonia	induce vomiting and nausea
ether, acetone, and alcohol	flammable
chloroform	carcinogen and volatile
mercuric chloride	poisonous (used as insecticide)
cyanide gas	extremely poisonous if breathed
acids	potent irritants
iodine	irritant; causes nausea, headaches, and dizziness
phosphene gas	poison, flammable (used as nerve gas)

Source: Kennedy, K. "Meth Mania: Even Cops Duck for Cover." *Salt Lake Tribune* (28 June 1999): B-1.

is called tweaking . The tweaker often has neither slept nor eaten much for 3 to 15 days and can be extremely irritable and paranoid and have an elevated body temperature, a condition known as hyperpyrexia . This is a potentially dangerous stage for medical personnel or law enforcement officers because if the tweaker becomes agitated, he or she can respond violently to the efforts of the others to help. In order to relieve some of the side effects of the extensive use of methamphetamine, tweakers often use a depressant such as alcohol, barbiturates, benzodiazepines, or opioid narcotics. The consequences of such a drug combination is to intensify negative feelings and worsen the dangers of the drug. Tweakers are frequently involved in domestic violence and motor vehicle accidents (Prevline 1999; Taylor 1999). Withdrawal follows for 30 to 90 days, including feelings of depression and lethargy. During this phase, craving can be intense and the abuser may even become suicidal. Because a dose of methamphetamine often relieves these symptoms, a high percentage of addicts in treatment return to abusing this stimulant (Prevline 1999).

After the first day or so of a run, unpleasant symptoms become prominent as the dosage is increased. Symptoms commonly reported at this stage are teeth grinding, disorganized patterns of thought and behavior, stereotypy, irritability, self-consciousness, suspiciousness, and fear. Hallucinations and delusions can occur that are similar to a paranoid psychosis and indistinguishable from schizophrenia (DSM-IV-TR 2000). The person is likely to show aggressive and antisocial behavior for no apparent reason. Severe chest pains, abdominal discomfort that mimics appendicitis, and fainting from overdosage are sometimes reported. "Cocaine bugs" represent one bizarre effect of high doses of potent stimulants such as amphetamines: the user experiences strange feelings, like insects crawling under the skin. The range of physical and mental symptoms from low to high doses is summarized in Table 11.1.

Toward the end of the run, the adverse symptoms dominate. When the drug is discontinued because the supply is exhausted or the symptoms become too unpleasant, an extreme crash can occur, followed by prolonged sleep, sometimes lasting several days. On awakening, the person is lethargic, hungry, and often severely depressed. The amphetamine user may overcome these unpleasant

KEY TERMS

ice
a smokable form of methamphetamine

rush
initial pleasure after amphetamine use that includes racing heartbeat and elevated blood pressure

high
4 to 16 hours after drug use; includes feelings of energy and power

run
intense use of a stimulant, consisting of multiple administrations over a period of days

binge
similar to a run, but usually of shorter duration

tweaking
repeated administration of methamphetamine to maintain the high

hyperpyrexia
elevated body temperature

effects by smoking ice or injecting speed, thereby initiating a new cycle (DSM-IV-TR 2000).

Continued use of massive doses of amphetamine often leads to considerable weight loss, sores in the skin, nonhealing ulcers, liver disease, hypertensive disorders, cerebral hemorrhage (stroke), heart attack, kidney damage, and seizures (Hall and Hando 1993). For some of these effects, it is impossible to tell whether they are caused by the drug, poor eating habits, or other factors associated with the lifestyle of people who inject methamphetamine.

Speed freaks are generally unpopular with the rest of the drug-taking community, especially "acid-heads" (addicts who use lysergic acid diethylamide [LSD]), because of the aggressive, unpredictable behavior associated with use of potent stimulants. In general, drug abusers who take high doses of these agents, such as amphetamines or cocaine, are more likely to be involved in violent crimes than those who abuse other drugs (McCafferty 1999) (see "Here and Now," Aftermath of a Stimulant-Driven Shooting, on page 271). Consequently, these individuals may live together in "flash houses" that are solely occupied by chronic amphetamine or stimulant addicts. Heavy users are generally unable

TABLE 11.1 Summary of the Effects of Amphetamines on the Body and Mind

	BODY	MIND
Low dose	Increased heartbeat	Decreased fatigue
	Increased blood pressure	Increased confidence
	Decreased appetite	Increased feeling of alertness
	Increased breathing rate	Restlessness, talkativeness
	Inability to sleep	Increased irritability
	Sweating	Fearfulness, apprehension
	Dry mouth	Distrust of people
	Muscle twitching	Behavioral stereotypy
	Convulsions	Hallucinations
	Fever	Psychosis
	Chest pain	
	Irregular heartbeat	
High dose	Death due to overdose	

to hold steady jobs because of their drug habits and often have a parasitic relationship with the rest of the illicit drug-using community.

Although claims have been made that amphetamines do not cause physical dependence, it is almost certain that the depression (sometimes suicidal), lethargy, muscle pains, abnormal sleep patterns, and, in severe cases, suicide attempts occur after high chronic doses as part of withdrawal (Cantwell and McBride 1998; NIDA Diagnosis 2000). During withdrawal from amphetamine use, the dependent user often turns to other drugs for relief (Cantwell and McBride 1998). Rebound from the amphetamines is opposite to that experienced with withdrawal from CNS depressants (see Chapter 7).

There is evidence that repeated high-dose use of amphetamines, such as methamphetamine, causes long-term and perhaps permanent damage to both dopamine and serotonin systems of the brain (Kita et al. 1999). This brain damage may result in persistent episodes of psychosis (Yui et al. 1999), as well as long-lasting memory and motor

impairment (Mathias 1998; McKetin and Mattick 1998). Abuse of amphetamine often seriously damages personal relationships with friends, associates, and even family members. The following was described by a sister of a methamphetamine addict:

Following a family intervention, my sister was diagnosed with methamphetamine psychosis. She was of the belief that she was contaminated by fiberglass fibers. Over the last six years, she lost custody of her children three times and became distanced from the family. She now writes hundreds of vindictive letters to government officials . . . The letters are almost impossible to decipher. (*Personal communication to Hanson, April 2000.*)

Treatment

Presently, the most effective treatments for amphetamine addiction are behavioral interventions to help modify thinking patterns, change expectations, and increase coping with life's stressors. Ampheta-

HERE AND NOW   Aftermath of a Stimulant-Driven Shooting

Remains of uneaten meals were still on the tables of the middle-class restaurant located in an upscale neighborhood outside of Salt Lake City as mourners and well-wishers drove by a day after a shooting spree. Quinn Martinez had been arrested by police for the rampage that left two people dead and another three seriously injured in what appeared to be senseless acts of violence. It began in a nearby hotel with an argument between Martinez and his girlfriend over car keys and ended after killing the manager of a restaurant because he wouldn't let Martinez use the business phone and a patron in the parking lot because he wouldn't give Martinez the keys to his car. Police described Martinez's actions as erratic and senseless and suggestive of someone under the influence of drugs. Because of a history of heavy methamphetamine abuse, it was suspected that this stimulant contributed to Martinez's irrational violent behavior.

Source: Burton, G., and M. Vigh. "Hotel Called Ideal Habitat for Crime." *Salt Lake Tribune* 26 (29 April 2000): B-1.

mine support groups also appear to be successful as adjuncts to behavioral therapies. There currently are no well-established pharmacological treatments for amphetamine dependency. Approaches used for cocaine have been tried with little success. Antidepressant medication may help relieve the depression that occurs during early stages of withdrawal (NIDA Research Report 2000).

Amphetamine Combinations

As just mentioned, amphetamines are frequently used in conjunction with a variety of other drugs such as barbiturates, benzodiazepines, alcohol, and heroin (Hall and Hando 1993). Amphetamines intensify, prolong, or otherwise alter the effects of LSD, and the two drugs are sometimes combined. The majority of speed users have also had experience with a variety of psychedelics or other drugs. In addition, people dependent on opiate narcotics frequently use amphetamines or cocaine. These combinations are called   speedballs .

"Designer" Amphetamines

Underground chemists can synthesize drugs that mimic the psychoactive effects of amphetamines.

Although the production of such drugs diminished in the early 1990s, a recent surge in use by American teens has resulted in an approximate 6% annual use rate in high school seniors (Johnston 1999). These substances have become known as "designer drugs" (Christophersen 2000).

Designer amphetamines sometimes differ from the parent compound by only a single element. These "synthetic spinoffs" pose a significant abuse problem because often several different designer amphetamines can be made from the parent compound and still retain the abuse potential of the original substance.

For many years the production and distribution of designer amphetamines were not illegal, even though they were synthesized from controlled substances. In the mid-1980s, however, the DEA actively pursued policies to curb their production

---

KEY TERMS

speedballs
combinations of amphetamine or cocaine with an opioid narcotic, often heroin

and sale. Consequently, many designer amphetamines were outlawed under the Substance Analogue Enforcement Act (1986), which makes illegal any substance that is similar in structure or psychological effect to any substance already scheduled, if it is manufactured, possessed, or sold with the intention that it be consumed by human beings (Beck 1990).

The principal types of designer amphetamines are listed:

- Derivatives from amphetamine and methamphetamine that retain the CNS stimulatory effects, such as methcathinone ("cat").

- Derivatives from amphetamine and methamphetamine that have prominent hallucinogenic effects in addition to their CNS stimulatory action, such as MDMA (Ecstasy).

Because the basic amphetamine molecule can be easily synthesized and readily modified, new amphetamine-like drugs continue to appear on the streets. Although these designer amphetamines are thought of as new drugs when they first appear, in fact, most were originally synthesized from the 1940s to the 1960s by pharmaceutical companies trying to find new decongestant and anorexiant drugs to compete with the other amphetamines. Some of these compounds were found to be too toxic to be marketed but have been rediscovered by "street chemists"

and are sold to unsuspecting victims trying to experience a new sensation. See Table 11.2 for a list of some of these designer amphetamines.

Some designer drugs of abuse that are chemically related to amphetamine include DOM (STP), methcathinone (Called "cat" or "bathtub speed"), MDA, and MDMA (or methylenedioxymethamphetamine, called *Ecstasy, X, E, XTC,* or *Adam*). All of these drugs are currently classified as Schedule I agents.

MDMA (Ecstasy) Among the designer amphetamines, MDMA continues to be the most popular. It gained widespread popularity in the United States throughout the 1980s, and its use peaked in 1987 despite its classification as a Schedule I drug in 1985 by the DEA. At the height of its use, 39% of the undergraduates at Stanford University reported having used MDMA at least once (Randall 1992a). In the late 1980s and early 1990s, use of MDMA declined in this country, but about this time it was "reformulated": this reformulation was not in a pharmacological sense but in a cultural context.

The "rave" scene in England provided a new showcase for MDMA or Ecstasy (Randall 1992a). Partygoers attired in "Cat in the Hat" hats and psychedelic jumpsuits paid $20 to dance all night to heavy electronically generated sound mixed with computer-generated video and laser light shows. An Ecstasy tablet could be purchased for the sensory enhancement caused by the drug (Randall 1992b).

TABLE 11.2 "Designer" Amphetamines

AMPHETAMINE DERIVATIVE	PROPERTIES
Methcathinone ("cat")	Properties like those of methamphetamine and cocaine
Methylenedioxy**methamphetamine** (MDMA, "Ecstasy")	Stimulant and hallucinogen
Methylenedioxy**amphetamine** (MDA)	More powerful stimulant and less powerful hallucinogen than MDMA
4-Methylaminorex	CNS stimulant like amphetamine
N, N-Dimethyl**amphetamine**	One-fifth potency of amphetamine
4-Thiomethyl-2, 5-dimethoxy**amphetamine**	Hallucinogen
Para-methoxy**methamphetamine**	Weak stimulant

Dancers at a "rave" often consume Ecstasy for sensory enhancement.

It is estimated that as many as 31% of English youth from 16 to 25 years old have used Ecstasy (Grob et al. 1996). The British rave counterculture and its generous use of Ecstasy was exported to the United States in the early 1990s. Its high-tech music and video trappings were encouraged by low-tech laboratories that illegally manufactured the drug and shipped it into this country. Ecstasy has rapidly become the drug of choice for many young people in the United States (Cloud 2000). The availability of Ecstasy tablets has dramatically escalated in the United States as demonstrated by the report that the DEA seized approximately 300,000 of these tablets in 1999 compared with only 196 tablets in 1993. Most of these illegal drugs originate in European countries such as the Netherlands (Fields 1999), and the association of Ecstasy with raves has continued and become even more popular (Farley 2000). Because of its frequent association with raves, clubs, and bars, MDMA has been referred to as a club drug (Leshner 2000). Recent surveys revealed that 5.6% of high school seniors used Ecstasy in 1999 compared with 3.6% in 1998. This dramatic increase in Ecstasy use by adolescents is very troubling (Johnston 1999; Stocker 2000).

Some have compared the rave culture of the past decade and its use of MDMA to the acid-test parties of the 1960s and the partygoers' use of LSD and amphetamines (Cloud 2000; Randall 1992a). This drug is said by some not to cause dependence, but more teenagers are experimenting with it than ever before. For instance, Karen, an 18-year-old, sometimes sneaks off with her friends to take Ecstasy. After the effects take hold, they smile at each other, oblivious to their surroundings. At night, they get together again to take more of the drug because they like how it makes them feel (Cloud 2000). This type of frequent use is being seen more and more, suggesting that under extreme circumstances, MDMA can cause dependence and high frequency use (Jansen 1999).

MDMA was first inadvertently discovered in 1912 by chemists at E. Merck in Darmstadt, Germany (Grob et al. 1996). No pharmaceutical company has ever manufactured MDMA for public marketing, and the FDA has never approved it for therapy. MDMA was first found by the DEA on the streets in 1972 in a drug sample bought in Chicago (Beck 1990). The DEA earnestly began gathering data on MDMA abuse a decade later, which led to its classification as a Schedule I substance in 1985 despite the very vocal opposition by a number of psychiatrists who had been giving MDMA to

KEY TERMS

club drug
drugs used by young adults at dance parties such as raves

patients since the late 1970s to facilitate communication, acceptance, and fear reduction (Beck 1990). Even today, some health professionals still believe that MDMA should be made available to clinicians for the treatment of some psychiatric disorders (Cloud 2000). MDMA and related designer amphetamines are somewhat unique from other amphetamines in that, besides causing excitation, they have prominent hallucinogenic effects as well (Leshner 2000) (see Chapter 13). These drugs have been characterized as combining the properties of amphetamine and LSD (Shifano et al. 1998). The psychedelic effects of MDMA are likely caused by release of the neurotransmitter serotonin. After using hallucinogenic amphetamines, the mind is often flooded with a variety of irrelevant and incoherent thoughts and exaggerated sensory experiences and is more receptive to suggestion.

MDMA is often viewed as a "smooth amphetamine" and does not appear to cause the severe depression, or "crash," often associated with frequent high dosing of the more traditional amphetamines. MDMA was originally thought to be nonaddictive; however, more recent reports suggest that addiction does occur when high doses of this drug are used (Jansen 1999). Many users tend to be predominantly positive when describing their initial MDMA experiences (Cloud 2000). They claim the drug causes them to dramatically drop their defense mechanisms or fear responses while they feel an increased empathy for others (Parrott 1997). Combined with its stimulant effects, this action often increases intimate communication and association with others (Cloud 2000; Goldstein 1995). However, heavy users often experience adverse effects, such as loss of appetite, grinding of teeth, muscle aches and stiffness, sweating, rapid heartbeat, hostility, anxiety, and altered sleep patterns (Gamma et al. 2000; Morland 2000; Parrott et al. 2000). In addition, fatigue can be experienced for hours or even days after use. In high doses, MDMA can cause paranoid psychosis, panic attacks, and seizures (Schifano et al. 1998). There is evidence that these high doses can seriously damage serotonin neurons in the brain and cause long-term memory deficits and psychological disturbances in people (Gerra 2000; Davison and Parrott 1997; McCann 1999; Schifano et al. 1998).

There also are reports of MDMA overdoses resulting in death: in most of these cases, this drug had been taken by the victim at a rave where crowds were packed together and dancing vigorously (Cloud 2000). The victims collapsed unconscious while dancing and started to convulse. The combination of rapidly rising body temperature (up to 110°F), racing pulse, and plummeting blood pressure resulted in death between 2 and 60 hours after hospital admission. The lethality of MDMA under these conditions appears to be related to its ability to elevate body temperature and cause dehydration (NIDA Notes 1999). Thus, mixed with the crowd, hot environment of a "rave" and extreme physical exertion while dancing, the drug causes a deadly episode of hyperthermia (Boot et al. 2000; Taylor 1994).

Methylphenidate: A Special Amphetamine

Methylphenidate (Ritalin) is related to the amphetamines but is a relatively mild CNS stimulant that has been used to alleviate depression. Research now casts doubt on its effectiveness for treating depression, but it is effective in treating narcolepsy (a sleep disorder). As explained previously, Ritalin has also been found to help calm children suffering from attention deficit hyperactivity disorder and is currently the drug of choice for this purpose. The stimulant potency of Ritalin lies between that of caffeine and amphetamine. Although it is not used much on the street by hard-core drug addicts, there have been reports of use by high school and college students because of claims that it helps them to "study better," "party harder," and experience a buzz (Hinkle and Winckler 1996). High doses of Ritalin can cause tremors, seizures, and strokes. Ritalin has been classified as a Schedule II drug, like the other prescribed amphetamines.

▪ COCAINE

In the so-called war against drugs, cocaine eradication is considered to be a top priority. The tremendous attention directed at cocaine reflects the fact that from 1978 to 1987, the United States experienced the largest cocaine epidemic in history. Antisocial and criminal activities related to the effects of this potent stimulant have been highly visible and widely publicized (Grinspoon 1993).

As recently as the early 1980s, cocaine use was not believed to cause dependency because it did not cause gross withdrawal effects, as do alcohol and narcotics (Goldstein 1994). In fact, a 1982 article in *Scientific American* stated that cocaine was "no more habit forming than potato chips" (Van Dyck and Byck 1982). This perception has clearly been proven false: cocaine is so highly addictive that it is readily self-administered not only by human beings but also by laboratory animals (Fischman and Johanson 1996). Surveys suggest that 1.5 million Americans are chronic cocaine users (NIDA 1999).

There is no better substance than cocaine to illustrate the "love-hate" relationship that people can have with drugs. Many lessons can be learned by understanding the impact of cocaine and the social struggles that have ensued as people have tried to determine their proper relationship with this substance.

The History of Cocaine Use

Cocaine has been used as a stimulant for thousands of years. Its history can be classified into three eras, based on geographic, social, and therapeutic considerations. Learning about these eras can help us understand current attitudes about cocaine.

The First Cocaine Era

The first cocaine era was characterized by an almost harmonious use of this stimulant by South American Indians living in the regions of the Andean Mountains and dates back to about 2500 B.C. in Peru. It is believed that the stimulant properties of cocaine played a major role in the advancement of this isolated civilization, providing its people with the energy and motivation to realize dramatic social and architectural achievements while being able to endure tremendous hardships in barren, inhospitable environments. The *Erythroxylon coca* shrub (cocaine found in the leaves) was held in religious reverence by these people until the time of the Spanish Conquistadors (Golding 1993).

The first written description of coca chewing in the New World was by explorer Amerigo Vespucci in 1499:

> They were very brutish in appearance and behavior, and their cheeks bulged with the leaves of a certain green herb which they chewed like cattle,

An Andean chews coca leaves.

so that they could hardly speak. Each had around his neck two dried gourds, one full of that herb in their mouth, the other filled with a white flour-like powdered chalk. . . . [This was lime, which was mixed with the coca to enhance its effects.] When I asked . . . why they carried these leaves in their mouth, which they did not eat, . . . they replied it prevents them from feeling hungry, and gives them great vigor and strength. (Aldrich and Barker 1976, p. 3)

It is ironic that there are no indications that these early South American civilizations had any significant social problems with cocaine, considering the difficulty it has caused contemporary civilizations. There are three possible explanations for their positive experiences with coca:

1. The Andean Indians maintained control of the use of cocaine. For the Incas, coca could only be

used by the conquering aristocracy, chiefs, royalty, and other designated honorables (Aldrich and Barker 1976).

2. These Indians used the unpurified, and less potent, form of cocaine in the coca plant.

3. Chewing the coca leaf was a slow, sustained form of administering the drug; therefore, the effect was much less potent than snorting, intravenous injection, or smoking techniques most often used today.

The Second Cocaine Era

A second major cocaine era began in the 19th century. During this period, scientific techniques were used to elucidate the pharmacology of cocaine and identify its dangerous effects. It was also during this era that the threat of cocaine to society—both its members and institutions—was first recognized

The "refreshing" element in Vin Mariani was coca extract.

POPULAR
FRENCH TONIC WINE
*Fortifies and Refreshes Body & Brain
Restores Health and Vitality*

(DiChiara 1993; Musto 1998). At about this time, scientists in North America and Europe began experimenting with a purified, white, powdered extract made from the coca plant.

In the last half of the 19th century, Corsican chemist Angelo Mariani removed the active ingredients from the coca leaf and identified cocaine. This purified cocaine was added into cough drops and into a special Bordeaux wine called Vin Mariani (Musto 1998). The Pope gave Mariani a medal in appreciation for the fine work he had done. The cocaine extract was publicized as a magical drug that would free the body from fatigue, lift the spirits, and cause a sense of well-being, and the cocaine-laced wine became widely endorsed throughout the civilized world (Fischman and Johanson 1996). Included in a long list of luminaries who advocated this product for an array of ailments were the Czar and Czarina of Russia; the Prince and Princess of Wales; the Kings of Sweden, Norway, and Cambodia; commanders of the French and English armies; President McKinley of the United States; H. G. Wells; August Bartholdi (sculptor of the Statue of Liberty); and some 8000 physicians.

The astounding success of this wine attracted imitators, all making outlandish claims. One of these cocaine tonics was a nonalcoholic beverage named Coca-Cola, which was made from African kola nuts and advertised as the "intellectual beverage and temperance drink"; it contained 4 to 12 milligrams per bottle of the stimulant (DiChiara 1993). By 1906, Coca-Cola no longer contained detectable amounts of cocaine, but caffeine had been substituted in its place.

In 1884, the esteemed Sigmund Freud published his findings on cocaine in a report called "Uber Coca." Freud recommended this "magical drug" for an assortment of medical problems, including depression, hysteria, nervous exhaustion, digestive disorders, hypochondria, "all diseases which involve degeneration of tissue," and drug addiction.

In response to a request by Freud, a young Viennese physician, Karl Köller, studied the ability of cocaine to cause numbing effects. He discovered that it was an effective local anesthetic that could be applied to the surface of the eye and permit painless minor surgery to be conducted. This discovery of the first local anesthetic had tremendous worldwide impact. Orders for the new local anesthetic, cocaine, overwhelmed pharmaceutical companies.

Sigmund Freud was an early advocate of cocaine, which he referred to as a "cure-all."

Soon after the initial jubilation over the virtues of cocaine came the sober realization that with its benefits came severe disadvantages. As more people used cocaine, particularly in tonics and patent medicines, the CNS side effects and abuse liability became painfully evident. By the turn of the 20th century, cocaine was being processed from the coca plant and purified routinely by drug companies. People began to snort or inject the purified form of this popular powder, which increased both its effects and its dangers. The controversy over cocaine exploded before the American public in newspapers and magazines.

As medical and police reports of cocaine abuse and toxicities escalated, public opinion demanded that cocaine be banned. In 1914, the Harrison Act misleadingly classified both cocaine and coca as narcotic substances (cocaine is a stimulant) and outlawed their uncontrolled use.

Although prohibited in patent and nonprescription medicines, prescribed medicinal use of cocaine continued into the 1920s. Medicinal texts included descriptions of therapeutic uses for cocaine to treat fatigue, vomiting, seasickness, melancholia, and gas-

tritis. However, they also included lengthy warnings about excessive cocaine use, "the most insidious of all drug habits" (Aldrich and Barker 1976).

Little of medical or social significance occurred for the next few decades (Fischman and Johanson 1996). The medicinal use of cocaine was replaced mostly by the amphetamines during World War II because cocaine could not be supplied from South America. (Cocaine is not easily synthesized so even today, the supply of cocaine, both legal and illegal, continues to come from the Andean countries of South America.) During this period, cocaine continued to be employed for its local anesthetic action, was available on the "black market," and was used recreationally by musicians, entertainers, and the wealthy. Because of the limited supply, the cost of cocaine was prohibitive for most would-be consumers. Cocaine abuse problems remained of minor concern until the 1980s.

The Third Cocaine Era

With the 1980s, came the third major era of cocaine use. This era started much like the second in that the public and even the medical community were naive and misinformed about the drug. Cocaine was viewed as a glamorous substance and portrayed by the media as the drug of celebrities. Its use by prominent actors, athletes, musicians, and other members of a fast-paced, elite society was common knowledge. By 1982, over 20 million Americans had tried cocaine in one form or another, compared with only 5 million in 1974 (Green 1985).

The following is an example of a report from a Los Angeles television station in the early 1980s, which was typical of the misleading information being released to the public:

> Cocaine may actually be no more harmful to
> your health than smoking cigarettes or drinking
> alcohol; at least that's according to a 6-year study
> of cocaine use [described in *Scientific American*].
> It concludes that the drug is relatively safe and,
> if not taken in large amounts, it is not addictive
> (Byck 1987).

With such visibility, an association with prestige and glamour, and what amounted to an indirect endorsement by medical experts, the stage was set for another epidemic of cocaine use. Initially, the high cost of this imported substance limited its use. With increased demand came increased supply, and prices tumbled from an unaffordable $100 per "fix" to an affordable $10. The epidemic began.

By the mid-1980s, cocaine permeated all elements of society. No group of people or part of the country was immune from its effects. Many tragic stories were told of athletes, entertainers, corporate executives, politicians, fathers and mothers, high school students, and even children using and abusing cocaine. It was no longer the drug of the laborer or even the rich and famous. It was everybody's drug and everybody's problem (Golding 1993). As one user recounted:

> I think I was an addict. I immediately fell in love with cocaine. I noticed right away it was a drug that you had power with, and I wanted more and more. (*From Venturelli's research files, interview with a 22-year-old male, 1995.*)

Cocaine Production

Because cocaine is derived from the coca plant, which is imported from the Andean countries, America's problems with this drug have had a profound effect on several South American countries. With the dramatic rise in U.S. cocaine demand in the early 1980s, coca production in South America increased in tandem. The coca crop is by far the most profitable agricultural venture in some of these countries. In addition, this crop is easily cultivated and easily maintained (the coca plant is a perennial and remains productive for decades) and can be harvested several times a year (on average, two to four). The coca harvest has brought many jobs and some prosperity to these struggling economies. According to National Geographic, coca exports bring between $500 million and $1 billion to Bolivia annually. In U.S. terms, this figure is a relatively small amount, but for a poor country such as Bolivia, this money can mean the difference between life and death for many impoverished families (Boucher 1991).

KEY TERMS

adulterated
contaminating substances are mixed in to dilute the drugs

In spite of U.S. efforts, coca production increased from 1994 to 1995 in Colombia, Peru, and Bolivia. The profits (1 kilogram of cocaine brings farmers $1000), combined with the traditional view held by the people in Latin American countries that coca is a desirable substance, have made it difficult to persuade farmers to change crops just to satisfy the demands of the United States (Haven 1996).

Cocaine Processing

Cocaine is one of several active ingredients from the leaves of *Erythroxylon coca* (its primary source). The leaves are harvested two or four times per year and used to produce coca paste, which contains up to 80% cocaine. The paste is processed in clandestine laboratories to form a pure, white hydrochloride salt powder (Hatsukami and Fischman 1996). Often purified cocaine is adulterated (or "cut") with substances such as powdered sugar, talc, arsenic, lidocaine, strychnine, and methamphetamine before it is sold on the streets. Adverse responses to street cocaine are sometimes caused by the additives, not the cocaine itself. The resultant purity of the cut material ranges from 10% to 85%.

Cocaine is often sold in the form of little pellets, called *rocks*, or as flakes or powder. If it is in pellet form, it must be crushed before used. Such exotic names as Peruvian rock and Bolivian flake are bandied about to convince the buyer that the "stash" is high grade. Other street names used for cocaine have included blow, snow, flake, C, coke, toot, white lady, girl, cadillac, nose candy, gold dust, and stardust.

■ CURRENT ATTITUDES AND PATTERNS OF ABUSE

Given contemporary medical advances, we have greater understanding of the effects of cocaine and its toxicities and the dependence it produces. The reasons for abusing cocaine are better understood, as well. For example, it is clear that as many as 30% of chronic cocaine users are self-medicating psychiatric disorders such as depression, attention deficit disorders, or anxiety (Grinspoon 1993). Such knowledge helps in identifying and administering effective treatment. The hope is that society will never again be fooled into thinking that cocaine abuse is glamorous or an acceptable form of entertainment.

Attempts are being made to use this understanding (either recently acquired or merely relearned) to educate people about the true nature of cocaine. Such education was likely responsible for trends of declining cocaine use observed from 1987 to 1991 (see Figure 11.1). Decreases occurred in virtually every age group evaluated during this period. Surveys during this time revealed that, in general, cocaine use became less acceptable; these changes in attitude almost certainly contributed to the dramatic reduction in use (Johnston 1994). However, since 1992, cocaine abuse has rebounded, especially in young populations. Although it is not clear why the declines reversed, some experts have speculated that attitudes about cocaine use are again changing and eventually may lead to a new era of cocaine problems (Johnston 1999). This is supported by the most recent increases in cocaine use by high school seniors (see Figure 11.1). A particularly disturbing finding is that cocaine-related deaths have been rising dramatically in some large metropolitan areas in the United States, suggesting increases in heavy cocaine abuse (CEWG Publications 2000).

Cocaine Administration

Cocaine can be administered orally, inhaled into the nasal passages, injected intravenously, or smoked. The form of administration is important in determining the intensity of cocaine's effects, its abuse liability, and the likelihood of toxicity (Nathan et al. 1998).

Oral administration of cocaine produces the least potent effects; most of the drug is destroyed in the gut or liver before it reaches the brain. The result is a slower onset of action with a milder, more sustained stimulation. This form is least likely to cause health problems and dependence (Grinspoon 1993). South American Indians still take cocaine orally to increase their strength and for relief from fatigue. Administration usually involves prolonged chewing of the coca leaf, resulting in the consumption of about 20 to 400 milligrams of the drug (DiChiara 1993). Oral use of cocaine is not common in the United States.

"Snorting" involves inhaling cocaine hydrochloride powder into the nostrils, where deposits form on the lining of the nasal chambers and approximately 100 milligrams of the drug passes through the mucosal tissues into the bloodstream (DiChiara 1993). Substantial CNS stimulation occurs in several minutes, persists for 30 to 40 minutes, and then subsides. The effects occur more rapidly and are shorter-lasting and more intense than those achieved with oral administration, because more of the drug enters the brain more quickly. Because concentrations of cocaine in the body are higher after snorting than after oral ingestion, the side effects are more severe. One of the most common consequences of snorting cocaine is rebound depression, or "crash," which is of little consequence after oral consumption. As a general

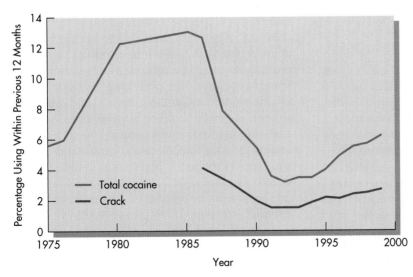

FIGURE 11.1

Trends in cocaine and crack use by high school seniors, 1975–1999. These data represent the percentages of high school seniors surveyed who reported using cocaine during the year.

Note: Crack cocaine did not become widely available until 1986.

Source: L. Johnston. "University of Michigan Annual National Surveys of Secondary Students." Lansing, MI: University of Michigan, 1999.

rule, the intensity of the depression correlates with the intensity of the euphoria (Goldstein 1995).

According to studies performed by the National Institute on Drug Abuse, about 10% to 15% of those who try intranasal (snorting) cocaine go on to heavier forms of dosing, such as intravenous administration. Intravenous administration of cocaine is a relatively recent phenomenon because the hypodermic needle was not widely available until the late 1800s. This form of administration has contributed to many of the cocaine problems that appeared at the turn of the 20th century. Intravenous administration allows large amounts of cocaine to be introduced very rapidly into the body and causes severe side effects and dependence. Within seconds after injection, cocaine users experience an incredible state of euphoria. The "high" is intense but short-lived; within 15 to 20 minutes, the user experiences dysphoria and is heading for a "crash." To prevent these unpleasant rebound effects, cocaine is readministered every 10 to 30 minutes. Readministration continues as long as there is drug available (NIDA 1998).

This binge activity resembles that seen in the methamphetamine "run," except it is usually shorter in duration. When the cocaine supply is exhausted, the binge is over (Goldstein 1994). Several days of abstinence may separate these episodes; the average cocaine addict binges once to several times a week, with each binge lasting 4 to 24 hours. Cocaine addicts claim that all thoughts turn toward cocaine during binges; everything else loses significance. This pattern of intense use is how some people blow all of their money on cocaine, as the following scenario illustrates:

> I'm working hard for my old man and I'm even selling [cocaine] at work a little bit, but now I'm starting to get to the point where you know the whole thing is one big lie. I didn't even know what the truth was anymore. I just started lying to everybody about things. I was making this kind of money, . . . but I got so f——— addicted to this stuff, you don't even know you're lying anymore. And I started doing so much of it that I started losing money and I started losing other people's as well. I had to lie to those people, and I started screwing those people just so I could get my next fix. (*From Venturelli's research files, interview with a 22-year-old male, 1995.*)

"Freebasing" paraphernalia. A water pipe is often used to smoke freebased cocaine, or "crack." Cocaine administered by smoking is very potent and fast acting; the effect lasts for 10 to 15 minutes, after which depression occurs. This is the most addicting form of cocaine.

Freebasing is a method of reducing impurities in cocaine and preparing the drug for smoking. It produces a type of cocaine that is more powerful than normal cocaine hydrochloride. One way to "freebase" is to treat the cocaine hydrochloride with a liquid base such as sodium carbonate or ammonium hydroxide. The cocaine dissolves, along with many of the impurities commonly found in it (such as amphetamines, lidocaine, sugars, and others). A solvent, such as petroleum or ethyl ether, is added to the liquid to extract the cocaine. The solvent containing the cocaine floats to the top and is drawn off with an eyedropper; it is placed in an evaporation dish to dry, and crystalized cocaine residue is then crushed into a fine powder, which can be smoked in a special glass pipe (DSM-IV-TR 2000).

The effects of smoked cocaine are as intense or more than those achieved through intravenous administration (Fischman and Johanson 1996). The onset is very rapid, the euphoria is dramatic, the depression is severe, the side effects are dangerous, and the chances of dependence are high (Grinspoon 1993). The reason for these intense reactions to inhaling cocaine into the lungs is that the drug passes rapidly through the lining of the lungs and into the many blood vessels present; it is then carried almost directly to the brain.

Freebasing became popular in the United States in the 1980s due to the fear of diseases such as AIDS and hepatitis, which are transmitted by sharing contaminated hypodermic needles. But freebasing involves other dangers. Because the volatile solvents required for freebasing are very explosive, careless people have been seriously burned or killed during processing (Seigel 1985). Street synonyms used for freebased cocaine include baseball, bumping, white tornado, world series, and snowtoke.

"Crack"

Between 1985 and 1986, a special type of freebased cocaine known as crack or "rock" appeared on the streets (Hatsukami and Fischman 1996). By 1988, approximately 5% of high school students had tried crack. As of 1992, this number had fallen to 2.6%, but as of 1999, it rose again to 4.6% (Johnston 1999). Crack is inexpensive and can be smoked without the dangerous explosive solvents mentioned earlier in the discussion of freebasing. It is made by taking powdered cocaine hydrochloride and adding sodium bicarbonate (baking soda) and water. The paste that forms removes impurities as well as the hydrochloride from the cocaine. The substance is then dried into hard pieces called rocks, which may contain as much as 90% pure cocaine. Other slang terms for crack include base, black rock, gravel, Roxanne, and space basing.

Like freebased cocaine, crack is usually smoked in a glass water pipe. When the fumes are absorbed into the lungs, they act rapidly, reaching the brain within 8 to 10 seconds. An intense "rush" or "high" results, and later a powerful state of depression, or "crash," occurs. The high may last only 3 to 5 minutes, and the depression may persist from 10 to 40 minutes or longer in some cases. As soon as crack is smoked, the nervous system is greatly stimulated by the release of dopamine, which seems to be involved in the rush. Cocaine prevents resupply of this neurotransmitter, which may trigger the crash.

Because of the abrupt and intense release of dopamine, smoked crack is viewed as a drug with tremendous potential for addiction (DSM-IV-TR 2000) and is considered by users to be more enjoyable than cocaine administered intravenously (Fischman and Johanson 1996). In fact, some people with serious cardiovascular disease continue using crack despite knowing their serious risk for heart attacks and strokes (Fischman and Foltin 1992).

Crack and cocaine marketing and use are often associated with criminal activity (DSM-IV-TR 2000). For example, at one time, it was reported that nearly 30% of the bodies of homicide victims in New York City had cocaine in them (Swan 1995).

In general, crack use has been more common among African American and Hispanic populations than among white Americans. However, the difference in prevalence does not appear to be racially related, but rather due to socioeconomic circumstances (Lillie-Blanton et al. 1993). Of special concern is the use of crack among women during pregnancy. Children born under these circumstances have been referred to as crack babies; their population is estimated to include as many as 900,000 infants born during 1989–1992 (Knight-Ridder News Service 1992). Even though the effects of crack on fetal development are not fully understood, many clinicians and researchers have predicted that these crack babies will impose an enormous social burden as they grow up. However, other experts have expressed concern that the impact of cocaine on the fetus is grossly overstated and have suggested that behavioral problems seen in these children are more a consequence of social environment than direct pharmacological effects (Fischman and Johanson 1996). This is discussed in greater detail later in this section.

It is not coincidental that the popularity of crack use paralleled the AIDS epidemic in the mid-

---

KEY TERMS

freebasing
conversion of cocaine into its alkaline form for smoking

crack
already processed and inexpensive "freebased" cocaine, ready for smoking

crack babies
infants born to women who use crack cocaine during pregnancy

1980s. Because crack administration does not require injection, theoretically, the risk of contracting HIV from contaminated needles is avoided. Even so, incidence of HIV infection in crack users is still very high because many crack smokers also use cocaine intravenously and 30% to 40% of the intravenous users are HIV-positive (Des Jarlais 1992) (see Chapter 17). Another reason for the high incidence of HIV infections (as well as other sexually transmitted diseases, such as syphilis and gonorrhea) among crack users is the dangerous sexual behavior in which these people engage (Castilla et al. 1999). Not only is crack commonly used as payment for sex, but also its users are much less inclined to be cautious about their sexual activities while under the influence of this drug (Des Jarlais 1992).

Major Pharmacological Effects of Cocaine

Cocaine has profound effects on several vital systems in the body (Nathan et al. 1998). With the assistance of modern technology, the mechanisms whereby cocaine alters body functions have become better understood today. Such knowledge will hopefully lead to better treatment of cocaine dependence.

Most of the pharmacological effects of cocaine use stem from enhanced activity of catecholamine (dopamine, noradrenaline, adrenaline) and serotonin transmitters. It is believed that the principal action of the drug is to block the reuptake and inactivation of these substances following their release from neurons. The consequence of such action is to prolong the activity of these transmitter substances at their receptors and substantially increase their effects. The summation of cocaine's effects on these four transmitters causes CNS stimulation (Woolverton and Johnston 1992). The increase of noradrenaline activity following cocaine administration increases the effects of the sympathetic nervous system and alters cardiovascular activity (see discussion later).

CNS Effects Because cocaine has stimulant properties, it has antidepressant effects as well. In fact, some users self-administer cocaine to relieve severe depression or the negative symptoms of schizophrenia (Mendelson and Mello 1996; Seibyl et al. 1992), but in general its short-term action and abuse liability make cocaine unsatisfactory for the treatment of depression disorders. The effects of stimulation appear to increase both physical and mental performance while masking fatigue. High doses of cocaine cause euphoria (based on the form of administration) and enhance the sense of strength, energy, and performance. Because of these positive effects, cocaine has intense reinforcing properties, which encourage continual use and dependence (Nathan et al. 1998).

Cocaine addicts can often distinguish between the two phenomena of the rush and high associated with cocaine administration. Both the rush and high peak about 3 minutes after use. The rush seems to be associated with elevated heart rate, sweating, and feelings of "speeding" or "being out of control," whereas the high includes feelings of euphoria, self-confidence, well-being, and sociability. Drug craving also occurs rapidly and is evident as soon as 12 minutes after administration. Interestingly, brain scans of cocaine users have demonstrated that specific brain regions are associated with these drug effects; thus, the rush and craving are linked with different regions of the limbic system in the brain (see Figure 5.6; Stocker 1999).

The feeling of exhilaration and confidence caused by cocaine can easily transform into irritable restlessness and confused hyperactivity (DSM-IV-TR 2000). In addition, high chronic doses alter personality, frequently causing psychotic behavior that resembles paranoid schizophrenia (DSM-IV-TR 2000; Nathan et al. 1998). For example, in an interview with Dr. Peter Venturelli, a 17-year-old-female explained that a cocaine-abusing friend ". . . was so coked up that he carved the word 'pain' in his arm and poured coke on it. He thought it symbolized something." In addition, cocaine use heightens the risk of suicide, major trauma, and violent crimes (DSM-IV-TR 2000). In many ways, the CNS effects of cocaine are like those of amphetamines, although perhaps with a more rapid onset, a more intense high (due partially to the manner in which the drugs are administered), and a shorter duration of action (DSM-IV-TR 2000).

Besides dependence, other notable CNS toxicities that can be caused by cocaine use include headaches, temporary loss of consciousness, seizures, and death (Nathan et al. 1998).

Cardiovascular System Effects Cocaine can initiate pronounced changes in the cardiovascular system by enhancing the sympathetic nervous system, increasing the levels of adrenaline, and causing vasoconstriction (Stocker 1998). The initial effects of cocaine are to increase heart rate and elevate blood pressure. While the heart is being stimulated and working harder, the vasoconstriction effects deprive the cardiac muscle of needed blood (Fischman and Johanson 1996). Such a combination can cause severe heart arrhythmia (an irregular contraction pattern) or heart attack. Other degenerative processes have also been described in the hearts and blood vessels of chronic cocaine users (Fischman and Johanson 1996). In addition, the vasoconstrictive action of this sympathomimetic can damage other tissues, prompting a stroke, lung damage in those who smoke cocaine, destruction of nasal cartilage in those who snort the drug, and injury to the gastrointestinal tract (Goldstein 1995).

Local Anesthetic Effect Cocaine was the first local anesthetic used routinely in modern-day medicine (Musto 1998). There is speculation that in ancient times, Andes Indians of South America used cocaine-filled saliva from chewing coca leaves as a local anesthetic for surgical procedures (Aldrich and Barker 1976). However, this assumption is contested by others (Byck 1987). Even so, cocaine is still a preferred local anesthetic for minor *pharyngeal* (back part of the mouth and upper throat area) surgery due to its good vasoconstriction (reduces bleeding) and topical, local numbing effects. Although relatively safe when applied topically, significant amounts of cocaine can enter the bloodstream and, in sensitive people, cause CNS stimulation, toxic psychosis, or even on rare occasions, death (Medical Letter 1996).

Cocaine Withdrawal

Considerable debate has arisen as to whether cocaine withdrawal actually happens and, if so, what it involves. With the most recent cocaine epidemic and the high incidence of intense, chronic use, it has become apparent that nervous systems do become tolerant to cocaine and that, during abstinence, withdrawal symptoms occur (DSM-IV-TR 2000). In fact, because of CNS dependence, the use of cocaine is less likely to be stopped voluntarily than is the use of most other illicit drugs (Schwartz et al. 1991). Certainly, if the withdrawal experience is adverse enough, a user will be encouraged to resume the cocaine habit.

The extent of cocaine withdrawal is proportional to the duration and intensity of use. The physical withdrawal symptoms are relatively minor compared with those caused by long-term use of CNS depressants and by themselves are not considered to be life-threatening (Woolverton and Johnston 1992). Short-term withdrawal symptoms include depression (chronic cocaine users are 60 times more likely to commit suicide than nonusers), sleep abnormalities, craving for the drug, agitation, and *anhedonia* (inability to experience pleasure). Long-term withdrawal effects include a return to normal pleasures, accompanied by mood swings and occasional craving triggered by cues in the surroundings (DSM-IV-TR 2000; Mendelson and Mello 1996).

Of particular importance to treatment of the chronic cocaine users is that abstinence after bingeing appears to follow three unique stages, each of which must be dealt with in a different manner if relapse is to be prevented. These phases are classified as phase 1, or "crash" (occurs 9 hours–4 days after drug use is stopped); phase 2, or withdrawal (1–10 weeks); and finally, phase 3, or extinction (indefinite). The basic features of these phases are outlined in Table 11.3 (DSM-IV-TR 2000; Gawin 1991).

Treatment of Cocaine Dependence

Cocaine dependency is classified as a psychiatric disorder by the American Psychiatric Association (DSM-IV-TR 2000). Treatment of this condition has improved as experience working with these patients has increased. Even so, success rates vary for different programs (Nathan et al. 1998). The problem with program assessments is that they often do not take into account patients who drop out. Also, no clear-cut criteria for qualifying success have been established. For example, is success considered to be abstaining from cocaine for 1 year, 2 years, 5 years, or forever?

No one treatment technique has been found to be significantly superior to others or universally effective (Mendelson and Mello 1996; SAMHSA News 1999); consequently, substantial disagreement exists as to what is the best strategy for treating cocaine dependency, and there is a major ongoing effort by federal agencies and scientists to find effective therapy for cocaine addiction. Most treatments are directed at relieving craving (Kleber 1992). Major differences in treatment approaches include

TABLE 11.3 Cocaine Abstinence Phases

	PHASE 1: "CRASH"	PHASE 2: WITHDRAWAL	PHASE 3: EXTINCTION
Time since last binge	24–48 hours	1–10 weeks	Indefinite
Features	*Initial*	*Initial*	
	Agitation, depression, anorexia, suicidal thoughts	Mood swings, sleep returns, some craving, little anxiety	Normal pleasure, mood swings, occasional craving, cues trigger craving
	Middle Fatigue, no craving, insomnia	*Middle and late* Anhedonia, anxiety, intense craving, obsessed with drug seeking	
	Late Extreme fatigue, no craving, exhaustion		

Source: Gawin, F. "Cocaine Addiction: Psychology and Neurophysiology." *Science* 251 (1991): 1580–6.

(1) whether outpatient or inpatient status is appropriate, (2) which drugs and what dosages should be used to treat patients during the various stages of abstinence, and (3) what length of time the patient should be isolated from cocaine-accessible environments. It is important to treat each individual patient according to his or her unique needs. Some questions that need to be considered when formulating a therapeutic approach include the following:

Why did the patient begin using cocaine, and why has dependency occurred?

What is the severity of abuse?

How has the cocaine been administered?

What is the psychiatric status of the patient; are there underlying or coexisting mental disorders, such as depression or attention deficit disorder?

What other drugs are being abused along with the cocaine?

What is the patient's motivation for eliminating cocaine dependence?

What sort of support system (family, friends, coworkers, and so on) will sustain the patient in the abstinence effort?

Outpatient Versus Inpatient Approaches The decision as to whether to treat a patient dependent on cocaine as an outpatient or inpatient is based on a number of issues. For example, inpatient techniques allow greater control than outpatient treatment; thus, the environment can be better regulated, the training of the patient can be more closely supervised, and the patient's responses to treatment can be more closely monitored. In contrast, the advantages of the outpatient approach are that supportive family and friends are better able to encourage the patient, the surroundings are more comfortable and natural, and potential problems that might occur when the patient returns to a normal lifestyle are more likely to be identified. In addition, outpatient treatment is less expensive.

Cocaine-dependent patients should be matched to the most appropriate strategy based on their personalities, psychiatric status, and the conditions of their addiction (Mendelson and Mello 1996). For instance, a cocaine addict who lives in the inner city, comes from a home with other drug-dependent family members, and has little support probably would do better in the tightly controlled inpatient environment. However, a highly motivated cocaine addict who comes from a supportive home and a neighborhood that is relatively free of drug problems would probably do better on an outpatient basis.

Therapeutic Drug Treatment Several drugs have been used to treat cocaine abstinence, some which are themselves active on dopamine systems, but none has been found to be universally effective (Smith et al. 1999). Table 11.4 lists some drugs that have been used in each of the three principal phases of cocaine abstinence. Besides relieving acute problems of anxiety, agitation, and psychosis, drugs can also diminish cocaine craving; this effect is achieved by giving drugs such as bromocriptine or levodopa that stimulate the dopamine transmitter system or the narcotic, buprenorphine. As mentioned, the pleasant aspects of cocaine likely relate to its ability to increase the activity of dopamine in the limbic system. When cocaine is no longer available, the dopamine system becomes less active, causing depression and anhedonia, which result in tremendous craving for cocaine. The intent of these cocaine substitutes is to stimulate dopamine activity and relieve the cravings. Although this approach sometimes works initially, it is temporary. In the third phase of cocaine abstinence, antidepressants such as desipramine are effective for many cocaine-dependent patients in relieving underlying mood problems and occasional cravings.

The beneficial effects of these drugs are variable and not well studied. There is some debate over their use. Drugs are, at best, only adjuncts in the treatment of cocaine dependence (Carroll et al. 1994). Successful treatment of cocaine abuse requires intensive counseling; strong support from family, friends, and coworkers; and a highly motivated patient. It is important to realize that a complete "cure" from cocaine dependence is impossible: ex-addicts cannot return to cocaine and control its use (Kleber 1992). The following is an example of the constant battle of one cocaine addict who is attempting to break the habit:

> I had several years of sobriety [from cocaine use] until recently when I relapsed on crack. . . . I don't know if I am addicted to crack. I still want the drug, perhaps to cover the sadness and make me feel happy again. . . . I love the excitement I felt with the drug. . . . My focus is one-tracked. . . . I need help but I don't know if I want it. (From America Online, Dewey CBS 1996.)

Recovery from Cocaine Dependence Although numerous therapeutic approaches exist for treating cocaine addiction, successful recovery is not likely unless the individual will substantially benefit by giving up the drug. Research has shown that treatment is most likely to succeed in patients who are middle-class, employed, and married; for example, 85% of addicted medical professionals recover from cocaine addiction. These people can usually be convinced that they have too much to lose in their personal and professional lives by continuing their cocaine habit. In contrast, a severely dependent crack addict who has no job, family, home, or hope for the future is not likely to be persuaded that abstinence from cocaine would be advantageous, so therapy usually is not successful (Grinspoon 1993). Unfortunately, there currently is no uniformly effective pharmacological treatment available to deal with long-term cocaine addiction, although intensive research to identify such therapeutic agents is underway (SAMHSA News 1999).

Polydrug Use by Cocaine Abusers Treatment of most cocaine abusers is complicated by the fact that they are *polydrug* (multiple drug) users. It is unusual

TABLE 11.4 Medications Used in Treatment of Cocaine Abstinence at Various Phases

PHASE	DRUG	DRUG GROUP (RATIONALE)
1. Crash	Benzodiazepines	Depressants (relieve anxiety)
2. Withdrawal	Bromocryptine, Levodopa	Dopamine agonist (relieve craving)
3. Extinction	Desipramine, imipramine	Antidepressant (relieve depression and craving)

Source: Mendelson, J., and N. Mello. "Management of Cocaine Abuse and Dependence." *New England Journal of Medicine* 334 (1996): 965–72.

to find a person who only abuses cocaine. For example, it has been reported that 60% to 90% of cocaine abusers also use alcohol (Fischman and Johanson 1996). In general, the more severe the alcoholism, the greater the severity of the cocaine dependence. For most cases, alcoholism develops after the cocaine abuse pattern (Carroll et al. 1993) because the alcohol is used to relieve some of the unpleasant cocaine effects, such as anxiety, insomnia, and mood disturbances (Sands and Ciraulo 1992). This drug combination is particularly dangerous for several reasons:

1. The presence of both cocaine and alcohol (ethanol) in the liver results in the formation of a unique chemical product called cocaethylene, which is created in the reaction of ethanol with a cocaine metabolite. Cocaethylene is often found in high levels in the blood of victims of fatal drug overdoses and appears to enhance the euphoria as well as the cardiovascular toxicity of cocaine (Fischman and Johanson 1996).

2. Both cocaine and alcohol can damage the liver; thus, their toxic effects on the liver are added together when the drugs are used in combination (Sands and Ciraulo 1992).

3. The likelihood of damaging a fetus is enhanced when both drugs are used together during pregnancy (Sands and Ciraulo 1992).

4. Cardiovascular stress is substantially enhanced in the presence of both drugs; thus, people with underlying coronary artery disease are 18 times more likely to suffer sudden death from cardiovascular factors when using this combination (Sands and Ciraulo 1992).

As with amphetamines, cocaine abusers also frequently coadminister narcotics, such as heroin; this combination is called a *speedball* and has been associated with an especially high risk for HIV infection (Mendelson and Mello 1996). Cocaine users often combine their drug with other depressants, such as benzodiazepines, or marijuana (Sands and Ciraulo 1992) to help reduce the severity of the crash after their cocaine binges. Codependence on cocaine and a CNS depressant can complicate treatment but must be considered.

Cocaine and Pregnancy

One of the consequences of widespread cocaine abuse is that thousands of babies are born each year in the United States having been exposed to cocaine in the womb. Cocaine use during pregnancy is highest in poor, inner-city regions; estimates of its prevalence range from 3% to 50% according to the metropolitan area (Mayes et al. 1992). It is likely that in the United States, more than $1 billion is spent annually for care of cocaine-using women

Infants born to crack-using mothers are often premature.

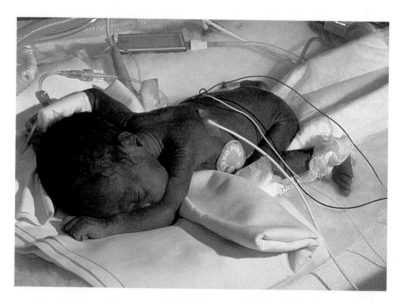

during their pregnancies. The majority of these cocaine babies are abandoned by their mothers and left to the welfare system for care.

It is still not clear exactly what types of direct effects cocaine has on the developing fetus. Some early studies have been criticized because (1) the pregnant populations examined were not well defined and properly matched, (2) use of other drugs (such as alcohol) with cocaine during pregnancy was often ignored, and (3) the effects of poor nutrition, poor living conditions, and a traumatic lifestyle were not considered when analyzing the results. Due to these problems, much of the earlier work examining prenatal effects of cocaine is flawed and the conclusions are questionable (Fischman and Johanson 1996; Grinspoon 1993).

It is known that cocaine use during pregnancy can cause vasoconstriction of placental vessels, thus interfering with oxygen and nutrient exchange between mother and child, or contraction of the uterine muscles, resulting in trauma or premature birth. Current data also suggest that infants exposed to cocaine during pregnancy are more likely to suffer a small head (microencephaly), reduced birth weight (Coles et al. 1992), and increased irritability and subtle learning and cognitive deficits (Fischman and Johanson 1996). Recent findings also suggest that children who had experienced prenatal cocaine exposure have problems with some motor skills, subtle deficits in I.Q., and some minor problems with language development, attention span, and ability to gather and use information (Bulletin Board 1999; Leshner 1999). Clearly, individuals exposed to cocaine during fetal development can function in society, but they frequently require special help. It remains to be seen how these individuals will cope as adults (Leshner 1999).

Minor Stimulants

Minor stimulants enjoy widespread use in the United States because of the mild lift in mood provided by their consumption. The most popular of these routinely consumed agents are methylxanthines (commonly called *xanthines*), such as caffeine, which are consumed in beverages made from plants and herbs. Other minor stimulants are con-

cocaine babies
infants born to women using cocaine during pregnancy

tained in OTC medications, such as cold and hay fever products; these will be mentioned briefly in this chapter but discussed at greater length in Chapter 17. Because of their frequent use, some dependence on these drugs can occur; however, serious dysfunction due to dependence is infrequent. Consequently, abuse of xanthines such as caffeine is not viewed as a major health problem by most health experts (Daly and Fredholm 1998).

■ CAFFEINELIKE DRUGS (XANTHINES)

Caffeine is the world's most frequently used stimulant and perhaps its most popular drug (Daly and Fredhom 1998). Beverages and foods containing caffeine are consumed by almost all adults and children living in the United States today (see Table 11.5). In this country, the average daily intake of caffeine is approximately 200 mg (the equivalent of

TABLE 11.5 Caffeine Content of Beverages and Chocolate

BEVERAGE	CAFFEINE CONTENT (MG/CUP)	AMOUNT
Brewed coffee	90–125	5 oz
Instant coffee	35–164	5 oz
Decaffeinated coffee	1–6	5 oz
Tea	25–125	5 oz
Cocoa	5–25	5 oz
Coca-Cola	45	12 oz
Pepsi-Cola	38	12 oz
Mountain Dew	54	12 oz
Chocolate bar	1–35	1 oz

~2 cups of coffee), with up to 30% of American consuming 500 mg or more per day (DSM-IV-R 2000). The most common sources of caffeine include coffee beans, tea plants, kola nuts, maté leaves, guaraná paste, and yoco bark.

Although the consumption of caffeine-containing drinks can be found throughout history, the active stimulant caffeine was identified by German and French scientists in the early 1820s. Caffeine was described as a substance with alkaloid (basic) properties that was extracted from green coffee beans and referred to as *kaffebase* by Ferdinand Runge in 1820 (Gilbert 1984). In the course of the next 40 to 60 years, caffeine was identified in several other genera of plants, which were used as sources for common beverages. These included tea leaves (originally the drug was called *thein*); guaraná paste (originally the drug was called *guaranin*); Paraguay tea, or maté; and kola nuts. Certainly, the popularity of these beverages over the centuries attests to the fact that most consumers find the stimulant effects of this drug desirable.

The Chemical Nature of Caffeine

Caffeine belongs to a group of drugs that have similar chemical structures and are known as the xanthines . Besides caffeine, other xanthines are *theobromine* (means "divine leaf"), discovered in cacao beans (used to make chocolate) in 1842, and *theophylline* (means "divine food"), isolated from tea leaves in 1888. These three agents have unique pharmacological properties (which are discussed later), with caffeine being the most potent CNS stimulant.

Beverages Containing Caffeine

To understand the unique role that caffeine plays in U.S. society, it is useful to gain perspective on its most common sources: unfermented beverages.

Coffee Coffee is derived from the beans of several species of coffea plants. The *Coffea arabica* plant grows as a shrub or small tree and reaches 4 to 6 meters in height when growing wild. Coffee beans are primarily cultivated in South America and East Africa and constitute the major cash crop for exportation in several developing countries.

The name *coffee* was likely derived from the Arabian word *kahwa* or named after the Ethiopian prince Kaffa. From Ethiopia, the coffee tree was carried to Arabia and cultivated (Kihlman 1977); it became an important element in Arabian civilization and is mentioned in writings dating back to A.D. 900.

Coffee probably reached Europe through Turkey and was likely used initially as a medicine. By the middle of the 17th century, coffeehouses had sprung up in England and France—places to relax, talk, and learn the news. These coffeehouses turned into the famous "penny universities" of the early 18th century where, for a penny a cup, you could listen to some of the great literary and political figures of the day.

Coffee was originally consumed in the Americas by English colonists, although tea was initially preferred. Tea was replaced by coffee following the Revolutionary War. Because tea had become a symbol of English repression, the switch to coffee was more a political statement than a change in taste. The popularity of coffee grew as U.S. boundaries moved west. In fact, daily coffee intake continued to increase until it peaked in 1986, when annual coffee consumption averaged 10 pounds per person. Although concerns about the side effects associated with caffeine use have since caused some decline in coffee consumption, this beverage still plays a major role in the lifestyles of most Americans (Sawynok and Yaksh 1993).

Tea Tea is made from the *Camellia sinensis* plant, which is native to China and parts of India, Burma, Thailand, Laos, and Vietnam. As mentioned, tea contains two xanthines: caffeine and theophylline. As with coffee, the earliest use of tea is not known.

Although apocryphal versions of the origin of tea credit Emperor Shen Nung in 2737 B.C., the first reliable account of the use of tea as a medicinal plant is from an early Chinese manuscript written around A.D. 350. The popular use of tea slowly grew. The Dutch brought the first tea to Europe in 1610, where it was accepted rather slowly; however, with time, it was adopted by the British as a favorite beverage and became an integral part of their daily

---

KEY TERMS

xanthines
the family of drugs that include caffeine

activities. In fact, the tea trade constituted one of the major elements of the English economy. Tea revenues made it possible for England to colonize India and also helped to bring on the Opium Wars in the 1800s, which benefited British colonialism (see Chapter 10).

The British were constantly at odds with the Dutch as they attempted to monopolize the tea trade. Even so, the Dutch introduced the first tea into America at New Amsterdam around 1650. Later, the British gained exclusive rights to sell tea to the American colonies. Because of the high taxes levied by the British government on tea being shipped to America, tea became a symbol of British rule.

Soft Drinks The second most common source of caffeine is soft drinks. In general, the caffeine content per 12-ounce serving ranges from 30 to 60 milligrams (see Table 11.5). Soft drinks account for most of the caffeine consumed by U.S. children and teenagers, and for many people, a can of cola has replaced the usual cup of coffee. Recently, caffeine has been added to juices and even water. These caffeine-containing products have alluring names such as "Surge," "Jolt," "Aqua Buzz," "Krank H2O," and "XTC" and are designed to target teenager consumers (*Consumer Reports* 1997).

Social Consequences of Consuming Caffeine-Based Beverages It is impossible to accurately assess the social impact of consuming beverages containing caffeine, but certainly the subtle (and sometimes not so subtle) stimulant effects of the caffeine present in these drinks have had some social influence. These beverages have become integrated into social customs and ceremonies and recognized as traditional drinks.

Today, drinks containing caffeine are consumed by many people with ritualistic devotion first thing in the morning, following every meal, and at frequent interludes throughout the day known as "coffee breaks" or "tea times." The immense popularity of these products is certainly a consequence of the stimulant actions of caffeine. Both the dependence on the "jump-start" effect of caffeine and the avoidance of unpleasant withdrawal consequences in the frequent user ensure the continual popularity of these products.

These effects are illustrated by the following comments from college students:

Tina (freshman, psychology major): "I get headaches if I do not have my . . . Coca-Cola. The tension builds up in my head and I feel nauseous . . . As soon as I drink Coke, it goes away. I'm definitely addicted."

Eric (senior, geology major): "I wake up and feel like I could fall asleep walking down the street. That's how I tell I need [coffee]."

Jesse (senior, biology major): "I have worked at a coffeehouse for 2 years. I see customers come in dragging their feet . . . Once [customers] get it, though, they go 'Now I can get through my day.' Some people are more . . . on the edge if they don't get it [coffee]."

(Source: http://www.thejack.nau.edu/ 0913/lige2.html/, 1996.)

Other Natural Caffeine Sources

Although coffee and tea are two of the most common sources of natural caffeine in the United States, other caffeine-containing beverages and food are popular in different parts of the world. Some of the most common include guaraná from Brazil; maté from Argentina, Southern Brazil, and Paraguay; and kola nuts from West Africa, West Indies, and South America (Kihlman 1977).

Chocolate

Although chocolate contains small amounts of caffeine (see Table 11.5), the principal stimulant in chocolate is the alkaloid theobromine, named after the cocoa tree, *Theobroma cacao*. (*Theobroma* is an Aztec word meaning "fruit of the gods.") The Aztecs thought very highly of the fruit and seed pods from the cacoa tree, and they used the beans as a medium of exchange in bartering. The Mayan Indians adopted the food and made a warm drink from the beans that they called *chocolatl* (meaning "warm drink"). The original chocolate drink was a very thick concoction that had to be eaten with a spoon. It was unsweetened because the Mayans apparently did not know about sugar cane.

Hernando Cortés, the conqueror of Mexico, took some chocolate cakes back to Spain with him in 1528, but the method of preparing them remained a secret for nearly 100 years. It was not until 1828 that the Dutch worked out a process to remove much of the fat from the kernels to make a chocolate powder that was the forerunner of the cocoa we know today. The cocoa fat, or cocoa butter as it is called, was later mixed with sugar and pressed into bars. In 1847, the first chocolate bars appeared on the market. By 1876, the Swiss had developed milk chocolate, which is highly popular in today's confectioneries.

OTC Drugs Containing Caffeine

Although the consumption of beverages is by far the most common source of xanthines, a number of popular OTC products contain significant quantities of caffeine. For example, many OTC analgesic products contain approximately 30 milligrams of caffeine per tablet (Anacin). Higher doses of 100 to 200 milligrams per tablet are included in stay-awake (Nō-Dōz, Caffedrine) and "picker-upper" (Vivarin) products (*PDR Nonprescription Drugs* 2000). The use of caffeine in these OTC drugs is highly controversial and has been criticized by clinicians who are unconvinced of caffeine's benefits. Some critics believe that the presence of caffeine in these OTC drugs is nothing more than a psychological gimmick to entice customers through mild euphoric effects provided by this stimulant.

Despite this criticism, it is likely that caffeine has some analgesic (pain-relieving) properties of its own (Sawynok and Yaksh 1993). Recent studies suggest that 130 milligrams, but not 65 milligrams, of caffeine is superior to a placebo in relieving nonmigraine headaches. In addition, the presence of caffeine has been shown to enhance aspirin-medicated relief from surgical pain (such as tooth extraction). Based on such findings, more clinicians are recommending the use of caffeine in the management of some types of headaches and minor to moderate pains (Health News 1997).

Physiological Effects of the Xanthines

The xanthines significantly influence several important body functions. Although the effects of these drugs are generally viewed as minor and short-term (Goldstein 1994), when used in high doses or by people who have severe medical problems, these drugs can be dangerous. The following sections summarize the responses of the major systems to xanthines.

CNS Effects Among the common xanthines, caffeine has the most potent effect on the CNS, followed by theophylline; for most people, theobromine has relatively little influence. Although the CNS responses of users can vary considerably, in general, 100 to 200 milligrams of caffeine enhances alertness, causes arousal, and diminishes fatigue (Daly and Fredholm 1998). Caffeine is often used to block drowsiness and facilitate mental activity, such as when cramming for examinations into the early hours of the morning. In addition, caffeine stimulates the formation of thoughts but does not improve learning ability in the wide-awake student. The effects of caffeine are most pronounced in unstimulated, drowsy consumers (Goldstein 1994). The CNS effects of caffeine also diminish the sense of boredom (*Consumer Reports* 1997). Thus, people engaged in dull, repetitive tasks, such as assembly-line work, or nonstimulating and laborious exercises, such as listening to a boring professor, often consume caffeine beverages to help compensate for the tedium. Most certainly, xanthine drinks are popular because they cause these effects on brain activity.

Adverse CNS effects usually occur with doses greater than 300 milligrams per day. Some of these include insomnia, increased tension, anxiety, and initiation of muscle twitches. Doses over 500 milligrams can be dysphoric (unpleasant) and can cause panic sensations, chills, nausea, and clumsiness. Extremely high doses of caffeine, from 5 to 10 grams, frequently result in seizures, respiratory failure, and death (DSM-IV-TR 2000).

Cardiovascular and Respiratory Effects Drugs that stimulate the brain usually stimulate the cardiovascular system as well. The response of the heart and blood vessels to xanthines is dependent on dose and previous experience with these mild stimulants. Tolerance to the cardiovascular effects occurs with frequent use (DSM-IV-TR 2000). With low doses (100–200 milligrams), heart activity can either increase, decrease, or do nothing; at higher doses (>500 milligrams), the rate of contraction of the heart increases. Xanthines usually cause minor vasodilation in most of the body. In contrast, the cerebral blood vessels are vasoconstricted by the action of caffeine. In fact, cerebral vasoconstriction likely accounts for this drug's effectiveness in relieving some minor vascular headaches caused by vasodilation of the cerebral vessels.

Among the xanthines, theophylline has the greatest effect on the respiratory system, causing air passages to open and facilitate breathing. Because of this effect, tea has often been recommended to relieve breathing difficulties, and theophylline is frequently used to treat asthma-related respiratory problems.

Other Effects The methylxanthines have noteworthy, albeit mild, effects on other systems in the body. They cause a minor increase in the secretion of digestive juices in the stomach, which can be significant to individuals suffering from stomach ailments such as ulcers. These drugs also increase urine formation (as any heavy tea drinker undoubtedly knows).

Caffeine Intoxication

Consuming occasional low doses of the xanthines (equivalent of two to three cups of coffee per day) is relatively safe for most users (Heishman and Hennington 1992; Margen 1994). However, frequent use of high doses causes psychological as well as physical problems called caffeinism . This condition is found in about 10% of the adults who consume coffee (DSM-IV-TR 2000; Heishman and Henningfield 1992).

The CNS components of caffeine intoxication are recognized as a "psychoactive substance-induced psychiatric disorder" in DSM-IV-TR (2000) criteria established by the American Psychiatric Association. The essential features of this disorder are restlessness, nervousness, excitement, insomnia, flushed face, diuresis, muscle twitching, rambling thoughts and speech, and stomach complaints. These symptoms can occur in some sensitive people following a dose as low as 250 milligrams per day. Caffeine doses in excess of 1 gram per day may cause muscle twitching, rambling thoughts and speech, heart arrhythmias, and motor agitation. With higher doses, hearing ringing in the ears and seeing flashes of light can occur.

Some researchers suggest consuming large quantities of caffeine is associated with cancers of the bladder, ovaries, colon, and kidneys. These claims have not been reliably substantiated (Gurin 1994; Margen 1994).

caffeinism
symptoms caused by taking high chronic doses of caffeine

One problem with many such studies is that they assess the effect of coffee consumption on cancers rather than the effect of caffeine itself. Because coffee contains so many different chemicals, it is impossible to determine specifically the effect of caffeine in such research (Gurin 1994). Other reports claim that caffeine promotes cyst formation in women's breasts. Although these conclusions also have been challenged, many clinicians advise patients with breast cysts to avoid caffeine (Margen 1994). Finally, some reports indicate that very high doses of caffeine given to pregnant laboratory animals can cause stillbirths or offspring with low birth weights or limb deformities. Studies found that moderate consumption of caffeine (<300 milligrams per day) did not significantly affect human fetal development (Mills 1993); however, intake of more than 300 milligrams per day during pregnancy has been associated with an increase in spontaneous fetal loss (*Consumer Reports* 1997). Mothers are usually advised to avoid or at least reduce caffeine use during pregnancy (Margen 1994).

Based on the information available, no strong evidence exists to suggest that moderate use of caffeine leads to disease (Margen 1994). There are, however, implications that people with existing severe medical problems—psychiatric disorders (such as severe anxiety, panic attacks, and schizophrenia), cardiovascular disease, and possibly breast cysts—are at greater risk when consuming caffeine. Realistically, other elements, such as alcohol and fat consumption and smoking, are much more likely to cause serious health problems (Gurin 1994).

Caffeine Dependence

Caffeine causes limited dependence, which, for most people, is relatively minor compared with that of the potent stimulants; thus, the abuse potential of caffeine is also much lower and dependence is less likely to interfere with normal daily routines (Daly and

Fredholm 1998). Consequently, 50% of those consuming one to three cups of coffee each day develop headaches when withdrawing and 10% become significantly depressed, anxious, or fatigued without their coffee. Some people experience elements of withdrawal every morning before their first cup (*Consumer Reports* 1997). However, caffeine is so readily available and socially accepted (almost expected) that the high quantity of consumption has produced many modestly dependent users (Holtzman 1990). The degree of physical dependence on caffeine is highly variable but related to dose. With typical caffeine withdrawal, adverse effects can persist for several days (see Table 11.6). Although these symptoms are unpleasant, they usually are not severe enough to prevent most people from giving up their coffee or cola drinks. It is noteworthy that two-thirds of those patients who are treated for caffeinism relapse into their caffeine-consuming habits (Heishman and Henningfield 1992).

Variability in Responses

Caffeine is eventually absorbed entirely from the gastrointestinal tract after oral consumption. In most users, 90% of the drug reaches the bloodstream within 20 minutes and is distributed into the brain and throughout the body very quickly (Sawynok and Yaksh 1993). The rate of absorption of caffeine from the stomach and intestines differs from person to person by as much as six-fold. Such wide variations in the rate at which caffeine enters the blood from the stomach likely account for much of the variability in responses to this drug.

■ OTC SYMPATHOMIMETICS

Although often overlooked, the sympathomimetic decongestant drugs included in OTC products such as cold, allergy, and diet aid medications have stimulant properties like those of caffeine (Appelt 1993). For most people, the CNS impact of these drugs is minor, but for those people who are very sensitive to these drugs, they can cause jitters and interfere with sleep. For such individuals, OTC products containing the sympathomimetics should be avoided before bedtime.

The common OTC sympathomimetics are shown in Table 11.7 and include ephedrine. In the past, OTC agents were packaged to look like amphetamines (called *look-alike drugs*) and legally sold on the "street," usually to children or high school students. Although much less potent than amphetamines (although they can be used as precursor chemicals to make methamphetamine), these minor stimulants can be abused and have caused deaths. Attempts to regulate look-alike drugs resulted in passage of the federal and state Imitation Controlled Substances Acts. These statutes prohibit the packaging of OTC sympathomimetics to look like amphetamines.

These laws have not resolved the problem, however. Other products containing the OTC sympathomimetics are promoted on the street as "harmless speed" and "OTC uppers." It is likely that use of such products can lead to the abuse of more potent stimulants.

■ HERBAL STIMULANTS

Some OTC sympathomimetics occur naturally and are also found in herbal stimulants sold by mail and in novelty stores, beauty salons, health food stores and on-line. (Gugliotta 2000; Lane 1996). These pills are sold under names such as "Cloud 9," "Ultimate Xphoria," and "Herbal Ecstasy;" and contain stimulants such as ephedrine, ephedra, or *ma huang* (Gugliotta 2000; *Pharmacy Times* 1996; Sprague et al. 1998). These products are particularly promoted

TABLE 11.6 Caffeine Withdrawal Syndrome

SYMPTOM	DURATION
Headache	Several days to 1 week
Decreased alertness	2 days
Decreased vigor	2 days
Fatigue and lethargy	2 days
Nervousness	2 days

Source: Based on Holtzman, S. "Caffeine as a Model Drug of Abuse." *Trends in Pharmacological Sciences* 11 (1990): 355–6.

TABLE 11.7 Common OTC Sympathomimetics

DRUG	OTC PRODUCT (FORM)
Ephedrine	Decongestant (oral, nasal spray or drops)
Levodesoxyephedrine	Decongestant (nasal inhalant)
Naphazoline	Decongestant (nasal spray or drops)
Oxymetazoline	Decongestant (nasal spray or drops)
Phenylephrine	Decongestant (oral, nasal spray or drops, eye drops)
Pseudoephedrine	Decongestant (oral)
Tetrahydrozoline	Decongestant (eye drops)
Xylometazoline	Decongestant (nasal spray or drops)

Source: Based on Knodel, L. C. "Cough, Cold and Allergy Products." In *Nonprescription Product. Formulations and Features,* '97–'98. Washington, DC: American Pharmaceutical Association, 1997.

to high school and college students as natural highs to be used as diet aids, energy boosters, or performance enhancers for athletics. Excessive use of these products can cause seizures, heart attacks, and strokes (Gugliotta 2000). In fact, several deaths and many cases of severe reactions have been reported in the United States from excessive use of these products (Gugliotta 2000). The FDA recently issued a warning about the dangers of these products but has not been able to remove herbal stimulants from the market because of a 1994 federal law that prohibits such action until the FDA conclusively proves the dangers of these substances (Gugliotta 2000). As of 2000, 12 states designated ephedrine-only products as controlled substances, but most states permit OTC dispensing of these products (Gugliotta 2000). However, even though the efforts of FDA to control distribution of these herbal stimulants have been curtailed, there have been numerous law suits filed against herbal companies that manufacture products containing *ma huang* and the drug ephedrine. These legal actions claim that such products have caused serious illness and even death. Several of these lawsuits have been settled out of court reportedly for millions of dollars (Gugliotta 2000). Because ephedrine can be converted into methamphetamine, the Comprehensive Methamphetamine Act passed in 1996 regulates the amount of ephedrine that can be purchased or sold at one time (Sprague et al. 1998).

Discussion Questions

1. Should the FDA continue to approve amphetamines for the treatment of obesity? Why?

2. How are methamphetamine and Ecstasy similar, and how do they differ?

3. What are the dangers of designer drugs in general, and of designer amphetamines in particular?

4. What have past experiences taught us about cocaine? Do you think we have finally learned our lesson concerning this drug?

5. Why does the method of cocaine administration make a difference in how a user is affected by this drug? Use examples to substantiate your conclusions.

6. Why do people use crack cocaine, and what are the major toxicities caused by use of high doses of this stimulant?

7. How is cocaine dependence treated? What are the rationales for the treatments?

8. How does caffeine compare with cocaine and amphetamine as a CNS stimulant?

9. Because of caffeine's potential for abuse, do you think the FDA should control it more tightly? Defend your answer.

10. Do you feel that herbal stimulants, such as ephedra and *ma huang* should be available OTC? Explain your answer.

Key Terms

uppers **264**

anorexiants **265**

behavioral stereotypy **265**

narcolepsy **266**

speed **267**

precursor chemicals **267**

ice **268**

rush **268**

high **268**

run **268**

binge **268**

tweaking **269**

hyperpyrexia **269**

speedballs **271**

club drug **273**

adulterated **278**

freebasing **280**

crack **281**

crack babies **281**

cocaine babies **287**

xanthines **288**

caffeinism **291**

Summary

1 Amphetamines, originally developed as decongestants, are potent stimulants. Some amphetamines have been approved by the FDA as (1) diet aids to treat obesity; (2) treatment for narcolepsy; and (3) treatment for attention deficit hyperactivity disorder in children.

2 In therapeutic doses, amphetamines can cause agitation, anxiety, and panic owing to their effects on the brain; in addition, they can cause an irregular heartbeat, increased blood pressure, heart attack, or stroke. Intense, high-dose abuse of these drugs can cause severe psychotic behavior, stereotypy, and seizures as well as the severe cardiovascular side effects just mentioned.

3 *Speed* refers to the use of intravenous methamphetamine. *Ice* is smoked methamphetamine. A *run* is a pattern of intense, multiple dosing over a period of days that can cause serious neurological, psychiatric, and cardiovascular consequences.

4 *Tweakers* are individuals who repeatedly self-administer methamphetamine to maintain the high. They often have not slept or eaten for days, are very irritable, and sometimes are paranoid or even violent.

5 "Designer" amphetamines are chemical modifications of original amphetamines. Some designer amphetamines, such as Ecstasy, retain abuse potential and are often marketed on the street under exotic and alluring names.

6 In the early 1980s, cocaine was commonly viewed by the U.S. public as a relatively safe drug with glamorous connotations. By the mid-1980s, however, it was apparent that cocaine was a very addicting drug with dangerous side effects.

7 The CNS and cardiovascular effects of both amphetamines and cocaine are similar. However, the effects of cocaine tend to occur more rapidly, be more intense, and wear off more quickly than those of amphetamines.

8 The intensity of the cocaine effect and the likelihood of dependence occurring are directly related to the means of administration. Going from least to most intense effect, the modes of cocaine administration include chewing, snorting, injecting, and smoking (or freebasing).

9 *Crack* is cocaine that has been converted into its "freebase" form and is intended for smoking.

10 Cocaine withdrawal goes through three main stages: (1) the "crash," the initial abstinence phase consisting of depression, agitation, suicidal

thoughts, and fatigue; (2) withdrawal, including mood swings, craving, anhedonia, and obsession with drug seeking; and (3) extinction, when normal pleasure returns and cues trigger craving and mood swings.

11 Treatment of cocaine dependence is highly individualistic and has variable success. The principal strategies include both inpatient and outpatient programs. Drug therapy often is used to relieve short-term cocaine craving and to alleviate mood problems and long-term craving. Psychological counseling and support therapy are essential components of treatment.

12 Caffeine is the most frequently consumed stimulant in the world. It is classified as a xanthine (methylxanthine) and is added to a number of beverages, including water. It is also included in some OTC medicines such as analgesics and "stay-awake" products. Caffeine causes minor stimulation of cardiovascular activity, kidney function (it is a diuretic), and gastric secretion.

13 Dependence on caffeine can occur in people who regularly consume large doses. Withdrawal can cause headaches, agitation, and tremors. Although unpleasant, withdrawal from caffeine dependence is much less severe than that from amphetamine and cocaine dependence.

14 OTC sympathomimetics such as ephedrine and phenylpropanolamine are consumed in high doses and used as "legal" highs. Although not as potent as the major stimulants, the recreational use of these drugs can be dangerous. Some of these drugs are also naturally found in herbal stimulant products.

References

Aldrich, M. and R. Barker. *Cocaine: Chemical, Biological, Social and Treatment Aspects*, edited by S. J. Mule. Cleveland, OH: CRC, 1976: 3–10.

Appelt, G. "Weight Control Products." In *Handbook of Nonprescription Drugs*, 10th ed., edited by T. Covington, 339–49. Washington, DC: American Pharmaceutical Association, 1993.

Beck, J. "The Public Health Implications of MDMA Use." In *Ecstasy*, edited by S. Peroutka, 77–103. Norwell, MA: Kluwar, 1990.

Boot, B., I. McGregor, and W. Hall. "MDMA (Ecstasy) Neurotoxicity: Assessing and Communicating the Risks." *The Lancet* 355 (2000): 1818–21.

Boucher, D. "Cocaine and the Coca Plant." *BioScience* 41 (1991): 72–6.

Byck, R. "Cocaine Use and Research: Three Histories." In *Cocaine: Chemical and Behavioral Aspects*, edited by S. Fisher, 3–17. London: Oxford University Press, 1987.

Bulletin Board. "Prenatal Cocaine Exposure Costs at Least $352 Million per Year." *NIDA Notes* 13 (1999): 14–5.

Cantwell, B. and A. McBride. "Self Detoxification by Amphetamine-Dependent Patients: A Pilot Study." *Drug and Alcohol Dependence* 49 (1998) 157–63.

Carroll, K., B. Rounsaville, and K. Bryant. "Alcoholism in Treatment-Seeking Cocaine Abusers: Clinical and Prognostic Significance." *Journal in Studies of Alcohol* 54 (1993): 199–208.

Carroll, K., B. Rounsaville, L. Gordon, C. Nich, P. Jatlow, R. Bisighini, and F. Gawin. "Psychotherapy and Pharmacotherapy for Ambulatory Cocaine Abusers." *Archives of General Psychiatry* 51 (1994): 177–87.

Castilla, J., G. Barrio, M. Belza, and L. de la Fuente. "Drug and Alcohol Consumption and Sexual Risk Behaviour Among Young Adults: Results from a National Survey." *Drug, Alcohol and Dependence* 56 (1999): 47–53.

CEWG Publications. "Epidemiological Trends in Drug Abuse. Advance Report, December 1999." National Institute on Drug Abuse (May 2000). Available 165.112 .78.61/CEWG/AdvancedRep/1299ADV/1299adv.html.

Christophersen, A. "Amphetamine Designer Drugs—An Overview and Epidemiology." *Toxicology Letters.* 112-113 (2000): 127–31.

Cloud, J. "The Lure of Ecstasy." *Time* 155 (5 June 2000): 60.

Coles, C., K. Platzman, I. Smith, M. James, and A. Falek. "Effects of Cocaine and Alcohol Use in Pregnancy on Neonatal Growth and Neurobehavioral Status." *Neurotoxicology and Teratology* 14 (1992): 22–33.

Consumer Reports. "Coffee Clutch: Should You Worry About All That Caffeine?" *Consumer Reports* 62 (1997): 52–3.

Daly, J., and B. Fredholm. "Caffeine—An Atypical Drug of Dependence." *Drug and Alcohol Dependence* 51 (1998): 199–206.

Davison, D. and A. Parrott. "Ecstasy (MDMA) in Recreational Users: Self-reported Psychological and Physical Effects." *Human Psychopharmacology* 12 (1997): 221–6.

Des Jarlais. "AIDS and HIV Infections in Cocaine Users." In *Cocaine: Scientific and Social Dimensions*, edited by Ciba, 181–95. Ciba Foundations Symposium 166. New York: Wiley, 1992.

DiChiara, G. "Cocaine: Scientific and Social Dimensions." *Trends in Neurological Sciences* 16 (1993): 39.

DMS-IV-TR. "Substance-Related Disorders." In *Diagnostic and Statistical Manual of Mental Disorders*, 4th ed., Text Revision [DSM-IV-TR], A. Francis, chairperson, 223–50. Washington, DC: American Psychiatric Association, 2000.

Farley, C. "Rave New World." *Time* 155 (5 June 2000): 69.

Fields, G. "An Explosion of Chemical 'Ecstasy.'" *USA Today* 18 (25 October 1999): 3-A.

Fischman, M. and R. Foltin. "Self-Administration of Cocaine by Humans: A Laboratory Perspective." In *Cocaine: Scientific and Social Dimensions*, edited by Ciba, 165–80. New York: Wiley, 1992.

Fischman, M. and C. Johanson. "Cocaine." In *Pharmacological Aspects of Drug Dependence: Towards an Integrated Neurobehavior Approach Handbook of Experimental Pharmacology.* edited by C. Schuster and M. Kuhar, 159–95. 1996.

Fumagalli, F., R. Gainetdinov, Y. Wang, K. Valenzano, G. Miller, and M. Caron. "Increased Methamphetamine Neurotoxicity in Heterozygous Vesicular Monoamine Transporter 2 Knock-Out Mice." *Journal of Neuroscience* 19 (1999): 2424–31.

Gamma, A., E. Lehman, R. Pasqual-Marqui, D. Hell, and F. Vollenweider. "Mood State and Brain Electric Activity in Ecstasy Users." *Clinical Neuroscienc and Neuropsychology* 11 (January 2000): 157–62.

Gerra, G., A. Zaimovic, M. Ferri, U. Zambelli, M. Timpano, E. Neri, G. Marzocchi, R. Delsignore, and F. Brambilla "Long-lasting Effects of 3,4-MDMA (Ecstasy) on Serotonin Systems in Humans." *Biologic Psychiatry* 47 (2000): 127–36.

Gilbert, R. "Caffeine Consumption." In *The Methylxanthine Beverages and Foods: Chemistry, Consumption, and Health Effects.* New York: Liss, 1984.

Golding, A. "Two Hundred Years of Drug Abuse." *Journal of the Royal Society of Medicine* 86 (May 1993): 282–6.

Goldstein, A. *Addiction from Biology to Drug Abuse.* New York: Freeman, 1994.

Goldstein, F. "Pharmacological Aspects of Substance Abuse." In *Remington's Pharmaceutical Sciences*, 19th ed., edited by A. R. Genaro, 780–94. Easton, PA: Mack, 1995.

Green, E. "Cocaine, Glamorous Status Symbol of the 'Jet Set,' Is Fast Becoming Many Students' Drug of Choice." *Chronicle of Higher Education* 13 (November 1985): 1, 34.

Grinspoon, L. "Update on Cocaine." Parts 1 & 2. *Harvard Mental Health Letter* 10 (August/September 1993): 1–4.

Grinspoon, L. and J. Bakalar. "The Amphetamines: Medical Use and Health Hazards." In *Amphetamines: Use, Misuse and Abuse*, edited by D. Smith, 18–33. Boston: Hall, 1978.

Grob, C., R. Poland, L. Chang, and T. Ernst. "Psychobiological Effects of 3.4-Methylenedioxymethamphetamine in Humans: Methodological Considerations and Preliminary Observations." *Behavioral Brain Research* 73 (1996): 103–7.

Gugliotta, G. "Ephedra Lawsuits Show Big Increase." *The Washington Post* (23 July 2000): A-1.

Gurin, J. "Coffee and Health." *Consumer Reports* (October 1994): 650–1.

Gygi, M., S. Gygi, M. Johnson, D. Wilkins, J. Gibb, and G. R. Hanson. "Mechanisms for Tolerance to Methamphetamine Effects." *Neuropharmacology* 35 (1996): 751–7.

Hall, W. and J. Hando. "Illicit Amphetamine Use Is a Public Health Problem in Australia." *Medical Journal of Australia* 159 (1993): 643–4.

Hatch, O. "Methamphetamines." (5 August 1999). Available www.orrinhatch.org/leading/legislation/meth.html.

Hatsukami, D. and M. Fischman. "Crack Cocaine and Cocaine Hydrochloride." *Journal of the American Medical Association* 276 (1996): 1580–8.

Haven, P. "Cocaine Still Colombia's Most Lucrative Cash Crop." *Salt Lake Tribune* 251 (24 March 1996): A-8.

Health News. "Caffeine Helps Tension Headaches." *Health News* (15 April 1997): 5.

Heishman, S. and J. Henningfield. "Stimulus Functions of Caffeine in Humans: Relation to Dependence Potential." *Neuroscience and Behavior Review* 16 (1992): 273–87.

Hinkle, J. and S. Winckler. "Vitamin R: The Expansion of Ritalin Abuse." *PRN (Pharmacy Recovery Network)* 4 (April/June 1996): 1.

Hoffman, B. and R. Lefkowitz. "Catecholamines, Sympathomimetics Drugs, and Adrenergic Receptor Antagonists." In *The Pharmacological Basis of Therapeutics*, 9th ed., edited by J. Hardman and L. Limbird, 199–248. New York: McGraw–Hill, 1995.

Holtzman, S. "Caffeine as a Model Drug of Abuse." *Trends in Pharmacological Sciences* 11 (1990): 355–6.

Jansen, K. "Ecstasy (MDMA)." *Drug and Alcohol Dependence* 53 (1999): 121–4.

Johnston, L. "Monitoring the Future." *Drug Trends in 1999 Among American Teens.* Lansing, MI: University of Michigan, 1999. Available from author at 412 Maynard, Ann Arbor, MI.

Johnston, L. University of Michigan Annual National Surveys of Secondary Students. Lansing, MI: University of Michigan, 1996. Available from author at 412 Maynard, Ann Arbor, MI.

Johnston, L. University of Michigan Annual National Surveys of Secondary Students. Lansing, MI: University of Michigan, 1994. Available from author at 412 Maynard, Ann Arbor, MI.

Kennedy, K. "Meth Mania: Even Cops Duck for Cover." *Salt Lake Tribune* (28 June 1999): B-1.

Kihlman, B. *Caffeine and Chromosomes.* Amsterdam: Elsevier, 1977.

Kita, T., M. Takahashi, K. Kubo, G. Wagner, and T. Nakashima. "Hydroxyl Radical Formation Following

Methamphetamine Administration to Rats." *Pharmacological Toxicology* 85 (1999): 133–7.

Kleber, H. "Treatment of Cocaine Abuse: Pharmacotherapy." In *Cocaine Scientific and Social Dimensions*, edited by Ciba, 195–206. Ciba Foundation Symposium 166. New York: Wiley, 1992.

Knight-Ridder News Service, "Experts Call War on Drugs a $32 Billion Stalemate." *Salt Lake Tribune* 244 (21 September 1992): A-2.

Lane, E. "On 'Cloud 9'? Loose Regulation of Ephedrine Raises Some Questions." *Ogden Standard-Examiner* (21 April 1996): 5-E.

Leshner, A. "A Club Drug Alert." *NIDA Notes* 14 (2000): 3–5.

Leshner, A. "Research Shows Effects of Prenatal Cocaine Exposure Are Subtle, but Significant." *NIDA Notes* 14 (1999): 3–4.

Lillie-Blanton, M., J. Anthony, and C. Schuster. "Probing the Meaning of Racial/Ethnic Group Comparisons in Crack Cocaine Smoking." *Journal of the American Medical Association* 269 (1993): 993–7.

Margen, S. "Caffeine: Grounds for Concern." *U.C. Berkeley Wellness Letter* 10 (March 1994): 4.

Mathias, R. "NIDA Initiative Tackles Methamphetamine Use." *NIDA Notes* 13 (1998): 1–4.

Max, B. "This and That: The Ethnopharmacology of Simple Phenethylamines and the Questions of Cocaine and the Human Heart." *Trends in Pharmacological Sciences* 12 (1991): 329–33.

Mayes, L., R. Granger, M. Bornstein, and B. Zucker. "The Problem of Prenatal Cocaine Exposure." *Journal of the American Medical Association* 15 (1992): 406–8.

McCafferty, B. "Methamphetamine." *ONDCP, Drug Policy Information Clearinghouse*. NCJ-1756677 (May 1999): 1–3.

McCann, U., M. Mertl, V. Eligulashvili, and G. Ricaurte. "Cognitive Performance in MDMA (Ecstasy) Users: A Controlled Study." *Psychopharmacology* 143 (1999): 417–25.

McKetin, R. and R. Mattick. "Attention and Memory in Illicit Amphetamine Users: Comparison with Non–drug-using Controls." *Drug and Alcohol Dependence* 50 (1998): 181–4.

Medical Letter. "Acute Reaction to Drugs of Abuse." *Medical Letter* 38 (1996): 43.

Mendelson, J. and N. Mello. "Management of Cocaine Abuse and Dependence." *New England Journal of Medicine* 334 (1996): 965–72.

Mills, J., L. Holmes, J. Aarons, J. Simpson, Z. Brown, L. Peterson, M. Conley, B. Graubard, and R. Knopp. "Moderate Caffeine Use and the Risk of Spontaneous Abortion and Intrauterine Growth Retardation." *Journal of the American Medical Association* 269 (1993): 593–602.

Morland, J. "Toxicity of Drug Abuse-Amphetamine Designer Drugs (Ecstasy): Mental Effects and Consequences of Single Dose Use." *Toxicology Letters* 112-113 (2000): 147–52.

Musto, D. "International Traffic in Coca Through the Early 20th Century." *Drug and Alcohol Dependence* 49 (1998): 145–56.

Nash, M. "How We Get Addicted." *Time* (5 May 1997): 69–76.

Nathan, K., W. Bresnick, and S. Battei. "Cocaine Abuse and Dependence." *CNS Drugs* 10 (1998): 43–59.

National Institute on Drug Abuse Notes. "Comparing Methamphetamine and Cocaine." *NIDA Notes* 13 (June 1998).

NIDA Diagnosis. "Diagnosis and Treatment of Drug Abuse in Family Practice." (May 2000). Available 165.112.78.61/ Diagnosis-Treatment/Diagnosis6.html

NIDA Notes. "Facts About MDMA (Ecstasy)." *NIDA Notes* 14 (1999): 15.

NIDA (National Institute on Drug Abuse). "Cocaine Abuse and Addiction." *NIDA Research Report*. NIH Publication No. 99-4342 (May 1999).

NIDA Research Report. "Methamphetamine Abuse and Addiction." (22 May 2000). Available 165.112.78.61/ ResearchReports/Methamph/methamp5.html.

Parrott, A., E. Sisk, and J. Turner. "Psychobiological Problems in Heavy 'Ecstasy' (MDMA) Polydrug Users." *Drug and Alcohol Dependence* 60 (2000): 105–10.

Parrott, A. "Ecstatic, but Memory-depleted." *The Psychologist* 10 (June 1997): 265.

Pharmacy Times. "New York County Bans Herbal Stimulants." *Pharmacy Times* 62 (1996): 8.

PDR Nonprescription Drugs. Physicians' Desk Reference for Nonprescription Drugs, 21st ed. Montvale, NJ: Medical Economics, 2000.

Prevention Pipeline. "Methamphetamine Update." *The Prevention Pipeline* 10 (September/October 1997): 13–6.

Prevline. "Methamphetamine." *Quick Docs. Prevline, Prevention Online*. (1999). Available http://www.health.org.

Randall, T. "Ecstasy-fueled 'Rave' Parties Become Dances of Death for English Youths." *Journal of the American Medical Association* 268 (1992a): 1505–6.

Randall, T. "'Rave' Scene, Ecstasy Use, Leap Atlantic." *Journal of the American Medical Association* 268 (1992b): 1506.

Reno, J. (U.S. Attorney General). "National Methamphetamine Strategy" (message to the President of the United States). U.S. Department of Justice, Office of the Attorney General (April 1996).

SAMHSA News. "Abuse Treatment Guidelines Released." *SAMHSA* 17 (Summer 1999) 17.

Sands, B. and D. Ciraulo. "Cocaine Drug-Drug Interactions." *Journal of Clinical Psychopharmacology* 12 (1992): 49–55.

Sawynok, J. and T. Yaksh. "Caffeine as an Analgesic Adjuvant: A Review of Pharmacology and Mechanisms of Action." *Pharmacological Reviews* 45 (1993): 43–85.

Schwartz, R., M. Lyenberg, and N. Hoffman. "Crack Use by American Middle-Class Adolescent Polydrug Users." *Journal of Pediatrics* 118 (1991): 150–5.

Seibyl, J., L. Brenner, J. Drystal, R. Johnson, and D. Charney. "Mazindol and Cocaine Addiction in Schizophrenia." *Biological Psychiatry* 31 (1992): 1172–83.

Seigel, R. K. "Treatment of Cocaine Abuse." *Journal of Psychoactive Drugs* 17 (1985): 52.

Shifano, F., L. Furia, G. Forza, N. Minicuci, N., and R. Bricolo. "MDMA ('Ecstasy') Consumption in the Context of Polydrug Abuse: A Report on 50 Patients." *Drug and Alcohol Dependence* 52 (1998): 85–90.

Smith, M., A. Hoeping, K. Johnson, M. Trzcinska, and A. Kozikovski. "Dopaminergic Agents for the Treatment of Cocaine Abuse." *Drug Discovery Technology* 4 (1999): 322–32.

Sprague, J., A. Harrod, and A. Teconchuk. "The Pharmacology and Abuse Potential of Ephedrine." *Pharmacy Times* (May 1998): 72–80.

Stocker, S. "Cocaine Abuse May Lead to Strokes and Mental Deficits." *NIDA Notes* 13 (August 1998): 10–3.

Stocker, S. "Cocaine Activates Different Brain Regions for Rush Versus Craving." *NIDA Notes* 13 (1999): 7–10.

Stocker, S. "Overall Teen Drug Use Stays Level, Use of MDMA and Steroids Increases." *NIDA Notes* 15 (2000): 5.

Swan, N. "Response to Escalating Methamphetamine Abuse Build on NIDA-funded Research." *NIDA Notes* 11 (November/December 1996) 1–12.

Swan, N. "31% of New York Murder Victims Had Cocaine in Their Bodies." *NIDA Notes* 10 (March/April 1995): 4.

Taylor, J. "All-New MDMA FAQ." *Usenet News* (27 May 1994). Available sci.med.pharmacy.

Taylor, K. "Meth Deals Death, Abuse to Children." *The Sunday Oregonian.* 149 (22 August 1999): 1.

USIS Washington File. "Senate Judiciary Committee Introduces New Anti-drug Bill." 1999. Available www.usia.gov/topical/global/drugs/bill.htm.

Van Dyck, C. and R. Byck. "Cocaine." *Scientific American* 246 (1982): 128–41.

Vigh, M. "Utah's Homegrown Meth Labs Creating an Epidemic of Addicted Tots." *Salt Lake Tribune* 260 (1 May 2000): A-1.

Woolverton, W. and K. Johnston. "Neurobiology of Cocaine Abuse." *Trends in Pharmacological Sciences* 13 (1992): 193–200.

Yui, K., et al. "Methamphetamine Psychosis: Spontaneous Recurrence of Paranoid-Hallucinating States and Monoamine Neurotransmitter Function." *Journal of Clinical Psychopharmacology* 17 (1999): 34–43.

Drugs and Society Online is a great source for additional drugs and society information for both students and instructors.
Visit **http://drugsandsociety.jbpub.com** to find a variety of useful tools for learning, thinking, and teaching.

Tobacco

Did You Know?

- ► Approximately 26% of the U.S. population age 12 and older smokes.

- ► Tobacco use is the leading preventable cause of death in the United States.

- ► Tobacco kills more than 430,000 United States citizens each year—more than alcohol, cocaine, heroin, suicide, homicide, fire, car accidents, and AIDS combined.

- ► Nearly 50% of all smokers aged 35 to 69 die prematurely.

- ► Tobacco farming is among the 10 largest legal cash crops in the United States.

- ► Nicotine is one of more than 4000 chemicals found in cigarette smoke.

- ► Nearly 3000 young people in the United States will begin smoking today. Of these individuals, 1000 will lose their lives to diseases caused by smoking.

- ► Individuals who stop smoking before age 50 reduce their risk of dying over the next 15 years by 50%.

- ► Several smoking cessation aids are now available, including nicotine gum, patches, nasal spray, and inhalers. In addition, antidepressants are now used to help with smoking cessation.

Chapter 12

Learning Objectives

On completing this chapter you will be able to:

▶ Describe the social and economic costs of smoking in the United States.

▶ Describe the history of tobacco use.

▶ Explain how the quality of leaf tobacco has changed since the mid-1950s.

▶ Describe the pharmacological effects of nicotine.

▶ List several disease states caused by cigarette smoking.

▶ Explain the consequences of environmental tobacco smoke on nonsmokers.

▶ List several reasons individuals smoke.

▶ List several strategies that aid in smoking cessation.

▶ List the four primary aspects of tobacco control laws at the state level.

Introduction

Tobacco Use: Scope of the Problem

If we do not act decisively today, a hundred years from now our grandchildren and their children will look back and seriously question how people claiming to be committed to public health and social justice will allow the tobacco epidemic to unfold unchecked.
— Dr. Gro Harlem Brundtland, Director General, World Health Organization (WHO), November 1999

Tobacco use is the leading preventable cause of death in the United States. The impact of nicotine addiction in terms of morbidity, mortality, and economic costs to society is staggering. Tobacco kills more than 430,000 United States citizens each year—more than alcohol, cocaine, heroin, suicide, homicide, fire, car accidents, and AIDS combined (NIDA 1998). The American Cancer Society (2000) estimated that nearly 50% of all smokers aged 35 to 69 die prematurely and that smoking may cost individuals 20 to 25 years of their lives.

In addition to these enormous health consequences, there is a significant economic burden; in 1999, tobacco use resulted in more than $50 billion in medical expenditures and another $50 billion in indirect costs (CDC 2000). These costs include hospital, physician, nursing home, prescription drug, and home health care expenditures. These high costs will likely continue and increase in the future because it is estimated that each day, nearly 3000 individuals under the age of 18 will start smoking (NIDA 1998) and many will become addicted. In fact, cigarette smoking is so addictive that 83% of smokers smoke every day; in contrast, only 10% of illicit drug users are daily users (USDHHS 1994).

Although much of this chapter deals with tobacco use in the United States, it is noteworthy that tobacco is used throughout the world and that markets for tobacco sales abroad have expanded in recent years. The WHO estimates that tobacco kills 4 million people a year. By about 2030, that number will escalate to 10 million a year, a figure greater

WHO estimates that by 2030, tobacco will kill 10 million people a year worldwide. Early exposure increases the chance that young people will become regular adult smokers.

than the combined death toll from tuberculosis, malaria, and maternal and major childhood conditions. Over 70% of the tobacco-associated deaths will occur in the developing world (WHO 2000).

■ CURRENT TOBACCO USE IN THE UNITED STATES

In 1999, 66.8 million Americans, or 30.2% of the population aged 12 years and older, reported current use of a tobacco product. Among these individuals, 2.4 million smoked tobacco in pipes, 7.6 million used smokeless tobacco, 12.1 million smoked cigars and 57 million smoked cigarettes (SAMHSA 2000). Smoking among adults decreased dramatically from 42% of the population in 1965 to 25% in 1995. During this period, the percentage of smokers among the adult male population declined from 52% to 27%;

the percentage of adult female smokers declined from 34% to 23%. Additional significant findings related to smoking include the following:

- Approximately 151 million people aged 12 years and older (68% of the population) have tried smoking cigarettes, and 67 million (30% of the population) have smoked cigarettes within the past year (SAMHSA 2000).

- People aged 18 to 25 have the highest rates of smoking. According to a recent SAMHSA survey, nearly 45% of persons aged 18 to 25 report the use of a tobacco product within the last month (SAMHSA 2000).

- Males are more likely than females to report the use of any tobacco product. In 1999, 36.5% of males aged 12 and older were current tobacco users compared with 24.3% of females (SAMHSA 2000).

Past month United States cigarette use among individuals aged 12 or older by region is as follows: approximately 28% of the population in the North Central region, 26% in the South region, 23% in the West region, and 25% in the Northeast region. Level of educational attainment was also correlated with tobacco usage: 30% of adults aged 26 or older who did not complete high school smoked cigarettes whereas only 13% of college graduates smoked. The data also show that the average age of people who began daily cigarette use was 17.6 years in 1993, whereas the average age was 20 years in 1998. Thus, daily cigarette use appears to be occurring at a later age (SAMHSA 2000). (Additional information on the groups that use tobacco is discussed later in this chapter.)

The year 1999 marked the first time that SAMHSA reported information on use of specific cigarette brands, especially among young people. Of current smokers aged 12 to 17 years, Marlboro was reported as their usual brand. Newport and Camel was reported by 21.6% and 9.8% of youths, respectively. No other cigarette brand was reported by even 2% of youths (SAMHSA 2000).

■ THE HISTORY OF TOBACCO USE

Like alcohol, tobacco has a long history of use in the Americas and is indigenous to the United States. In fact, tobacco was one of the New World's contribu-

tions to the rest of humanity. The word *tobacco* may have come from *tabacco*, which was a two-pronged tube used by the natives of Central America to take snuff. Columbus reported receiving tobacco leaves from the natives of San Salvador in 1492. However, the native peoples had been smoking the leaves for many centuries before Columbus arrived. Practically all native people, from Paraguay to Quebec, used tobacco. The Mayans regarded tobacco smoke as divine incense that would bring rain in the dry season. The oldest known representation of a smoker is a stone carving from a Mayan temple, which shows a priest puffing on a ceremonial pipe. The Aztecs used tobacco in folk medicine and religious ritual.

Indeed, Native Americans used tobacco in every manner known: smoked as cigars and cigarettes (wrapped in corn husks) and in pipes; as a syrup to be swallowed or applied to the gums; chewed and snuffed; and administered rectally as a ceremonial enema (O'Brien et al. 1992; Schultes 1978).

In the 1600s, Turkey, Russia, and China all imposed death penalties for smoking. In Turkey, smoking was introduced in the 1600s, spread in popularity, and instantly created two camps. On the one hand, poets praised tobacco as one of four elements of the world of pleasure: tobacco, opium, coffee, and wine. Priests, on the other hand, were violently opposed to this substance. They created the legend that tobacco grew from Mohammed's spittle, after he was bitten by a viper, sucked out the venom, and spat.

Murad (Amurath) IV, known as Murad the Cruel, who reigned during 1623–1640, executed many of his subjects caught smoking:

> Whenever the Sultan went on his travels or on a military expedition, his halting-laces were always distinguished by a terrible increase in the number of executions. Even on the battlefield, he was fond of surprising men in the act of smoking, . . . he would punish them by beheading, hanging, quartering, or crushing their hands and feet and leaving them helpless between the lines. . . . Nevertheless, in spite of all the horrors of this lust [smoking] that seemed to increase with age, the passion for smoking still persisted. . . . Even the fear of death was of no avail with the passionate devotees of the habit. (Corti 1931)

The Romanov tsars publicly tortured smokers and exiled them to Siberia. The Chinese decapitated anyone caught dealing in tobacco with the "outer barbarians." Yet smoking continued to grow to epidemic proportions. Despite their opposition to anything foreign, the Chinese became the heaviest smokers in Asia, thus facilitating the later spread of opium smoking. Thus, no nation whose population has learned to use tobacco products has been successful in outlawing use or getting people to stop.

Snuffing first became fashionable in France during the reign of Louis XIII and spread throughout the European aristocracy. Snuffing was regarded as daintier and more elegant than constantly exhaling smoke. King Louis XIV, however, detested all forms of tobacco and would not permit its use in his presence. (He would have banned it, but he needed the tax revenue that tobacco brought in.) His sister-in-law, Charlotte of Orleans, was one of the few at court who agreed with him. As she wrote to her sister, "It is better to take no snuff at all than a little; for it is certain that he who takes a little will soon take much, and that is why they call it 'the enchanted herb,' for those who take it are so taken by it that they cannot go without it." Napoleon is said to have used seven pounds of snuff per month (Corti 1931).

■ POPULARITY IN THE WESTERN WORLD

When tobacco reached Europe, it was at first merely a curiosity, but its use spread rapidly. Europeans had no name for the process of inhaling smoke, so they called this "drinking" smoke. Perhaps the first European to inhale tobacco smoke was Rodrig de Jerez, a member of Columbus's crew. He had seen people smoking in Cuba and brought the habit to Portugal. When he smoked in Portugal, his friends, seeing smoke coming from his mouth, believed he was possessed by the devil. As a result, he was placed in jail for several years (Heimann 1960; O'Brien et al. 1992).

In 1559, the French ambassador to Portugal, Jean Nicot, grew interested in this novel plant and sent one as a gift to Catherine de Medici, Queen of France. The plant was named *Nicotiana tabacum* after him.

The next several hundred years saw a remarkable increase in the use of tobacco. Portuguese sailors smoked it and left tobacco seeds scattered around the world. Over the next 150 years, the Portuguese introduced tobacco to trade with India, Brazil, Japan, China, Arabia, and Africa. Many large tobacco plantations around the world were started by the Portuguese at this time.

An early Christian religious leader, Bishop Bartolome de las Casas (1474–1566), reported that Spanish settlers in Hispaniola (Haiti) smoked rolled tobacco leaves in cigar form like the natives. When the bishop asked about this disgusting habit, the settlers replied that they found it impossible to give up.

As the use of tobacco spread, so did the controversy about whether it was bad or good. Tobacco use inspired the first major drug controversy of global dimensions. As a medicine, tobacco was at first almost universally accepted. Nicholas Monardes, in his description of New World plants (dated 1574), recommended tobacco as an infallible cure for 36 different maladies. It was described as a holy, healing herb—a special remedy sent by God to humans.

Opponents of tobacco use disputed its medical value. They pointed out that tobacco was used in the magic and religion of Native Americans. Tobacco was attacked as an evil plant, an invention of the devil. King James I of England was fanatically opposed to smoking. In an attempt to limit tobacco use, he raised the import tax on tobacco and also sold the right to collect the tax (Austin 1978; O'Brien et al. 1992).

Nevertheless, tobacco use increased. By 1614, the number of tobacco shops in London had mushroomed to over 7000, and demand for tobacco usually outstripped supply. Tobacco was literally worth its weight in silver; to conserve it, users smoked it in pipes with very small bowls. Use of tobacco grew in other areas of the world as well.

In 1642, Pope Urban VIII issued a formal decree forbidding the use of tobacco in church under penalty of immediate excommunication. This decree was in response to the fact that priests and worshippers had been staining church floors with tobacco juice. One priest in Naples sneezed so hard after taking snuff that he vomited on the altar in full sight of the congregation. In response, Pope Innocent X issued another edict against tobacco use in 1650, but the clergy and the laity continued to take snuff and smoke. Finally, in 1725, Pope Benedict XIII, himself a smoker and "snuff-taker," annulled all previous edicts against tobacco (Austin 1978).

■ HISTORY OF TOBACCO USE IN AMERICA

Tobacco played a significant role in the successful colonization of the United States (Langton 1991). In 1610, John Rolfe was sent to Virginia to set up a tobacco industry. At first, the tobacco planted in Virginia was a native species, *Nicotiana rustica*, that was harsh and did not sell well. But in 1612, Rolfe managed to obtain some seeds of the Spanish tobacco species *Nicotiana tabacum* , and by 1613, the success of the tobacco industry and the Virginia colony was ensured.

The history of tobacco smoking in the United States is rich in terms of the tremendous number of laws, rules, regulations, and customs that have arisen around the habit of smoking. Many states have had laws prohibiting the use of tobacco by young people as well as women of any age. In the 1860s, for instance, it was illegal in Florida for anyone under the age of 21 to smoke cigarettes. A 20-year-old caught smoking could be taken to court and compelled to reveal his source (the cigarette "pusher"). In Pennsylvania, as in South Carolina, any child not informing on his or her cigarette supplier was a criminal.

Up to the turn of the 20th century, chewing and snuffing were the most common ways of using tobacco in the United States. In 1897, half of all tobacco was prepared for chewing. Law required that spittoons be placed in all public buildings until 1945 ("Cigars" 1988).

An example of a spittoon from the early 1900s that would have been placed in a public building.

Cigars became popular in the United States in the early 1800s. Cigar manufacturers fought the introduction of cigarettes for many years. They spread rumors that cigarettes contained opium, were made with tobacco from discarded cigar butts, and were made with paper made by Chinese lepers, and so on. By about 1920, cigarette consumption started to exceed that of cigars. The introduction of the cigarette-rolling machine in 1883 spurred cigarette consumption because cigarettes became cheaper than cigars. By 1885, a billion cigarettes a year were being produced. Americans consumed more than 815 billion cigarettes in 1988. More recent estimates show that the number of cigarettes manufactured in the United States rose from 667 billion in 1983 to 695 billion in 1991 to 702 billion from 1992 to 1993. Although domestic consumption has dropped, the increases result from foreign demand of U.S. tobacco leaf and U.S. cigarette manufacturers offering discounted cigarettes and lower prices on premium brands.

Tobacco Production

Tobacco farming is among the 10 largest legal cash crops in the United States. Tobacco grown in North Carolina, Kentucky, Tennessee, South Carolina, and Virginia account for 89% of tobacco production (NCSE 1999). Although there are more than 60 species of plants, *Nicotiana tabacum* is the primary species of tobacco cultivated in the United States. Its mature leaves are 1 to 2.5 feet long. The nicotine content ranges from 0.3% to 7%, depending on the variety, leaf position on the stalk (the higher the position, the more nicotine), and growing conditions. The flavor of tobacco comes from nicotianin, also called *tobacco camphor.*

After harvesting and drying, tobacco leaves are shredded, blown clean of foreign matter and stems, remoistened with glycerine or other chemical agents, and packed in huge wooden barrels called *hogsheads.* These barrels are placed in storehouses for 1 to 2 years to age, during which time the tobacco becomes darker and loses moisture, nico-

KEY TERMS

Nicotiana tabacum
primary species of tobacco cultivated in the United States

tine, and other volatile substances. When aging has been completed, moisture is again added and the tobacco is blended with other varieties.

There are many types of tobacco, with varying characteristics of harshness, mildness, and flavor. Bright , also called flue-cured or Virginia , is the most common type used in cigarettes. (Flue-cured tobacco is heated in curing sheds to speed the drying process.) Developed just before the Civil War, this technique made tobacco smoke more readily inhalable.

The amount of leaf tobacco in a cigarette has declined by roughly 25% since 1956. There are two reasons for this drop, not including the introduction of filtertip cigarettes. (If a filtertip is the same size as a plain cigarette, it has about one-third less tobacco.) The first reason is the use of reconstituted sheets of tobacco. Parts of the tobacco leaves and stems that were discarded in earlier years are now ground up, combined with many other ingredients to control factors such as moisture, flavor, and color, and then rolled out as a flat, homogenized sheet of reconstituted tobacco. This sheet is shredded and mixed with regular leaf tobacco, thus reducing production costs. Nearly one-fourth of the tobacco in a cigarette comes from tobacco scraps made into reconstituted sheets.

A second technological advance has further reduced the amount of tobacco needed. This process, called puffing , is based on freeze-drying the tobacco and then blowing air or an inert gas, such as carbon dioxide, into it. The gas expands, or puffs up, the plant cells so they take up more space, are lighter, and can absorb additives better.

Tobacco additives are not controlled by the Food and Drug Administration (FDA) or any other government agency. Additives may include extracts of tobacco, as well as nontobacco flavors such as licorice, cocoa, fruit, spices, and floral compositions.

(Licorice was first used in tobacco as a preservative around 1830 and became appreciated only later as a sweetener.) Synthetic flavoring compounds also may be used.

In the 1870s, a "cigarette girl" could roll about four cigarettes per minute by hand. When James Duke leased and improved the first cigarette-rolling machine in 1883, he could make about 200 cigarettes per minute. This advance was the last link in the chain of development leading to the modern American blended cigarette. Today's machines make more than 3600 uniform cigarettes per minute.

Tar and nicotine levels in cigarettes have dropped considerably over the past 40 years (Bartecchi et al. 1995; Palfai and Jankiewicz 1991). Most cigarettes today are low-tar and low-nicotine types. The filtertip, in which the filter is made of cellulose or in some cases charcoal, has also become common; the vast majority of all cigarettes sold currently in the United States are filtertips. The filter does help remove some of the harmful substances in smoke, but most, such as carbon monoxide, pass through into the mouth and lungs. To date, 43 cancer-causing substances have been identified out of the 4700 substances used in cigarettes (Bartecchi et al. 1995). The health consequences of many more substances found in cigarettes have not been adequately analyzed.

U.S. cigarette consumption in 1998 was estimated at 470 billion cigarettes, 2% less than the previous year. Declines in consumption have been attributed to health concerns, aggressive anti-smoking campaigns, price increases, and decreased social acceptance of smoking. Figure 12.1 shows the relationship between smoking rates and major smoking and health events. Cigarette production fell 6% in 1998 to an estimated 680 billion pieces, about the 1990 level, due to a decline in exports and domestic consumption. Approximately two-thirds of U.S. cigarette output goes to the domestic market with the remainder going for export. Cigarette exports in 1998 totaled 201 billion pieces, down 7%. The leading U.S. cigarette export markets in 1998 were Japan, Belgium/Luxembourg (a major transshipment point for cigarettes destined to other European markets), Lebanon, Saudi Arabia, and the Russian Federation. The United States is not a significant importer of cigarettes (USDA 1999).

KEY TERMS

bright, flue-cured, or Virginia
the most common type of tobacco used in cigarettes

puffing
a method for reducing the amount of tobacco in cigarette production

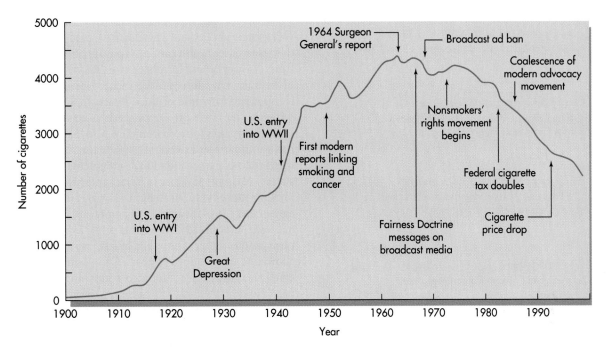

FIGURE 12.1

Adult per capita cigarette consumption and major smoking and health events, United States, 1900–1999.

Note: The 1999 data are preliminary.

Sources: Adapted from Warner 1985; U.S. Department of Health and Human Services 1989; Creek et al. 1994; U.S. Department of Agriculture 2000. U.S. Department of Health and Human Services. Reducing Tobacco Use: A Report of the Surgeon General. Atlanta, GA: USDHHS, CDC, National Center for Chronic Disease Prevention and Health Promotion, Office on Smoking and Health, 2000.

Government Regulation

In the early 1960s, attitudes toward tobacco use began to change in the United States. Before this time, tobacco was perceived as being devoid of any negative consequences. After years of study and hundreds of research reports about the effects of smoking, the Advisory Committee to the U.S. Surgeon General reported in 1964 that cigarette smoking is a cause of lung cancer and laryngeal cancer in men, a probable cause of lung cancer in women, and the most important cause of chronic bronchitis. The committee stated that "cigarette smoking is a health hazard of sufficient importance in the United States to warrant appropriate remedial action." In 1965, Congress passed legislation setting up the National Clearinghouse for Smoking and Health. This organization has the responsibility of monitoring, compiling, and reviewing the world's medical literature on the health consequences of smoking.

Reports were published by this clearinghouse in 1967, 1968, and 1969. The statistical evidence presented in 1969 made it difficult for Congress to avoid warning the public that smoking was dangerous to their health. Since November 1, 1970, all cigarette packages and cartons have had to carry this label: "Warning: The Surgeon General Has Determined That Cigarette Smoking Is Dangerous to Your Health." In 1984, Congress enacted legislation requiring cigarette advertisements and packages to post four distinct warnings (Figure 12.2), which are to be rotated every 3 months.

Further pressure on Congress prompted laws to be passed that prohibited advertising tobacco on radio and television after January 2, 1971. The intent

SURGEON GENERAL'S WARNING: Quitting Smoking Now Greatly Reduces Serious Risks to Your Health.

SURGEON GENERAL'S WARNING: Smoking Causes Lung Cancer, Heart Disease, Emphysema, and May Complicate Pregnancy.

SURGEON GENERAL'S WARNING: Smoking by Pregnant Women May Result in Fetal Injury, Premature Birth, and Low Birth Weight.

SURGEON GENERAL'S WARNING: Cigarette Smoke Contains Carbon Monoxide.

FIGURE 12.2

Warnings on cigarette labels. Four warnings must be rotated on cigarette packages. The messages are based on the reports of the U.S. Surgeon General on *The Health Consequences of Smoking* (1985) and went into effect on October 12, 1985.

was to limit the media's ability to make smoking seem glamorous and sophisticated. The loss in revenue to radio and television was enormous.

The 1979 publication *Smoking and Health: A Report of the Surgeon General* gave what was then up-to-date information on research about the effects of tobacco on cardiovascular disease, bronchopulmonary disease, cancer, peptic ulcer, and pregnancy. It also emphasized the increase in smoking by women and girls over the preceding 15 years. The 1981 U.S. Surgeon General's report, *The Changing Cigarette*, gave further information, and the 1985 report, *The Health Consequences of Smoking*, gave research findings showing the relationship of smoking, cancer, and chronic lung disease in the workplace.

KEY TERMS

nicotine
a colorless, highly volatile liquid alkaloid

Over the years, private insurance companies, as well as state and federal agencies, have paid billions of dollars to cover health care costs presumably resulting from diseases caused by tobacco use. Recently, a series of lawsuits have forced large tobacco companies to compensate for some of these losses. In a landmark settlement in 1998, 46 states reached an agreement with five major tobacco companies to pay a settlement estimated at exceeding $200 billion. This agreement follows earlier individual settlements with four states—Mississippi, Florida, Texas, and Minnesota—totaling more than $40 billion. As part of the 1998 agreement, "Big Tobacco" companies are no longer allowed outdoor advertisements such as billboards near stadiums or shopping malls, nor are they allowed to use cartoons (e.g., Joe Camel) in the packaging and advertising of tobacco-containing products (see "Holding the Line"). In addition, the sale and distribution of clothing and merchandise such as caps and T-shirts with brand name logos is no longer permitted (Master Settlement Agreement 1998). This settlement did not cover individual, federal, or class-action suits but instead only suits filed by the states themselves. In addition, the cigarette manufacturers that signed the settlement agreement also agreed to negotiate with the tobacco-growing states to establish a trust fund to compensate tobacco farmers for financial losses as a result of the anticipated decline in cigarette consumption.

Since 1985, numerous other reports on smoking and health by the U.S. Surgeon General have been issued; they invariably repeat the assertions about the devastating effects of cigarette smoking. For a historical summation of the developments between cigarette consumption and efforts to diminish cigarette use, see Table 12.1.

Pharmacology of Nicotine

■ NICOTINE ADMINISTRATION

In 1828, nicotine was discovered to be one component of tobacco. It is a colorless, highly volatile liquid alkaloid. It is one of more than 4000 chemicals found in the smoke from tobacco products such as cigarettes (NIDA 1998). When smoked, nicotine enters

(*text continued on page 314*)

HOLDING THE LINE

"Arming our children with the tools they need to say no to tobacco products is the most effective way I know to prevent them from picking up this deadly habit. As we work to pass comprehensive legislation to reduce youth smoking, President Clinton and I are committed to finding new ways to teach children that saying 'no' to tobacco means saying 'yes' to a longer, healthier life."—former Vice President Gore, April 1, 1998

In April 1998, former Vice President Gore attended a National "Kick Butts Day" event, joining more than 700 students in celebration of kids fighting back against the marketing and advertising of tobacco products to young people. Both Vice President Gore and President Clinton were strong proponents of comprehensive legislation to stop young Americans from smoking before they start; an effort that the White House claimed would save 1 million lives. In addition, the Vice President promoted several efforts aimed at reducing youth tobacco use: the National Education Association's "Kids Act to Control Tobacco" program that motivates and mobilizes teachers, students (grades 6–8), and parents to become tobacco control advocates at the grass-roots level; a Girl Scouts project to make resources available to kids and adults to show why smoking is so dangerous; Girls Incorporated's "teach-in" effort coordinated as part of their Stamp Out Smoking campaign; and new ads to deter teen smoking.

As announced in 1998, the Clinton-Gore plan for comprehensive tobacco legislation included five key principles:

1. A comprehensive plan to reduce youth smoking by raising the price of packs of cigarettes by up to $1.50 over 10 years through a

Former Vice President Al Gore stands with a student in Jacksonville, Florida in 1998 as he announces the federal government ad campaign to cut underage smoking.

combination of annual payments and tough penalties on the tobacco industry.

2. Full authority for the Food and Drug Administration to regulate tobacco products.

3. Changes in the way the tobacco industry does business, including ending marketing and promotion to kids.

4. Progress toward other public health goals, including biomedical and cancer research, reduction of second-hand smoke, promotion of smoking cessation programs, and other urgent priorities.

5. Protection for tobacco farmers and their communities.

It is very likely that reforms such as those mentioned above will be among the first of many regulating tobacco products in the years to come.

Source: The White House at Work; (2 April 1998). Available http://www.white-house.gov/WH/Work/040298.html.

TABLE 12.1 Significant Developments Related to Smoking and Health 1964–1996

1964	• *Smoking and Health: Report of the Advisory Committee to the Surgeon General,* the first major U.S. report on smoking and health, is published. It concludes that cigarette smoking is a cause of lung cancer in men and a suspected cause in women, and identifies many other causal relationships and smoking-disease associations. The report calls for "appropriate" remedial action. • The National Interagency Council on Smoking and Health, the first national antismoking coalition, is formed. • Cigarette manufacturers establish a voluntary Cigarette Advertising Code for television and radio. • The American Medical Association (AMA) officially calls smoking "a serious health hazard." • The State Mutual Life Assurance Company becomes the first company to offer life insurance to nonsmokers at discounted rates.
1965	• Congress passes the Federal Cigarette Labeling and Advertising Act, requiring the following health warning on all cigarette packages: "Caution: Cigarette Smoking May Be Hazardous to Your Health." • Public Health Service (PHS) establishes the National Clearinghouse for Smoking and Health.
1966	• A health warning label appears on all cigarette packages.
1967	• A report of the Surgeon General concludes that smoking is the principal cause of lung cancer. • The Federal Communications Commission (FCC) rules that the Fairness Doctrine applies to cigarette advertising. Stations broadcasting cigarette commercials must donate air time to anti-smoking messages. • The Federal Trade Commission (FTC) releases the first report on tar and nicotine yield in cigarette brands.
1968	• Action on Smoking and Health is formed to serve as a legal action arm for the antismoking community.
1969	• The National Association of Broadcasters (NAB) endorses phasing-out cigarette ads on television and radio.
1970	• The Public Health Cigarette Smoking Act of 1969 is enacted, banning cigarette advertising on television and radio and requiring a stronger health warning on cigarette packages: "Warning: The Surgeon General Has Determined That Cigarette Smoking Is Dangerous to Your Health." • The World Health Organization (WHO) takes a public position against cigarette smoking.
1971	• The Surgeon General proposes a government ban on smoking in public places. • Cigarette advertising ends on radio and television. Fairness Doctrine antismoking messages also end. • Cigarette manufacturers' voluntary agreement to list tar and nicotine yield in all advertising becomes effective.
1972	• A report of the Surgeon General identifies involuntary smoking as a health risk. • Under a consent order with the FTC, six major cigarette companies agree to include a "clear and conspicuous" health warning in all cigarette advertisements.
1973	• Congress enacts the Little Cigar Act of 1973, banning little cigar ads from television and radio. • The Civil Aeronautics Board requires "no smoking" sections on all commercial airline flights. • Arizona becomes the first state to restrict smoking in a number of public places and the first to do so explicitly because environmental tobacco smoke exposure is a public hazard.
1975	• Cigarettes are discontinued in K-rations and C-rations to soldiers and sailors.

1977
- The American Cancer Society (ACS) sponsors the first national "Great American Smokeout."
- Doctors Ought to Care is formed to provide a focal point for physicians' antismoking advocacy, especially through counteradvertising.

1978
- The National Clearinghouse for Smoking and Health is renamed the Office on Smoking and Health.
- Utah enacts the first state law banning tobacco advertisements on any billboard, streetcar sign, streetcar, or bus.

1979
- Minneapolis and St. Paul become the first cities to ban the distribution of free cigarette samples.

1980
- A report of the Surgeon General highlights health consequences of smoking to women.
- PHS announces "Health Objectives for the Nation," which include a goal to reduce smoking to below 25% of adults by 1990.
- The FTC begins testing cigarettes for carbon monoxide yields.

1981
- A report of the Surgeon General focuses on "The Changing Cigarette." It concludes that no cigarette or level of tobacco consumption is safe.

1982
- A report of the Surgeon General focuses exclusively on smoking and cancer.
- Congress temporarily doubles the federal excise tax on cigarettes to 16 cents per pack, to take effect from January 1, 1983, to October 1, 1985. It marks the first such increase since 1951.
- ACS, American Lung Association (ALA), and American Heart Association (AHA) form a tripartite Coalition on Smoking OR Health, primarily to coordinate federal legislative activities related to smoking control.
- The National Cancer Institute (NCI) reorganizes its smoking research program as the Smoking, Tobacco and Cancer Program to focus on smoking behavior research and interventions.

1983
- A report of the Surgeon General focuses exclusively on smoking and cardiovascular disease.
- San Francisco passes a law to include smoking restrictions in private workplaces.

1984
- A report of the Surgeon General focuses exclusively on smoking and chronic obstructive lung disease.
- Congress enacts the Comprehensive Smoking Education Act, requiring rotational health warnings on cigarette packages and advertisements.
- The FDA approves nicotine polacrilex gum as a "new drug."
- The Surgeon General announces his goal of a smoke-free society by 2000.

1985
- A report of the Surgeon General covers smoking and occupational exposures.
- Minnesota enacts the first state legislation to earmark a portion of the state cigarette excise tax to support antismoking programs.
- STAT (Stop Teenage Addiction to Tobacco) is formed to focus on teenage tobacco use.

1986
- A report of the Surgeon General focuses exclusively on the health consequences of involuntary smoking.
- A special report of the Surgeon General documents the health consequences of using smokeless tobacco.
- Congress enacts the Comprehensive Smokeless Tobacco Health Education Act of 1986. It requires rotation of three health warnings on smokeless tobacco packages and advertisements and bans smokeless tobacco advertising on broadcast media.
- Congress extends permanently the 16 cents per pack federal excise tax on cigarettes.
- Californians for Nonsmokers' Rights goes national, becoming Americans for Nonsmokers' Rights. It was originally formed as California GASP (Group Against Smoking Pollution) in 1976.
- Minnesota enacts the first state law to ban free distribution of smokeless tobacco samples.
- Congress imposes a federal excise tax on smokeless tobacco products.

(continued)

TABLE 12.1 *(continued)*

1987	• The Department of Health and Human Services (DHHS) establishes a smoke-free environment in its facilities, affecting 120,000 DHHS employees nationwide. • The Minnesota Sports Commission votes to ban tobacco advertising in the Metrodome Sports Stadium effective in 1992, the first such action in the United States.
1988	• A report of the Surgeon General concentrates exclusively on nicotine addiction. • A congressionally mandated smoking ban takes effect on domestic airline flights scheduled for 2 hours or less. Northwest Airlines voluntarily bans smoking on all flights in North America. • ALA sponsors the first annual "Non-Dependence Day." • California voters pass a referendum raising the state cigarette excise tax by 25 cents per pack, the largest cigarette excise tax increase in U.S. history. Revenues earmarked for public health purposes.
1989	• A report of the Surgeon General marks the 25th anniversary of the first Smoking and Health report; it focuses on progress since the first report.
1990	• The Environmental Protection Agency (EPA) issues a draft risk assessment on environmental tobacco smoke (ETS). • The Office of the Inspector General (OIG), DHHS, issues a report concluding that laws curtailing minors' access to tobacco are ignored. If proposes a minors' access to tobacco law for states. • The airline smoking ban goes into effect, banning smoking on all scheduled domestic flights of 6 hours or less. • The Secretary of the DHHS denounces "Uptown" cigarettes, a brand to be targeted to blacks—the manufacturer cancels its plans to market the cigarettes.
1991	• The National Institute for Occupational Safety and Health (OSH), part of the Centers for Disease Control and Prevention (CDC), issues a bulletin recommending that ETS be reduced to the lowest feasible concentration in the workplace. • The NCI and the ACS join together in the American Stop Smoking Intervention Study (ASSIST), funding 17 states over a period of 7 years at a cost of $165 million. • The federal cigarette excise tax increases to 20 cents.
1992	• The first federal legislation is enacted to require states to adopt and enforce restrictions on tobacco sales to minors. Penalties are to be imposed on state substance abuse funding without proper enforcement. • OIG, DHHS, issues a report documenting the widespread use of smokeless tobacco, particularly among young athletes. • A transdermal nicotine patch is introduced. • The Joint Commission on Accreditation of Healthcare Organizations (JCAHO) requires hospitals to be smoke-free as of January 1994 to maintain accreditation. • The FTC takes its first enforcement action under the Smokeless Tobacco Act, alleging that the Pinkerton Tobacco Company's Red Man brand name appeared illegally during a televised event. • The World Bank establishes a formal policy on tobacco, including discontinuing loans or investments for tobacco agriculture in developing countries.
1993	• The EPA releases final risk assessment of ETS, classifying it as a "Group A" carcinogen. • Representatives of the tobacco industry file a suit against the EPA related to the findings of its ETS risk assessment. • The OSH provides tobacco control resources to the remainder of states not funded under project ASSIST. • The FDA prohibits over-the-counter smoking-deterrent products because they have not been shown to be effective.

1993
- The U.S. Postal Service eliminates smoking in all of its facilities.
- The federal cigarette excise tax increases to 24 cents.
- Congress enacts a smoke-free policy for Women, Infants and Children (WIC) clinics.
- The Office of the U.S. Trade Representative and DHHS meet to discuss tobacco trade issues, creating the Task Force on Tobacco Exports to review the government's activities involving tobacco trade.
- Congress enacts legislation requiring all American cigarettes to contain at least 75% American-grown tobacco and requiring a tariff on imported tobacco to help finance the federal tobacco crop subsidy program.
- A working group of 16 state Attorneys General releases recommendations for implementing smoke-free policies in fast-food restaurants.

1994
- A report of the Surgeon General focuses on tobacco use among youth.
- Congress enacts the Pro-Children Act of 1994, requiring all federally funded children's services to become smoke-free.
- Occupational Safety and Health Administration (OSHA) announces proposed regulations to prohibit smoking in the workplace, except in separately ventilated smoking rooms.
- The six major domestic cigarette manufacturers testify before the U.S. House Subcommittee on Health and the Environment that they do not manipulate the nicotine levels in cigarettes.
- FDA Commissioner Kessler testifies that cigarettes may qualify as drug delivery systems, bringing them within the jurisdiction of the FDA.
- Mississippi becomes the first state to sue the tobacco industry to recover Medicaid costs for tobacco-related illnesses.
- The Department of Defense (DOD) bans smoking in all of its workplaces.
- The Robert Wood Johnson Foundation and the AMA launch the Smokeless States grant program to fund local initiatives for tobacco control and prevention.

1995
- *The Journal of the American Medical Association* publishes articles on documents from the Brown and Williamson Tobacco Corporation, indicating the industry's early knowledge of the harmful effects of tobacco use and the addictive nature of nicotine.
- The Philip Morris Company recalls its cigarette brands due to the presence of contaminants. The CDC investigates reports of possible health effects.
- FDA Commissioner Kessler declares tobacco use to be a pediatric disease.
- The Department of Justice reaches a settlement with Philip Morris to remove tobacco advertisements from the line of sight of TV cameras in sports stadiums to ensure compliance with the federal ban on tobacco ads on TV.
- The FTC reports that the cigarette industry spent $6 billion on advertising and promotions in 1993.

1996
- The Department of Transportation reports that about 80% of nonstop scheduled U.S. airline flights between the United States and foreign points will be smokefree by June 1, 1996.
- FDA approved nicotine gum and two nicotine patches for over-the-counter sale.
- The AMA calls for divestment of all tobacco stocks and mutual funds.
- Philip Morris and U.S. Tobacco Company offer a proposal for federal legislation to ban vending machines, partial-pack sales, free-samples to kids, and transit advertisements, among other things, in an effort to prohibit FDA regulation of tobacco.
- On August 23, 1996, President Clinton announces the nation's first comprehensive program to prevent children and adolescents from smoking cigarettes or using smokeless tobacco and beginning a lifetime of nicotine addiction.

Source: Tobacco Information and Prevention Source, National Center for Chronic Disease Prevention and Health Promotion, Centers for Disease Control and Prevention, 1996. Available http://www.cdc.gov/tobacco/chron96.htm.

(Text continued from page 308)

the lungs and is then absorbed into the bloodstream. When chewed (tobacco chewing) or dipped (also referred to as snuff dipping), nicotine is absorbed through the mucous lining of the mouth.

The amount of nicotine absorbed into the body varies according to several factors:

1. The exact composition of the tobacco used.

2. How densely the tobacco is packed in the cigarette and the length of the cigarette smoked.

3. Whether a filter is used and the characteristics of the filter.

4. The volume of smoke inhaled.

5. The number of cigarettes smoked throughout the day.

Depending on how tobacco is taken, the rate at which it enters the bloodstream varies widely. Cigarette smoking results in rapid distribution of nicotine throughout the body; it reaches the brain within 10 seconds of inhalation. A typical smoker will take 10 puffs on a cigarette during the 5 minutes that the cigarette is lit. Thus, a person who smokes two packs (40 cigarettes) each day gets 400 "hits" of nicotine to the brain each day. In contrast, cigar and pipe smokers typically do not inhale the smoke; nicotine is absorbed more slowly through the lining of the mouth.

■ EFFECTS ON THE CENTRAL NERVOUS SYSTEM

Nicotine produces an intense effect on the central nervous system. Research has demonstrated that nicotine activates the brain circuitry in regions responsible for regulating feelings of pleasure. In particular, nicotine increases the release of the neurotransmitter, dopamine, in the so-called reward or pleasure pathways of the brain. This effect likely contributes to the abuse potential of the stimulant.

The pharmacokinetic properties of nicotine also enhance its abuse potential. As just noted, cigarette smoking allows nicotine to enter the brain rapidly, with drug levels peaking within 10 seconds of inhalation. The acute effects of this rapid increase in brain concentration dissipate within a few min-

utes, causing the smoker to continue to dose frequently throughout the day in order to maintain the pleasurable effects of the drug.

■ OTHER EFFECTS OF NICOTINE

In addition to its direct effects in the brain, nicotine increases the respiration rate at low dose levels because it stimulates the receptors in the carotid artery (in the neck) that monitor the brain's need for oxygen. It also stimulates the cardiovascular system by releasing epinephrine, which increases coronary blood flow, heart rate, and blood pressure. The effect is to raise the oxygen requirements of the heart muscle. Initially, nicotine stimulates salivary and bronchial secretions, then inhibits them. The excess saliva associated with smoking is typically caused by the irritating smoke, not the nicotine itself.

Nicotine and perhaps other substances in tobacco smoke tend to inhibit hunger contractions in the stomach for up to 1 hour. At the same time, this substance causes a slight increase in blood sugar and deadens the taste buds. These factors may explain the decreased feelings of hunger experienced by many smokers. Smokers have often reported that they gain weight after they stop smoking and that their appetite increases. In addition, when someone who smokes one or more packs a day quits, there may be a decrease in heart rate (two to three beats per minute) and up to a 10% decrease in basal metabolic rate. The body is under less stress; therefore, it converts more food into fat.

Nicotine has been used as an insecticide, and at higher concentrations it can be extremely toxic. Symptoms of nicotine poisoning include sweating, vomiting, mental confusion, diminished pulse rate, and breathing difficulty. Respiratory failure from the paralysis of muscles usually brings on death. The fatal dose for adults is 60 milligrams. Most cigarettes in the U.S. market today contain 10 milligrams or more of nicotine, and through smoke, the average smoker takes in 1 to 2 milligrams nicotine from every cigarette (NIDA 1998). It is virtually impossible to overdose, in part because a smoker feels the effects before any lethal amount can accumulate in the body (Schelling 1992).

Nicotine and other products in smoke, such as carbon monoxide, produce still other effects. Up to

10% of all the hemoglobin in smokers may be in the form of carboxyhemoglobin. This type of hemoglobin cannot carry oxygen, so up to 10% of the smoker's blood is effectively out of circulation as far as normal oxygen–carbon dioxide exchange is concerned. This situation could easily cause a smoker to become breathless following exertion. It is a factor in heart attacks and in the lower birthweights and survival rate of infants born to women who smoke during pregnancy (discussed later in this chapter).

■ CLOVE CIGARETTES

Indonesian clove cigarettes were first used by young Americans in the 1980s. In 1980, 12 million clove cigarettes were sold in this country; by 1984, sales had increased to 150 million. The popularity of clove cigarettes has diminished, however.

The aroma of clove cigarettes masks the negative physical effects of nicotine. As a result, adolescent and adult smokers often assume that these cigarettes are safer than tobacco cigarettes. The truth is that eugenol, the organic chemical that gives the clove its aroma, anesthetizes the back of the throat, reducing the apparent harshness of the smoke and allowing deeper inhalation. Further, these cigarettes consist of more than 60% tobacco and possess a greater amount of tar, nicotine, and carbon monoxide than regular cigarettes manufactured in the United States. Users have reported excessive wheezing, fluid retention in the lungs, and bloody phlegm after smoking clove cigarettes.

Cigarette Smoking: A Costly Addiction

Today, nearly 3000 young people across our country will begin smoking regularly. Of these 3000 people, 1000 will lose that gamble to diseases caused by smoking. The net effect of this is that among children living in America today, 5 million will die an early, preventable death because of a decision made as a child. —Donna E. Shalala, Ph.D., former Secretary, U.S. Department of Health and Human Services (CDC 2000)

■ MORTALITY RATES

The past 25 years has been marked by a steady decline in cigarette consumption. Still, an estimated 48 million adults in the United States smoke cigarettes even though this single behavior will result in death or disability for half of all regular users (CDC 2000). As noted earlier, tobacco use is responsible for more than 430,000 deaths each year, or 1 in every 5 deaths—more than alcohol, cocaine, heroin, suicide, homicide, fire, car accidents, and AIDS combined. This includes 98,000 deaths from heart disease, 123,000 deaths from lung cancer, 32,000 deaths from other forms of cancer, 72,000 deaths from chronic lung disease, 24,000 deaths from stroke, and about 81,000 deaths from other diagnoses (CDC 2000; see Figure 12.3). In fact, tobacco use is the leading preventable cause of death in the United States (NIDA 1998).

A 35-year-old male who smokes two packs a day has a life expectancy that is 8.1 years shorter than his nonsmoking counterpart (Callahan 1987; USDHHS/CDC 1993; U.S. Surgeon General 1985). The death rate increases with the amount smoked: A two-pack-a-day smoker has a mortality rate twice as high as a nonsmoker. Overall mortality rates are greater for those who smoke longer; death rates are directly proportional.

Various cigarettes have different tar and nicotine contents; the effects they produce—and thus the mortality rates—vary as well. Smokers of low-

---

KEY TERMS

tobacco chewing
the absorption of nicotine through the mucous lining of the mouth

snuff dipping
placing a pinch of tobacco between the gums and the cheek

clove cigarettes
Indonesian aromatic-type cigarettes with more tobacco, tar, nicotine, and carbon monoxide than standard cigarettes in the United States

eugenol
the organic chemical in clove cigarettes that delivers the aroma when inhaled

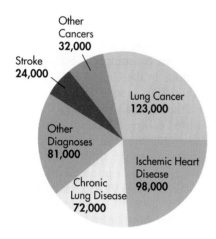

FIGURE 12.3

430,000 deaths attributable to cigarette smoking, United States, 2000.

··

Source: CDC, Tobacco Information and Prevention Source. *Targeting Tobacco Uses: The Nation's Leading Cause of Death*, 2000.

Cigarette smoking is the leading cause of bronchopulmonary disease.

tar and low-nicotine cigarettes have a mortality ratio 50% greater than that of nonsmokers but 15% to 20% less than that of cigarette smokers as a group (DeAngelis 1989; U.S. Surgeon General 1981).

Overall mortality rates decline the longer ex-smokers abstain from smoking. People who stop smoking before age 50 reduce their risk of dying over the next 15 years by 50%. The mortality rate for ex-smokers is related to the number of cigarettes they used to smoke per day and the age at which they started to smoke. The mortality rate for cigar smokers is somewhat higher than that for nonsmokers and is related to the number of cigars smoked daily. The mortality rate for pipe smokers is slightly greater than that for nonsmokers.

■ CHRONIC ILLNESSES

Cigarette smokers not only tend to die at an earlier age than nonsmokers but also have a higher probability of developing certain diseases, including cardiovascular disease, cancer, and bronchopulmonary disease.

Cardiovascular Disease

Overwhelming evidence shows that cigarette smoking increases the risk of cardiovascular disease. In fact, cigarettes caused almost 98,000 deaths per year from cardiovascular disease in the United States during the early 1990s (CDC 2000). Data collected for the United States, the United Kingdom, Canada, and other countries show that smoking is a major risk factor for heart attack. The probability of heart attack is related to the amount smoked, which has a synergistic relationship to other risk factors, such as obesity.

Smoking cigarettes is a major risk factor for arteriosclerotic disease and for death from arteriosclerotic aneurysm of the aorta (Palfai and Jankiewicz 1991). (An *aneurysm* is a weakened area in a blood vessel that forms a blood-filled sac and may rupture.) Smokers have a higher incidence of atherosclerosis of the coronary arteries that supply blood to the heart (the arteries become blocked with fat deposits), and the effect is dose-related. Both the carbon monoxide and the nicotine in cigarette smoke can precipitate *angina attacks* (painful spasms in the chest when the heart muscle does not get the blood supply it needs).

Smokers of low-tar and low-nicotine cigarettes have less risk of coronary heart disease, but their risk still exceeds that of nonsmokers. The risk goes down if the person quits; after about 10 years, the risk of coronary disease in ex-smokers approaches that in nonsmokers. Recovery time can be shorter or longer based on how long and frequently an individual smoked. Women who smoke and use oral contraceptives have a significantly higher risk of death or disability from stroke, heart attack, and other cardiovascular diseases than nonsmokers.

Cancer

Cigarette smoking is a major cause of cancers of the lung, bladder, pancreas, cervix, and kidney. The risk of cancer increases according to the number of cigarettes smoked each day, the number of years a person has smoked, and the age at which smoking began. For example, the risk of lung cancer in individuals who smoke two or more packs per day is nearly 20 times greater than the risk for nonsmokers (American Cancer Society 2000).

Use of filter cigarettes and of lower-tar and low-nicotine cigarettes decreases the lung cancer mortality rate, but it is still significantly higher than that for nonsmokers. If a smoker quits, the lung cancer mortality rate goes down but will not approach the nonsmoker rate until 10 years of abstinence.

Pipe and cigar smokers are more likely to contract lung cancer than nonsmokers but less likely to do so than habitual cigarette smokers. Common types of cancers among cigar and pipe smokers include cancers of the mouth, larynx, and esophagus. Cancer of the larynx is significantly higher in smokers compared with nonsmokers and is related to the amount smoked. A compounding effect has also been shown to exist between smoking and alcohol consumption and between exposure to asbestos and smoking, increasing the likelihood of developing cancer of the larynx. The risk of laryngeal cancer goes down if the person stops smoking; as with lung cancer, however, this form of cancer does not reach the level for nonsmokers until nearly 10 years following cessation.

Bronchopulmonary Disease

Cigarette smoking is the leading cause of bronchopulmonary disease, which includes a host of lung ailments. Cigarette smokers have higher death rates from pulmonary emphysema and chronic bronchitis and more frequently have impaired pulmonary function and other symptoms of pulmonary disease than nonsmokers.

Respiratory infections are more prevalent and more severe among cigarette smokers—particularly heavy smokers—than among nonsmokers. The risk of developing or dying from bronchopulmonary disease is higher among pipe or cigar smokers than nonsmokers but lower than for cigarette smokers. Ex-smokers have lower death rates from bronchopulmonary disease than do continuing smokers.

It is now understood how cigarette smoking causes one of the most common lung diseases, emphysema . Smoking produces inflammation of the lung tissue and increases the protein elastase in the tissue. Elastin, a structural material in the lungs, is broken down by elastase enzyme. In the long run, the lung tissue is damaged extensively, causing emphysema (USDHHS 1995; U.S. Surgeon General 1984).

■ EFFECTS WITHOUT SMOKING

The harmful effects of tobacco are not restricted to smokers. As described next, women who use tobacco during pregnancy are more likely to have adverse birth outcomes, including babies with low birth weight, which is linked with an increased risk of infant death and with a variety of infant health disorders. Individuals who chew or dip tobacco run the risk of adverse consequences as well. Finally, the health of individuals who neither smoke nor chew is also adversely affected by tobacco. As described next, exposure to environmental tobacco smoke (ETS) causes an estimated 3000 nonsmoking Americans to

Heavy smoking can severely damage the lungs and cause emphysema. Left, a diseased lung due to smoking. Right, a healthy nonsmoker's lung.

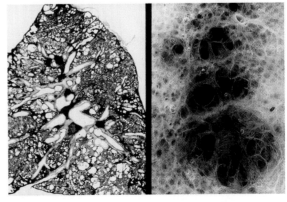

die of lung cancer and causes up to 300,000 children to suffer from lower respiratory tract infections each year (CDC 2000).

▪ EFFECTS ON THE FETUS

Cigarette smoking during pregnancy has a significantly harmful effect on the development of the fetus, the survival of the newborn infant, and the continued development of the child (see "Here and Now," Pregnant Smoking Mothers and Their Daughters). Adverse effects on pregnancy range from increased risk for spontaneous abortion to impaired fetal growth, stillbirth, premature birth, and neonatal death. Babies born to mothers who smoke have a lower average body weight and length and have a smaller head circumference (Bartecchi et al. 1995). The amount a woman smokes will affect the size of the child she bears. If a smoking woman gives up this habit for the entire duration of the pregnancy, her child will likely be of normal size and strength.

The below-average weight of babies born to smokers is caused by carbon monoxide and nicotine (Cook et al. 1990). Carbon monoxide reduces the oxygen-carrying capacity of the fetus's blood, just as it does the mother's. Fetal growth is retarded because the tissue becomes starved for oxygen. Inhaled nicotine enters the mother's blood from her lungs and rapidly constricts the blood flow to the placenta, reducing available oxygen and nutrients until the effect of the nicotine has worn off. In addition, nicotine crosses the blood-placenta barrier to the fetal bloodstream. It has the same effects on the fetus' nervous system and blood circulation as on the mother's. However, the fetus cannot metabolize nicotine efficiently; therefore, the effects last longer for the child than for the mother.

One known carcinogen in tobacco smoke, benzo(a)pyrene, crosses the placenta and enters the fetal blood. Experiments with pregnant mice exposed to benzo(a)pyrene showed that their offspring had a markedly higher incidence of cancer. The impact of smoking during pregnancy on the incidence of cancer in infants is not known. In addition, if the father smokes but the mother does not, the infant may still be affected by secondhand smoke.

Infants born to mothers who smoke have a reduced probability of survival. They are more likely to die from sudden infant death syndrome (SIDS) and other causes related to their retarded growth. Long-term effects may be observed in physical growth, mental development, and behavioral characteristics of those babies who survive the early weeks of life.

▪ TOBACCO USE WITHOUT SMOKING

Although it is customary to associate the effects of tobacco use with smoking, in fact, millions of non-smokers experience tobacco effects through their use of smokeless tobacco products.

Although a resurgence has occurred in the use of all forms of smokeless tobacco—plug, leaf, and snuff—the greatest cause for concern centers on the increased use of "dipping snuff." Dipping snuff, an act of placing tobacco between the gums and cheek, exposes the body to levels of nicotine equal to those obtained with cigarettes. Chewing tobacco and snuff are two types of smokeless tobacco products that are commonly referred to as "spit tobacco." Both types consist of tobacco leaves that are shredded and twisted into strands and then either chewed or placed in the cheek between the lower lip and gum. In this process, nicotine, along with a number of carcinogens, is absorbed through the oral tissue. In snuffing, tobacco is "snorted" instead of being chewed or placed in the cheek.

KEY TERMS

sudden infant death syndrome (SIDS)
unexpected and unexplainable death that occurs while infants are sleeping

dipping snuff
placing a pinch of smokeless tobacco between the gums and the cheek

chewing tobacco
tobacco leaves shredded and twisted into strands for chewing purposes

snuff
smokeless tobacco

snuffing
snorting chewing tobacco nasally

HERE AND NOW
Pregnant Smoking Mothers and Their Daughters

A 1994 study by Dr. Denise Kandel of Columbia University suggested a strong relationship between prenatal exposure to smoking and the exposed female child's likelihood to smoke later in life. Before this study, prenatal exposure to smoking had been linked to "impairments in memory, learning, cognition, and perception in the growing child." In addition, this study suggested that exposed female children are "four times as likely to begin smoking during adolescence and to continue smoking than daughters of women who did not smoke during pregnancy."

An article describing this work noted, "The study suggests that nicotine, which crosses the placental barrier, may affect the female fetus during an important period of development so as to predispose the brain to the addictive influence of nicotine more than a decade later" (Mathias 1995). Prenatal smoking, however, had no strong effect on the smoking of male children; the researchers did not find any strong evidence to explain this result, calling this odd relationship "speculative."

The disturbing number of female adolescents who smoke is illustrated in the accompanying chart. This trend had previously been linked to a number of factors, but Dr. Kandel's work was the first to document this possible connection between prenatal nicotine exposure and smoking later in life.

The researchers worked to ensure that later smoking was a result of prenatal—not postnatal—smoking by the mother. They found that "regardless of the amount or duration of current or past maternal smoking, the strongest correla-

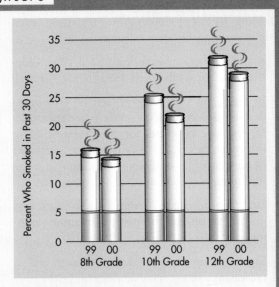

Trends in Adolescent Girls' Current Use of Cigarettes

According to NIDA's *Monitoring the Future* study, the percentage of adolescent girls who smoked cigarettes in the last 30 days remains significant. Although smoking among adolescent girls has been linked to many different factors, Dr. Kandel's study is the first to document a possible link between prenatal exposure to nicotine and an adolescent girl's tendency to smoke cigarettes.

Source: NIDA's Monitoring the Future Studies, 1999–2000.

tion between maternal smoking and a daughter's smoking occurred when the mother smoked during pregnancy."

Dr. Kandel plans to continue her research and probe into other aspects of prenatal exposure to nicotine.

Source: Mathias, R. "Daughters of Mothers Who Smoked During Pregnancy Are More Likely to Smoke, Study Says." *NIDA Notes* 10.5 (September/October 1995): 11, 14

Smokeless tobacco contains powerful chemicals—including nicotine, nitrosamines, polycyclic aromatic hydrocarbons, and dozens of other carcinogens—that can injure tissues in the mouth and throat (see "Here and Now," Think Twice About "Chewing"). The following findings have been made regarding smokeless tobacco:

- About 7.6 million Americans aged 12 or older used smokeless tobacco in 1999 (NHSDA 1999).

- In 1986, the U.S. Surgeon General concluded that smokeless tobacco is not a safe substitute for smoking cigarettes for three reasons: (1) it can cause cancer, (2) it can produce a number of noncancerous oral conditions, and (3) it can lead to nicotine addiction and dependence.

- Oral cancer occurs several times more frequently among snuff dippers than among nontobacco users.

- The prevelance of smokeless tobacco use is increasing among male adolescents and young adults (American Cancer Society 2000).

- According to the U.S. Department of Agriculture, U.S. output of moist snuff rose 50% from 1988, when it reached 41 million pounds, to 1993, when it reached an estimated 66 million pounds (USDA 1999).

The increasing popularity of snuff tobacco is largely due to more effective and persistent advertising campaigns depicting famous athletes using such products. Some experts also believe that the increasing popularity of this tobacco product relates to its ability to satisfy the addiction to nicotine where smoking is prohibited. Thus, snuffing is perceived as an alternative to smoking in smoke-free environments.

KEY TERMS

mainstream smoke
smoke drawn directly through the mouthpiece of a cigarette

sidestream smoke
smoke released into the air from a lighted cigarette

passive smoking
nonsmoker's inhalation of tobacco smoke

How safe are smokeless tobacco products compared with cigarettes? The likelihood of getting oral cancer increases significantly for anyone who uses smokeless tobacco daily for 3.5 years or longer (Perry 1990; USDHHS 1995) (see "Here and Now," Think Twice About "Chewing"). Other evidence has shown that continued use of smokeless products can cause cancer of the pharynx and esophagus. The incidence of developing these cancers is related to the duration of use and the type of product used because "long-term snuff users have a 50% greater risk of developing oral cancer than nonusers" ("Smokeless Tobacco" 1990). Other, less serious effects of using smokeless tobacco include severe inflammation of gum tissue, tooth decay, receding gums, and tooth loss (Giovino et al. 1994; "Smokeless Tobacco" 1990).

In response to these developments, Congress enacted the Comprehensive Smokeless Tobacco Health Education Act of 1986. It requires rotation of three health warnings on smokeless tobacco packages and advertisements and bans smokeless tobacco advertising on broadcasting media (see Table 12.2).

■ ENVIRONMENTAL TOBACCO SMOKE

Cigarette smoke drawn through the mouthpiece and inhaled directly from a cigarette is classified as mainstream smoke . Sidestream smoke , or secondhand smoke, refers to the smoke that comes directly from the lighted tip of a cigarette between puffs. Passive smoking refers to nonsmokers' inhalation of tobacco smoke. In addition, the term *ETS* is used to refer to the mixture of predominantly sidestream smoke and exhaled mainstream smoke that is inhaled by the passive smoker (USDHHS 1994).

Studies of smoking and its effects have directed increased attention to sidestream smoke because the burning tobacco smoke that pollutes the air is breathed in by smokers and nonsmokers alike. This type of smoke contains much higher concentrations of some irritating and hazardous substances—such as carbon monoxide, nicotine, and ammonia—than inhaled mainstream smoke. Because it contains more particles of smaller diameter, sidestream smoke is therefore more likely to be deposited deep in the lungs (Bartecchi et al. 1995).

As mentioned earlier, exposure to ETS causes an estimated 3000 nonsmoking Americans to die of

HERE AND NOW

Think Twice About "Chewing"

Dear Readers:

What follows is an edited version of an article by Susan Miller Degnan, a newspaper reporter for the *Miami Herald*. It was sent to me [Ann Landers] by an 84-year-old fan in Harlingen, Texas, who urged me to "keep up the good work." I hope you will be as moved by it as I was. Here it is:

There may never have been a quieter time in the 117-year history of the Philadelphia Phillies than when Rick Bender, a longtime sandlot ballplayer, walked into their clubhouse in early March with the U.S. Surgeon General.

Bender's face—what was left of it—jolted the Phillies so much that when they took the field that day, not a single cheek was filled with tobacco.

"Put it this way," said Bender, 31, a bee-keeper in Montana, "I have a face you will never forget."

Half a jaw. Partial tongue. Cavernous neck. Three remaining teeth. And scars he can't help but cut when he shaves the few hairs that still grow after radiation treatments. It took four operations to halt the mouth cancer doctors attributed to Bender's daily use of two cans of finely ground tobacco snuff, also known as dip, which he packed between his lower lip and gum.

"He scared me out of the chimney," said pitcher Terry Mulholland, who dipped for 17 years. "I thought, 'I'm 30 years old. It's time to grow up.' "

If major league baseball had its way, it would sever the growth at its roots. Smoking, dipping, and chewing tobacco neither promote physical health nor portray a wholesome image for young people who idolize athletes.

Mulholland quit dipping, but his team-mates couldn't last. By the ninth inning, cheeks were bulging.

Smokeless tobacco has been linked to baseball since the game's rules were roughed out in 1845. It was as easy to spit on the base-ball field as on the corn field. Still is. A 1988 study funded by the National Cancer Institute found that 40% of pro players dip or chew, a figure that dwarfs use in other sports.

Dipping half a tin of snuff daily is like inhaling 30 to 40 cigarettes. The nicotine is so addictive that it has been compared to heroin.

Along with alcohol and cigars, Babe Ruth chewed vigorously and dipped. He even snorted snuff and was advised to stop because of impacted nasal passages. Ruth continued to do it all and died of throat cancer in 1948. He was 53.

"A tobacco ban in baseball?" Pirates manager Jim Leyland responded with a cigar dangling from his mouth. "It's ridiculous, a total invasion of privacy. We have a lot of other things we should be paying attention to rather that telling some poor SOB he can't put chew in his mouth."

And now this is Ann talking: I hope every baseball player who uses smokeless tobacco will take this seriously. Youngsters look up to you and think everything you do is cool. Do you want to be responsible for some kid ending up like Rick Bender? Please think about it.

Other adverse medical reactions can result from an addiction to smokeless tobacco as illustrated by the following: In April 1997, Mets base-ball pitcher Pete Harnisch was removed from a weekend start because he was not "mentally" pre-pared to pitch (The Associated Press, 8 April 1997). Harnisch was placed on a 15-day disabled list by the New York Mets after having quit cold turkey his 13-year addiction to smokeless tobacco products on March 19.

After quitting, the major symptoms he experienced were night sweats, shakes, raw nerves, edginess, sleep deprivation, and shaking that lasted the day prior to his medical removal from pitching. Harnisch's physician said that his symptoms were common of tobacco withdrawal.

Source: Degnan, S. M., *Miami Herald,* (9 October 1993) [Living Section].

TABLE 12.2 Past-Month Use of Cigarettes, by Age Group, Race/Ethnicity, and Gender: 1985–1999

DEMOGRAPHIC CHARACTERISTICS	1985	1988	1991	1994	1999
Total	38.7	35.3	33.0	28.6	25.8
Age Group					
12–17	29.4	22.7	20.9	18.9	14.9
18–25	47.4	45.6	41.7	34.6	39.7
26–34	45.7	42.1	37.3	32.4	24.9*
≥35	35.5	32.4	31.6	27.9	
Race/Ethnicity					
White	38.9	35.2	33.5	29.4	27.0
Black	38.0	34.2	31.2	28.4	22.5
Hispanic	40.0	35.6	33.6	25.8	22.6
Gender					
Male	43.4	39.5	35.2	31.5	28.3
Female	34.5	31.4	31.1	26.0	23.4

Note: The population distributions for the 1994 and 1996 National Household Survey on Drug Abuse (NHSDAs) are post-stratified to population projections of totals based on the 1990 decennial census. NHSDAs from 1985 through 1992 used projections based on the 1980 census. The change from one census base to another has little effect on estimated percentages reporting drug use but may have significant effect on estimates of a number of drug users in some subpopulation groups.

Estimates for 1985 through 1991 may differ from estimates for these survey years that were published in other NHSDA reports. The estimates shown here for 1985 through 1991 have been adjusted to improve their comparability with estimates based on the new version of the NHSDA instrument that was fielded in 1994 and subsequent NHSDAs.

Because of the methodology used to adjust the 1985 through 1993 estimates, some logical inconsistency may exist between estimates for a given drug within the same survey year. For example, some adjusted estimates of past-year use may appear to be greater than adjusted lifetime estimates. These inconsistencies tend to be small, rare, and not statistically significant.

* Statistic reflects individuals aged 26 and older.

Source: National Household Survey on Drug Abuse: Population Estimates. Rockville, MD: U.S. Department of Health and Human Services, Substance Abuse and Mental Health Services Administration (SAMHSA).

lung cancer and causes up to 300,000 children to suffer from lower respiratory tract infections each year. If several people smoke in an enclosed area, the carbon monoxide level may exceed the safe limit recommended by the Environmental Protection Agency. Under conditions of heavy smoking and poor ventilation, high concentrations of carbon monoxide can occur from sidestream smoke. Carbon monoxide gas is not removed by most standard air filtration systems. It can be diluted only by increasing ventilation with fresh air containing low levels of carbon monoxide. Formation of carbon monoxide can be reduced by increasing the amount of oxygen available during the burning of the tobacco. This goal can be achieved by using perforated cigarette paper and perforated filtertips. Regular and small cigars produce more carbon monoxide than cigarettes because the tobacco leaf wrapper reduces the amount of oxygen available at the burning zone. The levels of carbon monoxide created by smokers may cause nonsmokers with coronary disease to have angina attacks.

Who Smokes?

Given what we know today about the effects of smoking, it can be difficult to understand why people smoke. Lifetime users are understandably addicted; quitting is hard. Following are some recent statistics from SAMHSA (2000) that describe who is smoking:

1. In 1999, an estimated 60 million Americans were current smokers. This number gives a smoking rate of 28% for the population age 12 and older.

2. Males were more likely than females to report past-month use of any tobacco product. In 1999, 36.5% of males (ages 12 and older) were current users of any tobacco product compared to 24.3% of females.

3. Current smokers are more likely to be heavy drinkers and illicit drug users. For instance, past-month cigarette use is highly correlated with illicit drug use, especially for adolescents. Among youths age 12 to 17 years, 41.1% of past-month smokers reported past-month use of an illicit drug as compared with 5.6% of the adolescent nonsmokers. Among persons 18 to 25 years of age, cigarette smokers were about four times as likely to report the past-month use of an illicit drug (31.0% compared with 8.0%). For past-month cigarette smokers 26 and older, 10.1% reported current use of an illicit drug as compared with 2.5% of nonsmokers. (More details about smoking and licit and illicit drug use are discussed in the section, "Tobacco as a Gateway Drug.")

4. Approximately 14.9% of youths aged 12 to 17 were current smokers in 1999. The current rate of smoking was highest in the 18- to 25-year-old age group (39.7%). Among adults age 26 and older, the rate was 24.9%. After age 25, rates generally decline, reaching 22.5% for persons age 50 to 64 years and 10.7% of persons age 65 and older.

5. In regard to smoking and racial and/or ethnic ancestry, Native Americans and Alaska Natives were more likely than any other race/ethnicity group to report the use of tobacco products. For past month use (age 12 and older), 43.1% of Native Americans and Alaska Natives reported using at least one form of tobacco. The next highest rates were for non-Hispanic whites and persons of multiple races (31.9% and 34.0% respectively). The lowest current tobacco use rates were observed for Asians.

6. Similar and other findings are shown in Table 12.3, which describes past-month use of cigarettes by age groups, race/ethnicity, and gender for the period 1985–1999. Since 1985, cigarette use has been steadily declining. Whites, blacks, and Hispanics have past-month smoking rates of 27%, 22.5%, and 22.6%, respectively (SAMHSA 2000). In addition, past-month use of cigarettes is higher for males (28.3%) than for females (23.4%).

7. Level of educational attainment was correlated with tobacco usage. Among persons 26 years of age and older, the prevalence of cigarette smoking decreased with increasing levels of education. College graduates were the least likely to report they smoked cigarettes (13.3%) compared with 29.7% of young adults age 26 years and older with only a high school diploma and 29.8% of persons who lacked a high school diploma (SAMHSA 2000).

■ REASONS FOR SMOKING

Nicotine dependency through cigarette smoking is not only the most common form of drug addiction but also the one that causes more deaths and disease than all other addictions combined (USDHHS 1994). Tobacco use continues despite the fact that, since the 1960s, medical research and government assessments have clearly proved that smoking leads to premature death.

If one asks tobacco users why they smoke, their answers are often quite similar:

1. It is relaxing.
2. It decreases the unpleasant effects of tension, anxiety, and anger.
3. It satisfies the craving.
4. It is a habit.
5. It provides stimulation, increased energy, and arousal.
6. It allows the manipulation of objects that have become satisfying habits (the cigarette, pipe, and so on).

TABLE 12.3
Kicking the Habit

To wean oneself from cigarettes means denying the central nervous system a substance that induces pleasure. There are a variety of methods to break the habit, but experts say wanting to break the habit is half the battle.

METHOD	DESCRIPTION	DURATION	PROS/CONS
Acupuncture Cost: About $200, but depends on program	Needles are placed primarily in the scalp and ears supposedly to stimulate production of enkephalins, the chemical messengers found at nerve endings. These chemicals have a morphine-like effect on the brain and theoretically override desire for nicotine.	From 1 month to 6 weeks. Patients come in once a week for a treatment. Relaxation tapes also are used.	Some people have an aversion to needles. But if patients can stomach it, the technique is 80% successful, practitioners say.
Cold Turkey Cost: None	The oldest method of breaking the smoking habit involves giving up cigarettes altogether.	Can take a week for some people, months for others. The time it takes to break the habit depends on how often the smoker "sneaks" a cigarette.	Because of a lack of supervision, there is often a tremendous desire to smoke, and each cigarette enhances the desire for nicotine. The technique can be 100% successful for individuals. There have been no studies conducted on this method versus medically supervised techniques.
Hypnosis Cost: $50 to $100 per session	The smoker is hypnotized to enhance the power of suggestion.	Some people need just a single session, whereas others need more.	National studies have not established the effectiveness of hypnosis. Smokers who have tried the technique often turn to medically supervised nicotine patch or nicotine gum programs.
Nicotine gum Cost: $36.99 for 96 pieces of gum	Smokers chew gum laced with nicotine to replace the substance found in cigarettes. The gum is often offered as part of behavioral modification programs.	From 10 to 12 pieces of the prescription gum are recommended per day, with a maximum of 30. Each piece is chewed for 30 minutes. The program lasts 3–6 months.	There have been complaints about the taste and texture of the gum, which some say is like cardboard. The effectiveness rate is 40%–50%.

METHOD	DESCRIPTION	DURATION	PROS/CONS
Nicotine patch Cost: $56.99 for a two-week supply	Smokers receive decreasing doses of nicotine from a patch that adheres to the body. A different patch is worn daily and is rotated to different parts of the body to prevent skin irritation.	Generally involves a 6-week program in which patches with decreasing amounts of nicotine are worn.	The patch has to be worn faithfully. Some people will forget to put on a patch; others on occasion sneak a cigarette, defeating the purpose because the amount of nicotine is increased in the body. National studies place the overall effectiveness at 60%.
Self-help with behavioral modification Cost: $10 refundable deposit for a 4-week program on how to quit	The American Medical Association (AMA) and the American Cancer Society (ACS) offer a "How to Quit" program of audio and video tapes. The program focuses on four areas: How to Keep My Mouth Busy; How to Keep My Hands Busy; Calm My Nerves; and Focus My Concentration.	A 4-week program.	The success of the program depends largely on the smoker's desire to quit. It is endorsed by the AMA and the ACS because it changes the smoker's need to have a cigarette. AMA studies show that the program is more effective than behavior modification alone.

Source: Ricks, D. "What a Drag: How Nicotine Gets Its Hammerlock on Users." *Salt Lake Tribune* 251 (21 March 1996): B-1, B-8.

A 1994 study by the University of Iowa showed that (1) two methods—hypnosis and acupuncture—worked well. Thirty-six percent of smokers using hypnosis and 30% who underwent acupuncture quit for approximately 3 months; (2) 16% of smokers using nicotine gum were not smoking 3 months later; (3) smokers who were told verbally to quit without any other assistance had a 7% success rate after 3 months; and (4) the best smoking cessation aid was the nicotine patch, with a 60% success rate.

In addition,

7. Female high school students smoke to lose weight (Rovner 1991; Wentz 1993).

8. Parents and/or siblings smoke (Rovner 1991; Wentz 1993).

9. A close friend or boyfriend/girlfriend smokes (USDHHS 1994).

Tobacco use fosters dependence for a number of reasons:

1. The habit can be rapidly and frequently reinforced by inhaling tobacco smoke (about 10 reinforcements per cigarette, or 200 with one pack).

2. The rapid metabolism and clearance of nicotine allows frequent and repeated use, which is encouraged by the rapid onset of withdrawal symptoms.

3. Smoking has complex pharmacological effects, both central and peripheral, that may satisfy a variety of the needs of the smoker.

4. Some groups offer psychological and social rewards for use, especially the peer groups of young people.

5. Smoking patterns can be generalized; that is, the smoker becomes conditioned to smoke with specific activities. For example, some smokers feel the need to smoke after a meal, when driving, and so on.

6. Smoking is reinforced by both pharmacological effects and ritual.

7. There is no marked performance impairment; in fact, smoking enhances performance in some cases. (Nicotine produces a state of alertness, prevents deterioration of reaction time, and improves learning.)

These reasons may not only explain why people continue to smoke but also reveal why it is often difficult for them to stop. (USDHHS 1994).

Smokers appear to regulate their intake of nicotine. For example, the smoker of a low-nicotine cigarette is likely to smoke more and inhale more deeply. The average one-pack-a-day smoker is estimated to self-administer thousands of pulses (one pulse per inhalation) of nicotine to specific nicotinic receptors in the brain per year. This rate greatly surpasses the stimulation rate of any other known form of substance abuse. A habit that is reinforced as frequently and easily as smoking is very hard to break.

Other factors responsible for creating the addiction to nicotine follow:

1. Cigarettes are readily available.
2. No equipment other than a lighter or match is needed.
3. Cigarettes are portable and easy to store.
4. Cigarettes are legal for individuals over age 18.
5. Other rewarding behaviors can occur while smoking (for example, drinking, socializing, and eating).

Relapse or Readdiction

Relapse or readdiction to tobacco can result if the ex-smoker does not use smoking cessation aids after overcoming nicotine withdrawal symptoms during the first few weeks of abstinence. Various internal and external stimuli may serve as triggers for craving or withdrawal symptoms. Stressful situations—an argument with a spouse, encounters with friends who smoke, and various types of social events—may prompt a response similar to withdrawal. This reaction sets the stage for readdiction.

The Motivation Not to Smoke

When habitual smokers stop smoking on their own, without the use of smoking cessation aids, they may experience a variety of unpleasant withdrawal effects, including craving for tobacco, irritability, restlessness, sleep disturbances, gastrointestinal disturbances, anxiety, and impaired concentration, judgment, and psychomotor performance. The onset of nicotine withdrawal symptoms may occur within hours or days after quitting and may persist from a few days to several months. Frustration over these symptoms leads many people to start smoking again. The intensity of withdrawal effects may be mild, moderate, or severe; it is not always correlated with the amount smoked.

Research shows that smoking cessation should be a gradual process because this type of withdrawal eliminates the severe symptoms of craving for nicotine. According to the National Institute on Drug Abuse, "rates of relapse are highest in the first few weeks and months and diminish considerably after three months" (NIDA 1995) (see Figure 12.4). The optimal treatment for smoking cessation also includes behavioral therapies (NIDA 1995). Behavioral modification treatments report 33% long-term abstinence with 50% recidivism. "Studies have shown that pharmacological treatment combined with psychological treatment, including psychological support and skill training to overcome high-risk situations, result in some of the highest long-term abstinence rates" (NIDA 1995).

■ ALTERNATIVE ACTIVITIES FOR SUCCESSFULLY QUITTING

The American Cancer Society has developed a list of alternative activities that the new ex-smoker might try as aids to get through the withdrawal period. When the craving for a cigarette arises, the smoker may engage in these behaviors:

- Nibble on fruit, celery, or carrots.
- Chew gum or spices such as ginger, cinnamon bark, or cloves.
- Use replacements in conjunction with quitting smoking, such as the nicotine patch or nicotine gum. (Such cessation smoking aids are discussed in greater detail in the next section.)
- Perform moderately strenuous physical activity, such as bicycling, jogging, or swimming (if the person's heart and lungs are not too badly damaged from smoking).

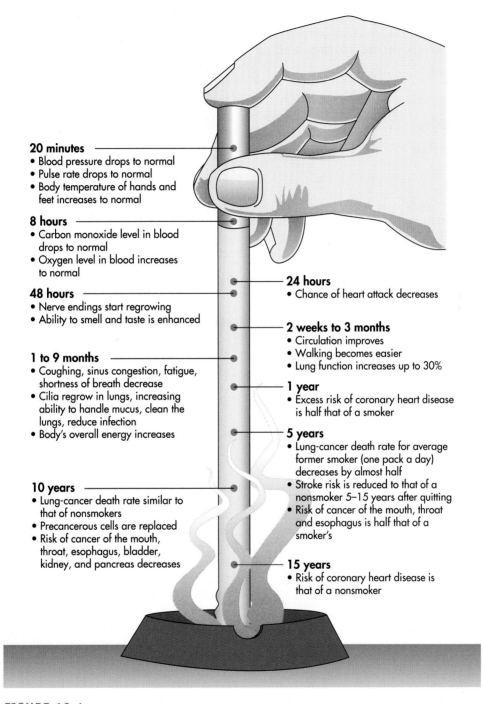

20 minutes
- Blood pressure drops to normal
- Pulse rate drops to normal
- Body temperature of hands and feet increases to normal

8 hours
- Carbon monoxide level in blood drops to normal
- Oxygen level in blood increases to normal

48 hours
- Nerve endings start regrowing
- Ability to smell and taste is enhanced

1 to 9 months
- Coughing, sinus congestion, fatigue, shortness of breath decrease
- Cilia regrow in lungs, increasing ability to handle mucus, clean the lungs, reduce infection
- Body's overall energy increases

10 years
- Lung-cancer death rate similar to that of nonsmokers
- Precancerous cells are replaced
- Risk of cancer of the mouth, throat, esophagus, bladder, kidney, and pancreas decreases

24 hours
- Chance of heart attack decreases

2 weeks to 3 months
- Circulation improves
- Walking becomes easier
- Lung function increases up to 30%

1 year
- Excess risk of coronary heart disease is half that of a smoker

5 years
- Lung-cancer death rate for average former smoker (one pack a day) decreases by almost half
- Stroke risk is reduced to that of a nonsmoker 5–15 years after quitting
- Risk of cancer of the mouth, throat and esophagus is half that of a smoker's

15 years
- Risk of coronary heart disease is that of a nonsmoker

FIGURE 12.4
When Smokers Quit
Within 20 minutes of smoking that last cigarette, the body begins a series of changes that continues for years. All benefits are lost by smoking just one cigarette a day, according to the American Cancer Society.

Source: The American Cancer Society, Washington Division; Centers for Disease Control.

- Spend as much time as possible in places where smoking is prohibited, such as movie theaters, libraries, and other smoke-free environments.

- Associate with nonsmokers for long periods of time.

▪ SMOKING CESSATION AIDS

> Quitting smoking is easy. I've done it a thousand times.
>
> —*Mark Twain*

There is no one "right" way to quit this habit. Successful cessation may include one or a combination of methods, including using step-by-step manuals, attending self-help classes or counseling, or using nicotine replacement therapy. A number of stop smoking aids are currently available, and they are discussed next.

Nicotine Gum

Nicotine gum can be purchased over-the-counter without a prescription. Chewing the gum allows the rapid absorption of nicotine through the mucous membranes of the mouth. Users chew the gum until noting a "peppery taste," and then hold it against the cheek to permit faster absorption. The user will chew on and off for about 20 to 30 minutes. Because food and drink can affect nicotine absorption, package instructions indicate that the user should avoid acidic foods and drinks such as soft drinks, coffee, or juices for at least 15 minutes before and during gum use.

Significant advantages afforded by nicotine gum are that it is easy to use and allows the user to control the dose of nicotine by controlling the number of pieces chewed each day. Nicotine gum is usually recommended for 1 to 3 months, with the maximum being 6 months. Individuals gradually decrease the number of pieces chewed each day, with a goal of complete abstinence from the drug. Side effects of the gum can include a bad taste, throat irritation, nausea (if the gum is swallowed), jaw discomfort (if chewed too rapidly), and racing heartbeat.

Nicotine Patches

Nicotine patches, also known as *transdermal nicotine systems*, are available without a prescription. The patch, which is directly applied and worn on the

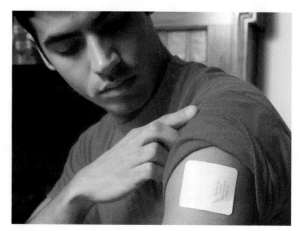

A transdermal patch, an example of a popular remedy for quitting smoking.

skin, releases a continuous flow of small doses of nicotine to quell the desire for cigarette-provided nicotine. The method of delivering nicotine to the skin reduces the withdrawal symptoms as the smoker attempts to quit. As the nicotine doses are lowered over a course of weeks, the smoker is weaned away from nicotine. The most common side effects are mild skin irritations such as redness and itching.

Nicotine Nasal Spray

Nicotine nasal sprays are available by prescription only. This form of administration rapidly delivers nicotine to the bloodstream as it is absorbed through the membranous lining of the nasal passages. It is easy to use and gives immediate relief of withdrawal symptoms. It is recommended for periods no longer than 6 months, tapering the dose at the end of 3 months. The most common side effects of using the spray include coughing, sinus irritation, runny nose, watery eyes, sneezing, and throat irritation. It is generally not recommended for individuals with asthma, allergies, or other pulmonary problems.

Nicotine Inhalers

Like nicotine nasal sprays, nicotine inhalers are only available by prescription. The nicotine inhaler is a small plastic tube that contains a nicotine plug. When the user puffs on the inhaler, the plug provides nicotine vapor into the mouth. One advantage to the inhaler is that the action of puffing it mimics some of the behaviors associated with smoking. Side effects associated with its use include coughing and throat irritation.

Buproprion

Buproprion is an antidepressant medication available only by prescription. In many individuals, this drug reduces symptoms of nicotine withdrawal. Individuals typically use the drug for 7 to 12 weeks, although the duration of therapy is generally individualized to the particular patient. Buproprion can be used alone or in combination with nicotine replacement therapies as just described.

Social Issues: Looking to the Future

■ TOBACCO AS A GATEWAY DRUG

Just recently, several research findings have indicated that tobacco is more of a serious gateway drug than previously expected. For example, nearly all heroin addicts initially began using gateway drugs such as alcohol and/or tobacco products. (Granted, most people who drink alcohol and use tobacco do not become heroin addicts.)

Biochemical evidence proving that the use of gateway drugs leads to the abuse of others is weak. However, some findings are quite interesting. "The decisions to use tobacco or other gateway drugs set up patterns of behavior that make it easier for a user to go on to other drugs" ("Non-smoking Youth" 1991). In other words, smokers have developed the behavioral patterns that may lead them to experiment with and use other licit and illicit drugs.

Research indicates that cigarette smokers are more likely to use alcohol, marijuana, and cocaine than are nonsmokers (Giovino et al. 1994). Figure 12.5 shows a strong association between cigarette smoking and the use of illicit drugs and alcohol by 12- to 17-year-old smokers. "[I]n the 12- through

FIGURE 12.5
Use of illicit drugs and alcohol by 12–17-year-old smokers and nonsmokers, 1998.

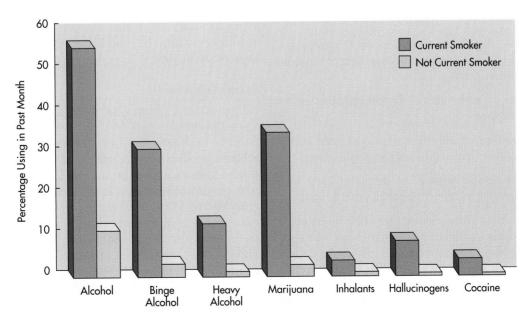

17-year-old group . . . those who smoked daily were approximately 14 times more likely to have binged on alcohol, 114 times more likely to have used marijuana at least 11 times, and 32 times more likely to have used cocaine at least 11 times than those who had not smoked" (USDHHS 1994). Other studies have shown similar relationships between cigarette smoking and the prevalence of other drug use. In addition, more smokable preparations are now available for various drugs such as cocaine (crack), methamphetamine (ice), phencyclidine (PCP), and heroin (USDHHS 1988; USDHHS 1995). Because smokers who become polydrug users report that tobacco is one of the first drugs they used, it is apparent that cigarette smoking skills can easily be transferred to other smokable drugs and may facilitate the process of experimenting with these drugs.

▪ SMOKING PROHIBITION VERSUS SMOKERS' RIGHTS

In response to the percentage of the U.S. population that has effectively banned smoking from certain public facilities, people who desire to continue smoking have formed action groups to press their right to smoke. Through mailing lists, newsletters, and magazine promotions, the groups advocate and report on the following issues:

- How the rights of smokers have been eroded in public and private places

- How to write to members of Congress and other political leaders to urge them to uphold smokers' rights

- How to lobby effectively for smoking in the workplace

- How the harmful effects of second-hand smoke have been exaggerated or remain unproven

- How people who enjoy smoking have won major battles, preserving their right to smoke

Although some modest gains have been made by these groups, the trend to restrict and ban cigarette smoking continues to be very strong. Antismoking groups have been highly successful in their own efforts, and restrictions on the sale of cigarettes and tobacco products remain very strong. The four

primary aspects of tobacco control laws in each state are smoke-free indoor air, youth access to tobacco products, advertising of tobacco products, and excise taxes on tobacco products.

Smoke-Free Indoor Air

As of 1998, 46 states and the District of Columbia required some variation of smoke-free indoor air. Forty-two states have laws restricting smoking in public work sites. In contrast, only 22 states have laws that restrict smoking in private workplaces. Many states have laws that regulate smoking in restaurants, and some have laws that regulate smoking in other locations, such as daycare centers, hospitals, public transportation facilities, grocery stores, and enclosed arenas.

Youth Access to Tobacco

All 50 states have enacted laws that restrict the purchase, possession, or use of tobacco products by minors. Although no state has completely banned the sale of tobacco products through vending machines, none allows such sales to minors. In fact, many states have created additional restrictions intended to reduce youth access to vending machines. Some have banned the placement of vending machines in areas accessible to young people and allow their placement only in bars, liquor stores, adult clubs, and other adult-oriented establishments.

Licensing

Forty-six states and the District of Columbia require some form of retail licensure for the sale of tobacco products.

Taxing Cigarettes

All states tax cigarettes. In 1998, the tax ranged from 25 cents per pack in Virginia to 65 cents per pack in Washington, D.C. In addition, smokeless tobacco products are taxed in 40 states. Thus, statewide enforcement, preemptive legislation (legislation prohibiting any local jurisdiction from enacting reductions that are more stringent than the state law or restrictions that may vary from state law), court decisions, and federal legislation all influence and control the impact of state tobacco control legislation (American Cancer Society 1998).

In short, the willingness of nonsmokers to speak up as firmly as necessary against smoking and exposure to second-hand smoke has inspired restrictive legislation against tobacco use, which in turn affects smoking habits. As stated earlier, a complete network of laws defines, controls, and restricts smoking, from the purchase of tobacco to the consumption of cigarettes or other types of tobacco products, such as smokeless and pipe tobacco, cigars, and the like.

Several organized groups of nonsmokers have made quite an impact, including Action on Smoking and Health (ASH), the Group Against Smokers' Pollution (GASP), the American Lung Association, the American Cancer Society, and medical and dental associations. These groups have been instrumental in passing legislation restricting or banning smoking in public places; banning cigarette commercials on television; and prohibiting smoking on commercial aircraft, on interstate buses, and in some restaurants, elevators, indoor theaters, libraries, art galleries, and museums.

Discussion Questions

1. If smoking is the most preventable cause of disease and premature death in the United States, why do people continue to smoke?

2. How effective are the health warning labels on cigarette packages? Interview two or three smokers about these warning labels.

3. List and define the diseases that cigarette smokers are most likely to contract.

4. What effects do cigarettes have on the fetus?

5. Why is smokeless tobacco perceived as safer than other forms of tobacco?

6. Who is most likely to smoke, and why?

7. Why do people who smoke become dependent on tobacco?

8. As tobacco markets in the United States have shrunk, what has happened abroad?

9. Assess the major methods for quitting smoking. Which methods are most likely to succeed?

10. Do you think smokers should have the right to smoke in public places? Explain.

Key Terms

Nicotiana tabacum **305**

bright, flue-cured, or Virginia **306**

puffing **306**

nicotine **308**

tobacco chewing **314**

snuff dipping **314**

clove cigarettes **315**

eugenol **315**

emphysema **317**

environmental tobacco smoke **317**

sudden infant death syndrome (SIDS) **318**

dipping snuff **318**

chewing tobacco **318**

snuff **318**

snuffing **318**

mainstream smoke **320**

sidestream smoke **320**

passive smoking **320**

gateway drug **329**

patterns of behavior **329**

Summary

1 Nicotine is by far one of the most addictive drugs.

2 Approximately 25.8% of the U.S. population age 12 and older smokes cigarettes.

3 The quality of leaf tobacco has changed throughout the years of production. Since 1956, the amount of leaf tobacco in a cigarette has declined by approximately 25%. Most cigarettes today are low-tar and low-nicotine types.

4 Nicotine is the substance in tobacco that causes dependence. This drug initially stimulates and then depresses the nervous system.

5 The amount of tobacco absorbed varies according to five factors: (1) the exact composition of tobacco being used; (2) how densely the tobacco is packed in the cigarette and the length of the cigarette smoked; (3) whether a filter is used and the characteristics of the filter; (4) the volume of the smoke inhaled; and (5) the number of cigarettes smoked throughout the day.

6 Cigarette smoking is an addiction that is costly in several ways. For instance, each year 430,000 deaths in the United States are attributed to cigarette smoking. In addition, in 1999, smoking-attributable costs for medical care totaled more than $100 billion.

7 Chewing tobacco and snuff are types of smokeless tobacco products that are commonly referred to as "spit tobacco." Both types consist of tobacco leaves that are shredded and twisted into strands and then either chewed or placed in the cheek between the lower lip and gum.

8 Research clearly shows that the tar and nicotine content of cigarettes affect mortality rates. Cigarette smokers tend to die at an earlier age than nonsmokers. They also have a greater probability of contracting various illnesses, including types of cancers, chronic bronchitis and emphysema, diseases of the cardiovascular system, and peptic ulcers. In addition, smoking has adverse effects on pregnancy and may harm the fetus.

9 Cigarette smoke is classified as either mainstream smoke, the smoke drawn directly through the mouthpiece of the cigarette, or sidestream smoke. Passive smoking refers to nonsmokers' inhalation of tobacco smoke. The term *environmental tobacco smoke (ETS)* is widely used to refer to the mixture of predominantly sidestream and exhaled mainstream that is inhaled by the passive smoker.

10 The primary methods for quitting smoking are step-by-step manuals, acupuncture, "cold turkey" techniques, hypnosis, nicotine gum, nicotine patches, and self-help with behavioral modification.

11 The four primary aspects of tobacco-control laws in each state are smoke-free indoor air, youth access to tobacco products, advertising of tobacco products, and excise taxes on tobacco products.

References

American Cancer Society. Tobacco and Cancer (2000). Available http://www.cancer.org/tobacco.

American Cancer Society. Smoking Legislation (1998). Available http://www.cancer.org.tobacco/legislation.html.

Austin, G. A. *Perspectives on the History of Psychoactive Substance Use.* Washington, DC: National Institute on Drug Abuse, 1978.

Bartecchi, C. E., T. D. MacKenzie, and R. W. Shrier. "The Global Tobacco Epidemic." *Scientific American* (May 1995): 49.

Callahan, M. "How Smoking Kills You." *Parade Magazine* 213 (December 1987): 209–11.

Centers for Disease Control and Prevention (CDC). Tobacco Information and Prevention Source (TIPS). Targeting Tobacco Use: The Nation's Leading Cause of Death (2 November 2000). Available http://www.cdc.gov.

"Cigars." *Encyclopedia Americana.* Danbury, CT: Grolier 1988.

Cook, P. S., R. C. Petersen, and D. T. Moore. *Alcohol, Tobacco, and Other Drugs May Harm the Unborn.* Rockville, MD: U.S. Department of Health and Human Services 1990.

Corti, E. C. *A History of Smoking.* London: Harrap and Company, 1931.

DeAngelis, T. "Behavior Is Included in Report on Smoking." *APA Monitor* 20, No. 3 (1989): 1, 4.

Giovino, G. A., M. W. Schooley, B. P. Zhu, J. H. Chrismon, S. L. Tambour, and J. P. Peddicord. "Trends and Recent Patterns in Selected Tobacco-Use Behaviors. Surveillance Summary." *Mortality and Morbidity Weekly Report* 43 (SS-3) (1994): 1–43.

Heimann, R. K. *Tobacco and Americans.* New York: McGraw–Hill, 1960.

Langton, P.A. *Drug Use and the Alcohol Dilemma.* Boston: Allyn and Bacon, 1991.

Master Settlement Agreement Between the Settling States of the United States of America and the Participating Tobacco Manufacturers, 1998.

National Council for Science and the Environment (NCSE). *PL30058: Tobacco Master Settlement Agreement (1998): Overview, Implementation by States, and Congressional Issues.* Washington DC: NCSE, November 1999.

National Household Survey on Drug Abuse, 1999 Chapter 2, National Estimates of Substance Abuse. Available at: http://www.samhsa.gov/oas.NHSDA/1999/Chapter2.htm#topofpage.

National Institute on Drug Abuse (NIDA). *Cigarette Smoking*. CAP 42. Rockville, MD: National Institute on Drug Abuse, January 1995.

National Institute on Drug Abuse (NIDA). NIDA Research Report—Nicotine Addiction (1998). Available http://165.112.78.61/research reports/nicotine.

"Non-Smoking Youth Better Resist Other Drugs." Prevention Newsline 4, No. 3 (Spring 1991), p. 5.

O'Brien, R., S. Cohen, G. Evans, and J. Fine. *The Encyclopedia of Drug Abuse*, 2nd ed. New York: Facts on File and Greenspring, 1992.

Palfai, T. and H. Jankiewicz. *Drugs and Human Behavior*. Dubuque, IA: Brown, 1991.

Perry, S. "Recognizing Everyday Addicts." *Current Health* 2, No. 16 (May 1990): 20–3.

Rovner, S. "Up in Smoke: Why Do So Many Kids Ignore All the Evidence Condemning Cigarettes?" *Washington Post, National Weekly Edition* (16–22 December 1991): 20–1.

Schelling, T. C. "Addictive Drugs: The Cigarette Experience." *Science* (24 January 1992): 430–3.

Schultes, R. E. "Ethnopharmacological Significance of Psychotropic Drugs of Vegetal Origin." In *Principles of Psychopharmacology*, 2nd ed., edited by W. G. Clark and J. del Giudice, 41–70. New York: Academic Press, 1978.

"Smokeless Tobacco, Think Before You Chew." (Leaflet). Chicago: American Dental Association, 1990.

Substance Abuse and Mental Health Services Administration (SAMHSA), Office of Applied Studies. *1999 National Household Survey on Drug Abuse*. 2000.

U.S. Department of Agriculture (USDA). *Tobacco: World Markets and Trade, Circular Series FT-12-99*. December 1999.

U.S. Department of Health & Human Services. "The Health Consequences of Smoking: Nicotine Addiction: A Report of the Surgeon General" 1988, DHHS Pub# CDC 88–8406. U. S. Department of Health & Human Services, Public Health Service, Centers for Disease Control, Center for Health Promotion and Education Office on Smoking and Health.

U.S. Department of Health & Human Services (USD HHS). *Preventing Tobacco Use Among Young People: A Report of the Surgeon General*. Atlanta: USDHHS, Public Health Service, Centers for Disease Control and Prevention, National Center for Chronic Disease Prevention and Health Promotion, Office on Smoking and Health, 1994.

U.S. Department of Health & Human Services (USD HHS). *Tobacco-Control Activities in the United States, 1992–1993: Biennial Report to Congress*. Atlanta: USD HHS, Public Health Service, Centers for Disease Control and Prevention, National Center for Chronic Disease Prevention and Health Promotion, Office on Smoking and Health, 1995.

U.S. Department of Health & Human Services (USD HHS) and Centers for Disease Control and Prevention (CDC). "Current Trends: Mortality Trends for Selected Smoking-Related Cancers and Breast Cancer—United States 1950–1990." *Morbidity and Mortality Weekly Report* 12, No. 44 (12 November 1993): 863–6.

U.S. Surgeon General. *The Changing Cigarette*. Publication No. PHS 81-51056. Washington, DC: U.S. Department of Health, Education, and Welfare, 1981.

U.S. Surgeon General. *The Health Consequences of Smoking*. Washington, DC: U.S. Department of Health, Education and Welfare, 1984.

U.S. Surgeon General. *The Health Consequences of Smoking: Cancer and Chronic Lung Disease in the Workplace*. Washington, DC: U.S. Government Printing Office, 1985.

Wentz, C. "22.2 Million American Women Just Don't Get It." (Editorial) *Journal of Women's Health* 3 (4 November 1993): 127–8.

World Health Organization, Tobacco Free Initiative Update (7 November 2000). Available http://tobacco.who.int/.

Hallucinogens (Psychedelics)

Did You Know?

- Many ancient mystics used hallucinogens as part of their religious ceremonies.
- Hallucinogens were abused by relatively few people in the United States until the social upheaval of the 1960s.
- The Native American Church in the United States has special permission by the federal government to use the psychedelic mescaline as part of its religious sacrament.
- Some hallucinogens—such as LSD, MDA, and Ecstasy—have been used by psychiatrists to assist in psychotherapy with certain patients.
- Hallucinogens such as LSD do not tend to be physically addicting.
- The senses are grossly exaggerated and distorted under the influence of hallucinogens.

- Ecstasy abuse has increased dramatically in the past few years due to its popularity as a "club drug" and its use at "rave" parties.
- For some users, hallucinogens can cause frightening, nightmarish experiences called *bad trips*.
- Phencyclidine (PCP) and ketamine were originally developed as general anesthetics.
- PCP is sometimes used as an additive in "street" hallucinogens.
- Intense use of PCP can cause psychotic episodes accompanied by tremendous strength, making management of users by medical or law enforcement personnel very dangerous.

Chapter 13

Learning Objectives

**On completing this chapter
you will be able to:**

► Explain why hallucinogens became so popular during the 1960s.

► Describe the nature of the sensory changes that occur due to the influence of hallucinogens.

► Outline how psychedelic, stimulant, and anticholinergic effects are expressed in the three principal types of hallucinogens.

► Describe why some psychotherapists believe that the use of MDMA on their patients may be beneficial.

► Explain the reason for Ecstasy's most recent popularity.

► Explain how hallucinogens differ from other commonly abused drugs in terms of their addicting properties and their ability to cause dependence.

► Describe the effects that environment and personality have on the individual's response to hallucinogens.

► Explain the term *club drugs* and describe their particular problems.

► Characterize how PCP differs from other hallucinogens.

Introduction

First time I tried [LSD], I was in college. I just saw tracers, no big visuals. Everything was enhanced or something. It made me jittery, but not tense. I could really drink. (*From Venturelli's files, Joe, age 24, 1996.*)

I was doing acid [LSD] on Thanksgiving. The turkey begged my Dad not to carve it. Another time my James Dean poster told me to kill myself and I wasn't worth living. So I tried. (*From Venturelli's files, Val, age 17, 1996.*)

These quotes from young adults illustrate the sensory and emotional distortions that can be caused by using hallucinogens. In this chapter, we begin with a brief historical review of the use of hallucinogens, tracing the trend in the United States from the 1960s to today. Next, the nature of hallucinogens and the effects they produce are examined. The rest of the chapter addresses the various types of psychedelic agents: LSD types, phenylethylamines (including Ecstasy), anticholinergics, and other miscellaneous substances.

Protests against the Vietnam War in the 1960s and 1970s often included the use of hallucinogens.

The History of Hallucinogen Use

People have known and written about drug-related hallucinations for centuries. Throughout the ages, individuals who saw visions or experienced hallucinations were perceived as being holy or sacred, as receiving divine messages, or possibly as being bewitched and controlled by the devil. There are many indications that medicine men, shamans, witches, oracles, and perhaps mystics and priests of various groups were familiar with drugs and herbs that caused such experiences and today are known as hallucinogens .

Before the 1960s, several psychedelic substances, such as mescaline from the peyote cactus, could be obtained from chemical supply houses with no restriction in the United States. Abuse of hallucinogens did not become a major social problem in this country until this decade of racial struggles, the Vietnam War, and violent demonstrations. Many individuals frustrated with the hypocrisy of "the establishment" tried to "turn on and tune in" by using hallucinogens as pharmacological crutches.

Psychedelic drugs became especially popular when some medical professionals such as then-Harvard psychology professor, Timothy Leary, reported that these drugs allowed users to get in touch with themselves and achieve a peaceful inner serenity (Associated Press 1999). At the same time, it became well publicized that the natural psychedelics (such as mescaline and peyote) were and had been for many years used routinely by some religious organizations of Native Americans for enhancing spiritual experiences. This factor contributed to the mystical, supernatural aura associated with hallucinogenic agents and added to their enticement to a so-called dropout generation.

With widespread use of LSD, it was observed that this and similar drugs may induce a form of psychosis-like schizophrenia (DSM-IV-TR 2000). The term psychotomimetic was coined to describe these compounds; it means "psychosis mimicking" and is still used in medicine today. The basis for the designation is the effects of these drugs that induce mental states that impair an individual's ability to recognize and respond appropriately to reality.

By the mid-1960s, federal regulatory agencies had become concerned with the misuse of hallucinogens and the potential emotional damage caused by these drugs. Access to hallucinogenic agents was restricted, and laws against their distribution were passed. Despite the problems associated with these psychedelics, some groups demanded that responsible use was possible and that they be allowed legal access to these substances.

■ THE NATIVE AMERICAN CHURCH

The hallucinogen peyote plays a central role in the ceremonies of Native Americans who follow a religion that is a combination of Christian doctrine and Native American religious rituals. Members of this Church are found as far north as Canada. They believe that God made a special gift of this sacramental plant to them so that they might commune more directly with Him. The first organized peyote church was the First-Born Church of Christ, incorporated in 1914 in Oklahoma. The Native American Church of the United States was chartered in 1918 and is the largest such group at present (approximately 100,000–200,000 members).

Because of the religious beliefs of the members of the Native American Church concerning the powers of peyote, when Congress legislated against its use in 1965, it allowed room for religious use of this psychedelic plant. The American Indian Religious Freedom Act of 1978 was an attempt by Congress to allow the members of the Native American Church access to peyote due to constitutional guarantees of religious freedom. Due to controversy inspired by the original piece of legislation, an amendment to the 1978 act was signed in 1994, which specifically protected the use of peyote in Native American Church ceremonies. This amendment also prohibits use of peyote for nonreligious purposes (Becenti 1994; Mims 2000).

Peyote is used as a sacramental plant by members of the Native American Church as part of their religious ceremonies.

KEY TERMS

hallucinogens
substances that alter sensory processing in the brain, causing perceptual disturbances, changes in thought processing, and depersonalization

psychedelics
substances that expand or heighten perception and consciousness

psychotomimetic
substances that cause psychosis-like symptoms

■ TIMOTHY LEARY AND THE LEAGUE OF SPIRITUAL DISCOVERY

In 1966, 3 years after being fired by Harvard because of his controversial involvement with hallucinogens (Associated Press 1999), Timothy Leary undertook a constitutional strategy intended to retain legitimate access to another hallucinogen, LSD. He began a religion called the League of Spiritual Discovery; LSD was the sacrament. This unorthodox religious orientation to the LSD experience was presented in a manual called *The Psychedelic Experience* (Leary et al. 1964), which was based on the *Tibetan Book of the Dead*. It became the "bible" of the psychedelic drug movement.

The movement grew, but most members used "street" LSD and did not follow Leary's directions. Leary believed that the hallucinogenic experience was only beneficial under proper control and guidance. But most members of this so-called religion merely used the organization as a front to gain access to an illegal drug. Federal authorities did not agree with Leary's freedom of religion interpretation and in 1969 convicted him for possession of marijuana and LSD and sentenced him to 20 years imprisonment (Stone 1991). Before being incarcerated, Leary escaped to Algeria and wandered for a couple of years before being extradited to the United States. He served several years in jail and was released in 1976.

Even in his later years, Leary continued to believe that U.S. citizens should be able to use hallucinogens without government regulation. He died in 1996 at the age of 75 years, revered by some but cursed by others (Associated Press 1999; Letters 1996).

Timothy Leary advocated legalization of LSD in the 1960s.

Hallucinogen Use Today

Today, the use of hallucinogens (excluding marijuana) is primarily a young adult phenomenon (Johnston 1999). Although the use rate has not returned to that of the late 1960s and early 1970s (approximately 16%), the increase in high school seniors lifetime use from 9.2% in 1992 to 14% in 1999 is very disturbing (Table 13.1). Of particular concern is the 50% increase in LSD use during this time (Johnston 1999). It has been speculated that this increase reflects the ignorance of a new generation about the potential problems of the hallucinogens and a shift from using the widely publicized drugs of abuse such as cocaine and heroin.

The Nature of Hallucinogens

Agreement has not been reached on what constitutes a hallucinogenic agent (O'Brien 1996), for several reasons. First, a variety of seemingly unrelated drug groups can produce hallucinations, delusions, or sensory disturbances under certain conditions. For example, besides the traditional hallucinogens (such as LSD), high doses of anticholinergics, cocaine, amphetamines, and steroids can cause hallucinations.

What's more, responses to even the traditional hallucinogens can vary tremendously from person to person and from experience to experience. It is

apparent that multiple mechanisms are involved in the actions of these drugs, which contribute to the array of responses that they can cause. These drugs most certainly influence the complex inner workings of the human mind and have been described as psychedelic, psychotogenic , or (as already mentioned) psychotomimetic. The features of hallucinogens that distinguish them from other drug groups are their ability to alter perception, thought, and feeling in such a manner that does not normally occur except in dreams or during experiences of extreme religious exaltation (Jaffe 1990). We examine these characteristics throughout this chapter.

■ SENSORY AND PSYCHOLOGICAL EFFECTS

In general, LSD is considered the prototype agent against which other hallucinogens are measured. Typical users experience several stages of sensory experiences; they can go through all stages during a single "trip" or, more likely, they will only pass through some. These stages follow:

1. Heightened, exaggerated senses

2. Loss of control

3. Self-reflection

4. Loss of identity and a sense of cosmic merging

The following illustrations of the stages of the LSD experience are based primarily on an account by Solomon Snyder (1974), a highly regarded neuroscientist (one of the principal discoverers of endorphins; see Chapter 5), who personally experienced the effects of LSD as a young resident in psychiatry.

Altered Senses

In his encounter with LSD, Snyder used a moderate dose of 100 to 200 micrograms and observed few discernible effects for the first 30 minutes except some mild nausea. After this time had elapsed, objects took on a purplish tinge and appeared to be vaguely outlined. Colors, textures, and lines achieved a richness Snyder had never before experienced. Perception was so exaggerated that individual skin pores "stood out and clamored for recognition" (Snyder 1974, p. 42). Objects became distorted; when Snyder focused on his thumb, it began to swell, undulate, and then moved forward in a menacing fashion. Visions filled

TABLE 13.1 Trends (shown in percentages) in the Use of LSD and all Hallucinogens by Eighth-graders Through Young Adults from 1992 to 1999

	USED DURING LIFETIME				USED DURING YEAR				USED DURING MONTH			
	1992	1994	1996	1999	1992	1994	1996	1999	1992	1994	1996	1999
Eighth-graders												
LSD	3.2	3.7	5.1	4.1	2.1	2.4	3.5	2.4	0.9	1.1	1.5	1.1
All hallucinogens	N.A.	3.8	4.3	5.9	4.8	2.5	2.7	4.1	2.9	1.1	1.3	1.9
Tenth-graders												
LSD	5.8	7.2	9.4	8.5	4.0	5.2	6.9	6.0	1.6	2.0	2.4	2.3
All hallucinogens	N.A.	6.4	8.1	10.5	9.7	4.3	5.8	7.8	6.9	1.8	2.4	2.8
Twelfth-graders												
LSD	8.6	10.5	12.6	12.2	5.6	6.9	8.8	8.1	2.0	2.6	2.5	2.7
All hallucinogens	N.A.	9.2	11.4	14.0	13.7	5.9	7.6	10.1	9.4	2.1	3.1	3.5
Young Adults												
LSD	13.8	13.8	15.0	N.A.	4.3	4.0	4.5	N.A.	1.1	1.1	0.7	N.A.
All hallucinogens	N.A.	15.9	15.4	16.4	N.A.	5.1	4.9	5.6	N.A.	1.6	1.4	1.2
Ecstasy	3.9	3.8	5.2	N.A.	1.0	0.7	1.7	N.A.	0.3	0.2	0.3	N.A.

Note: N.A., not available.

*For this survey, inhalants and marijuana were not considered as hallucinogens.

Sources: National Survey on Drug Abuse from The Monitoring the Future Study, 1975–1998; College and Young Adults; L. D. Johnston, P. M. O'Malley, J. G. Bachman; The University of Michigan Institute for Social Research, National Institute on Drug Abuse, U.S. Department of Human Services, National Institutes of Health, 1999.
The University of Michigan News and Information Services; 17 December 1999; citing the National Survey on Drug Abuse, The Monitoring the Future Study, 1999; L. D. Johnston, P. M. O'Malley, J. G. Bachman; The University of Michigan Institute for Social Research, National Institute on Drug Abuse, U.S. Department of Human Services, National Institutes of Health.

with distorted imagery occurred when his eyes were closed. The sense of time and distance changed dramatically; "a minute was like an hour, a week was like an eternity, a foot became a mile" (Snyder 1974, p. 43). The present seemed to drag on forever, and the concept of future lost its meaning. The exaggeration of perceptions and feelings gave the sense of more events occurring in a time period, giving the impression of time slowing.

An associated sensation described by Snyder is called synesthesia, a crossover phenomenon between senses. For example, sound develops visual dimensions and vice versa, enabling you to see sounds and hear colors. These altered sensory experiences are described as a heightened sensory awareness and relate to the first component of the psychedelic state (O'Brien 1996).

Loss of Control

The second feature of LSD also relates to altered sensory experiences and a loss of control (O'Brien 1996). The user cannot determine whether the psychedelic trip will be a pleasant, relaxing experience or a "bad trip," with recollections of hidden fears

KEY TERMS

psychotogenic
substances that initiate psychotic behavior

synesthesia
a subjective sensation of image of a sense other than the one being stimulated, such as an auditory sensation caused by a visual stimulus

and suppressed anxieties that can precipitate neurotic or psychotic responses. The frightening reactions may persist a few minutes or several hours and be mildly agitating or extremely disturbing. Some bad trips can include feelings of panic, confusion, suspicion, helplessness, and a total lack of control. The following scenario illustrates how terrifying a bad trip can be:

> I was having problems breathing [and] my throat was all screwed up. The things that entered my mind were that I was dead and people were saying good-bye, because they really meant it. I was witnessing my own funeral. I was thinking that I was going to wake either in the back seat of a cop car or in the hospital. (*From Venturelli's files, interview with a 19-year-old male, 1995.*)

Replays of these frightening experiences can occur at a later time, even though the drug has not been taken again; such recurrences are referred to as " flashbacks ."

It is not clear what determines the nature of the sensory response. Perhaps it relates to the state of anxiety and personality of the user or the nature of his or her surroundings. It is interesting that Timothy Leary tried to teach his "drug disciples" that "turning on correctly means to understand the many levels that are brought into focus; it takes years of discipline, training and discipleship" ("Celebration #1" 1966). He apparently felt that, with experience and training, you could control the sensory effects of the hallucinogens. This is an interesting possibility but has never been well demonstrated.

Self-Reflection

Snyder (1974) made reference to the third component of the psychedelic response in his LSD experience. During the period when sensory effects predominate, self-reflection also occurs. While in this state, Snyder explained, the user "becomes aware of thoughts and feelings long hidden beneath

the surface, forgotten and/or repressed" (p. 44). As a psychiatrist, Snyder claimed that this new perspective can lead to valid insights that are useful psychotherapeutic exercises.

Some psychotherapists have used or advocated the use of psychedelics for this purpose since the 1950s, as described by Sigmund Freud, to "make conscious the unconscious" (Snyder 1974, p. 44). It should be noted that, although a case can be made for the psychotherapeutic use of this group of drugs, the Food and Drug Administration (FDA) has not approved any of these agents for psychiatric use. The psychedelics currently available are considered to be too unpredictable in their effects and possess substantial risks (Abraham et al. 1996). Not only is their administration not considered to be significantly therapeutic but also their use is deemed a great enough risk that the principal hallucinogenic agents are scheduled as controlled substances (see Chapter 3).

Loss of Identity and Cosmic Merging

The final features that set the psychedelics apart as unique drugs were described by Snyder (1974) as the "mystical-spiritual aspect of the drug experience." He claimed, "It is indescribable. For how can anyone verbalize a merging of his being with the totality of the universe? How do you put into words the feeling that 'all is one,' 'I am of the all,' 'I am no longer.' One's skin ceases to be a boundary between self and others" (p. 45). Because consumption of hallucinogen-containing plants has often been part of religious ceremonies, it is likely that this sense of cosmic merging and union with all humankind correlates to the exhilaratingly spiritual experiences described by many religious mystics.

The loss of identity and personal boundaries caused by hallucinogens is not viewed as being so spiritually enticing by all. In particular, for individuals who have rigid, highly ordered personalities, the dissolution of a well-organized and well-structured world is terrifying because the drug destroys the individual's emotional support. Such an individual finds that the loss of a separate identity can cause extreme panic and anxiety. During these drug-induced panic states, which in some ways are schizophrenic-like, people have committed suicide and homicide. These tragic reactions are part of the risk

---

KEY TERMS

flashbacks
recurrences of earlier drug-induced sensory experiences in the absence of the drug

of using hallucinogenics and explains some of the FDA's hesitancy to legalize or authorize them for psychotherapeutic use.

■ MECHANISMS OF ACTION

As with most drugs, hallucinogens represent the proverbial "double-edged sword." These drugs may cause potentially useful psychiatric effects for many people. However, the variability in positive versus negative responses, coupled with lack of understanding as to what factors are responsible for the variables, have made these drugs dangerous and difficult to manage.

Some researchers have suggested that all hallucinogens act at a common central nervous system (CNS) site to exert their psychedelic effects. Although this hypothesis has not been totally disproven, there is little evidence to support it. The fact that so many different types of drugs can cause hallucinogenic effects suggests that multiple mechanisms are likely responsible for their actions.

The most predictable and typical psychedelic experiences are caused by LSD or similar agents. Consequently, these agents have been the primary focus of studies intended to elucidate the nature of hallucinogenic mechanisms. Although LSD has effects at several CNS sites, ranging from the spinal cord to the cortex of the brain, its effects on the neurotransmitter serotonin most likely account for its psychedelic properties (Aghajanian and Marek 1999). That LSD and similar drugs alter serotonin activity has been proven; how they affect this transmitter is not so readily apparent.

Although many experts believe changes in serotonin activity are the basis for the psychedelic properties of most hallucinogens, a case can be made for the involvement of norepinephrine, dopamine, acetylcholine, and perhaps other transmitter systems as well (see Chapter 5). Only additional research will be able to sort out this complex but important issue.

Types of Hallucinogenic Agents

Due to recent technological developments, understanding of hallucinogens has advanced; even so, the classification of these drugs remains somewhat arbitrary. Many agents produce some of the pharmacological effects of the traditional psychedelics, such as LSD and mescaline.

A second type of hallucinogen includes those agents that have amphetamine-like molecular structures (referred to as *phenylethylamines*) and possess some stimulant action; this group includes drugs such as DOM (dimethoxymethylamphetamine), MDA (methylenedioxyamphetamine), and MDMA (methylenedioxymethamphetamine or Ecstasy). These agents vary in their hallucinogen or stimulant properties. MDA is more like an amphetamine (stimulant), whereas MDMA is more like LSD (hallucinogen). In large doses, however, each of the phenylethylamines causes substantial CNS stimulation.

The third major group of hallucinogens is the anticholinergic drugs, which block some of the receptors for the neurotransmitter acetylcholine (see Chapter 5). Almost all drugs that antagonize these receptors cause hallucinations in high doses. Many of these potent anticholinergic hallucinogens are naturally occurring and have been known, used, and abused for millennia.

■ TRADITIONAL HALLUCINOGENS: LSD TYPES

The LSD-like drugs are considered to be the prototypical hallucinogens and are used as the basis of comparison for other types of agents with psychedelic properties. Included in this group are LSD itself and some hallucinogens derived from plants, such as mescaline from the peyote cactus, psilocybin from mushrooms, dimethyltryptamine (DMT) from seeds, and myristicin from nutmeg. Because LSD is the principal hallucinogen, its origin, history, and properties is discussed in detail, providing a basis for understanding the other psychedelic drugs.

Lysergic Acid Diethylamide (LSD)

LSD is a relatively new drug, but similar compounds have existed for a long time. For example, accounts from the Middle Ages tell about a strange affliction that caused pregnant women to abort and others to develop strange burning sensations in their extremi-

KEY TERMS

ergotism
poisoning by toxic substances from the ergot fungus
Claviceps purpurea

ties. Today, we call this condition ergotism and know that it is caused by eating grain contaminated by the ergot fungus. This fungus produces compounds related to LSD called the *ergot alkaloids* (Goldstein 1994; NIDA Infofax 1999). Besides the sensory effects, the ergot substances can also cause hallucinations, delirium, and psychosis.

In 1938, Albert Hofmann, a scientist for Sandoz Pharmaceutical Laboratories of Basel, Switzerland, worked on a series of ergot compounds in a search for active chemicals that might be of medical value. Lysergic acid was similar in structure to a com-

Albert Hofmann created LSD in 1938 while trying to synthesize a drug to study psychosis.

pound called *nikethamide,* a stimulant, and Hofmann tried to create slight chemical modifications that might merit further testing. The result of this effort was the production of lysergic acid diethylamide, or LSD. Hofmann's experience with this new compound gave insight to the effects of this drug.

Soon after LSD was discovered, the similarity of experiences with this agent to the symptoms of schizophrenia were noted, which prompted researchers to investigate correlations between the two. The hope was to use LSD as a tool for producing an artificial psychosis to aid in understanding the biochemistry of psychosis. Interest in this use of LSD has declined because it is generally accepted that LSD effects differ from natural psychoses (Abraham et al. 1996).

The use of LSD in psychotherapy has also been tried in connection with the treatment of alcoholism, autism, paranoia, schizophrenia, and various other mental and emotional disorders. Therapeutic use of LSD has not increased to any great extent over the years because of its limited success, legal aspects, difficulty in obtaining the pure drug, adverse reactions to the drug ("bad trips" can occur under controlled as well as uncontrolled conditions), and rapid tolerance buildup in some patients.

Nonmedical interest in LSD and related drugs began to grow during the 1950s and peaked in the 1960s, when LSD was used by millions of young Americans for chemical escape. Occasionally, a "bad trip" would cause a user to feel terror and panic; these experiences resulted in well-publicized accidental deaths due to jumping from building tops or running into the pathway of oncoming vehicles (U.S. Department of Justice 1991).

As with other hallucinogens, the use of LSD by teenagers declined somewhat over the 1970s and 1980s but began to rise again in the early 1990s. The reason for this rise is thought to relate to a decline in the perceived dangers of using LSD and an increase in peer approval (Johnston 1999). These changes in attitude may reflect the recent reduction in education concerning these drugs. Of high school seniors sampled in 1975, 11.3% had used LSD sometime during their life; that number declined to 8.6% in 1992 and rebounded to 12.2% in 1999 (Table 13.1). LSD users are typically college or high school students, white, middle-class, and risk-takers (Johnston et al. 1996).

Synthesis and Administration LSD is a complex molecule that requires about 1 week to be synthesized. Because of the sophisticated chemistry necessary for its production, LSD is not manufactured by local illicit laboratories. Because of LSD's potency, it has been difficult to locate the illicit LSD labs; small quantities of LSD are sufficient to satisfy the demand and can be easily transported without detection.

The physical properties of LSD are not distinctive. In its purified form, LSD is colorless, odorless, and tasteless. It can be purchased in several forms, including tiny tablets (about one-tenth the size of aspirins, called *microdots*), capsules, and occasionally even a liquid. The street names of LSD include *acid, blotter acid, microdot,* and *white lightning* (U.S. Department of Justice 1991). Although LSD usually is taken by mouth, it is sometimes injected.

LSD often is added to absorbent paper, such as blotter paper, that can be divided into small decorated squares. Each square is swallowed or chewed and represents a single dose. One gram of LSD can provide 10,000 individual doses and be sold on the streets for $50,000.

Physiological Effects Like many hallucinogens, LSD is remarkably potent. The typical dose today is 20 to 30 micrograms, compared with a typical dose of 150 to 300 micrograms in the 1960s. This difference in dose likely explains why today fewer users of LSD are experiencing severe side effects (NIDA Infofax 1999). In monkeys, the lethal dose has been

Small quantities of LSD are applied to squares of absorbent blotter paper to be chewed or swallowed.

determined to be about 5 milligrams per kilogram of body weight.

When taken orally, LSD is readily absorbed and diffused into all tissues. It will pass through the placenta into the fetus and through the blood-brain barrier. The brain receives about 1% of the total dose.

Within the brain, LSD is particularly concentrated in the hypothalamus, the limbic system, and the auditory and visual reflex areas. Electrodes placed in the limbic system show an "electrical storm," or a massive increase in neural activity, which might correlate with the overwhelming flood of sensations and the phenomenon of synesthesia reported by the user (Goldstein 1995). LSD also activates the sympathetic nervous system; shortly after the drug is taken, body temperature, heart rate, and blood pressure rise, the person sweats, and the pupils of the eyes become dilated. Its effects on the parasympathetic nervous system cause an increase in salivation and nausea (NIDA Infofax 1999). These systemic effects do not appear to be related to the hallucinogenic properties of the drug.

Pharmacokinetic experiments with LSD show that about half of the substance is cleared from the body within 3 hours, and more than 90% is excreted within 24 hours (Goldstein 1995). The effects of this hallucinogen can last 2 to 12 hours depending on the dose and previous experience with the drug (NIDA Infofax 1999). Tolerance to the effects of LSD develops more rapidly and lasts longer than tolerance to other hallucinogens. Tolerance develops very quickly to repeated doses, probably because of a change in sensitivity of the target cells in the brain rather than a change in its metabolism. Tolerance wears off within a few days after the drug is discontinued. Because there are no withdrawal symptoms, a person does not become physically dependent, but some psychological dependency on LSD can occur (NIDA Infofax 1999).

Behavioral Effects Because LSD alters a number of systems in the brain, its behavioral effects are many and variable among individuals (Goldstein 1995). The following sections address common CNS responses to this drug.

Creativity and Insight. A question often raised by researchers interested in experimenting with LSD is: Does it help expand the mind, increasing insight and creativity? This question is extremely difficult to answer because no one has ever determined the origin of insight and creativity. Moreover, each of us views these qualities differently.

Subjects under the influence of LSD often express the feeling of being more creative, but creative acts such as drawing and painting are hindered by the motor impairment caused by LSD. The products of artists under the influence of the drug usually prove to be inferior to those produced before the drug experience. Paintings done in LSD creativity studies have been described as reminiscent of "schizophrenic art."

In an often cited study, creativity, attitude, and anxiety tests on 24 college students found that LSD had no objective effect on creativity, although many of the subjects said they felt they were more creative (McGlothin et al. 1967). This paradox is noted in several studies of LSD use: the subjects believe they have more insight and provide better answers to life's problems, but they do not or cannot demonstrate this increase objectively. Overt behavior is not modified, and these new insights are short-lived unless they are reinforced by modified behavior.

This head was sculpted by a university student while under the influence of LSD.

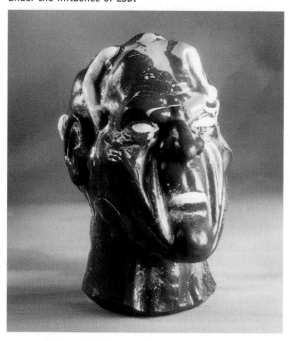

In spite of these results, some researchers still contend that LSD can enhance the creative process. For example, Oscar Janigar, a psychiatrist at the University of California, Los Angeles, claimed to have determined that LSD does not produce a tangible alteration in the way a painter paints; thus, it does not turn a poor painter into a good one. However, Janigar claimed that LSD does alter the way the painter appraises the world and allows the artist to "plunge into areas where access was restricted by confines of perceptions" and consequently becomes more creative (Tucker 1987, p. 16).

Adverse Psychedelic Effects. It is important to remember that there is no typical pattern of response to LSD. The experience varies for each user as a function of the person's *set*, or expectations, and *setting*, or environment, during the experience. Two of the major negative responses are described as follows (NIDA Infofax 1999; Pahnke et al. 1970):

1. The psychotic adverse reaction, or "freakout," is an intense, nightmarish experience. The subject may have complete loss of emotional control and experience paranoid delusions, hallucinations, panic attacks, psychosis, and catatonic seizures. In rare instances, some of these reactions are prolonged, lasting days.

2. The nonpsychotic adverse reaction may involve varying degrees of tension, anxiety, fear, depression, and despair but not as intense a response as the "freakout." A person with deep psychological problems or a strong need to be in conscious control or one who takes the drug in an unfavorable setting is more likely to have an adverse reaction than a person with a well-integrated personality.

Severe LSD behavioral toxicity can be treated with tranquilizers or a benzodiazepine.

Perceptual Effects. Because the brain's sensory processing is altered by a hallucinogenic dose of LSD, many kinds of unusual illusions can occur. Some users report seeing shifting geometrical patterns mixed with intense color perception; others observe the movement of stationary objects, such that a speck on the wall appears as a large blinking eye or an unfolding flower. Interpretation of sounds can also be scrambled; a dropped ashtray may become a gun fired at the user, for instance. In some cases, LSD alters perceptions to the extent that people feel they can walk on water or fly through the air. The sensation that the body is distorted and even coming apart is another common effect, especially for novice users. Thoughts of suicide and sometimes actual attempts can be caused by use of LSD as well (NIDA Infofax 1999; U.S. Department of Justice 1991).

Many LSD users find their sense of time distorted, such that hours may be perceived as years or an eternity. As discussed earlier, users may also have a distorted perception of their own knowledge or creativity; for instance, they may feel their ideas or work are especially unique, brilliant, or artistic. When analyzed by a person not on LSD, however, or explained after the "trip" is over, these ideas or creations are almost always quite ordinary.

In sum, LSD alters perception such that any sensation can be perceived in the extreme. An experience can be incredibly beautiful and uplifting. However, sometimes the experience can be very unpleasant.

The "flashback" is an interesting but poorly understood phenomenon of LSD use. Although usually thought of as being adverse, sometimes flashbacks are pleasant and even referred to as "free trips." During a flashback, sensations caused by previous LSD use return, although the subject is not using the drug at the time.

There are three broad categories of negative LSD-related flashbacks:

1. *"Body trip"*: recurrence of an unpleasant physical sensation

2. *"Bad mind trip"*: recurrence of a distressing thought or emotion

3. *Altered visual perception*: most frequent type of recurrence, consisting of seeing dots, flashes, trails of light, halos, false motion in the peripheral field, and other sensations

Flashbacks are most disturbing because they come on unexpectedly. Some have been reported years after use of LSD; for most people, however, flashbacks usually subside within weeks or months after taking LSD (NIDA Infofax 1999). The duration of a flashback is variable, lasting from a few minutes to several hours.

Although the precise mechanism of flashbacks is unknown, physical or psychological stresses and some drugs such as marijuana may trigger these experiences (Goldstein 1995). It has been proposed that flashbacks are an especially vivid form of memory that becomes seared into the subconscious mind due to the effects of LSD on the brain's transmitters. As one user described it:

> It was like watching a video of my past, except it was intensified greatly and the colors were extreme. Faces and objects were melting and I got really scared and started to flip out. (*From Venturelli's files, interview with a 19-year-old male, 1995.*)

Treatment consists of reassurance that the condition will go away and use of a sedative such as diazepam (Valium), if necessary, to treat the anxiety or panic that can accompany the flashback experience.

Genetic Damage and Birth Defects Experiments conducted in the mid-1960s suggested that LSD could cause birth defects, based on the observation that, when LSD was added to a suspension of human white blood cells in a test tube, the chromosomes of these cells were damaged. From this finding, it was proposed that, when LSD was consumed by human beings, it could damage the chromosomes of the male sperm, female egg, or the cells of the developing infant. Such damage theoretically could result in congenital defects in offspring (Dishotsky et al. 1971).

Carefully controlled studies conducted after news of LSD's chromosomal effects were made public have not supported this hypothesis. Experiments have revealed that, in contrast to the test tube findings, there is no chromosomal damage to white blood cells or any other cells when LSD is given to a human being (Dishotsky et al. 1971).

Studies have also shown that there are no carcinogenic or mutagenic effects from using LSD in experimental animals or human beings, with the exception of the fruit fly. (LSD is a mutagen in fruit flies if given in doses that are equivalent to 100,000 times the hallucinogenic dose for people.) Teratogenic effects occur in mice if LSD is given early in pregnancy. LSD may be teratogenic in rhesus monkeys if it is injected in doses (based on body weight) exceeding at least 100 times the usual hallucinogenic dose for humans. In other studies, women who took street LSD but not those given pure LSD had a higher rate of spontaneous abortions and births of malformed infants; this finding suggests that contaminants in adulterated LSD were responsible for the fetal effects and not the hallucinogen itself (Dishotsky et al. 1971).

Early Human Research In the 1950s, the U.S. government—specifically, the Central Intelligence Agency (CIA) and the army—became interested in reports of the effects of mind-altering drugs, including LSD. Unknown to the public at the time, these agencies conducted tests on human beings to learn more about such compounds and determine their usefulness in conducting military and clandestine missions. These activities became public when a biochemist, Frank Olson, killed himself in 1953 after being given a drink laced with LSD. Olson had a severe psychotic reaction and was being treated for the condition when he jumped out of a 10th-story window. His family was told only that he had committed suicide. The connection to LSD was not uncovered until 1975. The court awarded Olson's family $750,000 in damages in 1976.

In 1976, the extent of these studies was revealed: nearly 585 soldiers and 900 civilians had been given LSD in poorly organized experiments in which participants were coerced into taking this drug or not told that they were being given it. Powerful hallucinogens such as LSD can cause serious psychological damage in some subjects, especially when they are unaware of what is happening.

The legal consequences of these LSD studies continued for years. As recently as 1987, a New York judge awarded $700,000 to the family of a mental patient who killed himself after having been given LSD without an explanation of the drug's nature. The judge said that there was a "conspiracy of silence" among the army, the Department of Justice, and the New York State Attorney General to conceal events surrounding the death of the subject, Harold Blauer.

Mescaline (Peyote)

Mescaline is one of approximately 30 psychoactive chemicals that have been isolated from the peyote cactus and used for centuries in the Americas (see "Here and Now," Peyote: An Ancient Indian Way). One of the first reports on the peyote plant was made by Francisco Hernandez of the court of King Philip II of Spain. King Philip was interested in reports from the earlier Cortés expedition about strange medicines the natives used and sent Her-

---

HERE AND NOW   Peyote: An Ancient Indian Way

Members of the Native American Church use the buttons of the hallucinogenic peyote cactus to brew a sacramental tea as sacred to them as the bread and wine of the Christian Eucharist. As described by one member, "Peyote is a gift given to the Indians, but its ways cannot be obtained overnight. It has to be done with sincerity. It becomes part of your way of life. One has to walk that walk." Those that accept this form of worship believe that respectful use of peyote can be a gateway to the realm of the spirit, visions, and guidance. The use of peyote as part of the latest New Age craze is very disturbing to members of this church and is viewed almost as a form of sacrilege.

Source: Mims, B. "Peyote: When the Ancient Indian Way Collides with a New Age Craze." *Salt Lake Tribune* 258 (1 July 1999): A-10.

nandez to collect information about herbs and medicines. Hernandez worked on this project from 1570 to 1575 and reported the use of more than 1200 plant remedies, as well as the existence of many hallucinogenic plants. He was one of the first to record the eating of parts of the peyote cactus and the resulting visions and mental changes.

In the 17th century, Spanish Catholic priests asked their Indian converts to confess to the use of peyote, which they believed was used to conjure up demons. However, nothing stopped its use. By 1760, use of peyote had spread into what is now the United States.

Peyote has been confused with another plant, the mescal shrub, which produces dark red beans that contain an extremely toxic alkaloid called *cytisine*. This alkaloid may cause hallucinations, convulsions, and even death. In addition, a mescal liquor is made from the agave cactus. Partly because of misidentification with the toxic mescal beans, the U.S. government outlawed the use of both peyote and mescaline for everyone except members of the Native American Church (Mims 2000). Mescaline has been used for decades by this group as part of their religious sacrament.

Mescaline is the most active drug in peyote; it induces intensified perception of colors and euphoria in the user. However, as Aldous Huxley said in *The Doors of Perception* (1954), his book about his experimentation with mescaline, "Along with the happily transfigured majority of mescaline takers there is a minority that finds in the drug only hell and purgatory." After Huxley related his experiences with mescaline, it was used by an increasing number of people.

Physiological Effects The average dose of mescaline that will cause hallucinations and other physiological effects is from 300 to 600 milligrams. It may take up to 20 peyote (mescal) buttons (ingested orally) to get 600 milligrams of mescaline.

Based on animal studies, scientists estimate that a lethal dosage is 10 to 30 times greater than that which causes behavioral effects in human beings. (About 200 milligrams is the lowest mind-altering dose.) Death in animals results from convulsions and respiratory arrest. Mescaline is perhaps 1000 to 3000 times less potent than LSD and 30 times less potent than another common hallucinogen, psilocybin (Mathias 1993). Psilocybin is discussed later in this chapter.

Effects include dilation of the pupils (mydriasis), increase in body temperature, anxiety, visual hallucinations, and alteration of body image. The last effect is a type of hallucination in which parts of the body may seem to disappear or to become grossly distorted. Mescaline induces vomiting in many people and some muscular relaxation (sedation). Apparently, there are few after-effects or drug hangover feelings at low doses. Higher doses of mescaline slow the heart and respiratory rhythm, contract the intestines and the uterus, and cause headache, difficulty in coordination, dry skin with itching, and hypertension (high blood pressure).

Mescaline users report that they lose all awareness of time. As with LSD, the setting for the "trip" influences the user's reactions. Most mescaline users prefer natural settings, most likely due to the historical association of this drug with Native Americans and their nature-related spiritual experiences (often under the influence of this drug). The visual hallucinations achieved depend on the individual. Colors are at first intensified and may be followed by hallu-

The peyote cactus contains a number of drugs. The best known is mescaline.

KEY TERMS

mydriasis
pupil dilation

cinations of shades, movements, forms, and events. The senses of smell and taste are enhanced. Some people claim (as with LSD) that they can "hear" colors and "see" sounds, such as the wind. Synesthesia occurs naturally in a small percentage of cases.

At low to medium doses, a state of euphoria is reported, often followed by a feeling of anxiety and less frequently by depression. Occasionally, users observe themselves as two people and experience the sensation that the mind and body are separate entities. A number of people have had cosmic experiences that are profound, almost religious, in which they discover a sense of unity with all creation. People who have this sensation often believe they have discovered the meaning of existence (see "Point/Counterpoint," Selective Access).

Mechanism of Action Within 30 to 120 minutes after ingestion, mescaline reaches a maximum concentration in the brain. The effects may persist for up to 9 or 10 hours. Hallucinations may last up to 2 hours and are usually affected by the dose level. About half the dose is excreted unchanged after 6 hours and can be recovered in the urine for reuse (if peyote is in short supply). A slow tolerance builds up after repeated use, and there is cross-tolerance to LSD. As with LSD, mescaline intoxication can be alleviated or stopped by taking a dose of chlorpromazine (Thorazine), a tranquilizer, and to a lesser extent with diazepam (Valium). Like LSD, mesca-

line probably exerts much of its hallucinogenic effects by altering serotonin systems (Jaffe 1990).

Analysis of street samples of mescaline in a number of U.S. cities over the past decade shows that the chemical sold rarely is authentic. Regardless of color or appearance, these street drugs are usually other hallucinogens, such as LSD, DOM, or PCP. If a person decides to take hallucinogenic street drugs, "let the buyer beware." Not only is the actual content often different and potentially much more toxic than bargained for (they are frequently contaminated) but also the dosage is usually unknown even if the drug is genuine.

Psilocybin

The drug psilocybin has a long and colorful history. Its principal source is the *Psilocybe mexicana* mushroom of the "magic" variety (Goldstein 1994). It was first used by some of the early natives of Central America more than 2000 years ago. In Guatemala, statues of mushrooms that date back to 100 B.C. have been found. The Aztecs later used the mushrooms for ceremonial rites. When the Spaniards came into Mexico in the 1500s, the natives were calling the *Psilocybe mexicana* mushroom "God's flesh." Because of this seeming sacrilege, they were harshly treated by the Spanish priests.

Gordon Wasson identified the *Psilocybe mexicana* mushroom in 1955. The active ingredient was

POINT/COUNTERPOINT

Selective Access

A particularly difficult issue relating to the legalization of drugs with abuse potential is the policy of making some drugs legal to a selective minority of society, under a limited set of circumstances. In the case of peyote, lawmakers wrestled with the issue of how far can the drug laws infringe on religious beliefs and rights. In this example, the Native American Church was eventually allowed to continue its use of peyote as part of its religious ceremonies even though possession of this substance was illegal for the rest of society. Select a side either to defend or argue against this policy of selective access to drugs of abuse. Think about issues such as when are such policy exceptions acceptable, how can these special cases be controlled and enforced, and how should criteria be identified?

The psilocybe mushroom is the source of the hallucinogens psilocybin and psilocin.

extracted in 1958 by Albert Hofmann, who also synthesized LSD. Doing research, Hofmann wanted to make certain he would feel the effects of the mushroom, so he ate 32 of them, weighing 2.4 grams (a medium dose by Native American standards) and then recorded his hallucinogenic reactions (Burger 1968).

Timothy Leary also tried some psilocybin mushrooms in Mexico in 1960; apparently, the experience influenced him greatly. On his return to Harvard, he carried out a series of experiments using psilocybin with student groups. Leary was careless in experimental procedures and did some work in uncontrolled situations. His actions caused a major administrative upheaval, ending in his departure from Harvard.

One of Leary's questionable studies was the "Good Friday" experiment in which 20 theological students were given either a placebo or psilocybin in a double-blind study (that is, neither the researcher nor the subjects know who gets the placebo or the drug), after which all attended the same 2.5-hour Good Friday service. The experimental group reported mystical experiences whereas the control group did not (Pahnke and Richards 1966). Leary believed that the experience was of value and that, under proper control and guidance, the hallucinatory experience could be beneficial.

Psilocybin is not very common on the street. Generally, it is administered orally and is eaten either fresh or dried. Accidental poisonings are common for those who mistakenly consume poisonous mushrooms rather than the hallucinogenic variety.

The dried form of these mushrooms contains from 0.2% to 0.5% psilocybin. The hallucinogenic effects produced are quite similar to those of LSD, and there is a cross-tolerance among psilocybin, LSD, and mescaline. The effects caused by psilocybin vary with the dosage taken. Up to 4 milligrams will cause a pleasant experience, relaxation, and some body sensation. In some subjects, higher doses cause considerable perceptual and body image changes, accompanied by hallucinations, as illustrated in the following quote:

> The first time I 'shroomed, everything looked like it was made of plastic, like everything could be folded up or something. Whatever somebody told me, I would believe it to be true. Like if I was drinking a beer and someone told me it was tequila, I would taste tequila. (*From Venturelli's files, interview with a 20-year-old male, 1995.*)

In extreme cases, psyilocybin can even induce the first stages of schizophrenia-like psychosis (Vollenwelder et al. 1998). Psilocybin stimulates the autonomic nervous system, dilates the pupils, and increases the body temperature. There is some evidence that psilocybin is metabolized into psilocin, which is more potent and may be the principal active ingredient. Psilocin is found in mushrooms but in small amounts. Like the other hallucinogens, psilocybin apparently causes no physical dependence.

Dimethyltryptamine (DMT)

DMT is a short-acting hallucinogen found in the seeds of certain leguminous trees native to the West Indies and parts of South America (Schultes 1978). It is also prepared synthetically in illicit laboratories. For centuries, the powdered seeds have been used as a snuff called *cohoba* in pipes and snuffing tubes. The Haitian natives claim that, under the influence of the drug, they can communicate with their gods. Its effects may last under 1 hour, which has earned it the nickname "the businessman's lunch break" drug.

DMT has no effect when taken orally; it is inhaled either as smoke from the burning plant or in vaporized form. DMT is sometimes added to parsley leaves or flakes, tobacco, or marijuana to induce its hallucinogenic effect. The usual dose is 60 to 150 milligrams. In structure and action, it is similar to psilocybin although not as powerful. Like the other hallucinogens discussed, DMT does not cause physical dependence.

Nutmeg

High doses of nutmeg can be quite intoxicating, causing symptoms such as drowsiness, stupor, delirium, and sleep. Prison inmates have known about this drug for years, so in most prisons, use of spices such as nutmeg is restricted.

Nutmeg contains 5% to 15% myristica oil, which is responsible for the physical effects. Myristicin (about 4%), which is structurally similar to mescaline, and elemicin are probably the most potent psychoactive ingredients in nutmeg. *Myristicin* blocks release of serotonin from brain neurons. Some scientists believe that it can be converted in the body to MDMA (a close relative of MDA, discussed later), which also affects the CNS. Mace, the exterior covering of the nutmeg seed, also contains the hallucinogenic compound myristicin.

Two tablespoons of nutmeg (about 14 grams) taken orally cause a rather unpleasant "trip" with a dreamlike stage; rapid heartbeat, dry mouth, and thirst are experienced as well. Agitation, apprehension, and a sense of impending doom may last about 12 hours, with a sense of unreality persisting for several days (Claus et al. 1970).

■ PHENYLETHYLAMINE HALLUCINOGENS

The phenylethylamine drugs are chemically related to amphetamines. Phenylethylamines have varying degrees of hallucinogenic and CNS stimulant effects, which are likely related to their ability to release serotonin and dopamine, respectively. Consequently, the phenylethylamines that predominantly release serotonin are dominated by their hallucinogenic action and are LSD-like, whereas those more inclined to

release dopamine are dominated by their stimulant effects and are cocaine-like.

Dimethoxymethylamphetamine (DOM or STP)

The basic structure of DOM is amphetamine. Nonetheless, it is a fairly powerful hallucinogen that seems to work through mechanisms similar to those of mescaline and LSD. In fact, the effects of DOM are similar to those caused by a combination of amphetamine and LSD, with the hallucinogenic effects of the drug overpowering the amphetamine-like physiological effects.

"Designer" Amphetamines

"Designer" amphetamines are discussed in Chapter 11 but are presented again here owing to their hallucinogenic effects. Their hybrid actions as psychedelic stimulants not only make them a particularly fascinating topic for research but also provide a unique experience described by drug abusers as a "smooth amphetamine" or entactogens (implying that the pleasurable sensation of touch is enhanced). This characterization likely accounts for the popularity of the designer amphetamines (Drug Abuse USA Home 2000).

3,4-Methylenedioxyamphetamine (MDA) MDA, first synthesized in 1910, is structurally related to both mescaline and amphetamine. Early research found that MDA is an *anorexiant* (causing loss of appetite) as well as a mood elevator in some persons. Further research has shown that the mode of action of MDA is similar to that of amphetamine. It causes additional release of the neurotransmitters serotonin, dopamine, and norepinephrine.

MDA has been used as an adjunct to psychotherapy. In one study, eight volunteers who had previously experienced the effects of LSD under clinical conditions were given 150 milligrams of MDA. Effects of the drug were noted between 40 and 60 minutes following ingestion by all eight subjects. The subjective effects following administration peaked at the end of 90 minutes and persisted for approximately 8 hours. None of the subjects experienced hallucinations, perceptual distortion, or closed-eye imagery, but they reported that the feelings the drug induced had some relationship to those previously experienced with LSD. The sub-

---

KEY TERMS

entactogens
drugs that enhance the sensation and pleasure of touching

jects found that both drugs induced an intensification of feelings, increased perceptions of self-insight, and heightened empathy with others during the experience. Most of the subjects also felt an increased sense of aesthetic enjoyment at some point during the intoxication. Seven of the eight subjects said they perceived music as "three-dimensional" (Naranjo et al. 1967).

On the street, MDA has been called the *love drug* because of its effects on the sense of touch and the attitudes of the users. Users often report experiencing a sense of well-being (likely a stimulant effect) and heightened tactile sensations (like a hallucinogenic effect) and thus increased pleasure through sex and expressions of affection. Those under the influence of MDA frequently focus on interpersonal relationships and demonstrate an overwhelming desire or need to be with or talk to people. Some users say they have a very pleasant "body high"—more sensual than cerebral, and more emphatic than introverted.

The unpleasant side effects most often reported are nausea, periodic tensing of muscles in the neck, tightening of the jaw and grinding of the teeth, and dilation of the pupils. Street doses of MDA range from 100 to 150 milligrams. Serious convulsions and death have resulted from larger doses, but in these cases, the quantity of MDA was not accurately measured. Ingestion of 500 milligrams of pure MDA has been shown to cause death. The only adverse reaction to moderate doses reported is a marked physical exhaustion, lasting as long as 2 days (Marquardt et al. 1978).

An unpleasant MDA experience should be treated the same as a bad trip with any hallucinogen. The person should be "talked down" (reassured) in a friendly and supportive manner. Usually, the use of other drugs is not needed, although medical attention may be necessary. Under the Comprehensive Drug Abuse Prevention and Control Act of 1970, MDA is classified as a Schedule I substance; illegal possession is a serious offense.

Methylenedioxymethamphetamine (MDMA)

MDMA is a modification of MDA but is thought to have more psychedelic and less stimulant activity (for example, euphoria) than its predecessor. MDMA is also structurally similar to mescaline. This drug has become known as "Ecstasy," "XTC," and "Adam" (Zickler 2000). (Ecstasy is also discussed in Chapter 11.)

MDMA was synthesized in 1912, but it only became widely used in the 1980s (Drug Abuse USA Home 2000; Shulgin 1990). This designer amphetamine can be produced easily; the reaction can literally be set up in a cookie jar using a coffee filter. The synthesis can be done by local illicit laboratories (Hyslop 2000), but most of the MDMA supplies in this country are smuggled in from outlaw drug laboratories in European countries such as the Netherlands (Cloud 2000). The unusual psychological effects it produces are part of the reason for its popularity. The drug causes euphoria, increased sensitivity to touch, and lowered inhibitions. Many users claim it intensifies emotional feelings without sensory distortion and that it increases empathy and awareness both of the user's body and of the aesthetics of the surroundings (Farley 2000). Some consider MDMA to be an aphrodisiac. Because MDMA lowers defense mechanisms and reduces inhibitions, it has even been used during psychoanalysis (Cloud 2000).

MDMA—popularized in the 1980s by articles in *Newsweek* (Adler 1985), *Time* (Toufexis 1985), and other magazines—is again being touted on the national newstands as a drug with euphoric effects, potential therapeutic value, and lack of serious side effects. MDMA is extremely popular with college-age students and young adults (Farley 2000). Because of its effect of enhancing sensations, MDMA has been used as part of a countercultural "rave" scene, including high-tech music and laser light shows. Observers report that MDMA-linked rave parties are reminiscent of the "acid parties" of the 1960s and 1970s.

Because of the widespread abuse of MDMA, the DEA prohibited its use by placing it on Schedule I in 1985 (Greenhouse 1992). At the time of the ban, it was estimated that up to 200 physicians were using the drug in psychotherapy (Greer and Tolbert 1990) and an estimated 30,000 doses a month were being taken for recreational purposes (American Medical News 1985). Currently, MDMA is classified as a "club drug" because of its frequent use at rave dances, clubs, and bars (Zickler 2000). A dose of this drug is readily affordable at $10 to $20 (Hegadoran et al. 1999).

MDMA is usually taken orally, but it is sometimes snorted or even occasionally smoked (Taylor

Ecstasy is frequently used at "raves" to increase sensory stimulation and the pleasure of touching.

milligrams; toxic effects have been reported at higher doses (Randall 1992).

There is disagreement as to the possible harmful side effects of MDMA. Use of high doses can cause psychosis and paranoia (Parrott 2000a). Some negative physiological responses caused by recreational doses include dilated pupils, dry mouth and throat, clenching and grinding of teeth (in 76% of users), muscle aches and stiffness (in 28% of users), fatigue (in 80% of users), insomnia (in 38% of users), agitation, and anxiety. Some of these reactions can be intense and unpredictable. Under some conditions, death can be caused by hyperthermia (elevated body temperature), instability of the autonomic nervous system, and kidney failure (Greenhouse 1992; Hyslop 2000; Iwersen and Schmoldt 1996).

Several studies have demonstrated long-term damage to serotonin neurons in the brain following a single high dose of both MDMA and MDA, which may result in impaired memory, diminished ability to process information and heightened impulsivity (Parrott 2000b). Although the behavioral significance of this damage in people is not clear, at the present time, caution using this drug is warranted (Gerra et al. 2000) (see "Here and Now," MDMA's Casual User).

1994). After the high starts, it may persist for minutes or even an hour, depending on the person, the purity of the drug, and the environment in which it is taken. When "coming down" from an MDMA-induced high, people will often take small oral doses known as "boosters" to get high again. If they take too many boosters, they become very fatigued the next day. The average dose is about 75 to 150

HERE AND NOW   MDMA's Casual User

A study examined 15 regular Ecstasy users, 15 novice (first time) Ecstasy users, and 15 controls who attended a Saturday night rave. The regular users consumed, on average, 1.8 MDMA tablets, the novice users took 1.4 MDMA tablets, and the control had no drug except alcohol. All groups reported positive moods during the dance. However, 2 days later, the Ecstasy users felt significantly more depressed, unsociable, unpleasant and less good tempered than controls. Verbal recall was also diminished in MDMA users who remembered only 60% to 70% of the words remembered by the control subjects. Those who used Ecstasy regularly had the most difficulty remembering.

Source: Parrott, A., and J. Lasky. "Ecstasy (MDMA) Effects Upon Mood and Cognition: Before, During and After a Saturday Night Dance." *Psychopharmacology* 139 (1998): 261–68.

ANTICHOLINERGIC HALLUCINOGENS

The anticholinergic hallucinogens include naturally occurring alkaloid (bitter organic base) substances that are present in plants and herbs found around the world. These drugs are often mentioned in folklore and in early literature as being added to "potions." They are thought to have killed the Roman Emperor Claudius and to have poisoned Hamlet's father. Historically, they have been the favorite drugs used to eliminate inconvenient people (Marken et al. 1996). Hallucinogens affecting the cholinergic neurons also have been used by South American Indians for religious ceremonies (Schultes and Hofmann 1980) and were probably used in witchcraft to give the illusion of flying, to prepare sacrificial victims, and even to give some types of marijuana ("superpot") its kick.

The potato family of plants (Solanaceae) contain most of these mind-altering drugs. Three potent anticholinergic compounds are commonly found in these plants: (1) scopolamine, or hyoscine; (2) hyoscyamine; and (3) atropine. Scopolamine may produce excitement, hallucinations, and delirium even at therapeutic doses: with atropine, doses bordering on toxic levels are usually required to obtain these effects (Schultes and Hofmann 1973). All of these active alkaloid drugs block some acetylcholine receptors (see Chapter 5).

The alkaloid drugs can be used as ingredients in cold symptom remedies because they have a drying effect and block production of mucus in the nose and throat. They also prevent salivation; therefore, the mouth becomes uncommonly dry and perspiration may stop. Atropine may increase the heart rate by 100% and dilate the pupils markedly, causing inability to focus on nearby objects. Other annoying side effects of these anticholinergic drugs include constipation and difficulty in urinating. These inconveniences tend to discourage excessive abuse of these drugs for their hallucinogenic properties. Usually, people who abuse these anticholinergic compounds are receiving the drugs by prescription (Marken et al. 1996).

Anticholinergics can cause drowsiness by affecting the sleep centers of the brain. At large doses, a condition occurs that is similar to a psychosis, characterized by delirium, loss of attention, mental confusion, and sleepiness (Carlini 1993). Hallucinations may also occur at higher doses. At very high doses, paralysis of the respiratory system may cause death.

Although hundreds of plant species naturally contain anticholinergic substances and consequently can cause psychedelic experiences, only a few of the principal plants are mentioned here.

Atropa Belladonna: The Deadly Nightshade Plant

Knowledge of this plant is very old, and its use as a drug is reported in early folklore. The name of the genus, *Atropa*, is the origin for the drug name atropine and indicates the reverence the Greeks had for the plant. Atropos was one of the three Fates in Greek mythology, whose duty it was to cut the thread of life when the time came. This plant has been used for thousands of years by assassins and murderers. In *Tales of the Arabian Nights*, unsuspecting potentates were poisoned with atropine from the deadly nightshade or one of its relatives. Fourteen berries of the deadly nightshade contain enough drug to cause death.

The species name, *belladonna*, means "beautiful woman." In early Rome and Egypt, girls with large pupils were considered attractive and friendly. To create this condition, they would put a few drops of an extract of this plant into their eyes, causing the pupils to dilate (Marken et al. 1996). Belladonna has also had a reputation as a love potion.

Mandragora Officinarum: The Mandrake

The mandrake contains several active psychedelic alkaloids: hyoscyamine, scopolamine, atropine, and mandragorine. Mandrake has been used as a love potion for centuries but has also been known for its toxic properties. In ancient folk medicine, mandrake was used to treat many ailments in spite of its side effects. It was recommended as a sedative, to relieve nervous conditions, and to relieve pain (Schultes and Hofmann 1980).

The root of the mandrake is forked and, viewed with a little imagination, may resemble the human body. Because of this resemblance, it has been credited with human attributes, which gave rise to many superstitions in the Middle Ages about its magical powers. Shakespeare referred to this plant in *Romeo and Juliet*. In her farewell speech, Juliet says, "And shrieks like mandrakes torn out of the earth, that living mortals hearing them run mad."

Hyoscyamus Niger: Henbane

Henbane is a plant that contains both hyoscyamine and scopolamine. In A.D. 60, Pliny the Elder spoke of henbane: "For this is certainly known, that if one takes it in drink more than four leaves, it will put him beside himself" (Jones 1956). Henbane was also used in the orgies, or bacchanalias, of the ancient world.

Although rarely used today, henbane has been given medicinally since early times. It was frequently used to cause sleep, although hallucinations often occurred if given in excess. It was likely included in witches' brews and deadly concoctions during the Dark Ages (Schultes and Hofmann 1980).

Datura Stramonium: Jimsonweed

The Datura genus of the Solanaceae family (see earlier discussion) includes a large number of related plants found worldwide. The principal active drug in this group is scopolamine; there are also several less active alkaloids.

Throughout history, these plants have been used as hallucinogens by many societies. They are mentioned in early Sanskrit and Chinese writings and

Datura stramonium, or jimsonweed, is a common plant that contains the hallucinogenic drug scopolamine.

were revered by the Buddhists. There is also some indication that the priestess (oracle) at the ancient Greek Temple of Apollo at Delphi was under the influence of this type of plant when she made prophecies (Schultes 1970). Before the supposed divine possession, she appeared to have chewed leaves of the sacred laurel. A mystic vapor was also reported to have risen from a fissure in the ground. The sacred laurel may have been one of the Datura species, and the vapors may have come from burning these plants.

Jimsonweed gets its name from an incident that took place in 17th-century Jamestown. British soldiers ate this weed while trying to capture Nathaniel Bacon, who had made seditious remarks about the king. Although still abused occasionally by adventuresome young people, the anticholinergic side effects of jimsonweed are so unpleasant that it rarely becomes a long-term problem (Tiongson and Salen 1998).

■ OTHER HALLUCINOGENS

Technically, any drug that alters perceptions, thoughts, and feelings in a manner that is not normally experienced except in dreams can be classified as a hallucinogen. Because the brain's sensory input is complex and involves several neurotransmitter systems, drugs with many diverse effects can cause hallucinations (Jaffe 1990).

Three agents that do not conveniently fit into the principal categories of hallucinogens are discussed in the following sections.

Phencyclidine (PCP)

PCP is considered by many experts as the most dangerous of the hallucinogens (DSM-IV-TR 2000; U.S. Department of Justice 1991b). PCP was developed in the late 1950s as an intravenous anesthetic. Although it was found to be effective, it had serious side effects that caused it to be discontinued for human use. Sometimes when people were recovering from PCP anesthesia, they experienced delirium and manic states of excitation lasting 18 hours (DSM-IV-TR 2000). PCP is currently a Schedule II drug, legitimately available only as an anesthetic for animals but has even been banned from veterinary practice since 1985 because of its high theft rate. Most, if not all, PCP used in the United States today is produced illegally (U.S. Department of Justice 1991).

Street PCP is mainly synthesized from readily available chemical precursors in clandestine laboratories. Within 24 hours, "cooks" (the makers of street PCP) can set up a lab, make several gallons of the drug, and destroy the lab before the police can locate them. Liquid PCP is then poured into containers and ready for shipment (Sanchez 1988).

PCP first appeared on the street drug scene in 1967 as the *PeaCe Pill*. In 1968, it reappeared in New York as a substance called *hog*. By 1969, PCP was found under a variety of guises. It was sold as *angel dust* and sprinkled on parsley for smoking. Today it is sold on the streets under many different slang names, including *angel dust, ozone, wack, rocket fuel, killer joints,* and *crystal supergrass* (DSM-IV-TR 2000; NIDA Infofax 1999a).

In the late 1960s, PCP began to find its way into a variety of street drugs sold as psychedelics. By 1970, authorities observed that phencyclidine was used widely as a main ingredient in psychedelic preparations. It is still frequently substituted for and sold as LSD, mescaline, marijuana, and cocaine (Goldstein 1995).

One difficulty in estimating the effects or use patterns of PCP is caused by variance in drug purity. Also, there are about 30 analogs of PCP, some of which have appeared on the street. PCP has so many other street names that people may not know they are using it or they may have been deceived when buying what they thought was LSD or mescaline. Users may not question the identity of the substances unless they have a bad reaction.

PCP is available as a pure, white crystalline powder, as tablets, or as capsules. However, because it is usually manufactured in makeshift laboratories, it is frequently discolored by contaminants from a tan to brown with a consistency ranging from powder to a gummy mass (U.S. Department of Justice 1991). PCP can be taken orally, smoked, sniffed, or injected (NIDA Infofax 1999a). In the late 1960s through the early 1970s, PCP was mostly taken orally, but it is now commonly snorted or applied to dark brown cigarettes, leafy materials such as parsley, mint, oregano, marijuana, or tobacco and smoked (U.S. Department of Justice 1991b). By smoking PCP, the experienced user is better able to limit his or her dosage to a desired level. After smoking, the subjective effects appear within 1 to 5 minutes and peak within the next 5 to

KEY TERMS

jimsonweed
a potent hallucinogenic plant

analogs
drugs with similar structures

30 minutes. The high lasts about 4 to 6 hours, followed by a 6- to 24-hour "comedown" (DSM-IV-TR 2000).

In the 1979 national drug survey performed by the National Institute on Drug Abuse, about 7% of the U.S. high school seniors had used PCP in a 12-month period; however, in 1999, that rate had declined to 1.8% (Johnston 2000).

Physiological Effects Although PCP may have hallucinogenic effects, it can also cause a host of other physiological actions, including stimulation, depression, anesthesia, and analgesia. The effects of PCP on the CNS vary greatly. At low doses, the most prominent effect is similar to that of alcohol intoxication, with generalized numbness. As the dose of PCP is increased, the person becomes even more insensitive and may become fully anesthetized. Large doses can cause coma, convulsions, and death (DSM-IV-TR 2000).

The majority of peripheral effects are apparently related to activation of the sympathetic nervous system (see Chapter 5). Flushing, excess sweating, and a blank stare are common, although the size of the pupils is unaffected. The cardiovascular system reacts by increasing blood pressure and heart rate. Other effects include side-to-side eye movements (called *nystagmus*), muscular incoordination, double vision, dizziness, nausea, and vomiting (NIDA Infofax 1999a). These symptoms occur in many people taking medium to high doses.

Psychological Effects PCP has unpleasant effects most of the time it is used. Why, then, do people use it repeatedly as their drug of choice?

PCP has the ability to markedly alter the person's subjective feelings; this effect may be reinforcing, even though the alteration is not always positive. There is an element of risk, not knowing how the trip will turn out. PCP may give the user feelings of strength, power, and invulnerability (NIDA Infofax 1999a). One user described the effects of PCP as follows: "I felt like I didn't have a care in the world. It made me feel like God, like I was powerful. I felt superhuman" (Sanchez 1988, p. A-1). Other positive effects include heightened sensitivity to outside stimuli, a sense of stimulation and mood elevation, and dissociation from surroundings. Also, PCP is a social drug; virtually all users report taking it in groups rather than during a solitary experience. PCP also causes serious perceptual distortions. Users cannot accurately interpret the environment and as a result may do what appears to be absurd things such as jump out of a window thinking they can fly (DSM-IV-TR 2000).

Chronic users may take PCP in "runs" extending over 2 to 3 days, during which time they do not sleep or eat. In later stages of chronic administration, users may develop outright paranoia and unpredictable violent behavior, as well as auditory hallucinations (DSM-IV-TR 2000). Law enforcement officers claim to be more fearful of suspects on PCP than of suspects on other drugs of abuse. Often such people seem to have superhuman strength and are totally irrational and very difficult, even dangerous, to manage (NIDA Infofax 1999a).

PCP has no equal in its ability to produce brief psychoses similar to schizophrenia (Jentsch and Roth 1999). The psychoses—induced with moderate doses given to normal, healthy volunteers—last about 2 hours and are characterized by changes in body image, thought disorders, estrangement, autism, and occasionally rigid inability to move (catatonia , or catalepsy). Subjects report feeling numb, have great difficulty differentiating between themselves and their surroundings, and complain afterward of feeling extremely isolated and apathetic. They are often violently paranoid during the psychosis (DSM IV-TR 2000; Medical Letter 1996). When PCP was given experimentally to hospitalized chronic schizophrenics, it made them much

worse not for a few hours but for 6 weeks. "PCP is not just another hallucinogen, to be warned about in the same breath as LSD. . . . PCP is far more dangerous to some individuals than the other abused drugs" (Goldstein 1995; Luisada 1978).

Medical Management The diagnosis of a PCP overdose is frequently missed because the symptoms often closely resemble those of an acute schizophrenic episode.

Simple, uncomplicated PCP intoxication can be managed with the same techniques used in other psychedelic drug cases. It is important to have a quiet environment, limited contact with an empathic person capable of determining any deterioration in the patient's physical state, protection from self-harm, and the availability of hospital facilities. "Talking down" is not helpful; the patient is better off isolated from external stimuli as much as possible.

Valium is often used for its sedating effect to prevent injury to self and to staff and also to reduce the chance for severe convulsions. An antipsychotic agent (for example, haloperidol [Haldol]) is frequently administered to make the patient manageable (Jaffe 1990).

The medical management of a comatose or convulsing patient is more difficult. The patient may need external respiratory assistance and external cooling to reduce fever. Blood pressure may have to be reduced to safe levels and convulsions controlled. Restraints and four to five strong hospital aides are often needed to prevent the patient from injuring himself or herself or the medical staff. After the coma lightens, the patient typically becomes delirious, paranoid, and violently assaultive.

Effects of Chronic Use Chronic PCP users may develop a tolerance to the drug; thus, a decrease in behavioral effects and toxicity can occur with frequent administration. Different forms of dependence may occur when tolerance develops. Users may complain of vague cravings after cessation of the drug. In addition, long-term difficulties in memory, speech, and thinking persist for 6 to 12 months in the chronic user (NIDA Infofax 1999). These functional changes are accompanied by personality deficits such as social isolation and states of anxiety, nervousness, and extreme agitation (DSM-IV-TR 2000).

KEY TERMS

catatonia
a condition of physical rigidity, excitement, and stupor

Ketamine

Ketamine, like PCP, was originally developed because of its general anesthetic properties. Its effects resemble those of PCP except they are more rapid and less potent. Depending on the dose, ketamine can have many effects ranging from feelings of weightlessness to out-of-body or near-death experiences. Ketamine, often referred to as "Special K," and classified as a "club drug," has been abused as a "date rape" drug like other CNS depressants, such as Rohypnol or gamma hydroxybutyrate (GHB) (see Chapter 7). Abuse of ketamine has been reported in many cities throughout the United States and is sometimes snorted as a substitute for cocaine. Several deaths have been linked to ketamine overdoses (NIDA Infofax 1999b).

Marijuana

In high doses, marijuana use can result in image distortions and hallucinations (Abood and Martin 1992). Some users claim that marijuana can enhance hearing, vision, and skin sensitivity, although these claims have not been confirmed in controlled laboratory studies.

Although typical marijuana use does not appear to cause severe emotional disorders like the other hallucinogens, some experts suggest it can aggravate underlying mental illness such as depression. Each month, thousands of people seek professional treatment due to marijuana-related problems (Brown 1991). In contrast to other hallucinogens that have a combination of stimulant and psychedelic effects, high doses of marijuana cause a combination of depression and hallucinations and enhance the appetite (Goldstein 1995). Marijuana is discussed thoroughly in Chapter 14.

NATURAL SUBSTANCES
Naturally Occurring Hallucinogens

Many plants contain naturally occurring hallucinogens. As already discussed, examples of such substances include mescaline from the peyote cactus, psylocybin from psilocybe mushrooms, and anticholinergic drugs such as atropine, from the deadly nightshade plant, mandrake or jimsonweed. Although some of these plants have been used for medicinal purposes for centuries, typically, the therapeutic benefit has not been a consequence of the hallucinogenic effects of the substance. For example, anticholinergic drugs usually cause CNS depression and induce sleep; therefore, herbs that contain these drugs have been used as sleep potions. The hallucinogenic properties of some of these natural products, such as peyote, are viewed as positive by some cultures. As already mentioned, peyote is employed in a religious context as a sacrament for the Native American Church. In the United States today, the hallucinogen-containing natural substances are generally not viewed as therapeutic and are more likely to be used for their mind-altering properties as "recreational" drugs.

Discussion Questions

1. Why were substances with hallucinogenic properties used by ancient religions and cults?

2. Would you expect "natural" hallucinogens such as peyote to have any less adverse effects than other hallucinogens?

3. Why would a drug with both stimulant and hallucinogenic effects have abuse potential?

4. Why do some users find a psychedelic experience terrifying?

5. Do you think the federal government is justified in lying to the public about the dangers of hallucinogens to convince people to stop using these drugs? Defend your answer.

6. How do the side effects of LSD compare with those of the CNS stimulants?

7. Why is MDMA used as a "club drug"?

8. Why is PCP more dangerous than LSD?

9. What is the best way to convince people that hallucinogenic drugs of abuse can be harmful?

10. What is a flashback and how is it caused?

Key Terms

hallucinogens   336

psychedelics   336

psychotomimetic   336

psychotogenic   338

synesthesia   339

flashbacks   340

ergotism   342

mydriasis   347

entactogens   350

jimsonweed   354

analogs   355

catatonia   356

Summary

1 Many drugs can exert hallucinogenic effects. The principal hallucinogens include LSD types, phenylethylamines, and anticholinergic agents. The four major effects that occur from administering LSD include (1) heightened senses, (2) loss of sensory control, (3) self-reflection or introspection, and (4) loss of identity or sense of cosmic merging.

2 The recent resurgence in LSD abuse likely reflects its perceived safety and a lack of education about its dangers.

3 Hallucinogens exaggerate sensory input and cause vivid and unusual visual and auditory effects.

4 The classic hallucinogens, such as LSD, cause predominantly psychedelic effects. Phenylethylamines are related to amphetamines and cause varying combinations of psychedelic and stimulant effects. Anticholinergic drugs are also psychedelic in high doses.

5 One of the prominent effects of hallucinogens is self-reflection. The user becomes aware of thoughts and feelings that had been forgotten or repressed. Some experiences help to clarify motives and relationships and cause periods of greater openness. These effects have been claimed by some psychiatrists to provide valid insights useful in psychotherapy.

6 The classic hallucinogens do not cause physical dependence. Although some tolerance can build up to the hallucinogenic effects of drugs like LSD, withdrawal effects are usually minor.

7 The environment plays a major role in determining the sensory response to hallucinogens. Environments that are warm, comfortable, and hospitable tend to create a pleasant sensory response to the psychedelic effects of these drugs. In contrast, threatening, hostile environments are likely to lead to intimidating, frightening "bad trips."

8 In some users, high doses of LSD can cause a terrifying destruction of identity, resulting in panic and severe anxiety that resembles schizophrenia. Another psychological feature commonly associated with LSD is the "flashback" phenomenon. LSD use can cause recurring, unexpected visual and time distortions that last a few minutes to several hours. Flashbacks can occur months to years after use of the drug.

9 Designer amphetamines such as MDMA (Ecstasy) have been included in the "club drug" phenomenon. As such, MDMA is frequently used by young people to enhance the sensory experience of "raves" and the nightclub scene. Although viewed by some to be harmless and even therapeutic, evidence of potentially serious negative consequences suggest that these drugs can be extremely dangerous in high doses and under some conditions.

10 Hallucinogens purchased on the "street" are often poorly prepared and contaminated with adulterant substances. This practice of cutting with other substances also makes use of street hallucinogens very dangerous.

11 PCP differs from the other traditional hallucinogens in several ways: (1) It is a general anesthetic in high doses. (2) It causes schizophrenia-like psychosis. PCP can cause incredible strength and extreme violent behavior, making users very difficult to manage. (3) Management of the severe psy-

chological reactions to PCP requires drug therapy, whereas treatment of other hallucinogens often only requires reassurance, "talking down," and supportive therapy. (4) Reactions to overdoses include fever, convulsions, and coma.

References

Abood, M. and B. Martin, "Neurobiology of Marijuana Abuse." *Trends in Pharmacological Sciences* 13 (May 1992): 201–6.

Abraham, H., A. Aldridge, and P. Gogia. "The Psychopharmacology of Hallucinogens." *Neuropharmacology* 14 (1996): 285–98.

Adler, J. "Getting High on Ecstasy." *Newsweek* (15 April 1985): 15.

Aghajanian, G. and Marek, G.: "Serotonin and Hallucinogens." *Neuropsychopharmacology* 21 (1999): 165–235.

American Medical News (14 June 1985).

Associated Press. "60s Icon Timothy Leary Cooperated with the FBI." *Salt Lake Tribune* 258 (1 July 1999): A-10.

Becenti, D. "American Indians Get OK to Use Peyote." *Salt Lake Tribune* 249 (30 October 1994): A-10.

Brown, M. *Guide to Fight Substance Abuse*. Nashville, TN: International Broadcast Services, 1991.

Burger, A., ed. "Quotes from Albert Hofmann." *Drugs Affecting the Central Nervous System. Psychotomimetic Agents*, vol. 2. New York: Dekker, 1968.

Carlini, E. "Preliminary Note: Dangerous Use of Anticholinergic Drugs in Brazil." *Drugs and Alcohol Dependence* 32 (1993): 1–7.

"Celebration #1." *New Yorker* 42 (1966): 43.

Claus, E. P., V. E. Tyler, and L. R. Brady. *Pharmacognosy*, 6th ed. Philadelphia: Lea & Febiger, 1970.

Cloud, J. "The Lure of Ecstasy." *Time* 155 (5 June 2000): 62.

Dishotsky, N. I., W. D. Loughman, R. E. Mogar, and W. R. Lipscomb. "LSD and Genetic Damage." *Science* 172 (1971): 431–40.

Drug Abuse USA Home. "Entactogens: MDA, MDMA and MDEA." (25 April 2000). Available www.drug-abuse .com/information/mdma/mdma4.html.

DSM-IV-TR. *Diagnostic and Statistical Manual of Mental Disorders. 4th edition Text Revision.* Washington DC: APA, 2000.

Farley, C. "Rave New World." *Time* 15 (5 June 2000): 69.

Gerra, G. et al. "Long-lasting Effects of MDMA (Ecstasy) on Sertonin System Function in Humans." *Biological Psychiatry* 47 (2000): 127–36.

Goldstein, A. *Addiction from Biology to Drug Policy.* New York: Freeman, 1994.

Goldstein, F. "Pharmacological Aspects of Substance Abuse." In *Remington's Pharmaceutical Sciences*, 19th ed., edited by A. R. Genaro, 780–94. Easton, PA: Mack, 1995.

Greenhouse, C. "NIDA Lays Plans for Quicker Response to Drug Crises." *NIDA Notes* 7 (January/February 1992): 20–2.

Greer, G. and R. Tolbert. "The Therapeutic Use of MDMA." In *Ecstasy: The Clinical, Pharmacological and Neurotoxicological Effects of the Drug MDMA*, edited by S. J. Peroutka, 28. Boston: Kluwer, 1990.

Hegadoran, K., Baker, G., and Bourin, M. "3,4-Methylenedioxy Analogues of Amphetamine: Defining the Risks to Humans." *Neuroscience and Behavioral Review* 23 (1999): 539–53.

Huxley, A. *The Doors of Perception*. New York: Harper, 1954.

Hyslop, M. "Townsend Spearheads Campaign to Curb Rising Use of Ecstasy." *The Washington Times* (29 September 2000): C-1.

Iwersen, S. and H. Schmoldt. "Two Very Different Fatal Cases Associated with the Use of Methylenedioxyethylene." *Clinical Toxicology* 34 (1996): 241–4.

Jaffe, J. "Drug Addiction and Drug Abuse." In *The Pharmacological Basis of Therapeutics*, 8th ed., edited by A. Gilman, T. Rall, A. Nies, and P. Taylor, 522–73. New York: Pergamon, 1990.

Jentsch, J. and Roth, R. "The Neuropsychopharmacology of Phencyclidine: From NMDA Receptor Hypofunction to the Dopamine Hypothesis of Schizophrenia." *Neuropsychopharmacology* 20 (1999): 201–25.

Johnston, L. University of Michigan News Release (17 December 1999), citing the National Survey on Drug Abuse.

Johnston, L., P. O'Malley, and J. Bachman. *National Survey Results on Drug Use from Monitoring the Future Study, 1975–1994*, vol. 2. University of Michigan, NIDA, NIH Publication No. 96-4027. Washington, DC: National Institute on Drug Abuse, 1996.

Johnston, L., P. O'Malley, and J. Bachman. *National Survey Results on Drug Use from Monitoring the Future Study, 1975–1999*, vol. 1. University of Michigan, NIDA, NIH Publication No. 00-4802. Washington, DC: National Institute on Drug Abuse, 2000.

Jones, W. H. S. *Natural History.* Cambridge, MA: Harvard University Press, 1956.

Leary, T., R. Metzner, and R. Alpert. *The Psychedelic Experience.* New Hyde Park, NY: University Books, 1964.

Letters (to the editor). "Many Were Lost Because of Leary." *USA Today* 14 (3 June 1996): 12-A.

Luisada, P. V. "The Phencyclidine Psychosis: Phenomenology and Treatment." In *Phencyclidine (PCP) Abuse: An Appraisal*, edited by R. C. Petersen and R. C. Stillman.

NIDA Research Monograph No. 21. Washington, DC: National Institute on Drug Abuse, U.S. Department of Health, Education, and Welfare, 1978.

Marken, P., S. Stoner, and M. Bunker. "Anticholinergic Drug Abuse and Misuse." *CNS Drugs* 5 (1996): 190–9.

Marquardt, G. M., V. DiStefano, and L. L. Ling. "Pharmacological Effects of (S)-, and (R)-MDA." In *The Psychopharmacology of Hallucinogens*, edited by R. C. Stillman and R. E. Willette. New York: Pergamon, 1978.

Mathias, R. "NIDA Research Takes a New Look at LSD and Other Hallucinogens." *NIDA Notes* 8 (March/April 1993): 6.

McGlothin, W., S. Cohen, and M. S. McGlothin. "Long-Lasting Effects of LSD on Normals." *Archives of General Psychiatry* 17 (1967): 521–32.

Medical Letter. "Phencyclidine (PCP)." 38 (May 10, 1996): 45.

Mims, B. "Peyote: When the Ancient Indian Way Collides with a New Age Craze." *Salt Lake Tribune* 260 (12 August 2000): C-1.

Naranjo, C., A. T. Shulgin, and T. Sargent. "Evaluation of 3,4-Methylenedioxyamphetamine (MDA) as an Adjunct to Psychotherapy." *Medicina et Pharmacologia Experimentalis* 17 (1967): 359–64.

NIDA Infofax. Club Drugs (updated November 1999b). Available 165.112.78.61/Infofax/clubdrugs.html.

NIDA Infofax. LSD (updated November 1999). Available 165.112.78.61/Infofax/lsd.html.

NIDA Infofax. PCP (Phencyclidine) (updated November 1999a). Available 165.112.78.61/Infofax/pcp.html.

O'Brien, C. "Drug Addiction and Drug Abuse." In *The Pharmacological Basis of Therapeutics*, 9th ed., edited by J. Hardman and L. Limbird, 557–77. New York: McGraw–Hill, 1996.

Pahnke, W. N., A. A. Kurland, S. Unger, C. Savage, and S. Grof. "The Experimental Use of Psychedelic (LSD) Psychotherapy." In *Hallucinogenic Drug Research: Impact on Science and Society*, edited by J. R. Gamage and E. L. Zerkin. Beloit, WI: Stash, 1970.

Pahnke, W. N. and W. A. Richards. "Implications of LSD and Experimental Mysticism." *Journal of Religion and Health* 5 (1966): 175–208.

Parrott, A. "Human Research on MDMA Neurotoxicity: Cognitive and Behavioral Indices of Changes." *Neuropsychobiology* 43 (2000a): 17–24.

Parrott, A. "Psychobiological Problems in Heavy 'Ecstasy' (MMA) Polydrug Users." *Drug and Alcohol Dependence* 60 (2000b): 105–10.

Randall, T. "Ecstasy-Fueled 'Rave' Parties Become Dances of Death for English Youth." *Journal of the American Medical Association* 268 (1992): 1505.

Sanchez, E. "PCP Users Are Courting Fire." *Washington Post* (7 March 1988): A-1.

Schultes, R. E. "Ethnopharmacological Significance of Psychotropic Drugs of Vegetal Origin." In *Principles of Psychopharmacology*, 2d ed., edited by W. G. Clark and J. del Giudice. New York: Academic Press, 1978.

Schultes, R. E. "The Plant Kingdom and Hallucinogens (Part III)." *Bulletin on Narcotics* 22, No. 1 (1970): 25–53.

Schultes, R. E. and A. Hofmann. *The Botany and Chemistry of Hallucinogens.* Springfield, IL: Thomas, 1973.

Schultes, R. E. and A. Hofmann. *The Botany and Chemistry of Hallucinogens*, 2nd ed. Springfield, IL: Thomas, 1980.

Shulgin, A. "History of MDMA." In *Ecstasy: The Clinical, Pharmacological, and Neurotoxicological Effects of the Drug MDMA*, edited by S. J. Peroutka. Boston: Kluwer, 1990.

Snyder, S. H. *Madness and the Brain.* New York: McGraw–Hill, 1974.

Stone, J. "Turn On, Tune In, Boot Up." *Discover* 12 (June 1991): 32–3.

Taylor, J. "All-new MDMA FAQ." *Usenet News*, (27 May 1994). Available sci.med.pharmacy.

Tiongson, J. and Salen, P. "Mass Ingestion of Jimsonweed by Eleven Teenagers." *Delaware Medical Journal* 70 (1998): 1–6.

Toufexis, A. "A Crackdown on Ecstasy." *Time* (10 June 1985): 64.

Tucker, R. "Acid Test." *Omni* (November 1987): 16.

U.S. Department of Justice. "Let's All Work to Fight Drug Abuse." Pamphlet from DEA published by L.A.W. Publications and distributed with permission by International Drug Education Association, 1991.

Vollenwelder, F., M. Vollenweider-Scherpenhuyzen, A. Baber, N. Vogel and D. Nell "Psilocybin Induces Schizophrenia-like Psychosis in Human Via a Serotonin-2 Agonist Action." *NeuroReport* 9 (1998): 3897–902.

Zickler, P. "NIDA Launches Initiaive to Control Club Drugs." *NIDA Notes* 14 (2000): 1.

Marijuana

Did You Know?

- Marijuana contains hundreds of chemical compounds but only a few found in the resin are responsible for producing the euphoric "high."

- In the 1930s, one early belief about marijuana was that smokers turned into killers.

- In the 1930s, marijuana was brought across the U.S. borders by Mexican laborers who migrated into the United States seeking jobs.

- George Washington grew marijuana plants at Mount Vernon for medicine and rope making.

- Out of 13.6 million illicit drug users in the United States, 60% exclusively use marijuana.

- In some states, marijuana is one of the largest cash-producing crops.

- Marijuana still grows wild in many American states today.

- Research shows that many users have difficulty learning and remembering what they have learned when they are "high."

- Approximately 90% of most senior high school students report that marijuana is "very easy" to get.

- A typical "high" from one "joint" may last from 2 to 3 hours.

- Marijuana has been found to impair many skills required for safe driving: alertness, ability to concentrate, coordination, and reaction time.

- In June 2000, Hawaii became the first state to approve a medical marijuana bill.

- Tetrahydrocannabinol (THC) reaches the brain within 14 seconds after inhalation.

- Surveys indicate that 60% to 80% of marijuana users sometimes drive when "high."

- Cannabis has been used to treat extreme nausea, glaucoma, pain, depression, and convulsions.

- THC is stored for a long period in body fat; complete elimination can take up to 30 days.

Chapter 14

Learning Objectives

On completing this chapter you will be able to:

▶ Explain what marijuana is and why it remains so controversial.

▶ Differentiate between the effects of low and high doses of marijuana.

▶ List and explain the potential effects marijuana use has on the body.

▶ Describe how tolerance and dependence affect the response to marijuana and its use.

▶ Explain the medical uses of marijuana.

▶ Explain what age groups are most likely to use marijuana.

▶ Explain how the percentages of first-time users of marijuana have changed from 1994 to 1997.

▶ Explain how the perceived danger of marijuana use has changed with regard to high school seniors and younger age groups.

▶ Differentiate between prior and current beliefs regarding the effects of chronic marijuana use.

Since I was in college and tried my first hit, I have always been a connoisseur of what we used to call grass, now it's weed or even "the ganja." I first went through a period of using it a lot—it was a different way to get a buzz. Then I got married and my wife did not like me smoking it, and we had kids, so except for a few occasional puffs from my neighbor, I just about gave it up. Then I got divorced from [my wife] and I married a woman who does not object to me smoking a little weed every now and then, even though she does not do it herself. So sometimes on weekends, I will roll a joint before going to bed and take a few puffs off of it. I know it is illegal, but big deal, who knows about it? I used to watch that program "Cops" and just found it silly when police officers would arrest someone (usually a young kid) for possession. Big bust I would think. Isn't it silly to charge someone with possession of marijuana? I consider it to be like alcohol and cigarettes. I don't think it should be illegal anymore. I know so many people who do it and there are dozens of people who probably use this drug that I am not even aware of their using it. What happens if two-thirds of our population uses this drug? Are we going to charge and arrest all these people? The whole illegality of it is silly. *(From Venturelli's research files, interview with a 48-year-old male working as a restaurant owner, residing in Reno, Nevada, June 10, 2000.)*

We used to have one great big bong and fill it with dope [referring to marijuana], and all of us in someone's fraternity room would each take hits from the bong. Today, it's a different life altogether. I am working three different jobs, one teaching at a junior high school, [one] working at a film production studio, and my third claim to fame is my job as a part-time waiter. . . . I feel that I wasted many nights by just "smokin'," "dopin'," and "drinkin'" back during those college days. I sometimes think that I could have accomplished a lot more if I would not have inhaled so much dope. If I had to do it over again I would not have wasted so much time. *(From Venturelli's research files, interview with a 28-year-old male, August 9, 1996.)*

The interview excerpts above illustrate two contrasting views regarding marijuana usage as a subcultural phenomenon. The first interview presents a "die-hard" user who refuses to relinquish his use of this drug. This individual has been using marijuana for many years and considers it an essential recreational drug. Conversely, the second interviewee expresses some regret over the time "wasted" while becoming intoxicated with marijuana when he could have been pursuing other, more career-oriented activities.

Introduction

Although marijuana is potentially less addictive than other drugs such as cocaine, crack, heroin, and barbiturates (to name a few), it remains one of the few drugs that is controversial. It is difficult to wade through the emotion, politics, and rigidity found in the writings on marijuana to tease out the objective, clinical reality. In the United States, extreme views go back to the 1930s, when the film *Reefer Madness* portrayed an after-school marijuana "club" for high school students in suits and ties who became hallucinatory, homicidal, violent, and suicidal, such symptoms were highly exaggerated. As a complete contradiction, in the same decade, the Rastafarian religion spread among Jamaican agricultural workers, who named marijuana a *holy plant*.

[In], *Ganja in Jamaica* (Rubin and Comitas 1975) [the book] focused its findings to refute the claim that marijuana users damaged their productive capability. The study found that most rural Jamaicans who smoked ganja (marijuana) were extraordinarily diligent peasants who invested impressive amounts of time and energy in multiple income-bearing schemes every day of the year. Starting before sunrise, they tended livestock and poultry; farmed gardens; hired out their labor for wages; exchanged goods and services in an indigenous marketing system; maintained churches, self-help associations, political parties, guilds, schools, and households; and sometimes, at night, clandestinely cleared acres of forest to cultivate marijuana. They listened to the radio, watched television, and read newspapers to perform better as citizens in a modern democracy. These active, clear-sighted economic strategist and community builders depended on a heavy daily intake of ganja for nourishment as "brain food," and relied on it specifically to improve production. Adult Jamaican marijuana smokers consumed some six or more large "spliffs" (hand-rolled cigars) of ganja a day, or a few ounces. They also consumed it in teas, tisanes, and tonics. As employers, they preferred to pay their employees ganja rather than money and encouraged its use in the workplace. (Rubin and Comitas, 1975, cited in Hamid 1998, p. 61)

Marijuana is simply the hemp plant, *Cannabis sativa*, which has been cultivated for thousands of years. When smoked, the dried and crushed leaves, stems, and seeds of cannabis produce sedative and mind-altering effects, which vary according to the potency of the variety of plant used. Usage in the United States began in the 1920s, rose during the 1960s and 1970s, and fell in every year from 1978 until 1991. From 1991 on, however, usage began to climb.

In this chapter, we review the history, past and current usage trends, attitudes and controversies surrounding marijuana (including the amotivational syndrome and the recent debate inspired by proposals for medical legalization), and its physiological and behavioral effects on the user.

History and Trends in Marijuana Use

In many societies, marijuana has historically been a valued crop. It is called *hemp* because the woody fibers of the stem yield a fiber that can be made into cloth and rope. The term *cannabis* comes from the Greek word for hemp.

Initially, the Spaniards brought cannabis to the Western hemisphere as a source of fiber and seeds. For thousands of years, the seeds have been pressed to extract red oil used for medicinal and euphorigenic purposes (Abood and Martin 1992; Iversen 1993). The plant (both male and female) also produces a resin with active ingredients that affect the central nervous system (CNS). Marijuana contains hundreds of chemical compounds, but only a few found in the resin are responsible for producing the euphoric "high."

Even the original uses of marijuana remain controversial. Botanists have never been able to trace cannabis to its origins, although some think it originated in Asia. Ancient Chinese documents contain the earliest record name of hemp—*ma*, meaning fiber producing plant. In the late 1970s, during an archeological dig in Gansu, the seat of Chinese civilization, workers uncovered cannabis seed stored in an earthen jar.

Ayurvedic documents from 600 B.C. describe an intoxicating resin from the plant. The fifth-century B.C. Greek historian Herodotus recorded that the Scythians burned the tops of the plant, producing a narcotic smoke. And a first-century Greek physician wrote that hemp was made into intoxicating cakes, perhaps the forerunners of the marijuana brownies of 1960s fame. (Pollan 1998, p. 39)

Other sources report that the first known record of marijuana use is the *Book of Drugs* written about 2737 B.C. by the Chinese Emperor Shen Nung; he prescribed marijuana for treating gout, malaria, gas pains, and absentmindedness. The Chinese apparently had much respect for the plant. They obtained fiber for clothes and medicine from it for thousands of years. The Chinese named the plant *ma* (maw), which in the Chinese language can also mean "valuable" or "endearing." The term *ma* was still used as late as 1930.

Around 500 B.C., another Chinese book of treatments referred to the medical use of marijuana. Nonetheless, the plant got a bad name from the moralists of the day, who claimed that youngsters became wild and disrespectful from the recreational use of *ma*. They called it the "liberator of sin" because, under its influence, the youngsters refused to listen to their elders and did other scandalous things. Although the Chinese recognized *ma*'s medical usefulness, they eventually banned it because of unpredictable intoxicating effects. Later, because of rampant use, it was legalized again.

India also has a long and varied history of marijuana use. It was an essential part of Indian religious ceremonies for thousands of years. The well-known Rig Veda and other chants describe the use of *soma*, which some believe was marijuana. Early writings describe a ritual in which resin was collected from the plants. After fasting and purification, certain men ran naked through the cannabis fields. The clinging resin was scraped off their bodies, and cakes were made from it and used in feasts.

For centuries, missionaries in India tried to ban the use of marijuana, but they were never successful, because its use was too heavily ingrained in the culture. From India, the use of marijuana spread throughout Asia, Africa, Europe, and the Americas—English settlers brought it to the U.S. colonies.

Assyrian records dating back to 650 B.C. refer to a drug called *azulla* that was used for making rope and cloth and was consumed to experience euphoria. The ancient Greeks also knew about marijuana. Galen described the general use of hemp in cakes, which, when eaten in excess, produced narcotic effects. Herodotus described the Scythian custom of burning marijuana seeds and leaves to produce a narcotic smoke in steam baths. It was believed that breathing the smoke from the burning plants would cause frenzied activity. Groups of people stood in the smoke and laughed and danced as it took effect.

One legend about cannabis is based on the travels of Marco Polo in the 12th century. Marco Polo told of the legendary Hasan Ibn-Sabbah, who terrorized a part of Arabia in the early 1100s. His men were some of the earliest political murderers and he ordered them to kill under the influence of hashish, a strong, unadulterated cannabis derivative. The cult was called the *hashishiyya*, from which came the word *hashish*. (The word *assassin* may be derived from the name of Sheik Hasan, who was a political leader in the 10th century.)

It is unlikely, however, that using hashish can turn people into killers. Experience suggests that people tend to become sleepy and indolent rather than violent after eating or smoking hashish or another of the strong cannabis preparations available in Arabia (Abel 1989).

Napoleon's troops brought hashish to France after their campaign in Egypt at the beginning of the 19th century, despite Napoleon's strict orders to the contrary. By the 1840s, the use of hashish, as well as opium, was widespread in France, and efforts to curb its spread were unsuccessful.

In North America, hemp was planted near Jamestown in 1611 for use in making rope. By 1630, half of the winter clothing at this settlement was made from hemp fibers. There is no evidence that hemp was used medicinally at this time. Hemp was also valuable as a source of fiber for clothing and rope for the Pilgrims at Plymouth. To meet the demand for fiber, a law was passed in Massachusetts in 1639 requiring every household to plant hemp seed. How-ever, it took much manual labor to work the hemp fiber into usable form, resulting in a chronic shortage of fiber for fishnets and the like (Abel 1989).

George Washington cultivated a field of hemp at Mount Vernon, and there is some indication that it was used for medicine as well as for making rope. In his writings, Washington once mentioned that he forgot to separate the male and female plants, a process usually done because the female plant gave more resin if not pollinated.

In the early 1800s, U.S. physicians used marijuana extracts to produce a tonic intended for both medicinal and recreational purposes. This practice changed in 1937 with passage of the Marijuana Tax Act. The Marijuana Tax Act was modeled after the Harrison Act of 1914 in that marijuana was now considered a narcotic and subject to the same legal controls as cocaine and the opiates (see Chapter 3). Like these opiates, marijuana distributors had to register and pay a tax to legally import, buy, or sell this drug (Musto 1999). As a result, the Marijuana Tax Act prohibited the use of this drug as an intoxicant and regulated its use as a medicine.

Most of the abuse of marijuana in the United States during the early part of the 20th century took place near the Mexican border and in the ghetto areas of major cities. Cannabis was mistakenly considered a narcotic, like opium, and legal authorities treated it as such (Abood and Martin 1992). In 1931, Harry Anslinger, who was the first appointed head of the Bureau of Narcotics and later would become responsible for the enforcement of marijuana laws, believed that the problem was slight (Musto 1999). By 1936, however, he claimed that the increase in the use of marijuana was of great national concern (Anslinger and Cooper 1937) (see Figure 14.1). Anslinger set up an informational program that ultimately led to the federal law that banned marijuana. The following sensationalized statement was part of Anslinger's campaign to outlaw the drug:

> What about the alleged connection between drugs and sexual pleasure? . . . What is the real relationship between drugs and sex? There isn't any question about marijuana being a sexual stimulant. It has been used throughout the ages for that: in Egypt, for instance. From what we have seen, it is an aphrodisiac, and I believe that the use in colleges today has sexual connotations. (Anslinger and Cooper 1937, p. 19)

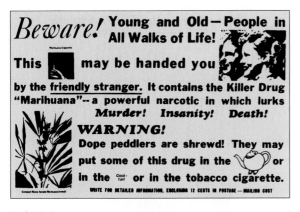

FIGURE 14.1
This antimarijuana poster was distributed by the Federal Bureau of Narcotics in the late 1930s.

In addition, during this time, some usually accurate magazines reported that marijuana was partly responsible for crimes of violence. In 1936, *Scientific American* reported that "marijuana produces a wide variety of symptoms in the user, including hilarity, swooning, and sexual excitement. Combined with intoxicants, it often makes the smoker vicious, with a desire to fight and kill" ("Marijuana Menaces Youth" 1936, p. 151). A famous poster of the day, called "The Assassination of Youth," was effective in molding attitudes against drug use.

Largely because of the media's influence on public opinion, Congress passed the Marijuana Tax Act in 1937. However, as a result of the discussions and debates before the passage of the 1970 Comprehensive Drug Abuse Prevention and Control Act, which replaced or updated all other laws concerning narcotics and dangerous drugs, the Marijuana Tax Act of 1937 was declared unconstitutional in 1969 because it classified marijuana as a narcotic. (For further historical details, see Chapter 3). Marijuana has not been classified as a narcotic since 1971.

In the early 1900s, marijuana was brought into the U.S. borders by Mexican laborers who entered the United States seeking jobs. From the border areas of the United States, recreational use of marijuana spread well into mainly the southwestern region of the United States. Such use spread to major cities in Texas and surrounding states as well as a number of African American communities in these cities. Heavy users of marijuana included a subpopulation of jazz musicians as well as other "bohemian types" who lead more of an unstructured existence in unconventional jobs and occupations (artists, entertainers, poets, criminals, and so on). Thus, before the 1960s, marijuana use was largely confined to small segments of African American urban youth, jazz musicians, and particularly artists and writers who belonged to the 1950s beat generation. Use rose tremendously in the 1960s, when it was closely associated with the hippie counterculture, in which marijuana was categorized as a psychedelic (consciousness-expanding) sacrament. It spread into other youth categories during the 1970s, until approximately 1978. In each year from 1978 until 1991, marijuana use fell. After 1991, researchers and prevention specialists were astounded to see a rise in usage among youth.

Marijuana still grows wild in many American states today. Curiously, one reason for the survival of this supply is that, during World War II, the fiber used to make rope (sisal) was hard to import, so the government subsidized farmers to grow hemp. Much of today's crop comes from these same plants. Another reason for the spread of the plants is that, until recently, the seeds were used in birdseed. Leftover seed was discarded in the garbage and thus spread to landfill dumps, where it sprouted. Birdseed containing marijuana seeds is still available, but the seeds are sterilized so that they cannot germinate.

The Indian Hemp Drug Commission Report in the 1890s and the 1930 Panama Canal Zone Report on marijuana stressed that available evidence did not prove marijuana to be as dangerous as it was popularly thought; these reports were given little publicity, however, and for the most part disregarded. In 1944, a report was issued by the LaGuardia Committee on Marijuana, which consisted of 31 qualified physicians, psychiatrists, psychologists, pharmacologists, chemists, and sociologists appointed by the New York Academy of Medicine. They stated in one key summary that marijuana was not the killer many thought it to be:

> It was found that marijuana in an effective dose impairs intellectual functioning in general. . . .
> Marijuana does not change the basic personality structure of the individual. It lessens inhibition and this brings out what is latent in his thoughts and emotions but it does not evoke responses that would otherwise be totally alien to him. . . .
> Those who have been smoking marijuana for

years showed no mental or physical deterioration that may be attributed to the drug. (Solomon 1966, p. 37)

Much of the early research conducted did not consider the potency of marijuana. As a result, findings from various studies are often conflicting and difficult to compare. Because the quality of marijuana varies so greatly, it is impossible to know the amount of drug taken without analyzing the original material and the leftover stub, or "roach." Conditions such as type of seed, soil moisture and fertility, amount of sunlight, and temperature all have an effect on the amounts of active ingredients found in the resulting marijuana plant.

Current Use of Marijuana

In 1998, there were 13.6 million Americans (12 years of age and over), who were current illicit drug users (SAMHSA 1999). *Current drug use* is defined as having used an illicit drug in the month before the interview. From this number, 81% had used marijuana in combination with other drugs and approximately 60% of current illicit drug users used only marijuana. Although 21% used marijuana and another illicit drug, the remaining 19% used an illicit drug but not marijuana in the past month (see Figure 14.2) (SAMHSA 1999). This makes marijuana the most commonly used illicit drug.

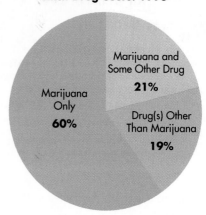

Types of Drugs Used by Past-Month Illicit Drug Users: 1998

Marijuana and Some Other Drug **21%**

Marijuana Only **60%**

Drug(s) Other Than Marijuana **19%**

13.6 Million Illicit Drug Users

FIGURE 14.2

Source: Substance Abuse and Mental Health Services Administration (SAMHSA), Office of Applied Studies (OAS). *Summary of findings from the 1998 National Household Survey on Drug Abuse.* Rockville, MD: SAMHSA and OAS, August 1999.

As Table 14.1 shows, the frequency of marijuana use is strongly correlated with age. The age group reporting the highest lifetime use was 26- to 34-year-olds (47.9%). For past-year and past-month usage, 18- to 25-year-olds reported the highest use. Marijuana use sharply dropped in the 35 and older

TABLE 14.1 **Marijuana Use Reported in 1998 by Americans During Lifetime, Past Year, and Past Month, According to Age**

AGE (YEARS)	LIFETIME (%)	PAST YEAR (%)	PAST MONTH (%)
12–17	17.0	14.1	8.3
18–25	44.6	24.1	13.8
26–34	47.9	9.7	5.5
35+	29.4	4.1	2.5

Source: National Household Survey on Drug Abuse: Population Estimates 1998, Rockville, MD. U.S. Department of Health and Human Services, Substance Abuse and Mental Health Services Administration (SAMHSA).

age group across all usage periods (lifetime 29.4%, past year 4.1%, and past month 2.5%). Overall, the heaviest users are between 18 and 34 years old. Table 14.2 shows the number of people who first used marijuana from 1994 to 1997 by mean age and age-specific rate of first use. In comparing Tables 14.1 with 14.2, we find that although drug use remains highest among youth, Table 14.2 shows that first use of marijuana is highest among 12- to 17-year-olds, fluctuating from 64.4% in 1997 to a high of 79.3% in 1996. Next highest rate of first users of marijuana are the 18- to 25-year-olds, ranging from 52.6% in 1995 to a low of 47.1% in 1997. The percentage of new "recruits" using marijuana for the first time remains high for people under 26 years of age. This indicates that the large percentages of young first-time users do not show any signs of less use.

Marijuana Use and Youth

■ TRENDS IN USE

Figure 14.3 demonstrates trends in annual use, perceived risk, disapproval, and availability for 8th, 10th, and 12th graders. Annual marijuana use peaked at 51% among 12th graders in 1979, following a rise that likely began in the 1960s. Then use declined steadily for 13 years, bottoming at 22% in 1992—a decline of more than half. In the 1990s,

there was resurgence in use of this drug. After a considerable increase in the 1990s (one that actually began among 8th graders a year earlier than among 10th and 12th graders), annual prevalence rates peaked in 1996 at 8th grade and in 1997 at 10th and 12th grades. Some decline followed, through there was no further specific decline observed in 1999 (Johnston et al. 2000).

■ PERCEIVED RISK

Perceived risk is a leading indicator of change in use. When the amount of risk associated with marijuana use decreases, a resurgence of use follows shortly. Similarly, when perceived risk increases, a decrease in use will soon follow. As seen in Figure 14.3, 10th and 12th graders reported lower perceived risks a year before the rise in use in the 1990s and a rise in perceived risk before dropping use rates in 1997 (Johnston et al. 2000).

■ DISAPPROVAL

Among 8th graders, between 1991 and 1996, personal disapproval of marijuana use slipped considerably. Among 10th and 12th graders, the same occurred between 1992 and 1997. There has since been a small increase in disapproval among 8th and 10th graders but not yet among 12th graders (Johnston et al. 2000).

TABLE 14.2 **Estimated Number (in Thousands) of Persons Who First Used Marijuana During 1994–1997, Their Mean Age at First Use and Annual Age-Specific Rates of First Use**

Year	Initiates (1000s)	Mean Age	AGE SPECIFIC RATE OF FIRST USE		
			12–17	18–25	26–34
1994	2380	16.9	72.8	47.9	2.5
1995	2409	16.6	74.1	52.6	1.8
1996	2462	16.6	79.3	52.1	2.4
1997	2114	17.1	64.4	47.1	1.4

Source: Substance Abuse and Mental Health Services Administration (SAMHSA). *Summary of Findings from the 1998 National Household Survey on Drug Abuse.* Rockville, MD: Office of Applied Studies. National Clearinghouse for Alcohol and Drug Information (NCADI), 1999.

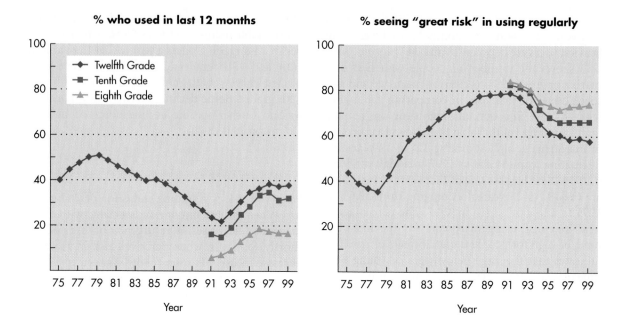

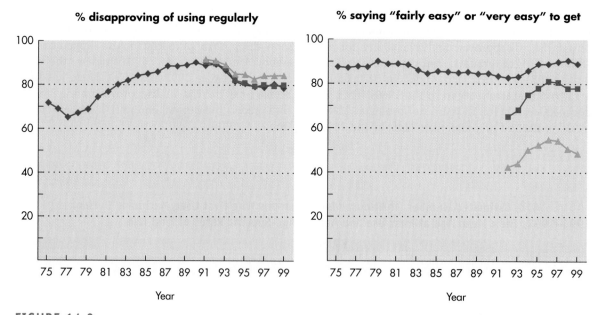

FIGURE 14.3

Marijuana: trends in annual use, risk, disapproval, and availability for eighth, tenth, and twelfth graders.

Source: Johnston, L., P. O'Malley, and J. Bachman. *The Monitoring the Future National Results on Adolescent Drug Use: Overview of Key Findings*, 1999. Bethesda, MD: National Institute on Drug Abuse, July 2000.

■ **AVAILABILITY**

Since 1975, between 83% and 90% of every senior class indicated that it was "fairly easy" or "very easy" to get marijuana. One interview that is believed to be typical at many of our nation's public schools reveals the following:

> What, weed? It's so easy to get. In fact, many times, I didn't even have to buy, it would be offered in the morning, at lunchtime, and whenever we get together, it's there after school. Among the users, (and we know each other real well), it's as common as sharing candy. *(From Venturelli's research files, 15-year-old-male, first year high school student residing in a medium-sized town in the Midwest, June 19, 2000.)*

Figure 14.3 also indicates that since 1991, marijuana tends to be less accessible to 8th and 10th graders. Nevertheless, in 1999 nearly half of all 8th graders (48%) and more than three-quarters of all 10th graders (78%) reported it as being accessible. This compares with 89% for seniors (Johnston et al. 2000).

Marijuana: Is It the Assassin of Youth?

In the late 1930s, the poster "Marijuana: Assassin of Youth" made a clever play on words, bringing up reminders of the Middle Eastern "hashashin" cult, whose terrible exploits were attributed to their use of hashish (marijuana resin).

At the time, marijuana was even incorrectly classified as a narcotic, like opium and morphine. Amotivational syndrome, lassitude, poor driving skills the day after smoking, educational failure, and dependence may not quite add up to "assassination," as wildly exaggerated in *Reefer Madness*. The poster was right, however, in associating use of this drug with young people among whom marijuana is popular both in local peer groups and broad youth cultures.

■ **PEER INFLUENCES**

As discussed in the beginning chapters of this text, the mass media and parental role models directly influence the development of youths' attitudes regarding drug use. However, beginning several years before age 13 (early adolescence), peers and peer groups exert the most influence (Greenblatt 1999; Heitzeg 1996; Tudor et al. 1987; Venturelli 2000).

Research shows that it is unlikely that an individual will use drugs when his or her peers do not use them. Marijuana use, in particular, is a group-motivated behavior that is strongly affected by peer pressure and influence. Thus, in effect, we can say that habitual drug users are likely to belong to drug-using groups. In contrast, people who do not use drugs belong to groups in which drug use is perceived as a deviant form of social recreation. Learning theory (see Chapter 2) shows how peers can influence one another; drug-using peer members serve as role models, legitimizing use. Peers in such groups are in effect saying, "It's perfectly normal to use drugs," and in turn, this justifies usage.

In addition to peer influences, four additional factors must be taken into account as influencing factors responsible for drug use:

1. Structural factors, such as age, gender, family background, religious beliefs.

2. Social and interactional factors, such as type of interpersonal relationships, friendship cliques, and drug use within the peer group setting.

3. Setting (physical location of drug use).

4. Attitudinal factors, such as personal attitudes toward the use of drugs.

Keep in mind these factors can easily overlap; they are not separate and distinct.

Sociologists have long studied "youth cultures" (Coleman 1961). In the 1970s, sociologists began to examine different subcultures of youth in terms of the behaviors that symbolically represent the group, where participation in drug use is a ritual that marks off entrance into the group and out of childhood—a "rite of passage." Typically, American high school culture includes a "leading" clique, often associated with team sports, whose members might be called "jocks," "collegiates," or "rah-rahs," and a marginal, deviant, or rebellious group (Eckert 1989). In some cases, the latter group is associated with marijuana use. In the mid-1960s, hippies were perceived as a group whose members were part of a counter-culture committed to unconventional values, pacifism, and communalism in addition to psychedelic drugs. By 1970, this name denoted broader segments of youth who adhered merely to hippie styles of clothing and drug use (Buff 1970). By the 1980s, marijuana use was identified with subgroups of youth often called "burnouts." In many communities that were studied by sociologists, "burnouts" came from all social levels, but were often over-represented in upper middle classes, and they were marginal and/or rebellious within the educational system, if not dropouts (Eckert 1989, Gaines 1992). Membership in such marijuana-using subcultures often bonds the youth to persistent drug use.

The Role of Marijuana as a Gateway Drug

Gateway drugs are drugs that serve as the "gate" or path that usually precedes the use of illicit drugs such as marijuana, heroin, and LSD. Gateway drugs, or drugs-of-entry, serve to initiate a novice user into the drug-using world. Although the linkage is not biochemical, common gateway drugs include tobacco, inhalants, alcohol, and anabolic steroids. The claim that marijuana use leads to the use of other more serious drugs, such as heroin, is controversial (Gardner 1992). Although it is true that many heroin addicts began drug use with marijuana, it is also true that many, if not most, also

used coffee and cigarettes. Millions of marijuana users never go beyond the gateway drugs used. "There are only a few thousand opiate addicts in Great Britain, yet there are millions who have tried cannabis" (Gossop 1987, p. 9).

Nevertheless, some explanation is needed for the small percentage of marijuana users who do progress to hard drugs such as heroin. Thus, it is unlikely that the use of marijuana is the principal cause of moving to harder drugs. Much more important factors are the personality of the users as well as their social environment. As described in Chapter 18, youths who turn to drugs are usually slightly to seriously alienated individuals. Thus, progression from marijuana to other drugs is more likely to depend on peer group composition, family relationships, social class, and the age at which drug use begins (Indiana Prevention Resource Center 1996).

It is important to note, however, that many, if not most, young drug users do eventually leave drug-using groups and abandon their drug-using behavior, a process sometimes called *maturing out*. An example that often typifies maturing out is found in the following interview:

> Sure, smoking dope and tripping on acid was a way of life when I was a teenager. But then, I graduated college and had to join the real world—that everyday work world that my dull parents lived in. *(From Venturelli's research files, 28 year-old female, working for a national private security firm, August 12, 2000.)*

Other research further documents some young "burnouts" quitting marijuana smoking without sacrificing group membership (Eckert 1989).

Misperceptions of Marijuana Use

In a world in which marijuana can be considered either an "assassin" or a "sacrament," and where it is associated with membership in prized or despised peer groups, it is not surprising that estimates of its use will vary widely and inaccurately. Parents, for example, tend to underestimate their children's use of drugs. Findings from one study indicated that, "only 14% of the parents interviewed thought their children had experimented with marijuana while

KEY TERMS

gateway drugs
drugs that often lead to the use of more serious drugs: alcohol, tobacco, and marijuana are the drugs most commonly believed to be gateway drugs

Cannabis sativa
biological species name for the variety of hemp plant known as marijuana

sinsemilla
meaning without seeds, this marijuana is made from the buds and flowering tops of female plants and is one of the most potent types

38% of the teenagers said they had tried it" (Wren 1996, p. 1). In the same survey, 52% of teenagers reported having been offered drugs, while 34% of the parents thought their children might have been offered drugs.

Interestingly, another report by the former president of the National Center on Addiction and Substance Abuse at Columbia University stated the following with regard to baby boomer parents (parents born between the late 1940s through late 1950s):

> Almost half know someone who uses illegal drugs; a third have friends who use marijuana. Almost half expect their children to try illegal drugs, and 65 percent of those who smoked pot regularly when young believe their kids will try drugs . . . almost half of the parents don't think they can have much influence on whether their kids will use drugs (Califano 1996, p. 19)

Even with regard to users' perceptions of other users, beliefs about marijuana remain distorted. College students tend to have exaggerated misperceptions of use, believing that their peers use marijuana much more than is true (Berkowitz 1991). For example, at one campus in northern New Jersey, two-thirds of students reported never using marijuana, yet most students polled believed that the average student uses marijuana once per week. Thus, with regard to marijuana users, interest in using remains persistently strong for the time being. In the early years of this millennium, high usage of marijuana remains stubbornly persistent.

Characteristics of Cannabis

In 1753, Carolus Linnaeus, a Swedish botanist, classified marijuana as *Cannabis sativa* . *Cannabis sativa* is a plant that grows readily in many parts of the world. Most botanists agree that there is only one species (*sativa*) and that all the variants (*indicia, Americana,* and *africana*) belong to that species, while others believe that the variants are three distinct species (Schultes 1978). *Indica* is considered to have the most potent resin, but climate, soil, and selective plant breeding all influence potency. The world's record marijuana plant was 39 feet tall, and its woody stem was nearly 3 inches in diameter.

Cannabis is *dioecious*, meaning that there are male and female plants (see Figure 14.4). After the male plant releases its pollen, it usually dies. In any case, even before the male plant dies cultivators of marijuana often eliminate or remove the male plants once the female plant has been pollinated.

There are more than 421 different chemicals in the cannabis plant, many of which have not yet been identified. Tetrahydrocannabinol, or THC, is the primary mind-altering (psychoactive) agent in marijuana (Abood and Martin 1996; Swan 1996) and appears to be important for the reinforcing properties of this substance (Kelly et al. 1994). THC is most highly concentrated in the flowering tops and upper leaves of the female plant. When crushed or beaten, these flowering tops produce a resin in which the psychoactive ingredient THC is found.

In cultivated marijuana crops, male plants are eradicated from the growing fields so that they cannot pollinate the female plants. The lack of pollination makes the potency of female plants increase dramatically. *Sinsemilla* (meaning "without seeds" in Spanish) is one of the most potent derivatives of the cannabis plant known in the United States, with an average of 7.5% and a range as high as 24% THC. *Sinsemilla* is made from the buds of flowering tops of female plants (NIDA 1998). Other known types that have a much higher THC content include "hydro" (which means grown in water) and "kine bud."

In the United States, the amount of THC found in "street" sold marijuana ranges broadly from 0.5% to 11%. Reports indicate that the amount of THC in marijuana has risen dramatically since the 1960s (Kaplan and Whitmire 1995; NIDA 1998). "More efficient agriculture—new methods of harvesting and processing marijuana plants—has made pot about 20 times more potent than the marijuana on the street in the 1960s and 1970s, drug treatment experts and law officials say" (Henneberger 1994, F-18). Further, the quantities of other more potent types of marijuana such as sinsemilla as well as hydroponic-types of marijuana (known as "hydro") are more readily available in illegal drug markets. The actual potencies of the more generic types of marijuana have remained the same in the past 30 years.

Native U.S. street variety marijuana, often referred to as "ditch weed" cannabis is sometimes

FIGURE 14.4
Male and female
marijuana plants.

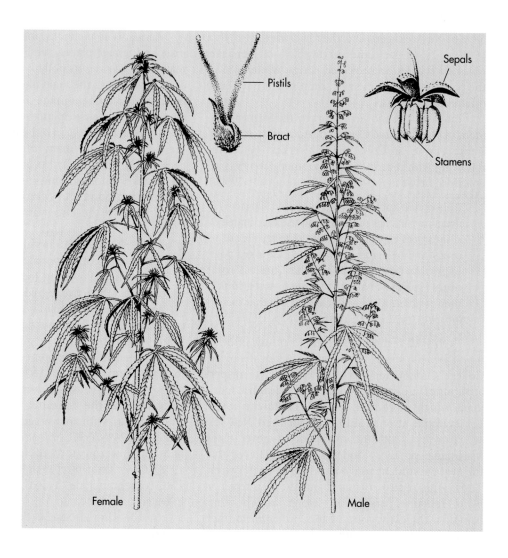

Female   Male

Pistils

Bract

Sepals

Stamens

considered inferior because of a low concentration of THC, usually less than 0.5%. THC levels in Jamaican, Colombian, and Mexican varieties range between 0.5% and 7%. It is made from parts of the cannabis plant that contain the least amount of THC. Some members of drug-using subcultures grind this type of marijuana (as well as more potent types of marijuana) into a powder and mix it into drinks, teas, and cookie and brownie batter.

Hashish (or hasheesh) is a second derivative of cannabis that contains the purest form of resin. This type of marijuana is the sticky resin from the female plant flowers and has an average THC level of 3.6%, which can go as high as 28% (NIDA 1998). Historically, hashish users have represented a somewhat small percentage of the cannabis user population in the United States, whereas in Europe, use is much more prevalent. Hashish is produced in Lebanon, Afghanistan, and Pakistan.

A third derivative of the cannabis plant is *ganja*, which is produced in India. This preparation consists of the dried tops of female plants.

KEY TERMS

hashish
sticky resin from the female plant flowers, which has an average THC level of 3.6%, and ranges as high as 28%

The Behavioral Effects of Marijuana Use

■ THE "HIGH"

The then widely held belief of the 1930s that marijuana is a destructive assassin of youth is no longer considered valid for casual or occasional users of this drug. In most individuals, low to moderate doses of cannabis produce euphoria and a pleasant state of relaxation (Goldstein 1994). What are the common effects experienced from marijuana use? After a few minutes of forcibly holding the smoke in the lungs, most users suddenly experience the "high." In this state of euphoria, the user experiences a dry mouth, elevated heartbeat, and some loss of coordination and balance, coupled with slower reaction times and a feeling of euphoria (mild to elevated intoxication). Blood vessels in the eyes expand, which accounts for reddening of the eyes. Some people experience slightly elevated blood pressure, which can double the normal heart rate. These effects can become intensified when other drugs, such as LSD and/or psychedelic ("magic") mushrooms, are combined with the marijuana.

The state of euphoria that results from the "high" is usually mild and short-lived; a typical high from one joint may last from 2 to 3 hours. Subjectively, the user experiences altered perception of space and time, impaired memory of recent events, and impaired physical coordination (more of these subjective effects are discussed at length in the next section) (Abood and Martin 1992). An occasional high is not usually hazardous unless the person attempts to drive a car, operate heavy machinery, fly a plane, or function in similar ways requiring coordination, good reflexes, or quick judgment (Nahas and Latour 1992). Even low doses of marijuana adversely affect perception, such as being able to judge the speed of an approaching vehicle or how much to slow down on an exit ramp. One interview revealed the following:

> In trying to describe the high, it's not like an alcohol high. In an alcohol high, you are a lot more uncoordinated if drinking a lot. With weed it's like reality changes, you add a lot more bass so-to-speak to what you see, hear, think, and feel. The reality is tempered with some distortion that to me and many others is pleasurable. You know how you feel after three or four very strong drinks [referring to alcoholic beverages]? Well take two more of those drinks and then look around the room you are in. Now, the difference between alcohol and weed is that you can walk to the bathroom quite well while under the influence of weed, while with alcohol, you walk carefully so that no one notices that you are just about drunk. Weed is a mind high while alcohol is more of a body high *(From Venturelli's research files, May 19, 2000, 23-year-old female, professionally employed residing in San Francisco.)*

Another two interviews (same interviewee on two different occasions) also attempted to compare the "high" from marijuana with the effects of alcohol:

> The marijuana high is also not nearly as harsh on the body. Being high doesn't give you that painful hangover as alcohol does. The actual high is very functional; I tend to do some of my best work (after burning a "dubbie") in that state [of mind]. It is part of the lifestyle of marijuana. [In contrast], alcohol, makes me (and most people I know) very unproductive when the "buzz" is reached. *(From Venturelli's research files, "Lectus Ferberger," 21-year-old male, undergraduate student at a Midwestern University, August 10, 2000.)*

> There seems to be a small misconception about the effects of marijuana and alcohol. For me, anyway, in looking at the physical "buzz" you get from alcohol; it is very physically disabling. You get drunk and stumble around, your lips loosen up, and you say things that you would not normally say. I find that marijuana has more of a calming effect. It makes you relaxed and a little more perceptive to some stimuli and obviously less perceptive to other stimuli. It is a light feeling, but not overwhelming to the equilibrium. *(From Venturelli's research files, same student as above, August 11, 2000.)*

An acute dose of cannabis can produce adverse reactions, ranging from mild anxiety to panic and paranoia in some users. These reactions occur most frequently in individuals who are under stress or who are anxious, depressed, or borderline schizophrenic (Nahas and Latour 1992). Such effects may also be seen in normal users who accidentally take much more than they feel they can handle.

Extreme reactions can also occur because of ingesting marijuana treated (or "laced") with such things as opium, PCP, or other additives. Based on limited evidence from survey studies, mild or often adverse, reactions are experienced on one or more occasions by more than one-half of regular users; they are mainly self-treated and usually go unreported (see "Case in Point," Specific Signs of Marijuana Use).

■ SUBJECTIVE EUPHORIC EFFECTS

Subjective euphoric effects associated with marijuana use are the ongoing social and psychological experiences incurred while intoxicated by marijuana. These effects of intoxication include both the user's altered state of consciousness and his or her perceptions.

Subjective effects also include a general sense of relaxation and tranquility, coupled with heightened sensitivity to sound, taste, and emotionality. Some users report occasional similarities to the typical hallucinogenic high. How closely the marijuana high resembles a hallucinogenic high depends on the amount of THC absorbed from marijuana. For example, higher amounts of THC found in more potent plants of marijuana, like *sinsemilla*, hydro,

and kine bud more clearly mimic a hallucinogenic high. These effects are especially evident when considering the extent to which the senses of hearing, vision, sound, and taste are distorted by use of highly potent forms of marijuana.

Among marijuana users, there are a proportion who are very attached to these euphoric effects (in search of re-experiencing these effects). Such users often pride themselves on their extensive knowledge of this drug and maintain interest in discussing past experiences of "when I was really high" or "let me tell you about that night we smoked hydro. . . . " Devotees stay current with developments in the marijuana field by avidly reading monthly issues of magazines devoted to marijuana (the "art" of marijuana use) and frequently scan the Internet for information and conversations in chat rooms about the best varieties of marijuana, best growing techniques, announcements of hemp festivals, advice and information regarding current laws, fines, and other information.

Why is marijuana so attractive to many individuals? One quote from an interview illustrates the extensive psychological and social reinforcement experienced by marijuana users:

CASE IN POINT

Specific Signs of Marijuana Use

- A sweet odor similar to burnt rope in room, on clothes, etc.
- Roach: The small butt end of a marijuana cigarette.
- Joint: Looks like a hand-rolled cigarette, usually the ends are twisted or crimped.
- Roach clips: Holders for the roach could be any number of common items such as paper clips, bobby pins, or hemostats. They could also be of a store-bought variety in a number of shapes and disguises.
- Seeds or leaves in pockets or possession.
- Rolling papers or pipes, usually hidden somewhere.

- Eye drops: For covering up red eyes.
- Excessive use of incense, room deodorizers, or breath fresheners.
- Devices for keeping the substance such as film canisters, boxes, or cans.
- Eating binges: An after-effect for some marijuana users.
- Appearance of intoxication, yet no smell of alcohol.
- Excessive laughter.
- Initial use (first hour): Animated behavior (loud or excessive talking).
- (Hours later): Fatigue or drowsiness.

It's the high that I particularly like. Everything becomes mellower. Everyday tensions are released or submerged by more inner-like experiences. I can review the day and how happy or miserable I feel. Actually, when I am thinking and I am high on grass, I always feel that my thoughts are profound. You think from another perspective, one that numbs the more reality-based everyday strains. On the other hand, there are moments when this drug affects your mood and channels it [in] different ways. You have moments when you either feel sad, happy, angry (in a more contemplative way), or worried. These moods are both good and bad. If for the moment you feel good, then your mood is positive. If you feel down, your mood is negative in a particular way. If I am with friends and we are all sharing the bong or joint or pipe, we laugh a lot together. It's a type of drug that makes you more jovial, more introspective, and friendly, gregarious.... *(From Venturelli's research files, 40-year-old male personnel manager, August 20, 1996.)*

Intense attachment to passionate feelings surrounding the use of marijuana is quite common. As explained in Chapter 2, largely through the reinforcement of pleasurable feelings, psychologists believe the drug user becomes attached and habituated to the drug. If these subjective euphoric experiences were to become largely negative, attachment to and repeated use of this drug would cease. Thus, the theory of differential association applies to the two interviewees. Developed by Edwin Sutherland in 1939 and revised in 1947, this theory attempts to explain delinquent behavior. Sociologists define the term differential association , as the process by which individuals are socialized into the perceptions and values of a group. The application of this concept can be redefined as differential association with respect to drug use. In the case of marijuana, the drug using group or even a fellow drug user rewards such behavior. It can include the perception that marijuana will relieve boredom, stress, or is the "perfect" drug for just "hanging out" or "partying" and "getting high." Specifically, the definition of differential association is the behavioral satisfaction derived from friends who use marijuana. Psychologically, the high with others is the positive reward that cements the user to his friends and the drug.

■ DRIVING PERFORMANCE

Evidence shows that the ability to perform complex tasks, such as driving, can be strongly impaired while under the influence of marijuana (Goldstein 1994; Mathias 1996). Research indicates, "Cannabis consumption impairs motor coordination, reaction time, sensory perceptions and glare recovery" (Teen Challenge 2000, p. 1). This effect has been demonstrated in laboratory assessments of driving-related skills such as eye-hand coordination and reaction time, in driver simulator studies, in test course performance, and in actual street driving situations (Chait and Pierri 1992; Mathias 1996; Teen Challenge 2000). Another study tested the effects of known amounts of marijuana, alcohol, or both on driving. The subjects drove a course rigged with various traffic problems. There was a definite deterioration in driving skills among those who had used either drug, but the greatest deterioration was observed in subjects who had taken both. In another test, 59 subjects smoked marijuana until they were intoxicated and then were given sobriety tests on the roadside by highway patrol officers. Overall, 94% of the subjects did not pass the test 90 minutes after smoking, and 60% failed at 150 minutes, even though the blood THC was much lower at this time (Hollister 1986). Other studies on driving show this same inability to drive for as long as 12 to 24 hours after marijuana use.

In limited surveys, from 60% to 80% of marijuana users indicate that they sometimes drive while high. A study of drivers involved in fatal accidents in the greater Boston area showed that marijuana smokers were over-represented in fatal highway accidents as compared with a control group of nonusers of similar age and gender. A 1998 study found that, of nearly 1800 blood samples taken from drivers arrested for driving while intoxicated, 19% tested positive for marijuana.

KEY TERMS

subjective euphoric effects
ongoing social and psychological experiences incurred while intoxicated with marijuana

differential association
behavioral satisfaction derived from friends who use marijuana

Further, "figures from previous studies of automobile accident victims show that from 6% to 12% of nonfatally injured drivers and 4% to 16% of fatally injured drivers had THC . . . in their bloodstream," (Mathias 1996, p. 6). Another study showed that 32% of drivers in shock trauma units had marijuana in their bloodstream. One problem with this study, however, is that individuals testing positive for THC also had alcohol in their bloodstream, making it impossible to determine whether THC or alcohol directly caused the car accident.

One notable interview presents us with a negative experience regarding use of marijuana and driving experiences:

> One time I smoked some real strong dope at my friend's house, then had to drive back home, which was 2 miles in one direction. I remember wigging' out (panicking) in trying to get home. There were moments where I did not know where I was until I would see the next marker of my neighborhood. I remember having seconds of panic because I did not know where I was then suddenly, I would notice a neighborhood restaurant or some other marker that said I was right around my neighborhood. I took smaller streets on the way home and even took a longer way home because I was freaking out about the cops—what if one would spot me? This was bogus thinking because how the hell would anyone suddenly spot me while driving home? Well, that's an example of wigging out on weed. But, I still don't think that even that time I would be getting into an accident. I was so freaked out that I was extra careful not to speed, pass stop signs, or violate any law for fear of being seen. If anything, I drive slower when I am really high, not more dangerously. *(From Venturelli's research files, 20-year-old male college student in a Midwestern town, July 19, 2000.)*

In contrast, more scientific research indicates that some perceptual or other performance deficits resulting from marijuana use may persist for some time after the high, and users who attempt to drive, fly, operate heavy machinery, perform surgery, and so on may not recognize their impairment because they do not feel intoxicated. States such as California have established testing procedures to detect the presence of THC in urine or blood samples from apparently intoxicated drivers.

If the use of marijuana becomes more socially acceptable (or perhaps even legal) and penalties for simple possession become more lenient, it is likely that individuals will feel less inclined to hide their drug use. Unfortunately, it follows that these individuals may also be more inclined to drive while high, endangering themselves and others.

■ CRITICAL THINKING SKILLS

Marijuana has been found to have a negative impact on critical thinking skills. Recent research by the NIDA shows that heavy marijuana use impairs critical skills related to attention, memory, and learning. Another study showed that even alertness, coordination, and reaction time were impaired by marijuana usage (NCADI 1998). Impairment continues even after discontinuing this drug's use for at least 24 hours (Brown and Massaro 1996).

In the same study, researchers compared 65 *heavy users* (using approximately every other day) with *light users* (using once or twice per week). Heavy users made more mistakes and had greater difficulty sustaining attention, shifting attention to meet demands of challenges in the environment, and registering, processing, and using information (Brown and Massaro 1996) compared with the group dubbed "light users." In addition, heavy users had greater difficulty completing the tests, which specifically measured aspects of attention, memory, and learning, such as intellectual functioning, abstraction ability, attention span, verbal fluency, and learning and recalling abilities (Brown and Massaro 1996; Teen Challenge 2000). One researcher stated, "If you could get heavy users to learn an item, then they could remember it; the problem was getting them to learn it in the first place" (Brown and Massaro 1996, p. 3). The researchers surmised that marijuana alters brain activity because residues of the drug persist in the brain or because a withdrawal syndrome follows after the euphoric effects of the marijuana wear off. In another study, researchers tested the cognitive functioning of 65 marijuana-using college students. Residual impairments were seen on the day (24 hours) after use in terms of sustaining attention, shifting attention, and hence in registering, organizing, and using information (Pope and Yurgulen-Todd 1996). This study, which was undertaken during the 1990s, is significant because it was carefully controlled. The unresolved question is whether these memory impairments are short-term or long-term. These noteworthy findings complement many other similar findings that identified protracted cognitive impairment among heavy users of marijuana (NCADI 1998).

■ THE AMOTIVATIONAL SYNDROME

The so-called amotivational syndrome (sometimes referred to as "antimotivational syndrome") is a flashpoint of controversy about marijuana, although not as newsworthy as that regarding medical legalization. *Amotivational syndrome* refers to a belief that heavy use of marijuana causes a lack of motivation and reduced productivity. Specifically, users show apathy, poor short-term memory, difficulty in concentration, and a lingering disinterest in pursuing goals (Abood and Martin 1992).

In the past, this syndrome received considerable attention. People who are high, or "stoned," lack the desire to perform hard work and are not interested in doing difficult tasks. There is some evidence of this behavior in regular marijuana users (Nahas and Latour 1992). Overall, although not solely the result of cannabis use, *chronic users* have lower grades in school, are more likely to be absent from classes, and are likely not to complete assignments and to drop out of school (Henneberger 1994; Liska 1997). In terms of age, the earlier someone begins smoking marijuana coupled with heavier use the more likely the amotivational characteristics will prevail and the more difficult it will be to cease using this drug.

Although the effects of marijuana *per se* are somewhat responsible for creating this syndrome, other factors contribute as well. For instance, is the lack of motivation caused by the drug itself or is it that poorly motivated people begin using marijuana then further exacerbate their lack of motivation? Surveys show that a sizeable number of marijuana users and their peer groups tend to be alienated from society and are likely to be classified as nonconformists and/or rebellious youths. They may in fact select to emphasize pleasure and nonconformity rather than goal-directed behavior.

Advocates of marijuana legalization stress data that tends to debunk research on amotivational syndrome. One institute that supports legalization, the Lindesmith Center, published a study asserting that college students who are users have higher grades than nonusers (Zimmer and Morgan 1997). How can we account for the discrepancies between this study and others, not to mention the clinical experiences of students, who often report academic repercussions of heavy use? One factor in the explanation is sociocultural:

> In the New York–New Jersey metro region, there are "druggy" schools and "drinking" schools. The "druggy" schools are more upper-middle-class, liberal arts schools, artsy types, latter-day hippies, etc. The boozer campuses are filled with blue-collar and lower middle class kids—sometimes big fraternity schools. Front-loading at basketball games, comas after pledge parties . . . Not as good educational backgrounds as the artsy potheads, who went to better schools, private schools, read a lot, or heard a lot at dinner before college, so they get by with their profs. But the potheads ratchet down into easier majors, and they get crummier grades as they get into regular use. (Interview with Pearl Mott, prevention specialist, Drug Prevention Programs in Higher Education, Washington, D.C., October 1994, for a prevention newsletter.)

A second methodological factor complicating drug research among such students is simply that academic failures stay in "F" categories for only one or two semesters. Many then disappear from statistics entirely, via academic attrition.

A more serious challenge to the notion of amotivational syndrome comes from the same ethnographic research that was mentioned at the beginning of this chapter. The most well known of these investigations was carried out by Vera Rubin and Labros Comitas, as reported in their book *Ganja in Jamaica* (1975). Follow-up studies were done in Jamaica (Hamid 1998; Dreher 1982) and Costa Rica (Carter 1980; Pollan 1998). None of these works found that chronic use impaired occupational or

---

KEY TERMS

amotivational syndrome
refers to a belief that heavy use of marijuana causes a lack of motivation and reduced productivity

other functioning; in fact, the main point of the Jamaican studies was that users defined this drug as helpful and motivating for work—a "motivational syndrome." This work is often cited to counter amotivational syndrome claims. By this logic, dropping out of the "rat race" is a cultural posture, with marijuana being secondary to, or, at most, reinforcing the drift away from a mainstream lifestyle. The Jamaican and Costa Rican subjects, however, were not observed engaging in an academic, cognitively complex, or rapid reflex activity, nor were they found in occupations that are competitive and striving for mobility. Rather, these subjects were involved in repetitive, physical labor such as sugar-cane cutting. In such a context, marijuana drug use functions to provide a pleasant sedation that counters the monotony and physical discomfort of such labor. When studies in other cultures contradict the largely American notion of amotivational syndrome, we are left to be cautious in making a direct assumption that marijuana use leads to such a syndrome. (For related information on how marijuana affects personality see "Case in Point," Marijuana Use May Lead to a Life of Trouble.)

CASE IN POINT

Marijuana Use May Lead to a Life of Trouble

Dear Ann Landers: Twenty years ago, when I was in my early 20s, you printed a column about marijuana. You expressed concern that marijuana may have "taken a generation of doers and turned them into a generation of dreamers."

I used to smoke pot daily. I somehow managed to get through college and hold down a job, but I wasn't getting anywhere. Every night, I would get high and write down in a journal all the things I planned to do. After reading your column, I realized I had been doing the same thing year after year and was getting nowhere. I decided to quit smoking pot.

I can't begin to tell you how my life changed. I became bored with my party-animal boyfriend and later married a wonderful man. I went back to school, earned a master's degree and got an excellent position with a Fortune 500 company. I also developed much needed self-esteem. It was your column on marijuana that helped me turn my life around, and I want to write a belated "thank you."—*Margie in Tennessee*

Dear Tennessee: I very much appreciate your generous letter. Please keep reading for one that should be of special interest to you:

Dear Ann Landers: Last fall, my teen-age son began smoking marijuana and was soon out of control. I sent him away to a special program. He is much better now, but I could not understand how my son got into so much trouble. Two weeks ago, the truth came out.

Last summer, I sent my two teen-agers to visit their uncle and aunt across the country. I decided it would be a good way for my brother and his wife to get to know their niece and nephew. I was mistaken. He and his wife smoked pot in front of my kids and offered it to them.

I believe that my brother and his wife contributed to my son's problems, and I am considering suing them for the cost of the special program I put my son in. I am so angry about this that I am considering a break with the entire family. Please advise.—*A Canadian Mom*

Dear Mom: Be thankful the "special program" was a success, and forget about a lawsuit and becoming estranged from the entire family. Mass retaliation is never a good idea.

Next summer, see that your son has a local job, and keep your eye on the companions he hangs out with.

Source: Ann Landers/*The Times of Northwest Indiana*, c/o Times Mirror, Los Angeles, CA 90053.

Therapeutic Uses and the Controversy over Medical Marijuana Use

In the last 6 years, new controversy about the medical uses of marijuana has begun to emerge. Basically, medical marijuana use involves using cannabis, primarily THC, as a drug to calm or to relieve symptoms of an illness. At the heart of this controversy is the use of an illicit drug for medical purposes. However, the desire to use cannabis in this fashion is nothing new. Between 1840 and 1900, European and American medical journals published more than 100 articles on the therapeutic use of the drug known then as *Cannabis indica* (or Indian hemp) and now as marijuana. It was recommended as an appetite stimulant, muscle relaxant, analgesic, hypnotic, and anticonvulsant. As late as 1913, Sir William Osler recommended it as the most satisfactory remedy for migraine (Grinspoon and Bakalar 1995).

Marijuana was used to treat a variety of human ills in folk and formal medicine for thousands of years in South Africa, Turkey, South America, and Egypt as well as such Asian countries as India, Malaysia, Myanmar, and Siam. Thus, marijuana, known as *cannabis* back then, has a 5000-year medical history that came to an abrupt end by passage of the Marijuana Tax Act of 1937. When the Marijuana Tax Act became law, marijuana was legally classified as a narcotic, and at this time, medical use of this substance effectively ceased. Only in the past decade has there been organized renewed interest in possible medical uses for cannabis. Because of potential clinical uses for marijuana, enforcement of laws prohibiting the use of this substance has been very controversial (see "Holding the Line," page 382).

Marijuana has been shown to be effective in the treatment of certain types of medical conditions; however, because medicines are available that are at least as effective and without abuse potential, none of these applications are currently approved by the Food and Drug Administration (FDA). According to researchers (Abood and Martin 1992; Consroe and Sandyk 1992; Iversen 1993) and proponents for the medical uses of marijuana, the following uses include:

Reduction in intraocular (eye) pressure. Marijuana lowers glaucoma-associated intraocular

pressure, even though it does not cure the condition or reverse blindness (Goldstein 1995). Glaucoma is the second leading cause of blindness, caused by uncontrollable eye pressure (Julian 1994).

Antiasthmatic effect. Some research indicates that short-term smoking of marijuana improves breathing for asthma patients. Marijuana smoke dilates the lungs' air passages (bronchodilation). Findings also show, however, that the lung-irritating properties of marijuana smoke seem to offset its benefits. Regardless, marijuana may still prove useful when other drugs are not effective because of a different mode of action in causing bronchodilation.

Muscle-relaxant effect. Some studies indicate that muscle spasms are relieved when patients with muscle disorders, such as multiple sclerosis, use marijuana.

Antiseizure effect. Marijuana has both convulsant and anticonvulsant properties and has been considered for use in preventing seizures associated with epilepsy. In animal experimentation, the cannabinoids reduced or increased seizure activities, depending on how the experiments were conducted. One or more of the marijuana components may be useful in combination with other standard antiseizure medication, although at present their value seems limited.

Antidepressant effect. Cannabis and the synthetic cannabinoid synhexyl have been used successfully in Great Britain as specific euphoriants for the treatment of depression.

Analgesic effect. Published testimonials have reported that marijuana can relieve the intense pain associated with migraine and chronic headaches or inflammation (Grinspoon and

Bakalar 1995). In South Africa, native women smoke cannabis to dull the pain of childbirth (Solomon 1966; Hamid 1998). The pain-relieving potency of marijuana has not been carefully studied and compared with other analgesics such as the narcotics or aspirin-type drugs.

Appetite stimulant. The stimulant affects on appetite are seen as useful for patients with HIV and some eating disorders (Sewester 1993) (see Chapter 17).

Arguments against using marijuana for medicinal purposes conclude that marijuana is a harmful substance for the following reasons:

1. It contains 421 chemicals.

2. It is stronger than it was 20 years ago, and this new, potent marijuana presents new dangers unrecognized years ago.

3. It is far worse for the lungs than tobacco.

4. THC and other components of marijuana are fat soluble and remain in the human body for a month.

5. It causes brain damage and a behavioral disorder known as "amotivational syndrome."

HOLDING THE LINE

In San Francisco, a small underground shop called the Cannabis Buyers' Club flourishes. Writer Richard C. Paddock describes a typical scene: "Dozens of people sit on rummage-sale couches and folding chairs, smoking high-grade marijuana. A dozen more line up at the counter, fingering the day's sample buds and buying their ration of weed." Although this setting may sound enticing to the average pot smoker, chances are he or she would be leery of partaking in this scene; as Paddock tells us, " . . . doing your shopping here means you are sick or dying."

The Cannabis Buyers' Club is just one flourishing underground trend directed toward granting sick or dying people the right to use marijuana. Thousands of people stricken with such ailments as AIDS, cancer, glaucoma, epilepsy, and multiple sclerosis use marijuana every day to treat their sicknesses or allay their pains. Regarding the San Francisco scene, 1995 Mayor Frank Jordan (formerly a police chief) said, "I have no problem whatsoever with the use of marijuana for medical purposes . . . we should bend the law."

Marijuana has been used for medical purposes for at least 5000 years, across cultures and generations; such a strong grounding in history would seem to grant a certain credibility to this drug as being medically beneficial. Unfortunately for proponents of medical cannabis use, the United States has been reluctant to permit studies on possible ways to allow open use of marijuana for medical reasons. For over 3 years, Donald Abrams of the University of California, San Francisco, a respected AIDS researcher, has been seeking government permission to conduct a " . . . clinical trial to determine whether smoking marijuana can help patients overcome the deadly AIDS wasting syndrome." To date, Abrams has been unsuccessful in his attempts and predicts that he will be able to do his research if science can survive the politics.

Bob Randall, one of the eight people in the United States who can legally smoke marijuana, is quoted by Paddock as saying, "In a sane society, the prospect of an easy-to-grow plant that could ease suffering and prolong life would be a cause for celebration."

Source: R. C. Paddock. "'Drug Stores' Fill Prescriptions with Pot, Not Pills." *Salt Lake Tribune* 249, (1 March 1995): A-1.

6. Any use of marijuana constitutes abuse, and marijuana has no medical value whatsoever (NORML 2000).

All of these reasons have either been disputed or shown to be exaggerated claims by proponents who are in favor of allowing marijuana to be medically used. Proponents for medical use argue that " . . . its illegality (marijuana), . . . imposes much anxiety and expense on suffering people, forces them to bargain with illicit drug dealers, and exposes them to the threat of criminal prosecution" (Grinspoon and Bakalar 1995, p. 1876).

In 1996, voters in Arizona and California approved propositions permitting physicians to prescribe marijuana for medical problems, with the idea that terminally ill patients could be given the option of smokable marijuana as opposed to the already-approved Marinol (dronabinol). This event triggered a major response by the federal government. Former President Clinton, the Secretary of Health and Human Services, and the U.S. Attorney General all made pronouncements reiterating the negative effects of marijuana, its abuse potential, and the danger of sending a "pro-use message" or one that suggested use was not outside the realm of accepted behavior (HHS 1996). The government warned that physicians who availed themselves of the permission given in these new state regulations would be prosecuted, lose their privilege of writing prescriptions, and be excluded from Medicare and Medicaid reimbursement. The entire legislative initiative was cast as being a smokescreen for legalization, with the federal government purporting that those who supported it were "closet" marijuana advocates or, at best, legalization advocates.

Physicians responded indignantly to what they considered a heavy-handed attempt to overrule their medical judgments and to smear them unfairly, especially when most of them were neither pro-use nor even pro-legalization, except in this one medical situation. An editorial in the prestigious *New England Journal of Medicine*, titled "Federal Foolishness and Marijuana" (Kassirer 1997), claimed that it was hypocritical to allow physicians to prescribe the highly addicting opiates morphine or meperidine, which cause death at doses not much greater than those that relieve pain, but not marijuana, which is far less addictive and does not cause death. The purpose of the legislative initiative, the editorial pointed

KEY TERMS

Marinol
FDA-approved THC in capsule form (dronabinol)

out, was to alleviate the suffering of terminally ill patients, for whom long-term abuse potential is irrelevant. Many of these patients perceive the smokable form of THC as being more effective than Marinol, a factor that is difficult to measure in experimental procedures. As far as the governmental reasons for prohibiting the drug for medical purposes, a few joked, it was a rerun of *Reefer Madness*.

In June 2000, Hawaii became the first state to pass a medical marijuana bill that approved the possession and use of marijuana for medical purposes. The Governor, Benjamin J. Cayetano, " . . . said it was one aspect of his effort to make Hawaii the health care center of the Pacific" (Associated Press 2000). Passage of this bill currently affects 500 to 1000 residents of Hawaii. The belief by the Governor is that " . . . Hawaii law will lead to similar legislation in

In July 2000, California began to issue cards that allow the users to purchase marijuana for medicinal purposes.

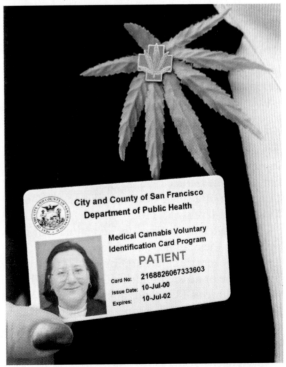

other states" (Associated Press 2000). This means that anyone found in possession of marijuana would be exempt if he or she can verify medical usage. This same article mentioned that Alaska, Arizona, California, Maine, Nevada, Oregon, Washington, and the District of Columbia have approved medical marijuana laws even though the Justice Department is challenging those laws. Also, in March 2000, London's conservative Tory party voted in favor of supporting an experiment in legalization by beginning to hold public debates on this matter (Hopps 2000). Members of the party were expecting to experiment with legalization. Interestingly, in England, cannabis possession carries up to a seven-year jail sentence, although such long sentences are rare. Time will tell what the final outcomes in both the United States and Britain will be.

The Physiological Effects of Marijuana Use

Although the literature on marijuana use repeatedly states that " . . . in 5,000 years of medical and non-medical use, marijuana has not caused a single overdose death" (Grinspoon and Bakalar 1995, p. 1875), the effects of marijuana use should not be overlooked. We begin with the effects of marijuana on the lungs.

When marijuana smoke is inhaled into the lungs, THC, the psychoactive ingredient, leaves the blood rapidly through metabolism and efficient uptake into the tissues. THC and its metabolites tend to bind to proteins in the blood and remain stored for long periods in body fat. Five days after a single dosage of THC, 20% remains stored, whereas 20% of its metabolites remain in the blood (Indiana Prevention Resource Center 1996; Kryger 1995). Complete elimination of a single dose can take up to 30 days. Measurable levels of THC in blood from chronic users can often be detected for several days or even weeks after their last marijuana cigarette (joint).

In smokers, lung absorption and transport of THC to the brain are rapid; THC reaches the brain within as little as 14 seconds after inhalation. Marijuana is metabolized more efficiently through smoking than intravenous injection or oral ingestion. Smoking is also three to five times more

potent than these two methods (Jones 1980; Kaplan and Whitmire 1995; Kryger 1995). Other findings that compare the amounts of marijuana with tobacco conclude, " . . . that three to four joints a day is about as harmful to your lungs as smoking a pack of cigarettes a day . . ." (Reaney 2000, p. 1).

Some effects of cannabis described in the following sections are unquestionably toxic in that they can either directly or indirectly produce adverse health effects. Other effects may be beneficial in treating some medical conditions. The uses of marijuana, THC, and synthetic cannabinoids, either alone or in combination with other drugs, are currently being investigated for use in treating pain, inflammation, glaucoma, nausea, and muscle spasms (Iversen 1993).

▪ EFFECTS ON THE CENTRAL NERVOUS SYSTEM

The primary effects of marijuana—specifically, THC—are on CNS functions. The precise CNS effects of consuming marijuana or administering THC can vary according to the expectations of the user, the social setting, the route of administration, and previous experiences (Abood and Martin 1992; Jaffe 1990). Smoking a marijuana cigarette can alter mood, coordination, memory, and self-perception. Usually, such exposure causes some euphoria, a sense of well-being, and relaxation. Marijuana smokers often claim heightened sensory awareness and altered perceptions (particularly a slowing of time), associated with hunger (the " munchies ") and a dry mouth (Swan 1994; Hubbard et al. 1999).

High doses of THC or greater exposure to marijuana can cause hallucinations, delusions, and paranoia (APA 1994; Goldstein 1995; Hubbard et al. 1999). Some users describe anxiety after high-dose exposure. Due to the availability and widespread use of marijuana, psychiatric emergencies from marijuana overdose are becoming somewhat common. Long-term, chronic users often show decreased interest in personal appearance or goals (part of the amotivational syndrome discussed earlier in this chapter) as well as an inability to concentrate, make appropriate decisions, and recall information from short-term memory (Abood and Martin 1992; Block 1996).

The precise classification of THC is uncertain because the responses to marijuana are highly variable and appear to have elements of all three major groups of drugs of abuse. Consequently, marijuana use can cause euphoria and paranoia (like stimulants), drowsiness and sedation (like depressants), and hallucinations (like psychedelics). It is possible that THC alters several receptor or transmitter systems in the brain and this action would account for its diverse and somewhat unpredictable effects. However, the recent dramatic discovery of a specific receptor site in the brain for THC, called the *cannabinoid* receptor, suggests that a selective endogenous marijuana system exists in the brain and is activated by THC when marijuana is consumed (Hudson 1990). Some researchers speculate that an endogenous fatty acid–like substance called anandamide naturally works at these marijuana sites; efforts are being made to characterize this substance, which perhaps is a neurotransmitter (Iversen 1993). It is possible that, from this discovery, a group of new therapeutic agents will be developed that can selectively interact with the marijuana receptors, resulting in medical benefits without the side effects that generally accompany marijuana use (Iversen 1993; Swan 1993).

■ EFFECTS ON THE RESPIRATORY SYSTEM

Marijuana is often smoked like tobacco and like tobacco can cause damage to the lungs (Adams and Martin 1996; Consroe and Sandyk 1992). When smoking tobacco, nearly 70% of the total suspended particles in the smoke are retained in the lungs. Because marijuana smoke is inhaled more deeply than tobacco smoke, even more tar residues may be retained with its use.

Smoke is a mixture of tiny particles suspended in gas, mostly carbon monoxide. These solid particles combine to form a residue called *tar*. Cannabis produces more tar (up to 50% more) than an equivalent weight of tobacco and is smoked in a way that increases the accumulation of tar (Jones 1980).

More than 150 chemicals have been identified in marijuana smoke and tar. A few are proven carcinogens; many others have not yet been tested for carcinogenicity. The carcinogen benzopyrene, for example, is 70% more abundant in marijuana smoke than in tobacco smoke. When cannabis tar is applied to the skin of experimental animals, it causes precancerous lesions similar to those caused by tobacco tar.

KEY TERMS

altered perceptions
changes in the interpretation of stimuli, resulting from marijuana

munchies
hunger experienced while under the effects of marijuana

anandamide
possible neurotransmitter acting at the marijuana (cannabinoid) receptor

Similarly, whenever isolated lung tissue is exposed to these same tars, precancerous changes result (Hollister 1986; Jones 1980; Turner 1980).

Special white blood cells in living lung tissue—alveolar macrophages—play a role in removing debris from the lungs. When exposed to smoke from cannabis, these cells are less able to remove bacteria and other foreign debris.

Smoking only a few marijuana cigarettes a day for 6 to 8 weeks can significantly impair pulmonary function. Laboratory and clinical evidence often indicates that heavy use of marijuana causes cellular changes and that users have a higher incidence of such respiratory problems as laryngitis, pharyngitis, bronchitis, asthma-like conditions, cough, hoarseness, and dry throat (Hollister 1986; Goldstein 1995). Some reports emphasize the potential damage to pulmonary function that can occur from chronic marijuana use (NIDA 1991). Evidence suggests that many 20-year-old smokers of both hashish and tobacco have lung damage comparable to that found in heavy tobacco smokers older than 40 years of age. It is believed that the tar from tobacco and marijuana has damaging effects, but it is not known whether smokers who use both products suffer synergistic or additive effects (Hollister 1986; Jones 1980).

■ EFFECTS ON THE CARDIOVASCULAR SYSTEM

In human beings, cannabis causes both *vasodilation* (enlarged blood vessels) and an increase in heart rate related to the amount of THC consumed (Abood and Martin 1992; NIDA 2000). The vasodilation is responsible for the reddening of the eyes often seen in marijuana smokers. In physically healthy users, these effects, as well as slight changes in heart rhythm, are transitory and do not appear to be significant. In patients with heart disease, however, the increased oxygen requirement due to the accelerated heart rate may have serious consequences. The effect of cannabis on people with heart rhythm irregularities is not known.

Because of vasodilation caused by marijuana use, abnormally low blood pressure can occur when standing. In addition, if a user stands up quickly after smoking, a feeling of lightheadedness or fainting may result. Chronic administration of large doses of THC to healthy volunteers shows that tolerance develops to the increase in heart rate and vasodilation.

People with cardiovascular problems seem to be at an increased risk when smoking marijuana (Hollister 1986). Marijuana products also bind hemoglobin, limiting the amount of oxygen that can be carried to the heart tissue. In few cases, this deficiency could trigger heart attacks in susceptible people (Palfai and Jankiewicz 1991). The National Academy of Sciences' Institute of Medicine recommends that people with cardiovascular disease avoid marijuana use because there are still many unanswered questions about its effects on the cardiovascular system.

■ EFFECTS ON SEXUAL PERFORMANCE AND REPRODUCTION

Drugs may interfere with sexual performance and reproduction in several ways. They may alter sexual behavior, affect fertility, damage the chromosomes of germ cells in the male or female, or adversely affect fetal growth and development.

The Indian Hemp Commission (Taylor 1963 and 1966), which wrote the first scientific report on cannabis, commented that it had a sexually stimulating effect, like alcohol. However, the report also said that cannabis was used by Asian Indian ascetics to destroy the sexual appetite. This apparent discrepancy may be a dose-related effect. Used occasionally over the short-term, marijuana may act as an aphrodisiac by releasing CNS inhibitions. In addition, the altered perception of time under the influence of the drug could make the pleasurable sensations appear to last longer than they actually do.

Marijuana affects the sympathetic nervous system, increasing vasodilation in the genitals and delaying ejaculation. High doses over a period of time lead to depression of libido and impotence—possibly due to the decreased amount of testosterone, the male sex hormone.

Cannabis has several effects on semen. The total number of sperm cells and the concentration of sperm per unit volume are decreased during ejaculation. Moreover, there is an increase in the proportion of sperm with abnormal appearance and reduced motility. These qualities are usually associated with lower fertility and a higher probability of producing an abnormal embryo should fertilization take place.

Despite these effects, there are *no* documented reports of children with birth defects in which the abnormality was linked to the father's smoking marijuana. It is possible that damaged sperm cells are incapable of fertilization (so that only normal sperm cells reach the egg) or that the abnormal sperm appearance is meaningless in terms of predicting birth defects. When marijuana use stops, the quality of sperm gradually returns to normal over several months.

Less reliable data are available on the effects of cannabis on female libido, sexual response (ability to respond to sexual stimulation with vaginal lubrication and orgasm), and fertile reproductive (menstrual) cycles (Consroe and Sandyk 1992; Grinspoon 1987). Preliminary data from the Reproductive Biology Research Foundation show that chronic smoking of cannabis (at least three times per week for the preceding six months) adversely affects the female reproductive cycle. Results with women were correlated with work in rhesus monkeys; it was found that THC blocks ovulation (due to effects on female sex hormones).

Data on effects of marijuana use during pregnancy and lactation are inconclusive. Some evidence suggests that the use of this drug by pregnant

---

KEY TERMS

aphrodisiac
refers to a compound that is believed to be the cause of sexual arousal

women can result in intrauterine growth retardation, which is characterized by increased fetal mortality, prolonged labor, low-birth weight babies, and behavioral abnormalities in newborns (Fernandez-Ruiz et al. 1992; Nahas and Latour 1992; Roffman and George 1988). THC and other cannabinoids pass through the blood-placenta barrier and concentrate in the fetus's fatty tissue, including its brain. Ethical considerations prevent duplication of the experiment in humans.

Women who smoke marijuana during pregnancy also often use other drugs—such as alcohol, tobacco, and cocaine—that are known to have adverse effects on the developing fetus. Because multiple drugs are used, it is difficult to isolate the specific effects of marijuana during pregnancy. Like many other substances, THC is taken up by the mammary glands in lactating women and is excreted in the breast milk. Effects of marijuana in the breast milk on human infants have not been determined (Christina 1994; Murphy and Bartke 1992).

In studies on mice and rats (but not humans), the addition of THC to pregnant animals lowered litter size, increased fetal reabsorption, and increased the number of reproductive abnormalities in the surviving offspring (Dewey 1986). The offspring of the drug-treated animal mothers had reduced fertility and more testicular abnormalities. The dose of cannabinoids used in these studies was higher than that used by humans. Clearly, pregnant women should be advised against using marijuana, even though there are few direct data on its prenatal effects in humans (Dewey 1986; Murphy and Bartke 1992).

■ TOLERANCE AND DEPENDENCE

It has been known for many years that tolerance to some effects of cannabis builds rapidly in animals—namely, the drug effect becomes less intense with repeated administration. Frequent use of high doses of marijuana or THC in humans produces similar tolerance. For example, increasingly higher doses must be given to obtain the same intensity of subjective effects and increased heart rate that occur initially with small doses (Abood and Martin 1992).

Frequent high doses of THC also can produce mild physical dependence. Healthy subjects who smoke several "joints" a day or who are given comparable amounts of THC orally experience irritability, sleep disturbances, weight loss, loss of appetite, sweating, and gastrointestinal upsets when drug use is stopped abruptly. However, all subjects do not experience this mild form of withdrawal. It is much easier to show psychological dependence in heavy users of marijuana (Abood and Martin 1992; Hollister 1986).

Psychological dependence involves an attachment to the euphoric effects of the THC content in marijuana and may include "craving" for the drug. The subjective psychological effects of marijuana intoxication include a heightened sensitivity to and distortion of sight, smell, taste, and sound; mood alteration; and diminished reaction time.

Diagnosis: Cannabis Dependence

In general, outright cannabis addiction, with obsessive drug seeking and compulsive drug-taking behavior, is relatively rare with low-THC cannabis. Contributing to this is the fact that the less potent forms of marijuana are most readily available in the United States, resulting in most chronic users in this country having little problem controlling or eliminating their cannabis habit if they so desired.

The Diagnostic and Statistical Manual of Mental Disorders, fourth edition (DSM-IV), recognizes a diagnosis of cannabis dependence. It is characterized by "compulsive use" and spending hours per day acquiring and using the substance. These users persist in their use despite knowledge of physical problems (for example, chronic cough related to smoking) or psychological problems (for example, excessive sedation resulting from repeated use of high doses) (APA 1994).

■ CHRONIC USE

Research on *chronic use of marijuana* (repeated daily use of this drug) in the 1970s indicated the possibility of three types of damage: (1) chromosomal damage (Stenchever et al. 1974); (2) *cerebral atrophy* (shrinking of the brain) (Campbell et al. 1971); and (3) lowered capacity of white blood cells to fight disease (Suciu-Foca et al. 1974). These findings have all been found to be contradicted or refuted by subsequent research. The only finding that appears very credible is that heavy use of this drug impairs lung capacity (Bloodworth 1987; Henneberger 1994; Kaplan and Whitmire 1995; Oliwenstein 1988; Swan 1994).

Other evidence indicates that chronic, heavy use of cannabis can lead to unforeseen calamities in some users (see "Case in Point," Chronic Marijuana Use). We have pointed out that marijuana produces a variety of psychoactive effects. One of those effects is sedation of unwanted emotional states such as anxiety, which are inevitable given the conflicts and turmoil of living in our fast-paced society today. As with the chronic use of any psychoactive drug that produces sedating effects, normal emotional and psychosocial development can be arrested by heavy marijuana consumption. For example, a youth who is usually "high" at a party will avoid the anxieties and embarrassments of introspective and critical interpersonal interactions, but instead will be interested in "thrill seeking" behavior, such as romantic and sexual involvements, experimentation with and heavy use of other drugs, and other types of more daring experiences.

From years of research with this drug, we find that heavy and chronic use of marijuana can very easily compromise cognitive functions such as short-term memory, concentration, moderately "taxing" problem-solving, and even spiritual growth and development. Often, the more serious costs in using this drug are that the individual

---

CASE IN POINT

Chronic Marijuana Use

The following comments show how marijuana use can become a disturbing habit:

I guess you could say it was peer pressure. Back in 1969, I was a sophomore in college, and everyone was smoking "dope." The Vietnam War was in progress, and most students on college campuses were heavily involved in the drug scene. I first started smoking marijuana when my closest friends did. I was taught by other students who already knew how to enjoy the effects of "pot."

I recall that one of my fellow students used to supply me with "nickel bags," and many users nicknamed him "God." How did he get such a name? Because he sold some very potent marijuana that at times caused us to hallucinate.

I used pot nearly every day for about a year and a half, and hardly an evening would pass without smoking dope and listening to music. Smoking marijuana became as common as drinking alcohol. I used it in the same manner a person has a cocktail after a long day. At first, I liked the effects of being "high," but later, I became so accustomed to the stuff that life appeared boring without it.

After graduating, my college friends went their separate ways, and I stopped using marijuana for a few years. A year later, in graduate school, a neighborhood friend reintroduced me to the pleasure of smoking pot. I began to use it again but not as often. Whenever I experienced some pressure, I would use a little to relax.

After finishing my degree, I found myself employed at an institution that at times was boring. Again, I started using pot at night to relax, and somehow it got out of control. I used to smoke a little before work and sometimes during lunch. I thought all was well until one day I got fired because someone accused me of being high on the job.

Soon afterward, I came to the realization that the use of marijuana can be very insidious. It has a way of becoming psychologically addictive, and you don't even realize it. When I was high, I thought that no one knew, and that I was even more effective with others. Little did I know, I was dead wrong and fooling no one.

Source: From Venturelli's files, interview with a 39-year-old man, May 1990.

acquires a poor record for development and advancement of learning, as often expected in educational settings (schools, colleges, trade school, and universities). Another cost that is more serious is the retardation in emotional development. Such types of development are often obscured by "being high all-the-time." Further, in such chronic use cases, much time is wasted seeking the pleasures and sometimes the longed for thrills derived from the habitual use of marijuana.

The amotivational syndrome can, in fact, be "deconstructed" into the sedation, depression, and cognitive impairment discussed throughout this chapter. The user who is experiencing a subjective euphoric effect, enjoying the presence and social reinforcement of peers, "feeling no pain," and remaining cognitively unfocused finds it difficult to intellectually grasp the learned experiences from such developmental delays. Although many do "mature out" of use, this step may occur only after years of development have slipped away, never to be regained. Sometimes treatment interventions are necessary to get the subject into a drug-free state and reunited with non–drug using peer groups.

In concluding this chapter, we saw that the history of this drug indicates that usage and availability remains widespread despite all the efforts to eradicate its existence. Despite all the prevention efforts to date, marijuana remains the most popular illicit drug, preceded by alcohol and tobacco, which are licit drugs.

Discussion Questions

1. What are the pharmacological, sociological, and psychological reasons why the very young continue to use marijuana at alarming rates despite the illegality of usage?

2. Do you believe that prosecution for marijuana possession should be more or less rigid than it currently is? Why?

3. Debate whether marijuana use adversely affects driving capabilities.

4. Either directly interview or imagine interviews of several users and non-users of marijuana.

How do you think they would answer the question of whether or not their critical thinking skills are adversely affected by this drug?

5. Among marijuana users, does the amotivational syndrome exist? Interview several users and try to either add to the characteristics of this syndrome from your interviews or modify the syndrome as explained in this chapter.

6. In light of the information in this chapter regarding medical marijuana use, do you believe in legalizing medical marijuana use? Why or why not?

7. What is your reaction to legalizing marijuana as a controlled substance like alcohol and tobacco products? Give reasons either for or against this statement.

8. Do you believe consistent use of marijuana changes personality? If so, how?

9. Summarize how marijuana affects: the CNS, respiratory system, cardiovascular system, and sexual performance and reproduction.

10. Debate how much family upbringing and attachment to a religion contributes to later drug use.

11. From reading this chapter, try to explain why most heroin users have used marijuana while the vast majority of marijuana users never advance to such highly addictive drugs?

12. Explain why a user of cannabis might develop psychological dependence.

13. Do you believe that use of marijuana is more or less harmful than use of tobacco products? Should they be regulated differently?

Key Terms

gateway drugs **372**

Cannabis sativa **373**

sinsemilla **373**

hashish **374**

subjective euphoric effects 376

differential association 377

amotivational syndrome 379

medical marijuana use 381

glaucoma 381

Marinol 383

altered perceptions 384

munchies 384

anandamide 385

aphrodisiac 386

Summary

1 Marijuana consists of the dried and crushed leaves, flowers, stems, and seeds of the *Cannabis sativa* plant. THC (tetrahydrocannabinol) is the primary mind-altering (psychoactive) ingredient in marijuana.

2 Marijuana continues to remain very controversial for the following reasons: (1) a high percentage of the U.S. population uses this drug; (2) it remains illegal; (3) several states, but not the federal government, have approved medical uses of marijuana; (4) marijuana accounts for too many arrests for simple possession; (5) it is one of the least addictive-type drugs; and (6) most marijuana users do not "graduate" to other more addictive illicit drugs.

3 Effects of marijuana can vary according to expectations and surroundings. At low doses, such as when smoked or eaten, marijuana often has a sedative effect. At higher doses, it can produce hallucinations and delusions.

4 As with tobacco, heavy use of marijuana can impair pulmonary function, cause chronic respiratory diseases (such as bronchitis and asthma), and promote lung cancer. Marijuana causes vasodilation and a compensatory increase in heart rate. The effects of marijuana on sexual performance and reproduction are controversial. Some studies have suggested this substance not only enhances sexual arousal but also promotes "risky" sexual behavior (unprotected sex).

5 Tolerance to the CNS and cardiovascular effects of marijuana develop rapidly with repeated use. Although physical dependence and associated withdrawal are minor, psychological dependence can be significant in chronic, heavy users.

6 The active ingredient in marijuana, THC, has been used for treating a variety of seemingly unrelated medical conditions. This drug is indicated for treatment of nausea and vomiting in cancer patients receiving chemotherapy and for treatment of anorexia (lack of appetite) in AIDS patients. Other potential therapeutic uses for THC include relief of intraocular pressure associated with glaucoma, as an antiasthmatic drug, for muscle relaxation, as prevention for some types of seizures, as an antidepressant, and as an analgesic to relieve migraines and other types of pain.

7 The age groups most likely to use marijuana are the following: (1) highest lifetime use, adults between 26 and 34 years of age (47.9%); (2) highest past-year and past-month use, 18 to 25-year-olds; and (3) sharp drop in use, 35 and older age group.

8 First use of marijuana is highest among 12- to 17-years olds, with an all-time high of 79.3% in 1996. Next highest first users of marijuana are the 18- to 25-year-olds, with a low of 47.1% in 1997.

9 Newer groups of seniors in high school (1997 and beyond) are less likely to perceive use of marijuana as dangerous than did high school seniors in the late 1980s and early 1990s. An even weaker perceived risk is occurring with younger age groups (grades 8, 10, and 12). Today, perceived risk is at its lowest point since the early 1980s in the youngest age groups.

References

Abel, E. L. *Marijuana: The First Twelve Thousand Years.* New York: Plenum, 1989.

Abood, M. and B. Martin. "Neurobiology of Marijuana Abuse." *Trends in Pharmacological Sciences* 13 (May 1992): 201–6.

Abood, M. E. and B. R. Martin. Molecular neurobiology of the cannabinoid receptor. *International Review of Neurobiology* 39 (May 1996): 197–219.

Adams, I. B. and B. R. Martin, "Cannabis: Pharmacology and Toxicology in Animals and Humans." *Addiction* 91 (1996): 1585–614.

American Psychiatric Association (APA). *Diagnostic and Statistical Manual of Mental Disorders,* 4th ed. [DSM-IV], chairman Allen Frances. Washington, DC: APA, 1994.

Anslinger, H. J. and C. R. Cooper. "Marijuana: Assassin of Youth." *American Magazine* 124 (July 1937): 19–20, 150–3.

Associated Press. "Hawaii Becomes First State to Approve Medical Marijuana Bill." *The New York Times on the Web* (15 June 2000). Available http://www.nytimes.com/library/national/science/health/061500hth-hawaii-marijuana.html.

Berkowitz, A. "Following Imaginary Peers: How Norm Misperceptions Influence Student Substance Abuse." In *Project Direction,* edited by G. Lindsay and G. Rulf, 12–15 (Module No. 2). Muncie, IN: Ball State University, 1991.

Block, R. I. "Does Heavy Marijuana Use Impair Human Cognition and Brain Function?" *Journal of the American Medical Association* 275 (1996): 560–61.

Bloodworth, R. C. "Major Problems Associated with Marijuana Use." *Psychiatric Medicine* 3 (1987): 173–84.

Brown, M. W. and S. Massaro. *Attention and Memory Impaired in Heavy Users of Marijuana.* Rockville, MD: NIDA, 20 February 1996. Available http://www.health.org pressrl/heavymar.html.

Buff, J. "Greasers, Dopers, and Hippies: Three Responses to the Adult World." In *The White Majority,* edited by L. Howe, 60–70. New York: Random House, 1970.

Califano, J. A. "Dangerous Indifference to Drugs." *Washington Post* (23 September 1996): A-19.

Campbell, A. G., M. Evans, J. L. Thomson, and M. J. Williams. "Cerebral Atrophy in Young Cannabis Smokers." *Lancet* 19 (1971): 1219–25.

Carter, E. *Cannabis in Costa Rica.* Philadelphia: Institute for the Study of Human Issues, 1980.

Chait, L. and J. Pierri. "Effect of Smoked Marijuana on Human Performance: A Critical Review." In *Marijuana/Cannabinoids, Neurobiology and Neurophysiology,* edited by L. Murphy and A. Bartke, 387–424. Boca Raton, FL: CRC Press, 1992.

Christina, D. *Marijuana: Personality and Behavior.* Tempe, AZ: Do It Now, 1994.

Coleman, J. S. *The Adolescent Society.* New York: Free Press of Glencoe, 1961.

Consroe, P. and R. Sandyk. "Potential Role of Cannabinoids for Therapy of Neurological Disorders." In *Marijuana/Cannabinoids, Neurobiology and Neurophysiology,* edited by L. Murphy and A. Bartke, 459–524. Boca Raton, FL: CRC Press, 1992.

Dewey, W. L. "Cannabinoid Pharmacology." *Pharmacological Reviews* 38 (1986): 48–50.

Dreher, M. C. "Working Men and Ganja: Marijuana Use in Rural Jamaica." Philadelphia: Institute for the Study of Human Issues, 1982.

Eckert, P. *Jocks and Burnouts: Social Categories and Identity in the High School.* New York: Teachers College, Columbia University, 1989.

Fernandez-Ruiz, J., F. Rodriguez de Fonseca, M. Navarro, and J. Ramos. "Maternal Cannabinoid Exposure and Brain Development: Changes in the Ontogeny of Dopaminergic Neurons." In *Marijuana/Cannabinoids, Neurobiology and Neurophysiology,* edited by L. Murphy and A. Bartke, 118–64. Boca Raton, FL: CRC Press, 1992.

Gaines, G. *Teenage Wasteland: Suburbia's Dead-End Kids.* New York: Harper Perennial, 1992.

Gardner, E. "Cannabinoid Interaction with Brian Reward Systems: The Neurobiological Basis of Cannabinoid Abuse." In *Marijuana/Cannabinoids, Neurobiology and Neurophysiology,* edited by L. Murphy and A. Bartke, 275–335. Boca Raton, FL: CRC Press, 1992.

Goldstein, A. *Addiction from Biology to Drug Policy.* New York: Freeman, 1994.

Goldstein, F. "Pharmacological Aspects of Substance Abuse." *Remington's Pharmaceutical Sciences,* 19th ed. Easton, PA: Mack, 1995.

Gossop, M. *Living with Drugs,* 2nd ed. Aldershot, England: Wildwood House, 1987.

Greenblatt, J. C. *Adolescent Self-Reported Behaviors and Their Association with Marijuana Use.* Office of Applied Studies (OAS) of the Substance Abuse and Mental Health Services Administration (SAMHSA). Rockville, MD: National Clearinghouse for Alcohol and Drug Information, July 1999.

Grinspoon, L. "Marijuana." *Harvard Medical School Mental Health Letter* 4, No. 5 (November 1987): 1–4.

Grinspoon, L. and J. B. Bakalar. "Commentary, Marijuana as Medicine: A Plea for Reconsideration." *Journal of the American Medical Association* 273 (1995): 1875–6. Available http://www.commonlink.com~olsen/medical/lester.html.

Hamid, A. *Drugs in America: Sociology, Economics, and Politics.* Gaithersburg, MD: Aspen Publishers Inc., 1998.

Harclerode, J. "The Effect of Marijuana on Reproduction and Development." In *Marijuana Research Findings: 1980,* edited by R. C. Petersen. NIDA Research Monograph No. 31. Washington, DC: National Institute on Drug Abuse, 1980.

Health and Human Services (HHS). "*Substance Abuse—A National Challenge.*" (6 May 1996). Available www.os.dhhs.gov/news/press/1996pres/960506b.html.

Heitzeg, N. *Deviance: Rulemakers and Rulebreakers.* St. Paul, MN: West Publishing, 1996.

Henneberger, M. "Pot Surges Back, It's Like a Whole New World." *New York Times* (6 February 1994): C19.

Hollister, L. E. "Health Aspects of Cannabis." *Pharmacological Reviews* 38 (1986): 39–42.

Hopps, J. "Tory Press Open to Reform on Cannabis." *Reuters* (30 March 2000). Available http://dailynews.yahoo.com/h/nm/20000330/wl/Britain_drugs_1.html.

Hubbard, J. R., S. E. Franco, and E. S. Onaivi. "Marijuana: Medical Implications." *American Family Physician* 283 (1999): 231–40.

Hudson, R. "Researchers Identify Gene That Triggers Marijuana's 'High.'" *Wall Street Journal* (9 August 1990): B-2.

Indiana Prevention Resource Center. *Factline on: Marijuana.* Bloomington, IN: Indiana Prevention Resource Center, 1996.

Iversen, L. "Medicinal Use of Marijuana." *Nature* 365 (1993): 12–3.

Jaffe, J. H. "Drug Addiction and Drug Abuse." In *The Pharmacological Basis of Therapeutics*, 8th ed., edited by A. Gilman, T. Rall, A. Nies, and P. Taylor. New York: Pergamon, 1990.

Johnston, L., P. O'Malley, and J. Bachman. *The Monitoring the Future National Results on Adolescent Drug Use: Overview of Key Findings, 1999.* Bethesda, MD: National Institute on Drug Abuse, 2000.

Jones, R. T. "Human Effects: An Overview." In *Marijuana Research Findings: 1980*, NIDA Research Monograph No. 31. Washington, DC: National Institute on Drug Abuse, 1980.

Julian, B. S. "alt.hemp CANNABIS/MARIJUANA FAQ." FAG Maintainer (online publication) Amherst, MA: The University of Massachusetts at Amherst, 1994. Available http://www.faqs.org/faqs/drugs/hemp-marijuana/

Kaplan, L. F. and R. Whitmire. "Pot—It's Potent, Prevalent and Preventable." *Salt Lake Tribune* 250 (21 May 1995): 9.

Kassirer, J. "Federal Foolishness and Marijuana" (editorial). *New England Journal of Medicine* 336 (1997): 14–32.

Kelly, T., R. Foltin, C. Enurian, and M. Fischman. "Effects of THC on Marijuana Smoking, Drug Choice and Verbal Report of Drug Liking." *Journal of Experimental Analysis of Behavior* 61 (1994): 203–11.

Kryger, A. H. *Preventive Medicine Clinic of Monterey: Marijuana Mental Disturbances.* Iowa: Virtual Hospital Home Page (24 October 1995): 1-6. Available http://vh.radiology.uiowa. edu.

Liska, K. *Drugs and the Human Body*, 5th ed. Upper Saddle River, NJ: Prentice Hall, 1997.

"Marijuana Menaces Youth." *Scientific American* 154 (1936): 151.

Mathias, R. "Marijuana Impairs Driving-Related Skills and Workplace Performance." *NIDA Notes* 11, no. 1 (January/February 1996a): 6.

Musto, D. F. *The American Disease: Origins of Narcotic Control*, 3rd ed. New York, NY: Oxford University Press, 1999.

Murphy, L. and A. Bartke. "Effects of THC on Pregnancy, Puberty, and the Neuroendocrine System." In *Marijuana/Cannabinoids, Neurobiology and Neurophysiology*, edited by L. Murphy and A. Bartke, 539. Boca Raton, FL: CRC Press, 1992.

Nahas, G. and C. Latour. "The Human Toxicity of Marijuana." *Medical Journal of Australia* 156 (1992): 495–7.

National Clearinghouse on Alcohol and Drug Information (NCADI). *Marijuana: Facts Parents Need to Know.* Quick Screen, At Home Drug Test. Rockville, MD: National Clearinghouse on Alcohol and Drug Information (revised November 1998). Available http://www.athomedrugtest.com/drugabusemarij.html.

National Institute on Drug Abuse (NIDA). *Drug Abuse and Drug Abuse Research*, DHHS Publication No. 91-1704. Washington, DC: U.S. Department of Health and Human Services, 1991.

National Institute on Drug Abuse (NIDA) (Infofax). *Marijuana.* Bethesda, MD: U.S. Department of Health and Human Services (USDHHS) (29 March 2000). Available http://www.nida.nih.gov/infofax/marijuana.html.

National Institute on Drug Abuse (NIDA). *Marijuana: Facts Parents Need to Know.* NIH Publication No. 95-4037. Rockville, MD: National Clearinghouse on Alcohol and Drug Information (1998). Available http://www.athomedrugtest.com/drugabusemarij.html.

NORML. *Marijuana and the Human Body.* NORML Common Sense Series, (June 2000). Available http://www.timesoft.com/ncnorml/common.

Oliwenstein, L. "The Perils of Pot." *Discover* 9, No. 6 (1988): 18.

Palfai, T. and H. Jankiewicz. *Drugs and Human Behavior.* Dubuque, IA: Brown, 1991.

Pollan, M. "Medical Marijuana: Can It Help You? Should It Be Legal? A Report From California." *Herbs for Health*, (March/April 1998): 38–50.

Pope, H. G., Jr. and D. Yurgulen-Todd. "The Residual Cognitive Effects of Heavy Marijuana Use in College Students." *Journal of the American Medical Association* 275 (1996): 521–7.

Reaney, P. *Getting High May Not Be So Harmless After All. Reuters Limited.* (20 March 2000). Available http://dailynews.yahoo.com/h/nm/20000320/sc/health_marijuana_1html.

Roffman, R. A. and W. H. George. "Cannabis Abuse." In *Assessment of Addictive Behaviors*, edited by D. M. Donovan and G. A. Marlatt. New York: Guilford, 1988.

Rubin, V. and L. Comitas. *Ganja in Jamaica: A Medical Anthropological Study of Chronic Marijuana Use.* Paris: Mouton, 1975.

Schultes, R. E. "Ethnopharmacological Significance of Psychotropic Drugs of Vegetal Origin." *Principles of Psy-*

chopharmacology, 2nd ed., edited by W. G. Clark and J. del Giudice. New York: Academic Press, 1978.

Sewester, S. *Drug Facts and Comparisons*. St. Louis: Kluwer, 1993: 259h–59k.

Solomon, D., ed. *The Marihuana Papers*. New York: New American Library, 1966.

Stenchever, M. A., T. J. Kunysz, and M. A. Allen. "Chromosome Breakage in Users of Marijuana." *American Journal of Obstetrics and Gynecology* 118 (January 1974): 106–13.

Substance Abuse and Mental Health Services Administration (SAMHSA), Office of Applied Studies. *Summary of Findings from the 1998 National Household Survey on Drug Abuse*. Rockville, MD: Substance Abuse and Mental Health Services Administration (SAMHSA) and Office of Applied Studies (OAS), August 1999.

Suciy-Foca, N., J. P. Armand and A. Morishima. "Inhibition of Cellular Immunity in Marijuana Smokers." *Science* 183 (1974): 419–20.

Swan, N. "A Look at Marijuana's Harmful Effects." *NIDA Notes 9* (February/March 1994): 3–4.

Swan, N. "Facts About Marijuana and Marijuana Abuse." *NIDA Notes 11* (March/April 1996): 15.

Swan, N. "Researchers Make Pivotal Marijuana and Heroin Discoveries." *NIDA Notes 8* (10 September 1993): 1.

Taylor N. *Narcotics: Nature's Dangerous Gifts*. New York: Dell, 1963.

Taylor, N. "The Pleasant Assassin: The Story of Marihuana." *The Marijuana Papers*, ed. D. Solomon. Indianapolis, 1966.

Teen Challenge. *Drugs: Frequently Asked Questions*. South Australia: Pragin Press, 2000. Available http://www.tc.sn .au/hoax2.asp.

Tudor, C. G., D. M. Petersen, and K. W. Elifson. "An Examination of the Relationships Between Peer and Parental Influences and Adolescent Drug Use." In *Chemical Dependencies: Patterns, Costs, and Consequences*, edited by C. D. Chambers, J. A. Inciardi, D. M. Petersen, H. A. Siegal, and O. Z. White. Athens, OH: Ohio University Press, 1987.

Turner, C. E. "Chemistry and Metabolism." In *Marijuana Research Findings: 1980*. NIDA Research Monograph No. 31. Washington, DC: National Institute on Drug Abuse, 1980.

Venturelli, P. J. "Drugs in Schools: Myths and Reality." *The Annals of the American Academy of Political and Social Science*, edited by W. Hinkle and S. Henry, 567 (January 2000): 72–87. Thousand Oaks, CA: Sage Publications, January 2000.

Wren, C. S. "Youth Marijuana Use Rises." Themes of the Times, *New York Times* (20 February 1996): 1.

Zimmer, L. and J. P. Morgan. *Marijuana Myths, Marijuana Facts: A Review of the Scientific Evidence*. New York: The Lindesmith Center, 1997.

Inhalants

Did You Know?

- More than 1000 different products are abused commonly in the United States.
- Ordinary household products are misused as inhalants: glues/adhesives, nail polish remover, gasoline, paint thinner, spray paint, butane lighter fluid, propane gas, typewriter correction fluid, household cleaners, cooking sprays, deodorants, whipping cream aerosols, marking pens, and air conditioning coolants.
- Every 46 seconds, someone in the United States will abuse an inhalant for the first time.
- Inhalant abuse is typically a problem of adolescents and teenagers. By the time a student reaches eighth grade, one in five will have misused inhalants.

- Although one in five young people have misused an inhalant, 9 out of every 10 parents refuse to believe their child would try it.
- Every year, young people in this country die of inhalant abuse, and hundreds suffer severe consequences including permanent brain damage and destruction of the heart, kidney, liver, and bone marrow.
- Inhalant abusers can die suddenly and without warning; even first-time abusers have died from sniffing inhalants.

Chapter 15

Learning Objectives

On completing this chapter you will be able to:

▶ Understand that inhalant use is not harmless and even one-time use could lead to "sudden sniffing death syndrome."

▶ List the household and commercial products that are most often abused as inhalants.

▶ Describe the principal means of using household and commercial products as inhalants.

▶ Identify signs of abuse.

▶ Examine the current patterns of abuse among various groups.

▶ List the dangers of inhalant abuse.

Introduction

Inhalants are volatile substances that elicit psychological or physiological changes when introduced into the body via the lungs. They are rarely administered by any other route. Most cause intoxicating and/or euphorigenic effects. Many of these substance were never intended to be used by humans as drugs; consequently, they are not often thought of as having abuse potential. However, abuse of inhalants is a serious public health problem: according to data derived from the 1998 National Household Survey on Drug Abuse population estimates, every 46 seconds, someone in the United States will abuse an inhalant for the first time (Dynatable 2000). This rate is nearly identical to the rate at which individuals abuse cocaine for the first time (the average elapsed time for each new cocaine user is 43 seconds [Dynatable 2000]) and resulted in more than 700,000 new users of inhalants in the year 2000. Use among adolescents is especially disturbing because nearly 20% of U.S. eighth graders have misused an inhalant at least once in their lifetime (Johnston et al. 1999). This frequency of inhalant abuse among eighth graders surpasses the frequency of use of such highly publicized drugs as cocaine and the amphetamines and is nearly equal to the lifetime prevalence of marijuana usage in this age group (Johnston et al. 1999).

A widespread misconception is that inhalant abuse is a harmless "phase" that occurs commonly during normal childhood and teenage development and as such is not worthy of significant concern because young people will "grow out of it" without experiencing harm. On the contrary, hundreds of adolescents and teenagers in the United States die or are seriously injured each year as a result of inhalant abuse (see "Case in Point," Sniffing Can Kill). Even first-time users die from a condition referred to as "sudden sniffing death syndrome" (SSDS), a condition characterized by serious cardiac arrhythmia occurring during or immediately after inhaling. Accurate statistics regarding the actual number of inhalant-associated deaths and injuries each year are unavailable, in part because medical examiners often attribute deaths from inhalant use to suicide, suffocation, or accidents, and in part because there is no national system for gathering data on the number of inhalant-related injuries (NIDA 1999). Still, it has been estimated that inhalants killed more than 1000 adolescents in 1994 (Vaughn 1995) and that many more suffer severe consequences such as permanent brain damage, loss of muscle control, and damage to the heart, blood, kidney, liver, and bone marrow (U.S. Consumer Product Safety Commission 2000).

Most inhalants are household or commercial products composed of several different chemicals. These can act alone or synergistically to exert toxic effects. The potential of these agents to cause harm is compounded by the high concentrations of these substances absorbed in the body by inhalation and the tendency for these often *lipid* (oil or fat)-rich substances to be retained in lipid-containing vital organs. Another important consideration is that the users are often developmentally immature and as such can be more susceptible to the toxic effects of inhalants. The summation of these factors makes inhalants dangerous substances of abuse.

History of Inhalants

The use of inhalants for recreational purposes is not a new phenomenon, as the ancient Greeks inhaled gases as part of their religious ceremonies (Evans 1998). During subsequent years, many different societies used inhalants for both religious and recreational purposes.

The modern era of inhalant abuse can be traced to 1776, when British chemist Joseph Priestly synthesized nitrous oxide (Kennedy and Longnecker 1990), a colorless gas with a slightly sweet odor and no noticeable taste. Roughly 20 years later, he and Humphry Davy suggested correctly that the

---

KEY TERMS

volatile
readily evaporated at low temperatures

euphorigenic
having the ability to cause feelings of pleasure and well-being

arrhythmia
an irregular heart beat

CASE IN POINT

"Sniffing" Can Kill

Wade Alan Heiss was a young boy described by his parents as being "full of life" and a "wonderful child." His father's first memory of a problem was a phone call from Wade's 18-year-old brother reporting that he had found his younger brother in a shed "sniffing out of an air freshener can." Dr. Heiss spoke with his son, and discovered that the boy had been introduced to sniffing by friends at school. He explained the dangers of inhalants to his son. Alan told his father that he didn't realize that sniffing was dangerous, and promised not to sniff again. His father believed Alan. Two weeks later, Alan was found lying next to a jacuzzi. His father administered cardiopulmonary resuscitation, but it was too late: Alan was dead.

Alan's mother reports wishing that she had paid more attention to her son's behavior. At one point, she found a butane lighter in his pocket and assumed he had been smoking. In fact, Alan and his friends had been sniffing from lighters. Today, Alan's parents actively educate other parents regarding the dangers of inhalant abuse in the hopes of preventing other families from experiencing the tragedy that their family shares.

Source: Educate: Creating Inhalant Abuse Awareness Together. Prevline, National Clearinghouse for Drug and Alcohol Information/The Substance Abuse and Mental Health Services Administration (February 2000). Available http://www.health.org./pubs/qdocs/inhal/index.html.

gas may be useful as an anesthetic, and experiments were conducted to test this possibility. Meanwhile, many people learned that inhalation of nitrous oxide produces a euphoria that lasts for minutes, and a general pleasurable feeling that lasts for hours. Hence, during the decades between its discovery and clinical use, the inhalant was abused (Evans 1998). Its abuse continued to be fashionable into the early 19th century because it served as a means of rapidly attaining drunkenness without consuming alcohol.

Dentists contributed greatly to the introduction of nitrous oxide as an anesthetic. At a stage show in the 1840s, Horace Wells, a dentist, noticed that one of the persons involved in the show injured himself while under the influence of nitrous oxide, and yet felt no pain. Wells was so impressed by this anesthetic effect that he subsequently allowed his own tooth to be extracted while under the influence of the gas. His experiment was a success as Wells felt no pain. He went on to attempt to demonstrate his discovery at Massachusetts General Hospital in Boston; unfortunately the patient cried out during the operation and the experiment was deemed unsuccessful. Nevertheless, word of this demonstration and others like it spread, ultimately leading to the use of nitrous oxide and other volatile anesthetics as legitimate medical therapy (Kennedy and Longnecker 1990).

Over the years, it was discovered that many chemicals, in addition to nitrous oxide, could be inhaled so as to alter psychological function. Such abuse of inhalants came to public attention in the 1950s when the news media reported that young people were getting "high" from sniffing glue. The term *glue sniffing* is still used today, but it is often used to describe inhalation of many products besides glue. In fact, there are more than 1000 different products that are currently misused as inhalants (U.S. Consumer Product Safety Commission 2000), some of which are listed in Table 15.1. These chemicals are not regulated like other drugs of abuse; hence, they are readily available to young people. This category of drugs can be classified into three major groups: volatile substances, anesthetics, and nitrites.

Types of Inhalants

■ VOLATILE SUBSTANCES

Over the past 50 years, the number of products containing volatile substances has increased substantially. This category of agents includes aerosols (e.g.,

TABLE 15.1 Inhalants and Their Chemical Contents (adapted from NIDA, 1999)

VOLATILE SOLVENTS	
Adhesives	
Airplane glue	Rubber cement
Polyvinylchloride cement	
Aerosols	
Spray paint	Hair spray
Deodorant, air freshener	Analgesic spray, asthma spray
Solvents and Gases	
Nail polish remover	Paint remover
Paint thinner	Typing correction fluid and thinner
Fuel gas	Cigarette lighter fluid
Gasoline	
Cleaning Agents	
Dry-cleaning fluid	Spot remover
Degreaser	
Dessert Topping Sprays	
Whipped cream, whippets	
ANESTHETICS	
Gas	Liquid
Local	
NITRITES	
Nitrite Room Odorizers	
"Poppers" and "rush"	

spray paints, hair sprays, deodorants, air fresheners), art or office supplies (e.g., correction fluids, felt-tip marker fluids), adhesives (e.g., airplane and other glues), fuels (e.g., propane, gasoline), and industrial or household solvents (e.g., nail polish remover, paint thinners, dry-cleaning fluids). Some volatile substances exist as gases (e.g., nitrous oxide; the propellant in whipping cream cans), and others as liquids that vaporize at room temperature (e.g., gasoline). In some cases, the abuser inhales vapors directly from their original containers (called *sniffing* or *snorting*). Still others inhale volatile solvents from plastic bags (called *bagging*) or from old rags or bandannas soaked in the solvent fluid and held in the mouth (called *huffing*).

Acute effects of the volatile chemicals that are commonly abused include initial nausea with some irritation of airways causing coughing and sneezing. Low doses often bring a brief feeling of light-headedness, mild stimulation followed by a loss of control, lack of coordination, and disorientation accompanied by dizziness and possible hallucinations. In some instances, higher doses can produce relaxation and depression leading to sleep or coma. If inhalation is continued, dangerous hypoxia may occur and cause brain damage or death. In other cases, SSDS can occur. Other potential toxic consequences of inhaling such substances include hypertension and damage to the cardiac muscle, peripheral nerves, brain, and kidneys. In addition, chronic users of inhalants frequently lose their appetite, are continually tired, and experience nosebleeds. If use of inhalants persists, some of the damage becomes irreversible.

Aerosols

Chemicals associated with aerosol sprays are popular among young inhalant abusers; so much so that one manufacturer (see Figure 15.1) of aerosol room deodorizers has added a warning to its label advising parents to keep their product out of the reach of children and teens (Prevline 2000). Aerosol sprays are often abused not because of effects produced by their principal ingredients but rather because of the effects of their propellant gases. In addition, some aerosol sprays (i.e., those necessary to suspend metallic paints) are inhaled because of the psychoactive effects caused by the solvents used to dissolve the product (NIDA 1999). Inhalation of aerosol preparations can be dangerous because these devises are capable of

FIGURE 15.1

S. C. Johnson, the manufacturer of products such as Glade air fresheners, now places this label on their products to warn users about the dangers of inhalant abuse.

generating very high concentrations of the inhaled chemicals, much greater than those released more slowly from liquid products. In addition to the toxic effects of the inhaled compound, aerosols can also cause respiratory injury through exposure to surprisingly cold temperatures. Contents of aerosol cans expand rapidly upon release, resulting in cooling to temperatures as low as 20° C (National Inhalant Prevention Coalition 2000).

Toluene

Aerosol preparations can contain a variety of chemicals. One such chemical is toluene. Toluene is found in some glues, paints, thinners, nail polishes, and typewriter correction fluid. It is a principal ingredient in "Texas shoe shine" (spray paint containing toluene). Toluene represents one of the more dangerous chemicals found in aerosols and other solvents. Because this molecule is highly lipid-soluble and has a low molecular weight, it is rapidly absorbed by the lungs, brain, heart, and liver. The brain has a large capacity to concentrate and store toluene as illustrated by the fact that shortly after inhalation, its concentration in the brain may be 10 times greater than levels in the blood (National Inhalant Prevention Coalition 2000). Accordingly, toluene abuse can cause damage to the brain resulting in incoordination, convulsions, behavioral abnormalities, and coma. In addition, chronic abuse of toluene-containing prod-

ucts can damage other organs, especially the liver and kidneys. Toluene inhalation can also cause heart arrhythmia, thereby leading to death by SSDS. A number of case reports describe neonatal effects that have been attributed to toluene abuse during pregnancy, including fetal growth retardation, congenital malformations, premature delivery, and postnatal developmental retardation.

Butane and Propane

Butane and propane are found commonly in aerosols (e.g., spray paints, air fresheners, hair sprays) and are used as fuel gas or in lighter fluid. Use of these agents is quite common among inhalant abusers. For instance, a recent survey of adolescents in a Virginia correctional facility reported that butane lighter fluid was the third most frequently used inhalant among members of that population (gasoline was the most frequently used, and Freon the second most commonly used [McGarvey et al. 1999]). These chemicals likely constitute the most common "sniffing death hazards" among U.S. students (NIDA 1999). Furthermore, these chemicals are highly flammable: fires and serious burn injuries have resulted when inhalation has been combined with smoking (see "Here and Now," Huffing and Cigarettes: A Deadly Combination, on page 400).

Gasoline

Because of its widespread availability, gasoline is abused commonly by young people, particularly in rural settings. Gasoline is a mixture of volatile chemicals, including toluene, benzene, and tri-orthocresyl phosphate (TCP). Its inhalation produces intoxication that peaks within 3 to 5 minutes and lasts up to 5 to 6 hours (National Inhalant Prevention Coalition 2000). As a mixture of chemicals, its intentional inhalation can be especially dangerous. Benzene is an organic compound that causes serious injury to the bone marrow and suppresses the immune system. TCP is a fuel additive that causes degeneration of motor neurons. Lead, formerly a common constituent of gasoline, can cause

KEY TERMS

hypoxia
a state of oxygen deficiency

HERE AND NOW

Huffing and Cigarettes: A Dangerous Combination

On November 24, 1996, two young residents, aged 17 and 19, were sniffing propane in a Hyannis shelter for homeless people who are working or attending school. When one of them lit a cigarette, the fumes were ignited causing an explosion that destroyed the residence. 19-year-old Jason sustained second and third degree burns over nearly half of his body. The other young man sustained burns to his hands and face.

"Now that we're certain of what caused the fire, we can now make sure the situations don't repeat themselves," said the administrator of the shelter. "My biggest concern is how we get this information out without encouraging a young person . . . It's the last thing I would have thought of, that a kid would huff any chemical, let alone propane. I'm afraid a kid will read this and say, 'Whoa, I didn't know I could get high off of that stuff.' The kid is going to be off and running to see what it's like. But they haven't seen how burned Jason is . . . "

Source: from the Cape Cod Times, January 19, 1997.

lead poisoning, which leads to long-term CNS degeneration. Furthermore, gasoline is highly flammable; as with butane and propane, fires and serious burn injuries have resulted when gasoline inhalation has been combined with smoking of marijuana, tobacco, or other drugs.

Freon

Freon and other fluorinated hydrocarbons are used in a number of products including refrigerators, air conditioners, and airbrushes. Their inhalation can cause not only serious liver damage but also SSDS. Inhaling these agents also poses other dangers; freeze injuries can occur when individuals inhaling Freon lose consciousness, leaving unprotected skin in close proximity to cold. In one recent case, a 16-year-old male attempted to "get high" by inhaling airbrush propellant. The patient lost consciousness. When he awoke, he discovered that his tongue and lips were frozen, and that he had suffered serious burns on his larynx, vocal cords, trachea, bronchi, and esophagus (Kuspis and Krenzelok 1999). In addition to freeze injuries, respiratory collapse can also occur as a result of sudden and dramatic cooling of the respiratory tract. When inhaled from a high-pressure source, the delicate air sacs in the lung can rupture resulting in life-threatening collapse of a segment of the lung.

■ ANESTHETICS

When used properly, other forms of inhalants with abuse potential are important therapeutic agents. Included in this category are anesthetics such as ether, chloroform, halothane and nitrous oxide. Although all the anesthetic gases work much like the central nervous system (CNS) depressants, only nitrous oxide is available enough to be a significant abuse concern.

Nitrous oxide is a colorless gas that is used frequently for minor outpatient procedures in offices of both physicians and dentists. It is often referred to as "laughing gas" because it can cause giggling and laughter in the patient receiving it. Nitrous oxide produces a unique profile of stimulant, hallucinogenic, and depressant effects. Because it is readily accessible, health professionals themselves or their staff are most likely to abuse nitrous oxide.

In addition to being found in a clinical setting, nitrous oxide is sold in large balloons from which the gas is released and inhaled for its mind-altering effects. It is also found in small cylindrical cartridges used as charges for whipped cream dispensers. These balloons, cylinders, and other plastic containers filled with nitrous oxide are referred to as "whippets." Although significant abuse problems of nitrous oxide are infrequent, there are occasional reports of severe hypoxia (i.e., a lack of oxygen) or death due to acute overdoses or psychosis and neuronal disorders developing after chronic abuse (Dohrn et al. 1993). For the most part, nitrous oxide does not pose a significant abuse problem for the general public.

■ NITRITES

Nitrites are chemicals that cause vasodilation. Owing to this property, the prototype of this group, amyl nitrite, is available by prescription to treat angina; however, it is seldom employed currently because of its expense and inconvenience. Nitrites were first abused in the 1960s when ampules of the compound were available over-the-counter (OTC). The ampules were "popped" between the fingers (hence, the name "poppers") and held to the nostrils for inhalation. They have been abused by only a few, selective groups, such as some homosexual men, to enhance "sexual stamina and pleasure."

Before the cause of AIDS was known, early reports suggested that the cause might be related to homosexual lifestyle practices, including the use of recreational drugs such as nitrites. With the discovery that HIV causes AIDS, concern about nitrite use diminished. Some studies indicate that the early attribution of risk may have been caused by an association between nitrite use and certain behaviors associated with enhanced AIDS virus transmission (AHFS 1999). Nitrite use has been suggested to be a possible cofactor in the development of AIDS-related Kaposi sarcoma (a rare form of cancer affecting the immune system) (Haverkos and Drotman 1996).

Following restriction of the availability of OTC nitrites in 1968, small companies began developing alternative nitrite forms that could be sold legally (Balster 1998). These products often contained butyl nitrite and were sold as aromas or incense under names such as "rush", "locker room", and "bullet" (NIDA 1999). Amyl and butyl nitrite are also found in room odorizers. Their use has declined because

many of these chemicals were banned in 1991 (NIDA 1999) and since the launching of an advertising campaign by the Partnership for a Drug Free America in 1996 (Johnston et al., 1999). According to a recent survey, only 0.9% of 12th graders reported any nitrite use in 1999 (Johnston et al. 1999).

Current Patterns and Signs of Abuse

Inhalant abuse is the fourth most common form of substance abuse among high school students in the United States, behind alcohol, tobacco, and marijuana (Johnston et al. 1999). The inhalants are popular for several reasons:

- They are legally obtained.
- They are readily available in most households and workplaces.
- They are inexpensive.
- They are easy to conceal.
- Most users are uninformed about the potential dangers.

In addition, inhalation is popular because it causes feelings of intoxication and euphoria much more rapidly than does the consumption of agents such as alcohol. Furthermore, the withdrawal ("hangover") is often less severe than with alcohol.

■ ADOLESCENT AND TEENAGE USAGE

Inhalant abuse is typically a problem of adolescents and teenagers. According to the Substance Abuse and Mental Health Services Administration (SAMHSA), in 1998, 1.1% of 12- to 17-year-olds (253,000 individuals) reported having used an inhalant in the past month, as compared with only 0.1% of adults aged 26 to 34 (37,000 individuals) (SAMHSA 1999). Adolescents most commonly use inhalants, with usage decreasing as students grow older. For example, according to the 1999 Monitoring the Future Study (Johnston et al.), 5% of 8th graders reported using inhalants within the past month, whereas only 2.6% of 10th graders and 2% of high school seniors reported a similar pattern of use (see Table 15.2). One reason for this age difference is that older individuals often view use of inhalants with disdain and consider it unsophisticated and a "kid's" habit.

Inhalants were used by high percentages of 10th and 12th graders in 1999. Lifetime inhalant use among 12th graders in 1999, which had increased steadily for most of the 1980s, was 15.4%, compared with 17% among 10th graders (see Table 15.2).

Of considerable concern are recent reports that inhalant abuse can begin as early as the preschool years (Spiller and Krenzelok 1997). Researchers and poison information centers have described cases of 2- to 6-year old children inhaling gasoline vapors. Imitation of older siblings or neighbors often accounts for this initial exposure. At least one study indicates that many 7 and 8 year olds are familiar with the psychological effects of inhaling gasoline (Kaufman 1973). Hence, education efforts should be directed at very young children as well as adolescents and their parents (see Figure 15.1).

There has been a recent trend of decreasing inhalant abuse among young people. For instance, in 1999, 10.3% of 8th graders used an inhalant in the last year and 5% in the last month compared with 12.8% and 6.1%, respectively, in 1995 (Johnston et al. 1999). These numbers may be decreasing, in part, because of educational campaigns directed toward educating parents regarding the dangers of inhalant abuse. Increasing parental awareness is especially important: although approximately one in every five young people have abused an inhalant, statistics show that 9 of every 10 parents refuse to believe their child would even try it (Prevline 2000). Moreover,

while over 90% of parents claim to have talked to their children about substance abuse, less than half of those parents have specifically mentioned inhalants (Prevline 2000). One campaign to educate parents about the dangers of inhalant abuse is currently being advanced by Deloris Jordan (author of *Family First*, and mother of basketball star Michael), consumer products manufacturer S. C. Johnson, the Office of National Drug Control Policy, and the U.S. Consumer Product Safety Commission.

■ GENDER, RACE, SOCIOECONOMICS, AND ABUSE

According to the 1998 National Household Survey on Drug Abuse, a greater number of men (7.9%) than women (3.7%) have used an inhalant at least once in their lifetime. However, that gender difference is diminishing as evidenced by recent findings that a near equal percentage (approximately 1%) of females and males aged 12 to 17 report having used an inhalant in the past month. White, non-Hispanic individuals are more likely than Hispanic or black, non-Hispanic individuals to have used an inhalant at least once in their lifetime (i.e., 6.6%, 4.1%, and 2.2%, respectively). Moreover, more white, non-Hispanic and Hispanic teenagers (1.2% and 1.4%, respectively) used inhalants during the preceding 30 days than black, non-Hispanic teenagers (0.5%) (SAMHSA 1998).

TABLE 15.2 Inhalant Use Among Eighth, Tenth, and Twelfth Graders
Data show the percentages of eighth, tenth, and twelfth graders who used inhalants in the past three years.

	8TH GRADERS			10TH GRADERS			12TH GRADERS		
	1997	1998	1999	1997	1998	1999	1997	1998	1999
Inhalants									
Lifetime	21.0%	20.5%	19.7%	18.3%	18.3%	17.0%	16.1%	15.2%	15.4%
Annual	11.8	11.1	10.3	8.7	8.0	7.2	6.7	6.2	5.6
30-Day	5.6	4.8	5.0	3.0	2.9	2.6	2.5	2.3	2.0

Sources: National Survey on Drug Abuse from the Monitoring the Future Study, 1975–1998; College and Young Adults; L. D. Johnston, P. M. O'Malley, J. G. Bachman; The University of Michigan Institute for Social Research, National Institute on Drug Abuse, US Department of Human Services, National Institutes of Health, 1999.
The University of Michigan News and Information Services; Dec. 17, 1999; citing the National Survey on Drug Abuse, The Monitoring the Future Study, 1999; L. D. Johnston, P. M. O'Malley, J. G. Bachman; The University of Michigan Institute for Social Research, National Institute on Drug Abuse, US Department of Human Services, National Institutes of Health.

In 1998, Deloris Jordan, mother of Washington Wizzard star Michael Jordan, joined manufacturer S. C. Johnson and government agencies to introduce *EDUCATE: Create Inhalant Abuse Awareness Together*, an education video that gives important information to parents, teachers, and caregivers on discussing inhalant use with children.

Chronic inhalant users frequently have a profile like that associated with other substance abusers. That is, often they live in unhappy surroundings with severe family or school problems, they have poor self-images, and sniffing gives them an accessible escape. Inhalant abuse tends to occur in episodic outbreaks that may happen at a particular school or in a particular geographic region (NIDA 1999). These isolated incidents reflect the faddish nature of inhalant use and result in a continually fluctuating level of abuse. The problem of inhalant abuse is not unique to the United States. According to research data reported by the National Institute on Drug Abuse (NIDA), inhalant abuse is of world-wide concern. Low prices and easy access make inhalants as problematic in Asia, Africa and Latin America as in the United States (NIDA 1999).

■ SIGNS OF INHALANT ABUSE

Individuals under the influence of inhalants are often uncoordinated and disoriented and appear "drunken" as if having consumed alcohol. Red and watery eyes, slurred speech, nausea, headaches, and nosebleeds are also common. Rashes around the nose and mouth or unexplained paint on the hands and mouth can be signs of inhalant abuse. Other signs include smelling a chemical odor in the room or in unusual containers (e.g., soda cans, plastic bags), finding cans of aerosol whipped cream that will not foam, or discovering air conditioners that do not work. In addition, children who are frequent users of inhalants have the following characteristics:

* Often collect an unusual assortment of chemicals (such as glues, paints, thinners and solvents, nail polish, liquid eraser, and cleaning fluids) in bedrooms or with belongings

* Have breath that occasionally smells of solvents

* Often have the "sniffles" similar to a cold but without other symptoms of the ailment

* Appear drunk for short periods of time (15–60 minutes) but recover quickly

* Do not do well in school and are usually unkempt.

Other signs of inhalant abuse can include the following:

* Sitting with a pen or marker near nose

* Constantly smelling clothing sleeves

* Hiding rags, clothes, or empty containers of the potentially abused products in closets, boxes, and other places

* Possessing chemical-soaked rags, bags, or socks

* Abusable household items missing

Dangers of Inhalant Abuse

The dangers of inhalant abuse stretch beyond simply the direct physical damage to the heart, lungs, liver, and brain. Other dangers include choking on vomitus, asphyxiation, and suffocation. Damage to an unborn child, similar to that observed in fetal alcohol syndrome, can also occur if inhalants are used during pregnancy (National Inhalant Prevention Coalition 1999). In addition, abusers can seriously injure themselves or others while in an "intoxicated" state caused by the inhalant. In particular, frequent falls or accidents involving impaired driving occur in individuals under the influence of inhalants.

Another significant concern with inhalants is that these agents are considered gateway drugs because they are easy to obtain, inexpensive, and difficult to detect. According to Dr. Fred Beauvais, Tri-Ethnic Center for Prevention Research at Colorado State University, "children as young as 4th graders who begin to use volatile solvents also will start experimenting with other drugs, usually alcohol and marijuana" (NIDA 1999, p. 7).

Treatment of Abuse

As with most substances of abuse, the fewer times volatile inhalants are used, the easier it is to stop and the less likely it is that severe physiological damage has been done. Although the inhalants do not tend to cause dangerous physical dependence, their chronic use can lead to an addiction, which requires professional counseling or even hospitalization. Frequently, young inhalant users resist treatment for their addiction because of peer pressure (U.S. Department of Justice 1991).

Treatment programs for inhalant users are rare and difficult to find. Compounding this difficulty is the fact that chronic inhalant abusers are often resistant to treatment efforts. These individuals exhibit high rates of treatment failure and relapse when compared with other forms of substance abuse. In particular, chronic inhalant abusers may require longer-term treatment efforts to produce a satisfactory outcome (National Inhalant Prevention Coalition 1999).

Discussion Questions

1. Name the three types of inhalants, and list examples of each type. List the dangerous side effects associated with the misuse of each type of inhalant.

2. Why are inhalants widely abused?

3. What is sudden sniffing death syndrome?

4. What chemical properties of inhalants make these agents particularly dangerous?

5. Who is most likely to abuse inhalants?

6. List several signs of inhalant abuse.

7. List several dangers of inhalant abuse other than the direct physical damage done by the chemical itself.

Key Terms

volatile   **396**

euphorigenic   **396**

arrhythmia   **396**

hypoxia   **398**

Summary

1 Inhalants are volatile substances that cause intoxicating and/or euphorigenic effects. Most were never intended to be used as drugs and are not often thought of as having abuse potential. However, inhalant abuse is a serious public health problem. Hundreds of adolescents and teenagers in the United States die or are seriously injured each year as a result of inhalant abuse. Even first-time users die from a condition referred to as "sudden sniffing death syndrome" (SSDS).

2 Most inhalants are household or commercial products composed of several different fat-soluble chemicals that can act alone or synergistically to exert toxic effects. These agents can be classified into three groups: volatile substances, anesthetics, and nitrites.

3 Volatile substances include aerosols, adhesives, fuels, and household solvents. Abusers inhale vapors directly form their original containers (called *sniffing* or *snorting*), from plastic bags (called *bagging*), or from old rags or bandannas soaked in the solvent fluid and held in the mouth (called *huffing*). Abuse of these agents can cause damage to the liver, brain, kidney, and immune system, as well as SSDS.

4 Anesthetics include ether, chloroform, halothane and nitrous oxide. When used properly, these forms of inhalants are important therapeutic agents. However, misuse can cause severe hypoxia and death.

5 Nitrites are vasodilators abused by only a few, selective groups to enhance "sexual stamina and pleasure." Their use has declined since many of these chemicals were banned in 1991.

6 Inhalant abuse is the fourth most common form of substance abuse among high school students in the United States, behind alcohol, tobacco, and marijuana. The inhalants are popular because they are legally obtained, readily available, inexpensive, and easy to conceal.

7 Inhalant abuse is typically a problem of adolescents and teenagers, although it can begin as early as the preschool years. There has been a recent trend of decreasing inhalant abuse among young people. Nevertheless, one in every five 8th graders have abused an inhalant.

8 Signs of inhalant abuse include a "drunken" appearance, watery eyes, nausea, headaches, and nosebleeds. Rashes around the nose and mouth or unexplained paint on the hands and mouth can be signs of inhalant abuse. Other signs can include smelling a chemical odor in the room or in unusual containers (e.g., soda cans, plastic bags), finding cans of aerosol whipped cream that will not foam, or discovering air conditioners that do not work.

9 Dangers of inhalant abuse beyond those caused by the chemicals per se include choking on vomitus, asphyxiation, and suffocation. Individuals under the influence of inhalants also have frequent falls, accidents involving impaired driving, and accidents involving fires.

References

American Hospital Formulary Service (AHFS) Drug Information—1999, edited by McEvoy, G. K. Bethesda, MD: American Society of Health-System Pharmacists.

Balster, R. L. "Neuroal Basis of Inhalant Abuse." *Drug and Alcohol Dependence* 51 (1998): 207–14.

Dohrn, C., J. Lichtor, A. Coalson, H. Uitvlugt, H. deWit, and J. Zachny. "Reinforcing Effects of Extended Inhalation of Nitrous Oxide in Humans." *Drugs and Alcohol Dependence* 31 (1993): 265–80.

Dynatable, Prevline, National Clearinghouse for Drug and Alcohol Information/The Substance Abuse and Mental Health Services Administration (February 2000). Available http://www.health.org/dynatable/nsu-appxtest.asp#NewUsersTime.

Evans, E. B. "Pharmacology of Inhalants." In: *Handbook of Substance Abuse: Neurobehavioral Pharmacology*, edited by R. E. Tarter, R. T. Ammerman, and P. J. Ott. New York: Plenum Press, 1998.

Haverkos, H. W. and D. P. Drotman. "NIDA Technical Review: Nitrite Inhalants" *Biomedical Pharmacotherapy* 50 (1996): 228–30.

Johnston, L. D., J. G. Bachman, and P. M. O'Malley. "Monitoring the Future" (press release). Ann Arbor: Institute for Social Research, University of Michigan (December 1999). (The University of Michigan News and Information Services; 17 December 1999; citing the National Survey on Drug Abuse, The Monitoring the Future Study, 1999; L. D. Johnston, P. M. O'Malley, J. G. Bachman; The University of Michigan Institute for Social Research, National Institute on Drug Abuse, U.S. Department of Human Services, National Institutes of Health.)

Kaufman, A. "Gasoline Sniffing Among Children in a Pueblo Indian Village." *Pediatrics* 51 (1973): 1060–64.

Kennedy, S. K. and D. E. Longnecker, "History and Principles of Anesthesiology." In *The Pharmacological Basis of Therapeutics*, edited by A. G. Gilman, T. W. Rall, A. S. Nies, and P. Taylor. New York: Pergamon Press, 1990.

Kuspis, D. A. and E. P. Krenzelok. "Oral Frostbite Injury from Intentional Abuse of a Fluorinated Hydrocarbon." *Journal of Toxicology and Clinical Toxicology* 37 (1999): 873–5.

McGarvey, E. L., G. J. Calvet, W. Mason, and D. Waite. "Adolescent Inhalant Abuse: Environments of Use." *American Journal of Drug and Alcohol Abuse* 25 (1999): 731–41.

National Inhalant Prevention Coalition (February 2000). Available http://www.inhalants.org/.

National Institute on Drug Abuse (NIDA). *Research Report Series—Inhalant Abuse*, NIH Publication No. 94–3818. July 1999.

Prevline. National Clearinghouse for Drug and Alcohol Information/The Substance Abuse and Mental Health Services Administration. (February 2000). Available http://www.health.org./pubs/qdocs/inhal/index.html.

Spiller, H. A. and E. P. Krenzelok. "Epidemiology of Inhalant Abuse Reported to Two Regional Poison Centers" *Clinical Toxicology* 35 (1997) 167–73.

Substance Abuse and Mental Health Services Administration (SAMHSA), *National Household Survey on Drug Abuse: Population Estimates 1998*. Rockville, MD: Department of Health and Human Services.

U.S. Consumer Product Safety Commission. *A Parent's Guide to Preventing Inhalant Abuse*. (February 2000). Available http://www.cpsc.gov/cpscpub/pubs/inhalant.html.

U.S. Department of Justice, "Let's All Work to Fight Drug Abuse" (Pamphlet) DEA. L. A. W. Publications, 1991.

Vaughn, K. (Knight-Ridder News Service). "Inhalants Killing Teens by Hundreds." *Salt Lake Tribune* 249 (13 April 1995): A-7.

Over-the-Counter (OTC), Prescription, and Herbal Drugs

Did You Know?

► Pharmacists can provide useful counseling in selecting appropriate over-the-counter (OTC) products.

► Careless, excessive use of some OTC medications can cause addiction, physical dependence, tolerance, and withdrawal symptoms.

► When used together, prescription drugs can interact with OTC or herbal drugs in a dangerous and sometimes even lethal manner.

► There are really only three different types of active analgesic ingredients found in OTC pain relievers.

► OTC cold medications do not cure the common cold but might temporarily relieve symptoms such as nasal congestion, muscle aches, and coughing.

► Herbal remedies are very popular products that, despite containing drugs, are available without a prescription and are not regulated by the Food and Drug Administration (FDA).

► More people die in the United States from adverse reactions to legal medications than succumb to all illegal drug use.

► Most generic drugs are as effective as, but substantially less expensive than, their proprietary counterparts.

► Pharmacists are required by law to counsel patients concerning the use and safety of prescriptions that they fill.

Chapter 16

Learning Objectives

On completing this chapter you will be able to:

▶ Outline the general differences between prescription and nonprescription drugs.

▶ Explain why the FDA occasionally switches prescription drugs to OTC status.

▶ Identify some of the drugs that have been switched to OTC.

▶ Discuss the potential problems of making more effective OTC drugs available to the public for self-care.

▶ Describe the type of information that is included on the labels of nonprescription medicines.

▶ Discuss the rules for safe use of nonprescription drugs.

▶ Determine the difference between herbal products and OTC medications.

▶ Explain why the FDA is considering regulating some herbal products.

▶ Discuss the type of information that should be communicated between doctor and patient to avoid unnecessary side effects.

▶ Explain the advantages and disadvantages of generic and proprietary drugs.

Introduction

Prescription and nonprescription (over-the-counter, or OTC) drugs have been viewed differently by the public since these classifications were formally established by the Durham-Humphrey Amendment of 1951. In general, we view OTC medications as less effective, relatively free from side effects, and rarely abused; in contrast, we often consider prescription drugs as much more potent and frequently dangerous. However, distinctions between prescription and nonprescription drugs, which at one time appeared to be obvious, have become blurred by changes in public demand and federal policies. Because of escalating health costs and a growing interest in self-care, people today want access to effective medications, and governmental agencies such as the Food and Drug Administration (FDA) are responding to their demands. Consequently, the FDA is actively involved in switching effective and relatively safe prescription medications to OTC status. It is clear that in the future, many more drugs will be removed from behind the pharmacist's counter and made available for public access as nonprescription medications. These changes emphasize the arbitrary nature of classifying drugs as prescription and OTC and remind us that similar care should be taken with all medications to achieve maximal benefit and minimal risk.

In this chapter, we begin by discussing OTC or nonprescription drugs. The first topic encompasses policies regarding OTC drug regulation and is followed by a discussion of safe self-care with nonprescription drug products. Explanations of some of the most common medications in this category, including herbal remedies, conclude the section on OTC drugs. The second part of this chapter gives a general overview of prescription drugs. The consequences of misusing prescription drugs, as well as ways for you to avoid such problems, are discussed. A brief presentation of some of the most commonly prescribed drugs ends the chapter.

OTC Drugs

Each year the United States spends more than $14 billion on drug products that are purchased OTC, and this market is projected to reach $28 billion by the year 2010 (Covington 1993; Greenberg 1996). Today, more than 300,000 different OTC products are available to treat everything from age spots to halitosis; they comprise 60% of the annual drug purchases in this country (Greenberg 1996). An estimated three out of four people routinely self-medicate with these drug products (Greenberg 1996). The major drug classes currently approved for OTC status are shown in Table 16.1.

OTC remedies are nonprescription drugs that may be obtained and used without the supervision of a physician or other health professional. Nevertheless, for some people, certain OTC products can be dangerous when used alone or in combination with other drugs. Although some OTC drugs are very beneficial in the self-treatment of minor to moderate uncomplicated health problems, others are of questionable therapeutic value, and their usefulness is often misrepresented by manufacturers.

■ ABUSE OF OTC DRUGS

During 1996 spring break, Peter Schlendorf, a 20-year-old student, was found dead in his motel room in Panama City, Florida, only hours after consuming eight pills of Ultimate Xphoria. This herbal stimulant was manufactured by Alternate Research (Tempe, Arizona) and contained the amphetamine-related drug, ephedrine. Although a medical examiner's report on the Schlendorf case was not made public, friends and family claimed that Peter was in good health and had not used other drugs or alcohol before consuming the stimulant. Because herbal medicines are generally exempt from FDA regulation and available as OTC products through mail order, at counterculture shops, or in health nutrition stores, the possible abuse of these potentially dangerous drugs is of concern to federal and state authorities (Lane 1996; "New York County" 1996).

This account gives only one example of problems associated with misuse or abuse of OTC products. Because these drugs are usually available on demand, perceived as being exceptionally safe, and poorly understood by the general public, their abuse patterns differ somewhat from those seen with the so-called hard-core drugs of abuse; nevertheless, they can be equally harmful. Even though the OTC products generally have a greater margin of safety than their prescription counterparts, issues

TABLE 16.1 **Major Drug Classes Approved by the FDA for OTC Status**

DRUG CLASS	EFFECTS
Analgesics and anti-inflammatories	Relieve pain, fever, and inflammation
Cold remedies	Relieve cold symptoms
Antihistamines and allergy products	Relieve allergy symptoms
Stimulants	Diminish fatigue and drowsiness
Sedatives and sleep aids	Promote sleep
Antacids	Relieve indigestion from rebound acidity
Laxatives	Relieve self-limiting constipation
Antidiarrheals	Relieve minor, self-limiting diarrhea
Gastric secretion blockers	Relieve heartburn
Topical antimicrobials	Treat skin infections
Bronchodilators and antiasthmatics	Assist breathing
Dentrifices and dental products	Promote oral hygiene
Acne medications	Treat and prevent acne
Sunburn treatments and sunscreens	Treat and prevent skin damage from ultraviolet rays
Dandruff and athlete's foot medications	Treat and prevent specific skin conditions
Contraceptives and vaginal products	Prevent pregnancy and treat vaginal infections
Ophthalmics	Promote eye hygiene and treat eye infections
Vitamins and minerals	Provide diet supplements
Antiperspirants	Promote body hygiene
Hair growth stimulators	Promote hair growth

Source: Gilbertson, W. "The FDA's OTC Drug Review." In *Handbook of Nonprescription Drugs*, 10th ed. Washington, DC: American Pharmaceutical Association, 1993.

of abuse need to be considered. For example, many OTC drugs, when misused, can cause physical and psychological dependence. Nonprescription products that can be severely habit-forming include nasal and ophthalmic (eye) decongestants, laxatives, antihistamines, sleep aids, and antacids. Of particular abuse concern are the OTC stimulants, such as ephedrine, which can either be severely toxic by themselves (see the account in the previous paragraph) or can be used as precursors to the synthesis of the extremely addicting and dangerous amphetamines.

Because use of OTC products is unrestricted, the patterns of abuse are impossible to determine accurately. However, these products are more likely to be abused by members of the unsuspecting general public who inadvertently become dependent due to excessive self-medication than by hard-core drug addicts who obtain the most potent drugs of abuse by illicit means.

■ FEDERAL REGULATION OF OTC DRUGS

In the United States, the FDA is responsible for regulating OTC drugs. Under direction of the FDA, the active ingredients in OTC drugs have been, and continue to be, evaluated and classified according to their effectiveness and safety (Gilbertson 1993; Holt 1996). At this time, the principal ingredients included in nonprescription drug products are category I (that is, they are considered safe and effective). On the one hand, as recently as August 1992, the FDA banned more than 400 ingredients from seven categories of OTC products (Lamy 1993).

On the other hand, the FDA is attempting to make even more drugs available to the general public by switching some frequently used and safe prescription medications to OTC status. This policy is in response to public demand to have access to effective drugs for self-medication and has resulted in approximately 100 switched active ingredients (White-Sax 1998). This policy helps to cut medical costs by eliminating the need for costly visits to health providers for treatment of minor, self-limiting ailments (Hsu 1994). A few of the more notable drugs that have been switched from prescription to nonprescription status since 1985 (Slezak 1996; White-Sax 1998) are naproxen (analgesic, anti-inflammatory: Aleve); ketoprofen (analgesic: Orudis); hydrocortisone (anti-inflammatory steroid: Cortaid); loperamide (antidiarrheal: Imodium); tioconazole (vaginal antifungal: Vagistat-1); epinephrine (bronchodilator: Bronkaid Mist); miconazole (antifungal: Monistat 7); cimetidine (heartburn medication: Tagamet); increased strength minoxidil (hair growth stimulant: Rogaine); nicotine patch (smoking cessation aid: Nicotrol); cromolyn (allergy medication: Nasalcrom); and triclosan (antibacterial for gum disease: Colgate Total toothpaste).

A major concern of health professionals is that reclassification of safe prescription drugs to OTC status will result in overuse or misuse of these agents. The reclassified drugs may tempt individuals to self-medicate rather than seek medical care for potentially serious health problems or encourage the use of multiple drugs at the same time, increasing the likelihood of dangerous interactions (Stewart 1995). However, the FDA has proceeded cautiously, and the majority of consumers support the switching policy (Slezak 1996). As of yet, few major problems have

been identified, and the reclassified products have been well received by the public.

It is likely that effective and safe prescription drugs will continue to be made available OTC, and it is hoped that the public will be prepared to use them properly. In fact, the FDA is considering another group of drugs currently available by prescription for OTC status in the next several years. Drugs being evaluated for reclassification include those that lower cholesterol, inhaled nasal steroids for allergies, new topical antibiotics, antivirals (to treat skin viral infections), and nonsedating antihistamines (to treat allergies) (White-Sax 1998).

■ OTC DRUGS AND SELF-CARE

Of approximately 3.5 billion health problems treated in the United States annually, almost 2 billion can be treated with an OTC drug (OTC Observations 1998). This fact demonstrates that the public frequently engages in medical self-care with OTC products. Self-care with nonprescription medications occurs because we decide that we have a health problem that can be adequately self-medicated without involving a health professional. Proper self-care assumes that the individual has made a correct diagnosis of the health problem and is informed enough to select the appropriate OTC product. If done correctly, self-care with OTC medications can provide significant relief from minor, self-limiting health problems at minimal cost. However, a lack of understanding about the nature of the OTC products—what they can and cannot do—and their potential side effects can result in harmful misuse. For this reason, it is important that those who consume OTC medications be fully aware of their proper use. This goal usually can be achieved by reading product labels carefully and asking questions of health professionals such as pharmacists and physicians (Klein-Schwartz and Hoopes 1993).

OTC Labels

Information about proper use of OTC medications is required to be cited on the drug label and is regulated by the FDA. Required label information includes (1) approved uses of the product, (2) detailed instructions on safe and effective use, and (3) cautions or warnings to those at greatest risk when taking the medication. Recent FDA regulations require that this information be readily intelligible to the lay public and easily read (Nordenberg 1999) (see Figure 16.1).

Many consumers experience adverse side effects because they either choose to ignore the warnings on OTC labels or simply do not bother to read them. For example, excessive or inappropriate use of some nonprescription drugs can cause drug dependence; consequently, people who are always dropping medication in the eyes "to get the red out"

or popping antacids like dessert after every meal are likely addicted. They continue to use OTC products to avoid unpleasant eye redness or stomach acidity, which are likely withdrawal consequences of excessive use of these medications.

Rules for Proper OTC Drug Use

The OTC marketplace for drugs operates differently than does its prescription counterpart. The use of OTC drugs is not restricted, and consumers are responsible for making correct decisions about these products. Thus, the consumer sets policy and determines use patterns.

Because there are no formal controls over the use of OTC drugs, abuse often occurs. In extreme situations, the abuse of OTC medication can be very troublesome, even causing structural damage to the body. Proper education about the pharmacological features of these agents is necessary if consumers are to make intelligent and informed decisions about OTC drug use. To reduce the incidence of problems, the following rules should be observed when using nonprescription products:

FIGURE 16.1
OTC Label
Certain information must appear on the labels of an OTC medicinal product: (a) Front of label, and (b) back of label.

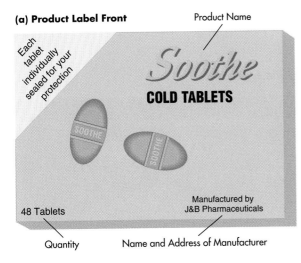

1. Always know what you are taking. Identify the active ingredients in the product.

2. Know the effects. Be sure you know both the desired and potential undesired effects of each active ingredient.

3. Read and heed the warnings and cautions. The warnings are not intended to scare but to protect.

4. Do not use OTC drug products for more than 1 to 2 weeks. If the problem being treated persists beyond this time, consult a health professional.

5. Be particularly cautious if you are also taking prescription or herbal drugs. Serious interactions between OTC and these medications frequently occur. If you have a question, be sure to find out the answer.

6. If you have questions, ask a pharmacist. Pharmacists are excellent sources of information about OTC drugs. They possess up-to-date knowledge of OTC products and can assist consumers in selecting correct medications for their health needs. Ask them to help you.

7. Most importantly: If you don't need it, don't use it!

■ TYPES OF OTC DRUGS

It is impossible to provide a detailed description of the hundreds of active ingredients approved by the FDA for OTC distribution; however, the following includes a brief discussion of the most common OTC drugs available in this country.

Internal Analgesics

We spend more than $2 billion on internal (taken by mouth) analgesics , the largest sales category of OTC drugs in the United States. Most of the money is for salicylates (aspirin products—Anacin, Bayer), acetaminophen (Tylenol, Datril, Pamprin, Panadol), ibuprofen (Advil, Nuprin), and ibuprofen-like drugs such as naproxen (Aleve) and ketoprofen (Orudis). The compositions of common OTC internal analgesics are given in Table 16.2.

Therapeutic Considerations The internal analgesic products are effective in treating several common ailments.

- *Analgesic Action.* The OTC analgesics effectively relieve mild to moderate somatic pain associated with musculoskeletal structures such as bones, skin, teeth, joints, and ligaments. Pains that are relieved by the use of these drugs include headaches, toothaches, earaches, and muscle strains. In contrast, these drugs are not effective in the treatment of severe pain or pain associated with internal organs, such as the heart, stomach, and intestines (AHFS 2000).

- *Anti-inflammatory Effects.* Use of high doses (two to three times the analgesic dose) of the salicylates and ibuprofen relieves the symptoms of inflammation such as those associated

TABLE 16.2 **Compositions of OTC Internal Analgesics (dose per unit)**

PRODUCT	ASPIRIN (MG)	ACETAMINOPHEN (MG)	IBUPROFEN (MG)	OTHER
Anacin	400	—	—	Caffeine
Bayer Aspirin	325	—	—	—
Empirin	325	—	—	—
Alka-Seltzer, Extra Strength	500	—	—	Antacid
Ecotrin	325	—	—	Coated tablet
Excedrin, Extra Strength	250	250	—	Caffeine
Tylenol, Children's	—	80	—	—
Advil	—	—	200	—
Motrin IB	—	—	200	—
Motrin, Children's	—	—	100	—
Nuprin	—	—	200	—
Aleve	—	—	—	Naproxen (200 mg)
Orudis	—	—	—	Ketoprofen (12.5 mg)

Source: Walsh, P. *Physician's Desk Reference for Nonprescription Drugs*, 21st ed. Oradell, NJ: Medical Economics Data, 2000.

with arthritis (AHFS 2000). In contrast, even high doses of acetaminophen have little anti-inflammatory action. Because of this anti-inflammatory effect, these drugs are frequently compared with a group of natural, very potent anti-inflammatory compounds, the steroids. To distinguish drugs such as the salicylates and ibuprofen from steroids, these drugs are often called nonsteroidal anti-inflammatory drugs (NSAIDs).

- *Antipyretic Effects.* The OTC analgesics, such as aspirin and acetaminophen, reduce fever but do not alter normal body temperature (AHFS 2000). Such drugs are called antipyretics. The frequent use of these drugs to eliminate fevers is very controversial. Some clinicians believe that low-grade fever may be a defense mechanism that helps destroy infecting microorganisms such as bacteria and viruses; thus, interfering with fevers may hamper the body's ability to rid itself of infection-causing microorganisms. Because no serious problems are associated with fevers of 102°F or less, they are probably better left alone.

- *Side Effects.* When selecting an OTC analgesic drug for relief of pain, inflammation, or fever, possible side effects should be considered. Although salicylates such as aspirin are frequently used, they can cause problems for both children and adults (see Table 16.3). Because of their side effects, salicylates are not recommended for (1) children, because of the potential for Reye's syndrome; (2) people suffering gastrointestinal problems, such as ulcers; or (3) people with bleeding problems, who are taking anticlot medication, who are scheduled for surgery, or who are near term in pregnancy, because salicylates interfere with blood clotting and prolong bleeding.

For minor aches and pains, acetaminophen substitutes adequately for salicylates, has no effect on blood clotting, and does not cause stomach irritation. In addition, acetaminophen does not influence the occurrence of Reye's syndrome, a potentially deadly

KEY TERMS

analgesics
drugs that relieve pain while allowing consciousness

salicylates
aspirin-like drugs

anti-inflammatory
relieves symptoms of inflammation

steroids
potent hormones released from the adrenal glands

nonsteroidal anti-inflammatory drugs (NSAIDs)
anti-inflammatory drugs that do not have steroid properties

antipyretics
drugs that reduce fevers

Reye's syndrome
potentially fatal complication of colds, flu, or chickenpox in children

TABLE 16.3 Common Side Effects of OTC Nonsteroidal Antiinflammatory Drugs (NSAIDs)

DRUGS	SYSTEM AFFECTED	SIDE EFFECTS
Salicylates (aspirin-like)	Gastrointestinal	Cause irritation, bleeding; aggravate ulcers
	Blood	Interfere with clotting; prolong bleeding
	Ears	Chronic high doses cause ringing (tinnitus) and hearing loss
	Pediatric	Cause Reye's syndrome
Acetaminophen	Liver	High acute doses or chronic exposure can cause severe damage
Ibuprofen (includes other, newer NSAIDs)	Gastrointestinal	Similar to salicylates but less severe
	Blood	Similar to salicylates but less severe
	Kidneys	Damage in elderly or those with existing kidney disease

complication of colds, flu, and chickenpox in children up to the age of 16 to 18 years who are using salicylates (AHFS 2000).

Caffeine and Other Additives   A number of OTC analgesic products contain caffeine. Caffeine may relieve the aversion of pain due to its stimulant effect, which may be perceived as pleasant and energizing. The combination of caffeine with OTC analgesics may enhance pain relief (AHFS 2000) and be especially useful in treating vascular headaches because of the vasoconstrictive properties on cerebral blood vessels caused by this stimulant. In most OTC analgesic products, for example, Anacin, Excedrin, the amount of caffeine is less than that found in one-fourth to one-half cup of coffee (about 30 milligrams/tablet). Other ingredients—such as antacids, antihistamines, and decongestants—sometimes included in OTC pain-relieving products have little or no analgesic action and usually add little to the therapeutic value of the medication.

A recent development for OTC analgesic products was FDA permission to advertise pain-relieving products effective in the relief of migraine headaches. Although these products have been found to provide relief from minor migraine headaches, they do not contain any new breakthrough drugs: these products contain previously available ingredients, such as aspirin, ibuprofen, and caffeine, but just in higher doses (e.g., Migraine Extra Strength Excedrin).

Cold, Allergy, and Cough Remedies

At any one time, almost 5% of the population has a common cold. This adds up to billions of colds per year in the United States, at a cost of almost $5 billion annually (Dale 2000).

The incidence of the common cold varies with age. Children between 1 and 5 years are most susceptible; each child averages 6 to 12 respiratory illnesses per year, most of which are common colds. Individuals 25 to 30 years old average about 6 respiratory illnesses a year, and older adults average two or three. The declining incidence of colds with age is owing to the immunity that occurs after each infection with a cold virus; thus, if reinfected with the same virus, the microorganism is rapidly destroyed by the body's defense and the full-blown symptoms of a cold do not occur (Sause and Mangione 1991).

Most colds have similar general symptoms: in the first stage, the throat and nose are dry and scratchy; in the second stage, secretions accumulate in the air passages, nose, throat, and bronchial tubes. The second stage is marked by continuous sneezing, nasal obstruction, sore throat, coughing, and nasal discharge. There may be watering and redness of the eyes and pain in the face (particularly near the sinuses) and ears. One of the most bothersome symptoms of the common cold is the congestion of the mucous membranes of the nasal passages, due in part to capillary dilation, which causes these blood vessels to enlarge and become more permeable. Such vascular changes allow fluids to escape, resulting in drainage and also inflammation due to fluid-swollen tissues (Mackowiak 1999).

Decongestants   The cold and allergy products we use are formulated with such drugs as decongestants (sympathomimetics), antihistamines (chlorpheniramine and pheniramine), analgesics (aspirin and acetaminophen), and an assortment of other substances (vitamin C, alcohol, caffeine, and so on). Table 16.4 lists the ingredients found in many common OTC cold and allergy products.

Antihistamines reduce congestion caused by allergies, but their effectiveness in the treatment of virus-induced colds is controversial (Mackowiak 1999). In high doses, the anticholinergic action of antihistamines (see Chapter 5) also decreases mucus secretion, relieving the runny nose; however, this action is probably insignificant at the lower recommended doses of OTC preparations (Mackowiak 1999). An anticholinergic drying action may actually be harmful because it can lead to a serious coughing response. Due to anticholinergic effects, antihistamines also may cause dizziness, drowsiness, impaired judgment, constipation, and dry mouth; they sometimes are abused because of psychedelic effects resulting from high-dose consumption. Because of the limited usefulness and the side effects of antihistamine for treating colds, decongestant products without such agents are usually preferred for these viral infections. In contrast, antihistamines are very useful in relieving allergy-related congestion and symptoms.

The sympathomimetic drugs used as decongestants cause nasal membranes to shrink because of their vasoconstrictive effect, which reduces the con-

TABLE 16.4 Compositions of Common OTC Cold and Allergy Products (dose per tablet)

PRODUCT	SYMPATHOMIMETIC (MG)	ANTIHISTAMINE (MG)	ANALGESIC (MG)
Actifed	Pseudoephedrine (30)	Triprolidine (2.5)	—
Chlor-Trimeton Allergy	—	Chlorpheniramine (4)	—
Dristan Cold Multi-Symptom Formula	Phenylephrine (5)	Chlorpheniramine (2)	Acetaminophen (325)
Sudafed Sinus	Pseudoephedrine (30)	—	Acetaminophen (325)

Source: Walsh, P. *Physician's Desk Reference for Nonprescription Drugs*, 21st ed. Oradell, NJ: Medical Economics Data, 2000.

gestion caused by both colds and allergies. Such drugs can be used in the form of sprays or drops (topical decongestants) or systemically (oral decongestants) (see Table 16.5). FDA-approved sympathomimetics include pseudoephredrine, phenylephrine (probably the most effective topical), naphazoline, oxymetazoline, and xylometazoline (Mackowiak 1999). Until recently, phenylpropanolamine was also included in OTC products and was one of the more popular system decongestant ingredients available without a prescription; however, in November 2000, the FDA requested that this mild stimulant be withdrawn from all OTC medications due to its association with strokes in women under the age of 50 years (Public Health Advisory 2000).

If you use decongestant nasal sprays frequently, you can experience   congestion rebound   due to tissue dependence. After using a nasal spray regularly for longer than the recommended period of time, the nasal membranes adjust to the effect of the vasoconstrictor and become very congested when the drug is not present. You may become "hooked" and use the spray more and more with less and less relief until your tissues no longer respond and the sinus passages become almost completely obstructed (Mackowiak 1999). Allergists frequently see new patients who are addicted to nasal decongestant sprays and are desperate for relief from congestion. This problem can be prevented by using nasal sprays sparingly and for no longer than the recommended time.

Orally ingested sympathomimetic drugs give less relief from congestion than the topical medications but do not cause rebound effects. In contrast, systemic administration of these drugs is more likely to cause cardiovascular problems (that is, stimulate the heart, cause arrhythmia, increase blood pressure, and cause stroke) as just described for phenylpropanolamine.

Antitussives Other drugs used to relieve the common cold are intended to treat coughing. The cough reflex helps clear the lower respiratory tract of foreign matter, particularly in the later stages of a cold. There are two types of cough: productive and nonproductive. A *productive cough* removes mucus

TABLE 16.5 Compositions of OTC Topical Decongestants (Drug Concentrations)

PRODUCT	SYMPATHOMIMETIC
Afrin nasal spray	Oxymetazoline (0.05%)
Neo-Synephrine, 12 Hour	Oxymetazoline (0.05%)
Vicks Sinex, 12-Hour	Oxymetazoline (0.05%)

Source: Walsh, P. *Physician's Desk Reference for Nonprescription Drugs*, 21st ed. Oradell, NJ: Medical Economics Data, 2000.

KEY TERMS

congestion rebound
withdrawal from excessive use of a decongestant, resulting in congestion

secretions and foreign matter so that breathing becomes easier and the infection clears up. A *nonproductive, or dry, cough* causes throat irritation; this type of cough is of little cleansing value. Some types of cough suppressant (antitussive) medication are useful for treating a nonproductive cough but should not be used to suppress a productive cough ("A Hacker's Guide" 1995).

Two kinds of OTC preparations are available to treat coughing:

- Antitussives —such as codeine, dextromethorphan, and diphenhydramine (an antihistamine)—that act on the central nervous system (CNS) to raise the threshold of the cough-coordinating center, thereby reducing the frequency and intensity of a cough

- Expectorants —such as guaifenesin and terpin hydrate—which theoretically (but not very effectively) increase and thin the fluids of the respiratory tract in order to soothe the irritated respiratory tract membranes and decrease the thickness of the accumulated secretions so that coughing becomes more productive.

Table 16.6 lists commonly used OTC antitussives and their compositions.

Often the tickling sensation in the throat that triggers a cough can be eased by sucking on a cough drop or hard candy, which stimulates saliva flow to soothe the irritated membranes. Unless the cough is severe, sour hard candy often works just as well as more expensive cough lozenges.

Cough remedies, like other medications, have a psychological value. Many patients with respiratory tract infections claim they cough less after using cough remedies, even when it is objectively demon-

The common cold accounts for 20% of all acute illnesses in the United States.

TABLE 16.6 Compositions of Common OTC Antitussives (dose per unit)

PRODUCT	DEXTROMETHORPHAN (MG)	EXPECTORANT	OTHER
Comtrex Maximum Strength	15	—	Sympathomimetic; antihistamine; analgesic
Cheracol D Cough	10	Guaifenesin	Alcohol
Novahistine DMX	10	Guaifenesin	Sympathomimetic; alcohol
Robitussin CF	10	Guaifenesin	Sympathomimetic
Vicks NyQuil	10	—	Sympathomimetic; antihistamine; analgesic

Source: Walsh, P. *Physician's Desk Reference for Nonprescription Drugs*, 21st ed. Oradell, NJ: Medical Economics Data, 2000.

strated that the remedies reduce neither the frequency nor the intensity of the cough. Cough remedies work in part by reducing patients' anxiety about the cough and causing them to believe that their cough is lessening. If you believe in the remedy, you often can get as much relief from a simple, inexpensive product as from the most sophisticated and costly one. If a cough does not ease in a few days, you should consult a doctor ("A Hacker's Guide" 1995).

Although not widely known, abuse of antitussive products by teenagers is a significant problem in some regions of this country. This abuse likely relates to the fact that the antitussive ingredient, dextromethorphan, in high doses can have a phencyclidine (PCP)-like effect (Schultz 2000; White 1995) (see "Here and Now," The Dextromethorphan Trip).

What Really Works? With all the advances in medicine today, there is still no cure for the common cold. In most cases, the best treatment is plenty of rest, increased fluid intake to prevent dehydration and to facilitate productive coughing, humidification of the air if it is dry, gargling with diluted salt water (2 teaspoons per quart), an anal-

gesic to relieve the accompanying headache or muscle ache, and perhaps an occasional decongestant if nasal stuffiness is unbearable. Allergy symptoms, in contrast, are best relieved by antihistamines.

Sleep Aids

In 1995, an estimated 49% of the U.S. population experienced insomnia (the inability to fall asleep or stay asleep) at least 5 nights each month (Gill 1999). About 1% of the adult population routinely self-medicate their insomnia with OTC sleep aids that are advertised as inducing a "safe and restful sleep" (Eggert and Crismon 1992). Described as nonbarbiturate and non–habit-forming, these low-potency

HERE AND NOW The Dextromethorphan Trip

Dextromethorphan is the antitussive ingredient frequently found in nonprescription cough medicine. Because of pharmacological properties that resemble those of PCP, OTC cough medicines are sometimes abused by teenagers. One such person, who had consumed almost an entire bottle of a popular anticough product, described his experience. He related that the effects of the drug hit first with lightheadedness and slight disorientation. After 1 hour, the disorientation became severe. He explained that it felt as though he were outside of himself looking in. The hallucinations were somewhat subtle with things appearing grainy and distorted. He found that breathing was sometimes constricted as though he were wearing a tight shirt collar. Then came hot flashes, which caused him to turn on a fan to cool down. He found walking was difficult, and time became distorted. The trip lasted 1 to 2 hours for the strong effects, but it seemed to continue forever. This person was an experienced user of acid (LSD) and mushrooms, but he had never been on a trip as scary as the one with the cough medicine. Several times he thought he was going to die. He found that coming down took a while. He decided that he would never do "dex" (dextromethorphan) again.

products are frequently misused (Shuster 1996). For example, the parents of a young child were traveling cross-country. They knew the trip would be long and the child likely would grow tired and cranky. In order to keep the child quiet and manageable, the parents used a cough syrup that contained an antihistamine to cause sedation (personal communication to Hanson, 2000). Use of these products in young children is inappropriate and can be dangerous.

The drugs commonly used in OTC sleep aids are antihistamines, particularly diphenhydramine (Gill 1999). Although antihistamines have been classified as OTC category I sleep aid ingredients (see Chapter 3), their usefulness in treating significant sleep disorders is highly questionable (Gill 1999). At best, some people who suffer mild, temporary sleep disturbances caused by problems such as physical discomfort, short-term disruption in daily routines (such as jet lag), and extreme emotional upset might experience temporary relief. However, even for those few who initially benefit from these agents, tolerance develops within 2 to 4 days. For long-term sleep problems, OTC sleep aids are of no therapeutic value and are rarely recommended by health professionals. Actually, their placebo benefit is likely more significant than their actual pharmacological benefit. Usually counseling and psychotherapy are more effective approaches for resolving chronic insomnia than OTC or even prescription sleep aid drugs (Gill 1999).

Because antihistamines are CNS depressants, in low doses they can cause sedation and antianxiety action (see Chapter 7). Although in the past, some OTC products containing antihistamines were promoted for their relaxing effects (e.g., Quietworld and Compoz), currently, no sedatives are approved for OTC marketing. The FDA decided that the earlier products relieved anxiety by causing drowsiness, so, in fact, they were not legitimate sedatives. Because of this ruling, medications that are promoted as antianxiety products are no longer available without a prescription. However, antihistamines have been added to an array of other OTC drug products marketed for the purpose of causing relaxation or promoting sleep; such products include analgesics (Excedrin P.M.) and cold medicines (Tylenol Allergy Sinus NightTime). The rationale for such combinations is questionable, and their therapeutic value unsubstantiated.

Melatonin The hormone melatonin is currently being used by millions to induce sleep or to help the body's natural clock readjust after the effects of jet lag. Melatonin was referred to as the "all-natural nightcap of the 1990s." Although most users of this hormone want assistance in falling asleep, melatonin is also claimed to slow the aging process, stimulate the immune system, and enhance the sex drive. Melatonin is a naturally occurring hormone, also found in some foods. Under the 1994 Dietary Supplement and Education Act, melatonin is considered a dietary supplement and is not regulated by the FDA. Despite the popularity of melatonin products, little is known about the benefits or the potential adverse effects of this hormone; consequently, these products should be used cautiously, if at all (Gill 1999).

Stimulants

Some OTC drugs are promoted as stay-awake (NōDōz) or energy-promoting (Vivarin) products (Walsh 2000). In general, these medications contain high doses of caffeine (100–200 milligrams per tablet). (Caffeine and its pharmacological and abuse properties are discussed at length in Chapter 11.) Although it is true that CNS stimulation by ingesting significant doses of caffeine can increase the state of alertness during periods of drowsiness, the usefulness of such an approach is highly suspect.

For example, college students sometimes rely on such products to enhance mental endurance during cramming sessions for examinations. In fact, at one western U.S. university, the back page of a quarterly class schedule, printed and distributed by the university, included a full-page advertisement for the OTC stimulant Vivarin with the caption, "Exam Survival Kit." The implications of such promotions are obvious and disturbing. Due to the objections of the faculty, the advertisement was not run again at the university.

Routine use of stay-awake or energy-promoting products to enhance performance at work or in school can lead to dependence, resulting in withdrawal when the person stops using the drug. Most health professionals agree that there are more effective and safer ways to deal with fatigue and drowsiness—for example, managing time efficiently and getting plenty of rest.

"Look-Alike" and "Act-Alike" Drugs Mild OTC stimulants have been marketed as safe substitutes for more potent and illicit stimulants of abuse. Known as "look-alike" or "act-alike" stimulants, in the past, these products were made to appear as real amphetamines and were intended to give a mild lift or sense of euphoria. The principal drugs found in the look-alikes are mild stimulants such as ephedrine and caffeine. The same drugs are also found in OTC decongestants and diet aids (Walsh 2000). Until recently, these products also contained the sympathomimetic phenylpropanolamine, but due to a link with strokes (see the earlier discussion in "Cold, Allergy, and Cough Remedies"), the FDA has required that this mild stimulant be withdrawn from all OTC products (Public Health Advisory 2000).

Although much less potent than amphetamines, when used in high doses, these OTC stimulants can cause anxiety, restlessness, throbbing headaches, breathing problems, and tachycardia (rapid heartbeat). There have been reports of death due to heart arrhythmia, cerebral hemorrhaging, and strokes, as discussed earlier. The availability of these drugs encourages their routine use and the development of dependence. Thus, they can serve as "gateway" drugs, leading to abuse of more potent compounds.

The manufacturers of these OTC stimulants unscrupulously advertise in college newspapers, handbills posted at truckstops, and unsolicited literature from mail order companies.

Gastrointestinal Medications

The gastrointestinal (GI) system consists principally of the esophagus, stomach, and intestines and is responsible for the absorption of nutrients and water into the body, as well as the elimination of body wastes. The function of the GI system can be altered by changes in eating habits, stress, infection, and diseases such as ulcers and cancers. Such problems may affect appetite, cause discomfort or pain, result in nausea and vomiting, and alter the formation and passage of stools from the intestines.

A variety of OTC medications are available to treat GI disorders such as indigestion (antacids), heartburn (gastric secretion blockers), constipation (laxatives), and diarrhea (antidiarrheals) (Walsh 2000). However, before individuals self-medicate with nonprescription drugs, they should be certain that the cause of their GI problem is minor, self-limiting, and does not require professional care. Because antacids are the most frequently used of the GI nonprescription drugs, they are discussed.

Antacids and Anti-heartburn Medication More than $1 billion is spent annually on antacid preparations that claim to give relief from heartburn and indigestion caused by excessive eating or drinking and to provide long-term treatment of chronic peptic ulcer disease. It is estimated that as much as 50% of the population has had one or more attacks of gastritis, often referred to as "acid indigestion, heartburn, upset stomach, and sour or acid stomach." These attacks are often due to acid rebound, occurring 1 to 2 hours after eating; by this time, the stomach contents have passed into the small intestines, leaving the gastric acids to irritate or damage the lining of the empty stomach. Heartburn, or gastroesophageal reflux, occurs after exposure of the lower esophagus to these very irritating gastric chemicals.

Some cases of severe, chronic acid indigestion may progress to peptic ulcer disease. Peptic ulcers (open sores) most frequently affect the duodenum (first part of the intestine) and the stomach. Although this condition is serious, it can be treated effectively with antacids, which are often combined with drugs available OTC or by prescription such as cimetidine (Tagamet), ranitidine (Zantac), and famotidine (Pepcid). A person with acute, severe stomach pain; chronic gastritis; blood in the stools (common ulcer symptoms); diarrhea; or vomiting should see a physician promptly and should not attempt to self-medicate with OTC antacids (Walsh 2000).

Most bouts of acid rebound, however, are associated with overeating or consuming irritating foods or drinks; these self-limiting cases can usually be managed safely with OTC antacids (such as sodium bicarbonate, calcium carbonate, aluminum salts, and magnesium salts). Because of their alkaline (opposite of acidic) nature, the nonprescription products neutralize gastric acids and give relief.

KEY TERMS

gastritis
inflammation or irritation of the gut

Generally speaking, OTC antacid preparations are safe for occasional use at low recommended doses, but excessive use can cause serious problems. In addition, all antacids can interact with other drugs; they may alter the GI absorption or renal elimination of other medications. For example, some antacids inhibit the absorption of tetracycline antibiotics; thus, these products should not be taken at the same time. Consequently, patients using prescription drugs should consult with their physicians before taking OTC antacids (Walsh 2000).

Heartburn can be treated effectively with low doses of Tagamet, Zantac, or Pepcid. These drugs were switched to OTC status in the mid-1990s and help reduce gastric secretions (Walsh 2000).

Diet Aids

In U.S. society, being slim and trim are prerequisites to being attractive. It is estimated that approximately 33% of the people in the United States are *obese* (body fat in excess of 20% of normal) and 50% are overweight (Sprague and Cubertson 1997). Being obese has been linked to cardiovascular disease, some cancers, diabetes, chronic fatigue, and an array of aches and pains, not to mention psychological disorders such as depression (Sprague and Culbertson 1997). Popular remedies for losing weight often include fad diets advertised in supermarket journals, expensive weight loss programs, or both prescription and OTC diet aids.

Approximately 25% to 30% of the people in the United States are obese and 50% are overweight.

Using drugs as diet aids is highly controversial (Sprague and Culbertson 1997). Most experts view them as useless or even dangerous. These drugs are supposed to depress the appetite, which helps users maintain low-calorie diets. The most effective of these agents are called anorexiants . Potent anorexiants, such as amphetamine-like drugs (including the once popular diet aid, Phen-fen), can cause dangerous side effects (see Chapter 11) and are available only by prescription. The appetite suppression effects of prescription anorexiants are usually temporary, after which tolerance often builds. Thus, even prescription diet aid drugs are usually effective for only a short period. There are no wonder drugs to help the obese lose weight permanently (Doheny 1993).

The most potent and most frequently used OTC diet aid ingredient used to be the sympathomimetic phenylpropanolamine. Since the FDA required that this drug be removed from all OTC products (Public Health Advisory 2000), it is not clear what sympathomimetic will replace it in OTC diet aids. The OTC diet aids are minimally effective and of no value in the treatment of significant obesity. Despite their questionable value, frequent use of high doses of the OTC diet aid products is a common practice by weight-conscious female high school and college students. As one college sophomore who routinely carried a package of Dexatrim in her purse said, "Popping two or three of these before an important date helps me to eat like a bird and appear more petite" (from Hanson's files, interview, 1996). Interestingly, this same woman also occasionally induced vomiting after eating because of her fear that she was gaining weight. Such weight-management practices are extremely worrisome.

Skin Products

Because the skin is so accessible and readily visible, most people are sensitive about its appearance. These cosmetic concerns are motivated by attempts to look good and preserve youth. Literally thousands of OTC skin products with cosmetic and health objectives are available to consumers (Walsh 2000). Only a few of the most commonly used products are mentioned here: acne medications, sun products, and basic first-aid products.

Acne Medications Acne is the most common skin disorder affecting adolescents (Krowchuk 2000) and typically occurs during puberty in response to the secretion of the male hormone androgen (both males and females have this hormone) (Tatro 1998). Acne is usually chronic inflammation caused by bacteria trapped in plugged sebaceous (oil) glands and hair follicles. This condition consists of whiteheads, pimples, nodules, and in more severe cases, pustules, cysts, and abscesses. Moderate to severe acne can cause unsightly scarring on the face, back, chest, and arms and should be treated aggressively by a dermatologist with drugs such as antibiotics (tetracycline) and potent keratolytics , such as Retin A (retinoic acid) or vitamin A or Accutane (isotretinoin). Usually, minor to moderate acne does not cause scarring or permanent skin damage and often can be safely self-medicated with over-the-counter acne medications (Tatro 1998).

Several nonprescription approaches to treating mild acne are available:

1. *Sebum removal.* Oil and fatty chemicals (*sebum*) can accumulate on the skin and plug the sebaceous glands and hair follicles. Use of OTC products such as alcohol wipes can help remove such accumulations (e.g., Stri-Dex).

2. *Peeling agents.* The FDA found several keratolytic agents safe and effective for treatment of minor acne: benzoyl peroxide (Oxy 5 and Oxy 10), salicylic acid (Oxy Medicated Pads), resorcinol, and sulfur (Acnemol), alone or in combination. These drugs help to prevent acne eruption by causing the keratin layer of the skin to peel or by killing the bacteria that cause inflammation associated with acne. If multiple concentrations of a keratolytic are available (such as Oxy 5 and Oxy 10 Advanced Formula), it is better to start with a lower concentration and move up to the higher one, allowing the skin to become accustomed to the caustic action of these products. The initial exposure may worsen the appearance of acne temporarily; however, with continual use, the acne usually improves.

Sun Products The damaging effects of sun exposure on the skin have been well publicized in recent

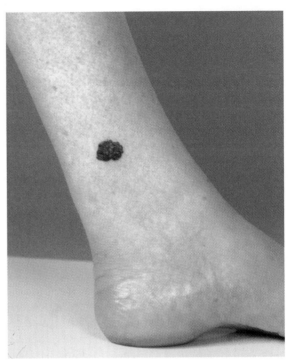

This skin cancer is melanoma and is caused by excessive exposure to ultraviolet light.

years. It is now clear that the ultraviolet (UV) rays associated with sunlight have several adverse effects on the skin. It has been demonstrated that almost 1 million cases of skin cancer each year in the United States are a direct consequence of exposure to UV rays (White-Sax 2000). Almost one of six people will experience some form of skin cancer during his or her lifetime (Simonsen 1993).

The majority of these will be cancers of skin cells called basal cell or squamous cell carcinomas

---

KEY TERMS

anorexiants
drugs that suppress the activity of the brain's appetite center, causing reduced food intake

keratolytics
caustic agents that cause the keratin skin layer to peel

keratin layer
outermost protective layer of the skin

(White-Sax 2000). These cancers usually are easily removed by minor surgery and patients have a good prognosis for recovery. About 0.5% of the population will suffer a much more deadly form of skin cancer called *melanoma.* Melanomas are cancers of the pigment-forming cells of the skin, called *melanocytes,* and spread rapidly from the skin throughout the body, causing death in 20% to 25% of patients (White-Sax 2000).

Another long-term concern related to UV exposure is premature aging. Skin frequently exposed to UV rays, such as during routine tanning, experiences deterioration associated with the aging process. Elastin and collagen fibers are damaged, causing a loss of pliability and elasticity in the skin and resulting in a leathery, wrinkled appearance (White-Sax 2000).

Because of these damaging effects of sun exposure, an array of protective sunscreen products are available OTC. Most sunscreens are formulated to screen out the shorter UVB rays. These products have deliberately been designed to allow passage, in varying degrees, of the UVA rays because researchers once thought that these longer rays would help skin to tan without causing damage. Now it appears scientists were mistaken, and due to deep penetration in the skin, UVA rays likely contribute to melanoma as well as chronic skin damage, causing skin to wrinkle, sag, and lose tone (White-Sax 2000).

The protection afforded by sunscreens is designated by an SPF (sun protection factor) number. This designation tells users the relative length of time they can stay in the sun before burning and includes ratings of 2 to 11 (*minimum*), 12 to 30 (*moderate*) and greater than 30 (*high*) (Schwartz 1999). For example, proper application of a product with an SPF of 10 allows users to remain in the sun without burning 10 times longer than if it was not applied. It is important to remember that the SPF designation does not indicate protection against UVA rays.

Although there currently is no convenient rating system to assess UVA screening, products with SPF ratings of 15 or greater usually offer some protection against the longer UV radiation. In addition, a compound called *avobenzone* appears to offer the fullest protection against UVA rays (Medical Letter 1999). If a product also protects against UVB and has an SPF designation of 15 it is classified as a broad-spectrum sunscreen ("Full Sun Protection" 1993).

Because the natural pigment in the skin affords some UV protection, people with fair complexions (less skin pigmentation) require products with higher SPF numbers than do dark-skinned people.

People who want complete protection from UVB exposure can use OTC sunblockers, which prevent any tanning. Sunscreen ingredients in high concentrations essentially become sunblockers. In addition, an opaque zinc oxide ointment is a highly effective and inexpensive sun-blocking product and is available OTC.

Skin First-Aid Products

A variety of unrelated OTC drugs are available as first-aid products for the self-treatment of minor skin problems. Included in this category of agents are the following products:

1. Local anesthetics, such as benzocaine (e.g., Dermoplast) to relieve the discomfort and pain of burns or trauma

2. Antibiotics and antiseptics, such as bacitracin (Polysporin), neomycin (Neosporin), betadine, and tincture of iodine to treat or prevent skin infections

3. Antihistamines (Benadryl) or corticosteroids (hydrocortisone [Cortaid]) to relieve itching or inflammation associated with skin rashes, allergies, or insect bites

These first-aid skin products can be effective when used properly. In general, side effects to such topical products are few and minor when they occur.

■ OTC HERBAL (NATURAL) PRODUCTS

Herbal products are a unique category of OTC remedies that account for almost $1.5 billion a year in U.S. sales (Foreman 1997). They are unique because, despite the presence of active ingredients,

---

KEY TERMS

SPF (sun protection factor) number
designation to indicate a product's ability to screen ultraviolet rays

Herbal products have become very popular and widely accepted.

there is little or no federal regulation due to a 1994 law, supported by the dietary supplement industry, called the Dietary Supplement Health and Education Act (Frontlines 2000; Tatro 1999). This law requires the government to demonstrate that substances in the herbal products are harmful before such products can be removed from the market, and the burden of proof lies with the FDA not the manufacturer (Tatro 1999).

This act also (1) makes the manufacturers responsible for product safety; (2) explains how product literature is used for product promotion; and (3) describes what can be included on labels. Due to these regulations, manufacturers cannot use terms such as *diagnose, treat, prevent,* or *cure.* But companies can make claims about affecting body function. For example, manufacturers of glucosamine cannot claim their product helps cure arthritis, but they can say products with glucosamine help the joints function better (Tatro 1999). Because of the lack of regulation, these products often are not scientifically tested, and they vary considerably in both the quantity and quality of active ingredients (Frontlines 2000a; Tatro 1999). These products have been viewed with considerable skepticism by many experts who argue that "assertions, speculation and testimonials do not substitute for evidence" when it comes to establishing the value of a drug (Slezak 1998, p. 38).

However, in the past few years, a change in attitude toward herbal products has occurred. More people, including health professionals, have become convinced that some herbs may be useful in the treatment of minor health problems (Consumer Report 2000). In fact, it has become quite common for doctors, nurses, and other formally trained health professionals to recommend herbal treatments for medical problems (Consumer Report 2000). Despite greater acceptance, the fact that most people who use herbs to treat medical conditions still consider prescription drugs to be considerably more effective suggests persistent skepticism regarding these products (Consumer Report 2000).

Frequent uses of herbal products include treatment of anxiety, chronic fatigue, arthritis, and digestive problems (Druglinks 1998). Another common use of these natural products is to elevate mood. The most popular herbs for the purpose are St. John's wort, S-adenosyl-methionine (SAM-e), and kava kava (see "Here and Now," Herbal Options, on page 424). It is generally thought that while these products do have some effect in the treatment of minor to moderate depression, there is no evidence they elevate a normal, undisturbed mood nor are particularly effective against severe mood disturbances. A major risk of self-administering these remedies for mood disorders is that some of the people self-treating their depression are severely emotionally unstable. Overall, depression leads to approximately 20,000 suicides in this country each year (Frontlines 2000). Another considerable problem of self-medicating with herbal products for mood disorders is the lack of standardization for these substances. A recent survey revealed that the actual amount of active SAM-e per pill in products claiming to contain 200 mg active ingredient ranged from 80 to 250 mg. For these reasons, it is almost universally recommended that patients with serious emotional disturbances, especially depression, be diagnosed by a mental-health professional even though some of these professionals may find use of the natural products to be acceptable for treatment of mild emotional problems (Frontlines 2000).

Other concerns with herbal products include the possibility of interaction with other OTC and prescription medications (Consumer Report 2000). This can be more problematic as the routine use of herbs becomes common, especially because unscrupulous manufacturers deceive customers into thinking that these products are perfectly safe and do not really contain any drugs. Some interactions identified occur between products containing

HERE AND NOW   Herbal Options

With the increasing popularity of herbal products, an array of choices has become available for dealing with many common, usually self-limiting health problems. The following is a list of some of the most popular of these medicinal herbs.

Echinacea
Common Claim: Stimulates immune system and helps fight infections.
Common Use: Reduce cold symptoms and help accelerate recovery.
Effectiveness: May shorten duration of cold, but does not prevent it; however, even this is controversial*
Concerns: Relatively well tolerated, but fatigue and sleepiness occasionally occur.

Garlic
Common Claim: Inhibits production of cholesterol and reduces blood sugar.
Common Use: Treat diabetes and prevent cardiovascular disease.
Effectiveness: Most studies do not find garlic effective against serious diseases.
Concerns: Mild stomach discomfort and possible interaction with blood-thinning (anticlotting) prescription drugs occur.

Ginkgo Biloba
Common Claim: Improves memory.
Common Use: Often promoted to enhance memory for patients with Alzheimer's disease.
Effectiveness: At best helps to prevent some mental decline in Alzheimer's patients but does not appear to reverse memory loss or help normal or age-related memory losses.
Concerns: Can interact with blood-thinning medications such as aspirin.

Glucosamine and Chondroitin
Common Claim: Contributes to joint strength.
Common Use: Relieve the discomfort of arthritis.
Effectiveness: Provides moderate relief from the pain of arthritis and may help to slow progress of the disease.

Concerns: May interact with blood thinners and adversely affect adult-onset diabetes.

Saw Palmetto
Common Claim: Relieves discomforts associated with prostate gland.
Common Use: Shrink enlarged prostate and facilitate urination.
Effectiveness: Provides relief for most men within a month of use.
Concerns: Well tolerated by most men.

SAM-e
Common Claim: Helps regulate brain transmitters such as dopamine.
Common Use: Relieve symptoms of depression.
Effectiveness: Some evidence that it relieves moderate depression.
Concerns: Side effects are typically mild, such as stomach upset, insomnia and nervousness. Can be very expensive, ranging from $55 to $260 a month.

St. John's Wort
Common Claim: Elevates mood.
Common Use: To treat mild to moderate depression.
Effectiveness: Appears to relieve some cases of mild depression for the short-term.
Concerns: Recent alert from the FDA warns about interactions with numerous medications, such as birth-control pills and other antidepressants.

Ginseng†
Common Claim: Increases energy
Common Use: Treat fatigue and enhance performance.
Effectiveness: There may be some mild stimulation, but there is no evidence of enhanced performance.
Concerns: Well tolerated for the most part, although there are some reports of minor addiction.

*Grimm, W. and H. Muller, "A Randomized Control Trial of the Effect of Fluid Extract of Echinacea Purpurea on the Incidence and Severity of Colds and Respiratory Infections."
†*Drug Facts and Comparison News* (October 1999), 74–8.

herbs such as garlic, ginkgo biloba, ephedra, and ginseng (Fugh-Berman 2000). A notable example of drug interactions has been reported with St. John's wort, which increases the metabolism and inactivates drugs used to treat heart failure, asthma, infections, or blood clots (Fugh-Berman 2000).

Finally, lack of regulation has encouraged such a lackadaisical attitude concerning herbs that their use has been trivialized to the extent that they and their associated active drugs are now being included in foods and marketed in both health-food stores and supermarkets. Recent snacks, cereals, and beverages spiked with medicinal herbs include ginseng ginger ale, kava kava corn chips, echinacea fruit drinks, and ginkgo-biloba chocolate bars (Frontlines 2000a). These products, sometimes referred to as "functional foods," are typically packaged in colorful containers with cartoon figures that are likely to appeal to kids and accompanied by subtle suggestive promotions implying that these products can "support emotional and mental balance." The exact quantities of herbal substances added to such food and snack products and their actual effects (if any) are difficult to monitor. Although concerned, regulator agencies are uncertain as to how to deal with the potential problems associated with this marketing strategy (Frontline 2000a).

Herbals and Abuse

Drugs found naturally in plants or herbs can have serious side effects or can be abused. In fact, some of the most powerful substances of abuse are extracted from plants and include drugs such as cocaine (*Erythroxylum coca*), marijuana (*Cannabis sativa*), peyote (*Lophophora williamsii*), and tobacco (*Nicotiana tabacum*). Because these substances are reviewed elsewhere in this book, they will not be discussed further here: they are mentioned to emphasize the point that being associated with herbs and natural products does not exclude a drug from being abused. Of concern in this section are unregulated herbal products and their potential for abuse and addiction. As a general rule, if a substance (including natural products) elevates mood, causes a feeling of energy, or brings on a feeling of relaxation and relief from stress, it likely has potential for abuse (Tinsley 1999). Based on these principles, the herbal products most likely to be abused include those containing ma huang, ginseng, kava kava, and ephedrine (Gruber and Pope 1998;

Tinsley 1999). Of course, with addiction typically comes high-quantity use and a greater chance of serious side effects, for example, the anorexia, thought disturbances, insomnia, racing heart and loss of sensation in the limbs sometimes experienced by users addicted to "Herbal Ecstasy," a product containing caffeine, kava kava, and ephedrine (Yates et al. 2000). Even though serious abuse of herbal products is possible, it does not occur frequently and when it does occur, it is generally relatively easy to treat.

Prescription Drugs

The Durham-Humphrey Amendment of 1951 established the criteria that are still used today to determine if a drug should be used only under the direction of a licensed health professional, such as a physician. According to this piece of legislation, drugs are controlled with prescriptions if they are (1) habit-forming, (2) not safe for self-medication, (3) intended to treat ailments that require the supervision of a health professional, or (4) new and without an established safe track record. There currently are more than 10,000 prescription products sold in the United States, representing approximately 1500 different drugs, with 20 to 50 new medications approved each year by the FDA (*Physician's Desk Reference* 2000).

Because of their specialized training, physicians, dentists, and, under certain conditions, podiatrists, physician assistants, nurse practitioners, pharmacists, and optometrists are granted drug-prescribing privileges. The health professionals who write prescriptions are expected to accurately diagnose medical conditions requiring therapy, consider the benefits and risks of drug treatment for the patient, and identify the best drug and safest manner of administering it. The responsibility of the health professional does not conclude with the writing of a prescription; in many ways, it only just begins. Professional monitoring to ensure proper drug use and to evaluate the patient's response is crucial for successful therapy.

■ PRESCRIPTION DRUG ABUSE

Dealing with suspected abuse of prescription medication can pose a difficult management problem for physicians and pharmacists. It has become such a major issue that some third-party payers (that is, health insurance companies) have implemented tight monitoring procedures. Abusing patients often employ manipulative tactics to gain access to drugs for which they have developed severe dependence. For example, a woman who became loud and abusive when a pharmacist questioned the validity of her prescription for a narcotic claimed a taxicab was waiting in the front to take her to a family emergency; her prescription was subsequently found to be fraudulent (Wick 1995). Illicit use of prescription drug products may be prompted by any of several reasons (Longo et al. 2000; Wick 1995): (1) to relieve withdrawal caused by drug habits (e.g., benzodiazepines are used to relieve alcohol withdrawal); (2) to treat infections caused by drug abuse (e.g., antibiotics are used to treat injection infections); (3) to provide a source of fresh, clean needles for injecting drugs of abuse (e.g., via insulin syringes); and (4) to prolong the high caused by drugs of abuse (e.g., appetite suppressants are taken to enhance effects of stimulants of abuse).

Abusers of prescription drugs often have multiple addictions, including dependence on caffeine, nicotine, or both. In addition, once a pharmacy is recognized as an easy target, word spreads and other abusers often begin to frequent the same store (Wick 1995). Signs of patients with drug-seeking behavior include the following:

- Use of altered or forged prescriptions

- Claims that a prescription has been lost and a physician is unavailable for confirmation

- Frequent visits to emergency rooms or clinics for poorly defined health problems

- Visits made to a pharmacy late in the day, on weekends, or just before closing

- Alteration of doses on a legitimate prescription

- Loud, abusive, and insulting behavior

- Use of several names

- Being particularly knowledgeable about drugs

■ PROPER DOCTOR-PATIENT COMMUNICATION

Many unnecessary side effects and delays in proper care are caused by poor communication between the health professional and the patient when a drug is prescribed. The smaller a drug's margin of safety (the difference between therapeutic and toxic doses), the greater the need for direction from a health professional concerning its proper use. The following is a brief overview of principles to help ensure that satisfactory communication takes place between the health professional and the patient.

Doctor-patient communication must be reciprocal. We tend to think that patients listen while doctors talk when it comes to deciding on the best medication for treatment. To ensure a proper diagnosis, precise and complete information from the patient is also essential. In fact, if a doctor is to select the best and safest drug for a patient, he or she needs to know everything possible about the medical problems to be treated. In addition, the patient should provide the doctor with a complete medical and drug history, particularly if there has been a problem with the patient's cardiovascular system, kidneys, liver, or mental functions. Other information that should be shared with the doctor includes previous drug reactions as well as a complete list of drugs routinely being used, including prescription, nonprescription, and herbal products.

The patient needs to be educated about proper drug use. If the doctor does not volunteer this information, the patient should insist on answers to the following questions:

- What is being treated? This question does not require a long, unintelligible scientific answer. It should include an easy-to-understand explanation of the medical problem.

- What is the desired outcome? The patient should know why the drug is prescribed and what the drug treatment is intended to accomplish. It is difficult for the patient to become involved in therapy if he or she is not aware of its objectives.

- What are the possible side effects of the drug? This answer does not necessitate an exhaustive list of every adverse reaction ever recorded in the medical literature; however, it is important to realize that adverse drug reactions to prescription drugs are very common. In the United States, more people die from adverse reactions to legal medications than succumb to all illegal drug use. It is estimated that approximately 100,000 people die while another 2.1 million are seriously injured in this country each year from reactions to legal medications (MacDonald 1998). In general, if adverse reactions occur in more than 1% of users, this should be mentioned to the patient. In addition, the patient should be made aware of ways to minimize the occurrence of side effects (e.g., an irritating drug should not be taken on an empty stomach to minimize nausea) as well as what to do if a side effect occurs (e.g., if a rash occurs, call the doctor immediately).

- How should the drug be taken to minimize problems and maximize benefits? This answer should include details on how much, how often, and how long the drug should be taken.

Although it is a health professional's legal and professional obligation to communicate this information, patients frequently leave the doctor's office with a prescription that gives them legal permission to use a drug but without the knowledge of how to use it properly. Because of this all-too-common problem, pharmacists have been mandated by legislation referred to as the Omnibus Budget Reconciliation Act of 1990 (OBRA '90) to provide the necessary information to patients on proper drug use (Waroholak-Juarez et al. 2000; Zak 1993) (see "Here and Now," OBRA '90, on page 428). Patients should be encouraged to ask questions of those who write and fill prescriptions.

■ DRUG SELECTION: GENERIC VERSUS PROPRIETARY

Although it is the primary responsibility of the doctor or health care provider to decide which drug is most suitable for a treatment, often an inexpensive choice can be as effective and safe as a more costly option. This statement frequently is true when choosing between generic and proprietary drugs. The term generic is used by the public to refer to the common name of a drug that is not subject to trademark rights; in contrast, proprietary denotes medications marketed under specific brand names (Vasquez and Vasquez 2000). For example, diazepam is the generic designation for the proprietary name Valium. Often, the most common proprietary name associated with a drug is the name given when it is newly released for marketing. Because such drugs are

KEY TERMS

generic
official, nonpatented, nonproprietary name of a drug

proprietary
brand or trademark name that is registered with the U.S. Patent Office

almost always covered by patent restrictions for several years when first sold to the public, they become identified with their first proprietary names. After the patent lapses, the same drug often is also marketed by its less-known generic designation (Dighe 1999).

Because usually the pharmaceutical companies that market the generic products have not invested in the discovery or development of the drug, they often charge much less for their version of the medication. This situation contrasts with that of the original drug manufacturer, which may have invested up to $500 million for research and development (see Chapter 3). Even though the generic product frequently is less expensive, the quality usually is not inferior to the related proprietary drug; thus, substitution of generic for proprietary products rarely compromises therapy (Dighe 1999). It should be noted that occasionally an inferior generic drug product is marketed in order to increase profit margins for the manufacturer and is not therapeutically equivalent to the proprietary drug product; however, physicians and pharmacists should be aware of these differences and prescribe accordingly. If a patient alerts the physician to concerns about drug costs, less expensive generic brands often can be substituted.

Because of reduced cost, generic products have become very popular. Currently, generic drugs account for over 30% of all prescription drug sales amounting to approximately $10 billion (CDER 2000). Because of the great demand, all states have laws that govern the use and substitution of generic drugs; unfortunately, the laws are not all the same. Some states have "positive laws" that require pharmacists to substitute a generic product unless the physician gives specific instructions not to do so. Other states have "negative laws" that forbid substitution without the physician's permission. Some physicians use convenient prescription forms with "May" or "May Not" substitution boxes that can be checked when the prescription is filled out.

■ COMMON CATEGORIES OF PRESCRIPTION DRUGS

Of the approximately 10,000 different prescription drugs available in the United States, the top 50 drugs in sales account for almost 30% of all new and refilled prescriptions ("Top 200 Drugs" 2000). As an example, a list of the 30 top-selling prescription drugs in 1999 is shown in Table 16.7. The following includes a brief discussion of some drug groups represented in the 30 most frequently pre-scribed medications. This list is not intended to be all-inclusive, but gives only a sampling of common prescription products.

Analgesics

The prescription analgesics consist mainly of narcotic and NSAID (nonsteroidal anti-inflammatory drug) types. The narcotic analgesics most often dispensed to patients by prescription are (1) the low-potency agents propoxyphene (Darvon) and codeine, (2) the

HERE AND NOW — OBRA '90—The Evolving Role of Pharmacists in Drug Management

In 1990, the U.S. Congress passed section 4401 of the Omnibus Budget Reconciliation Act (commonly referred to as OBRA '90), which substantially altered the role of pharmacists in drug management. This act designated the pharmacist as the key player in improving the quality of drug care for patients in this country. Because OBRA '90 is federal legislation, it can require drug-related services for Medicare patients only; however, most states have recognized that similar services should be made available to all patients and have enacted legislation to that end. OBRA '90 requires pharmacists to conduct a drug use review (DUR) for each prescription to improve the outcome of drug therapy and reduce adverse side effects. The DUR program describes four basic professional services that a pharmacist must render whenever a drug prescription is filled:

1. Prescriptions and patients' records must be screened to avoid problems caused by drug duplications, adverse drug-drug interactions, medical complications, incorrect drug doses, and incorrect duration of drug treatment.

2. Patients should be counseled regarding the following:
   - How to safely and effectively administer the drug
   - Common adverse effects and interactions with other drugs, food, and so forth
   - How to avoid problems with the drug
   - How to monitor the progress of drug therapy
   - How to store the drug properly
   - Whether a refill is intended
   - What to do if a dose is missed

3. Patient profiles, including information on disease, a list of medications, and the pharmacist's comments relevant to drug therapy, must be maintained. This information should be stored in computer files for future reference.

4. Documentation must record if the patient refuses consultation from the pharmacist, or if a potential drug therapy problem is identified and the patient is warned.

Source: Abood, R. "OBRA '90: Implementation and Enforcement." *NABP U.S. Pharmacists, State Boards—A Continuing Education Series*. Park Ridge, IL: National Association of Boards of Pharmacy, 1992.

TABLE 16.7 **The 30 Top-Selling Prescription Drugs of 1999 (based on new and refill prescriptions)**

RANKING	PROPRIETARY NAME	GENERIC NAME	PRINCIPAL CLINICAL USE
1	Premarin	Estrogen	Estrogen replacement therapy
2	Synthroid	Levothyroxine	Replace thyroid hormone
3	Lipitor	Atorvastatin	Reduce cholesterol
4	Prilosec	Omeprazole	Relieve ulcers
5	Hydrocodone	Same	Narcotic analgesic
6	Albuterol	Same	Open air passages
7	Norvasc	Amlodipine	Treat high blood pressure
8	Claritin	Loratiadine	Decongestant
9	Trimox	Amoxicillin	Antibiotic
10	Prozac	Fluoxetine	Antidepressant
11	Zoloft	Sertraline	Antidepressant
12	Glucophage	Metformin	Lower blood sugar
13	Lanoxin	Digoxin	Relieve heart failure
14	Prempro	Estrogen/Progestin	Hormone replacement
15	Paxil	Paroxetine	Relieve depression
16	Zithromax	Azithromycin	Antibiotic
17	Zestril	Mannitol	Reduces blood pressure
18	Zocor	Simvastatin	Reduce cholesterol
19	Prevacid	Lansoprazole	Treatment of ulcers
20	Augmentin	Amoxicillin	Antibiotic
21	Celebrex	Celecoxib	Anti-inflammatory
22	Coumadin	Warfarin	Prevent blood clots
23	Vasotec	Enalapril	Reduce hypertension
24	Amoxicillin	Same	Antibiotic
25	Furosemide	Same	Diuretic
26	Levoxyl	Levothyroxine	Replace thyroid hormone
27	Cipro	Ciprofloxacin	Antibiotic
28	Cephalexin	Same	Antibiotic
29	K-Dur	Potassium	Potassium replacement
30	Prednisone	Same	Anti-inflammatory

Source: "Top 200 Drugs of 1999." *Pharmacy Times* (April 2000): 24.

moderate-potency agents pentazocine (Talwin) and oxycodone (Percodan), and (3) the high-potency drug meperidine (Demerol). All narcotic analgesics are scheduled drugs because of their abuse potential and are effective against most types of pain. The narcotic analgesic products are often combined with aspirin or acetaminophen (e.g., Percocet is a combination of oxycodone and acetaminophen) to enhance their pain-relieving actions. For additional information about the narcotics, see Chapter 10.

The NSAIDs constitute the other major group of analgesics available by prescription. The pharmacology of these drugs is very similar to that of the OTC compound ibuprofen, discussed earlier in this chapter. These medications are used to relieve inflammatory conditions such as arthritis and are effective in relieving minor to moderate *musculoskeletal pain* (pain associated with body structures such as muscles, ligaments, bones, teeth, and skin). These drugs have no abuse potential and are not scheduled; several are also available OTC (see the discussion of OTC analgesics). The principal adverse side effects include stomach irritation, kidney damage, *tinnitus* (ringing in the ears), dizziness, and swelling from fluid retention. Most prescription NSAIDs have similar pharmacological and side effects. Included in the group of prescription NSAIDs are ibuprofen (Motrin), naproxen (Anaprox), indomethacin (Indocin), sulindac (Clinoril), mefenamic acid (Ponstel), tolmetin (Tolectin), piroxicam (Feldene), and ketoprofen (Orudis) (*Drug Facts and Comparisons* 2000).

Antibiotics

Drugs referred to by the layperson as "antibiotics" are more accurately described by the term *antibacterials*, although the more common term will be used here. For the most part, *antibiotics* are effective in treating infections caused by microorganisms classified as bacteria. Bacterial infections can occur anywhere in the body, resulting in tissue damage, loss of function, and, if untreated, ultimately death. Even though bacterial infections continue to be the most common serious diseases in the United States and throughout the world today, the vast majority of these can be cured with antibiotic treatment. There are currently close to 100 different antibiotic drugs, which differ from one another in (1) whether they kill bacteria (*bactericidal*) or stop their growth (*bacteriostatic*), and (2) the species of bacteria that are sensitive to

their antibacterial action (*Drug Facts and Comparisons* 2000). Antibiotics that are effective against many species of bacteria are classified as broad-spectrum types, whereas those antibiotics that are relatively selective and effective against only a few species of bacteria are considered narrow-spectrum drugs. Although most antibiotics are well tolerated by patients, they can cause very serious side effects, especially if not used properly. For example, the penicillins have a very wide margin of safety for most patients, but 5% to 10% of the population is allergic to these drugs and life-threatening reactions can occur in sensitized patients if penicillins are used. The most common groups of antibiotics include penicillins (e.g., amoxicillin—Amoxil, Augmentin, and Trimox), cephalosporins (e.g., cephalexin), fluoroquinolones (e.g., ciprofloxacin—Cipro), tetracyclines (e.g., minocycline—Minocin), aminoglycosides (e.g., streptomycin), sulfonamides (e.g., sufamethoxazole—Bactrim and Septra), and macrolides (e.g., erythromycin—E-Mycin).

Antidepressants

Severe depression is characterized by diminished interest or pleasure in normal activities accompanied by feelings of fatigue, pessimism, and guilt as well as sleep and appetite disturbances and suicidal desires (American Psychiatric Association 2000). Severe depression afflicts approximately 5% to 6% of the population at any one time, and it is estimated that about 17% of the population will become severely depressed during their life (Cooper 1998). This high prevalence makes depression the most common psychiatric disorder (Cooper 1998). According to the classification of the *Diagnostic and Statistical Manual of Mental Disorders* (DSM-IV-TR) of the American Psychiatric Association, several types of depression exist, based on their origin:

1. *Endogenous major depression,* a genetic disorder that can occur spontaneously and is due to transmitter imbalances in the brain.

2. *Depression associated with bipolar mood disorder* (that is, manic-depressive disorder).

3. *Reactive depression,* the most common form of depression, which is a response to situations of grief, personal loss, illness, or other very stressful situations.

Antidepressant medication is typically used to treat endogenous major depression, although on occasion these drugs also are used to treat other forms of depression if they are resistant to conventional therapy (Cooper 1998).

Several groups of prescription antidepressant medication are approved for use in the United States (*Drugs Facts and Comparisons* 2000). The most commonly used category is the tricyclic antidepressants . Included in this group are drugs such as amitriptyline (Elavil), imipramine (Tofranil), and nortriptyline (Pamelor). Although usually well tolerated, the tricyclic antidepressants can cause annoying side effects due to their anticholinergic activity. These adverse reactions include drowsiness, dry mouth, blurred vision, and constipation. Tolerance to these side effects usually develops with continued use.

The second group of drugs used to treat depression is referred to as the monoamine oxidase inhibitors (MAOIs) . Historically, these agents have been backup drugs for the tricyclic antidepressants. Because of their annoying and sometimes dangerous side effects as well as problems interacting with other drugs or even food, the MAOIs have become less popular with clinicians. Drugs belonging to this group include phenelzine (Nardil) and tranylcypromine (Parnate).

Agents from a third, somewhat disparate, group of antidepressants that are safer and with fewer side effects than the tricyclic or MAOI antidepressants are very poplar. They include fluoxetine (Prozac), sertraline (Zoloft), paroxetine (Paxil), fluvoxamine (Luvox), bupropion (Wellbutrin), and trazodone (Desyrel). Although side effects and the margin of safety of these groups of antidepressants may differ, in general they all appear to have similar therapeutic benefits. Of this third group of antidepressants, Prozac is the best known and the most frequently prescribed antidepressant; in 1999, it was the 10th most frequently prescribed drug in the United States (see Table 16.7). Although most commonly used to treat depression, Prozac has also been prescribed by physicians to treat more than 30 other conditions ranging from drug addiction (such as cocaine dependence) to kleptomania. The vast majority of these uses are not proven to be effective nor are they approved by the FDA (Sewester 1995).

Antidiabetic Drugs

Diabetes mellitus afflicts 3% of the people in the United States and is the result of insufficient activity of insulin, a hormone secreted from the pancreas (Gasbarro 1999). Due to the lack of insulin, untreated diabetics have severe problems with metabolism and elevated blood sugar (called hyperglycemia). The two major types of diabetes are type I (or juvenile type) and type II (or adult-onset type). Type I diabetes is caused by total destruction of the insulin-producing cells in the pancreas and usually begins in juveniles, but it occasionally begins during adulthood. In contrast, type II diabetes occurs most often after 40 years of age and is frequently associated with obesity: in these patients, the pancreas is able to produce insulin, but insulin receptors no longer respond normally to this hormone (Gasbarro 1999). In both types of diabetes mellitus, drugs are administered to restore proper insulin function.

Because of the inability to produce or release insulin in the type I diabetic, these patients are universally treated with subcutaneous injections of insulin one to three times a day, depending on their needs. Usually the levels of sugar (glucose) in the blood are evaluated to determine the effectiveness of treatment. Insulin products are characterized by

---

KEY TERMS

tricyclic antidepressants
most commonly used group of drugs to treat severe depression

monoamine oxidase inhibitors (MAOIs)
group of drugs used to treat severe depression

diabetes mellitus
disease caused by elevated blood sugar due to insufficient insulin

hyperglycemia
elevated blood sugar

type I diabetes
associated with complete loss of insulin-producing cells in the pancreas

type II diabetes
usually associated with obesity; does not involve a loss of insulin-producing cells

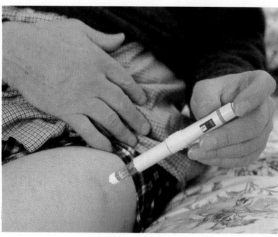

Insulin is self-administered by diabetic patients in subcutaneous injections.

rological condition characterized by recurring seizures (that is, uncontrolled hyperactivity of the brain). Seizures are classified according to the region of the brain involved and how far the hyperactivity spreads. Thus, seizures are considered to be either *partial* (brain involvement stays local) or *generalized* (brain involvement is widespread) and can involve severe motor activity (e.g., grand mal seizures) or few motor symptoms (e.g., petit mal seizures). Because of the diverse nature of different types of epilepsy, several drugs are used as antiepileptics. Thus, phenytoin (Dilantin), carbamazepine (Tegretol), and phenobarbital are prescribed to control partial and grand mal seizures, whereas ethosuximide (Zarontin) and valproic acid (Depakene) are used to treat generalized and petit mal seizures (*Drugs Facts and Comparisons* 2000).

their onset of action and duration of effects. Two types of insulin are used: *short-acting* (regular) and *medium-acting* (NPH and lente) types.

The strategy for treating type II diabetics is somewhat different. For many of these patients, the symptoms of diabetes, and problems of insufficient insulin function, subside with proper diet, weight, and exercise management. If an appropriate change in lifestyle does not correct the diabetes-associated problems, drugs called oral hypoglycemics (meaning they are taken by mouth and lower blood sugar) are often prescribed. These drugs, which stimulate the release of additional insulin from the pancreas, include popular drugs such as metformin (Glucophage). If the diabetic symptoms are not adequately controlled with the oral hypoglycemic drugs, type II diabetics are treated with insulin injections, as are type I patients. There has been substantial improvement in the treatment of diabetes in the past few years due to new, more selective and effective drugs that control glucose blood levels (Kim et al. 1999).

Antiepileptic Drugs

Approximately 1% of the population in the United States has some form of epilepsy . Although appropriate medication can control the disease in 80% of these patients, many people in this country with epilepsy are inadequately treated. Epilepsy is a neu-

Antiulcer Drugs

Peptic ulcers are sores that recur in the lining of the lower stomach (*gastric ulcer*) or most often in the upper portion of the small intestines (*duodenal ulcer*). It is apparent that secretions of gastric acids and digestive enzymes are necessary for ulcer development. Because gastric secretions are involved in developing peptic ulcers, several drug types are useful in ulcer treatment.

Antacids help to relieve acute discomfort due to ulcers by neutralizing gastric acidity. These drugs are discussed in greater detail in the OTC section of this chapter. Prescription drugs that block gastric secretion have been the mainstay of ulcer treatment. Because the endogenous chemical histamine is important in regulating gastric secretions, drugs that selectively block the activity of gastric histamine (called *H$_2$ blockers*) substantially reduce secretion of gastric acids and digestive enzymes. The very popular prescription drugs cimetidine (Tagamet), ranitidine (Zantac), and Pepcid function in this manner (Bernardi 1999). Because Tagamet, Zantac, and Pepcid are used so frequently, they have been switched to OTC status by the FDA—not to treat ulcers, but to relieve heartburn (*esophageal reflux*) (White-Sax 1999).

Although the exact causes of peptic ulcers are not completely understood, a role for the bacteria *Helicobacter pylori* is now widely accepted. Because of the involvement of these microorganisms, most clinicians treat patients with recurring ulcers with multiple antibiotics to eliminate these bacteria (Feldman 2001).

Bronchodilators

In 1999, the sixth leading drug for sales in this country was Albuterol, which widens air passages (*bronchi*) to facilitate breathing in patients with air passage constriction or obstruction ("Top 200 Drugs" 2000). Such drugs are called bronchodilators and are particularly useful in relieving respiratory difficulty associated with asthma. Asthmatic patients frequently experience bouts of intense coughing, shortness of breath, tightness in the chest, and wheezing. Many of the symptoms of asthma are due to an increased sensitivity of the airways to irritating substances and can result in serious asthma attacks that are life-threatening if not treated promptly. Two major categories of bronchodilators include sympathomimetics known as β-adrenergic stimulants —for example, isoproterenol (Isuprel) and albuterol (Proventil and Ventolin)—and xanthines (caffeine-like drugs) such as theophylline and its derivatives. These drugs relax the muscles of the air passages, cause bronchodilation, and facilitate breathing. In the early 1990s, some bronchial dilator medications were switched to OTC status, such as Bronkaid Mist and Primatene Mist.

Cardiovascular Drugs

Cardiovascular disease has been the number one cause of death in the United States for the past several decades. Consequently, of the 30 top-selling drugs in this country, 6 are medications for diseases related to the cardiovascular system ("Top 200 Drugs" 2000). The following are brief discussions of the major categories of cardiovascular drugs.

Antihypertensive Agents It is estimated that 15% of American adults require treatment for hypertension (persistent elevated high blood pressure) (Smith 2000). Because hypertension can result in serious damage to heart, kidneys, and brain, this condition needs to be treated aggressively. Treatment should consist of changes in lifestyle, including exercise and diet, but usually also requires drug therapy. Two of the principal antihypertensive agents are diuretics and direct vasodilators (Smith 2000):

1. *Diuretics* are drugs that lower blood pressure by eliminating sodium and excess water from the body. Included in this category is hydrochlorothiazide (Dyazide).

2. *Direct vasodilators* reduce blood pressure by relaxing the muscles in the walls of blood vessels that cause vasoconstriction, thereby dilating the blood vessels and decreasing their resistance to the flow of blood. Drugs included in this category are calcium-channel blockers (diltiazem [Cardizem], verapamil [Calan], nifedipine [Procardia]); inhibitors of the enzyme that synthesizes the vasoconstricting hormone, angiotensin II (enalapril [Vasotec]); and drugs that block the vasoconstricting action of the sympathetic nervous system (clonidine [Catapre]; prazosin [Minipres]).

Antianginal Agents When the heart is deprived of sufficient blood (a condition called ischemia), the oxygen requirements of the cardiac muscle are not met and the breakdown of chemicals caused by the continual activity of the heart results in pain; this viselike chest pain is called angina pectoris . The

---

KEY TERMS

oral hypoglycemics
drugs taken by mouth to treat type II diabetes

epilepsy
disease consisting of spontaneous, repetitive seizures

peptic ulcers
open sores that occur in the stomach or upper segment of the small intestine

bronchodilators
drugs that widen air passages

β-adrenergic stimulants
drugs that stimulate a subtype of adrenaline and noradrenaline receptors

hypertension
elevated blood pressure

ischemia
tissue deprived of sufficient blood and oxygen

angina pectoris
severe chest pain usually caused by a deficiency of blood to the heart muscle

most frequent cause of angina is obstruction of the large coronary vessels (Katzung and Chatterjee 1995). Angina pectoris frequently occurs in patients with hypertension; left untreated, the underlying blockage of coronary vessels can result in heart attacks. All the drugs used to relieve or prevent angina decrease the oxygen deficit of the heart by either decreasing the amount of work required of the heart during normal functioning or by increasing the blood supply to the heart (Katzung and Chatterjee 1995). The three types of drugs prescribed for treating angina pectoris are (1) calcium-channel blockers (e.g., verapamil [Calan], and diltiazem [Cardizem]), (2) nitrates and nitrites (e.g., amylnitrite [Vaporate], and nitroglycerin [Transderm-Nitro]), and (3) blockers of the sympathetic nervous system, specifically classified as β-adrenergic blockers (e.g., atenolol [Tenormin], and propranolol [Inderal]).

Drugs to Treat Congestive Heart Failure When the cardiac muscle is unable to pump sufficient blood to satisfy the oxygen needs of the body, congestive heart failure occurs. This condition causes an enlarged heart, decreased ability to exercise, shortness of breath, and accumulation of fluid (edema) in the lungs and limbs (Katzung and Parmley 1995). The principal treatment for congestive heart failure consists of drugs that improve the heart's efficiency, such as digoxin (Lanoxin).

Drugs that cause vasodilation are also sometimes used successfully to reduce the work required of the heart as it pumps blood through the body. Among the drugs causing vasodilation are those already discussed in conjunction with other heart conditions such as hypertension and angina pectoris (e.g., enalapril [Vasotec], and captopril [Capoten]).

KEY TERMS

congestive heart failure
heart is unable to pump sufficient blood for the body's needs

edema
swollen tissue

hypothyroidism
thyroid gland does not produce sufficient hormone

Cholesterol and Lipid-Lowering Drugs Cholesterol and some types of fatty (*lipid*) molecules can accumulate in the walls of arteries and narrow the openings of these blood vessels. Such arterial changes cause hypertension, heart attacks, strokes, and heart failure and are the leading cause of death in the United States and other Western countries (Witztum 1995). These health problems can often be avoided by adopting a lifestyle that includes a low-fat and low-cholesterol diet combined with regular, appropriate exercising. However, sometimes lifestyle changes are insufficient; in such cases, cholesterol-lowering drugs can be used to prevent the damaging changes in blood vessel walls. The drugs most often used include lovastatin (Mevacor), cholestyramine (Questran), and niacin (vitamin B_3).

Hormone-Related Drugs

As explained in Chapter 5, hormones are released from endocrine (ductless) glands and are important in regulating metabolism, growth, tissue repair, reproduction, and other vital functions. When there is a deficiency or excess of specific hormones, body functions can be impaired, causing abnormal growth, imbalance in metabolism, disease, and often death. Hormones, or hormone-like substances, are sometimes administered as drugs to compensate for an endocrine deficiency and to restore normal function. This is the case for (1) insulin used to treat diabetes (see the earlier discussion for more details), (2) levothyroxine (Synthroid, an artificial thyroid hormone) to treat hypothyroidism (insufficient activity of the thyroid gland), and (3) conjugated estrogens (Premarin) to relieve the symptoms caused by estrogen deficiency during menopause.

Hormones can also be administered as drugs to alter normal body processes. Thus, drugs containing the female hormones, estrogen and progesterone (norethindrone, ethinyl estradiol [Ortho Novum]), can be used as contraceptives to alter the female reproductive cycles and prevent pregnancy. Another example involves drugs related to *corticosteroids* (hormones from the cortex of the adrenal glands), which are often prescribed because of their immune-suppressing effects. In high doses, the corticosteroid drugs (e.g., triamcinolone [Kenalog]) reduce symptoms of inflammation and are used to treat severe forms of inflammatory diseases, such as arthritis (*Drug Facts and Comparisons* 2000).

Sedative-Hypnotic Agents

The sedative-hypnotics are discussed in considerable detail in Chapter 7. Because of the high incidence of anxiety and sleep disorders in the United States (Shuster 1996), drugs that encourage relaxation and drowsiness are frequently prescribed and are usually included in the list of top-selling prescription drugs ("Top 200 Drugs" 2000). Benzodiazepines commonly prescribed are clonazepam (Klonapin) and lorazepam (Ativan) ("Top 200 Drugs" 2000).

Drugs to Treat HIV

Although not included in the top 30 list of prescription drugs (see Table 16.7), medications to treat HIV infection are of special relevance to drug abuse because of the high prevalence of infection by this deadly virus in intravenous drug addicts. The issue of AIDS and drug abuse is discussed at length in Chapter 18; of relevance to our discussion on prescription drugs are recent advances in pharmacological management of this disease. Although no cure for HIV or immunization against this virus is available yet, some drug therapies can delay the onset or slow the progression of this infection. The first drugs to be used effectively in AIDS therapy are the "transcriptase inhibitors" such as AZT (zidovudine) and Stavudine, which block a unique enzyme essential for HIV replication (*Drug Facts and Comparisons* 2000). Another group of anti-AIDS drugs called the *protease inhibitors* prevent HIV maturation; they include the recently approved drug, Saquinar. The protease inhibitors are particularly effective when used in combination with the transcriptase inhibitor drugs (*Drug Facts and Comparisons 2000*).

Common Principles of Drug Use

Probably the most effective way to teach people not to use drugs improperly is to help them understand how to use drugs correctly. This goal can be achieved by educating the drug-using public about both prescription and OTC drug products. If people can appreciate the difference between the benefits of therapeutic drug use and the negative consequences of drug misuse or abuse, they are more likely to use medications in a cautious and thoughtful manner. To reach this level of understanding, patients must be able to communicate freely with health professionals. Before prescription or OTC drugs are purchased and used, patients should have all questions answered about the therapeutic objective, the most effective mode of administration, and side effects. Education about proper drug use greatly diminishes drug-related problems and unnecessary health costs.

To minimize problems, before using any drug product, the patient should be able to answer the following questions:

1. Why am I using this drug?
2. How should I be taking this drug?
3. What are the active ingredients in this drug product?
4. What are the most likely side effects of the drug?
5. How long should the drug be used?

Discussion Questions

1. Why are some prescription drugs appropriate for switching to OTC status?
2. What should the FDA use as a standard of safety when evaluating OTC and prescription drugs?
3. What role should the pharmacist play in providing information about OTC and prescription drugs to patients?
4. What type of formal training should be required before a health professional is allowed to prescribe drugs?
5. What kinds of questions should be asked by a health professional to ensure that a patient has sufficient understanding concerning a drug to use it properly and safely?

6. What are the basic rules for using OTC drugs properly?

7. Should the FDA require that generic and proprietary versions of the same drug be exactly the same?

8. Even though some antibiotics have a wide margin of safety, currently there is no systemic antibiotic available OTC. Why is the FDA not willing to make some of these drugs nonprescription?

9. Should herbal remedies be required to be safe and effective by the FDA like other OTC drug products?

Key Terms

analgesics 412

salicylates 412

anti-inflammatory 413

steroids 413

nonsteroidal anti-inflammatory drugs (NSAIDs) 413

antipyretics 413

Reye's syndrome 413

congestion rebound 415

antitussive 416

expectorants 416

gastritis 419

anorexiants 420

keratolytics 421

keratin layer 421

SPF (sun protection factor) number 422

generic 427

proprietary 427

tricyclic antidepressants 431

monoamine oxidase inhibitors (MAOIs) 431

diabetes mellitus 431

hyperglycemia 431

type I diabetes 431

type II diabetes 431

oral hypoglycemics 432

epilepsy 432

peptic ulcers 432

bronchodilators 433

β-adrenergic stimulants 433

hypertension 433

ischemia 433

angina pectoris 433

congestive heart failure 434

edema 434

hypothyroidism 434

Summary

1 Prescription drugs are available only by recommendation of an authorized health professional, such as a physician. Nonprescription (OTC) drugs are available on request and do not require approval by a health professional. In general, OTC medications are safer than their prescription counterparts but often less effective.

2 The switching policy of the FDA is an attempt to make available more effective medications to the general public on a nonprescription basis. This policy has been implemented in response to the interest in self-treatment by the public and in an attempt to reduce health care costs.

3 Drugs recently switched by the FDA to OTC status include ulcer medications, such as Tagamet and Zantac, and medications for asthma.

4 Potential problems that come by making more effective drugs available OTC include overuse

and inappropriate use, leading to dependence and other undesirable side effects. For example, these more effective drugs could encourage self-treatment of medical problems that require professional care.

5 Information on OTC product labels is crucial for proper use of these drugs and thus is regulated by the FDA. Product labels must list the active ingredients and their quantities in the product. Labels must also provide instructions for safe and effective treatment with the drug as well as cautions and warnings.

6 Many herbal products contain active drugs and have become very popular. The lack of regulation make these remedies difficult to assess for either efficacy or safety.

7 Although OTC drug products can be useful for treatment of many minor to moderate, self-limiting medical problems, when used without proper precautions, they can cause problems.

8 The principal drug groups available OTC are used in the treatment of common, minor medical problems and include analgesics, cold remedies, allergy products, mild stimulants, sleep aids, antacids, laxatives, antidiarrheals, antiasthmatics, acne medications, sunscreens, contraceptives, and nutrients.

9 In order for drugs to be prescribed properly, patients need to provide complete and accurate information about their medical condition and medical history to their physicians. In turn, the provider needs to communicate to the patient what is being treated, why the drug is being used, how it should be used for maximum benefit, and what potential side effects can occur.

10 Proprietary drug names can only be used legally by the drug company that has trademark rights. Often, the original proprietary name becomes the popular name associated with the drug. Because the pharmaceutical manufacturer that develops a drug is trying to recover the investment, a newly marketed proprietary drug is expensive. Once the patent rights expire, other drug companies can also market the drug but under a different name; often, the common, generic name is used because it cannot be trademarked. The generic brands are less expensive because the manufacturers do not need to recover any significant investment. Generally, the less expensive generic drug is as effective and safe as the proprietary counterpart.

11 Of the approximately 1500 different prescription drugs currently available in the United States, the most commonly prescribed groups are analgesics, antibiotics, antidepressants, drugs used for diabetes, antiulcer drugs, antiepileptic drugs, bronchodilators, drugs used to treat cardiovascular diseases, hormone-related drugs, and sedative-hypnotics.

12 Abuse of prescription drugs is a serious problem in the United States. Some patients try to persuade clinicians or pharmacists to make prescription medication available by using deceit or intimidation. Legal drugs obtained in this manner are often used to relieve drug dependence or to reduce withdrawal symptoms from illicit substances.

References

"A Hacker's Guide to Cough Remedies." *Wellness Letter* (UC Berkley) (October 1995): 3.

AHFS. *American Hospital Formulary Service Drug Information.* Bethesda, MD: American Society of Health-System Pharmacists, Inc., 2000.

American Psychiatric Association. *Diagnostic and Statistical Manual of Mental Disorders*, 4th ed. revised [DSM-IV-TR]. American Psychiatric Association, Washington, D.C. (2000).

CDER. "Office of Generic Drugs." *FDA, Center for Drug Evaluation and Research* (November 2000). Available www.fda.gov/cder/ogd/index.htm.

Consumer Report. The Mainstreaming of Alternative Medicine (May 2000): 17–24.

Consumer Report Books. *The New Medicine Show.* New York: Consumer Report Books, 1989.

Cooper, C. "The Pharmacist's Role in Treating Clinical Depression." *Pharmacy Times* (June 1998): 39–42.

Covington, T. "Trends in Self-Care: The Rx to OTC Switch Movement." *Drug Newsletter* 12 (February 1993): 15–6.

Dale, J. "The Common Cold." *Pharmacy Times.* Patient Education Colds (November 2000). Available www.pharmacytimes.com/patedcold.html.

Dighe, S. V. "A Review of the Safety of Generic Drugs." *Transplant Proceedings* 31 (3A suppl) (1999): 23S–4S.

Doheny, K. "The Skinny on Diet Pills." *American Druggist* (February 1993): 32–6.

Drug Facts and Comparisons. St Louis: Wolters Kluwer Co., 2000.

Druglinks. "Why Patients Use Alternative Medicines." *Druglinks* (July 1998): 54.

Eggert, A. and L. Crismon. "Dealing with Insomnia." *American Druggist* (May 1992): 83–96.

Feldman, M., B. Cryer, D. Mallat, and M. Go. "Role of Helicobacterpylori infection in gastroduodenal injury and gastric prostaglandin synthesis during long term/low dose aspirin therapy: a prospective placebo-controlled double-blind randomized trial." *Amer. J. Gastroenterology* 96 (2001) 1751–7.

Frontlines. "Emotional 'Aspirin' " *Consumer Reports* (December 2000): 60–2.

Frontlines. "Herbal Supplements, What's in the Chips?" *Consumer Reports* (December 2000a): 8.

Foreman, J. "Ginseng: $350 Million for Not Much." *Boston Globe* (3 February 1997): C-4.

Fugh-Berman, A. "Herb-drug Interactions." *Lancet* 355 (2000): 134–8.

"Full Sun Protection." *Wellness Letter* (June 1993): 4–5.

Gasbarro, R. "Counseling the Patient with Diabetes." *Pharmacy Times* (October 1999): 53–66.

Gilbertson, W. "The FDA's OTC Drug Review." In *Handbook of Nonprescription Drugs*, 10th ed., edited by T. Covington, 21–37. Washington, DC: American Pharmaceutical Association, 1993.

Gill, M. "The Pharmacist's Role in Sleep Disorders." *Pharmacy Times* (August 1999): 103–16.

Greenberg, S. *Physician's Desk Reference for Nonprescription Drugs*, 17th ed. Oradell, NJ: Medical Economics Data, 1996.

Gruber, A. J. and Pope, H. G. "Ephedrine Abuse Among 36 Female Weightlifters." *American Journal of Addiction* 7 (1998): 256–61.

Holt, C. "The Evolution of the OTC Drug History." *American Druggist* 213 (1996): 51–60.

Hsu, I. "Prescription to Over-the-Counter Switches." *American Druggist* (July 1994): 57–64.

Katzung, B., and K. Chatterjee. "Vasodilators and the Treatment of Angina Pectoris." In *Basic and Clinical Pharmacology*, 4th ed., edited by B. Katzung, 171–87. Norwalk, CT: Appleton & Lange, 1995.

Katzung, B. and W. Parmley. "Cardiac Glycosides and Other Drugs Used in Congestive Heart Failure." In *Basic and Clinical Pharmacology*, 6th ed., edited by B. Katzung, 188–204. Norwalk, CT: Appleton & Lange, 1995.

Kim, Y., A. An and E. Deng. "Advances in the Treatment of Type 2 Diabetes Mellites: Focus on Insulin Resistance." *Pharmacy Times* (June 1999): 78–86.

Klein-Schwartz, W. and J. Hoopes. "Patient Assessment and Consultation." In *Handbook of Nonprescription Drugs*, 10th ed., edited by T. Covington, 11–20. Washington, DC: American Pharmaceutical Association, 1993.

Krowchuk, D. "Managing Acne in Adolescents." *Pediatric Clinics of North America* 47 (2000): 841–57.

Lamy, P. ". . . And on Nonprescription Products." *Elder Care News* 9 (Summer 1993): 17.

Lane, E. "On 'Cloud 9'? Loose Regulation of Ephedrine." *Ogden Standard-Examiner* (21 April 1996): 5-E.

Longo, L. P., T. Parran, B. Johnson, and W. Kinsey. "Addiction: Part II. Identification and Management of the Drug-seeking Patient." *American Family Physician* 61 (2000): 2401–81.

MacDonald, S. "Use with Care: Medicines Can Cure, or Kill." *Salt Lake Tribune* (3 September 1998): B-1.

Mackowiak, E. "The Common Cold: Prevention and Treatment." *Pharmacy Times* (November 1999): 95–106

McCormick, E. "Rx to OTC: A Growth Industry?" *Pharmacy Times* (December 1992): 69–74.

Medical Letter. "Sunscreens: Are They Safe and Effective?" *The Medical Letter* 41 (7 May 1999): 43–4.

"New York County Bans Herbal Stimulant." *Pharmacy Times* 62 (May 1996): 8.

Nordenberg, T. "New Drug Label Spells It Out Simply." *FDA Consumer Magazine* (July/August 1999): Publication No. (FDA) 99-3232.

OTC Observations. "Facts and Figures About OTC Medicines." *Pharmacy Times* (suppl) (September 1998): 3.

Physician's Desk Reference, 54th ed. Oradell, NJ: Medical Economics Data, 2000.

Public Health Advisory. "Phenylpropanolamine Advisory." FDA Center for Drug Evaluations (November 2000). Available www.fda.gov/cder/drug/infopage/ppa/advsory.htm.

Sause, R. and R. Mangione. "Cough and Cold Treatment with OTC Medicine." *Pharmacy Times* (February 1991): 108–17.

Schultz, S. "Turning to Anything, Just to Get High. A Cough Syrup Ingredient Is a Popular Drug." *U.S. News and World Report* 128 (2000): 60.

Schwartz, R. "FDA Torches Sunscreen SPFs Greater than 30." *American Druggist* (July 1999): 22.

Sewester, S. "Fluoxetine: Unlabeled Uses and Dosage Range." *Drug Newsletter* 14 (March 1995): 24.

Shuster, J. "Insomnia: Understanding Its Pharmacological Treatment Options." *Pharmacy Times* 62 (August 1996): 67–76.

Simonsen, L. "Sun Exposure: The Stakes Are Rising." *Pharmacy Times* (May 1993): 25–31.

Slezak, M. "New England Journal Slaps 'Alternative' Industry." *American Druggist* (November 1998): 38.

Slezak, M. "Steering Patients to Switches." *American Druggist* (July 1996): 32–5.

Smith, S. "Treatment of Hypertension." *Pharmacy Times, ACPE Program* (November 2000). Available erpinfo.com/PTCE/content/Hypertension_CE.html.

Sprague, J. and J. Culbertson, "Weight Loss: An Overview of Anorexia Agents." *Pharmacy Times* (June 1997): 65–74.

Stewart, R. "Adverse Drug Reactions." In *Remington's Pharmaceutical Sciences*, 19th ed., edited by A. Gennaro, Easton, Pennsylvania, 1995.

Tatro, D. "Drug Interactions with Natural Product." *Drug Facts and Comparison News* (May 1999): 34–8.

Tatro, D. "Drug Therapy for Acne Vulgaris." *Druglink* (February 1998): 12–4.

Tinsley, J. A. "The Hazards of Psychotropic Herbs." *Minnesota Medicine* 82 (1999): 29–31.

"Top 200 Drugs of 1999." *Pharmacy Times* 66 (April 2000): 16.

Vasquez, C. and R. Vasquez. "Frequently Asked Questions About Generic Drugs." *GPR Patient Education* (November 2000). Available www.pharmacytimes.com/GPRpated.html.

Walsh, P. *Physicians's Desk Reference for Nonprescription Drugs and Dietary Supplements*, 21st ed. Montvale, NJ: Medical Economics, 2000.

Warholak-Juarez, T., M. Rupp, T. Salazar, and S. Foster. "Effect of Patient Information on the Quality of Pharmacists' Drug Use Review Decisions." *Journal of American Pharmaceutical Association* (Washington) 40 (2000): 500–8.

White, W. "The Dextromethorphan FAQ." (1995). Available Usenet alt.drugs.

White-Sax, B. "Educating Consumers About Sun Protection." *Pharmacy Times* (May 2000): 48–50.

White-Sax, B. "Help for Heartburn." *Pharmacy Times* (February 1999): 17–8.

White-Sax, B. "The Year in Review: OTCs of 1997." *Pharmacy Times* (March 1998): 42–6.

Wick, J. "Outsmarting Prescription Fraud." *Pharmacy Times* 61 (April 1995): 33–6.

Witztum, J. "Drugs Used in the Treatment of Hyperlipoproteinemias." In *The Pharmacological Basis of Therapeutics*, 9th ed., edited by J. Hardman and L. Limbird, 875–97. New York: McGraw–Hill, 1995.

Yates, K. M., A. O'Connor, and C. A. Horsley. "Herbal Ecstasy: A Case Series of Adverse Reactions." *New Zealand Medical Journal* 113 (2000): 315–7.

Zak, J. "OBRA '90 and DUR." *American Druggist* (October 1993): 57.

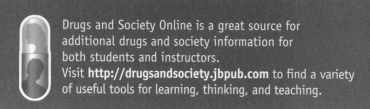
Drug Use Within Major Subcultures

Did You Know?

- Doping among world-class sports competitors is rampant.
- Athletes are much more likely than other subcultural groups to take drugs that enhance physical attributes.
- Approximately 500,000 teenagers use steroids and 52 million American children (12 and under) are using anabolic steroids.
- Women express greater concern about drug use than men.
- Overall, women consistently use fewer licit and illicit drugs than men.
- Drinking rates among adolescents are increasing more for girls than for boys.
- In general, in contrast to men, women are more likely to become addicted to tobacco.
- Approximately 70% of women in drug abuse treatment report histories of physical and sexual abuse with victimization beginning before 11 years of age and occurring repeatedly.
- Adolescents usually learn their attitudes about drug use from family models.
- Today, a significant rising number of adolescents report drug use with family members.
- Compared with adults who abuse drugs, drug-using adolescents are more likely to be involved in criminal activity.
- Research shows that teenage gangs are major players in the drug trade.
- Alcohol use is implicated in one-third to two-thirds of sexual assaults and acquaintance or date rape cases among teens and college students.
- Among drug using college students, 24% report using MDMA (Ecstasy) and psilocybin (mushrooms).
- Twenty-five to twenty-seven percent of all AIDS cases report injection drug use.
- Approximately 80% of all people with AIDS who are currently alive are male and 20% are female.
- African Americans comprise 47% of all reported U.S. AIDS cases, white Americans comprise 32%, and Hispanic Americans comprise 19%.
- An HIV-infected individual may not manifest symptoms of AIDS for as many as 10 to 20 years after the initial infection.
- Ninety-eight percent of movies depict illicit drug use, alcohol, tobacco, or over-the-counter/prescription medicines.

Chapter 17

Learning Objectives

On completing this chapter you will be able to:

▶ Know which drugs are most likely to be abused by athletes and why.

▶ Describe the use of drug testing in athletic competitions.

▶ Determine where anabolic steroids come from.

▶ Describe the purpose and goals of Adolescents Training and Learning to Avoid Steroids (ATLAS) prevention program.

▶ Explain the key differences between males and females regarding drug use.

▶ Explain two major ways women's history differs from men with regard to drug abuse.

▶ Explain the unique requirements that must be recognized and considered if women are to receive adequate treatment for drug dependence.

▶ Explain why adolescents use substances of abuse.

▶ Explain what types of parents are more likely to raise drug-abusing adolescents.

▶ List what type of drugs adolescents are most likely to abuse.

▶ Know the main factors motivating adolescents to join delinquent gangs.

▶ Know the major reasons why college students use drugs.

▶ List two major findings from research regarding drug use by college student subcultures.

▶ Know what "club drugs" are and how they are used.

▶ Explain how drug abuse contributes to the spread of AIDS.

▶ Know the key statistics regarding AIDS.

▶ List the major strategies to prevent contracting HIV.

▶ Know how the use of alcohol and other drugs is presented in popular movies and songs.

SEOUL 1988

Introduction

Although similarities appear in the patterns of addiction among drug users, the development of initial use and eventual abuse varies immensely from individual to individual. When attempting to understand common causes and patterns of drug use, examining subcultures often provides a semblance of group commonalities. A subculture is defined as a subgroup within the population whose members share similar values and patterns of related behaviors that differ from other subcultures and the larger population. Even though many subcultures can be so broad and diverse that all members may not be consciously aware of one another, nevertheless, from an outsider's perspective they qualify as subcultures because they share similar behavior patterns. For example, sport, gender, age, and drug subcultures are often very large across the United States, and all members of such subcultures cannot be aware of one another. However, from an outsider's perspective, they have similar patterns of behavior. When we refer to an insider's perspective, we are looking at a subculture from the inside and therefore expect the members to be aware of one another as a distinct group. An *insider's perspective* refers to viewing the subculture from the inside, just as members experience the ongoing activity. For example, a group of adolescents using drugs from a particular locality in a city or town and divorced women meeting to discuss coping with separation and being single qualify as distinct subcultures. Both insiders' and outsiders' perspectives include similar behavior patterns, just from different perspectives—inside and outside.

When defining a subculture, some sociologists refer to it as a "world within a world." Subcultures create and provide their members with lifestyle patterns that are observable, fairly consistent, and interwoven. Although it is a general perspective, viewing a group as a subculture offers a way to look at general distinctive patterns of drug use.

First, we examine why individuals within various subcultures would initially turn to drugs. The two types of forces that affect members of a subculture are internal and external forces, both of which affect these individuals' drug use behavior. *Internal subcultural forces* include:

1. Shared attitudes about drug users and nonusers.

2. Compatibility with other members of the peer group (often peer members share complementary personality traits).

3. Shared attitudes favorable to drug use despite conventional society's view that such behavior is deviant.

4. Addiction to drugs or, at minimum, habitual drug usage.

5. A common secrecy about drug use.

External subcultural forces include:

1. Preoccupation with law enforcement while procuring the drugs and while under the effects of illicit drugs.

2. Desire to identify other users and sellers of illicit drugs such as verifying the dependability of the drug dealer (who best to "hook-up" with).

3. Constant preoccupation regarding when more difficult-to-acquire–type drugs are available and seizing this opportunity.

4. Preoccupation with being caught using or acting high in public, at work, at school, or at a social function where drug use would be perceived as deviant social behavior.

To further understand how similar patterns of drug use and/or abuse occur, in this chapter we look at drug users from both outsiders' and insiders' perspectives, from the vantage point of the members belonging to a distinct subculture. This chapter examines drug use and potential abuse in the following seven *drug-using* subcultures:

1. Sports/athletics

2. Women

3. Adolescents

4. College students

5. HIV and AIDS carriers

6. A certain percentage of professional actors, actresses and entertainers who perform in movies

7. A certain percentage of internet users focused on illicit-drug use.

Athletes and Drug Abuse

Using performance-enhancing drugs for increased athletic ability is known as "doping". Current reports reveal that "'Doping' among world-class competitors is rampant, admit many athletes, and the governing bodies of individual sports, as well as the International Olympic Committee, turn a blind eye" (Begley et al. 1999, p. 49). Further, the reasons boil down to winning in sports, especially when millisecond differences exist between gold and silver medals. The differences between the two medals " . . . can amount to millions in endorsement contract and appearance fees..." (Begley et al. 1999, p. 49), and apparently the world of professional sports and " . . . drugs [performance enhancing drugs] go together like socks and sweat" (Begley et al. 1999, p. 49). To understand why athletes are willing to risk using these drugs, it is necessary to further explore the sports mind-set.

Young athletes receive exaggerated attention and prestige in almost every university, college, high school, and junior high school in the United States. Pressure to excel or be "the best" is placed on athletes by parents, peers, teachers, coaches, school administrators, the media, and surrounding community. The importance of sports is frequently distorted and even used by some to evaluate the quality of educational institutions (Lawn 1984) or the quality of living conditions in a city. Athletic success can determine the level of financial support these institutions receive from local and state governments, alumni, and other private donors; thus, winning in athletics often translates into fiscal stability and institutional prosperity.

For the athlete, success in sports means psychological rewards such as the admiration of peers, school officials, family, and community. In addition, athletic success can mean financial rewards such as scholarships, paid living expenses in college, advertising endorsement opportunities, and, for a few, incredible salaries as professional athletes. With the rewards of winning, athletes have to deal with the

> ### KEY TERMS
>
> **subculture**
> subgroup within the population whose members share similar values and patterns of related behaviors that differ from other subcultures and the larger population
>
> **outsider's perspective**
> viewing a group or subculture from outside the group and viewing the group and its members as an observer; looking "in" at the members
>
> **insider's perspective**
> viewing a group or subculture from inside the group; seeing members as they perceive themselves
>
> **"doping"**
> the use of performance enhancing drugs to increase athletic ability
>
> **ergogenic**
> drugs that enhance athletic performance

added pressures of not winning: "What will people think of me if I lose?" "When I lose, I let everybody down." "Losing shows that I am not as good as everyone thinks." These pressures on young, immature athletes can result in poor coping responses. Being better than competitors, no matter the cost, becomes the driving motivation, and doing one's best is no longer sufficient. Such attitudes may lead to serious risk-taking behavior in order to develop an advantage over the competition; this situation can include using drugs to improve performance.

The Canadian sprinter, Ben Johnson, once known as the fastest human in history, was banned for life from competitive running in March 1993 (Begley et al. 1999; Hoberman and Yesalis 1995). Five years earlier, at the 1988 Seoul Olympics, Johnson was stripped of a world's record for the 100-meter dash and forfeited the gold medal when his urine tested positive for steroids. Because of the first incident, Johnson was suspended from competition for 2 years. However, in 1992, the 31-year-old sprinter was attempting a comeback, with speeds that approached his world record times. In January 1993, a routine urine test determined Johnson was again using steroids to enhance his athletic performance (Ferrente 1993). Widely publicized incidents such as this one concerning illicit use of so-called ergogenic

(performance-enhancing) drugs by professional and amateur athletes have created intense interest in the problems of drug abuse in sports (Begley et al. 1999; Merchant 1992).

■ DRUGS USED BY ATHLETES

Yes, the steroids I used certainly made me get bigger. I was going out for football and I had just made the team, so I kept using them and the results were phenomenal. Now 2 years later, I won't be graduating. Several months ago, they removed a tumor on my liver, but they didn't get all the cancer. I am going home at the end of this semester. My parents want me to stay with them for the time I have left. When I go, I only have one wish—I want to die big and always be known as big Jim. (From Venturelli's research files, interview with a 20-year-old male, December 13, 1996.)

Studies have shown that athletes are not more likely than nonathletes to use some drugs of abuse such as marijuana, alcohol, barbiturates, cocaine, and hallucinogens (Hoberman and Yesalis 1995; Samples 1989). However, athletes *are* much more likely than other populations to take drugs that enhance (physically or psychologically), or are thought to enhance, competitive performance; these drugs include stimulants such as amphetamines and cocaine and an array of drugs with presumed ergogenic effects, such as anabolic steroids (Bell 1987). Some of the drugs that are abused by athletes are listed in Table 17.1, along with their desired effects. The following sections discuss the drugs that are most frequently self-administered by athletes in an effort to improve their competitive performance.

Anabolic Steroids

Anabolic steroids consist of a group of natural and synthetic drugs that are chemically similar to cho-

lesterol and related to the male hormone testosterone (Lukas 1993) and its artificial derivatives. Steroids are used for treatment of certain diseases such as specific types of anemia, some breast cancers, and testosterone deficiency. Although illegal when taken for nonmedical purposes, steroids have been illegally used by both athletes and nonathletes since the late 1950s to improve athletic ability and physical appearance because steroids have performance-enhancing and body-building properties. Steroids are taken orally or injected into the muscles. Although males and females use steroids, males have higher rates of use (SAMSA 1999).

Naturally occurring male hormones, or androgens , are produced by the testes in males. These hormones are essential for normal growth and development of male sex organs as well as secondary sex characteristics such as muscular development, male hair patterns, voice changes, and fat distribution. The androgens are also necessary for appropriate growth spurts during adolescence (*Drug Facts and Comparisons 1994*). The principal accepted therapeutic use for androgens is for hormone replacement in males with abnormally functioning testes. In such cases, the androgens are administered prior to puberty and for prolonged periods during puberty to stimulate proper male development (*Drug Facts and Comparisons* 1994).

Abuse of Anabolic Steroids by Athletes Under some conditions, androgen-like drugs can increase muscle mass and strength; for this reason, they are referred to as anabolic (able to stimulate the conversion of nutrients into tissue) steroids (because chemically, they are similar to the steroids produced in the adrenal glands) and are used by many athletes to improve performance (Burke and Davis 1992). It is estimated that as many as 1 million Americans have used or are currently using these drugs to achieve a "competitive edge" or for other purposes (Welder and Melchert 1993) (see Figure 17.1). Studies suggest that approximately 2% of college-age men and 6.7% of male high school students use anabolic steroids (Harlan and Garcia 1992).

Further, approximately 500,000 adolescents use steroids, and 52 million American *children* are using anabolic steroids " . . . a study in the journal *Pediatrics* last year found that 2.7% of Massachusetts middle-school athletes were using steroids" (Begley et al. 1999, p. 54). Another source indicates that

TABLE 17.1 **Partial List of Ergogenic Substances and Expected Effects**

DRUGS	EXPECTED RESULTS
Amino acids	Stimulate natural production of growth hormone
Amphetamines and cocaine	Increase strength, alertness, and endurance
Anabolic steroids	Increase muscle mass and strength
B-complex vitamins	Enhance body metabolism and increase energy
Caffeine	Reduce fatigue
Chromium	Enhance carbohydrate metabolism
Ephedrine	Improve breathing
Asthma medication	Improve breathing
OTC decongestants	Increase endurance
Thyroid hormone	Enhance metabolism and energy
β-blockers	Reduce hand tremor and stimulate growth hormone
Methylphenidate	Enhance alertness and endurance
Furosemide	Mask steroid use and enable rapid weight loss

Source: Harlan, R., and M. Garcia. "Neurobiology of Androgen Abuse." In *Drugs of Abuse,* edited by R. Watson, 185–201. Boca Raton, FL: CRC Press, 1992.

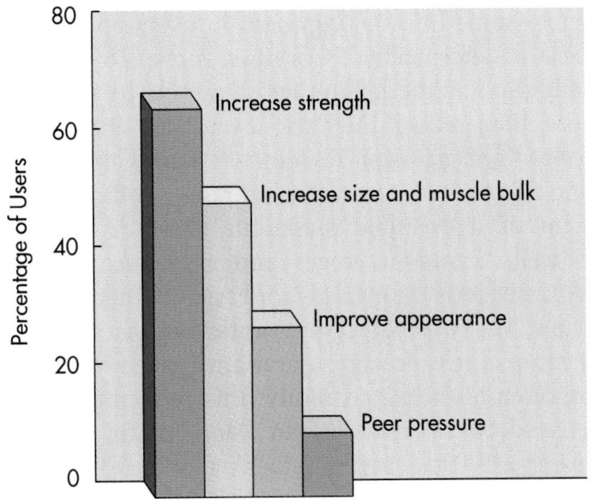

FIGURE 17.1

Reasons for nonmedicinal steroid use by college students.

Source: Harlan, R., and M. Garcia. "Neurobiology of Androgen Abuse." In *Drugs of Abuse*, edited by R. Watson, 186. Boca Roton, FL: CRC Press, 1992.

males are more likely to use and abuse steroids than females (NIDA 2000b), while " . . . steroid abuse is growing most rapidly among young women" (NIDA 2000, p. 2). In a much larger nationwide study, *The Monitoring the Future* 1999 survey reports that 2.7% of 8th and 10th graders and 2.9% of 12th graders reported that they had taken anabolic steroids at least once in their lives (NIDA 2000). Competition for scholarships and entry into professional sports are major factors that influence young athletes to use steroids (Scott et al. 1996).

Although the vast majority of anabolic steroid users are male, women involved in body building and strength and endurance sports also abuse these drugs. Among seniors in high school, 2.5% of the males reported steroid use in the past year compared with 0.5% of the females. These statistics are much lower among the 19 to 32 year olds—0.4%—with males accounting for all steroid use (Johnston et al. 1999).

The first report of use of anabolic steroids to improve athletic performance was in 1954 by the

Besides risking their health, athletes who choose to dope should remember that they are role models. Seventy-three percent of youth want to be like a famous athlete; 53% of youth say it is common for famous athletes to use banned substances to get ahead.

Russian weight-lifting team. These drugs' performance-enhancing advantages were quickly recognized by other athletes, and it has been estimated that as many as 90% of the competitors in the 1960 Olympic games used some form of steroid (Toronto 1992). Because of the widespread misuse and associated problems with the use of these drugs, anabolic steroids were classified as Schedule III controlled drugs (see Chapter 3 for drug schedules) in 1991 (Merchant 1992).

Due to federal regulations, individuals convicted of a first offense of trafficking with anabolic steroids can be sentenced to a maximum prison term of 5 years and a $250,000 fine. For a second offense, the prison term can increase to 10 years with a $500,000 fine. Even possession of illicitly obtained anabolic steroids can result in a 1-year term with at least a $1000 fine (U.S. Department of Justice 1991–1992).

Patterns of Abuse Geographical factors appear to have little to do with the use of anabolic steroids among athletes. In both inner-city and suburban schools, all are equally attracted to these drugs. However, some athletes are more inclined to abuse anabolic steroids than others. For example, football players have the highest rate of abuse; 9% self-reported out of 11 National Collegiate Athletic Association (NCAA) colleges and universities—a survey conducted by the NCAA—whereas track and field athletes have the least (4% reported) (NIH/NIDA 1998). Another study using a more indirect method of interviewing found rates three times higher than the percentages just reported. In addition, the likelihood of abusing these drugs increases as the level of competition increases. Usage rates were approximately 14% in the NCAA Division I athletes and 30% to 75% in professional athletes (Lukas 1993). In general, we find that usage patterns for the anabolic steroids can vary considerably according to athletes' motivation, the level of competition, the type of sport, and the pressure for winning. A survey of the athletes at 11 NCAA colleges and universities found that heaviest steroid use was by football players (9%) and that 4% of male track and field athletes also acknowledged use (NIH/NIDA 1998).

The pattern usually consists of self-administering doses that are 10 to 200 times greater than dosages used for legitimate medical conditions (Welder and Melchert 1993). Users take nonmedical anabolic-androgenic steroids in *cycles*, periods of use lasting 6 to 12 weeks or longer. "Stacking" these drugs means taking more than one at a time, which is common. The use of different steroids taken singly but in sequence is called "cycling". To avoid developing tolerance to a particular steroid ("plateauing"), athletes often stagger the various drugs, sometimes taking them in overlapping patterns or alternately. Users often move from a low daily dose at the beginning of a cycle to a higher dose, then reduce their use toward the end of the cycle ("pyramiding"). To combat steroids' unwanted side effects, such as severe skin rashes and development of irreversible masculine traits in women, as well as sudden anger and explosive physical aggressiveness (known as "roid rage" in men), other drugs such as diuretics, antiestrogens, human chorionic gonadotropin, and antiacne medication are often taken concurrently (this pattern of use is referred to by users as an "array"). In general, power athletes prefer stacking, whereas body builders prefer cycling.

Now that steroid use has been prohibited by almost all legitimate sporting organizations, urine testing just before the athletic event has become commonplace (Lukas 1993). Steroid-using athletes attempt to avoid detection by trying to fool the tests. These highly questionable strategies include the following (Lukas 1993; Merchant 1992):

- Using the steroid only during training for the athletic events, but discontinuing its use several weeks before the competition to allow the drug to disappear from the body. Because oral steroids are cleared from the body faster than the injectable types, they are usually discontinued 2 to 4 weeks and the injection steroids are stopped 3 to 6 weeks before competition.

- Taking drugs, such as probenecid, that block the excretion of steroids in the urine. Probenecid inhibits substance from reaching the urine. And urine tests are all that the International Olympic Committee (IOC) requires (Begley et al. 1999).

- Using diuretics and drinking large quantities of water to increase the urine output and dilute the steroid so that it cannot be detected by the test.

- Adding adulterant chemicals to the urine, such as Drano, Clorox, ammonia, or eye drops to invalidate the tests.

Recent Developments in Evading Detection One serious problem today according to Prince Alexandre de Merode, who has been in charge of the IOC's Medical Commission for 31 years is that:

> . . . the newest doping agents pose the risk of serious health problems, and even death. But a larger reason is that it is ridiculously easy to dope and not get caught. Doping and detection are like an arms race. First trainers discover a performance-enhancing drug. Then, sports officials develop a test for it. Trainers retaliate by inventing a way to elude the detectors. So far, doping has stayed a lap ahead.

Other comments from the same source include:

> "Undetectable drugs are 90 percent of estimated doping cases," said Hein Verbruggen, head of International Cycling Union (Begley et al. 1999, p. 50).

Chemists constantly use the 72 banned steroids to change the testosterone molecule. "All you have to do is take a steroid not on the list. Or, simply by going cold turkey a few weeks before competition, an

KEY TERMS

"stacking"
use of several types of steroids at the same time
"cycling"
use of different types of steroids singly, but in sequence
"plateauing"
developing tolerance to the effects of anabolic steroids
"pyramiding"
moving from a low daily dose at the beginning of the cycle to a higher dose, then reducing use toward the end of the cycle
"array"
use of other drugs while taking anabolic steroids to avoid possible side effects

athlete can get the muscle-bulking effects without getting caught" (Begley et al. 1999, p. 51). (See Table 17.2 for a list of new types of performance-enhancing substances that are invisible to official tests.)

Effects of Anabolic Steroids Low to moderate doses of anabolic steroids have little effect on the strength or athletic skills of the average adult. However, when high doses are used by athletes during intense training programs, these drugs cause significant gains in lean body mass (i.e., muscle) and strength while decreasing fat (Lukas 1993). Because most of these effects are transient and will disappear when steroid use is stopped, athletes feel compelled to continue using, and become psychologically hooked (Toronto 1992). The drugs are most likely to benefit athletes in contact and strength sports where increased muscle mass provides an advantage, such as weightlifting and football; anabolic steroids are less likely to benefit athletes involved in sports requiring dexterity and agility, such as baseball or tennis.

The risks caused by anabolic steroids are not completely understood. Most certainly, the higher the doses and the longer the use, the greater the potential damage these drugs can do to the body. Some of the adverse effects thought to occur with heavy steroid use (10 to 30 times the doses used therapeutically) include the following:

- Increased "bad" blood cholesterol levels, which could eventually clog arteries and cause heart attacks and strokes (NCADI 1999).

TABLE 17.2 **New Breed of Performance-Enhancing Substances That Are Invisible to Official Tests**

DRUG	WHAT DOES IT DO?	MASKING/ DETECTION	RISKS
Human growth hormone (HGH)	Stimulates the intracellular breakdown of body fat, allowing more to be used for energy.	This is a natural hormone, so added amounts don't show up in blood or urine tests.	Muscle and bone disfigurement—jutting forehead, elongated jaw. Also: heart and metabolic problems.
Erythropoletin (EPO)	Increases the number of red blood cells without having to "dope" using one's own blood.	It's extremely difficult to detect because the extra blood cells are the athlete's own.	Extra cells can make blood the consistency of yogurt. This can lead to a clot, heart attack, or stroke.
Testosterone	Used to build muscles. It lets the body recover quickly from strenuous exercise.	Rules allow up to five times the natural body level, giving athletes latitude.	Unnatural levels can cause heart disease, liver cancer, and impotence.
Steroids/ androstenedione	Anabolic steroids are incarnations of testosterone; androstenedione is a precursor molecule.	Water-based steroids (most common) are undetectable in urine after several weeks.	Synthetic testosterone carries the same risks as naturally occurring testosterone.
Stimulants	The first category the IOC tested for. They delay the symptoms of fatigue.	Stimulants such as amphetamines can be detected; diuretics can dilute them in urine.	Fatigue is the body saying "stop"—overriding that message can be dangerous.

Source: Begley, S. and M. Brant with Dickey, C., K. Helmstaedt, R. Nordland, and T. Hayden. "The Real Scandal." *Newsweek* (15 February 1999): 49.

- Increased risk of liver disorders, such as jaundice and tumors (Lukas 1993).

- Psychological side effects, including irritability, outbursts of anger ("roid rage"), mania, psychosis, and major depression.

- Possible psychological and physical dependence with continual use of high doses, resulting in withdrawal symptoms such as steroid craving (52%), fatigue (43%), depression (41%), restlessness (29%), loss of appetite (24%), insomnia (20%), diminished sex drive (20%), and headaches (20%) (Lukas 1993).

- Alterations in reproductive systems and sex hormones, causing changes in gender-related characteristics (Burke and Davis 1992): breast enlargement in males, breast reduction and bodily hair growth in females, infertility in both genders, and changes in genitalia—atrophy (shrinkage) of the penis and testicles in males and enlargement of external genitalia in females (Street et al. 1996).

- Changes in skin and hair in both genders: increased incidence and severity of acne, male pattern baldness, and increased body hair (Burke and Davis 1992).

- Persistent unpleasant breath odor (NCADI 1999).

- Swelling of the feet or lower limbs (NCADI 1999).

- Other changes, including stunted growth in adolescents, deepening of voice in females, and water retention, causing bloating (Burke and Davis 1992; Street et al. 1996).

Sources of Steroids Where do the anabolic steroids come from? About 50% of the anabolic steroids used in this country are prescribed by doctors; the other 50% are obtained from the black market.

Black market sources of steroids include drugs diverted from legitimate channels, smuggled from foreign countries—Brazil, Italy, Mexico, Great Britain, Portugal, France, and Peru (NIDA 1996)—are designated for veterinarian use, or inactive counterfeits (U.S. Department of Justice 1991–1992). Another source reports that recently, it was discovered that the primary source for steroids in the United States is the Baja, California area of Mexico (Yesalis and Cowart 1998). The steroids are manufactured in Mexico City and shipped to pharmacies in the Baja region. Some health food stores and mail-order firms also offer products with names similar to the prescription anabolic steroids, such as Dynabdin, Metrobolin, and Diostero. These "sham steroids" contain only vitamins, amino acids, or micronutrients (Merchant 1992).

Most steroids used for nonmedical purposes are illegally obtained. A major federal report indicates that sources of illicit steroids fall into three rough categories: (1) smuggled steroids manufactured licitly or illicitly abroad, (2) drugs legally manufactured in this country and diverted to illicit sales at various places in the distribution chain, and (3) drugs clandestinely produced domestically. A small minority of users obtain their drugs by prescription. Actual doses are often difficult to estimate because the product may have been produced in an uncontrolled laboratory with unknown quality control, may have been intended for veterinary use with its human equivalent doses not known, or may be counterfeit (NIH/NIDA 1998). Another report found that the majority of young people report that steroids are easily available through their friends and coaches (McCaffrey 1999).

Stimulant Use Among Athletes

There are often reports in the media of football, basketball, or baseball players who have tested positive in a drug-screening evaluation or who have been suspended from competition due to drug abuse. In 1986, reports of cocaine-related deaths of sports figures included basketball star Len Bias and professional football player Don Rogers. Perhaps such sports tragedies helped convince some U.S. youth of the dangers of stimulant abuse and contributed to the decline in drug abuse in the late 1980s (Johnston et al. 1993). Clearly, no one—not even an athlete—is immune from the risks of these drugs.

Amphetamines and cocaine are abused to improve athletic skills (McDonald 1995). However, it is not clear if stimulants actually enhance athletic performance or merely the athlete's perception of performance. Many athletes believe these drugs promote quickness, enhance endurance, delay fatigue, increase self-confidence and aggression, and mask pain (Hoberman and Yesalis 1995). In fact, some studies have shown that stimulants can improve some aspects of athletic performance, especially in the presence of fatigue (NIDA 1996). However, the risk of using stimulants in sports is substantial because these drugs mask extreme fatigue, increase the risk of heat exhaustion, and can have severe cardiovascular consequences, such as heart attacks and strokes (Bell 1987) (see "Case in Point," When Drugs Enter the Boxing Ring, on page 450).

Although some athletes would never consider using the hard stimulants, such as cocaine and amphetamines, milder stimulants that are legal and available over-the-counter (OTC) may be thought to be acceptable. Such stimulants include caffeine and OTC decongestants (for example, phenylpropanolamine and phenylephrine). These drugs can be a double-edged sword for the athlete. Their use can reduce fatigue, give a sense of energy, and even mask pain. But in high doses, especially when combined, they can cause nervousness, tremors, and restlessness, impair concentration, accelerate dehydration, and interfere with sleep ("OTC Drugs and Athletes" 1992). Some athletic competitions limit permissible blood levels of caffeine and do not allow the use of OTC stimulants such as decongestant drugs.

Miscellaneous Ergogenic Drugs

Most athletic organizations have banned the use of anabolic steroids and stimulants and are using more effective screening procedures to detect offenders. A result of this clamp-down has been the search for alternative performance-enhancing drugs by athletes who feel a need for such pharmacological assistance. The following are brief discussions of a few of these substitute ergogenic substances (for a more complete list, see Table 17.1).

Clenbuterol At the 1992 Olympic Games in Barcelona, Spain, at least four athletes, including German world sprint champion Katrina Krabbe,

CASE IN POINT

When Drugs Enter the Boxing Ring

When Oliver McCall entered the boxing ring to fight for the heavyweight championship on February 7, 1997, he was not alone. With him came the spectre of years of drug abuse.

Just 7 weeks before, McCall had been arrested for swinging a Christmas tree around a hotel lobby while in a drug-induced haze. A few years earlier, he was found in a crack house after having been mugged by a fellow addict, to whom he lost the $1.5 million check he had carried with him in a sock to buy drugs. These events were just two of many drug-related occurrences on his record. His most recent arrest, however, had been followed by a drug treatment program, which he attended daily.

But something went wrong the night of February 7. After having announced to a friend, "I want my title. I'm fighting for my life," McCall seemed to want to get knocked out. In the third round, in the middle of the ring, in front of a packed audience, he listlessly walked around as his opponent, Lennox Lewis, threw punches at

him. McCall dodged and bobbed his head, yet refused to fight back. After the fourth round, McCall stood alone, away from his corner, sobbing uncontrollably, seemingly having a nervous breakdown in front of a worldwide cable television audience. Fifty-five seconds into the fifth round, referee Mills Lane stopped the fight. Lewis was the winner. McCall, in more ways than one, was not.

While drugs have been an unwelcome part of sports in recent years, there are few cases where the consequences became more publicly evident. Here was a great contradiction for the world to see: Oliver McCall, the athlete who had never been knocked down, and Oliver McCall, the man floored by the pain and drugs in his life. McCall's trainer, George Benton, said, "It was hard to watch, but it could be the best thing that ever happened to the human race. Now a father can tell his kids, 'You see what you saw on T.V.? You see what happens on drugs?' It was a hell of a lesson."

Sources: Boston Globe (8 February 1997). New York Times (9 February 1997).

---

were disqualified from competition for using the drug clenbuterol to enhance their athletic performance (Merchant 1992). Not available in the United States, this drug is known as "Doper's Delight" and is supposed to improve breathing and increase strength. Currently, most athletic urine examinations test for it.

Erythropoietin Clinically, erythropoietin is a drug used to treat patients with anemia. Because it stimulates the production of *red blood cells* (the oxygen-carrying cells in the blood), it is thought that this drug enhances oxygen use and produces additional energy. Erythropoietin is being used as a substitute for blood doping. *Blood doping* is when athletes attempt to increase their number of red blood cells

by re-infusing some of their own blood (which has been stored) before an athletic event.

Erythropoietin is impossible to detect and has been reported to be used by athletes engaged in endurance activities such as long-distance cycling. The use of erythropoietin by athletes is extremely dangerous and is thought to be responsible for several deaths. It is also very expensive, which likely has helped to limit its abuse (Merchant 1992).

Human Growth Factor and Human Growth Hormone Relatively recently, athletes have begun to abuse two types of steroids: human growth factor (HGF) and its "designer drug" synthetic version, human growth hormone (HGH) . HGF, also known as *somatotropin*, is a hormone naturally secreted by the pituitary gland at the base of the brain that helps to achieve normal growth potential of muscles, bones, and internal organs. Some athletes claim that release of natural HGF can be simulated by using drugs such as levadopa (used to treat Parkinson's disease), clonidine (used to treat hypertension), and amino acids. Athletes use commercially prepared HGF because it cannot be distinguished from naturally occurring HGF.

Use of this hormone by athletes is limited, however, by its high cost. The benefits of HGF to athletic performance are very controversial, although the potential side effects are substantial, including abnormal growth patterns (called *acromegaly*), diabetes, thyroid gland problems, heart disease, and loss of sex drive (Merchant 1992).

In recent years, the synthetic HGH has become available in the form of a newly structured steroid-type analog sold in vials; this product is used to build muscle tissue, with corresponding decreases in body fat, without exercise (McDonald 1995). HGH is probably the most potent anabolic agent ever discovered, but it also one of the most expensive. In fact, HGH is so expensive that until the mid 1990s, " . . . its use in the United States was confined to pediatric endocrinologists who used it to treat undersized children" (McDonald 1995, p. C1). To date, no tests have proved capable of detecting HGH in the blood or urine. Also, the side effects of this drug remain largely unknown. As a result, this drug is highly vulnerable to abuse.

β (Beta)-Adrenergic Blockers The β-adrenergic blockers are drugs that affect the cardiovascular system and are frequently used to treat hypertension. They have been used in sports because they reduce the heart rate and signs of nervousness, which in turn quiets hand tremors. Consequently, these drugs are most likely to be used by individuals participating in sports that require steady hands, such as competitive shooting. The use of these drugs is prohibited by most athletic organizations (Merchant 1992).

Gamma-Hydroxybutyrate The substance gamma-hydroxybutyrate (GHB) is found naturally in the brain and has been used in England to treat insomnia. Athletes and body builders have used GHB to increase muscle mass and strength. Although the actual effects of the compound are

| KEY TERMS |

human growth factor (HGF)
a hormone that stimulates normal growth

human growth hormone (HGH)
a "designer drug" synthetic version of HGF

ATLAS program
Adolescents Training and Learning to Avoid Steroids (ATLAS) is an anabolic abuse prevention educational program that empowers student athletes to make the right choices about steroid use

not known, it has been reported to cause euphoria and increase the release of growth hormone. Acute poisoning with GHB has occurred, causing hospitalization; other adverse effects can include headaches, nausea, vomiting, muscle jerking, and even short-term coma, though full recovery has been universal ("Bodybuilding Drug" 1992; "Multistate Outbreak" 1994). Prolonged use may cause withdrawal (insomnia, anxiety, and tremor). GHB is especially dangerous when combined with central nervous system (CNS) stimulants such as amphetamines and cocaine.

■ PREVENTION AND TREATMENT

If the problem of drug abuse among athletes is to be dealt with effectively, sports programs must be designed to discourage inappropriate drug use and assist athletes who have developed drug abuse problems. Coaches and administrators should make clear to sports participants that substance abuse will never give an athlete a competitive advantage in their program and will not be tolerated. The Adolescents Training and Learning to Avoid Steroids (ATLAS) program , which was developed by Dr. Linn Goldberg of Oregon Health Sciences at the University of Portland, is one of the most successful prevention programs for steroid abuse. Athletes, coaches and team leaders are trained to educate team members about the effects of anabolic steroid abuse. Because adolescents already know that anabolic steroids build muscles and can increase athletic abilities, both desirable and adverse effects of steroid use are taught. Research has shown that information about anabolic steroids that fails to acknowledge potential benefits creates a credibility gap that can make youths distrustful of the prevention program. The program consists of three components: classroom, weight training, and parent information components to " . . . give the student athletes the knowledge and skills to resist steroid use and achieve their athletic goals in more effective, healthier ways . . . " (Goldberg et al. 1996, p. 1555):

1. The classroom component consists of football coaches and student leaders conducting highly interactive sessions that explore the effects of steroids, the elements of sports nutrition, and strength training alternatives to steroid use. In this setting, while the coaches introduce topics and act as leaders, the students are exploring and learning from one another (Goldberg et al. 1996).

2. In the weight-training component, research staff members conduct seven hands-on sessions that teach the students proper weight training techniques. (Goldberg et al. 1996).

3. The parent information component consists of discussions and information sessions with parents. The staff provides nutrition guidelines and seeks compliance while stressing the very best nutrition for the athletes and their families. Parents become more vigilant against steroid use and learn to enjoy well-balanced, nutritional meals (Goldberg et al. 1996).

Briefly summarized, results indicate that the students who participated in this program in comparison with the control group (a group of students not participating in the program), showed they (1) knew more about proper exercise, (2) had a clear understanding of the dangers of using steroids and had become much more sensitized to the harmful effects of such drugs, (3) held more unfavorable views of others' use of anabolic steroids, and (4) were more likely to avoid unhealthy eating (such as frequenting fast food restaurants) (Goldberg et al. 1996).

Drug Use Among Women

Until recently, little was known about the patterns of female drug abuse. In general, most clinical drug abuse research, including treatment and rehabilita-

tion outcomes, was either conducted in male populations and the results were extrapolated to women or the research was done in general populations with little regard to gender influences (Alexander et al. 2001, Dicker and Leighton 1994; Lin 1994). Most researchers considered drug abuse to be a male problem. Today, the research focusing on women and drug use is better, but a greater amount of research is still needed. We still find that scientists performing even basic research with animals generally prefer male animal models in order to avoid the hormonal complexities of female animals. However, a growing concern for the importance of unique emotional, social, biochemical, and hormonal features in females has caused researchers to acknowledge the importance of gender differences.

■ WOMEN MORE CONCERNED ABOUT DRUG USE THAN MEN

Women are expressing greater concerns about drug use than men. Regarding the question of whether drugs abuse is a greater problem now than 5 years earlier, 51% of women and 42% of men answered "yes" (Drug Strategies 1998). Responding to whether drug use is a big concern among youth, 58% of women and 48% of men answered "yes" (Drug Strategies 1998). Further, 58% of women and 50% of men thought it was wrong to reduce prevention funds while increasing prison funds (Drug Strategies 1998). One reason for this may be that women traditionally have been primary caregivers; therefore, they feel more responsible about issues that can plague their communities and their families and often feel the need to be more vocal and be in positions that maintain harmony within the family setting. Women also generally express more concerns about safety issues than men because they are more likely to be victims of violent crimes, such as muggings or sexual assaults.

■ PATTERNS OF DRUG USE: COMPARING FEMALES WITH MALES

Recent surveys comparing male and female drug use patterns confirm that differences exist among the licit and illicit drug-using populations. Table 17.3 compares annual female and male drug use.

In addition, other research findings indicate the following gender-related differences in drug use:

1. Overall, females consistently use fewer licit and illicit drugs (24% of females versus 31% of males use illicit drugs).

2. More males (5.2%) than females (2.1%) use marijuana daily. Also, on a daily basis, males consume alcohol more often (1.9% of females and 6.8% of males) and binge drink (five or more drinks in a row) more frequently (23% of females and 44% of males) (Johnston et al. 1999)

3. Steroid use among young adults is much more prevalent among males than females. Among high school seniors, 2.8% of the males reported

TABLE 17.3 Annual Use of Various Types of Drugs, by Gender, 1998 (percent of population)

	FEMALES	MALES	TOTAL
Any illicit drug	24.5	31.0	27.3
Any illicit drug other than marijuana	10.0	14.9	12.1
Marijuana	21.9	28.4	24.7
Inhalants	1.4	2.1	1.7
Hallucinogens	2.6	6.3	4.2
LSD	1.7	4.3	2.8
PCP	0.8	0.1	0.5
Cocaine	3.3	6.5	4.7
Crack	0.6	1.5	1.0
Other cocaine	3.1	6.0	4.3
MDMA (Ecstasy)	1.9	2.5	2.2
Heroin	0.3	0.5	0.4
Other opiates	2.5	3.7	3.0
Stimulants	3.8	4.1	3.9
Crystal methamphetamine (ice)	0.8	1.3	1.0
Barbiturates	1.8	2.6	2.2
Tranquilizers	3.3	4.1	3.6
Steroids	0.0	0.8	0.4
Alcohol	83.4	84.6	83.9
5+ drinks in a row in the last 2 weeks	22.9	43.9	31.8
Cigarettes	37.4	39.4	38.3
Half-pack or more per day	13.6	16.8	15.0

Source: National Survey on Drug Abuse from *The Monitoring the Future Study*, 1975–1998; College and Young Adults; L. D. Johnston, P. M. O'Malley, J. G. Bachman; The University of Michigan Institute for Social Research, National Institute on Drug Abuse, U.S. Department of Human Services, National Institutes of Health, 1999.

steroid use in the past year versus 0.3% of females (Johnston et al. 1999).

One finding that is often hidden by *current* drug use statistics is that nationwide surveys confirm that drug use is increasing among women, often more rapidly than among men (Drug Strategies 1998). From 1990 through 1996, the number of women seeking emergency treatment rose more rapidly than the number of men seeking such emergency treatment. Hospital records indicate that there were more women seeking emergency treatment for heroin and marijuana (Drug Strategies 1998). Other gender differences are that older women (over 60) tend to abuse tranquilizers, sedatives, and antidepressants (Drug Strategies 1998) and in some cases, girls in junior high and high school are now surpassing boys with regard to alcohol and tobacco use. Drinking rates are increasing more for girls than for boys (Drug Strategies 1998), and women in general are more likely than men to become addicted to tobacco. Two factors that make smoking attractive to women (and girls) are that they believe it reduces stress and controls weight (Drug Strategies 1998).

Although some similarities appear between genders in drug usage rates for specific types of drugs, the general differences in the prevalence rates for females and males compel researchers to look for explanations so that we can better understand and deal with gender-related drug abuse problems.

■ FEMALE ROLES AND DRUG ADDICTION

Women are expected to take on more responsibilities than in my mother's days. Not only are we expected to work like men but also take care of the house, worry about the children, and get dinner on the table. If the house needs cleaning, everyone looks at the woman of the house. Men still have these expectations. I know things are changing with more equality between the sexes, but *real* equality of responsibilities has yet to occur. After everyone gets to bed on weekdays, I have a few drinks in order to calm me down before I go to bed. *(From Venturelli's research files, interview with a 43-year-old female, employed full-time, June 30, 1996.)*

Another interview revealed the following:

My boyfriend does vacuum when I ask, but not much else. Of course, if his boss is coming to visit, then he appears concerned about cleaning the house. How many times is he fast asleep and I am having some hard liquor and a few puffs from a joint after cleaning everything before we get up the next morning. I used to complain but he does not really care about the housework, so I compensate by getting buzzed before going to sleep. *(From Venturelli's research files, interview with a 29 year-old female, employed part-time.)*

To appreciate the impact of drug abuse on women, it is necessary to understand the uniqueness of female roles in our society. Relative to drug abuse problems, women today are often judged by a double standard. Women suffering from drug addictions are often perceived less tolerantly than comparably addicted men (Erickson and Murray 1989). Because of these social biases, women are afraid of being condemned and are less likely to seek professional help for their own personal drug abuse problems. In addition, family, friends, and associates are less inclined to provide drug-dependent women with important emotional support (Alexander et al. 2001).

The image of the alcoholic woman has always been that of one who is boisterous, flirtatious, effusive, and sometimes, loud mouthed. This may be the person she might become on occasion, but more often, she is secluded in the privacy of her apartment or home after getting the kids off to school or having just come home from the office, classroom, or business. She is shy, reclusive to a point, alienated, retrospective, and lacking in self-esteem. Later in her drinking, she will become self-pitying, resentful, and even childishly cruel as a consequence of the drug alcohol (Kirkpatrick 1999).

Due to their unique socioeconomic and family roles, women are especially vulnerable to emotional disruptions resulting from divorce, loneliness, and professional failures. Studies suggest that such stresses aggravate tendencies for women to abuse alcohol and other substances (Korolenko and Donskih 1990; Kirkpatrick 1999). More specifically, " . . . women drink from a feeling of inadequacy and from a need for love, the kind of love not found within a sexual relationship but, rather, a love that is deeper and more primal" (Kirkpatrick 1999, p. 1).

In addition, drug addiction can occur in some women as a result of domestic adversities. Consequently, there is a high prevalence of drug dependence in women who are victims of sexual and/or physical abuse (Ladwig and Anderson 1989). "Approximately 70% of women in drug abuse treatment report histories of physical and sexual abuse, with victimization beginning before 11 years of age and occurring repeatedly" (SAMHSA 1999, p. 1). These physical and emotional traumas result in, or are precursors to factors leading to drug abuse, such as low self-esteem, self-condemnation, anxiety and personal conflicts, dysfunctional dependencies, and overwhelming feelings of guilt (Kirkpatrick 1999). In addition, because of the crucial nurturing roles women hold, drug abuse problems can be particularly damaging to family stability.

Another unique role for women in drug abuse situations is that of a spouse, significant other, or mother to a drug addict. Often, in both traditional and nontraditional family relationships, women are expected to be nurturing, understanding, and willing to sacrifice in order to preserve the family integrity. If a family member becomes afflicted by drug dependence, the wife or mother is viewed as a failure. In other words, if the woman had maintained a good home and conducted her domestic chores properly, the family member would not have been driven to drugs (Alexander et al. 2001).

Despite the disruption and considerable stress caused by drug addiction in the home, women continue to bear the burden of raising children, performing domestic chores, and keeping the family together. In addition, women in such circumstances are frequently put at great physical risk. The risk is from an addicted spouse who becomes abusive to his partner or from exposure to sexually transmitted diseases, such as HIV or hepatitis, transmitted by a careless infected partner. The anxiety and frustrations resulting from these stressful circumstances can encourage women themselves to become dependent as they seek emotional relief by using drugs.

■ WOMEN'S RESPONSE TO DRUGS

Research continues to lag regarding how women respond to substances of abuse. Although slowly changing, the trend in drug abuse studies is still to avoid female populations; the effects of the drugs in men are still extrapolated to women. Even when drug abuse research is conducted on women, frequently the woman's response is not of primary concern; the objective is to determine the effects on a fetus during pregnancy or an infant during nursing (Alexander et al. 2001).

Although it generally can be assumed that the physiological and drug responses of men and women are similar, some distinctions should be recognized. For example, a recent study compared the risk for lung cancer in men and women after a lifetime of cigarette smoking. It was found that female smokers were twice as likely to get lung cancer as males who had smoked an identical number of cigarettes in their lifetimes ("Women Smokers" 1994). Another study indicated that women are *three* times more likely to contract lung cancer than men when smoking the same amount of cigarettes (Kirkpatrick 1999). These differences clearly indicate that cigarette smoking is far more dangerous for women than men. Finally, women's unique response to drugs includes a finding discovered by researchers at the University of California at San Francisco that women respond to a class of painkillers called kappa-opioids which are ineffective in men (*Science Daily* 2000).

Drug Abuse and Reproduction

A very important physiological distinction that sets women apart from men in regard to taking drugs is their ability to bear children. Because of this unique function, men and women have different endocrine (hormone) systems, organs, and structures, and women have varied drug responses according to their reproductive state. The unique features of women have a substantial impact on the response to drug abuse in the presence and absence of pregnancy.

Drug abuse patterns can influence the outcome of pregnancy even if they occur before a woman becomes pregnant. For example, women who are addicted to heroin are more likely to have poor health, including chronic infections, poor nutrition, and sexually transmitted diseases such as HIV, which can damage the offspring if pregnancy occurs. If substances are abused during pregnancy, they may directly affect the fetus and adversely alter its growth and development. The incidence of substance abuse during pregnancy is not known precisely, but undoubtedly hundreds of thousands of children have been exposed to drugs in utero. The effects of individual drugs of abuse taken during pregnancy are discussed in detail in the corresponding chapters, but several specific observations merit reiteration.

1. Cocaine is a substantial threat for both the pregnant woman and the fetus. Although a number of specific claims for the fetal effects of cocaine are controversial (see Chapter 11), several observations appear legitimate: cocaine use increases the likelihood of miscarriage when used during pregnancy; cocaine use in the late stages of pregnancy can cause cardiovascular or CNS complications in the baby at birth and immediately thereafter; and due to its vasoconstrictor effects, cocaine may deprive the fetal brain of oxygen, resulting in strokes and permanent physical and mental damage to the child.

2. The impact of alcohol consumption during pregnancy has been well documented and publicized (Mathias 1995). When alcohol is consumed by the mother, it crosses the placenta, but the effect of this drug on the fetus is highly variable and depends on the quantity of alcohol consumed, timing of exposure, maternal drug metabolism, maternal state of health, and presence of other drugs. A particularly alarming consequence of high alcohol intake during pregnancy is an aggregate of physical and mental defects called *fetal alcohol syndrome* (FAS). Characteristics of this syndrome include low birth weight, abnormal facial features, mental retardation, and retarded sensorimotor development. For additional details, see Chapters 8 and 9.

   In addition to direct effects on the fetus, alcohol has played a major role in many unwanted pregnancies or has resulted in women's exposure to sexually transmitted diseases. As a CNS depressant, alcohol impairs judgment and reason, and in turn encourages sexual risk-taking that normally would not occur. The results are all too frequently tragic for women (SAMHSA 1999).

3. Tobacco use during pregnancy is particularly rampant in the United States. Specifically, 20% of the smoking female adult population is pregnant. Some experts suggest smoking cigarettes during pregnancy may pose a greater risk to the fetus than taking cocaine. Tobacco use by pregnant women may interfere with blood flow to the fetus, deprive it of oxygen and nutrition, and disrupt development of its organs, particularly the brain. Also of significant concern is the possibility that exposure of nonsmoking pregnant women to second-hand tobacco smoke may be damaging to the fetus.

4. Other drugs of abuse that have been associated with abnormal fetal development when used during pregnancy include barbiturates, benzodiazepines, amphetamines, marijuana, lysergic acid diethylamide (LSD), and even caffeine when consumed in high doses. Clearly, women should be strongly urged to avoid all substances of abuse, especially during pregnancy.

Women and Alcohol

Alcohol is the drug most widely used and abused by women in the United States. According to the 1999 *National Household Survey on Drug Abuse* among women aged 15 to 44, 49.3% used alcohol in the past month and 19.4% reported binge drinking (SAMHSA 1999). Alcohol abuse is also a major problem for women on college campuses, even though male college students are more likely than their female counterparts to use alcohol on a daily basis.

As a rule, women are less likely than men to develop severe alcohol dependence; thus, only 25% of the alcoholics in America are female. Women are also likely to initiate their drinking patterns later in life than men (Alexander et al. 2001). Interesting ethnic patterns of alcohol consumption have been reported in females, with black and white women manifesting similar drinking patterns. Although the proportions are similar, black women are more likely to completely abstain from alcohol than white women are.

Women who are dependent on alcohol are usually judged more harshly than men with similar difficulties. Alcoholic males are more likely to be excused because their drinking problems are often perceived as being caused by frustrating work conditions, family demands, economic pressures, or so-called nagging wives and children. In contrast, women with drinking problems are often perceived as spoiled or pampered, weak, deviant, or immoral.

Such stigmas, referred to as labels in Chapter 2 (see labeling theory), cause women to experience more guilt and anxiety about their alcohol dependence and discourage them from admitting their drug problems and seeking professional help (Kirkpatrick 1999).

The principal reasons for excessive alcohol consumption in women range from loneliness, boredom, and domestic stress in the "housewife drinker" to financial problems, sexual harassment, lack of challenge, discrimination, and powerlessness in the career woman. Depression is often associated with alcohol problems in women, although it is not clear whether this condition is a cause or an effect of the excessive use.

Women's Physiological Responses to Alcohol

Health consequences for excessive alcohol consumption appear to be more severe for women than for men. For example, alcoholic women are more likely to suffer premature death than alcoholic men. In addition, liver disease is more common and occurs at a younger age in female drinkers than in male alcoholics. In general, higher morbidity rates are experienced by alcoholic women than their male counterparts.

Several explanations have been suggested for the greater adverse effects seen in female alcoholics. Their higher blood alcohol concentrations may be due to a smaller blood volume and more rapid absorption into the bloodstream after drinking. Alternatively, slower alcohol metabolism in the stomach and liver might cause more alcohol to reach the brain and other organs as well as prolong exposure to the drug following consumption (Goldstein 1995). Studies have shown that for a woman of average size, one alcoholic drink has effects equivalent to two drinks in an average-size man (see Chapter 8).

Dealing with Women's Alcohol Problems Alcoholic consumption varies considerably in women, ranging from total abstinence or an occasional drink to daily intake of large amounts of alcohol. Clearly, much is yet to be learned about the cause of some women's excessive drinking and dependence on alcohol. The role of genetic factors in predisposing women to alcohol-related problems is still unclear. The environment is certainly a major factor contributing to excessive alcohol consump-

tion in women. It is well established that depression, stress, and trauma encourage alcohol consumption because of the antianxiety and amnesic properties of this drug. Because of unreasonable societal expectations and numerous socioeconomic disadvantages, women are especially vulnerable to the emotional upheavals that encourage excessive alcohol consumption.

As with all drug dependence problems, prevention is the preferred solution to alcohol abuse by women. Alcohol usually becomes problematic when it is no longer used occasionally to enhance social events but used daily to deal with personal problems. Such alcohol dependence can best be avoided by using constructive techniques to manage stress and frustrations. Because of unique female roles and society's expectations, women especially need to learn to be assertive with family members, associates in the workplace (including bosses), and other contacts in their daily routines (see Chapter 4). By expecting and demanding equitable treatment and consideration in personal and professional activities, stress and anxiety can often be reduced. Education, career training, and development of communication abilities can be particularly important in establishing a sense of self-worth (see Chapter 18). With these skills and confidence, women are better able to manage problems associated with their lives and less likely to resort to drugs for an escape.

Women and Prescription Drugs

Women are more likely than men to suffer depression, anxiety, and panic attacks (Kirkpatrick 1999); be unable to express anger; be victims of physical and sexual abuse; and be subject to overwhelming guilt feelings (Kirkpatrick 1999). Consequently, they are also more likely to take and become addicted to the prescription drugs used in treating these disorders. Because these drugs are used as part of psychiatric therapy and under the supervision of a physician, drug dependence frequently is not recognized and may be ignored for months or even years. This type of "legitimate" drug abuse occurs most often in elderly women and includes the use of sedatives, antidepressants, and antianxiety medications. A recent study found that one in four women over age 60 takes at least one of these drugs daily and that some of them develop serious drug problems (Drug Strategies 1998). Excessive use of these drugs by older women results in side effects such as insomnia, mood fluctuations, and disruption of cognitive and motor functions that can substantially compromise the quality of life.

■ TREATMENT OF DRUG DEPENDENCY IN WOMEN

As previously discussed, women are less likely than men to seek treatment for, and rehabilitation from, drug dependence (Kirkpatrick 1999). Possible reasons for their reluctance are as follows:

1. In more traditional families, women have unique roles with high expectations. They are expected to assume demanding and ongoing responsibilities, such as motherhood, child rearing, and family maintenance, that cannot be postponed and often cannot be delegated, even temporarily, to others. Consequently, many women feel that they are too essential for the well-being of other family members to leave the home and seek time-consuming treatment for drug abuse problems.

2. Drug treatment centers often are not designed to handle the unique health requirements of females—thus, women face more obstacles. These obstacles involve barriers to treatment entry, treatment engagement, and long-term recovery (NIDA 1999). Women have been shown to have greater health needs than men due to more frequent respiratory, genitourinary (associated with the sex and urinary organs), and circulatory problems. If drug treatment centers are not capable of providing the necessary physical care, women are less likely to participate in associated drug abuse programs.

3. Drug-dependent women are more inclined to be unemployed than their male counterparts and more likely to be receiving public support. The implications of this difference are twofold. First, because concerns about one's job often motivate drug-dependent workers to seek treatment, this issue is less likely to be a factor in unemployed women. Second, without the financial security of a job, unemployed women may feel that good treatment for their drug problems is unaffordable. (For more on treatment, see Chapter 4.)

The unique female requirements must be recognized and considered if women are to receive adequate treatment for drug dependence. Some considerations on how to achieve this objective include the following: (1) availability of female-sensitive services; (2) nonpunitive and noncoercive treatment that incorporates supportive behavior change approaches; and (3) treatment for a wide range of medical problems, mental disorders, and psychosocial problems (NIDA 1999). The role of motherhood needs to be used in a positive manner in drug treatment strategies. For most women, motherhood is viewed with high regard and linked to self-esteem. Approximately 90% of female drug abusers are in their childbearing years, and many have family responsibilities. Consequently, treatment approaches need to be tailored to allow women to fulfill their domestic responsibilities and satisfy their maternal obligations.

Women dependent on drugs often lack important coping skills. Because many women lead restricted, almost isolated lives that focus entirely on domestic responsibilities, they face limited alternatives for dealing with stressful situations. Under these restrictive circumstances, the use of drugs to cope with anxieties and frustrations is very appealing. In order to enhance their ability to cope, drug-dependent women need to develop communication and assertiveness skills. Further, they also need to be encouraged to control situations rather than allowing themselves to be controlled by the situation. Specific techniques that have proven useful in coping management are exercise (particularly relaxation types), relaxing visual imagery, personal hobbies, and outside interests that require active participation. Many drug-dependent women require experiences that divert their attention from the source of their frustrations while affording them an opportunity to succeed and develop a sense of self-worth.

Finally, one research study found that the most effective treatment for women included a mutually supportive therapeutic environment that addressed the following issues: psychopathology (such as depression); a woman's role as mother; interpersonal relationships; and the need for parenting education. Another study found that cocaine-using women whose children were living with them during residential treatment remained in the treatment programs significantly longer than women whose children were not living with them at the facility.

Thus, having the children in the treatment facility provides opportunities to assess and meet women's needs, which in turn affects the mother's prognosis (NIDA 1999).

Prevention of Drug Dependence in Women

The best treatment for drug addiction is prevention. To help prevent drug problems in women as opposed to men, socioeconomic disadvantages need to be recognized as factors that make women more vulnerable to drug dependence, especially from prescription medication. Women need to learn that nondrug approaches are often more desirable for dealing with situational problems than prescribed medications. For example, for older women suffering loneliness, isolation, or depression, it is better to encourage participation in outside interests, such as hobbies and service activities. In addition, social support and concern should be encouraged from family, friends, and neighbors. Such nonmedicinal approaches are preferred over prescribing sedatives and hypnotics to cope with emotional distresses. Similarly, medical conditions such as obesity, constipation, or insomnia should be treated by changing lifestyle, eating, and exercise habits rather than using drug "bandage therapy."

When women are prescribed drugs, they should ask about the associated risks, especially as they relate to drug abuse potential. Frequently, drug dependency develops insidiously and is not recognized by either the patient or attending physician until it is already firmly established. If a woman taking medication is aware of the potential for becoming dependent and is instructed on how to avoid its occurrence, the problems of dependence and abuse can frequently be averted. (See Chapter 18 for more on prevention and education.)

Drug Use in Adolescent Subcultures

I love waking up in the morning and smoking a nice fat joint. I live above the garage now, and my mom lives across the yard from the garage. This is a great living arrangement! I go to my room a few hours before crashing on many school nights, get high, drink some vodka that my older brother buys for me, then finally crash. In the morning, I always wake myself up so my mom stays away from my room, and my hideaway stash box is always locked. I roll me a joint and get a little high before I greet mom in the morning for a quick breakfast. I think she gets high too, but if I ask her and she says "no," what if she then asks me and gets all suspicious and shit? Besides, my Uncle Prentice always gets high with me, so I still think my mom really does not care about smoking weed. In fact, I know she is more worried about me drinking and driving than my friend "Mary Jane" [nickname for marijuana]. That's just my private life and no one needs to know. *(From Venturelli's research files, male, age 18, residing in Chicago, July 10, 2000.)*

From ages 13 through 18, adolescents are more likely to experience heightened psychological, social, and biological changes. Oftentimes, such internal and external changes are manifested by emotional outbursts. Why do such changes and urges arise? The adolescent's body is stretching, growing, and sometimes appearing out of control due to the hormonal changes of puberty.

Adolescents are uncertain and confused about not knowing who or what they are becoming. They are often confused as to their worth to family, peers, society, and even to themselves (Kantrowitz and Wingert 1999). Adding to the frustration of growing up, the cultural status of adolescents is poorly defined. They find themselves trapped in a "no-man's land" between the acceptance, simplicity, and security of childhood, and the stress, complexities, expectations, independence, and responsibilities of adulthood. Not only do adolescents have difficulty deciding who and what they are but also adults are equally unsure as to how to deal with these transitional human beings. While the grownup world tries to push adolescents out of the secure nest of childhood, it is not willing to bestow the full membership and rights of adulthood (Johnson et al. 1996; Kantrowitz and Wingert 1999).

Because of their uniquely rapid development, several developmental issues are particularly important to evolving adolescents (Elmen and Offer 1993; Johnson et al. 1996; Kantrowitz and Wingert 1999):

- Discovering and understanding their distinctive identities

- Forming more intimate and caring relationships with others

- Establishing a sense of autonomy

- Coming to terms with the hormone-related feelings of puberty and expressing their sexuality

- Learning to become productive contributors to society

- Feeling alone and alienated

Due to all this developmental confusion, "normal" behavior for the adolescent is difficult to define precisely. Experts generally agree that persistent low self-esteem, depression, feelings of alienation, and other emotional disturbances can be troublesome for teenagers. Most adolescents are relatively well adjusted and are able to cope with sociobiological changes . Emotionally stable adolescents relate well to family and peers and function productively within their schools, neighborhoods, and communities. The majority of adolescents experience transient problems, which they are able to resolve, whereas others become deeply disturbed and are unable to grow out of their problems without counseling and therapy. Those adolescents who are unable or unwilling to ask for assistance often turn to destructive devices, such as drugs or violence (Kantrowitz and Wingert 1999), for relief from their emotional dilemmas.

■ WHY ADOLESCENTS USE DRUGS

Although there is no such thing as a "typical" substance-abusing adolescent, there are physiological, psychological, and sociological factors that are often associated with drug problems in this subculture (Johnson et al. 1996). However, it is important to remember that not all drug use by adolescents means therapy is necessary or even desirable. Most excessive drug use and often eventual abuse by adolescents result from the desire to experience new behaviors and sensations, a passing fancy of maturation, an attempt to relieve peer pressure, feelings

of alienation, or an inclination to enhance a social setting with chemistry. (Kantrowitz and Wingert 1999) Most of these adolescent users will not go on to develop problematic dependence on drugs and, for the most part, should be watched but not aggressively confronted or treated. The adolescents who usually have significant difficulty with drug use are those who turn to drugs for extended support as coping devices and become drug-reliant because they are unable to find alternative, less destructive solutions to their problems. Several major factors can contribute to serious drug dependence in adolescents (Archambault 1992; Johnson et al. 1996; Walsh and Scheinkman 1992).

Research indicates that the most important factor influencing drug use among adolescents is peer drug use (Bahr et al. 1995; Kandel 1980; NIDA 1999; Swadi 1992; Winters 1997). Consequently, eventual transition to heavier substance use also directly correlates with peer use (Steinberg et al. 1994). Conversely, individuals whose peer groups do not use or abuse drugs are less likely to use drugs themselves (Venturelli 2000). Research has identified a correlation between strong family bonds and non–drug-using peer groups (NIDA 1999). "Adolescents with higher [stronger] family bonds are less likely than adolescents with lower [weaker] bonds to have close friends who use drugs" (Bahr et al. 1995, p. 466). In addition, family bonding is highly correlated with educational commitment. In essence, family bonding influences choice of friends and educational goals and aspirations (Bahr et al. 1995).

Three noteworthy differences exist between male and female adolescents: (1) males demonstrate a stronger association between educational achievement and family bonds; (2) among females, peer drug use is negatively associated with family bonds, so peer drug use and family bonds are not likely to influence the use of licit and illicit drugs by females; and (3) the impact of age on peer drug use (the younger the age, the more vulnerable to peer pressure) and on the amount of alcohol consumed can be predicted with slightly greater accuracy for males than females (Teen Challenge 2000).

Many adolescents use drugs to help cope with boredom, unpleasant feelings, emotions, and stress or to relieve depression, reduce tension, and reduce alienation (Teen Challenge 2000). Psychological differences among adolescents who are frequent

---

KEY TERMS

sociobiological changes
the belief that biological forces (largely genes) have a direct influence on the root causes of social psychological behavior

drug users, experimenters, and abstainers often can be traced to early childhood, the quality of parenting in their homes, and their home environment. It has been suggested that certain types of parents are more likely to raise children at high risk for substance abuse (Archambault 1992). For example, an alcoholic adolescent usually has at least one parent of the following types:

Alcoholic. This parent serves as a negative role model for the adolescent. The child sees the parent dealing with problems by consuming drugs. Even though drinking alcohol is not illegal for adults, it sends the message that drugs can solve problems. The guilt-ridden alcoholic parent is unable to provide the child with a loving supportive relationship. In addition, the presence of the alcoholic parent is often disruptive or abusive to the family and creates fear or embarrassment in the child.

Nonconsuming and condemning. This type of parent not only chooses to abstain from drinking but also is very judgmental about drinkers and condemns them for their behavior. Such persons, who are often referred to as *teetotalers*, have a rigid, moralistic approach to life. Their black-and-white attitudes frequently prove inadequate and unforgiving in an imperfect, gray world. Children in these families can feel inferior and guilty when they are unable to live up to parental expectations, and they may resort to drugs to cope with their frustrations.

Overly demanding. This type of parent forces unrealistic expectations on his or her children. These parents often live vicariously through their children and require sons and daughters to pursue endeavors in which the parents were unable to succeed. Particular emphasis may be placed on achievements in athletics, academics, or career selections. Even though the parents' efforts may be well intended, the children get the message that their parents are more concerned about "what they are" than "who they are." These parents frequently encourage sibling rivalries to enhance performance, but such competitions always yield a loser.

Overly protective. These types of parents do not give their children a chance to develop a sense of self-worth and independence. Because the parents deprive their children of the opportunities to learn how to master their abilities within their surroundings, the children are not able to develop confidence and a positive self-image. Such children are frequently unsure about who they are and what they are capable of achieving. Parents who use children to satisfy their own ego needs or who are trying to convince themselves that they really do like their children tend to be overly protective.

The principal influence for learned behavior is usually the home; therefore, several other family-related variables can significantly affect adolescents' decision to start, maintain, or cease a drug habit (Kinney 2000; Lawson and Lawson 1992). For example, adolescents usually learn their attitudes about drug use from family models. In other words, what are the drug-consuming patterns of parents and siblings? Adolescents are more likely to develop drug problems if other members of the family (1) are excessive in their drug (legal or illegal) consumption, (2) approve of the use of illicit drugs, or (3) use drugs as a problem-solving strategy.

Sociological factors that damage self-image can also encourage adolescent drug use. Feelings of rejection cause poor relationships with family members, peers, school personnel, or co-workers. Ethnic differences sometimes contribute to a poor self-image because people of minority races or cultures are frequently socially excluded and are sometimes viewed as being inferior and undesirable by the majority population. This type of negative message is very difficult for adolescents to deal with. Sometimes to ensure acceptance, adolescents adopt the attitudes and behavior of their affiliated groups. If a peer group, or a gang, views drug use as cool, desirable, or even necessary, members (or those desiring membership) feel compelled to conform and become involved in drugs.

■ PATTERNS OF DRUG USE IN ADOLESCENTS

A growing minority of younger aged teenagers are exposed to drug use within their own families. A recent finding reported that "20% of . . . 600 teens in drug treatment in New York, Texas, Florida and California said they have shared drugs other than alcohol with their parents, and that about 5% of the teens actually were introduced to drugs—usually marijuana—by their moms and dads" (Leinwand 2000, p. 1). In 1999, Partnership for a Drug-Free America reported similar shocking findings (Leinwand 2000).

Jason, 17, a recovering addict from an upper middle-class family in Simi Valley, California, says he wishes his father had been more of a parent and less of a buddy when it came to marijuana. " . . . [Jason] made his drug purchase: a $5 bag of pot. Jason says his father walked by his room's open door as he was stashing it in a dresser drawer. [His father then] ' . . . told about his marijuana use,' Jason says. 'We went into his [dad's] office, and he had a (water pipe) and we got high together.' [Jason reports that at the time, he] ' . . . thought it was *sooo* cool' " (Leinwand 2000, p. 2).

In another example, La'kiesha, 15, of Southern California, is the third generation of a family in which members have become addicted to drugs. La'kiesha said her grandmother smoked pot regularly and gave her a few puffs when she was 5 years old, to settle her down before bedtime (Leinwand 2000).

Teenagers being introduced to drugs or using drugs with parents, especially illicit drugs in middle- and upper-middle class families, is a relatively recent phenomenon. Years ago, alcohol may have been shared between parents and their children in a low percent of cases; however, today there are parents who either have been or are currently using illicit drugs and they appear to be influencing the use of these drugs by their children. Currently, this occurs in a small minority of families, nevertheless, it remains shocking.

Recent surveys regarding drug use patterns found that by eighth grade, approximately 52% of children had used alcohol, 44% had used cigarettes, 20% had used inhalants, and 22% had used marijuana (see Table 17.4). The 2000 *Monitoring the Future Study* conducted by the National Institute on Drug Abuse (NIDA) reported the following findings (Johnston et al. 2000a).

1. The use of illicit drugs such as marijuana, cocaine, heroin, and amphetamines did not change for 8th, 10th and 12th graders from 1999. Use of cigarettes also remained the same.

2. Use of alcohol for 8th, 10th and 12th graders also remained the same, even though use remains high: 24% of 8th graders, 40% of 10th graders, and 51% of 12th graders have used alcohol recently (past month when survey was taken).

3. Crack cocaine use by 8th graders declined from a high of 2.1% in 1998 to 1.8% in 1999.

4. Among high school seniors, 8% reported trying Ecstasy at least once; this percentage increased from 5.8% in 1998.

5. As reported earlier, use of steroids by male teens increased with 2.7% of 10th graders saying they used steroids in the past year—in 1998, it was 2%.

■ ADOLESCENT VERSUS
ADULT DRUG ABUSE

Adolescent patterns of drug abuse are very different from drug use patterns in adults (Moss et al. 1994). The uniqueness of adolescent drug abuse means that drug-dependent teenagers usually are not successfully treated with adult-directed therapy. For example, compared with adults who abuse drugs, drug-using adolescents are (1) more likely to be involved in criminal activity and at earlier ages; (2) more likely to have other members of the family who abuse drugs; (3) more likely to be associated with a dysfunctional family that engages in emotional and/or physical abuse of its members; and (4) more likely to begin drug use because of curiosity or peer pressure (Bahr et al. 1995; Daily 1992b; Hoshino 1992; Steinberg et al. 1994; Teen Challenge 2000). Such differences need to be considered when developing adolescent-targeted treatment programs.

■ CONSEQUENCES AND
COINCIDENTAL PROBLEMS

Researchers have concluded that the problem of adolescent drug use is a symptom and not a cause of personal social maladjustment. Even so, because of the pharmacological actions of drugs, routine use can contribute to school and social failures, unintended injuries (usually automobile-related), criminal and violent behavior, sexual risk taking, depression, and suicide (Curry and Spergel 1997).

TABLE 17.4 Drug Use among Eighth-, Tenth-, and Twelfth-graders

Data shows the percentages of 8th, 10th, and 12th graders who used drugs, including alcohol and tobacco, in 1997, 1998, and 1999.

| | 8TH GRADERS | | | 10TH GRADERS | | | 12TH GRADERS | | |
	1997	1998	1999	1997	1998	1999	1997	1998	1999
Alcohol†									
Lifetime	53.8%	52.5%	52.1%	72.0%	69.8%	70.6%	81.7%	81.4%	80.0%
Annual	45.5	43.7	43.5	65.2	62.7	63.7	74.8	74.3	73.8
30-Day	24.5	23.0	24.0	40.1	38.8	40.0	52.7	52.0	51.0
Daily	0.8	0.9	1.0	1.7	1.9	1.9	3.9	3.9	3.4
Cigarettes (any use)									
Lifetime	47.3	45.7	44.1	60.2	57.7	57.6	65.4	65.3	64.6
30-Day	19.4	19.1	17.5	29.8	27.6	25.7	36.5	35.1	34.6
Daily	9.0	8.8	8.1	18.0	15.8	15.9	24.6	22.4	23.1
1/2 Pack+ per day	3.5	3.6	3.3	8.6	7.9	7.6	14.3	12.6	13.2
Marijuana/hashish									
Lifetime	22.6	22.2	22.0	42.3	39.6	40.9	49.6	49.1	49.7
Annual	17.7	16.9	16.5	34.8	31.1	32.1	38.5	37.5	37.8
30-Day	10.2	9.7	9.7	20.5	18.7	19.4	23.7	22.8	23.1
Daily	1.1	1.1	1.4	3.7	3.6	3.8	5.8	5.6	6.0
Inhalants									
Lifetime	21.0	20.5	19.7	18.3	18.3	17.0	16.1	15.2	15.4
Annual	11.8	11.1	10.3	8.7	8.0	7.2	6.7	6.2	5.6
30-Day	5.6	4.8	5.0	3.0	2.9	2.6	2.5	2.3	2.0
Daily	N.A.	N.A.	N.A.	N.A.	N.A.	N.A.	N.A.	0.2	N.A.
Stimulants									
Lifetime	12.3	11.3	10.7	17.0	16.0	15.7	16.5	16.4	16.3
Annual	8.1	7.2	6.9	12.1	10.7	10.4	10.2	10.1	10.2
30-Day	3.8	3.3	3.4	5.1	5.1	5.0	4.8	4.6	4.5
Daily	N.A.	N.A.	N.A.	N.A.	N.A.	N.A.	0.3	0.3	N.A.
Hallucinogens									
Lifetime	5.4	4.9	4.8	10.5	9.8	9.7	15.1	14.1	13.7
Annual	3.7	3.4	2.9	7.6	6.9	6.9	9.8	9.0	9.4
30-Day	1.8	1.4	1.3	3.3	3.2	2.9	3.9	3.8	3.5
Daily	N.A.	N.A.	N.A.	N.A.	N.A.	N.A.	0.3	0.1	N.A.
Cocaine									
Lifetime	4.4	4.6	4.7	7.1	7.2	7.7	8.7	9.3	9.8
Annual	2.8	3.1	2.7	4.7	4.7	4.9	5.5	5.7	6.2
30-Day	1.1	1.4	1.3	2.0	2.1	1.8	2.3	2.4	2.6
Daily	N.A.	N.A.	N.A.	N.A.	N.A.	N.A.	0.2	0.2	N.A.

(continued)

TABLE 17.4 *(continued)*

| | 8TH GRADERS | | | 10TH GRADERS | | | 12TH GRADERS | | |
	1997	1998	1999	1997	1998	1999	1997	1998	1999
Crack cocaine									
Lifetime	2.7	3.2	3.1	3.6	3.9	4.0	3.9	4.4	4.6
Annual	1.7	2.1	1.8	2.2	2.5	2.4	2.4	2.5	2.7
30-Day	0.7	0.9	0.8	0.9	1.1	0.8	0.9	1.0	1.1
Daily	N.A.	N.A.	N.A.	N.A.	N.A.	N.A.	0.1	0.1	N.A.
Steroids									
Lifetime	1.8	2.3	2.7	2.0	2.0	2.7	2.4	2.7	2.9
Annual	1.0	1.2	1.7	1.2	1.2	1.7	1.4	1.7	1.8
30-Day	0.5	0.5	0.7	0.7	0.6	0.9	1.0	1.1	0.9
Daily	N.A.	N.A.	N.A.	N.A.	N.A.	N.A.	0.3	0.3	N.A.
Heroin									
Lifetime	2.1	2.3	2.3	2.1	2.3	2.3	2.1	2.0	2.0
Annual	1.3	1.3	N.A.	1.4	1.4	N.A.	1.2	1.0	N.A.
30-Day	0.6	0.6	N.A.	0.6	0.7	N.A.	0.5	0.5	N.A.
Daily	N.A.	N.A.	N.A.	N.A.	N.A.	N.A.	0.1	0.1	N.A.

Note: N.A., not available. (†) indicates that a "drink" means "more than a few sips."

Sources: National Survey on Drug Abuse from *The Monitoring the Future Study,* 1975–1998; College and Young Adults; L. D. Johnston, P. M. O'Malley, J. G. Bachman; The University of Michigan Institute for Social Research, National Institute on Drug Abuse, U.S. Department of Human Services, National Institutes of Health, 1999 / The University of Michigan News and Information Services; 17 December 1999; citing the National Survey on Drug Abuse, *The Monitoring the Future Study,* 1999; L. D. Johnston, P. M. O' Malley, J. G. Bachman; The University of Michigan Institute for Social Research, National Institute on Drug Abuse, U.S. Department of Human Services, National Institutes of Health.

It is important to realize that, because serious drug abuse is usually the result of emotional instability, consequences of the underlying disorders may be expressed with chemical dependence, making diagnosis and treatment more difficult. The undesirable coincidental problems may include self-destruction, risk taking, abuse, or negative group behaviors. Some of these adolescent problems and their relationship to drug abuse are discussed in the following sections.

Adolescent Suicide

Current research shows that although no cause-and-effect relationship exists between use of alcohol and/or other drugs and suicide, such drugs are often contributing factors (Minnesota Institute of Public Health 1995). Adolescents are particularly vulnerable to suicide actions; in fact, white males between 14 and 20 years old are the most likely to commit suicide in the United States (Daily 1992b). Further, the teenage suicide rate has doubled since 1980 (Siegel and Senna 1997). The result is that suicide is now the second leading cause of death among persons 15 to 24 years of age. Twenty percent to 36% of suicide victims have a history of alcohol abuse or were drinking shortly before their suicide. There are approximately 1800 teen suicides per year, approximately 8 or 9 per 100,000 living teens (ABC News 2000). Some experts have described severe chemical dependence as a form of slow drug-related suicide. For clinicians, every case of serious drug addiction conceals a suicidal individual because all drug abuse inevitably constitutes a game of life and death very similar to "Russian roulette," which comes back into fashion at certain times and under certain circumstances (Bergeret 1981).

Clearly, many teenagers who abuse alcohol and other drugs possess a self-destructive attitude as this quote from an online chat with Dr. David Shaffer, a teen suicide expert, demonstrates. "... [T]wo-thirds of all suicides amongst boys occur in boys who are abusing alcohol or other drugs; so the link between suicide and alcohol and certain drugs, like cocaine and Ecstasy and other stimulant drugs, is a very close one" (Schaefer, et al., p. 39).

Also according to Shaffer, adolescents who attempt suicide are more likely to (1) have disciplinary problems, then abuse alcohol and feel even more depressed; (2) be very anxious and not display any bad behavior problems; or (3) have a perfectionist attitude and are never satisfied with their outcomes. Nearly all suffer from depression before their suicide attempts and females generally differ from males in that they are prone to even greater amounts of depression with fewer cases of alcohol or other drug abuse (ABC News 2000).

Besides posing a direct health threat because of their physiological effects, drugs of abuse can precipitate suicide attempts due to their pharmacological impact. A number of studies have found a very high correlation between acute suicidal behavior and drug use (Buckstein et al. 1993). One report noted that adolescent alcoholics have a suicide rate 58 times greater than the national average. In another study, 30% of adolescent alcoholics had made suicide attempts, although 92% admitted to a history of having suicidal thoughts (Daily 1992b).

It has been speculated that the incidence of suicide in drug-consuming adolescents is high because both types of behavior are the consequence of an inability to develop fundamental adult attributes of confidence, self-esteem, and independence. When drug use does not make up for their need for these characteristics, the resulting frustrations are intensified and ultimately played out in the suicide act.

Most adolescents experiment with drugs for reasons not related to antisocial or deviant behavior but rather due to curiosity, desire for recreation, boredom, desire to gain new insights and experiences, or urge to heighten social interactions. These adolescents are not likely to engage in self-destructive behavior. In addition, adolescents from "healthy" family environments are not likely to attempt suicide. Specifically, Daily (1992b) stated that families least likely to have suicidal members are those that:

- Express love and show mutual concern.
- Are tolerant of differences and overlook failings.
- Encourage the development of self-confidence and self-expression.
- Have parents who assume strong leadership roles but are not autocratic.
- Have interaction characterized by humor and good-natured teasing.
- Are able to serve as a source of joy and happiness to their members.

Suicide is more likely to be attempted by those adolescents who turn to alcohol and other drugs to help them cope with serious emotional and personality conflicts and frustrations. These susceptible teenagers represent approximately 5% of the adolescent population (Beschner and Friedman 1985; Siegel and Senna 1997).

Wright (1985) found that four features significantly contribute to the likelihood of suicidal thought in high school students:

1. Parents with interpersonal conflicts who often use an adolescent child with drug problems as the scapegoat for family problems.

2. Fathers who have poor, and often confrontational, relationships with their children.

3. Parents who are viewed by their adolescent children as being emotionally unstable, usually suffering from perpetual anger and depression.

4. A sense of frustration, desperation, and inability to resolve personal and emotional difficulties through traditional means.

Clearly, it is important to identify those adolescents who are at risk for suicide and to provide immediate care and appropriate emotional support.

Sexual Violence and Drugs

Alcohol use has been closely associated with almost every type of sexual abuse in which the adolescent is victimized. "For the perpetrator, being under the influence may remove both physical and psychological inhibitors which keep people from acting out violently. They may also use alcohol or drugs as an excuse for criminal behavior" (WCASA 1997, p.

13). For example, alcohol is by far the most significant factor in date, acquaintance, and gang rapes involving teenagers (Parrot 1988; Prendergast 1994). The evidence for alcohol involvement in incest is particularly overwhelming. Approximately 4 million children in America live in incestuous homes with alcoholic parents. In addition, 42% of drug-abusing female adolescents have been victims of sexual abuse (Daily 1992a). It is estimated that almost half of the offenders consume alcohol before molesting a child and at least a third of the perpetrators are chronic alcoholics. Finally, 85% of child molesters were sexually abused themselves as children, usually at the same age as their victims, and the vast majority of these molesters abused drugs as adolescents (Daily 1992a).

These very disturbing associations illustrate the relationship between drugs and violent sexual behavior both in terms of initiating the act and as a consequence of the act. The effects of such sexual violence are devastating and far reaching. Thus, incest victims are themselves more likely than the general population to abuse drugs as adolescents and engage in antisocial delinquency, prostitution, depression, and suicide (Daily 1992a).

Gangs and Drugs

The very disturbing involvement of adolescents in gangs and gang-related activities and violence is a social phenomenon that first became widely recognized in the 1950s and 1960s. Hollywood, for example, introduced America to the problems of adolescent gangs in the classic movies *Blackboard Jungle* and *West Side Story*. Although the basis for gang involvement has not changed over the years, the level of violence and public concern have increased dramatically. Many communities consider gang-related problems to be their number one social issue. Access to sophisticated weaponry and greater mobility have drawn unsuspecting neighborhoods and innocent bystanders into the often violent clashes of intragang and intergang warfare. Individuals and communities have been reacting angrily to this growing menace. To deal effectively with the threats of gang-initiated violence and crime, however, it is important to understand why gangs form, what their objectives are, how they are structured, and how to discourage adolescent involvement.

Children often join gangs because they are neglected by their parents, lack positive role models, and fail to receive adequate adult supervision. Other motivations for joining a gang include peer pressures, low self-esteem, and perceived an easy acquisition of money from gang-related drug dealing and other criminal activities.

In comparison to traditional, formal youth organizations, juvenile gangs may appear disorganized. Research shows, however, that verbal rules, policies, customs, and hierarchies of command are rigidly observed within the gang. Thus, common values and attitudes exist:

1. Gang membership is usually defined in socioeconomic, racial, and ethnic terms, and adolescents involved have similar backgrounds.

2. Gang members are distinguished by a distinctive and well-defined dress code. Violation of this code by members, or mimicking of the dress code by nongang members can result in ostracism, ridicule, physical abuse, and violence.

3. Leadership and seniority within the gang are defined by vested time in belonging to the gang, age, loyalty, and demonstrated delinquent cleverness (often related to drug dealing and other crimes).

4. Gang members use gang slang to ensure camaraderie and group loyalty.

Although a stable home life does not ensure that an adolescent will not become involved with gang-related activity, a strong family environment and guidance from respected parents and guardians are clearly deterrents (Lale 1992). Many gang members are children from dysfunctional, broken, or single-parent homes. Many parents are aware of their children's gang involvement but they lack the skill, confidence, and authority to deter the gang or curtail drug involvement of their teenagers. To make matters worse, ineffective parents often discourage or even interfere with involvement by outside authorities due to misdirected loyalty to their children and/or to avoid embarrassment to their family and community.

Because troubled adolescents are often estranged from their families, they are particularly influenced by their peer groups. These teenagers are most likely to associate with groups who have similar backgrounds and problems and who make them feel accepted. Because of this vulnerability, adolescents may become involved with local gangs.

In summary, gangs offer the following:

- Fellowship and camaraderie
- Identity and recognition
- Membership and belonging
- Family substitution and role models
- Security and protection
- Diversion and excitement
- Friendships and structure
- Money and financial gain for relatively little effort
- Ability to live the crazy life (*vida loca*) (Sanders 1994; Shelden et al. 2001).

In the United States, estimates of the total number of existing gangs vary widely. For example, in Chicago, estimates range from 12,000 to 120,000 gang members. Spergel (1990) provided the following percentages of those who are reportedly in gangs within a particular school population in the Chicago area: 5% of the elementary school youths, 10% of all high school youths, 20% of those in special school programs, and, more alarmingly perhaps, 35% of those between 16 and 19 years of age who have dropped out of school (Shelden et al. 2001). Keep in mind this is an example of one city alone.

Research shows that teenage gangs are becoming major players in the drug trade (Siegel and Senna 1997). Two of the largest gangs in Los Angeles, the Bloods and Crips, are examples of this trend. Estimated membership in these two gangs exceeds 20,000. In the past, organized crime families maintained a monopoly on the Asian heroin market. Today, youth gangs have entered this trade, for two reasons: (1) recent efforts and successes in prosecuting top mob bosses by criminal justice officials have created opportunities for new players, and (2) demand has grown for cocaine and synthetic drugs that are produced locally in many U.S. cities. In Los Angeles and most major larger cities as well, drug-dealing gangs maintain "rock houses" or "stash houses" (where "crack" cocaine is used and

KEY TERMS

intragang
between members of the same gang
intergang
between members of different gangs

sold) that serve as selling and distribution centers for hard drugs. The "crack" cocaine found in these "rock houses" is often supplied or run by gang members (Siegel and Senna 1997).

To a lesser extent, other less violent gangs with smaller memberships are also involved in drug dealing. Recent research shows that the media may exaggerate the percentage of gangs involved in drug dealing. Citywide drug dealing by tightly organized "super" gangs appears to be on the decline and is being superseded by the activities of loosely organized, "neighborhood-based groups" (Siegel and Senna 1997). The main reason for this shift is that federal and state law enforcement of drug laws forced drug dealers to become " . . . flexible, informal organizations [rather] than rigid vertically organized gangs with . . . [leaders] . . . who are far removed from day-to-day action [on the street]" (Siegel and Senna 1997, p. 409).

Drug use and gang-related activities are often linked but the relationship is highly variable (Curry and Spergel 1997; Fagan 1990). Clearly, problems with drugs exist without gangs and gang-related activities can occur despite the absence of drugs; however, because they have common etiologies, their occurrences are often intertwined. Most adolescents who are associated with gangs are knowledgeable about drugs. Many gang members have experimented with drugs, much like other adolescents their age. However, the hard-core gang members are more likely to be engaged not only in drug use, but also in drug dealing as a source of revenue to support the gang-related activities (Lale 1992; Siegel and Senna 1997). The types of drugs used and their significance and functions vary from gang to gang (Fagan 1990; Siegel and Senna 1997). For example, many Latino gangs do not profit from drug trafficking but are primarily interested in using hard-core drugs such as heroin and phecyclidine (PCP). In contrast, African American gangs tend to be more interested in the illicit commercial value of drugs and often engage in dealing "crack" and other cocaine forms.

■ PREVENTION, INTERVENTION, AND TREATMENT OF ADOLESCENT DRUG PROBLEMS

The most effective way to prevent adolescent gang involvement is to identify, at an early age, those children at risk and provide them with lifestyle alternatives. Important components of such strategies are as follows:

- Encourage parental awareness of gangs and teach parents how to address problems in their own families that may encourage gang involvement.

- Provide teenagers with alternative participation in organizations or groups that satisfy their needs for camaraderie, participation, and emotional security in a constructive way. These groups can be organized around athletics, school activities, career development, or service rendering.

- Help children to develop coping skills that will enable them to deal with the frustration and stress in their personal lives.

- Educate children about gang-related problems and help them understand that, like drugs, gangs are the result of problems and are not the solutions.

As with most health problems, the sooner drug abuse is identified in the adolescent, the greater the likelihood that the problem can be resolved. It can be difficult to recognize signs of drug abuse in teenagers because their behavior can be erratic and unpredictable even under the best of circumstances. In fact, many of the behavioral patterns that occur coincidentally with drug problems are also present when drugs are not a problem. However, frequent occurrence or clustering of these behaviors may indicate the presence of substance abuse. The behaviors that can be warning signs include the following (Archambault 1992):

- Abruptly changing the circle of friends

- Experiencing major mood swings

- Continually challenging rules and regulations

- Overreacting to frustrations

- Being particularly submissive to peer pressures

- Sleeping excessively

- Keeping very late hours

- Withdrawing from family involvement

- Letting personal hygiene deteriorate

- Becoming isolated

- Engaging in unusual selling of possessions

- Manipulating family members

- Becoming abusive toward other members of the family

- Frequently coming home at night "high"

Prevention of Adolescent Drug Abuse

Logically, the best treatment for drug abuse is to prevent the problem from starting. This approach, referred to as primary prevention, has been typically viewed as total abstinence from drug use (see Chapter 18). Informational scare tactics are frequently used as a component of primary prevention strategies. These messages often focus on a dangerous (although in some cases, rare) potential side effect and presenting the warning against drug use in a graphic and frightening fashion. Although this approach may scare naïve adolescents away from drugs, many adolescents today, especially if they are experienced, question the validity of the scare tactics and ignore the message.

Another form of primary prevention is to encourage adolescents to become involved in formal groups, such as structured clubs or organizations, in order to reduce the likelihood of substance abuse (Howard 1992). Group memberships can help adolescents develop a sense of belonging and contributing to a productive, desirable objective. This involvement can also provide the adolescent with strength to resist undesirable peer pressures. In contrast, belonging to informal groups such as gangs—groups with loose structures and ill-defined, often antisocial, objectives—can lead to participation in poorly chaperoned parties, excessive sexual involvement, and nonproductive activities. Adolescent members of such poorly defined organizations tend to drink alcohol at an earlier age and are more likely to use other substances of abuse.

Some experts claim that primary prevention against drug use is unrealistic for many adolescents. They believe that no strategy is likely to stop adolescents from experimenting with alcohol or other drugs of abuse, especially if these substances are part of their home environment (e.g., if alcohol or tobacco is routinely used) and are viewed as normal, acceptable, and even expected, behaviors (Howard 1992). For these adolescents, it is important to recognize when drug use moves from experimentation or a social exercise to early stages of a problem and to prevent serious dependence from developing. This approach, referred to as secondary prevention , consists of (1) teaching adolescents about the early signs of abuse, (2) teaching adolescents how to assist peers and family members with drug problems, and (3) teaching adolescents how and where help is available for people with drug problems (Archambault 1992). Regardless of the prevention approach used, adolescents need to understand that drugs are never the solution for emotional difficulties nor are they useful for long-term coping.

Treatment of Adolescent Drug Abuse

To provide appropriate treatment for adolescent drug abuse, the severity of the problem must be ascertained. The criteria for such assessments include the following:

- Differentiating between abuse and normal adolescent experimentation with drugs.

- Distinguishing between minor abuse and severe dependency on drugs.

- Distinguishing among behavioral problems resulting from (1) general behavioral disorders, such as juvenile delinquency; (2) mental retardation; and (3) drugs of abuse.

There is no single best approach for treating adolescent substance abuse. Occasionally the troubled adolescent is admitted to a clinic and treated on an inpatient basis. The inpatient approach is very expensive and creates a temporary "artificial" environment that may be of limited value in preparing adolescents for the problems to be faced in their real homes and neighborhoods. However, the advantage of an inpatient approach is that adolescents can be managed better and their behavior can be more tightly monitored and controlled (Hoshino 1992).

A more practical and routine treatment approach is to allow adolescents to remain in their natural environment and to provide the necessary life skills to be successful at home, in school, and in the community. For example, adolescents being treated for drug dependence should be helped with

- Schoolwork, so that appropriate progress toward high school graduation occurs.

- Career skills, so that adolescents can become self-reliant and learn to care for themselves and others.

- Family problems and learning to communicate and resolve conflicts.

If therapy is to be successful, it is important to improve the environment of the drug-abusing adolescent. This aspect of treatment includes disassociation of the adolescent from groups (such as gangs) or surroundings that encourage drug use and encourages association with healthy and supportive groups (such as a nurturing family) and experiences (such as athletics and school activities). Although desirable, such separation is not always possible, especially if the family and home environment are factors that encourage abuse; the likelihood of therapeutic success is substantially diminished under these circumstances.

Often, therapeutic objectives are facilitated by positive reinforcement that encourages life changes that eliminate access to and use of drugs. This goal can frequently be achieved by association with peers who have similar drug and social problems but are motivated to make positive changes in their life. Group sessions with such peers are held under the supervision of a trained therapist and consist of members sharing problems and solutions (Hoshino 1992). Some other recent options include holistic therapies such as acupuncture, homeotherapy, massage therapy, aromatherapy, yoga, nutrition therapy, and many more options that were once marginalized by the medical profession (Apostolides 1996).

Another useful approach is to discourage use of drugs by reducing their reinforcing effects. This result can sometimes be achieved by substituting a stronger positive or negative reinforcer. For example, if adolescents use drugs because they believe these substances cause good feelings and help them cope with emotional problems, it may be necessary to replace the drug-taking behavior with other activities that make the adolescent feel good without the drug (such as participation in sports or recreational activities). Negative reinforcers, such as parental discovery and punishment or police apprehension, may discourage drug use by teenagers who are willing to conform and respect authorities. However, negative approaches are ineffective deterrents for nonconforming, rebellious adolescents. Negative reinforcers also do not tend to discourage adolescent use of substances that are more socially acceptable, such as alcohol, tobacco, and even marijuana (Howard 1992).

Regardless of the treatment approach, adolescents must meet several basic objectives if therapy for their drug dependence is to be successful (Daily 1992b):

- Realize that "drugs do not solve problems"—they only make the problems worse.

- Understand why they turned to drugs in the first place.

- Be convinced that abandoning drugs grants them greater independence and control over their own lives.

- Understand that drug abuse is a symptom of underlying problems that need to be resolved.

■ SUMMARY OF ADOLESCENT DRUG ABUSE

Drug abuse by adolescents is particularly problematic in the United States. The teenage years are filled with experimentation, searching, confusion, rebellion, poor self-image, and insecurity. These attributes, if not managed properly, can cause inappropriate coping and lead to problems such as drug dependence, gang involvement, violence, criminal behavior, and suicide. Clearly, early detection of severe underlying

emotional problems and application of effective early preventive therapy are important for proper management. Approaches to treatment of drug abuse problems must be individualized because each adolescent is a unique product of physiological, psychological, and environmental factors.

Almost as important as early intervention for adolescent drug abuse problems is recognizing when treatment is *unnecessary*. We should not be too quick to label all young drug users as antisocial and emotionally unstable. In most cases, teenagers who have used drugs are merely experimenting with new emotions or exercising their new-found freedom. In such situations, nonintervention is usually better than therapeutic meddling. For the most part, if adolescents are given the opportunity, they will work through their own feelings, conflicts, and attitudes about substance abuse, and they will develop a responsible philosophy concerning the use of these drugs.

Drug Use in College Student Subcultures

Chapter 9 includes a lengthy discussion of alcohol use and abuse by college students. This section focuses on college undergraduate use of alcohol not discussed in that chapter, with additional emphasis on the use and abuse of illicit drugs by college students currently attending institutions of higher education. Table 17.5 compares trends in the annual use of various licit and illicit drugs by full-time college students with trends in other groups. Overall, full-time college students were as likely to use any illicit drugs in 1998 as others with whom they were compared.

Table 17.6 shows yearly trends in drug use among U.S. college students from 1980 through 1998. This population of students consisted of 1200 full-time college students 1 to 4 years past high school. The study measured the percentage who used licit and illicit drugs anytime within the past 12 months before the survey was administered. The main finding was that, with exceptions for some slight increases in the use of marijuana/hashish since 1991 and in the use of hallucinogens and LSD since 1993, use of all licit and illicit drugs by college

TABLE 17.5 **Annual Prevalence for Various Types of Drugs, 1998: Full-Time College Students Versus Others (Among respondents 1 to 4 years beyond high school)**

	FULL-TIME COLLEGE STUDENTS	OTHERS
Any illicit drug*	37.8%	36.4%
Any illicit drug* other than marijuana	14.0	19.0
Marijuana	35.9	32.9
Inhalants[†]	3.0	3.5
Hallucinogens	7.2	7.7
LSD	4.4	6.1
Cocaine	4.6	7.1
Crack	1.0	1.8
MDMA (Ecstasy)[#]	3.9	3.9
Heroin	0.6	0.9
Other opiates[§]	4.2	4.3
Stimulants, adjusted[§,°]	5.1	7.8
"Ice"[#]	1.0	2.3
Barbiturates[§]	2.5	4.6
Tranquilizers[§]	3.9	4.8
Alcohol	84.6	81.0
Cigarettes	44.3	49.5
Approximate weighted N=	(1440)	(1120)

(*) Use of "any illicit drug" includes use of marijuana, hallucinogens, cocaine, or heroin, or any use of other opiates, stimulants, barbiturates, or tranquilizers not under a doctor's orders.
(†) This drug was included in five of the six questionnaire forms. Total N in 1998 for colleges students was approximately 1200.
(#) This drug was included in two of the six questionnaire forms. Total N in 1998 for colleges students was approximately 480.
(§) Only drug use that was not under a doctor's orders is included here.
(°) Based on the data from a revised question, which attempts to exclude the inappropriate reporting of nonprescription stimulants.

Source: National Survey on Drug Abuse from *The Monitoring the Future Study,* 1975–1998; College and Young Adults; L. D. Johnston, P. M. O'Malley, J. G. Bachman; The University of Michigan Institute for Social Research, National Institute on Drug Abuse, U.S. Department of Human Services, National Institutes of Health, 1999.

students steadily declined from 1980 through 1994. From 1994 to 1998, increases in the overall use of illicit drugs, including marijuana, MDMA, and opioids were noted.

The latest 1999 statistics do not show much change from 1998 (Johnston et al. 2000b). For example, in comparing 1998 with 1999, past year usage rates indicate slight decreases and increases; for example: marijuana, from 35.9% to 35.2%; inhalants, from 7.2% to 7.8%; hallucinogens (slightly more significant), from 4.4% to 5.4%; stimulants/crystal methamphetamine, from 1.0% to 0.5%; alcohol, from 84.6% to 83.6% (Johnston, et al. 2000b).

TABLE 17.6 Trends in Annual Prevalence of Various Types of Drugs Among College Students 1 to 4 Years Beyond High School (Percentage who used in the past 12 months)

This table shows partial results from the nationwide survey of drug use among high school students and young adults, conducted annually for the National Institute on Drug Abuse by the University of Michigan Institute for Social Research. Each year since 1977, some participants from all previously graduated high school classes have been followed through the use of mailed questionnaires. The follow-up surveys include a sample of about 1200 full-time college students 1 to 4 years past high school.

	1980	1985	1990	1995	1998
Approximate weighted N =	(1040)	(1080)	(1400)	(1450)	(1440)
Any illicit drug	56.2%	46.3%	33.3%	33.5%	37.8%
Any illicit drug other than marijuana	32.3	26.7	15.2	15.9	14.0
Marijuana/hashish	51.2	41.7	29.4	31.2	35.9
Inhalants	3.0	3.1	3.9	3.9	3.0
Hallucinogens	8.5	5.0	5.4	8.2	7.2
LSD	6.0	2.2	4.3	6.9	4.4
Cocaine	16.8	17.3	5.6	3.6	4.6
Crack	N.A.	N.A.	0.6	1.1	1.0
MDMA (Ecstasy)	N.A.	N.A.	2.3	2.4	3.9
Heroin	0.4	0.2	0.1	0.3	0.6
Other opiates	5.1	2.4	2.9	3.8	4.2
Amphetamines ([§])	22.4	N.A.	N.A.	N.A.	N.A.
Amphetamines ([°])	N.A.	11.9	4.5	5.4	5.1
Crystal methamphetamine	N.A.	N.A.	0.1	1.1	1.0
Sedatives	8.3	2.5	N.A.	N.A.	N.A.
Barbiturates	2.9	1.3	4.4	2.0	2.5
Methaqualone	7.2	1.4	N.A.	N.A.	N.A.
Tranquilizers	6.9	3.6	3.0	2.9	3.9
Alcohol	90.5	92.0	89.0	83.2	84.6
Cigarettes	36.2	35.0	35.5	39.3	44.3

Note: N.A., not available. ([§]) Only drug use that was not under a doctor's orders is included here. ([°]) Excludes the inappropriate reporting of non-prescription stimulants.

Source: National Survey on Drug Abuse from *The Monitoring the Future Study*, 1975–1998; College and Young Adults; L. D. Johnston, P. M. O'Malley, J. G. Bachman; The University of Michigan Institute for Social Research, National Institute on Drug Abuse, U.S. Department of Human Services, National Institutes of Health, 1999.

■ REASONS FOR COLLEGE STUDENTS' DRUG USE

Figure 17.2 shows the primary reasons why a sample survey of 1232 male and female college students used alcohol and other drugs. The major reasons cited in this sample survey were (1) to have fun (78.9%), (2) to relieve stress (63.9%), and (3) to ease social interactions (53.8%). This sample also reveals that within the past 12 months, approximately 89% used alcohol, 37% used marijuana (or hash or hash oil), and 40% used cigarettes. Approximately 74% of respondents were white, 12% were Hispanic, and 12% were African American (Campus Alcohol Drug Resource Center 2000). This survey alone indicates that the use of alcohol and other drugs on most larger state universities continues to be rampant.

■ ADDITIONAL NOTEWORTHY FINDINGS REGARDING DRUG USE BY COLLEGE STUDENTS

The following sections describe the most recent significant studies and findings regarding the use of drugs by college students.

Patterns of Alcohol and Other Drug Use

Recent literature reviews about undergraduates' substance use and abuse and the prevalence patterns of alcohol and other drug use found that the most popular substance used by undergraduates is alcohol, which was used by about 90% of students at least once a year. Heavy alcohol use, which includes binge drinking, ranged from 20% to 40% in this group: " . . . while binge drinking decreased by 6% among dormitory residents between 1993 and 1999, it increased by about the same amount among those living off campus. Nearly 80% of binge drinkers live in a fraternity or sorority house, often off campus" (Marklein 2000, p. 1). Other results showed that alcohol use was associated with serious and acute problems such as alcoholism, poor academic performance, drinking and driving, and criminal behavior. From 1997 to 1998, alcohol arrests in the nation's colleges increased by 24.3%; this is reported as the largest increase in 7 years. In comparing the same 2 years, drug law violations on our nation's campuses increased by 11.1% (Nicklin 2000).

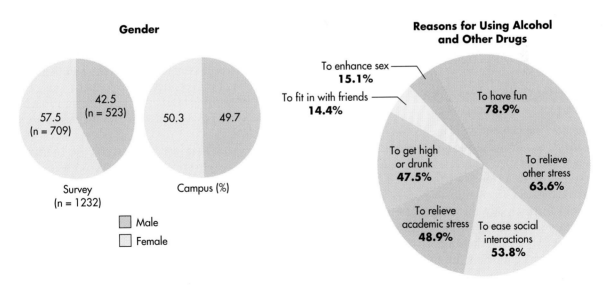

FIGURE 17.2

Sample of reasons for using alcohol and other drugs from the Campus Alcohol and Drug Resource Center at the University of Florida, 1999.

Source: Campus Alcohol Drug Resource Center at the University of Florida, Alcohol and Other Drug Use, 1999. University of Florida, 2000. Available http://www.health.ufl.edu/shcc/cadrc.htm.

Summarized below are other significant findings regarding alcohol and other drug use:

- During the 2 weeks before the survey, 39% of college students had "binged" on alcohol (Johnston et al. 2000b).

- Among college students, rates of binge drinking were highest among whites—43.3% for males and 24.4% for females; among African Americans, the rates were 24.8% for males and 5.4% for females; and among Asians, the rates were 32% for males and 20% for females.

- Young adults ages 18 to 25 are most likely to binge or drink heavily; 54% of the drinkers in this age group binge and about one in four are heavy drinkers.

- A clear relationship exists between alcohol use and grade-point average (GPA) among college students: students with GPAs of a "D" or "F" equivalent drink three times as much as those who earn "A" equivalent GPAs.

- Almost half of college students who were victims of campus crimes said they were drinking or using other drugs when they were victimized.

- Researchers estimate that alcohol use is implicated in one- to two-thirds of sexual assault and acquaintance or date rape cases among teens and college students.

Predicting Drug Use for First-Year College Students

The best predictor of drug use for first-year college students was drug use during a typical month in the senior year of high school. Overall, college students responding to a questionnaire were found to use marijuana less frequently than they did in high school. Further, alcohol use increased early in the college years. Although the frequency of alcohol use increased, however, the number of times that college students got drunk did not rise. Most of these students found new friends in college with whom they got drunk. Alcohol and drug use depended on the choice of new college friends (Leibsohn 1994).

Dormitories for Non–Drug Using Students

In 1988, Rutgers University was one of the first universities to create a dormitory for students who are recuperating addicts and who want to stay away from the alcohol-charged atmosphere of conventional dormitories. The dormitory at Rutgers maintains strict rules and careful management (Witham 1995). Other universities offer similar variations for on-campus living. In 1989, the University of Michigan opened a substance-free housing facility and set aside 500 dormitory spaces; 1,200 applied for these spaces (Belsie 1995).

Increasing Popularity of Certain Types of "Softer" Drugs

Marijuana and psilocybin mushrooms are two types of illicit recreational drugs whose popularity appeared to grow in the 1990s. Referred to as "soft drugs," these substances are commonly used on most college campuses (Ravid 1995). Nationwide surveys showed that in yearly drug use averages from 1984 through 1999, there was a steady progressive increase in the use of hallucinogens, which includes psilocybin mushrooms, Ecstasy, and LSD. In 1984 (the first year of the survey), 3.7% of college students used LSD; in 1999, 5.4% used this same drug. Similarly, in 1984, 6.2% used hallucinogens (excluding LSD) and in 1999, 7.8% used these same hallucinogenic-type drugs (Johnston et al. 2000b).

According to a 1990 study, with the exception of marijuana, psilocybin mushrooms and Ecstasy/MDMA were the most used illicit drugs among first- and second-year full-time college students. A fair number of universities reported that about 24% of their drug-using students use psilocybin mushrooms. Use of Ecstasy/MDMA also increased from 16% to 24%.

The occasional use of cocaine (a "harder" drug), increased from 5.9% in 1995 to 6.7% in 1996 (Bennett et al. 1999). This increase occurred in a sample of 2710 students at an undergraduate university in the Southwest. More than likely, the high cost of cocaine maintains the "occasional use" from becoming frequent use. Nevertheless, cocaine is another drug that appeared to be part of the drug scene on most campuses in the 1990s and in the beginning of the 21st century.

Steroid Usage Patterns

A study of 58,625 college students from 78 colleges and universities in the United States (Meilman et al. 1995) concluded the following:

- Steroid users consumed dramatically more alcohol and demonstrated higher rates of binge drinking than other students.

- A significantly higher percentage of steroid users than nonusers reported using tobacco, marijuana, cocaine, amphetamines, sedatives, hallucinogens, opiates, inhalants, and designer drugs.

- A higher percentage of steroid users than nonusers reported experiencing negative consequences as a result of substance abuse. Such negative consequences included arrest, public intoxication, driving under the influence, court ordered community service, and disciplinary actions by university officials.

- A greater percentage of steroid users than nonusers reported family histories of alcohol abuse and other drugs.

Rohypnol and Date Rape

Rohypnol , also known as the date-rape drug, is one of six drugs recently referred to as a club drug . Other club drugs are MDMA (Ecstasy), gamma hydroxybutyrate (GHB), ketamine, methamphetamine, and LSD. Club drugs are used by individuals at all-night dance parties such as "raves" or "trances," dance clubs, and bars. All of these drugs are colorless, tasteless, and odorless. They can be added unobtrusively to beverages by individuals who may want to intoxicate or sedate others (NIDA 2000a). In cases of sexual assault or rape, the small white Rohypnol pills are slipped into a person's drink causing the person to black out and have no memories of events that occurred while he or she was under the influence of the drug. A minority of undergraduates also use the drug to intensify the effects of marijuana and alcohol. One problem with identifying whether this drug has been given to an unwilling recipient is that Rohypnol can be detected only for 60 hours after ingestion (Lively 1996). Rohypnol (flunitrazepam) belongs to a class of drugs known as benzodiazepines (such as Valium and Xanax). Although this drug is not approved for prescription use in the United States, it is approved and used in more than 60 countries as a treatment for insomnia, as a sedative, and as a presurgery anesthetic (NIDA 2000a).

> **KEY TERMS**
>
> **Rohypnol**
> known as the "date rape drug," used on many college campuses
>
> **club drugs**
> refers to a new class of illicit drugs used on college campuses, at bars, in night clubs, and at "raves" where drinking and dancing occur; club drugs include MDMA (Ecstasy), GHB, Rohypnol, ketamine, methamphetamine, and LSD

HIV and AIDS: The Disease

AIDS came to the attention of medical authorities in the United States on June 4, 1981 in a newsletter from the Centers for Disease Control in Atlanta, Georgia (Zuger 2000). HIV, the virus that causes AIDS, was not discovered until 1983. Since 1981, 733,374 cases of AIDS have been reported to the Centers for Disease Control and Prevention (CDC 2000b). Of these cases, 83% were males and 17% were females. Worldwide, more than 18 million people have died of AIDS, almost 15 million of them in sub-Saharan Africa. About 34 million people are living with AIDS, with about 70% of them living in South Africa, and a million more were infected last year (Sternberg 2000). The disease has created about 13 million orphans.

As of December 1999, the CDC reported that 113,002 adults, adolescents, and children are living in the United States with HIV and 290,542 are living with AIDS. Between 1997 to 1999, 367,965 males and 62,476 females died from AIDS (CDC 1999). The CDC estimates that approximately 900,000 people in the United States are infected with HIV, but one-third have yet to be diagnosed.

■ NATURE OF HIV INFECTION AND RELATED SYMPTOMS

AIDS is caused by the human immunodeficiency virus. An HIV-infected individual may not manifest symptoms of AIDS for as many as 10 to 20 years after the initial infection. Although the HIV-infected individual may experience no symptoms, he or she is highly contagious.

After an individual has become infected, he or she may have a brief flu-like illness usually within 6 to 12 weeks. It is not known what determines the length of the latency period, when symptoms are not present. The asymptomatic period eventually ends, however, and signs of immune disorder appear. Initial symptoms of this disease include night sweats, swollen lymph glands, fever, and/or headaches.

The immune systems of HIV-positive individuals become severely compromised as important immune cells called CD4+ helper T-lymphocytes and macrophages are destroyed (see Figure 17.3). Because these immune cells are crucial in identifying and eliminating infection-causing microorganisms such as bacteria, fungi, and viruses, their deficiency substantially increases the likelihood and severity of infectious diseases. Progression of the disease brings weight loss, infections in the throat ("thrush") and skin (shingles), and other, opportunistic infections and/or cancer (e.g., Kaposi's sarcoma). A person with HIV is diagnosed with AIDS when the helper T-cell count in his or her blood falls below 200/mm^3.

Infections become increasingly difficult to control with medication, and consequently, severe opportunistic infections, such as pneumonia, meningitis, hepatitis, and tuberculosis, occur and eventually lead to death. The likelihood of introducing these opportunistic infections in the body increases in patients who are injection drug users because they often share injection equipment, such as needles and syringes, that are contaminated with disease-causing microorganisms.

■ DIAGNOSIS AND TREATMENT

It is crucial that HIV-infected people be aware of their condition to avoid activities that might transmit the infection to others. Testing for the presence of infection has been available since 1985 and is done by determining whether the body is producing antibodies against HIV. Further, since 1996, newspaper, magazine, radio, and television have been advertising a take-at-home HIV antibody test. The presence of these specific antibodies indicates

FIGURE 17.3
Disrupting the Assembly Line
HIV survives by invading white blood cells and turning them into virus factories. The process involves several steps, and each offers a potential target for therapy. This diagram shows how HIV does its work and how antiviral drugs do theirs.

....

Source: Crowley, G. "Targeting a Deadly Scrap of Genetic Code." *Newsweek* (2 December 1996): 69.

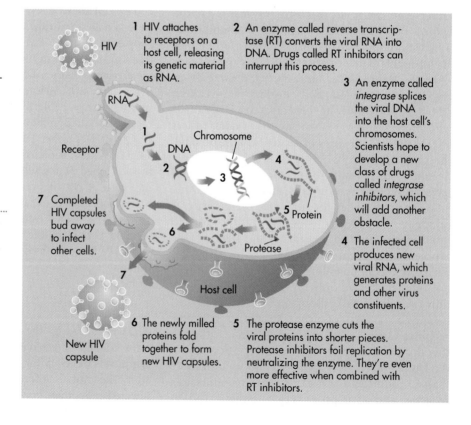

1 HIV attaches to receptors on a host cell, releasing its genetic material as RNA.

2 An enzyme called reverse transcriptase (RT) converts the viral RNA into DNA. Drugs called RT inhibitors can interrupt this process.

3 An enzyme called *integrase* splices the viral DNA into the host cell's chromosomes. Scientists hope to develop a new class of drugs called *integrase inhibitors*, which will add another obstacle.

4 The infected cell produces new viral RNA, which generates proteins and other virus constituents.

5 The protease enzyme cuts the viral proteins into shorter pieces. Protease inhibitors foil replication by neutralizing the enzyme. They're even more effective when combined with RT inhibitors.

6 The newly milled proteins fold together to form new HIV capsules.

7 Completed HIV capsules bud away to infect other cells.

HIV
RNA
Receptor
DNA
Chromosome
Protein
Protease
Host cell
New HIV capsule

HIV infection. If an individual is infected, it takes 6 to 12 weeks after the HIV exposure before the body produces enough antibodies to be detected in currently available tests. If the antibody is not present within 6 months after HIV exposure, it is likely that infection did not occur (Pietroski 1993).

Although the tests for HIV infection are reliable, false negatives (i.e., the test says no HIV is present even though the individual is infected) and false positives (i.e., the test says the individual is infected even though no HIV is present) occurs in only 1 out of 30,000 tests. Because testing positive for HIV is currently perceived as eventually life-threatening and is a highly emotional diagnosis, great effort is made to ensure confidentiality of the test results. The blood specimens to be tested are coded, and the personnel conducting the tests are not allowed to divulge the results to anyone but the individual who was tested. The issue of confidentiality is very controversial, however. It is often difficult to decide who has the right to know when HIV has been detected (see "Point/Counterpoint," Who Should Know the Results of Your HIV Test *If* You Test Positive?, on page 478).

After a positive HIV diagnosis, the best way to lengthen one's life is to immediately begin drug treatments. The first prescription drug treatment for AIDS, AZT, was introduced in 1987. In 1996, protease inhibitors came on the market. When combined with AZT and other drugs, protease inhibitors result in miraculous remissions of desperately ill AIDS patients (Zuger 2000). Further, it appears that with such drug combinations, HIV blood levels in newly infected patients remain at exceedingly low levels (Zuger 2000). Although the drug combinations do not rid the body of infected cells, results indicate that HIV infections could become as manageable as diabetes (Cowley 1996).

> I take the famous drug "cocktail" and have to wake myself up in the middle of the night around 4 in the morning then go back to sleep. I am used to it, I know it is a pain in the neck, but I think that despite this, the side effects can even be worse at times. I really don't want to go into it, it's depressing. The bright side, I am still alive after 9 years since diagnosed with AIDS, I am not dead yet. (*Interview with a 52 year-old male, working as a bartender in Chicago, May 18, 2000.*)

Patients take approximately 37 pills per day, which absolutely must be taken at regular daily intervals to be effective. The cost of the cocktail can be up to $2000 to $3000 per month. Unfortunately, many health insurance companies are actively issuing restrictive amendments on their policies that cap reimbursement for such expensive drug therapies. Often, infected individuals with extensive debt obligations and patients without health insurance are therefore unable to afford the latest drug therapy.

Some HIV infected persons taking the current treatment regimens suffer side effects that are so severe they choose to stop taking some of the drugs necessary to hold off the development of AIDS. Side effects can include diarrhea, bone-marrow suppression, an inability to tolerate the drugs, and tumor-like growths on the neck and other parts of the body. However, the overall success in treating HIV-positive patients has resulted in a 23% drop in HIV deaths in 1996 and a 40% drop in deaths in 1997. Because the drugs halt the progression of HIV to AIDS, the rates of new AIDS cases fell 25% by 1998 (Zuger 2000).

A successful prognosis for HIV infection and AIDS relies on three factors: (1) initiation of a drug regimen as soon as possible after an HIV-positive diagnosis, (2) strict adherence to medical advice and treatment, and (3) maintenance of a healthy diet without drug use or abuse so as to avoid taxing the immune system.

Scientists are optimistic that eventually there will be a vaccine against HIV/AIDS. Although approximately 30 types of vaccines are being studied, the development of such a vaccine after clinical trial can take more than a decade (Fischer 2000). The key is to invent "killer" T cells to shut down or destroy HIV-infected cells (Fischer 2000).

Who Is at Risk for AIDS?

Although anyone can become infected with HIV, its routes of transmission are limited to blood, semen, vaginal fluid, and possibly some other body fluids (Grinspoon 1994). Before AZT, mothers were more

KEY TERMS

protease inhibitors
recently discovered class of drugs used to treat HIV-infected individuals

likely to the pass the virus to their children prenatally or through breast milk. HIV is a virus that is not likely to survive outside of the body. Consequently, it is not spread by casual contact, such as by shaking hands, touching, hugging, or kissing (although "deep" kissing with an infected person is not recommended). In addition, it is not spread through food or water, by sharing cups or glasses,

POINT/COUNTERPOINT

Who Should Know the Results of Your HIV Test *If* You Test Positive?

Most people would probably want to keep such results private, but consider the following. Would your opinion about HIV+ people maintaining their results confidential change in the following circumstances:

- You require first aid after a serious auto accident and the emergency medical technician assisting is HIV+?
- Your doctor is HIV+?
- Your dentist is HIV+?
- Your manicurist is HIV+?
- Your massage therapist is HIV+?
- Your severely handicapped daughter's elementary school teacher is HIV+?
- Your lover is HIV+?
- Your tattoo artist is HIV+?
- Your jeweler who is about to pierce your daughter's ears is HIV+?
- Your boxing partner is HIV+?
- Your jail cellmate is HIV+?

Arguments for *not* disclosing HIV+ results to anyone other than the person undergoing HIV screening are that reporting such results to others would (1) force many people not to take the test for fear of disclosure to others; (2) possibly cause loss of employment (if the results require mandatory reporting to supervisors or managers); (3) unnecessarily stigmatize the HIV+ person, exposing an infected person to social ostracism and gossip and potentially creating fear and panic in others; and (4) potentially destroy a partner or marriage relationship if the significant other or spouse is notified.

Arguments *for* mandatory disclosure to others potentially affected by the results of this disease include (1) to protect domestic or marital partners, (2) to protect others from HIV+ workers who could infect them (such as surgeons who are involved in invasive bodily care or procedures), and (3) to honor the public's right to know of the threat of contracting this terminal disease.

Currently, employers cannot legally terminate a worker for being HIV+. In cases of direct potential threat to the public, an HIV+ worker can be reassigned to a different position. Also, in most cases, employers cannot legally inquire about HIV test results. An exception to this is the military and prison, where mandatory testing is required (Atlanta Legal Aid Main Page 1999).

What is your opinion about this issue?

The sooner an HIV+ person begins drug treatment, the more effective the treatment may be. Knowing this, should HIV+ individuals be required to inform past sexual partners and people with whom they have shared needles with so that these people can be tested (known as "partner notification" or "contact tracing")?

If an HIV+ surgeon is going to operate on you, your mother, father, or child—do you have the right to know? What are the rights of the HIV+ individual versus the rights of the public?

Source: Atlanta Legal Aid Main Page. *Should You Tell Your Employer That You're HIV Positive?* Atlanta: Emory University, 1999. Available http://www.law.emory.edu/PI?ALAS?disclosure.htm.

by coughing and sneezing, or by using common toilets. It is not spread by mosquitoes or other insects.

The following populations are at greatest risk for contracting AIDS: (1) men with a history of having had multiple homosexual or bisexual partners, (2) injecting drug users and their sexual partners, (3) heterosexuals with multiple partners, (4) infants born to HIV-infected women (approximately 25% of all HIV-positive mothers have HIV-positive babies), and (5) people who receive contaminated blood products, such as for transfusions or treatment of blood disorders (blood banks have nearly completely improved the screening of their blood supplies in the last decade). (See Figures 17.4 and 17.5 for a detailed breakdown of categories of U.S. AIDS cases by type of HIV exposure.)

Figure 17.4 shows that approximately 53% of all adult/adolescent men with AIDS report sex with men, and another approximately 27% report injection drug use. An estimated 13% of male cases are attributed to heterosexual contact, and other risk

exposures account for the remaining 7% of cases. Figure 17.5 shows that 62% of women with AIDS attribute their exposure to heterosexual contact, and 36% attributed their exposure to injection drug use.

Other findings regarding age at diagnosis of HIV infection and AIDS reported through 1999 follow:

- HIV is the fifth leading cause of death for all Americans between the ages of 25 and 44.

- Among African American men and women between the ages of 25 and 44, HIV is the number one cause of death.

- In the United States, approximately 80% of all current people with AIDS are male and 20% are female. Worldwide, 73 women are infected for every 100 infected men.

- African Americans comprise 47%, white Americans comprise 32%, and Hispanic Americans comprise 19% of all reported AIDS patients in the United States (CDC 2000a).

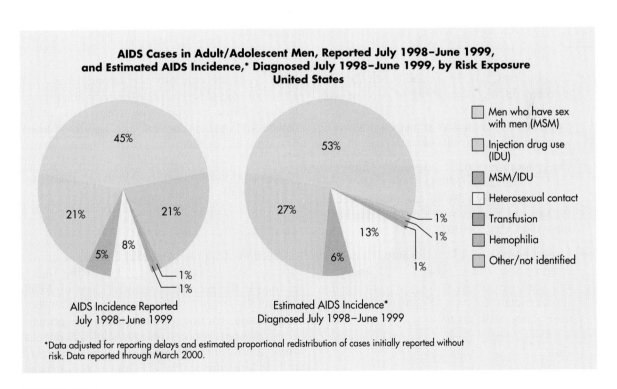

AIDS Cases in Adult/Adolescent Men, Reported July 1998–June 1999, and Estimated AIDS Incidence,* Diagnosed July 1998–June 1999, by Risk Exposure United States

AIDS Incidence Reported July 1998–June 1999

Estimated AIDS Incidence* Diagnosed July 1998–June 1999

Men who have sex with men (MSM)
Injection drug use (IDU)
MSM/IDU
Heterosexual contact
Transfusion
Hemophilia
Other/not identified

*Data adjusted for reporting delays and estimated proportional redistribution of cases initially reported without risk. Data reported through March 2000.

FIGURE 17.4

Source: Centers for Disease Control and Prevention (CDC). *HIV/AIDS Surveillance—General Epidemiology L178 slide series through 1999, Slide 9 of 24.* Atlanta: National Center for HIV, STD, and TB Prevention, August 1999.

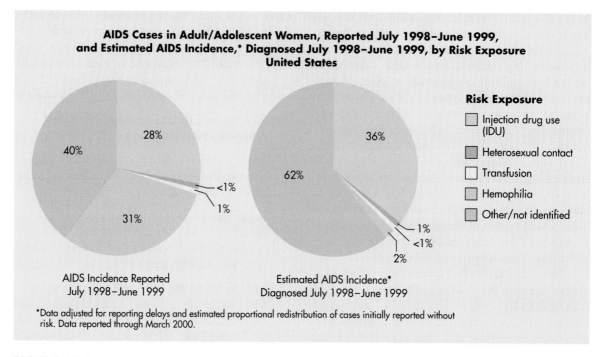

AIDS Cases in Adult/Adolescent Women, Reported July 1998–June 1999, and Estimated AIDS Incidence,* Diagnosed July 1998–June 1999, by Risk Exposure United States

Risk Exposure
- Injection drug use (IDU)
- Heterosexual contact
- Transfusion
- Hemophilia
- Other/not identified

AIDS Incidence Reported July 1998–June 1999: 40%, 28%, 31%, <1%, 1%

Estimated AIDS Incidence* Diagnosed July 1998–June 1999: 36%, 62%, 1%, <1%, 2%

*Data adjusted for reporting delays and estimated proportional redistribution of cases initially reported without risk. Data reported through March 2000.

FIGURE 17.5

Source: Centers for Disease Control and Prevention (CDC). *HIV/AIDS Surveillance—General Epidemiology L178 slide series through 1999, Slide 10 of 24.* Atlanta: National Center for HIV, STD, and TB Prevention, August 1999.

- Florida, Texas, New Jersey, and North Carolina reported the highest number of persons with HIV infection in 1999 (CDC 2000a). Most people with AIDS are found in metropolitan areas with populations of 500,000.

- The proportion of AIDS cases among men who have sex with men (MSM) has decreased over time from nearly 65% of cases diagnosed in 1985 to approximately 40% of cases diagnosed since 1998 (CDC 2000a).

- The proportion of AIDS cases among injection drug users increased between 1985 and 1994 and has remained stable, accounting for approximately 25% to 29% of recently diagnosed cases (CDC 2000a).

■ AIDS AND DRUGS OF ABUSE

During the past several years, the AIDS epidemic has become closely associated with drug abuse problems. As mentioned earlier, individuals addicted to illicit drugs are currently the second largest risk group for contracting AIDS. AIDS in women is particularly linked to drug abuse. Nearly 70% of the female AIDS patients are infected because of injection drug use by themselves or by a sexual partner (Glave 1994). Several reasons account for the high incidence of this deadly infection in the drug-abusing population.

Intravenous Drugs

Intravenous drug use has become the most important factor in the spread of AIDS in the United States. Of the recently diagnosed cases of AIDS, 29% resulted from injection drug use (CDC 2000c), with heroin, cocaine, or both being the primary drugs injected. Among severely addicted populations, intravenous drug use is often undertaken with little regard to hygiene, and injection paraphernalia such as needles, syringes, and cotton are frequently shared with other drug addicts (Millstein 1993). Sharing HIV-contaminated injection equipment can easily result in the transmission of this virus. The likelihood of an intravenous drug user contracting AIDS is directly correlated with (1) the frequency of drug injections, (2) the number of partners with whom injection equipment is shared, (3) the frequency of needle sharing, and (4) the frequency of injections in locations where there are high AIDS infection rates, such as in shooting galleries or crack houses (Booth et al. 1993).

Crack

Use of drugs such as crack (Ciba Foundation 1992) and alcohol (Colthurst 1993) tends to compromise judgment and encourage high-risk activities such as injection drug use or sexual risk taking (Beard and Kunsman 1993; Inciardi et al. 1993). In particular, the use of crack has been associated with high rates of HIV infection. Crack addicts often exchange sex for drugs or money to purchase drugs (Inciardi et al. 1993; Mathias 1993). These dangerous activities frequently occur in populations with an already high rate of HIV infection. Once infected, almost half of crack users continue to use sex to obtain their drugs and become a source of HIV infection for others (Diaz and Chu 1993).

■ ADOLESCENTS AND AIDS

It is estimated that out of the 40,000 new cases of HIV infection each year in the United States, as many as 50% of these may be among young people under the age of 25, and as many as 25% may be among young people under age 22 (CDC 1998). Some of the major findings summarized from the CDC in 1998 include the following:

- In 1986, 53 adolescents were reported with AIDS. By 1996, the number of HIV-positive adolescents reported had risen to 403. Through June 1997, a total of 2953 AIDS cases among adolescent had been reported.

- Although African Americans and Hispanic Americans represent approximately 25% of the U.S. population, they account for 56% of adolescent males with AIDS and 82% of adolescent females with AIDS.

- The proportion of females with AIDS among U.S. adolescents has more than tripled in the

past 10 years—from 14% of the reported cases in 1987 to 46% in 1996.

- Among male adolescents reported with HIV infection in 1996, 49% were among young men who had sex with men (MSM), 6% were among young men infected through heterosexual contact, 5% were among injection drug users, and 4% were among MSM who also injected drugs.

- For adolescents, those most at risk are young gay and bisexual males, particularly young men of color.

- Adolescents who are most vulnerable to HIV infection also include those who are homeless or runaways, juvenile offenders, and school dropouts.

Research shows that three of the principal ways adolescents become infected with HIV are as follows: (1) high-risk sexual activity (unprotected sexual intercourse is reported by over half of adolescents by the age of 17 years); (2) injection of substances of abuse; and (3) sex with multiple partners (Schafer et al. 1993). Clearly, young people must be better educated about HIV, its transmission, and potential consequences before this infection becomes disastrous to adolescents.

■ WHAT TO DO ABOUT HIV AND AIDS

What can I do about being HIV-positive? I was diagnosed 3 years ago, and so far I am basically okay. I have started taking medication to slow down the rate of infection, but one never knows when the first symptoms suddenly pop up. My lover is clear of the infection and we are careful—usually. I am worried about my condition, but nothing can be done about it. Life is full of good luck and bad luck; so far I have been spared. Regarding tomorrow, who knows. (From Venturelli's research files, interview with a 32-year-old male hospital administrator, October 10, 1996).

To date, the current use of combining various types of protease inhibitors and other antiviral drugs is the most promising treatment for remaining relatively healthy with HIV. Although protease inhibitors do not appear to completely rid the body of HIV antibodies, this category of drugs is usually successful in holding the HIV virus at low levels in the bloodstream. The current lack of a permanent cure makes prevention the most important element in dealing with the AIDS problem. There are two main strategies for preventing HIV:

- People should be encouraged to adopt safer sexual behavior. Some of the steps to help achieve this include (1) avoiding multiple sex partners, especially if they are strangers or only casual acquaintances; (2) avoiding risk-taking sexual behavior that may allow HIV transmission, such as unprotected vaginal, oral, and anal intercourse; and (3) encouraging individuals who choose to continue high-risk sexual behaviors to use condoms or insist that their sexual partner use a condom.

- Drug abusers should be educated about their risk of contracting AIDS. They should be encouraged to reduce their risk by (1) abstaining from injecting drugs; (2) not sharing injection paraphernalia or always using clean needles (if available through "needle exchange programs"); (3) not sharing drugs with groups with high rates of HIV infection such as those in shooting galleries or crack houses; and (4) disinfecting the equipment (cleaning and boiling equipment for at least 15 minutes) between uses if they continue to share injection equipment.

One of the major difficulties in controlling the AIDS epidemic is to identify where preventive efforts should be focused. Because of limited resources, it is impossible to personally educate everyone in this country about HIV and AIDS. Consequently, our most intense efforts must be targeted at populations and neighborhoods with particularly high HIV infection rates. The National Research Council has declared that, although anyone can acquire AIDS, a handful of neighborhoods have been devastated by this infection whereas most of the nation remains relatively unscathed (Kolata 1993). It has been speculated that some 35 to 45 large neighborhoods in the United States fuel the AIDS epidemic throughout the country; if HIV infection could be controlled in these areas, the national epidemic would diminish significantly.

Because of this hypothesis, it has been proposed that AIDS prevention efforts particularly be focused on younger gay men and injection drug users who have multiple sex partners in the high-density AIDS neighborhoods found in many large metropolitan cities throughout the United States. Even with this focused approach, no one should be fooled into thinking that the HIV/AIDS problem will be eliminated. Everyone should approach potential sexual partners with some degree of caution, especially because the carrier of HIV may be unaware of infection or be reluctant to admit being a carrier for fear of abandonment. One thing is evident: If any doubt exists, we strongly recommend getting tested several times in a row before engaging in potentially life-threatening sexual contact.

The Entertainment Industry and Drug Use

Musicians sing about guzzling liquor and movie stars puff cigarettes and take drugs on the big screen. But federal officials ask: Where is the unglamorous side of substance use—like hangovers, slurred speech, or trouble with the law? (*News Tribune* 1999) Drug use has a tendency to be displayed or fueled (depending on your perspective) by popular culture. In this section, we discuss three important genres of popular culture—movies, music, and the Internet—as one electronic "subculture" that depicts and promotes drug use.

At the Lollapalooza music festival held in July 1997 in an amphitheater in Massachusetts, the mostly white, suburban teen crowd cheered wildly when rap group Cypress Hill pushed a 6-foot-tall *bong*, or water pipe, onstage. The group sold 5 million copies of its first two albums, one of which included songs titled "Legalize It," "Hits from the Bong," and "I Wanna Get High" (Winters 1997).

In a research study for Columbia's Center on Addiction and Substance Abuse, 76% of 12- to 17-year-olds indicated that the entertainment industry encourages illegal drug use. One 16-year-old daily marijuana user said, "All I know is that almost every song you listen to says something about [drug use].

It puts it into your mind constantly. . . . When you see the celebrities doing it, it makes it seem okay" (Winters 1997, p. 41).

Approximately 5 years ago, rock and rap music industries experienced a heroin epidemic. Although many other rock stars before Kurt Cobain used and abused drugs, Cobain's struggle with heroin and his 1994 suicide appear to have glamorized the use of this drug. "The number of top alternative bands that have been linked to heroin through a member's overdose, arrest, admitted use, or recovery is staggering: Nirvana, Hole, Smashing Pumpkins, Everclear, Blind Melon, Skinny Puppy, 7 Year Bitch, Red Hot Chili Peppers, Stone Temple Pilots, Breeders, Alice in Chains, Sublime, Sex Pistols, Porno for Pyros, and Depeche Mode." (Schoemer 1996, p. 50).

Together these bands have sold more than 60 million albums—"that's a heck of a lot of white, middle-class kids in the heartland" (Schoemer 1996, p. 50). Despite some factions in the music industry attempting to curtail heroin use by rock stars, many claim that the music industry still glamorizes heroin and other drug use.

How pervasive is drug use in today's popular movies and music? Recent research indicates that there is much substance abuse in popular movies and music. Findings revealed that 98% of movies studied depicted illicit drugs, alcohol, tobacco, or OTC and prescription medicines. Alcohol and tobacco appeared in more than 90% of movies, and illicit drugs appeared in 22%. About one-quarter (26%) of the movies that depicted illicit drugs contained explicit, graphic portrayals of their preparation and/or ingestion. Substance use was almost never a central theme, and very few movies ever specified motivations for use. Less than one-half (49%) of the movies portrayed short-term consequences of substance use, and about 12% depicted long-term consequences. Of the 669 adult major characters featured in the 200 movies studied, 5% used illicit drugs, 25% smoked tobacco, and 65% consumed alcohol. At least two major characters used illicit drugs in 12% of the movies, tobacco in 44%, and alcohol in 85% (ONDCP 1999).

In summarizing main findings from a study conducted by the Office of National Drug Control Policy (1999) regarding substance use in both movies and songs, the following results were found:

- Alcohol appeared in 93% of the movies and 17% of the songs; tobacco appeared in 89% of the movies but only 3% of the songs.

- Alcohol use was associated with wealth or luxury in 34% of the movies in which it appeared, with sexual activity in 19%, and with crime or violence in 37%.

- Alcohol use was associated with wealth or luxury in 24% of the songs in which it was referenced, with sexual activity in 3%, and with crime or violence in 13%.

- 63% of rap songs contained references to substances; only 10% of songs in other categories did.

- In movies depicting illicit drugs, marijuana appeared most frequently (51%), followed by powder cocaine (33%); hallucinogens, heroin or other opiates, and miscellaneous others (each 12%); and crack cocaine (2%).

- In songs referring to illicit drugs, marijuana appeared most frequently (63%), followed by crack cocaine (15%); powder cocaine (10%); and hallucinogens, heroin or other opiates, and miscellaneous others (4% each).

These findings clearly indicate that both movies and songs continue to reflect widespread use of alcohol and other drugs in our culture. Furthermore, their influence on the public viewing audiences continues to have an impact on values and attitudes about the use and/or abuse of drugs. One executive director of a Washington, D.C. area youth group, said: "It's becoming increasingly difficult to administer our preventive drug programs because the youth culture has changed in a manner that a lot of more popular music idolizes the use of marijuana and hallucinogens and that has a profound effect on young people" (Haywood 1996, p. 14).

Another top administrator at the Center for Substance Abuse Prevention of the Substance Abuse and Mental Health Services Administration, agreed, and said, "Our pop culture is sending a lot of pro-drug messages" (Haywood 1996). In addition to these observations, the major findings noted earlier with regard to substance use in movies and songs support the amount of alcohol and other drugs used in these two major types of electronic and audio mediums.

■ MORE RECENT PROMOTER OF DRUG USE: THE INTERNET

According to the UCLA Center for Communication Policy, for those who use online technology, the Internet is considered the most important source for information—more important than TV or radio. Further, "Some 55% of Internet users said 'most' or 'all' information in cyberspace is reliable and accurate, while only a third of non-users agreed" (Reuters and CNN.com 2000a). A survey of 55,000 Internet users performed by a market research firm called Media Matrix discovered that low income worldwide web users are now the fastest-growing U.S. market (Reuters and CNN.com 2000b).

There is no question that pro-drug messages and detailed information are readily available over the Internet. The Internet maintains a unique subculture of drug enthusiasts. Drug use information found online includes how to roll super joints, bake marijuana-laced brownies, grow "magic" psilocybin mushrooms, and create formulas for making amphetamine-like drugs; where to purchase the latest equipment for indoor growing of marijuana; and where to obtain catalogs that offer drug paraphernalia for sale. Similarly, magazines such as *High Times* and *Hemp Times* claim growing numbers of subscribers. Such magazines devote most of their articles, features, advice columns, hemp festival information, and advertisements to the pleasures of drug consumption. Further, chat rooms devoted to finding, growing, purchasing, and making drug substances are growing in popularity. Oftentimes, chat rooms and exchange of information on the Internet remains oblivious to non illicit drug users.

Although the Internet serves as an immensely valuable medium for learning, conducting business, communicating, and making information available, and it is also used by a growing number of drug users as a forum for exchanging and learning about the latest information and techniques of drug consumption. Individuals who use the Internet for this type of information should be particularly wary because it is difficult if not impossible for harmful myths and fallacies posted on the web to be regulated.

Discussion Questions

1. What are two strengths and two weaknesses of studying subcultures from (1) an insider's perspective and (2) an outsider's perspective?

2. What are the principal drugs abused by athletes?

3. What are the principal effects and side effects of steroids?

4. What factors encourage drug use by athletes?

5. From the "world" of steroid abusers, define and give an example of the following terms: stacking, cycling, plateauing, pyramiding, and array.

6. Argue both for and against drug testing in sports.

7. What type of penalties do you think should be used against athletes who abuse drugs?

8. Review the ATLAS steroid prevention program. Can you improve its methods for lessening steroid use among adolescents? How effective do you think this program would be at your college or university?

9. List the reasons why women are more concerned about drug use and abuse than men. Can you add several additional reasons not mentioned in this chapter?

10. Do you believe that drug prevention programs should be created uniquely for males and females?

11. What factors in the unique female roles encourage the use of substances of abuse?

12. Should childbearing women who abuse drugs be punished? Why or why not?

13. Why are women who have been or are sexually abused more likely to become addicted to drugs?

14. Why are adolescents especially vulnerable to drug abuse problems?

15. List and explain three reasons why you think adolescents from upper-middle class socioeconomic backgrounds become drug abusers.

16. What types of parents are most likely to have children who develop drug abuse problems?

17. How do adolescent drug abuse patterns differ from those in adults?

18. In what way are drugs of abuse associated with juvenile gang activity?

19. Should all adolescents who use drugs of abuse be treated for drug dependence? Explain your answer.

20. Do you think that it is realistic to expect drug abusers to change their habits in order to prevent the spread of AIDS? Why or why not?

21. Should prisoners who test positive for HIV be segregated from the non–HIV positive populations? Should prisoners be given free access to condoms in prisons? Why or why not?

22. John was caught by campus or city police growing psilocybin (hallucinogenic) mushrooms in his off-campus college apartment. Should John be punished by his college or university in addition to the punishment that will be determined by the criminal justice system? Why or why not?

23. What if you discover that your roommate is HIV positive? How would you handle this situation?

24. Do you think that the excessive use of alcohol and other drugs in movies influences viewers? Further, are people who enjoy rap music affected by the lyrics that refer to drug use and/or abuse? Why or why not?

25. Do you believe that drug information over the Internet, such as chat rooms devoted to the use of certain drugs, (e.g., where to purchase equipment for growing marijuana, OTC stimulant pills, and the spores of psilocybin mushrooms) promotes drug use? Why or why not?

Key Terms

subculture 442

outsider's perspective 442

insider's perspective 442

"doping" 443

ergogenic 443

androgens 444

anabolic steroids 444

"stacking" 446

"cycling" 446

"plateauing" 446

"pyramiding" 446

"array" 446

human growth factor (HGF) 450

human growth hormone (HGH) 450

ATLAS program 451

sociobiological changes 460

intragang 466

intergang 466

primary prevention 468

secondary prevention 469

Rohypnol 475

club drugs 475

protease inhibitors 477

Summary

1 The most common drugs abused by athletes are the ergogenic (performance-enhancing) substances. They include the anabolic steroids, for building muscle mass and strength, and the CNS stimulants, to achieve energy, quickness, and endurance.

2 Drug testing is conducted for most professional athletic competitions and usually includes screens for steroids and stimulants. However, some performance-enhancing drugs, such as erythropoietin and HGF, are undetectable. Yet, undetectable drugs are 90% of the estimated doping cases. Athletes who use

performance-enhancing drugs often go to great lengths to avoid detection by these drug tests.

3 About 50% of the anabolic steroids used in the United States are prescribed by doctors; the other 50% are obtained from the black market. Black market steroids include drugs diverted from legitimate channels smuggled from foreign countries—for example, Brazil, Italy, Mexico, Great Britain, Portugal, France, and Peru—designated for veterinarian use, or inactive counterfeits.

4 The ATLAS prevention program uses athletes, coaches, and team leaders who are trained to educate team members about the effects of anabolic steroid abuse. They emphasize both desirable and adverse effects of steroid use. Presenting a balanced perspective is stressed because adolescents know very well how anabolic steroids build muscles and can increase athletic abilities.

5 Women are (1) more concerned about drugs and drug use than men; (2) more likely to believe in drug prevention programs, such as needle exchange and testing reckless drivers for drug use than men; and (3) more likely to speak with their children about drug use than men (Drug Strategies 1998).

6 There is a high prevalence of drug dependence in women who are victims of sexual and/or physical abuse. Approximately 70% of women in drug abuse treatment report histories of physical abuse with victimization beginning at 11 years of age and occurring repeatedly. Further, women and men have different endocrine (hormone) systems, organs, and structures, and women's responses to drugs vary according to their reproductive states.

7 In order for women to receive adequate treatment for drug dependence, certain considerations must be met: (1) availability of female-sensitive services, (2) nonpunitive and noncoercive treatment that incorporates supportive behavior change approaches, and (3) treatment for a wide range of medical problems, mental disorders, and psychosocial problems.

8 Most adolescents who use substances of abuse are going through normal psychosocial development and will not develop problematic dependence on these drugs. The adolescent users who have difficulty with drugs often lack coping skills to deal with their problems, have dysfunctional families, possess poor self-images, and/or feel socially and emotionally insecure.

9 Parents who are most likely to raise drug-abusing adolescents are (1) drug abusers, (2) non–drug using coupled with being constantly condemning, (3) overly demanding, (4) overly protective, and (5) unable to communicate effectively with their children.

10 The substances adolescents are most likely to abuse are alcohol, cigarettes, inhalants, marijuana, LSD, Ecstasy, and prescription stimulants. High-frequency use is most likely to occur with cigarettes, alcohol, and marijuana.

11 People who become gang members were often neglected by their parents, lacked positive role models, and failed to receive adequate adult supervision. Other motivations for joining a gang include peer pressures, low self-esteem, and perceived easy acquisition of money from gang-related drug dealing and other criminal activities.

12 The major reasons cited by college students for their use of drugs were (1) to have fun, (2) usually to relieve stress, (3) to ease social interactions, (4) to relieve academic stress, and (5) to get high or drunk.

13 Two interesting findings from research regarding drug use by college student subcultures are that (1) the best predictor of drug use for first-year college students is drug use during a typical month in the senior year of high school, and (2) usually recreational drug use does not begin in college but has already been established in high school.

14 Club drugs include MDMA (Ecstasy), GHB, Rohypnol, ketamine, methamphetamine, and LSD. The phrase *club drug* is derived from the use of these drugs at all-night dance parties such as raves or trances, dance clubs, and bars. All these drugs are colorless, tasteless, and odorless. Individuals who may want to intoxicate, sedate, and later sexually take advantage of others can add them unobtrusively to beverages.

15 Next to homosexual men, individuals who are addicted to illicit drugs are the second largest risk group for contracting AIDS. This risk results from sharing of blood-contaminated nee-

dles and syringes and increased involvement in sexual risk taking because of the effects of drugs or in securing payment for drugs.

16 In the United States alone, since 1981, 733,374 cases of AIDS have been reported to the CDC (CDC 2000b). Of these cases, 83% were males and 17% were women. Worldwide, " . . . more than 18 million people have died of AIDS, almost 15 million of them in sub-Saharan Africa. About 34 million people are living with AIDS, most of them in Africa, and a million more were infected last year" (Sternberg 2000, p. 1) and has caused 13 million children to be orphaned. Sadly, South Africa, which in large part is poverty stricken, has more than 70% of the World's 34 million people with HIV/AIDS.

17 Major ways to prevent contracting HIV include (1) engaging in safe (protected) sexual behavior, (2) avoiding use of contaminated drug paraphernalia and especially use of intravenous drugs, (3) avoiding use of drugs in groups with high rates of HIV infection, and (4) frankly discussing past sexual histories with potential sexual partners and, if in any doubt, being tested for HIV several times in a row.

18 The extent of alcohol and drug use in movies and songs is startling. Overall, findings revealed that 98% of movies studied depicted illicit drugs, alcohol, and tobacco or OTC/prescription medicines. In this same detailed study, alcohol appeared in 93% of the movies and in 17% of the songs; tobacco appeared in 89% of movies but only 3% of songs. The lyrics of 63% of rap songs versus about 10% of the lyrics in other categories had substance references.

19 The music industry has been setting up drug-using celebrities as teen role models. The message conveyed by much of the music and by many bands is that drug use is acceptable. After several drug-related deaths of celebrities over the past few years, the industry is working on changing such perceptions.

20 New media influences contribute to drug use. The Internet is considered to be the latest source of information where knowledge about use of illicit drugs is burgeoning.

References

ABC News. "Suicide's Young Victims: A Chat with Teen Suicide Expert Dr. David Shaffer." *Talk City and ABCNEWS.Com* (12 April 2000). Available http://www.abcnews.go.com/onair/dailynews/chat_teensuicide.html.

Alexander, L., J. LaRosa, and H. Bader. *New Dimensions in Women's Health,* 2nd ed. Boston: Jones and Bartlett, 2001.

Altman, L. K. "Focusing on Prevention in Fight Against AIDS." *New York Times* (31 August 1999). Available http://www.nytimes.com/library/national/science/aids/083199hth-aids-prevention.html.

Apostolides, M. "How to Quit the Holistic Way." *Psychology Today* 29 (September/October 1996): 30–43, 75–6.

Archambault, D. "Adolescence, a Physiological, Cultural and Psychological No Man's Land." In *Adolescent Substance Abuse, Etiology, Treatment and Prevention,* edited by G. Lawson and A. Lawson, 11–28. Gaithersburg, MD: Aspen, 1992.

Associated Press. "British Begin Human Testing of HIV Vaccine." The *New York Times* (1 September 2000). Available http://www.nytimes.com/library/national/science/aids/090100aids-test.html.

Bahr, S. J., A. C. Marcos, and S. L. Maughan. "Family, Educational and Peer Influences on Alcohol Use of Female and Male Adolescents." *Journal of Studies on Alcohol* 56 (1995): 457–69.

Beard, B. and V. Kunsman. "A Cause for Concern: Alcohol-Induced Risky Sex on College Campuses." *Prevention Pipeline* 6 (September/October 1993): 24.

Begley, S. and M. Brant with Dickey, C.; K. Helmstaedt; R. Nordland, and T. Hayden. "The Real Scandal." *Newsweek* 133 (15 February 1999): 48–54.

Bell, J. "Athletes' Use and Abuse of Drugs." *The Physician and Sports Medicine* 15 (March 1987): 99–108.

Belsie, L. "Temperance Movement Hits College Dorms." *The Christian Science Monitor* 87 (30 August 1995): 1.

Bennett, M. E., J. Miller, and W. Gill. "Drinking, Binge Drinking, and Other Drug Use Among Southwestern Undergraduates: Three-Year Trends." *American Journal of Drug and Alcohol Abuse* 25 (1999): 331–46.

Bergeret, J. *Young People, Drugs . . . and Others.* Rockville, MD: United Nations Office for Drug Control Office for Drug Control and Crime Prevention (UN/ODCCP) (1 January 1981). Available http://www.undep.org/bulletin/bulletin_1981-01-01_4_page002.html.

Beschner, G. and A. Friedman. "Treatment of Adolescent Drug Abusers." *International Journal of the Addictions* 20 (1985): 977–93.

"Bodybuilding Drug Yields 'High.'" *Pharmacy Times* (June 1992): 14.

Booth, R., J. Watters, and D. Chitwood. "HIV Risk-Related Sex Behaviors Among Injection Drug Users, Crack Smokers, and Injection Drug Users Who Smoke Crack." *American Journal of Public Health* 83 (1993): 1144–8.

Buckstein, D., D. Brent, J. Perper, G. Moritz, M. Baugher, J. Schweers, C. Roth, and L. Balach. "Risk Factors for Completed Suicide Among Adolescents with a Lifetime History of Substance Abuse: A Case-Control Study." *Acta Psychiatry Scandinavia* 88 (1993): 403–8.

Burke, C. and S. Davis. "Anabolic Steroid Abuse." *Pharmacy Times* (June 1992): 35–40.

Campus Alcohol Drug Resource Center at the University of Florida 2000. *Alcohol and Other Drug Use, 1999.* University of Florida. Available http://www.health.ufl.edu.shcc/cadrc. htm.

Centers for Disease Control and Prevention (CDC). *Facts About Adolescent and HIV/AIDS.* Atlanta, GA: CDC, March 1998. Available http://www.thebody.com/cdc/hivteen.html.

Centers for Disease Control and Prevention (CDC). "HIV/AIDS." *Surveillance Reports* 11 (1999): 1–3.

Centers for Disease Control and Prevention. *Age at Diagnosis of HIV Infection or AIDS, Reported Through 1999, United States.* HIV/AIDS Surveillance: General Epidemiology 178 Slide Series Through 1999, Slide 24 of 24. Atlanta, GA: National Center for HIV, STD, and TB Prevention, January 2000a.

Centers for Disease Control and Prevention. *AIDS Cases by Age and Sex Reported 1981–1999, United States.* HIV/AIDS Surveillance: General Epidemiology 178 Slide Series Through 1999, Slide 2 of 24. Atlanta, GA: National Center for HIV, STD, and TB Prevention, January 2000b.

Centers for Disease Control and Prevention. *Adult/Adolescent AIDS Cases by Exposure Category and Year of Diagnosis, 1985–June 1999, United States.* HIV/AIDS Surveillance: General Epidemiology 178 Slide Series Through 1999, Slide 8 of 24. Atlanta, GA: National Center for HIV, STD, and TB Prevention, January 2000c.

Ciba Foundation. "AIDS and HIV Infection in Cocaine Users." In *Cocaine: Scientific and Social Dimensions,* 181–94. New York: Wiley, 1992.

Colthurst, T. "HIV and Alcohol Impairment: Reducing Risks." *Prevention Pipeline* 6 (July/August 1993): 24.

Cowley, G. "Targeting a Deadly Scrap of Genetic Code." *Newsweek* 128 (2 December 1996): 68–9.

Curry, D. G. and I. A. Spergel. "Gang Homicide, Delinquency, and Community." In *Gangs and Gang Behavior,* edited by G. Larry Mays. Chicago, IL: Nelson-Hall, 1997: 314–36.

Daily, S. "Alcohol, Incest, and Adolescence." In *Adolescent Substance Abuse, Etiology, Treatment and Prevention,* edited by G. Lawson and A. Lawson, 251–66. Gaithersburg, MD: Aspen, 1992a.

Daily, S. "Suicide Solution: The Relationship of Alcohol and Drug Abuse to Adolescent Suicide." In *Adolescent Substance Abuse, Etiology, Treatment and Prevention,* edited by G. Lawson and A. Lawson, 233–50. Gaithersburg, MD: Aspen, 1992b.

Diaz, T. and S. Chu. "Crack Cocaine Use and Sexual Behavior Among People with AIDS." *Journal of the American Medical Association* 269 (1993): 2845–6.

Dicker, M., and E. A. Leighton. "Trends in the U.S. Prevalence of Drug-Using Parturient Women and Drug-Affected Newborns, 1979 Through 1990." *American Journal of Public Health* 84 (September 1994): 1433.

Drug Facts and Comparisons. St. Louis, MO: Kluwer, 1994.

Drug Strategies. *Keeping Score 1998, Drug Use and Attitudes.* Washington, DC: 1998. Available http://www.drugstrategies.org/ks1998/index.html.

Elmen, J., and D. Offer. "Normality, Turmoil and Adolescence." In *Handbook of Clinical Research and Practice with Adolescents,* edited by P. Tolan and B. Cohler, 5–19. New York: Wiley, 1993.

Erickson, P. G. and G. F. Murray. "Sex Differences in Cocaine Use and Experiences: A Double Standard Revived?" *American Journal of Drug and Alcohol Abuse* 15 (1989): 135–52.

Fagan, J. "Social Processes of Delinquency and Drug Use Among Urban Gangs." In *Gangs in America,* edited by C. R. Huff, 183–213. Newbury Park, CA: Sage, 1990.

Ferrente, R. "Ben Johnson Retires from Running After Positive Test." *Morning Edition* on National Public Radio (8 March 1993).

Fischer, J. S. "Searching for That Ounce of Prevention: Promising Strategies for an AIDS Vaccine." *U.S. News and World Report* (17 July 2000). Vol. 129 #3: pgs. 45–6.

Glave, J. "Betty Ford Got Help, but Addiction Stalks Thousands of Women." *Salt Lake Tribune* 248 (3 June 1994): A-1.

Goldberg, L, D. Elliot, G. N. Clarke, D. P. MacKinnon, E. Moe, L. Zoref, C. Green, S. L. Wolf, E. Greffrath, D. J. Miller, and A. Lapin. "Effects of a Multidimensional Anabolic Steroid Prevention Intervention: The Adolescents Training and Learning to Avoid Steroids (ATLAS) Program. *Journal of the American Medical Association* 276 (1996): 1555–62.

Goldstein, F. "Pharmacological Aspects of Substance Abuse." In *Remington's Pharmaceutical Sciences,* 19th ed. Easton, PA: Mack, 1995.

Grinspoon, L. "AIDS and Mental Health—Part 1." *Harvard Mental Health Letter* 10 (January 1994): 1–4.

Harlan, R. and M. Garcia. "Neurobiology of Androgen Abuse." In *Drugs of Abuse,* edited by R. Watson, 185–201. Boca Raton, FL: CRC Press, 1992.

Haywood, R. L. "Why More Young People Are Using Drugs." *Jet* 90 (9 September 1996): 14.

Hoberman, J. M. and C. E. Yesalis. "The History of Synthetic Testosterone." *Scientific American* 272 (February 1995): 76–81.

Hoshino, J. "Assessment of Adolescent Substance Abuse." In *Adolescent Substance Abuse, Etiology, Treatment and Prevention*, edited by G. Lawson and A. Lawson, 87–104. Gaithersburg, MD: Aspen, 1992.

Howard, M. "Adolescent Substance Abuse: A Social Learning Theory Perspective." In *Adolescent Substance Abuse, Etiology, Treatment and Prevention*, edited by G. Lawson and A. Lawson, 29–40. Gaithersburg, MD: Aspen, 1992.

Inciardi, J. A., D. Lockwood, and A. E. Pottieger. *Women and Crack-Cocaine*. New York: MacMillian, 1993.

Johnson, R. A., J. P. Hoffmann, and D. R. Gerstein. *The Relationship Between Family Structure and Adolescent Substance Use*. Rockville, MD: SAMHSA, Office of Applied Studies, July 1996.

Johnston, L. D., P. O'Malley, and J. G. Bachman. *National Survey Results from the Monitoring the Future Study, 1975–1992; 1975–1994*. Rockville, MD: National Institute on Drug Abuse, 1993, 1996.

Johnston, L. D., P. O'Malley, and J. G. Bachman. *National Survey on Drug Abuse from the Monitoring the Future Study, 1975–1998; College and Young Adults*. The University of Michigan Institute for Social Research, National Institute on Drug Abuse, Rockville, MD: U.S. Department of Human Services, National Institutes of Health, 1999.

Johnston, L. D., P. O'Malley, and J. G. Bachman. *The Monitoring the Future National Results on Adolescent Drug Use: Overview of Key Findings, 1999*. The University of Michigan Institute for Social Research, National Institute on Drug Abuse, U.S. Department of Human Services, National Institutes of Health, 2000a.

Johnston, L. D., P. O'Malley, and J. G. Bachman. *National Survey Results on Drug Use from the Monitoring the Future Study, 1975–1999. Vol. 2, College Students and Young Adults*. U.S. Department of Health and Human Services (USDHHS), National Institute on Drug Abuse (NIDA). Washington, DC: United States Government Printing Office, 2000b.

Kandel, D. B. "Drug and Drinking Behavior Among Youth." *Annual Review of Sociology* 6 (1980): 235–85.

Kantrowitz, B. and P. Wingert. "Beyond Littleton: How Well Do You Know Your Kid?" *Newsweek* 133 (10 May 1999): 36–40.

Kinney, J. *Loosening the Grip*, 6th ed. Boston, MA: McGraw–Hill, 2000.

Kirkpatrick, J. *The Woman Alcoholic*. Quakertown, PA: Women for Sobriety, 1999. Available http://www.womenforsobriety.org/articles/wfs_leadstory12.html.

Kolata, G. "Targeting Urged in Attack on AIDS." *New York Times* 142 (7 March 1993): 1.

Korolenko, C. P. and T. A. Donskih. "Addictive Behavior in Women: A Theoretical Perspective." *Drugs and Society* 4 (1990): 39–65.

Ladwig, G. B. and M. D. Anderson. "Substance Abuse in Women: Relationship Between Chemical Dependency of Women and Past Reports of Physical and/or Sexual Abuse." *International Journal of the Addictions* 24 (1989): 739–54.

Lale, T. "Gangs and Drugs." In *Adolescent Substance Abuse, Etiology, Treatment and Prevention*, edited by G. Lawson and A. Lawson, 267–81. Gaithersburg, MD: Aspen, 1992.

Lawn, J. *Team Up for Drug Prevention with America's Young Athletes*. Washington, DC: Drug Enforcement Administration, U.S. Department of Justice, 1984.

Lawson, G. and A. Lawson, "Etiology." In *Adolescent Substance Abuse, Etiology, Treatment and Prevention*, edited by G. Lawson and A. Lawson, 1–10. Gaithersburg, MD: Aspen, 1992.

Leinwand, D. "20% Say They Used Drugs with Their Mom or Dad. Among Reasons: Boomer Culture and Misguided Attempts to Bond." *USA Today* (27 August 2000). Available http://www.usatoday.com/usatonline/20000824/25790504s.htm.

Leibsohn, J. "The Relationship Between Drug and Alcohol Use and Peer Group Associations of College Freshmen as They Transition from High School." *Journal of Drug Education* 24 (1994): 177–92.

Lin, A. Y. F. "Should Women Be Included in Clinical Trials?" *Pharmacy Times* 10 (November 1994): 27.

Lively, K. "The 'Date-Rape Drug': Colleges Worry About Reports of Growing Use of Rohypnol, a Sedative." *Chronicle of Higher Education* 42 (28 June 1996): A-29.

Lukas, S. "Urine Testing for Anabolic-Androgenic Steroids." *Trends in Pharmacological Sciences* 14 (1993): 61–8.

Marklein, M. B. "College Binge Drinking Heads off Campus." *USA Today* (14 March 2000). Available http://www.usatoday.com/life/health/addiction/lhadd029.htm.

Mathias, R. "NIDA Survey Provides First National Data on Drug Use During Pregnancy." *NIDA Notes* 10 (January/February 1995): 6–7.

Mathias, R. "Sex-for-Crack Phenomenon Poses Risk for Spread of AIDS in Heterosexuals." *NIDA Notes* 8 (May/June 1993): 8–11.

McCaffrey, B. R. "McCaffrey Announces Strategy to Fight Drug Use in Sports." *Daily Washington File* (21 October 1999). Available http://www.usis.it/wireless/wf991021/99102114.htm.

McDonald, M. "Fast, Strong, Dead?" *Salt Lake Tribune* 250 (22 June 1995): C-1, C-8.

Meilman, P. W., R. K. Grace, C. A. Presley, and R. Lyerla. "Beyond Performance Enhancement: Polypharmacy Among Collegiate Users of Steroids." *Journal of American College Health* 44 (November 1995): 98–104.

Merchant, W. "Medications and Athletes." *American Druggist* (October 1992): 6–14.

Millstein, R. *Community Alert Bulletin.* Rockville, MD: National Institute on Drug Abuse, U.S. Department of Health and Human Services, (25 March 1993).

Minnesota Institute of Public Health. *Alcohol and Other Drugs and Suicide.* Anoka, MN: Spring 1995. Available http://www.mikph.org/area/fs8.html.

Moss, H., L. Kirisci, H. Gordon, and R. Tarter. "A Neuropsychological Profile of Adolescent Alcoholics." *Alcoholism: Clinical and Experimental Research* 18 (1994): 159–63.

"Multistate Outbreak of Poisonings Associated with Illicit Use of GHB." *Prevention Pipeline* 7 (May/June 1994): 95–96.

National Clearinghouse for Alcohol and Drug Information (NCADI). *Drugs of Abuse.* Rockville, MD: Substance Abuse and Mental Health Services Administration, 1999. Available http://www.health.org/pubs/catalog/rpos.htm.

National Institute of Mental Health. *The Number Count: Mental Disorders in America,* January 2001. Available http://www.nimh.nih.gov/publicat/numbers.pdf.

National Institutes of Health (NIH) and National Institute on Drug Abuse (NIDA). *Drug Abuse and Drug Abuse Research: Executive Summary.* Rockville, MD: Substance Abuse and Mental Health Services Administration, 1998.

National Institute on Drug Abuse (NIDA). *Anabolic Steroid Abuse.* Capsule 43. Rockville, MD: NIDA, 1996.

National Institute on Drug Abuse (NIDA). *Drug Abuse and Addiction Research: The Sixth Triennial Report to Congress.* Rockville, MD: U.S. Department of Health and Human Services (USDHHS), 1999.

National Institute on Drug Abuse (NIDA). "Club Drugs: Community Alert Bulletin." *NIDA Notes* 14 (30 March 2000a).

News Tribune. "Alcohol, Tobacco or Drugs Used in 98% of Popular Movies." *News Tribune* (29 April 1999). Available http://www.newstribune.com/stories/042999/ent_0429990069.html.

Nicklin, J. L. "Arrests at Colleges Surge for Alcohol and Drug Violations." *The Chronicle of Higher Education* XLVI, No. 40 (9 June 2000) A48–A58.

Office of National Drug Control Policy (ONDCP). *Substance Use in Popular Movies and Music.* Media Campaign, Campaign Publications. Rockville, MD: ONDCP Drugs and Crime Clearinghouse, 1999.

"OTC Drugs and Athletes." *Pharmacy Times* (June 1992): 16.

Parrot, A. *Date Rape and Acquaintance Rape.* New York: Rosen, 1988.

Pietroski, N. "Counseling HIV/AIDS Patients." *American Druggist* (August 1993): 50–6.

Prendergast, M. L. "Substance Use and Abuse Among College Students: A Review of Recent Literature." *Journal of American College Health* 43 (1994): 99–113.

Ravid, J. "The Hard-core Curriculum." *Rolling Stone* 719 (19 October 1995): 99.

Reuters and CNN.com. *Users See Internet as Key Information Source.* (16 August 2000a). Available http://www.cnn.com/2000/TECH/computing/08/16/internet.study.reut/index.html.

Reuters and CNN.com. *Study: Lower-income Web Users Now Fastest-growing U.S. Market.* (22 August 2000b). Available http://www.cnn.com/2000/TECH/computing/08/22/internet.incomes.reut/index.html.

Substance Abuse and Mental Health Services Administration (SAMHSA). *1999 Household Survey on Drug Abuse.* Available http://www.samhsa.gov/statistics/statistics.html.

Science Daily. "Pain Drug Reveals What Most Already Know—Men's and Women's Brains Are Simply Different. (15 March 2000). Available http://www.sciencedaily.com/releases/2000/03/000315075845.htm.

Substance Abuse and Mental Health Services Administration (SAMHSA). *Making the Connection Between Substance Abuse and HIV/AIDS Prevention for Women of Color and Youth.* Rockville, MD: U.S. Department of Health and Human Services, 1999.

Sanders, W. B. *Gangbangs and Drive-bys.* New York: Aldine De Gruyter, 1994.

Samples, P. "Alcoholism in Athletes: New Directions for Treatment." *The Physician and Sports Medicine* (17 April 1989): 193–202.

Schafer, M. A., J. F. Hilton, M. Ekstrand, and J. Keogh. "Relationship Between Drug Use and Sexual Behaviors and the Occurrence of Sexually Transmitted Diseases Among High-Risk Male Youth." *Sexually Transmitted Diseases* 20 (November/December 1993): 39–47.

Schoemer, K. "Rockers, Models and the New Allure of Heroin." *Newsweek* 128 (26 August 1996): 50–4.

Scott, D. M., J. C. Wagner, and T. W. Barlow. "Anabolic Steroids Use Among Adolescents in Nebraska Schools." *American Journal of Health-system Pharmacy* 53: 2068–72, 1996.

Shelden, R. G., S. Tracy, and W. Brown. *Youth Gangs in American Society.* Belmont, CA: Wadsworth/Thomson Learning, 2001.

Siegel, L., and J. Senna. *Juvenile Delinquency,* 6th ed. St. Paul, MN: West, 1997.

Spergel, I. A. *Youth Gangs: Problem and Response.* Chicago: University of Chicago, School of Social Service Administration, 1990

Steinberg, L., A. Fletcher, and N. Darling. "Parental Monitoring and Peer Influences on Adolescent Substance Use." *Pediatrics* 93 (1994): 1060–4.

Sternberg, S. "AIDS Apocalypse Expanding." *USA Today* (28 June 2000). Available at http://www.usatoday.com/life/health/aids/Africa/lhafr008.htm.

Street, C., J. Antonio, and D. Cudlipp. "Androgen Use by Athletes: A Reevaluation of the Health Risks." *Canadian Journal of Applied Physiology* 2 (1996): 421–40.

Substance Abuse and Mental Health Services Administration (SAMHSA). *Tips for Teens: About Steroids.* Center for Substance Abuse Prevention. Rockville, MD: U.S. Department of Health and Human Services, 1999.

Swadi, H. "Relative Risk Factors in Detecting Adolescent Drug Abuse." *Drug and Alcohol Dependence* 29 (1992): 253–4.

Teen Challenge. *Drugs: Frequently Asked Questions.* South Australia: Pragin Press, 2000. Available http://www.tc.sn.au/hoax2.asp.

Toronto, R. "Young Athletes Who Use 'Enhancing' Steroids Risk Severe Physical Consequences." *Salt Lake Tribune* 244 (6 July 1992): C-5.

U.S. Department of Justice. *Anabolic Steroids and You.* Washington, DC: Demand Reduction Section, Drug Enforcement Administration, 1991–1992.

Venturelli, P. J. "Drugs in Schools: Myths and Reality." *The Annals of the American Academy of Political and Social Science* 567, (special editions of this volume edited by W. H. Hinkle and S. Henry) January 2000: 72–87.

Walsh, F. and M. Sheinkman. "Family Context of Adolescence." In *Adolescent Substance Abuse, Etiology, Treatment and Prevention,* edited by G. Lawson and A. Lawson, 149–71. Gaithersburg, MD: Aspen, 1992.

Welder, A. and R. Melchert. "Cardiotoxic Effects of Cocaine and Anabolic-Androgenic Steroids in the Athlete." *Journal of Pharmacological and Toxicological Methods* 29 (1993): 61–8.

Winters, P. A. *Teen Addiction.* San Diego: Greenhaven Press, 1997.

Wisconsin Coalition Against Sexual Assault (WCASA). *Sexual Violence and Sexual Abuse.* Madison, WI: WCASA, 1997.

Witham, D. "Recovery in the Dorm: Rutgers University's Special Housing for Addicted Students." *Chronicle of Higher Education* 42 (10 November 1995): A-33.

"Women Smokers Run High Risk for Lung Cancer." *Prevention Pipeline* 7 (May/June 1994): 7.

Wright, L. "Suicidal Thoughts and Their Relationship to Family Stress and Personal Problems Among High School Seniors and College Undergraduates." *Adolescence* 20 (1985): 575–80.

Yesalis, C. E. and J. S. Cowart. *The Steroids Game.* Champaign, IL: Human Kinetics, 1998.

Zuger, A. "Epidemic: An Overview." *New York Times* (8 August 2000). Available http://www.nytimes.com/library/national/science/aids/aids-overview.html.

Drug Use/ Abuse Prevention

Did You Know?

▶ Comprehensive prevention programs involving the community, school, and family are more effective than single unit programs.

▶ The targeted audience of drug prevention programs must distinguish between early experimenters, non–problem drug users, nondetected committed or secret users, problem users, and former users.

▶ Drug prevention programs must first decide if they will stress total abstinence or responsible use.

▶ Students in drug prevention programs who do not know how to say no need refusal skills training or peer resistance training.

▶ Drug education actually began in the 1830s with the temperance movement.

▶ Family risk factors that often lead to drug use include being raised in a chaotic home environment, having parents with ineffective parenting skills, and having a lack of mutual attachments and nurturing.

▶ Information-only drug prevention programs increase the knowledge about drugs but have little or no effect on habitual use.

▶ Peer-based drug prevention uses fellow students as educators, mentors, counselors, or facilitators of prevention and out-reach work.

▶ D.A.R.E. drug prevention programs are in approximately 70% of the nation's school districts and reach approximately 25 million students.

▶ Drug courts are the newest form of drug prevention where drug defendants are more likely to undergo treatment (rehabilitation) than incarceration (punishment).

▶ Other alternatives to drug use include the alternatives approach and meditation.

Learning Objectives

On completing this chapter you will be able to:

▶ List the 10 most prominent factors influencing alcohol and other drug use surrounding the individual (see Figure 18.1).

▶ List and briefly explain the three major types of drug prevention programs.

▶ List the five different types of drug users that have to be considered *before* implementing a drug prevention program.

▶ List the three levels of comprehensive prevention programs for drug use and abuse.

▶ List the three family factors that can prevent initiation to drugs or extensive drug use.

▶ List four existing prevention programs largely found in higher education.

▶ Understand the main goals of the following large-scale drug prevention programs: BACCHUS and GAMMA Peer Education Network, D.A.R.E. and Drug Courts.

▶ Describe two other alternatives to drug use.

Introduction

When someone tells another person "just don't do drugs" and if that person is addicted to, say, cocaine like I was, that comes across as a retarded answer. You cannot just quit when you are addicted because even the idea of addiction continually blocks the possibility of casually deciding to stop using the drug. A lot has to go into the day you actually stop using the drug. First of all, the craving for the drug continually reminds you to do it maybe just a few more times. Then, your life appears to be less engaging because your body is missing the chemical properties of the drug that it became accustomed to and this affects your level of depression. So you have to sort of go through that slow abstinence period— you are without the drug and sometimes you can only deal with abstaining 1 hour at a time for the first week or so. Then slowly, ever so slowly, for me at least, the addict has to rebuild her or his daily living without the drug. It's just not easy. If it were, most people addicted to drugs would probably quit on their own. Especially when you realize that you are not controlling the drug, the drug is controlling you. Just remember, most addicts continually deceive (lie) to themselves and others that they are not "really" addicted. Do you know how hard it is to become aware that these lies are part of the addiction? Before the extended therapy I had, no one could convince me that the daily cocaine I was snorting and smoking was bad. *(From Venturelli's research files, female, age 37, academic administrator in higher education, who for the past 3 years has been drug free, 21 June 2000).*

After having read so much information on drug use, this final chapter concludes with one of the most important topics in drug information and research. Thus far, the chapters have examined: (1) risk factors for initial use (Chapter 2); (2) risk factors that generate habitual use and abuse and vicious cycles moving abusers toward addiction (Chapter 4); (3) legal ramifications of drug use (Chapter 3); (4) pharmacological effects of drug use (Chapters 5 and 6); and (5) the key drugs of abuse (Chapters 7 through 16). From all this information, you have now become familiar with the dozens, if not hundreds, of reasons why people experiment with, habitually use, abuse, and become dependent on psychoactive substances. You also know that the attraction to drug use involves genetic, pharmacological, personality (psychological), family, peer, subcultural, immediate environmental, societal (sociological), and cultural factors.

With so many potential causes for the unnecessary and nonmedical use of psychoactive substances, it becomes increasingly important to discuss methods, programs, and strategies that prevent, delay, or at the very least moderate the habitual use of drugs. This chapter explores and provides information on doing *something* about drug use and abuse.

Figure 18.1 shows many of the potential environmental factors involved in what influences alcohol and other drug use (AOD). The beginning core in this figure starts with the individual, and each concentric "zone" represent clusters of factors that influence an individual's views, attitudes, and behaviors toward drug use. With so many factors, each having an independent potential effect on the individual, you can see why comprehensive prevention programs involving the community, school, and family are more effective than single-unit programs, such as having a mandatory drug education program in elementary grades without other complementary and overlapping drug programs in the community and the family. Prevention research clearly shows that " . . . we must attend to all factors; prevention that focuses on only one or two factors and ignores or discounts the rest is likely to fail to have a long-term, permanent impact" (Tinzmann and Hixson 1992, p. 3).

Through comprehensive prevention programs that are multifaceted and complimentary, we are able to more effectively "tease-out" which factors are most influential. The televised commercial in the early 1990s that showed two eggs frying in a

---

KEY TERMS

AOD
refers to alcohol and other drug use

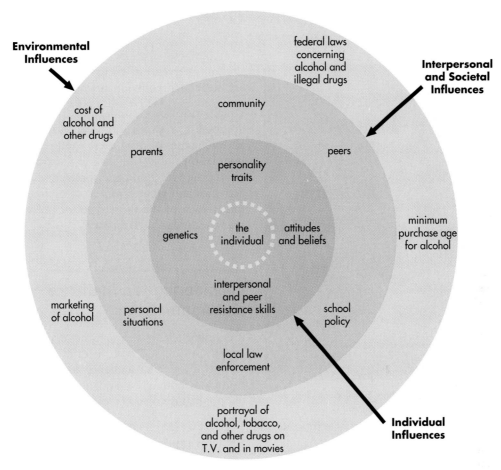

FIGURE 18.1
Potential factors that influence alcohol and other drug use.

Source: Tinzmann, M. B., and J. Hixson. *What Does Research Say About Prevention?* Oak Brook, IL: North Central Regional Educational Laboratory, 1992. Available http://www.ncrel.org/sdrs/areas/stw_esys/6prevntn.htm.

pan: "This is your brain . . . this is your brain on drugs," sponsored by the Partnership for a Drug-Free America, was an early attempt at prevention through a disturbing analogy. Although its effect was poor on drug users, who had never felt their brains frying, it was an initial step toward innovative prevention efforts. Was it worth the airtime? Can the success of these programs be adequately measured?

In 1997, 15 states thought prevention of alcohol and other drug abuse was important enough to maintain certified prevention specialist credential-

ing. Today, a bewildering variety of programs exist from coast to coast in school districts, churches, and other communities, all with the goal of preventing initial drug use or halting use before it becomes a problem ("Be Smart, Don't Start").

Drug Prevention Programs

There are three levels of drug prevention programs, each suited to different types of drug users.

AS A PARENT, YOU WANT TO DO EVERYTHING YOU CAN TO KEEP YOUR KIDS FROM EXPERIMENTING WITH DRUGS LIKE POT. IT WOULD BE A WHOLE LOT EASIER IF THEY CAME WITH INSTRUCTIONS. BUT THEY DON'T. WE CAN HELP. PLAY WITH THEM. READ TO THEM. SING WITH THEM. TEACH THEM A JOKE. LAUGH. LISTEN. TALK. BE INVOLVED. CALL 1-800-729-6866. WE'LL SEND YOU INFORMATION ON WHAT ELSE PARENTS CAN DO. ALSO VISIT OUR WEB SITE AT DRUGFREEAMERICA.ORG. YOU CAN MAKE A DIFFERENCE. PARENTS. THE ANTI-DRUG.

PARENTS. THE ANTI-DRUG.

Example of a current advertisement aimed at alerting parents about the dangers of early drug use.

Primary drug prevention programs are aimed at nonusers, and the goal is to "inoculate" potential users against drug use. Primary prevention is often targeted toward at-risk youth who may live in areas where licit- and illicit-type drugs are rampant, may come from problem families, or are surrounded by peers who use drugs.

Secondary drug prevention programs are aimed at newer drug users with a limited history of use.

Tertiary drug prevention programs usually have an intervention focus and target chemically dependent individuals who need treatment.

Usually primary, secondary, and tertiary programs are used in combination because, in most settings, all three types of drug users comprise the targeted population. Table 18.1 further illustrates these levels of drug prevention and corresponding suggested activities and what can be accomplished are listed under each of the three types of prevention (primary, secondary, and tertiary).

Considering the Audience and Approach

It is important to be aware that drug users vary in their exposure and past histories of substance use and/or abuse. The audience for drug prevention comprises both users and nonusers. In analyzing the population of users, categories include the following:

- Early experimenters
- Non–problem drug users—those who abuse drugs on occasion, mostly for recreation
- Nondetected, committed, or secret users—those who abuse drugs and have no interest in stopping
- Problem users
- Former users

It is important that role models, counselors, teachers, and anyone else involved in drug prevention programs take into consideration that there are different types of substance users/abusers. Therefore, drug prevention programs must cater to the specific needs of these groups. For nonproblem users, drug education programs should examine the abuse of drugs and reinforce the message that uncontrolled use leads to abuse. For committed users, drug education should aim to prevent or delay drug abuse. Former users should be given information that will reinforce their decision to stop abusing drugs.

TABLE 18.1 Levels of Drug Prevention and Suggested Activities

Primary Prevention (risk reduction before abuse)	

Intrapersonal Factors	Affective education (emotional literacy)
	Resilience training
	Values clarification
	Personal and social skills development
	    Assertiveness skills training
	    Refusal skills
	Drug information and education

Small Group Factors	Peer mentoring, counseling, outreach, modeling Conflict resolution Curriculum infusion Activities demonstrating misperception of peer norms Alternatives to use: recreational, cultural, athletic Strengthening families
Systems Level	Strengthening school–family links Strengthening school–community group links Strengthening community support systems Media advocacy efforts, reduce alcohol marketing
Secondary Prevention (intervening in early abuse)	
	Assessment strategies: identification of abuse subgroups and individual diagnoses Early intervention coupled with sanctions Teacher–counselor–parent team approach Developing healthy alternative youth culture Recovering role models
Tertiary Prevention (intervening in advanced abuse)	
	Assessment and diagnosis Referral into treatment Case management Reentry

A number of questions should be considered by a professional planning a prevention program. To what type of audience should the drug information be targeted: youths or adults? Peers or parents? Should information focus on knowledge, attitudes, or behavior? Should the program emphasize and recommend abstinence or responsible use?

In most cases, it is appropriate for drug prevention to focus on knowledge, attitudes, and behavior; the three are clearly related. For instance, if the goal is to increase knowledge, should we assume that attitudes and behavior will change accordingly, or should knowledge about the harmful effects of drugs be kept separate from attitudes and behavior?

For example, if you learn that smoking marijuana is a health hazard, equal to or more destructive than smoking cigarettes, does this knowledge limit the satisfaction you derive from smoking marijuana with friends? Some would say "yes." Unfortunately, many would say "no." In fact, knowledge about the harmful effects of certain types of drugs has very little effect on the personal attitudes and habits of most people. Most cigarette smokers are aware of the health hazards before they start smoking but this does not always stop them from starting or becoming addicted.

Drug education programs have to direct their attention to a small range of behavioral objectives. They will not be effective if they address too many issues.

Finally, drug prevention programs must decide if they will stress total abstinence or responsible use. Abstinence is radically different from responsible use. A program cannot advocate both. Information and "scare tactics" alone have no effect on drug use. Educational prevention models have been modified lately to achieve the following goals:

- Convey the message that society is inconsistent concerning drug use. For example, certain drugs that cause serious harm to a large percentage of the population are legal, whereas other drugs that have less impact are illegal.

- Convey that the reasons for drug use are complex and that drug users vary.

- Demonstrate to youth that young and old alike are affected by role models, in that attitudes regarding drug use are often patterned from family members who are role models.

- Acknowledge that other influential role models in music, sports, art, drama, business, and education who use and abuse drugs can affect attitudes toward drug use (see Chapter 17).

■ AN EXAMPLE OF DRUG PREVENTION AT CENTRAL HIGH IN ELMTOWN

This section describes how a school-based prevention program is implemented and demonstrates that programs must be comprehensive and multifaceted to be successful.

Let's stand in the shoes of a parent and teacher committee trying to design a primary prevention program for students at Central High in Elmtown. The group has some prevention research materials that it received from the National Clearinghouse for Alcohol and Drug Information. After some thought, most members of the committee decide not to address individual, personal risk factors (discussed in Chapters 2 and 4) that may generate anxieties or conflicts or painful or threatening feelings. They have spoken with some students and ascertained that most of the 9th- and 10th-graders, even those who tend toward rebelliousness and avant-garde styles, are against taking drugs. Although many students feel this way, there are trends in the school that worry the committee members. Some popular 11th- and 12th-grade peer group leaders are drug users, and drug sales have been occurring on school grounds. The presence and availability of drugs and the beginning of a drug-using atmosphere make it more likely that some of the younger students will initiate use. In brainstorming sessions, different committee members suggested ways to help these students avert initiation of drug use. Depending on their thinking, theoretical bent, and exposure to prevention models, members came up with the following ideas:

- Students need to be grounded in good, solid knowledge about the negative effects and dangers of drugs (1) as provided in a drug education course or (2) more subtly, in a curriculum concerning drug effects and drug-using behaviors (also covered later, in the section on higher education).

- Students with low self-esteem will feel uncomfortable asserting individual choices or points of view that deviate from those held by peers or peer leaders. Bolstering a positive self-image would allow such students to refuse drugs.

- Students who have low expectations regarding their ability to refuse drugs will be least likely to actually refuse. We might try to increase their "self-efficacy"—that is, their belief that their behaviors are powerful and will have results.

- Students just don't know how to say "no" and need refusal skills training or peer-resistance training.

- Although a clique leadership may set a pro-use tone, it is probable that the quiet antidrug students represent a silent majority. They may misperceive the amount of drug use that occurs in their school. If the antidrug students are shown that their own attitudes and beliefs are actually in the majority, they will see that the "emperor has no clothes."

- A more confrontational approach involves removing drugs from the school environment by infiltrating the student body or using informants to gather information about who is distributing drugs. Dealers and users can then be identified or counseled and their parents notified. The school could make the decision to go as far as having the student arrested or expelling him or her.

With so many options put forth, some of the committee members become frustrated and fear that a sufficient program will never be created. Some of them have experienced alcoholism in their families and fear that many of the above approaches are too "wishy-washy" to help the students who are already experimenting.

Seeing a disaster brewing, the committee chair makes a call to the Division of Substance Abuse Services in the state Department of Health to inquire about drug prevention programs. The operator refers the call to the prevention specialists at the agency, who are linked to the National Prevention Network, which is part of the National Association of State Alcohol and Drug Abuse Directors. The specialist schedules a meeting with the committee, where she makes the following points:

1. A prevention needs assessment is helpful, and necessitates using validated survey instruments to determine the patterns of behavior and attitudes regarding drug use among the student body.

2. A combination of primary and secondary prevention would be good for the majority of the student body, and group treatment for substance abuse should be made available at an adolescent outpatient clinic. The outpatient clinic will assess some students who are well on their way to addiction and refer them into inpatient treat-

ment. Because this intervention occurs when the student is at an advanced abuse state, this is considered tertiary prevention.

Notice how all three types of approaches (primary, secondary, and tertiary) are necessary to implement a comprehensive prevention strategy.

The specialist brought along a staff member of the Local Council on Alcoholism and Drug Dependence, an affiliate of the National Council on Alcoholism and Drug Dependence (NCADD) branch serving a three-county region of the state. Thousands of branches of NCADD exist in the United States, and their goal is to help local groups design and implement prevention programs. Many branches have developed specialized programs for teens, children, women, and the elderly. The staff member conducts preliminary sessions with the prevention committee and arranges to sign an affiliation agreement with the school administration, whereby NCADD will act as consultants to the school, aiding it in designing a prevention program to fit its particular needs. It will design a project, which will be based on a needs assessment that incorporates a survey of chemical attitudes and use and interviews with parents, teachers, and students. The project design will include the program objectives, a methods and management plan, a timeline, and an evaluation component. To help those members bewildered by the many possible factors identified by the committee in its brainstorming session (such as self-esteem, self-efficacy, and refusal skills), the staff member invites the committee to sample a number of available, attractive packages of "user-friendly" activities such as the following:

- "Broad-brush" packages, which cover a variety of personal choice and primary prevention areas (Holstein et al. 1995)

- More targeted strategies, which might include a training package to be implemented by a consultant hired by the school district to address issues such as assertiveness training

Assertiveness training skills, which include a variety of personal and social skills, enable people to communicate their needs and feelings in an open, direct, and appropriate manner, while still recognizing the needs and feelings of others. They make people feel more powerful and better about themselves (less like "doormats"), and they offer strategies for saying "no" without hurting, provoking, or manipulating others (Alberti and Emmons 1988). Assertive behavior contrasts with hostile or belligerent behavior, passive and helpless behavior, and passive–aggressive or indirect manipulation. The exercises included in assertiveness training are nonthreatening, concrete, direct, and enjoyable.

Many intrapersonal prevention concepts, or personal and social skills development concepts, have come and gone, with a trendy "buzz word" accompanying each in the year it was introduced. Many of these concepts overlap, such as life skills training, self-esteem, self-efficacy, resilience training, and assertiveness training (McIntyre et al. 1990; Norman 1994). The danger lies in employing them as gimmicks or slogans that accomplish little. Nevertheless, as Botvin and others have shown, personal and skills training that is carefully based on known cognitive and behavioral change factors, if carefully put into place, can indeed make a difference (Botvin and Wills 1985; Shiffman and Wills 1987). It is also true that almost any positive lifestyle activity is likely to act as an alternative to participating in a drug-using subculture.

Comprehensive Prevention Programs for Drug Use and Abuse

■ **COMMUNITY-BASED DRUG PREVENTION**

Community-based programs are very broad and take into account the community's youth, parents, businesses, media, schools, law enforcement, religious or fraternal groups, civic or volunteer groups, health care professionals, and government agencies with expertise in the field of substance abuse. The primary goal of community-based prevention is to provide coordinated programs among the numerous agencies and organizations involved in prevention. Prevention requires communities to conduct a structured review of current prevention programs to determine (1) whether the programs in place were examined and tested according to rigorous scientific standards during their development, and (2) whether these programs incorporate the basic prin-

ciples of prevention that have been identified in research. Usually, prevention programs at the community level ask the following questions (Sloboda and David 1999):

- Does the program have components for the individual, the family, the school, the media, community organizations, and healthcare providers? Are the program components well integrated in theme and content so that they reinforce rather than duplicate each other?

- Does the prevention program use media and community education strategies to increase public awareness, attract community support, reinforce the school-based curriculum for students and parents, and keep the public informed of the program's progress?

- Are interventions carefully designed to reach different at-risk populations, and are they of sufficient duration to make an impact?

- Does the program follow a structured organizational plan that progresses from needs assessment through planning, implementation, and review to refinement, with feedback to and from the community at all stages?

- Are the objectives and activities specific, time-limited, feasible (in terms of available resources), and integrated so that they work together across program components and can be used to evaluate program progress and outcomes?

Often, these programs set up prevention policy boards to oversee planning and implementation. Boards should include representatives from law enforcement, juvenile justice, education, recreation, social services, private industry, health and mental health agencies, churches, civic organizations, and other community agencies that serve youth and families. The board should also include one or several youth members. In such a program, "The community can be a target group, especially when there is extensive community denial or lack of awareness, lack of clear policies, poor law enforcement, and so on. Public awareness campaigns, political action, and similar efforts are appropriate at this level of prevention" (Tinzmann and Hixson 1992, pp. 2, 3).

Community prevention programs can also direct their attention to changing the legal and social environment regarding alcohol, tobacco, and other drug supplies (ATOD) and toward youth (CPRD 2000):

- Strengthening the enforcement of existing legal regulations of ATOD sales and use.

- Educating merchants and servers about alcohol and tobacco sales laws.

- Regulating legislation regarding the sale of alcohol and tobacco to minors.

- Implementing "use and lose" laws, which allow for the suspension of the driver's license of a person under 21 years of age following a conviction for any alcohol or drug violation (e.g., use, possession, or attempt to purchase with or without false identification).

- Imposing regulations on location and density of retail outlets—that is, monitoring the number of unsupervised vending machines dispensing cigarettes to minors in a given community and monitoring the number of retail establishments selling alcohol and tobacco near schools.

In conclusion, community prevention emphasizes comprehensive drug abuse prevention programs that include multiple components, such as the use of media, drug education in schools, parent education, community organizations, and formulation of drug-related health policy. In essence, community drug prevention seeks to reduce drug abuse by informing, coordinating, and increasing the level of drug use at the community level.

■ SCHOOL-BASED DRUG PREVENTION

Education has been used extensively in the past to control the use and abuse of drugs, especially alcohol and tobacco. Drug education actually began in the late 1800s, when most states required that the harmful effects of certain drugs be taught. An example of an early educational attempt to curb or stop drug abuse is the temperance movement in the late 19th century. The Women's Christian Temperance Union (WCTU) and the Anti-Saloon League taught that alcohol consumption was harmful and contrary to Christian morality.

Years ago, when drug prevention was first attempted, most substance abuse experts thought

KEY TERMS

ATOD
refers to alcohol, tobacco and other drugs

scare tactic approach
drug prevention information based on emphasizing the extreme negative effects of drug-use—scaring the audience of potential and current drug users/abusers into not using drugs

that schools should be responsible for educating the public about the dangerous use and eventual abuse of drugs because education is school's main objective. Schools began teaching about drug use, but in the beginning, drug prevention focused on individual factors such as the dangers of particular types of drugs, the dangers of trusting individuals who sell drugs, and other scare tactics. One problem with this approach was that students varied enormously with regard to drug experience. Often the students had already tried the "dangerous" drugs and had only experienced pleasurable effects with few negative consequences. Their experiences occurred *before* their exposure to drug prevention programs that relied on negative information, which is generally known as the scare tactic approach . Many self-reported use surveys revealed that these programs were not successful. With such audiences of drug users, the warnings are short-lived, not believed, or perceived as exaggerations. Table 18.2 summarizes the most popular common school-based drug prevention programs by including the premise, strategies, and effectiveness of the following approaches: (a) cognitive, (b) affective, (c) combined cognitive and affective, (d) social learning/cognitive behavioral, and (e) normative education. Table 18.2 also details the strengths (if any) and weaknesses of each approach.

Curriculum-Based Drug Education Objectives

In an effort to educate students about the dangers of drug use, school-based drug education programs and objectives have been implemented in most U.S. school curriculums. Specific educational topics have been established for elementary, junior high, and senior high and college levels:

TABLE 18.2 Summary of Common School-Based Drug Prevention Approaches

APPROACH	PREMISE	STRATEGIES	EFFECTIVENESS
Cognitive	If youths understand the dangers of AOD, they will not use them.	Teach pharmacology of alcohol and other drugs, how they are used, long-range consequences of use—usually through scare tactics.	Seldom effective; sometimes detrimental—arouses curiosity and encourages experimentation. "Dire facts" are not credible, knowledge alone does not counteract peer pressure. Knowledge is necessary, but not sufficient; focus on more immediate physical/social consequences may work.
Affective	High self-esteem, values consistent with non-use, and good problem-solving and decision-making skills help youth avoid AOD.	Raise self-esteem. Teach values and life skills. Typically, do not include AOD information.	Do not decrease rate of use. Some community members and parents protest teaching values and decision-making. Need to include AOD information.
Combined Cognitive and Affective	Students need both information and life skills to avoid AOD use.	Teach problem-solving, decision-making, peer pressure resistance skills; and provide explicit information about AOD to connect life skills and AOD use and consequences.	Little consistent effect on reducing AOD use, although some successes have been reported.
Social Learning/ Cognitive-Behavioral Approach	AOD use usually begins in a social setting between grades 5 and 9, usually with peers, but sometimes adults; youth need skills for resisting these pressures. (Based on Bandura's social learning theory.)	Teach how to identify pressures from peers, media, advertising, families. Teach resistance skills, model counterarguments. Students role play pressure situations and actively practice resisting.	Sometimes effective, especially if peers are involved in instruction and when students already have other fairly well-developed social skills. Little evidence that effects last.
Normative Education Approach	Youth overestimate the extent of AOD use among peers and thus may use AOD in order to feel part of the group.	Correct misconceptions, demonstrate actual norms through discussion, etc., develop non-use norms.	Success with some drugs; not very effective with alcohol. Some youngsters may believe that fewer peers use AOD than actually do, and may come to feel AOD use is more acceptable than they did before entering the program.

AOD, alcohol and other drugs.

Source: Tinzmann, M. B., and J. Hixson. *What Does Research Say About Prevention?* Oak Brook, IL: North Central Regional Educational Laboratory, 1992. Available http://www.ncrel.org/sdrs/areas/stw_esys/6prevntn.htm.

Elementary Level

Drugs versus poisons

Effects of alcohol, tobacco, and marijuana on the body

Differences between candy and drugs

Drug overdoses

Dangers of experimentation

How to say "no" to peers using drugs

Reasons for taking drugs: curing illness, pleasure, escape, parental use, and ceremony

Junior High Level

How peer pressure works

How to say "no" to peer pressure

How drugs affect the body, physiologically and psychologically

Where to seek help when needed

Attitudes toward drug use

How to have fun without drugs

Harmful effects of tobacco, alcohol, and marijuana on the body

Stress management and building positive self-esteem

How advertisers push drugs

Consequences of breaking drug laws

Differences between wine, beer, and distilled spirits

Family drug use

Family drinking problems and family members who may have drug addiction problems

Images of violence and drug use in rock and rap music

Teenage drug abuse and associated problems

Senior High and College Level

Responsible use of medications

How drugs affect the body and the mind

Legal versus illegal drugs

Drinking and driving

Drug effects on the fetus

Recreational drug use

Ways of coping with problems: anger and stress management

How to detect problem drug users

Drug education, prevention, and treatment

Positive and negative role models

How to build positive self-esteem

Criminal sanctions for various types of drug use

"Binge" drinking

Drugs and driving

Date rape

Addiction to drugs and alcoholism

Principal Questions for School-Based Programs

The following questions should be asked to improve the outcomes of drug education programs:

- Do the school-based programs reach children from kindergarten through high school? If not, do they at least reach children during the critical middle school or junior high years?

- Do the programs contain multiple years of intervention (all through the middle school or junior high years)?

- Do the programs use a well-tested, standardized intervention with detailed lesson plans and student materials?

- Do the programs use age-appropriate interactive teaching methods (modeling, role playing, discussion, group feedback, reinforcement, extended practice)?

- Do the programs foster prosocial bonding to the school and community?

- Do the programs
  - teach social competence (communication, self-efficacy, assertiveness) and drug resistance skills that are culturally and developmentally appropriate?
  - promote positive peer influence?
  - promote antidrug social norms?
  - emphasize skills-training teaching methods?
  - include an adequate "dosage" (10–15 sessions in year 1 and another 10–15 booster sessions)?
- Is there periodic evaluation to determine whether the programs are effective?

■ FAMILY-BASED PREVENTION PROGRAMS

Primary family risk factors that predispose youth to find drugs attractive include the following:

- Chaotic home environments, particularly in which parents abuse substances or suffer from mental illnesses

- Ineffective parenting, especially with children with difficult temperaments and conduct disorders

- Lack of mutual attachments and nurturing

Research indicates "Results from longitudinal studies of children particularly those children most at risk for problems, indicate that families can protect children and youth against drug use and abuse through effective family management practices that impart skills young people can use in resisting social pressures to use drugs" (NIH and NIDA 1998, p. 49).

If the just listed risk factors are the primary risk factors, *protective factors*—the factors that can insulate against drug use—include the following:

- Strong parent-child bonds
- Parental monitoring with clear rules of conduct within the family unit and involvement of parents in the lives of their children
- Open communication of values within the family
- High levels of supervision and monitoring

- No inconsistent disciplining from lackadaisical to extreme enforcement of rules, and no "say one thing then do another"
- Consistent high levels of parental warmth, affection, and emotional support

Additionally, research shows that protective family factors can moderate the effects of risk factors. The risk of associating with peers who use drugs can be offset by protective family factors such as parent conventionality, maternal adjustment, and strong parent-child attachment.

Prevention at the family level needs to stress parent-child interaction strategies, communication skills, child management practices, and family management skills. Research has also shown that parents need to take a more active role in their children's lives. This includes talking to their children about drugs, monitoring their activities, getting to know their friends, and understanding their problems and personal concerns (NIH and NIDA 1998).

Prevention Principles for Family-Based Programs

In conclusion, family-based prevention programs need to do the following:

- Reach families of children at each stage of development.

- Train parents in behavioral skills to
  - reduce conduct problems in children.
  - improve parent-child relations, including positive reinforcement, listening and communication skills, and problem solving.
  - provide consistent discipline and rulemaking.
  - monitor children's activities during adolescence.

- Include an educational component for parents with drug information for them and their children.

- Focus on families whose children are in kindergarten through 12th grade to enhance protective factors.

- Provide access to counseling services for families at risk.

Drug Prevention Programs in Higher Education

The seriousness of alcohol and other drug use on college campuses is underscored by the following findings (Phoenix House 2000):

- According to the Core Institute, an organization that surveys college drinking practices, 300,000 of today's college students will eventually die of alcohol-related causes such as drunk driving accidents, cirrhosis of the liver, various cancers, and heart disease.

- 159,000 of today's first-year college students will drop out of school next year because of alcohol or other drug-related reasons.

- Almost one-third of college students admit to having missed at least one class because of their alcohol or drug use.

- One night of heavy drinking can impair a person's ability to think abstractly for up to 30 days, limiting the ability to relate textbook reading to classroom discussions or to think through processes such as football plays.

As we can see, the use of alcohol and other drugs is a serious problem within the college or university environment. Major problems on college campuses resulting from such drug abuse include property damage, poor academic performance, damaged relationships, unprotected sexual activity, physical injuries, date rape, and suicide (Perkins 1997).

It is obvious that with all these negative findings regarding alcohol and other drug use on college campuses, prevention programs are vital. Next we review the major prevention programs that currently exist in higher education.

■ OVERVIEW AND CRITIQUE OF EXISTING PREVENTION PROGRAMS

Information-only or Awareness Model

This is one of the earliest preventive interventions. It is based on the belief that if people are given extensive information about the harmful effects of drugs, such information will change their attitudes about use and abuse. This model assumes that peo-

ple are rational enough to seriously curtail or stop drug use based on information. Obviously, today we know that, at most, the majority of drug users exposed to the information-only or awareness model become more knowledgeable about the effects of drugs, but this approach has very little influence on the use of habitual or addictive-type drugs.

Attitude Change Model or Affective Education Model

The attitude change model or affective education model assumes that people use drugs because they have poor self-esteem (Gonzalez and Clement 1994). As a result, prevention focuses on strengthening self-image, building up positive self-esteem, and boosting self-confidence. A problem with this model is that attitudes often are resistant to change and fluctuate depending on such environmental influences as peer and party settings. Attitudes that were formed in an educational setting (drug and alcohol classes) are abandoned in substance use settings.

Social Influences Model

The social influences model assumes that substance abuse results from multiple influences. Although "outside" influences are perceived as major influences, "inner" influences are also taken into account. Inner influences such as prior socialization, a vulnerability to please others, and a need to be accepted by friends and peers are likewise taken into account. This prevention strategy emphasizes peer resistance and "inoculation" techniques. Techniques primarily include the following (Gonzalez and Clement 1994):

1. Offering factual information about the consequences of drug use.

KEY TERMS

information-only or awareness model
assumes that teaching about the harmful effects of drugs will change attitudes about use and abuse

attitude change model or affective education model
assumes people use drugs because of lack of self-esteem

social influences model
assumes that drug users lack resistance skills

2. Guiding development of skills to recognize outer and inner pressures to use drugs and methods and techniques to resistance usage.

3. Communicating correct information about the extent of drug use by students of similar ages.

4. Modeling, rehearsing, and reinforcing skills for resisting drugs when friends or peers expect compliance.

5. Persuading students to try these resistance approaches and techniques in classroom or group settings and in peer group settings away from the classroom.

By far, this method has been more successful than the information-only and attitude change models. Although it works best when it begins at the junior high school level, refresher courses should be administered at least every 2 years. Some research findings indicate that although this method is least effective with alcohol consumption, it *is* effective with marijuana and cigarette smoking (Gonzalez and Clement 1994).

Ecological or Person-in-Environment Model

This is one of the most recent types of prevention programs. "Interventions based on this model have multiple components and are designed to address both individuals and the policies, practices, and social norms that affect students on campus or in the community" (Gonzalez and Clement 1994, p. 3). Developed from human ecology, the ecological or person-in-environment model stresses that changes in the environment change people. Although the ecological or person-in-environment model does not ignore substance use from individual causes, such as personal beliefs and perception of risk, it does primarily focus on the causes from the social environment (Hansen 1997, p. 6). "The central tenet [beliefs] of social ecology is that individual behavior is mainly the result of socialization; to change the behavior, we must change the social institutions that shape it" (Hansen 1997, p. 6). Hansen also stated "the strongest predictors of alcohol and drug abuse among young people are social."

This perspective emphasizes that it is important to take into account all of the environments that may have an impact on drug use. Students can be influenced by friends, acquaintances, room-mates, and classmates in dorms, sororities, and fraternities, at parties, cafes, and nightspots.

As a result, this model advocates the following drug prevention strategies (Gonzalez and Clement 1994):

1. Dissemination of drug information

2. Cognitive and behavioral skills training for youth, parents, and professionals

3. Mass media programming

4. Development of grassroots citizen interest groups

5. Leadership training for key organization and community officials

6. Policy analysis and reformulation

The college campus has long served as an initiator and perpetuator for drug use and abuse. Fraternity drunkenness, for example, was decried as early as 1840 (Horowitz 1987). In 1988, an 18-year-old student attending Rutgers University died of alcohol poisoning at a fraternity party. In a television interview following the incident, the now late Chancellor Edward Bloustein described fraternities as "organized conspiracies dedicated to the consumption of alcohol." (Hansen 1997, p. 5).

Chemical abuse on campus is linked to the vast majority of vandalism, fights, accidents, sexually transmitted diseases, unplanned pregnancies, racial bias incidents, and date rape, and at least one-third of academic attrition (Koss et al. 1987). Although campus prevention programs and research date back several decades, such efforts remained isolated and sporadic until the late 1970s. To date, all campuses now have medium to extensive alcohol and other drug prevention programs in effect.

Examples of Several Current Large-scale Drug Prevention Programs

■ BACCUS AND GAMMA PEER EDUCATION NETWORK

In 1975, an organization known as BACCHUS (Boosting Alcohol Consciousness Concerning the Health of University Students) was developed as a national student organization. Soon BACCHUS realized that many of their affiliates were members of sororities and fraternities; therefore, they renamed the organization BACCHUS and GAMMA (Greeks Advocating Mature Management of Alcohol) Peer Education Network . Currently, there are approximately 1000 international BACCHUS and GAMMA peer education affiliates with approximately 25,000 active members (BACCHUS and GAMMA 2000a). In the United States, there are approximately 850 affiliates.

The original goal of this program was to prevent alcohol abuse. Today, this program has broadened its goals to include other student health and safety issues such as sexual responsibility, tobacco use, marijuana use, and sexual assault. The mission of this organization is to actively promote peer education as a useful element of campus health education and wellness efforts (BACCHUS and GAMMA 2000b). Drug education and activities are created to increase awareness, development, and promotion of positive lifestyles and decision-making skills (BACCHUS and GAMMA 2000b).

Each campus affiliate group plans programs according to the needs of their specific campus. "Some members choose to focus on National Collegiate Awareness Week, Sexual Responsibility Week, Safe Spring Break programs or tobacco prevention. Others use formal peer education training to present programs to the campus community" (BACCHUS and GAMMA 2000b, p. 1).

■ FUND FOR THE IMPROVEMENT OF POST-SECONDARY EDUCATION DRUG PREVENTION PROGRAMS

In the year 1987, a huge explosion of campus drug prevention programs began. It was spawned by a $14 billion annual budget for college drug prevention placed in the Drug-Free Schools and Communities Act of 1986 (now titled the Safe and Free Schools and Communities Act). The funding was parceled out by the Department of Education, Fund for the Improvement of Post-Secondary Education (FIPSE). FIPSE Drug Prevention Programs awarded about 100 grants per year from 1987 until 1996 via a grant competition that called for colleges to mount institution-wide programs. The guiding philosophy included the following points:

- A small, isolated program was seen as making little difference, but a comprehensive and insti-

> **KEY TERMS**
>
> **ecological or person-in-environment model**
> stresses that changes in the environment changes people's attitudes about drugs
>
> **BACCHUS and GAMMA peer education network**
> a national and international association of college and university peer education programs focused on alcohol abuse prevention and other related student health and safety issues

tution-wide program reaching into several areas of the institution could send many consistent antiuse messages that would eventually reach "critical mass" and change the campus environment.

- There should be well-known, top-down administrative support for prevention programming.

- There should be well-written and carefully implemented policies about chemical use on campus.

The hundreds of new programs, whose administrators met and interacted in annual grantee conferences, generated the sense that there was a national prevention movement in higher education. The Network of Colleges and Universities Dedicated to Prevention of Alcohol and Other Drug Abuse was founded, incorporating 900 institutions. The Network is supported by a new Higher Education Center for Alcohol and Other Drug prevention funded by the U.S. Department of Education, which provides a range of materials and newsletters (Ryan et al. 1995).

In 1989, FIPSE initiated a grant program for regional campus prevention consortia. By joining a consortium, colleges and universities could pool scarce resources, create support networks, and train new workers. In 1994, more than 100 regional consortia were listed on a database maintained by the Higher Education Center. In 1999, more than two-thirds of all 3300 institutions of higher education were affiliates of the Network, belonged to a regional consortium, or had started other programs under the aegis of FIPSE.

Out of this decade-long experience, several exemplary approaches emerged. These strategies might be the predominant focus of a program, or one of a number of complementary components of a comprehensive effort. The strategies are addressed next.

Peer-based Efforts

Student peers can be involved in a number of ways: as educators, mentors, counselors, or facilitators of prevention and outreach work. Such an approach multiplies manpower tremendously, reaches the students who are apt to become lost in the flow, is not perceived as an outside or authoritarian intrusion, speaks the language of students, and works to change the predominant cultural tone on campus. Peers can conduct classroom presentations, work informational tables or drop-in centers, create prevention newsletters, and establish links to community groups. It is important to carefully train and supervise peer facilitators. Many peer programs are residence hall–based, taking advantage of the training of residence hall assistants and peer facilitators (BACCHUS-GAMMA 1994).

Curriculum Infusion

Infusion of a skill or topic across the curriculum has been used in conjunction with classes on writing skills, gender issues, and other areas. Curriculum infusion can be undertaken at individual institutions or as a consortium project. The advantage of curriculum infusion is that it involves faculty members, achieves open discussion of drug issues in the classroom as part of the normal educational process, and stimulates critical thinking about drug issues.

Improvisational Theater Groups

Improvisational theater groups that tackle health and wellness issues can be lively, stimulating, and provocative, often breaking through peer and institutional denial and bringing issues home to students with a dramatic emotional impact. Improvisational topics can include date rape, sexually transmitted disease, children of alcoholics on campus, and denial of chemical dependency.

Strategies to Change Misperceptions of Use

Social psychologists Alan Berkowitz and Wesley Perkins, both of Hobart and William Smith Colleges, have conducted influential research illustrating that students often have incorrect estimates (exaggerated misperceptions) of drug use by their peers (Perkins 1991 and 1997; Perkins and Berkowitz 1986). Thus, they misperceive the peer norms governing drug use, which may lead them to "follow imaginary peers." This idea is a modification of the traditional understanding that peers influence peers. It follows logically that activities demonstrating the accurate use pattern to students and correcting misperceptions will indirectly affect overall use patterns. These efforts have included simply publicizing the results of alcohol and drug use surveys and awarding prizes for coming up with correct estimates.

Alternative Events

Alternative events, such as "mocktail" parties, alcohol-free discos, and indoor rock climbing, especially as alternatives to pre-sporting events and holiday parties, help avoid some events that are traditionally associated with chemical abuse.

Programs That Change Marketing of Alcohol on and Near Campuses

Institutions of higher education are a major focus of alcohol marketing. Many campus events are sponsored by alcoholic beverage producers, and these companies also buy considerable newspaper advertising. The National College Magazine *U*, for example, had a 3-year advertising contract with Anheuser-Busch (Magnum and Taylor 1990). This publicity sends many pro-use messages. Prevention programs have recruited business and advertising majors to work on curtailing such marketing projects.

Finally, it is better to imbed prevention messages within an overall wellness perspective. Students are concerned about health and wellness issues, not programs that come off as dogmatic or preachy, moralizing, exaggerating, and nagging—perhaps reminding them of life at home.

■ D.A.R.E. (DRUG ABUSE RESISTANCE EDUCATION)

One of the most popular school-based drug education programs incorporated in approximately 70% of the nation's school districts is D.A.R.E. (Drug Abuse Resistance Education) . D.A.R.E. reaches 25 million students and has been adopted in 44 foreign countries (*Law Enforcement News* 1996). Recent evaluations of this program show that, on a short-term basis, D.A.R.E. improved students' views of themselves and increased their sense of personal responsibility. However, the program has not yielded a measurable, significant change in drug use (Rosenbaum and Hanson 1998). Moreover, this drug education program showed an inconsistency and non-significant results between students' self-reported attitudes about use and actual use behaviors (Clayton et al. 1991, Ennett et al. 1994). (See "Holding the Line," on page 510, for more information on D.A.R.E. and several other programs that attempt to prevent drug use.) One major problem that has been identified is that the D.A.R.E. drug education program is presented in the classroom by fully uniformed police officers. Although the officers are well intentioned and their efforts are commendable, they are hardly a mechanism for transmitting new norms that would find converts among students, except perhaps those already successfully socialized (Gopelrud 1991). More importantly, uniformed police officers used as teachers " . . . sends the wrong message that drugs are a law enforcement issue, rather than a public health issue" (Zeese and Lewin 1998).

■ DRUG COURTS

Although these courts of law vary in organization, in scope, and at what point intervention occurs, the underlying premise is that drug possession and use is not only a law enforcement/criminal justice problem but also a public health problem (Sherin and Mahoney 1996). In drug court programs, criminal justice agencies collaborate closely with the substance abuse treatment community and other societal institutions to design and operate the program. Thus, the key goal is to divert substance abusers into supervised community treatment centers in order to eliminate the destructive behavior. Whether treatment is needed and the type and length of treatment are determined by a committee usually comprised of a judge, the district attorney, a public defender, the probation department, and treatment center officials. At the first National Drug Court Conference, one researcher reported, "These courts rely on strong collaboration among judges, prosecutors, defense lawyers and related supporting agencies (such as case management, corrections, pretrial ser-

D.A.R.E. (Drug Abuse Resistance Education)
drug education program presented in elementary and junior high schools nationwide by police officers

drug courts
court designed to focus on treatment programs and options in place of punishment for drug offenses

vices, probation, etc.), on the one hand, and a partnership with treatment agencies (or providers) and other community organizations and representatives on the other" (Goldkamp 1993, p. 33).

> The treatment phase generally consists of: (1) detoxification (removal of physical dependence on drugs from body), (2) stabilization (treating the psychological craving for the drug), and (3) aftercare (helping the defendant obtain education or job training, find a job, and remain drug free). To date there are 46 states that have implemented courts and four additional states are planning drug courts. Currently, in the U.S., there are 264 drug courts that have operated for two years, 176 have recently been implemented, and 279 drug courts are classified as "being planned" (OJP 2000).

Overall, there have been lower re-arrest rates for defendants participating in drug court sentencing and there were statistically significant differences in disposition between those assigned to drug court and the comparison groups. Those assigned to drug court were more likely not to face further prosecution and less likely to serve probation or short jail terms. Finally, using drug court and its system of administering treatment within a legal atmosphere is more cost-effective than criminal courts: between $1200 and $3500 per participant compared with approximately $5000 to incarcerate the same defendant (OJP DCCTAP 1999). Research shows, however, that we should be cautious for two reasons: (1) the research on the effectiveness of these courts was done very early—the courts were in operation fewer than 10 months, and (2) these courts were very selective of the defendants allowed to participate—the criticism being that the courts tended to select violators who would have a better chance for rehabilitation.

HOLDING THE LINE

In 1995, a disturbing study published by a group of researchers at the University of Michigan and backed by the U.S. Department of Health and Human Services (HHS) and the National Institute on Drug Abuse (NIDA) showed that the use of illicit drugs by young people had been rising steadily since 1992. The results of this study were even more confounding because drug use overall had been declining for the same period. The increase was happening despite several seemingly successful efforts to combat drug abuse with high-powered prevention programs.

Since the 1980s, the most funds in drug prevention have been spent in three areas: criminal justice, major advertising campaigns, and D.A.R.E. (Drug Abuse Resistance Education). Compulsory preventive programs have been favored by law enforcement professionals for hard-core addicts, especially in poor urban neighborhoods. According to William N. Brownsberger, Assistant State Attorney General in the Massachusetts Narcotics and Special Investigations Division, addicts who are forced against their will to enter and remain in therapy can overcome their addiction. Roughly 90% of all addicts are arrested at least once every year, giving the criminal justice system plenty of opportunities to help them kick their habits.

One highly visible persuasive effort to end drug abuse has been the publicity and advertising campaign created by the Partnership for a Drug-Free America. The nation's advertising industry developed the Partnership and funded it by collaborating with advertisers and a variety of health and educational agencies. The goal was to promote images designed to make drug use look "uncool," especially to younger people. In addition to the creative services donated by advertising agencies, media organizations donated more than $2 billion worth of public service and advertising space to the Partnership between the late 1980s and 1990s.

In the early 1990s, the Partnership commissioned surveys to measure the effect of its media campaign on students in the Los Angeles and New York City school systems. On both coasts, increased exposure to the Partnership's messages appeared to dramatically change students' attitudes toward drugs. At the same time, however, the number of students who admitted using drugs actually increased.

Another high-visibility persuasive effort has been the nationwide D.A.R.E. program that was launched in Los Angeles in 1983. Using role-playing techniques and resistance training, uniformed police officers become social workers, talking with students in their classrooms, educating them about the dangers of drugs, and giving them the tools to resist temptation or peer pressure. They generally teach 17 classroom sessions.

Although D.A.R.E. is the most popular drug education program ever developed for children, increasing numbers of critics claim that its effects, if any, are short-lasting. Most D.A.R.E. training begins in the fifth grade. At this age, students accept most of what they hear. By middle school, however, the impact of D.A.R.E. begins to erode. By high school, many students resist participation in the program. According to a researcher from the Research Triangle Institute in Durham, North Carolina, which conducted a $300,000 study on the impact of D.A.R.E., "Unless there's some sort of booster session that reinforces the original curriculum, the effects of most drug use prevention programs decay rather than increase over time." From numerous research studies conducted on D.A.R.E.'s effectiveness, findings suggest that ". . . D.A.R.E. students were no less likely to use drugs than students who had not gone through the program (Ennett et al. 1994).

In light of diminishing returns from various drug prevention programs, in late 1996 the Clinton administration proposed a compulsory drug test for teenagers who are applying for their driver's licenses. Like everything else, the proposal had both supporters and critics. Although it may be part of the answer, the search for prevention programs that have measurable, long-lasting effects is far from over.

Sources: Brownsberger, W. N. "Just Say 'Criminal Justice.'" *Boston Globe* (20 October 1996).
Ennett, S. T, N. S. Tobler, C. L. Ringwalt, and R. L. Flewelling. "How Effective Is Drug Abuse Resistance Education? A Meta-analysis of Project D.A.R.E. Outcome Evaluations." *American Journal of Public Health* 84 (1994): 1394–1401.
Gordon, P. "Can Madison Avenue Really Save America by Making Illegal Drugs Totally Uncool?" *Buzz Magazine* (August 1996).
P. Gordon. "The Truth About D.A.R.E." *Buzz Magazine* (July 1996).

It is apparent that drug courts need more time to operate, and more evaluation research needs to be conducted. The most promising aspect of these courts is the emphasis on treating drug addiction in place of simply punishing without treating as has been the case historically.

Problems with Assessing Successes of Drug Prevention Programs

Both the National Institute on Drug Abuse (NIDA) and several individual researchers have evaluated the multitude of drug abuse prevention programs in the United States. The general conclusions of these studies are as follows:

- Very few programs have demonstrated clear success or have adequately evaluated themselves.

- The relationships among information about drugs, attitudes toward use, and actual use are unclear in these programs.

Some factors that are key to developing successful programs include the following:

- Prevention must be coordinated at different levels. Successful programs involve families, schools, and communities. In some cases, these efforts are not coordinated.

- The program must be integrated into the ongoing activities of schools, families, and community organizations. Superficial introduction of drug prevention strategies has limited effects. For instance, distributing literature door-to-door, making in-class presentations of the harmful effects of drugs, and posting banners and slogans warning of the consequences of drug abuse in communities are not successful methods. Instead, programs that are comprehensive and community-wide, integrated into neighborhood clubs, organizations, and church activities, are more likely to have a long-term impact on preventing drug use. A clear example is the yearly Great American Smokeout launched against tobacco use.

- Personal autobiographical and social experience accounts of former drug abusers should be included in drug information that is distributed. Recipients of drug prevention information should be given real-life accounts of use, abuse, despair, and successful drug rehabilitation. Just receiving drug information alone has little impact, either initially or over the long-term.

Other Alternatives to Drug Use

It has been suggested that people have an innate need to alter their conscious state. This belief is based on the observation that, as part of their normal play, preschoolers deliberately whirl themselves dizzy and even momentarily choke each other to lose consciousness (Wilson and Wilson 1975). Some young children progress to discovering and using chemicals (such as sniffing shoe polish or gasoline) to alter consciousness and learn to be very secretive about this behavior. They learn to be circumspect or come to feel guilty and repress the desire to alter consciousness when adults catch them in these activities.

If this desire to alter the state of consciousness is inherent in human beings, then the use of psychoactive drugs, legal or illegal, in adulthood is natural. Drug abuse is thus a logical continuation of a developmental sequence that goes back to early childhood (Carroll 1977, Weil 1972).

Other researchers question why, even if there is an innate desire to alter consciousness, only some people progress to abusing chemical substances. It appears that people who do not abuse psychoactive drugs have found positive alternatives to altering consciousness; they feel no need to take chemical substances for this purpose. Involvement in activities such as Boy Scouts and Girl Scouts, youth sports teams, music groups, the YMCA and YWCA, drug-free video game centers, drug-free dances, environmental and historical preservation projects, and social and service projects are viable alternatives to drug use. The rationale for these programs is that youth will find these activities engaging enough to forgo alcohol and drug use (Forman and Linney 1988).

This strategy is known as the alternatives approach . Workers in the drug abuse field tend to agree on its effectiveness. They note that young ex-abusers of common illicit drugs are more likely to stop when they gain satisfaction from exploring positive alternatives rather than from a fear of consequent harm. The alternatives approach assumes the following (Cohen 1971):

1. People abuse drugs voluntarily to fill a need or basic drive.

2. Most people abuse drugs for negative reasons. They may be dealing with negative feelings or situations, such as relieving boredom, anxiety, depression, tension, or other unpleasant emotional and psychological states. They may be rebelling against authority, trying to escape feelings of loneliness or inadequacy, or trying to be accepted by peers. Peer pressure is extremely important as an inducing force.

3. Some people who abuse drugs believe the experience is positive. They may feel that their sensual experiences or music enjoyment is enhanced, that they have achieved altered states of consciousness, or they may simply experience a sense of adventure. Some people may want to explore their own consciousness and reasons for the attraction to drug use.

Whether the reasons for drug use are positive or negative, the effects sought can be achieved through alternative, nondrug means. Such means are preferable to drug use and more constructive because the person is not relying on a psychoactive substance for satisfaction; rather, he or she is finding satisfaction based on personal achievements.

KEY TERMS

alternatives approach
an approach emphasizing the exploration of positive alternatives to drug abuse, based on replacing the pleasurable feelings gained from drug abuse with involvement in social and educational activities

meditation
a state of consciousness in which there is a constant level of awareness focusing on one object; for example, yoga and Zen Buddhism

---

Ideally, this approach should lead to a lifetime of self-satisfaction.

Table 18.3 lists various types of experiences, the motives for such experiences, the probable drugs of abuse with which they are associated, and alternatives to these drugs. As shown, any constructive activity can be considered an alternative to drug abuse. For example, a young person who needs an outlet for increased physical energy might respond better to dance and movement training or a project in preventive medicine than to work on ecological projects. In a large alternatives program established in Idaho, the following activities were planned during a month: arts and crafts, karate, re-forestation, backpacking, Humane Society dog show, horseback riding, artwork for posters for various programs, astronomy, camping, and volunteering in a local hospital.

■ **MEDITATION**

Some of the most intriguing research about the brain is being done on the state of the mind during meditation . In certain countries, like India, people have long histories of being able to achieve certain goals through meditation. The word *yoga* is derived from the Sanskrit word for union, or yoking, meaning "the process of discipline by which a person attains union with the Absolute." In a sense, it refers to the use of the mind to control itself and the body.

Meditation involves brain wave activity centered on ponderous, contemplative, and reflective thought. An individual who meditates is able to decrease oxygen consumption within a matter of minutes as much as 20%, a level usually reached only after 4 to 5 hours of sleep. However, meditation is physiologically different from sleep, based on the electroencephalograph (EEG) pattern and rate of decline of oxygen consumption. Along with the decreased metabolic rate and changes in EEG there is also a marked decrease in blood lactate. Lactate is produced by metabolism of skeletal muscle, and the decrease is probably due to the reduced activity of the sympathetic nervous system during meditation. Heart rate and respiration are also slowed.

■ **THE NATURAL MIND APPROACH**

Some people who take drugs eventually look for other methods of maintaining the valuable parts of the drug experience. These people may learn to

TABLE 18.3   **Experiences, Motives, and Possible Alternatives for a Drug Abuser**

EXPERIENCE	CORRESPONDING MOTIVES	DRUGS ABUSED	POSSIBLE ALTERNATIVES
Physical	Desire for physical well-being: physical relaxation, relief from sickness, desire for more energy	Alcohol, sedative-hypnotics, stimulants, marijuana	Athletics, dance, exercise, hiking, diet, carpentry, outdoor work, swimming, hatha yoga
Sensory	Desire to magnify sensorium: sound, touch, taste, need for sensual/sexual stimulation	Hallucinogens, marijuana, alcohol	Sensory awareness training, sky diving, experiencing sensory beauty of nature, scuba diving
Emotional	Relief from psychological pain: attempt to resolve personal problems, relief from bad mood, escape from anxiety, desire for emotional insight, liberation of feeling and emotional relaxation	Narcotics, alcohol, barbiturates, sedative-hypnotics	Competent individual counseling, well-run group therapy, instruction in psychology of personal development
Interpersonal	Desire to gain peer acceptance, break through interpersonal barriers, "communicate"; defiance of authority figures	Any, especially alcohol, marijuana	Expertly managed sensitivity and encounter groups, well-run group therapy, instruction in social customs, confidence training, emphasis on assisting others, e.g., YMCA or YWCA volunteers
Social	Desire to promote social change, find identifiable subculture, tune out intolerable environmental conditions, e.g., poverty	Marijuana, psychedelics	Social service community action in positive social change; helping the poor, aged, inform, or young; tutoring handicapped; ecology action; YMCA or YWCA Big Brother/Sister programs
Political	Desire to promote political change (out of desperation with the social-political order) and to identify with antiestablishment subgroup	Marijuana, psychedelics	Political service, lobbying for nonpartisan projects, e.g., Common Cause; field work with politicians and public officials
Intellectual	Desire to escape boredom, out of intellectual curiosity, to solve cognitive problems, gain new understanding in the world of ideas, research one's own awareness	Stimulants, sometimes psychedelics	Intellectual excitement through reading, debate, and discussion; creative games and puzzles; self-hypnosis; training in concentration
Creative-aesthetic	Desire to improve creative performance, enhance enjoyment of art already produced, e.g., music; enjoy imaginative mental productions	Marijuana, stimulants, psychedelics	Nongraded instruction in producing and/or appreciating art, music, drama, and creative hobbies
Philosophical	Desire to discover meaningful values, find meaning in life, help establish personal identity, organize a belief structure	Psychedelics, marijuana, stimulants	Discussions, seminars, courses on ethics, the nature of reality, relevant philosophical literature; explorations of value systems
Spiritual-mystical	Desire to transcend orthodox religion, develop spiritual insights, reach higher levels of consciousness, augment yogic practices, take a spiritual shortcut	Psychedelics, marijuana	Exposure to nonchemical methods of spiritual development; study of world religions, mysticism, meditation, yogic techniques

value the meditation "high" and abandon drugs. Long-term drug users sometimes credit their drug experiences with having given them a taste of their potential, even though continued use has diminished the novelty of drug use. Once these individuals become established in careers, they claim to have grown out of chemically induced altered states of consciousness. As Andrew Weil (1972, p. 67) put it, "One does not see any long-time meditators give up meditation to become acid heads."

Although chemical highs are effective means of altering the state of consciousness, they interfere with the most worthwhile states of altered consciousness because they reinforce the illusion that highs come from external, material agents rather than from within your own nervous system.

Some people have difficulty using meditation as an alternative to drugs because, in order to be effective, meditation takes practice and concentration; in contrast, the effects of drugs are immediate. Nevertheless, it is within everyone's potential to meditate.

Discussion Questions

1. Figure 18.1, "Potential Factors That Influence Alcohol and Other Drug Use," lists many factors that can influence drug use. Design a drug prevention program by selecting any one of the concentric circles and include all factors within that circle.

2. What would you emphasize in a primary prevention program for junior high school students? High school students? College students?

3. How would you design a drug prevention program for nondetected committed or secret users? What would you emphasize?

4. What do you think is more likely to work today in drug prevention programs for America's youth: teaching moderate use or total abstinence? Why?

5. Your boss says, "We received a much smaller amount of money from the federal government to create a drug prevention program. I want you to focus on a community-based approach,

school-based approach, or family-based prevention program." Which would you select and why?

6. How effective has BACCHUS and GAMMA Peer Education Network been on your campus? Examples?

7. List and explain two potential strengths and two potential weaknesses of drug courts in comparison with traditional criminal courts in the United States.

8. What is your assessment of using the alternatives approach and meditation for preventing drug use? Do you think it works? Why or why not?

Key Terms

AOD   **494**

primary drug prevention programs   **496**

secondary drug prevention programs   **496**

tertiary drug prevention programs   **496**

ATOD   **501**

scare tactic approach   **501**

information-only or awareness model   **505**

attitude change model or affective education model   **505**

social influences model   **505**

ecological or person-in-environment model   **506**

BACCHUS and GAMMA Peer Education Network   **507**

D.A.R.E. (Drug Abuse Resistance Education)   **508**

drug court   **509**

alternatives approach   **512**

meditation   **512**

Summary

1 The 10 most prominent factors affecting an individual's use of drugs are (1) genetics, (2) personality traits, (3) attitudes and beliefs, (4) interpersonal and peer resistance skills, (5) community, (6) peers, (7) school policy, (8) local law enforcement, (9) personal situations, and (10) parents.

2 Three major types of prevention programs are: (1) primary, (2) secondary, and (3) tertiary prevention.

3 Five major types of drug users that drug prevention programs have to recognize before assembling a program are (1) early experimenters, (2) non–problem drug users/recreational users, (3) nondetected committed or secret users, (4) problem users, and (5) former users.

4 The three levels of comprehensive prevention programs for drug use and abuse are (1) community-based, (2) school-based, and (3) family-based.

5 Proactive family factors can moderate the effects of drug risk factors. The risk of associating with peers who use drugs can be offset by protective family factors such as parent conventionality, maternal adjustment, and strong parent-child attachment.

6 Four primary prevention programs that exist in higher education are (1) information-only or awareness model, (2) attitude change model or affective education model, (3) social influence model, and (4) ecological or person-in-environment model.

7 The main goals of three more recent large-scale prevention programs include (1) BACCHUS and GAMMA Peer Education Network—a national and international association of college and university peer educating programs focused on alcohol abuse prevention and other related student health and safety issues; (2) D.A.R.E.—a nationwide drug prevention program presented in junior high schools by police officers; and (3) drug courts—a newer nationwide approach to prevention in which the primary purpose is to focus on treatment programs and options in place of punishment for drug offenses.

8 Two additional possibilities for lessening or eliminating drug use are the alternatives approach and meditation. Alternatives to drug abuse are based on replacing the euphoria and pleasure gained by being high with involvement in social, recreational, and educational activities. Meditation is producing a state of consciousness in which there is a constant level of very satisfying awareness that is rewarding in itself without artificial inducements (drugs). Yoga and Zen Buddhism are examples.

References

Alberti, R. E. and M. L. Emmons. *Your Perfect Right.* San Luis Obispo, CA: Impact Publishers, 1988.

BACCHUS and GAMMA. *Community College Guide to Peer Education.* Denver, CO: The BACCHUS and GAMMA Peer Education Network, 1994.

BACCHUS and GAMMA. *Energy, Education, Support.* Denver, CO: BACCHUS and GAMMA Peer Education Network, 2000a. Available http://www.bacchusgamma.org/contact.asp.

BACCHUS and GAMMA. *What Is BACCHUS and GAMMA Network?* Denver, CO: BACCHUS and GAMMA Peer Education Network 2000b. Available http://www.bacchusgamma.org/tour_2.asp.

Botvin, G. J. and T. A. Wills. "Personal and Social Skills Training: Cognitive-Behavioral Approaches to Substance Abuse Prevention." In *Prevention Research: Deterring Drug Abuse Among Children and Adolescents.* NIDA Research Monograph 64. Rockville, MD: NIDA (U.S. HHS, PHS, ADAMHA), 1985.

Carroll, E. "Notes on the Epidemiology of Inhalants." In *Review of Inhalants,* edited by C. W. Sharp and M. L. Brehm. NIDA Research Monograph No. 15. Washington, DC: National Institute on Drug Abuse, 1977.

Clayton, R. R., R. Cattarello, L. E. Cay, and K. P. Walden. "Persuasive Communication and Drug Prevention: An Evaluation of the D.A.R.E. Program." In *Persuasive Communication and Drug Abuse Prevention,* edited by L. Donohew, H. Sypepher, and W. Bukowski. Hillsdale, NJ: Erlbaum, 1991.

Cohen, A. Y. "The Journey Beyond Trips: Alternatives to Drugs." *Journal of Psychedelic Drugs* 3, No. 2 (Spring 1971): 7–14.

Center for Prevention Research and Development (The) (CPRD). *Research Based Approaches in The Community Domain.* Champaign, IL: University of Illinois Urbana Champaign, 2000. Available http://www.cprd.uiuc.edu/publications/principles/community_domain.html.

Ennett, S. T., N. S. Tobler, C. L. Ringwalt, and R. L. Flewelling. "How Effective is Drug Abuse Resistance Education? A Meta-Analysis of Project D.A.R.E. Outcome Evaluations." *American Journal of Public Health* 84 (1994): 1394–1401.

Forman, S. G. and J. A. Linney. "School-Based Prevention of Adolescent Substance Abuse: Programs, Implementation and Future Direction." *School Psychology Review* 17, No. 4 (1988): 550–58.

Goldkamp, J. *Justice and Treatment Innovation: The Drug Court Movement.* Washington, DC: National Institute of Justice and the State Justice Institute, 1993.

Gonzalez, G. M. and V. V. Clement, eds. *Preventing Substance Abuse,* U.S. Department of Education. Washington, DC: U.S. Government Printing Office, 1994.

Gopelrud E. N., ed. *Preventing Adolescent Drug Use: From Theory to Practice.* OSAP Monograph #8, DHHS Publication No. (ADM) 91-1725. Rockville, MD: Office of Substance Abuse Prevention, 1991.

Hansen, W. B. "A Social Ecology Theory of Alcohol and Drug Use Prevention Among College and University Students." In *Designing Alcohol and Other Drug Prevention Programs in Higher Education.* Newton, MA: The Higher Education Center for Alcohol and Other Drug Prevention, U.S. Department of Education, 1997. Available http://www.edc.org/hec/pubs/theorybook/Hansen.html.

Holstein, M. E., W. E. Cohen, and P. Steinbroner. *A Matter of Balance: Personal Strategies for Alcohol and Other Drugs.* Ashland, OR: CNS Productions, 1995.

Horowitz, H. L. *Campus Life.* New York: Knopf, 1987.

Koss, M. P., C. A. Gidycz, and R. Wisniewski. "The Scope of Rape: Incidence and Prevalence of Sexual Aggression and Victimization in a National Sample of Higher Education Students." *Journal of Consulting and Clinical Psychology* 34 (1987): 186–96.

Law Enforcement News 1996. "When it Comes to the Young, Anti-Drug Efforts Are Going to Pot." *Law Enforcement Nve* 22: 441–7.

Magnum, A. and P. Taylor. "Peddling Booze on Campus: How to Spot It, How to Fight It." *Eta Sigma Gamman* 22 (1990): 1.

McIntyre, K., D. White, and R. Yoast. *Resilience Among High-Risk Youth.* Madison, WI: University of Wisconsin, 1990.

National Institutes of Health (NIH) and National Institute on Drug Abuse (NIDA*). Drug Abuse and Drug Abuse Research.* Washington, DC: U.S. Government Printing Office, 1998.

Norman, E. "Personal Factors Related to Substance Misuse: Risk Abatement and/or Resiliency Enhancement." In *Substance Abuse in Adolescence,* edited by T. P. Gulotta, G. R. Adamds, and R. Montemayor. Thousand Oaks, CA: Sage Publications, 1994.

Office of Justice Programs (OJP). *OJP Drug Court Clearinghouse and Technical Assistance Project: Summary of Drug Court Activity by State and County.* Washington, DC: U.S. Government Printing Office, 10 January 2000.

Office of Justice Programs (OJP) Drug Court Clearinghouse and Technical Assistance Project (DCCTAP). *Looking at a Decade of Drug Courts.* Washington, DC: Drug Court Clearinghouse and Technical Assistance Project, 1999.

Perkins. H. W. "College Student Misperceptions of Alcohol and Other Drug Norms Among Peers: Exploring Causes, Consequences, and Implications for Prevention Programs." In *Designing Alcohol and Other Drug Prevention Programs in Higher Education.* Newton, MA: U.S. Department of Education. The Higher Education Center for Alcohol and Other Drug Prevention, 1997. Available http://www.edc.org/hec/pubs/theorybook/perkins.html.

Perkins, H. W. "Confronting Misperceptions of Peer Use Norms Among College Students: An Alternative Approach for Alcohol and Other Drug Education Programs." In *The Higher Education Leaders/Peers Network Peer Prevention Program Resource Manual.* Washington, DC: Texas Christian University, U.S. Department of Education (FIPSE), 1991: 18–32.

Perkins H. W. and A. D. Berkowitz. "Perceiving the Community Norms of Alcohol Use Among Students: Some Research Implications for Campus Alcohol Education Programming." *International Journal of the Addictions* 21, Nos. 9 and 10 (1986): 861–976.

Phoenix House. *School Daze? 2000.* Available http://www.factsontap.org/collexp/Stats.htm.

Rosenbaum, D. P. and S. Hanson. "Assessing the Effects of School-Based Drug Education; A Six-Year Multi-Level Analysis of Project D.A.R.E." Department of Criminal Justice and Center for Research in Law and Justice, Chicago: University of Illinois at Chicago, 6 April 1998. Available http://www.tfy.drugsense.org/uic.htm.

Ryan, B. E., T. Colthurst, and L. Segars. *College Alcohol Risk Assessment Guide.* San Diego: UCSD Extension, University of California at San Diego, 1995.

Sherin, K. M. and B. Mahoney. *Treatment Drug Courts: Integrating Substance Abuse Treatment with Legal Case Pro-*

cessing. Rockville, MD: U.S. Department of Health and Human Services, 1996.

Shiffman, S. and T. A. Wills, eds. *Coping and Substance Abuse.* New York: Academic Press, 1987.

Sloboda, Z., and S. L. David. *Preventing Drug Use Among Children and Adolescents: A Research-Based Guide.* Washington, DC: National Institute on Drug Abuse (NIDA) and National Institutes of Health, April 1999.

Tinzmann, M. B. and J. Hixson. *What Does Research Say About Prevention?* Oak Brook, IL: North Central Regional Educational Laboratory, 1992. Available http://www.ncrel.org/sdrs/areas/stw_esys/6prevntn.htm.

Weil, A. *The Natural Mind.* Boston, MA: Houghton Mifflin, 1972.

Wilson, M. and S. Wilson, eds. *Drugs in American Life,* Vol. 1. New York: Wilson, 1975.

Zeese, K. B. and P. M. Lewin. *The Effective Drug Control Strategy.* Washington, DC: Network of Reform Group and the National Coalition for Effective Drug Policies, 1998. Available http://www.csdp.org/edcs/edc.htm.

Appendix A

Federal Agencies with Drug Abuse Missions

Drug Enforcement Administration (DEA)

Because of the unique problems of drug abuse in 1930, Congress authorized the establishment of the Bureau of Narcotics in the Treasury Department to administer the relevant laws. This agency remained in the Treasury Department until 1968, when it became part of a new group in the Justice Department, the Bureau of Narcotics and Dangerous Drugs. Harry Anslinger served as head of the bureau for over 30 years, from its creation until his retirement in 1962. Anslinger was an agent during Prohibition, and later, as head of the bureau, he played an important role in getting marijuana outlawed by the federal government. In 1973, the Bureau of Narcotics and Dangerous Drugs became the Drug Enforcement Administration (DEA). Today, the DEA has the responsibility of infiltrating and breaking up illegal drug traffic in the United States, as well as controlling the use of Scheduled substances.

Special Action Office for Drug Abuse Prevention (SAODAP)

In 1971, President Richard Nixon set up a temporary agency, SAODAP, to initiate short-term and long-term planning of programs and to coordinate antidrug abuse programs with the states so that proper funding procedures and policies were followed. This office was located in the White House and was intended to advise the president. One major reason for establishing this organization was the initial report of a high heroin addiction rate in returning Vietnam veterans. The program was supposed to fight the increase in addiction in the United States. SAODAP was abolished, as planned, with most of its education, research, treatment, and rehabilitation functions going to a new agency, the National Institute on Drug Abuse (NIDA). An expert on the staff of advisors to the president, the domestic policy staff, assumed the duties of advising the president on drug-related matters and drug abuse programs. The advisor was to keep track of budgets for drug programs and coordinate policy with law enforcement groups. Under the administration of Ronald Reagan, further changes were proposed. A pattern of federal policy was established; that is, control and management of drug programs in the United States changed with each new "crisis."

Alcohol, Drug Abuse, and Mental Health Administration (ADAMHA)

In 1973, a new agency was formed after the Department of Health, Education, and Welfare Secretary Casper Weinberger stripped the alcohol and drug abuse sections from the National Institute of Mental Health (NIMH). This action formed the National Institute of Alcohol Abuse and Alcoholism (NIAAA) and the NIDA (see previous section). NIAAA, NIDA, and NIMH were under the agency ADAMHA (Alcohol, Drug Abuse and Mental Health Administration). This shuffling and redesign was part of federal attempts to bring the post-Vietnam War heroin crisis under control and to address the perennial problems of alcoholism and dependence on other drugs. The mission of NIAAA and NIDA was and still is to coordinate both clinical and basic research directed at drugs of abuse. Today, these institutes support 80% to 90% of all drug dependence research conducted in the United States. During fiscal year 1996, these institutes controlled budgets of $490 (NIDA) and $212 (NIAAA) million.

In October 1992, ADAMHA was reorganized, and both NIDA and NIAAA officially became Institutes of the National Institutes of Health (NIH) as mandated by the ADAMHA Reorganization Act of 1992 (Greenhouse 1992).

The Substance Abuse and Mental Health Services Administration (SAMHSA)

With passage of the ADAMHA Reorganization Act of 1992, the services programs of NIDA, NIAAA, and NIMH were incorporated into the newly created SAMHSA. This agency was given the lead responsibility for prevention and treatment of addictive and mental health problems and disorders. Its overall mission is to reduce the incidence and prevalence of substance abuse and mental disorders by ensuring the best therapeutic use of scientific knowledge and improving access to high-quality, effective programs (*SAMHSA Bulletin* 1992).

State Regulations

There have always been questions regarding the relative responsibilities of state versus federal laws and their respective regulatory agencies. In general, the U.S. form of government has allowed local control to take precedence over national control. Because of this historic attitude, states were the first to pass laws to regulate the abuse or misuse of drugs. Federal laws developed later, after the federal government gained greater jurisdiction over the well-being and lives of the citizens and it became apparent that, due to interstate trafficking, national drug abuse problems could not be effectively dealt with on a state-by-state basis. Some early state laws banned the use of smoking opium, regulated the scale of various psychoactive drug substances, and in a few instances, set up treatment programs. However, these early legislative actions made no effort to *prevent* drug abuse. Drug abuse was controlled to a great extent by social pressure rather than by law. It was considered morally wrong to be an alcoholic or an addict to opium or some other drug.

The drug laws varied considerably from state to state in 1932, so the National Conference of Commissioners on Uniform State Laws set up the Uniform Narcotic Drug Act (UNDA), which was later adopted by nearly all states. The UNDA provided for the control of possession, use, and distribution of opiates and cocaine. In 1942, marijuana was included under this act because it was classified as a narcotic.

In 1967, the Food and Drug Administration proposed the Model Drug Abuse Control Act and urged the states to adopt it on a uniform basis. This law extended controls over depressant, stimulant, and hallucinogenic drugs, similar to the 1965 federal law. Many states set up laws based on this model.

The federal Controlled Substances Act of 1970 stimulated the National Conference of Commissioners to propose a new Uniform Controlled Substances Act (UCSA). The UCSA permits enactment of a single state law regulating the illicit possession, use, manufacture, and dispensing of controlled psychoactive substances. At this time, most states have enacted the UCSA or modifications of it.

Today, state law enforcement of drug statutes does not always reflect federal regulations, although for the most part, the two statutory levels are harmonious. For example, marijuana has tentatively been approved for medicinal use in California and Arizona but is considered a Schedule I substance by federal regulatory agencies (as of this writing).

Appendix B

Some National Organizations in the Addictions

■ FEDERAL RESEARCH ENTITIES

National Institute on Drug Abuse

National Institute on Alcohol and Alcoholism

■ FEDERAL FUNDING AND COORDINATING ENTITIES

Center for Substance Abuse Treatment

Center for Substance Abuse Prevention (of the Substance Abuse, Mental Health Services Administration, HHS)

National Clearinghouse for Alcohol and Drug Information (NCADI, the source of all governmental literature and information on alcohol and drug subjects)

■ PRIVATE ADVOCACY, INFORMATIONAL, AND PROFESSIONAL ORGANIZATIONS

National Council on Alcoholism and Drug Dependency (a national association of the local councils on alcoholism and drug dependency in thousands of counties, municipalities, providing referral, information, and prevention services)

National Association of Drug Abuse and Alcoholism Counselors (NAADAC)*

International Certification Reciprocity Consortium (ICRC)*(a consortium of state boards certifying addictions counselors)

International Coalition of Addiction Studies Educators

(addiction studies and counselor training programs in higher education)

National Association of State Alcohol and Drug Abuse Directors

Therapeutic Communities

* NAADAC and ICRC certify alcohol, drug, and addictions counselors.

Appendix C

Drugs of Use and Abuse

The table that follows provides detailed information about the drugs listed. Note that the heading *CSA Schedules* refers to categorization under the Controlled Substances Act (CSA). The roman numeral(s) to the right of each drug name specifies each as a Schedule I, II, III, IV, or V drug. See Chapter 3, for more information on scheduling.

DRUGS	CSA SCHEDULES	MEDICAL USES	TRADE OR OTHER NAMES	SLANG NAMES
Narcotics				
Opium	II III V	Analgesic, antidiarrheal	Dover's Powder, Paregoric, Parepectolin	Opium
Morphine	II III	Analgesic, antitussive	Morphine, MS-Contin, Roxanol, Roxanol-SR	M, Morpho, Morph, Tab, White, Stuff, Miss, Emma, Monkey
Codeine	II III V	Analgesic, antitussive	Tylenol w/Codeine, Empirin w/Codeine, Robitussin A-C, Fiorinal w/Codeine	School Boy
Heroin	I	None	Diacetylmorphine	Horse, Smack, H, Stuff, Junk
Hydromorphone	II	Analgesic	Dilaudid	Little D, Lords
Meperidine (Pethidine)	II	Analgesic	Demerol, Mepergan	Isonipecaine, Dolantol
Methadone	II	Analgesic	Dolophine, Methadone, Methadose	Dollies, Dolls, Amidone
Other Narcotics	I II III IV V	Analgesic, antidiarrheal, antitussive	Numorphan, Percodan, Percocet, Tylox, Tussionex, Fentanyl, Darvon, Lomotil, Talwin*	T. and Blue's, Designer Drugs (Fentanyl Derivatives), China White

* Not designated as a narcotic under C.S.A. (Controlled Substances Act).

Source: Adapted from Drug Enforcement Administration, U.S. Dept. of Justice, Drugs of Abuse. 1989 Edition. Washington, DC: Government Printing Office, 1989: and "Let's All Work to Fight Drug Abuse." Dallas, TX: L.A.W. Publications, 1991.

DEPENDENCE PHYSICAL/ PSYCHOLOGICAL	TOLERANCE	DURATION (HOURS)	ADMINISTRATION METHODS	POSSIBLE EFFECTS	EFFECTS OF OVERDOSE	WITHDRAWAL SYNDROME
High/High	Yes	3–6	Oral, smoked			
High/High	Yes	3–6	Oral, smoked, injected	Euphoria, drowsiness, respiratory depression, constricted pupils, nausea	Slow and shallow breathing, clammy skin, convulsions, coma, possible death	Watery eyes, runny nose, yawning, loss of appetite, irritability, tremors, panic, cramps, nausea, chills and sweating
Mod./Mod.	Yes	3–6	Oral, injected			
High/High	Yes	3–6	Injected, sniffed, smoked			
High/High	Yes	3–6	Oral, injected			
High/High	Yes	3–6	Oral, injected			
High/High–Low	Yes	12–24	Oral, injected			
High–Low/ High–Low	Yes	Variable	Oral, injected			

(continued)

DRUGS	CSA SCHEDULES	MEDICAL USES	TRADE OR OTHER NAMES	SLANG NAMES
Depressants				
Chloral Hydrate	IV	Hypnotic	Noctec	—
Barbiturates	II III IV	Anesthetic, anti-convulsant, sedative, hypnotic, veterinary euthanasia agent	Amytal, Butisol, Fiorinal, Lotusate, Nembutal, Seconal, Tuinal, Phenobarbital	Yellows, Yellow Jackets, Barbs, Reds, Redbirds, Tooies, Phennies
Benzodiazepines	IV	Antianxiety, anticonvulsant, sedative, hypnotic	Ativan, Dalmane, Diazepam, Paxipam, Librium, Xanax, Serax, Valium, Tranxene, Verstran, Versed, Halcion, Restoril	Downers, Goof Balls, Sleeping Pills, Candy
Methaqualone	I	Sedative, hypnotic	Quaalude	Lude, Quay, Guad, Mandrex
Glutethimide	III	Sedative, hypnotic	Doriden	—
Other Depressants	III IV	Antianxiety, sedative, hypnotic	Equanil, Miltown, Noludar, Placidyl, Valmid	Tranquilizers, Muscle Relaxants, Sleeping Pills
Stimulants				
Cocaine†	II	Local anesthetic		Bump, Toot, C, Coke, Flake, Snow, Candy, Crack
Amphetamines	II	Attention deficit disorders, narcolepsy, weight control	Biphetamine, Desoxyn, Dexedrine	Pep Pills, Bennies, Uppers, Truck Drivers, Dexies, Black Beauties, Speed
Phenmetrazine	II	Weight control	Preludin	Uppers, Peaches, Hearts
Methylphenidate	II	Attention deficit disorders, narcolepsy	Ritalin	Speed, Meth, Crystal, Crank, Go Fast
Other Stimulants	III IV	Weight control	Apidex, Cylert, Didrex, Ionamin, Melfiat, Plegine, Sanorex, Tenuate, Tepanil, Prelu-2	—
Hallucinogens				
LSD	I	None		Acid, Microdot, Cubes
Mescaline and Peyote	I	None		Mesc Buttons, Cactus
Amphetamine Variants	I	None	2, 5-DMA, PMA, STP, MDA, MDMA, TMA, DOM, DOB	Ecstasy, Designer Drugs
Phencyclidine	II	None	PCP	PCP, Angel Dust, Hog, Peace Pill
Phencyclidine Analogues	I	None	PCE, PCPY, TCP	—
Other Hallucinogens	I	None	Bufotenine, Ibogaine, DMT, Det, Psilocybin, Psilocyn	Sacred Mushrooms, Magic Mushrooms, Mushrooms

† Designated as a narcotic under C.S.A.

DEPENDENCE PHYSICAL/ PSYCHOLOGICAL	TOLERANCE	DURATION (HOURS)	ADMINISTRATION METHODS	POSSIBLE EFFECTS	EFFECTS OF OVERDOSE	WITHDRAWAL SYNDROME
Mod./Mod.	Yes	5–8	Oral			
High–Mod./ High–Mod.	Yes	1–16	Oral	Slurred speech, disorientation, drunken behavior without odor of alcohol	Shallow respiration, clammy skin, dilated pupils, weak and rapid pulse, coma, possible death	Anxiety, insomnia, tremors, delirium, convulsions, possible death
Low/Low	Yes	4–8	Oral			
High/High	Yes	4–8	Oral			
High/Mod.	Yes	4–8	Oral			
Mod./Mod.	Yes	4–8	Oral			
Possible/High	Yes	1–2	Sniffed, smoked, injected	Increased alertness, excitation, euphoria, increased pulse rate and blood pressure, insomnia, loss of appetite	Agitation, increase in body temperature, hallucinations, convulsions, possible death	Apathy, long periods of sleep, irritability, depression, disorientation
Possible/High	Yes	2–4	Oral, injected			
Possible/High	Yes	2–4	Oral, injected			
Possible/Mod.	Yes	2–4	Oral, injected			
Possible/High	Yes	2–4	Oral, injected			
None/Unknown	Yes	8–12	Oral	Illusions and hallucinations, poor perception of time and distance	Longer, more intense "trip" episodes, psychosis, possible death	Withdrawal syndrome not reported
None/Unknown	Yes	8–12	Oral			
Unknown/Unknown	Yes	Variable	Oral, injected			
Unknown/High	Yes	Days	Smoked, oral, injected			
Unknown/High	Yes	Days	Smoked, oral, injected,			
None/Unknown	Possible	Variable	Smoked, oral, injected, sniffed			

(continued)

DRUGS	CSA SCHEDULES	MEDICAL USES	TRADE OR OTHER NAMES	SLANG NAMES
Cannabis				
Marijuana	I	None		Pot, Grass, Reefer, Roach, Maui Wowie, Joint, Weed, Loco Weed, Mary Jane
Tetrahydrocannabinol	I II	Cancer chemo-therapy antinauseant	THC, Marinol	THC
Hashish	I	None		Hash
Hashish Oil	I	None		Hash Oil
Inhalants		None	Gasoline, Airplane Glue, Veg. Spray, Hairspray, Deodorants, Spray Paint, Liquid Paper, Paint Thinner, Rubber Cement	Sniffing, Glue Sniffing, Snorting

DEPENDENCE PHYSICAL/ PSYCHOLOGICAL	TOLERANCE	DURATION (HOURS)	ADMINISTRATION METHODS	POSSIBLE EFFECTS	EFFECTS OF OVERDOSE	WITHDRAWAL SYNDROME
Unknown/Mod.	Yes	2–4	Smoked, oral	Euphoria, relaxed inhibitions, increased appetite, disoriented behavior	Fatigue, paranoia, possible psychosis	Insomnia, hyperactivity and decreased appetite occasionally reported
Unknown/Mod.	Yes	2–4	Smoked, oral			
Unknown/Mod.	Yes	2–4	Smoked, oral			
Unknown/Mod.	Yes	2–4	Smoked, oral			
None/Unknown	Yes	30 min.	Sniffed	Euphoria, headaches, nausea, fainting, stupor, rapid heartbeat	Damage to lungs, liver, kidneys, bone marrow, suffocation, choking, anemia, possible stroke, sudden death	Insomnia, increased appetite, depression, irritability, headache

Index

AA. *See* Alcoholics Anonymous (AA)
abstinence programs, 100
abuse. *See* drug abuse
Accutane, 421
acetaminophen, 412, 413, 414
acetylcholine, 116, 120–121
   receptors for, antihistamines and, 171
ACh. *See* acetylcholine
"acid." *See* LSD
acid heads, 269
acid rebound, 419
acne medications, 421
ACOAs (Adult Children of Alcoholics), 102, 226
acquaintance and date rape, alcohol and, 225
acquired immunodeficiency syndrome. *See* AIDS
acromegaly, 451
ACS (American Cancer Society), 311, 331
"act-alike" OTC drugs, 419
Action on Smoking and Health (ASH), 310, 331
acupuncture, quitting smoking through, 324
acute alcohol withdrawal syndrome, 227
acute response, 143
ADAMHA Reorganization Act (1992), 76
adaptive processes, 146–150
addiction, 7, 40, 92–109, 152–153
   causes of, 94–96
   characteristics necessary for, 19–20
   costs of, 21–28
   cycle of, 96–97
   definitions, 7, 19, 92–93
   dependence *vs.*, 19, 92
   drug laws and, 74–76
   family therapy for, 227–230
   models of, 93–94
   nondrug, 96–97
   origin and nature of, 92–96
   phases of, 19–20, 21
   risk factors for, 94–96
   stages of, 93–94
   treatment of, 97–109
"addiction to pleasure" theory, 42
additive interactions, 138
ADHD (attention deficit hyperactivity disorder), 266
adhesives, inhalation of, 398
adolescents, drug abuse among, 46–53, 459–470. *See also* college students, drug use among

adult drug abuse *vs.*, 462
AIDS and, 476–477
amphetamines, 266
antitussive products, 417
consequences and coincidental problems of, 462–468
data on, 463–464
developmental issues, 459–460
divorce and, 49
gangs and, 466–468
marijuana use, 369–371
patterns of, 461–462
PCP, 355
prevention of, 468–469
programs for, 498–504
reasons for, 460–461
risk factors for, 94
sexual violence and, 465–466
suicide and, 464–465
tobacco, 303, 322, 323, 324, 330
treatment of, 469–470
warning signs, 468
adrenaline. *See* epinephrine
Adult Children of Alcoholics, 102, 226
adulteration, 278
advertising, drug, 17, 71, 72–74
   alcohol, 17, 508
   OTC drugs, 17, 72–73
Advil. *See* ibuprofen
aerosols, 388–389, 398
affective education model, 505
age, drugs and, 12, 13, 145. *See also* adolescents, drug abuse among
agonistic substances, 119
AHA (American Heart Association), 311
AIDS
   adolescents and, 476–477, 481
   diagnosis of, 476–477
   drug abuse and, 21, 480–481
   drug "cocktail" for, 477
   drugs to treat, 435
   heroin addicts and, 249
   incidence of, 475
   marijuana therapy and, 382
   men and, 479
   nature of, 475–476
   needle sharing and, 480–481
   nitrite use and, 401
   populations at greatest risk for, 477–480
   symptoms of, 475–476
   treatment, 476–477
   women and, 477–478
ALA (American Lung Association), 311, 331

AL-Anon, 102
Alateen, 102
alcohol (ethanol), 8, 182–234
   absorption in body, 186
   advertising and marketing, 16
      on college campuses, 508
   benzodiazepines with, 175
   ceremonial meaning of, 218
   as CNS depressant, 160–161
   CNS depressants with, 174–175, 176
   college students' use of, 204 220–222
   common interactions with, 139
   concentration in common alcoholic beverages, 185
   consumption of, 202–203, 207
   culture and, 212–213, 216–226
   dependence on, 148, 191
   domestic violence and, 224–225
   drinking age and, 205–206
   family and, 225–226
   fetal alcohol syndrome and, 21, 195–196
   with heroin, 246
   highway fatalities and, 207
   history of, 182–183, 208–212
   impact of, 27, 28, 184
   metabolism of, 188
   nature of, 182
   organ system and bodily function effects, 191–196
   physical effects of, 185–191
   poly drug use and, 188–189
   pregnancy and, 456
   properties of, 184–185
   sex and, 225
   short-term effects of, 189–191
   as social drug, 184
   tolerance to, 148, 188
   U. S. attitudes toward, 208–212
   use in U. S. population groups, 202–206
   withdrawal from, 148, 227
   women and, 456–457
alcohol abuse
   among women, 222–224, 456
   defining, 213
   economic costs of, 207
   sexual violence and, 465–466
   in specific U.S. groups, 202–206
   symptoms of, 47
alcohol dehydrogenase, 187
alcohol dependence syndrome, 213
alcoholic cardiomyopathy, 194
alcoholic fatty liver, 191

alcoholic hepatitis, 192
alcoholic parent, 461
  adult children of, 102, 226
alcoholics
  benzodiazepine use in, 167, 174
  defining, 212–213
  victims of, 225–226
Alcoholics Anonymous (AA), 93, 96,
    100–102
  twelve steps for recovery, 101
alcoholism
  defining, 213
  family therapy for, 227–230
  treatment, 226–230
  treatment of, 100–102
  types of, 215–216
allergic reactions, 134
allergy remedies, OTC, 414–415
alpha alcoholism, 215
altered perceptions, 384
  visual, 345
alternatives approach, to drug use, 512
AMA (American Medical Associa-
    tion), 313
American Cancer Society (ACS), 311,
    331
American Heart Association (AHA),
    311
American Indian Religious Freedom
    Act of 1978, 337
American Lung Association (ALA),
    311, 331
American Medical Association
    (AMA), 313
American Psychiatric Association, 39,
    41, 92, 173, 283
Americans for Nonsmoker's Rights
    (1986), 311
amnesiac, 162
amotivational syndrome, 46, 379–380
amphetamines, 135, 264–274
  abuse of, 266–270
  addiction to, treatment of, 270–271
  approved uses for, 266
  athletes use of, 449
  combinations of, 271
  dependence on, 148
  designer, 271–274
  high-dose patterns, 268–270
  history of, 264–265
  mechanism of action of, 265
  misuse of, 266–270
  for narcolepsy, 267
  side effects of, 265–266, 266
  tolerance to, 148
  withdrawal from, 148
anabolic steroids, 9, 128, 443, 444–449
  effects of, 447–448
  evading detection of, 477
  patterns of abuse of, 446–447
  sources of, 448–449
Anacin. See aspirin
analgesic drugs, 238

caffeine and, 414
endogenous, 152
internal, 412
marijuana as, 381–382
narcotics as, 238, 241–242, 428
prescription of, 428–430
side effects of, 413–414
analogs, 355
Analogue (Designer Drug) Act (1986),
    75
anandamide, 385
Andean Indians, 275–276
androgens, 127, 444. See also anabolic
    steroids
  abuse of, 128
  athletes abuse of, 444–446
anesthetics, 162, 185
  inhalant, 397, 400–401
  local, 276, 283
aneurysm, 316
angina pectoris, 433
anorexiants, 265, 420
ANS (autonomic nervous system),
    124–126
Antabuse (disulfiram), 108–109, 227
antacids, 419–420
antagonists, 108–109, 119, 138
antianginal agents, 433–434
antibacterials, prescription of, 430
anticholinergic drugs, 123, 341
  hallucinogens, 353–354
antidepressants, 430
antidiabetic drugs, 431–432
Anti-Drug Abuse Act, 76
antiepileptic drugs, 431
antihistamines, 162, 171
  therapeutic usefulness and side ef-
      fects of, 171–172
antihypertensive agents, 433
anti-inflammatory drugs, 412–413
  nonsteroidal. See nonsteroidal anti-
      inflammatory drugs
antipyretics, 413
antiseptic agent, 185
antisocial behavior, drug abuse and,
    151
antitussives, 415–417
antiulcer drugs, 432–433
anxiolytic, 162
aphrodisiac, 386
"array," 446
Arrestee Drug Abuse Monitoring
    (ADAM) program, 24
arrhythmia, inhalant abuse and, 396
ASH (Action on Smoking and
    Health), 310, 331
aspirin, 412, 413, 414
asthma, THC therapy for, 381
athletes, drug abuse among, 443–452
  anabolic steroids, 128, 443, 444–449
  ergogenic drugs, 449–451
  prevention and treatment of,
      451–452

smokeless tobacco, 310
stimulants, 449
ATLAS program, 452
ATOD (alcohol, tobacco, and other
    drugs), 501
Atropa belladonna, 353
attention deficit hyperactivity disor-
    der, 266
attitude change model, 505
autonomic nervous system, 124–126
awareness model, 505
axon, 115, 117
AZT (zidovudine), 435, 477
azulla, 366

BAC or BAL (blood alcohol concen-
    tration level), 185, 187, 189,
    190
BACCHUS (Boosting Alcohol Con-
    sciousness Concerning the
    Health of University Students),
    506–507
"bad mind trip," 345
"bagging," 398
barbiturates, 161, 167–170
  CNS depressants used with, 175
  combinations of, 169
  dependence on
    physical, 148, 170
    psychological, 148
  effects of, 168–169
  elimination from body, 169–170
  history of, 161, 167–168
  mechanism of action, 169
  medical uses of, 168–169
  most frequently abused, 169
  tolerance to, 148
  withdrawal from, 148, 170
basal ganglia, 123
"bathtub speed" (methcathinone), 272
Bayer Aspirin. See aspirin
Bayer Pharmaceuticals, 241
behavior
  culture and drinking, 216–217
  patterns of, 329
behavioral compensation, 149
behavioral modification, self-help
    with, 325
behavioral stereotypy, 265
behavioral tolerance, 188
belladonna (deadly nightshade), 353
benzodiazepines, 161, 163–167
  abuse of, 167
  with alcohol, 164
  combinations of, 175
  dependence on, 148
  half-lives of, 165
  history of, 161
  mechanisms of action of, 164
  medical uses for, 163–164
  receptor for, 118, 164
  side effects of, 164–166
  tolerance to, 148

types of, 164
withdrawal from, 166–167
benzoyl peroxide, 421
beta alcoholism, 215
β-adrenergics
blockers, 451
stimulants, 433
"Big Tobacco," 308
binge, 268
binge drinking, 202, 221–222
biological explanation, of drug abuse, 38–40, 95
biotransformation, 144
birth defects, LSD and, 345–346
blood, alcohol's effect on, 194
blood alcohol concentration level, 185, 187, 189, 190
blood doping, 450
blood-brain barrier, 143
Bloustein, Edward, 506
bodily functions, effects of alcohol on, 191–196
body, drug distribution in, 142–144
"body trip," 345
bong, 482
Book of Drugs, 365
Boosting Alcohol Consciousness Concerning the Health of University Students (BACCHUS), 506–507
bootlegging, 210
brain. See also nervous system
alcohol's effect on, 191, 195
breast cysts, caffeine consumption and, 291
bright tobacco, 306
bronchodilators, 433
bronchopulmonary disease, tobacco and, 317
Buproprion, 329
Bush, George, 82
butane, inhalation of, 399

caffeine, 12, 287–292. See also xanthines
as analgesic, 290
analgesic products and, 414
beverages containing, 288–289
chemical nature of, 288
consumption of, 12
social consequences of, 289
dependence on, 148, 291–292
over-the-counter drugs containing, 290
physiological effects of, 290–291
pregnancy and, 291
social consequences of consumption of, 289
in soft drinks, 289
tolerance to, 148
withdrawal from, 148
caffeine intoxication, 291
caffeinism, 291

calcium-channel blockers, 433
cancer, tobacco and, 317, 320, 322
cannabinoid receptor, 118
cannabis, 9, 365. See also marijuana
characteristics of, 373–374
decriminalization of, Dutch policy on, 80
dependence on, 387
Cannabis Buyers' Club, 382
Cannabis sativa, 9, 365, 372
cardiovascular disease
drug treatment for, 433
tobacco and, 316
cardiovascular system
alcohol and, 194
caffeine and, 290
cocaine and, 282–283
drug abuse effects on, 135–136
marijuana and, 385–386
cartels, 25–26
"cat" (methcathinone), 272
Catapres (clonidine), 108, 257
catatonia, 356
catecholamines, 121
Center for Substance Abuse Prevention, 483
Central High drug prevention program, 498–500
central nervous system, 6, 122, 123–124
caffeine and, 290
cocaine and, 282
depressants of. See CNS depressants
marijuana and, 384–385
nicotine and, 314
cerebral cortex, 148
certification, of qualified counselors, 105
cessation methods, smoking, 324–325
The Changing Cigarette (report), 311
characterological model, 93
chemical toxins, meth labs and, 267, 268
chewing tobacco, 314, 318, 321
Children of Alcoholics, 226
as adults, 102, 226
family therapy and, 227–230
Children's Health Act (2000), 76
China
marijuana history of, 365–366
opium in, 238–239
"chippers," 15
chloral hydrate (Noctec), 170
chocolate, 289–290
cholesterol, and lipid-lowering drugs, 434
cholinergic drugs, 126
chromosome damage, LSD and, 345–346
chronic response, 143
"cigarette girl," 306
cigarettes, 306–308

consumption of, 307–308
government regulation of, 307–308
taxing of, 330–331
women and, 455
cigars, 305
cirrhosis, 192
cleaning agents, inhalation of, 398
clenbuterol, 449–450
clinical pharmacological evaluation stage, 70
clinical research and development, 70–71
Clinton, Bill, 81, 383
Clinton-Gore plan, for tobacco legislation, 309
clonidine (Catapres), 108, 257
closed meetings, 102
clove cigarettes, 315
club drug, 475
GHB as, 172
MDMA as, 273
Rohypnol as, 167
CNS depressants, 158–178. See also alcohol (ethanol)
abuse of, 166–167
dependence on, 166–167, 173–175
effects of, 161–162
history of, 160–161
over-the-counter, 418
patterns of abuse with, 173–176
side effects of, 164–166
tolerance to, 162, 166–167
types of, 162–173
withdrawal from, 166–167, 175–176
COAs. See Children of Alcoholics
Cobain, Kurt, 249
Coca-Cola, cocaine in, 276
cocaine, 274–287, 425
administration of, 279–281
AIDS and, 480–481
athletes use of, 449
cardiovascular system effects of, 282–283
central nervous effects of, 282
crack, 14, 281–282
dependence on, 148
recovery from, 285
therapeutic drugs for, 285–286
treatment for, 283–284
with heroin, 246
history of, 275–278
patterns of abuse of, 278–282
pharmacological effects of, 282
pregnancy and, 456
processing of, 278
production of, 278
student use of, 474
tolerance to, 148
withdrawal from, 148, 283
cocaine babies, 287
cocaine cartel, Colombian, 26
"cocktail," for AIDS, 477

Code of Hammurabi, 10
codeine, 239, 256
codependency, 96, 225
coffee, 288
cohoba, 349
cold remedies, OTC, 414
cold turkey, 324
college students, drug use among, 470–475
    alcohol, 204, 220–222, 473–474
        marketing of, on campuses, 508
    illicit, 474
    OTC stimulants, 418
    patterns of, 473–474
    predicting, for first-year students, 474
    prevalence of, 471
    prevention programs, 505–506
    reasons for, 473
    Rohypnol and date rape, 475
    "soft drugs," 474
    steroid usage patterns in, 472
    trends in, 472
Columbia, cocaine cartel in, 26
community-based drug prevention programs, 500–501
Comprehensive Alcohol Abuse and Alcoholism Prevention, Treatment, and Rehabilitation Act Amendments (1974), 75
Comprehensive Drug Abuse Prevention and Control Act (1970), 75
Comprehensive Methamphetamine Control Act (1996), 267
Comprehensive Smoking Education Act (1984), 311
compulsive users, 15
conditioning, 43
congestion rebound, 415
congestive heart failure, 434
contextual factors, 5
contraceptives, 434
    tobacco and, 316
control, of drug abuse, factors in, 78–79
control theory, 55–57
Controlled Substances Act, 9
    categorization under, 77
conventional behavior, 54
Coonce, John, 22
CORE Institute survey, 221
Cortéz, Hernando, 289
corticosteroids. See steroids
cost
    societal, of drug addictions, 21–28, 76–78
    of tobacco use, 302
cough
    OTC remedies for, 414, 416
    productive, 415–416
counseling, 105
crack, 14, 281–282
    HIV infection and, 481

crack babies, 281
"crank," 22. See also speed (methamphetamine)
"crash" (rebound depression), 279, 280
craving, drug, 153
crime
    drug-related, 21–26, 76–79, 247
    organized, 26
    violent, 24
critical thinking skills, marijuana and, 378–379
cross-dependence, 150
cross-tolerance, 149
CSA. See Controlled Substances Act
cultural factors, 5
    addiction and, 95
    alcohol use and, 216–226
    in drug abuse development, 94–96
    drug use attitudes, 66–67
cultural support perspective, 53
cumulative effect, 144
current drug use, 368
curriculum infusion, in drug prevention programs, 508
curriculum-based objectives, drug prevention and, 501–502
"cycling," 446

danger signals, of drug abuse, 57–58
D.A.R.E. (Drug Abuse Resistance Education), 508–509, 510
date rape, drugs and, 167, 225, 475. See also Rohypnol
Datura Stramonium, 354
de las Casas, Bishop Bartolome, 304
DEA (Drug Enforcement Administration), 18, 21, 75, 242
deadly nightshade, 353
decongestants, OTC, 414–415
decriminalization, of cannabis, 80
Delinquent Boys: The Culture of the Gang (Cohen), 53
delirium tremens, 227
delta alcoholic, 215
delta-9-tetrahydrocannabinol. See tetrahydrocannabinol
demand reduction strategy, 79, 81–82
demanding parent, 461
Demerol, 219, 255
dendrites, 117
Department of Health and Human Services, 312, 510
Department of Justice, 312
Department of Transportation, 313
dependence, 19–20, 35, 134, 146, 149–150. See also physical dependence; psychological dependence; *specific drugs*
    addiction *vs.*, 19, 92, 152
    alcohol, 148, 191, 213
    amphetamines, 148
    barbiturates, 148, 170

benzodiazepines, 148
caffeine, 148, 291–292
cannabis, 387
CNS depressants, 166–167, 173–175
cocaine. See cocaine, dependence on commonly abused drugs, properties of, 148
cross-dependence, 150
defined, 146
heroin, 248
LSD, 148
marijuana, 148, 387
narcotics, 244–252
nicotine, 148, 323
phencyclidine, 148
physical, 19, 149–150
psychological, 19, 150–151
tetrahydrocannabinol, 387
tobacco, 323–326
depressants, 8. See also CNS depressants
depression, 430
    bipolar mood disorder and, 430
    drug treatment of, 431
    endogenous major, 430
    reactive, 430
    rebound "crash," 279, 280
    self-medication with cocaine for, 278, 282
    THC therapy for, 381
"designer" drugs, 8, 9–10
    amphetamines, 271–274, 350
    MPTP as, 255–256
Desoxyn (methamphetamine), 22, 267
dessert topping sprays, inhalation of, 398
deterrence, drug laws and, 76–78
detoxification, 100, 102–103, 175
deviance, 50–51
Dexatrim, 421
dextromethorphan, 257
DHHS (Department of Health and Human Services), 312, 510
diabetes, 431
Diagnostic and Statistical Manual of Mental disorders (DSM-IV), 39, 41, 92–93, 173–174, 387, 430
diazepam (Valium), 118, 163, 427
diet aids, OTC, 420
differential association theory, 46, 377
differential reinforcement, 42, 43
digestive system, alcohol's effect on, 193–194
Dilaudid, 255
dimethoxymethylamphetamine, 341, 350
dimethyltryptamine, 349–350
diphenoxylate, 239
dipping snuff, 318
direct vasodilators, 433

discretionary enforcement, of drug laws, 85
disease, alcoholism as, 38
disease model, 93
disinhibition/disinhibitor, 189
    alcohol as, 217
distillation, 182–183
disulfiram (Antabuse), 108–109, 227
diuretics, 433
    alcohol as, 189
divorce, adolescent drug use and, 49
DMT (dimethyltryptamine), 349–350
doctor-patient communication, 426–427
DOM (dimethoxymethylamphetamine), 341, 350
domestic violence, role of alcohol in, 224–225
The Doors of Perception (Huxley), 347
dopamine, 38, 116, 120, 121
"doping," 443
Doriden (glutethimide), 170
dormitories, for non-drug using students, 474
dose, required, 143
dose-response relationship, 136–167
"double wall" of encapsulation, 93
driving
    alcohol use and, 207, 377
    marijuana and, 377–378
drug abuse. *See also specific drugs and specific populations*
    adaptive processes in, 146–150
    AIDS and, 21. *See also* AIDS
    antisocial behavior and, 151
    biological explanations of, 38–40
    common types of, 7–10
    controlling, 78–79
    danger signals of, 57–58
    defined, 7, 19
    law and, 74–79
    patterns of, 17–19
    psychological theories of, 40–43
    seriousness of, 37–38
    sociological theories of, 43–59
    statistics and trends in, 12–17, 36–37
    strategies for preventing, 79–87
    symptoms of, 19–20, 47
Drug Abuse Control Amendments (1965), 75
Drug Abuse Office and Treatment Act (1972), 75
Drug Abuse Resistance Education (D.A.R.E.), 508–509, 510
drug abuser, inpatient treatment of adolescent, 469
    for cocaine abuse, 284
drug abusers
    common characteristics of, 46–49
    experiences, motives, and alternatives for, 513
    testing to identify, 85–86
    types of, 15

drug addiction. *See* addiction
drug choices
    high-risk, 58, 268
    low-risk, 58
drug court, 509
drug dependence. *See* dependence
drug distribution, in body, 142–144
Drug Efficacy Study, 69
Drug Enforcement Administration, 18, 21, 75, 242
drug interactions, 137–140, 161, 167, 174–175. *See also specific drugs*
    common examples of, 139
    dealing with, 139–140
drug laws. *See* laws and regulations
drug misuse, 7. *See also* drug abuse
drug prevention programs. *See* prevention of drug abuse
drug receptors, 118–119
    agonistic and antagonistic effects on, 119
drug testing, 27–28
    to identify users, 85–86
drug use
    alternatives to, 511–514
    attraction of, 17–19, 37–38
    common principles of, 435
    costs of, 21–28
    cultural attitudes toward, 66–67
    current and future, 82–86
    dimensions of, 5–7
    experiences in, factors responsible for, 5
    extent and frequency of, 11–12
    gangs and, 466–468
    gender differences in, 14
    Internet as promoter of, 484
    mass media influences on, 15–17
    misperceptions of, 508
    statistics and trends in, 12–14
drug users
    employed, 26–28
    personality of, 41–42
    types of, 15
drug war, fighting, 83–85
    alcohol, 209–212
    D.A.R.E., 508–509
    drug trafficking, 239
    Herbal Ecstasy, 351
    KEY-CREST program, 107
    in Netherlands, 80
    prescription drugs, 425
    Rohypnol, 167
    smoking, 303–304
    supply reduction strategy, 79–80
drugs
    commonly abused, 7–10
    definition of, 6, 67
    designer, 8, 9–10, 255–256, 271–274, 350
    effects of, 134–136
    forms and methods of taking, 140–142

gateway, 7, 37, 329–330, 372
generic *vs.* proprietary, 427
drunken comportment, 217
DSM-IV classification of psychiatric disorders, 39, 41, 92, 282, 336
duodenal ulcer, 432
Durham-Humphrey Amendment, 68, 71, 425
dysphoria, 153

EAPs (employee assistance programs), 28
ecological model, 506
Ecotrin. *See* aspirin
Ecstasy (MDMA), 18, 272–274, 341
    as club drug, 475
    student use of, 474
edema, 434
educational drug prevention programs, 81, 498–506. *See also* prevention of drug abuse
    curriculum-based objectives of, 501–502
elixir, 67
emphysema, 317
Empirin. *See* aspirin
employee assistance programs (EAPs), 28
enablers, 225
encapsulation, double wall of, 93
endocrine system, 114
    alcohol's effect on, 195
    drugs and, 126–128
    regulation of, 126–128
endogenous analgesics, 152
endogenous messenger substances, 118
endorphins, 116, 118, 120, 152
    narcotics and, 241–242
entactogens, 350
entertainment industry, promotion of drug use by, 482–484
Environmental Protection Agency, 312
environmental tobacco smoke, 312, 317–318
EPA (Environmental Protection Agency), 312
epilepsy, 432
    THC therapy for, 381
epinephrine, 120, 121, 127
epsilon alcoholic, 215
equal-opportunity affliction, 11
ergogenic substances, 443–444
    expected effects of, 445
ergotism, 342
erythropoietin, 450
Erythroxylon coca, 275, 278
ethanol. *See* alcohol (ethanol)
ethical drugs. *See* prescription drugs
ethnic and racial groups
    AIDS incidence and, 479, 481
    alcohol consumption and, 219–220
    college students, drug use among, 473

ethnic and racial groups (*continued*)
  inhalant abuse, 402–403
  smoking, 323
ethylene glycol, 185
ETS (environmental tobacco smoke),
  312, 317–318
eugenol, 315
euphorigenic effects of inhalants, 396
Excedrin. *See* acetaminophen; aspirin
excitatory synapse, 118
Executive Order 12564 (1986), 76
expectorants, 416, 417
experimenters, 15
extended clinical evaluation, 70–71
extraversion, 41

false advertisement, 73
family, alcohol and, 225–226
family therapy/counseling, 227–230
family-based drug prevention programs, 504
FAS (fetal alcohol syndrome), 21,
  195–196, 456
FCC (Federal Communications Commission), 310
FDA. *See* Food and Drug Administration
Federal Cigarette Labeling and Advertising Act (1965), 310
Federal Communications Commission,
  310
federal laws. *See* laws and regulations
Federal Trade Commission, 73
fentanyls, 255
fermentation, 182
fetal alcohol syndrome, 21, 195–196,
  456
fetus
  alcohol and, 21, 195–196, 456
  cocaine and, 281. *See also* preg-
    nancy
  tobacco and, 318
FIPSE (Fund for the Improvement of
  Post-Secondary Education),
  507
First- Born Church of Christ, 337
first-aid products, OTC, 422
"flashbacks," 340
floaters, 15
flue-cured tobacco, 306
flunitrazepam (Rohypnol), 167, 475
Food, Drug, and Cosmetic Act (1938),
  68
Food and Drug Administration,
  67–72, 306, 381, 408
  history of, 67–69
  regulation of drugs and advertising
    by, 69–72, 410
"freakout," 344
free radicals, amphetamines and, 266
"freebasing," 280–281
Freon, inhalation of, 400

Freud, Sigmund, 40, 276
FTC (Federal Trade Commission), 73
Fund for the Improvement of Post-
  Secondary Education (FIPSE),
  507

GABA (gamma-aminobutyric acid),
  116, 120, 172
GAMMA (Greeks Advocating Mature
  Management of Alcohol), 507
gamma alcoholism, 215
gamma butyrolactone, 173
gamma-aminobutyric acid, 116, 120,
  172
gamma-hydroxybutyrate, 172–173,
  451
gangs, drugs and, 466–468
ganja, 374
gases, inhalation of, 398
gasoline, inhalation of, 399–400
GASP (Group Against Smokers' Pollution), 331
gastric ulcer, 432
gastritis, 419
gastrointestinal medications, OTC,
  419
gastrointestinal reflux (heartburn),
  419–420
gateway drugs, 8, 37, 329–330
  marijuana as, 372
GBL (gamma butyrolactone), 173
gender differences, in drug abuse. *See
  also* women, drug abuse
    among
  in adolescents, divorce affecting, 49
  alcohol use, 222–224
  drug effects, 145
  trends in, 14
generation gaps, 55
generic drugs, 427
genetic damage, LSD and, 345–346
genetic theories, of drug abuse, 38,
  39–40, 152
  alcoholism and, 40
genogram, 230
GHB (gamma-hydroxybutyrate),
  172–173, 451
glaucoma, THC therapy for, 381
glue sniffing, 397. *See also* inhalants
glutethimide (Doriden), 170
gonads, 127
Great American Smokeout, 311, 511
Greeks Advocating Mature Management of Alcohol (GAMMA),
  507
Group Against Smokers' Pollution
  (GASP), 331

habituation, 42
Halcion, 165
half-life, 144
hallucinogens, 8, 14, 336–357. *See also
  specific types*

defined, 336
effects of, 339–341
history of, 336–337
mechanisms of action of, 341
Native American religious use of,
  337
nature of, 338–341
types of, 341–357
use today, 338, 339
Hammurabi, 36–37
hangover, 189–190
Harrison Act of 1914, 74, 75, 240, 366
hashish, 366, 374
hashishiyya, 366
heartburn (gastrointestinal reflux),
  419–420
heavy drinkers, 203
Helicobacter pylori, 432–433
hemp, 365, 366, 367
henbane, 354
hepatitis
  alcoholic, 192
  drug effects and, 145
  needle sharing and drug abuse and,
    21
hepatotoxicity, 192
herbal medicines
  over-the-counter, 422–425
  as stimulants, 292–293
hereditary factors. *See* genetic theories,
  of drug abuse
heroin, 239
  abuse of, 244–246
    patterns, 247–248
    treatment for, 251–252
  administration methods for,
    248–249
  AIDS and, 249, 480–481
  combinations of, 245–246
  crime and, 247
  dependence on, stages of, 248
  history of, 241
  pregnancy and, 250
  profile of, 246–247
  tobacco use and, 330
  withdrawal symptoms, 250
Heroin Act (1924), 75
HGF (human growth factor), 450–451
HGH (human growth hormone),
  450–451
"high," 375
high-risk drug choices, 58, 268
HIV infection. *See also* AIDS
  drug abuse and, 21
  drugs to treat, 435
  marijuana use in, 382
  nature of, 475–476
  pregnancy and, 477–478
  symptoms of, 475–476
  transmission of, 477–480
  women and, 455
HIV-positive subcultures, drug use in,
  475–482

Hofmann, Albert, 342
hogsheads, 305
holistic approach, 28–29
holistic health, 28–29
holy plant, marijuana as, 364
homeostasis, 114
homeostatic systems and drug actions,
    114–128
    explanation of, 116–122
    overview of, 114–116
hormone(s), 114, 126–128
    abuse of, 128
hormone-related drugs, 434–435
5HT. *See* 5-hydroxytryptamine
"huffing," 398
human growth factor (HGF), 450–451
human growth hormone (HGH),
    450–451
human immunodeficiency virus. *See*
    HIV infection
Huxley, Aldous, 347
hydromorphone (Dilaudid), 255
5-hydroxytryptamine, 116, 120,
    121–122
hyoscine, 353
hyoscyamine, 353
Hyoscyamus niger, 354
hyperglycemia, 431
hyperpyrexia, 269
hypersensitive reactions, 134
hypertension, 433
hypnosis, smoking cessation and, 324
hypnotic-sedative agents, 162, 435
    common interactions with, 139
hypoglycemics, oral, 432
hypothalamus, 124
hypothyroidism, 434
hypoxia, inhalant use and, 398

ibuprofen, 412, 413, 430
ice, 268. *See also* methamphetamine
illicit drugs, 6
    use trends in, 12–13
IM (intramuscular) injection, 142
improvisational theater groups, 508
Indian Hemp Commission Report,
    367, 386
industrial alcoholism programs, 106
information-only model, 505
inhalants, 9, 396–405
    adolescent use of, 401–402
    anesthetics, 400–401
    chemical contents of, 398
    dangers of, 403–403
    history of, 396–397
    nitrites, 401
    signs of abuse, 401, 403
    socioeconomics and use of, 402
    treatment of abuse of, 404
    use of
        by gender, 402
        by race, 402–403
    volatile substances, 398–400

inhalation/inhalers, 141
    nicotine, 328–329
inhibitory effects, 138
inhibitory synapse, 118
initial clinical stage, 70
inoculation strategy, 79, 82
inpatient treatment, of drug abuser,
    adolescent, 469
insomnia, 417–418
instrumental use of drugs, 11–12
interaction of drugs. *See* drug interac-
    tions
interdiction, 79
intergang, 466
Internet, pro-drug messages and, 484
intoxication, 41
    caffeine, 291
    pseudointoxication, 217
intragang, 466
intramuscular injection, 142
intraocular pressure, 381
intravenous injection, 142
    AIDS and, 480–481
introversion, 41
ischemia, 433
isopropyl alcohol, 185
IV. *See* intravenous injection

James I (King of England), 304
jimsonweed, 354
Joe Camel, 308
Johnson, Ben, 443

Kefauver and Harris Amendment
    (1962), 69
keratin layer, 421
keratolytics, 421
ketamine, 357
KEY-CREST program, 107
"Kick Butts Day," 309
kidneys, alcohol's effect on, 195
Köller, Karl, 276

LAAM (long-acting methadone ana-
    logue), 108
labeling theory, 49–52
laughing gas (nitrous oxide), 396–397,
    400–401
laws and regulations, 67–87
    on advertising, 72–74
    deterrent effect of, 76–78
    discretionary enforcement of, 85
    drug abuse and, 74–79
    evolution of, 67–69
    history of, 67–69
    new prescription drugs and, 70–71
    nonprescription OTC drugs and,
        71–72
    pragmatic, 86–87
    quality assurance and, 74–75
Leary, Timothy, 337
legalization, of drugs
    debate on, 83–85

marijuana, 383
    in Netherlands, 80
    selective, 84–85
licit drugs, 6
limbic system, 124
lipid-lowering drugs, 434
Little Cigar Act of 1973, 310
liver
    alcohol's effect on, 191–192
    function of, 141
local anesthetic, 276, 283
Local Council on Alcoholism and
    Drug Dependence, 499
long-acting methadone analogue, 108
"look-alike" OTC drugs, 419
loperamide, 239
Louis XIII and Louis XIV (Kings of
    France), 304
LSD, 269, 338–339, 341–346
    altered senses from, 338–339
    behavioral effects of, 343–345
    creative effects of, 343–344
    cross-tolerances to, 348, 349
    dependence on, 148
    genetic damage and birth defects
        from, 345–346
    history of, 337
    League of Spiritual Discovery, 337
    loss of control from, 339–340
    loss of identity and cosmic merging
        from, 340–341
    mechanisms of action of, 341
    perceptual effects of, 344–345
    physiological effects of, 343
    psychedelic effects of, 344
    self-reflection from, 340
    sensory experiences from, stages of,
        338–341
    street names for, 343
    student use of, 339, 474
    synthesis and administration of,
        343
    tolerance to, 148
    withdrawal from, 148
lysergic acid diethylamide. *See* LSD

ma, 365
ma huang, 293
McCall, Oliver, 450
"magic bullet," 136
"magic mushrooms." *See* psilocybin
mainline, 248–249
mainstream smoke, 320. *See also* envi-
    ronmental tobacco smoke
maintenance programs, 106–108
    methadone, 107–108
malnutrition, alcoholism and, 188,
    196
Mandragora officinarum, 353
mandrake, 353
MAOs (monoamine oxidase in-
    hibitors), 431
margin of safety, 136–137

Mariani, Angelo, 276
marijuana, 9, 14, 118, 364–390, 425
    amotivational syndrome and, 46,
        379–380
    behavioral effects of, 375–380
    critical thinking skills and, 378–379
    current use of, 368–369
    dependence on, 148, 387
    driving and, 377
    as gateway drug, 372
    hallucinogenic effects of, 357
    history of, 365–368
    legalization of, 80, 383
    peer influences and, 371–372
    physiological effects of, 384–389
    subjective euphoric effects of,
        376–377
    tolerance to, 148, 387
    use of
        chronic, 387–389
        misperceptions of, 372–373
        signs of, 376
        by students, 369–371
        therapeutic, 381–384
        trends of, 365–368
    withdrawal from, 148
Marijuana Tax Act (1937), 75, 366
Marinol (THC capsule), 383
marketing of new drugs. See advertis-
    ing, drug
mass media, influences on drug use,
    15–17
master gland (pituitary gland),
    126–127
Master Settlement Agreement (1998),
    308
master status, 51
MDA (methylenedioxyamphetamine),
    341, 350–351
MDMA (methylenedioxymetham-
    phetamine), 18, 272–274, 341
    as club drug, 475
    student use of, 474
mead, 182
medical marijuana, 381–384
medicinal drugs, effectiveness of, 68
medicines, 7
meditation, 512
melanocytes, 422
melanoma, 422
melatonin, 418
member assistance programs, 106
memory, marijuana use and, 378
mental alertness, changes in, 134
mental disorders, substance abuse vs.,
    41. See also psychiatric disor-
    ders
mental set, 150
mentally ill chemical abusers, 105
meperidine (Demerol), 239, 255
mescaline (peyote), 8, 346–348
    mechanism of action of, 348
    physiological effects of, 347–348

    tolerance to, 348
    treatment for, 348
metabolism, 144
    of alcohol, 188
metabolites, 144
"meth." See methamphetamine
methadone, 239, 254–255, 251-252
    maintenance for, 107–108
Methadone Control Act (1973), 75
methamphetamine, 22, 267
methaqualone, 171
methcathinone ("cat" or "bathtub
    speed"), 272
methyl alcohol, 185
3,4-methylenedioxyamphetamine,
    341, 350–351
methylenedioxymethamphetamine,
    18, 272–274, 341, 351–352
methylphenidate (Ritalin), 266, 274
methyprylon (Noludar), 171
MICAs (mentally ill chemical
    abusers), 105
Mickey Finn, 170
Minnesota model, 102
minorities, alcohol use among,
    219–220
mokus, 227
Monardes, Nicholas, 304
Monitoring the Future 1999 Survey,
    445
monoamine oxidase inhibitors, 431
moral model, 93
morphine, 239, 253–254
    side effects of, 135
Motrin. See ibuprofen
MPTP, 255–256
multiple sclerosis, THC therapy for,
    381
"munchies," 384
Murad (Amurath) IV, 303
muscarinic receptors, 120
mydriasis, 347

naloxone, 257–258
Napoleon, 304
narcolepsy, 266
    amphetamines in treatment of, 267
Narcotic Addict Rehabilitation Act
    (1966), 75
Narcotic Addict Treatment Act (1974),
    75
Narcotic Drug Import and Export Act
    (1922), 75
narcotic fentanyl, heroin and, 245
narcotics, 9, 238–259
    abuse of, treatment for, 252–252
    as analgesics, 241–242
    antagonists for, 108–109
    classification of, 244
    common interactions with, 139
    commonly used, 239
    defined, 238
    dependence on, 244–252

    history of, 238–241
    mechanisms of action of, 243
    pharmacological effects of,
        241–243
    side effects of, 243–244
    therapeutic uses of, 241–243
    tolerance to, 148
    withdrawal from, 148
Narcotics Control Act (1956), 75
nasal sprays
    nicotine, 328
    OTC, 415
National Cancer Institute, 311
National Clearinghouse for Smoking
    and Health, 311
National Council on Alcoholism and
    Drug Dependence (NCADD),
    27–28, 499
National Drug Court Conference, 509
National Household Survey on Drug
    Abuse, 14, 27, 79, 82, 456
National Institute for Occupational
    Safety and Health, 312
National Institute of Drug Abuse
    (NIDA), drug addiction treat-
    ment goals, 97–99
National Institute of Justice (NIJ),
    ADAM program of, 24
National Institute on Drug Abuse
    (NIDA), 13, 21, 355, 510
    goals for treatment of drug addic-
        tion, 97–99
Native American Church, 337
Native Americans
    hallucinogen use and, 337
    tobacco use and, 303
nausea, 134
NCADD (National Council on Alco-
    holism and Drug Depen-
    dence), 27–28, 499
NDA (new drug application), 71
needle sharing, 480–481
nervous system, 114–126. See also cen-
    tral nervous system
    alcohol's effect on, 191
    autonomic, 124–126
    building blocks of, 116–122
    major divisions of, 123–124
    peripheral, 123, 124
Netherlands, drug policy in, 80
neurons, 114–118
neurotransmitters, 38, 114, 115,
    119–120
new drug application, 71
Nicot, Jean, 304
Nicotiana tabacum, 304, 305
nicotine, 8–9, 308–314
    administration of, 308, 314
    clove cigarettes and, 315
    CNS effects of, 314
    dependence on, 148, 323
    pharmacology of, 304, 308,
        314–315

physiological effects of, 314–315
tolerance to, 148
withdrawal from, 148
nicotine gum, 325, 328
nicotine inhalers, 328–329
nicotine nasal spray, 328
nicotine patch, 325, 328
nicotine polacrilex gum, 311
nicotinic receptors, 120
NIDA. *See* National Institute on Drug Abuse (NIDA)
NIJ (National Institute of Justice), ADAM program of, 24
nikethamide, 342
nitrite room odorizers, inhalation of, 398
nitrous oxide, 396–397, 400–401
Noctec (chloral hydrate), 170
NoDoz, 418
Noludar (methyprylon), 171
non-drug using students, dormitories for, 474
noneuphoric opiate, 106
nonprescription drugs. *See* over-the-counter drugs
nonsteroidal anti-inflammatory drugs, 413
common side effects of, 413
prescription, 428–430
norepinephrine, 120, 121
NSAIDs. *See* nonsteroidal anti-inflammatory drugs
Nuprin. *See* ibuprofen
nutmeg, 350
nystagmus, 355

Occupational Safety and Health Administration (OSHA), 312
Office of National Drug Control Policy (ONDCP), 12, 80, 83
Office of the Inspector General, DHHS, 312
Office on Smoking and Health (1978), 311
Olson, Frank, 346
ONDCP (Office of National Drug Control Policy), 12, 80, 83
open meetings, 102
opiates, 9
antagonists, 108–109
noneuphoric, 106
receptors for, 118, 119
opioids. *See* narcotics
opium
history of, 238–241
societal reactions to, 6
Opium Poppy Control Act (1942), 75
opium tincture, 239
Opium War, 239
oral hypoglycemics, 432
oral ingestion, 140–141

organ systems, effects of alcohol on, 191–196
organic solvents, 9
organized crime, drug use and, 26
Orphan Drug law, 71
OSHA (Occupational Safety and Health Administration), 312
OTC drugs. *See* over-the-counter drugs
outpatient treatment, 103–105
for cocaine abuse, 284
outsider's perspective, 442
overdose, of phencyclidine, first aid for, 356
over-the-counter drugs, 6, 7, 11, 12, 17, 408–425
abuse of, 408–410
advertising of, 17, 72–73
athlete use of, 449
caffeine in, 290
FDA-approved, 409
labeling of, 410–411
prescription drugs *vs.*, 67–68
regulation of, 71–72
review process and, 72
self-care and, 410
sympathomimetics, 292–293
types of, 412–425
use of
common principles for, 435
guidelines for, 411
oxycodone, 239

pain
somatic, 241
visceral, 241
panacea, 6
Panama Canal Zone Report, 367
panic disorder, 165
panpathogen, 6
Papaver somniferum, 238, 258
paradoxical effects, 149, 164
parents, 461
alcoholic, adult children of, 102, 226
Parkinson's disease, 123
MPTP and, 255–256
Partnership for a Drug Free America, 401
passive smoking, 320. *See also* environmental tobacco smoke
patent medicines, 67, 211. *See also* over-the-counter drugs
pathological variables, drug effects and, 145–146
patient placement criteria, 105–106
PCP. *See* phencyclidine
peeling agents, 421
peer pressure, 42–43, 44–45
adolescent drug use and, 43, 94
marijuana use and, 369–371
peer-based drug prevention programs, 508

penalties, for drug trafficking, 78
pentazocine, 256
peptic ulcers, 432
peptides, 152
personality
addictive, psychosocial/developmental factors in, 95
disorders of, 93
drug use and, 41–42
predisposition model, 93
person-in-environment model, 506
peyote. *See* mescaline (peyote)
pharmacist, drug management and, 428
pharmacokinetics, 134, 140
drug effects and, 140–146
pharmacological factors, 5
phencyclidine, 8, 354–356
chronic use effects of, 356
dependence on, 148
medical management of, 356
physiological effects of, 355
psychological effects of, 355–356
street names for, 355
tolerance to, 148
withdrawal from, 148
Phen-fen, 421
phenylethylamines, 341, 350–352
phenylpropanolamine (Dexatrim), 421
Philip Morris Company, 313
phocomelia, 69
physical dependence, 19, 149–150
physiological effects
of marijuana use, 384–389
variable, 145
pituitary gland, 126–127
placebo effect, 151
placental barrier, 143
plateau effect, 143
"plateauing," 446
PNS (peripheral nervous system), 124
Polo, Marco, 366
polydrug use, 188. *See also* drug interactions
cocaine and, 285–286
positive reinforcers, 38–39
posttraumatic stress disorder, 230
potency, 137
toxicity *vs.*, 137
potentiative (synergistic) effects, 138–149
pragmatic drug policy, 86–87
preclinical research and development, 70
precursor chemicals, 267
pregnancy
caffeine and, 291
cocaine use in, 281, 286–287
drug effects and, 145, 455–456
heroin and, 250
marijuana use in, 387

---

pregnancy (*continued*)
  smoking and, 318
  thalidomide use in, 68–69
  tobacco use in, 456
preoccupation phase, of addiction, 21
Prescription Drug User Fee Act of 1992, 71
prescription drugs, 7, 12, 425–435
  abuse of, 425–426
  advertising of, 73
  common categories of, 428–430
  common principles of use, 435
  doctor-patient communication and, 426–427
  generic *vs.* proprietary, 427
  illegal drugs as, availability of, 84–85
  over-the-counter drugs *vs.*, 67–68
  regulatory steps for, 70–72
  top-selling, 429
  women and, 457–458
prevention needs assessment, 499
prevention of drug abuse, programs for, 81, 494–514
  alternatives approach, 512
  assessing, 511
  audience and approach considerations in, 496–500
  community-based, 500–501
  comprehensive, 500–504
  demand reduction strategy and, 81–82
  educational prevention models, 498–506
  inoculation strategy in, 82
  large-scale, 506–511
  meditation and, 512
  natural mind approach to, 512–514
  primary, 496, 497
  school-based, 501–504
  secondary, 496, 497
  strategies in, 79–87
  supply reduction strategy in, 79–81
  tertiary, 496, 497
Priestly, Joseph, 396
primary deviance, 50
primary groups, 44
primary prevention, 468
Pro-Children Act of 1994, 313
productive cough, 415–416
Prohibition era, 210–212
"proof," 185
propane, inhalation of, 399
propoxyphene, 239, 256
proprietary drugs, 427
protease inhibitors, 435, 477
protective parent, 461
Prozac, 431
pseudointoxication, 217
psilocin, 349
psilocybin, 8, 348–349
  student use of, 474

Psychedelic Experience (Leary), 337
psychedelics, 8. *See also* hallucinogens
psychiatric disorders
  drug abuse and, 39
  substance-related mental disorders *vs.*, 41
psychoactive drugs/substances, 6, 115–116. *See also* alcohol (ethanol)
  effects of, 38
  mental set and, 151
psychoanalysis, 93
psychodrama genogram, 230
psychological dependence, 19, 150–151
psychological disorders. *See* psychiatric disorders
psychological theories, 40–43
psychosocial/developmental factors, in addictive personality, 95
psychotogenic, 338
psychotomimetic, 336
PTSD (posttraumatic stress disorder), 230
Public Health Cigarette Smoking (1969), 310
puffing, 306
Pure Food and Drug Act (1906), 67–68
"pyramiding," 446

quality assurance, federal regulation and, 73–74
quinine, heroin and, 245

race. *See* ethnic and racial groups
rapid eye movement sleep, 164
RAS (reticular activating system), 123
Rastafarian religion, marijuana use and, 364
"raves," 272, 274
Reagan, Ronald, 82
rebound depression ("crash"), 279, 280
rebound effect, 149
receptors, 40, 115
  drug, 118–119
recovery, from cocaine dependence, 285
recreational use of drugs, 11
Reefer Madness, 364, 371
regulation of drugs. *See* laws and regulations
reinforcement
  differential, 42, 43
  positive, 38–39
relapsing syndrome, 226
REM (rapid eye movement) sleep, 164, 168
replacement therapy, 81–82

reproduction
  drug abuse and, 455–456
  marijuana use and, 386–387
research and development, 70–71
resorcinol, 421
respiratory system, marijuana and, 385
reticular activating system, 123
Retin A (retinoic acid), 421
retrospective interpretation, 51
reverse tolerance, 149
Reye's syndrome, 413
risk factors
  for addiction, 94–96
  for drug abuse, 57, 58–59
risk-reduction process, 58–59
Ritalin, 266, 274
"roach," 368
Rohypnol, 167, 475
"roid rage," 128, 446
role playing (psychodrama) genogram, 230
Rolfe, John, 304–305
Romonov tzars, tobacco use and, 303–304
run, 268
rush, 268
Rutgers University, dormitories at, 474

safety margin, 136–137
salicylates, 412
salicylic acid, 421
SAMHSA (Substance Abuse and Mental Health Services Administration), 48, 98, 202
SAPs (student assistance programs), 106
SC (subcutaneous) injection, 142
scare tactic approach, 501
schedule classification, of abused drugs, 76, 77
school-based drug prevention programs, 501–504
  curriculum-based, 501–503
  D.A.R.E., 508–509
  in higher education, 505–508
  questions for, 503–504
sebum removal, OTC drugs for, 421
secondary deviance, 50–51
secondary groups, 44
secondary prevention, 469
second-hand drinking, 221
second-hand smoke, 320. *See also* environmental tobacco smoke
sedative-hypnotic agents, 162, 435
  common interactions with, 139
selective legalization, 84–85
self-help, with behavioral modification, 325
self-medication, for psychiatric disorders, 278, 282
sensation-seeking individuals, 42

sensitization, 134, 149
serotonin. *See* 5-hydroxytryptamine
setting, 217
sexual abuse
    alcohol abuse and, 224–225
    CNS depressants and, 174–175
sexual activity
    alcohol and, 222
    amphetamines and, 265
    "crack" and, 282
    marijuana and, 386–387
sexual organs, alcohol's effect on,
    194–195
sexual violence, drugs and, 465–466
Sherley Amendment, 67
side effects, of drugs. *See individual
    drugs*
sidestream smoke, 320. *See also* envi-
    ronmental tobacco smoke
SIDS (sudden infant death syndrome),
    318
significant others, role of, 45–46
Sinsemilla, 373
skin cancer, 421–422
skin products, 420
sleep aids, OTC, 417–418
sleep disorders, 417–418
smoke-free indoor air, 330
smokeless tobacco, 310, 317–318
Smokeless Tobacco Act, 312
smokers, tobacco
    characteristics of, 323–326
    rights of, 330–331
    youth and, 330
smoking. *See also* tobacco
    cessation methods, 324–325
    as costly addiction, 315–326
    government regulation of, 307–308
    health and, 308, 314–315
    laws restricting, 330–331
    marijuana cigarettes. *See* marijuana
    passive, 317–318
    prevalence of, 303
    reasons for, 323–324
    stopping, 324–325, 326–329
Smoking and Health (report), 308,
    310
"sniffing," 398
"snorting"
    cocaine, 279
    inhalants, 398
snuff, 318
snuff dipping, 314
"snuff taker," 304
snuffing, 318
social disorganization theory, 53–54
social drugs, 12
social environment, addiction and, 95
social factors, 5
social influence
    model, 505–506
    theories, 44–57

social learning theory, 42, 44–45
social lubricant, 184
social psychological learning theories,
    43
social support perspective, 53
socialization, 53
    defined, 56
society
    drugs in, 10–17
    and social change, 54–55
sociobiological changes, adolescents
    and, 460
sociological explanations, of substance
    abuse, 43–59
soft drinks, caffeine content of, 289
solvents, inhalation of, 398
soma, 365
somatic pain, 241
South American Indians, cocaine use
    by, 275
speakeasies, 210
special focus programs, 106
speed (methamphetamine), 22, 267
speedballing, 246
speedballs, 271
SPF (sun protection factor) number, 422
spittoons, 305
"stacking," 446
STAT (Stop Teenage Addiction to
    Tobacco), 311
steroids, 127–128, 413
    anabolic, 9, 128
stimulants, 8, 264–295. *See also* am-
    phetamines; caffeine; cocaine;
    nicotine
    abuse among athletes, 449
    common interactions with, 139
    herbal, 292–293
    major, 264–287
    minor, 287–293
    over-the-counter, 418
Stop Teenage Addiction to Tobacco
    (STAT), 311
stress management, support groups
    for, 104
structural influence theories, 44
student assistance programs, 106
subculture(s)
    defined, 442
    drug use within, 442–487
        adolescents. *See* adolescents,
            drug abuse among
        athletes, 443–452
        college students, 204, 220-222,
            470–475
        entertainment and media sub-
            culture, 482–484
        HIV-positive subcultures,
            477–482
        women. *See* women, drug abuse
            among
    theory of, 52–53

subcutaneous injection, 142
subjective euphoric effects, 376–377
substance abuse, 92
    mental disorders *vs.,* 41
Substance Abuse and Mental Services
    Administration (SAMHSA),
    48, 98, 202
substance dependence, 92
substance dependence disorder, 174
sudden infant death syndrome, 318
suicide, adolescent, 464–465
sulfur, 421
sun products, OTC, 421
sun protection factor number, 422
supply reduction strategy, 79–81
Surgeon General, reports by, 308, 311,
    312, 313
switching policy, 72
sympathomimetic drugs, 121, 126, 265
    over-the-counter, 292–293
synapse, 117, 118
synaptic cleft, 117
synergism, 138–139
synesthesia, 339

TC (therapeutic communities), 103
tea, 288–289
teenagers, drug use among. *See* adoles-
    cents, drug abuse among
teetotalers, 204, 461
temperance movement, 209
teratogenic, 145
tetrahydrocannabinol, 373–374, 381.
    See also marijuana
    dependence on, 387
    physiological effects of, 384–389
    sexual performance and reproduc-
        tion effects of, 386–387
    subjective euphoric effects of, 376
    therapeutic uses of, 381–384
    tolerance to, 387
"Texas shoe shine," 399
thalidomide, 68–69
THC. *See* tetrahydrocannabinol
theobromine, 288
    in chocolate, 289
theophylline, 288
therapeutic communities, 103
threshold, 143
time-response factors, 143–144
tobacco, 302–332, 425
    adolescents and, 319, 323, 324, 329,
        329-330
    advertising of, 307–308
    bronchopulmonary disease and,
        317
    characteristics of, 323
    chewing, 314, 318, 321
    chronic illness and, 316–317
    common interactions with, 139
    contraceptives and, 316
    cost of use of, 302

tobacco (*continued*
  current use in United States,
      302–303
  dependence on, reasons for,
      323–326
  developments related to smoking
      and health, 310–313
  economic costs of, 302
  as gateway drug, 329–330
  government regulation of, 307–308
  health consequences of, 302
  heroin and, 330
  history of, 303, 304–308
  mortality rates and, 315–316
  popularity of, 304
  pregnancy and, 318
  production of, 305–306
  prohibition of, 330
  readdiction to, 326
  scope of problem of, 302–308
  sidestream/second-hand smoke
      from, 320–323
  smokeless, 310, 317–318
  taxing of, 330–331
  withdrawal from, 326
tobacco camphor, 305
tobacco chewing, 314, 318, 321
tobacco smokers
  characteristics of, 323–326
  rights of, 330–331
  youth and, 330
tolerance, 92, 136, 146, 147
  alcohol, 148, 188
  amphetamines, 148
  barbiturates, 148
  behavioral, 188
  benzodiazepines, 148
  caffeine, 148
  CNS depressants, 162, 166–167
  cocaine, 148
  LSD, 148, 348, 349
  marijuana, 148, 387
  mescaline, 348
  narcotics, 148
  nicotine, 148
  phencyclidine, 148
  reverse, 149
  tetrahydrocannabinol, 387
toluene, inhalation of, 399
topical application, 142

toxicity, 137
  in liver, 192
  potency *vs.*, 137
trafficking penalties, federal, 67
"transcriptase inhibitors," 435
transdermal nicotine systems, 328
treatment for drug addiction, 97–109
  for adolescents, 469–470
  Alcoholics Anonymous, 93, 96
  Alcoholics Anonymous and,
      100–102
  alcoholism, 100–102
  for athletes, 451–452
  current trends in, 105–109
  detoxification units for, 102–103
  goals of, 97–99
  on inpatient basis, 284, 469
  on outpatient basis, 103–105
  rehabilitation facilities for, 97, 102
  therapeutic communities in, 103
  for women, 458–459
tricyclic antidepressants, 431
tweaking, 269
Tylenol. *See* acetaminophen

U. S. Tobacco Company, 312
ulcers, 432
uppers, 264
Urban VIII (Pope), 304

Valium, 118, 163, 427. *See also* benzo-
      diazepines
vasodilators, direct, 433
Vespucci, Amerigo, 275
violence, drug related, 21–28
  sexual, 465–466
Virginia tobacco, 306
visceral pain, 241
vitamin A, 421
Vivarin, 418
volatile substances, 386, 398–400. *See
      also* inhalants
vomiting, 134

"War on Drugs," 83–85. *See also* drug
      war, fighting
Washington, George, 366
weight reduction, amphetamines and,
      266

WHO (World Health Organization),
      310
withdrawal, 21, 41, 92, 134, 146
  alcohol, 148, 227
  amphetamines, 148
withdrawal
  barbiturates, 148, 170
  benzodiazepines, 166–167
  caffeine, 148
  CNS depressants, 166–167,
      175–176
  from CNS depressants, 175–176
  cocaine, 148, 283
  heroin, 250
  LSD, 148
  marijuana, 148
  narcotics, 148
  nicotine, 148
  phencyclidine, 148
  tobacco, 326
women, drug abuse among, 14,
      452–459. *See also* pregnancy
  AIDS and, 455, 477–478
  alcohol and, 222–224, 456–457
  female roles and, 454–455
  patterns of, 453–455
  prescription drugs and, 457–458
  prevention of, 459
  reproduction and, 455–456
  response to, 455–458
  tobacco use and, 455, 456
  treatment of, 458–459
Women's Christian Temperance
      Union (WTCU), 501
Wood, Alexander, 240
workplace, drugs in, 26–28
World Health Organization (WHO),
      310
Wren, Christopher, 240
WTCU (Women's Christian Temper-
      ance Union), 501

Xanax, 165–166
xanthines, 287–293. *See also* caffeine
  physiological effects of, 290

zeta alcoholic, 215
zidovudine, 435, 477